MAGPIES IN

From Antwerp

By Kev Fletcher

This book is dedicated to Denis Taylor … a lifelong friend, and a Toon fan who never stops believing.

Contents

Tino Asprilla

Foreword

JOHN McNAMEE

Being part of Newcastle United's Fairs Cup triumph in 1969 was the highlight of my football career, because we gave the fabulous Geordie crowd the success they deserved.

I had already played in Europe with Hibs and Celtic, but that 1968/9 season was remarkable because we won the competition after just about every critic had written us off.

We started the campaign well with the 4-0 thrashing of Feyenoord, and an amazing individual performance from Geoff Allen. But the Dutch were a different proposition in Rotterdam, and we had to fight all the way to get through. I had my own personal battle with Dutch hard-man Marinus Israel, who made all sorts of threats to me at the start of the game. He had already punched Tommy (Gibb) in an off-the-ball incident and he had a go at me, but we had a clash of heads when we both went for a high ball and he accused me of breaking his jaw. I said to him: "Where I come from you don't make threats, you just do it!"

The Vitoria Setubal tie was another memorable evening, played in a snow storm at St James' Park. As we walked out I said to the players "roll up your sleeves, and show them the weather doesn't bother us". We won 5-1.

I wasn't expected to play at Ibrox (against Rangers) in the semi-final because I was injured with a pulled hamstring, but Joe Harvey insisted that I start. He said: "I need you in the side because the fans will give you stick because you played for Celtic, and that will take the pressure off the other players. You can handle it".

I was up against my old pal from my Hibs days, Colin Stein, and I hobbled though the game on one leg trying to keep up with him. It was probably my best performance for Newcastle, but it took its toll, and I aggravated the injury and missed the return game at St James' Park.

My major regret was that I missed the final against Ujpest Dozsa in Budapest. I was substitute and I hoped to get on near the end but Joe didn't use me. It would have been extra special to have played that evening, as it was also my birthday. But we won the cup, after trailing 2-0 at half-time, and the reception back home from the fabulous fans was unforgettable.

I'm not suggesting we were a brilliant team. Yes we had good players - Wyn Davies was always a handful for any defender; David Craig was probably the best full-back in the country at the time; Tommy Gibb could run all day; and Pop Robson was the perfect strike partner for Big Wyn. But it was the Newcastle supporters who won the Fairs Cup for us. How could any player walk out at St James' Park and not give 100% with the backing they gave us?

They are quite simply … magnificent!

(* I would like to thank "Big Bad John" for his contribution to this book. He was my hero back in 1969 … and he remains my hero, even more so, today.)

Magpies in Europe…and beyond

Introduction

Although Newcastle United don't have the European record of giants Barcelona, Real Madrid, Liverpool or AC Milan, the Magpies have to date (2011) played an impressive 120 games on the continental stage, and can at least boast that they have made their own little imprint on foreign shores.

Newcastle United are recognised as one of the biggest clubs in the country, yet nobody can be accused of following them because of their success. There are no 'Glory Seekers' on this nostalgia trip. Anyone who has been privileged to take an excursion around the beautiful St James' Park will have been a little disappointed when they reached the trophy room and found it full of stuffed magpies and memorabilia from a bygone age. No sign of Premiership wins or anything that you would see in the hallowed halls of Old Trafford or The Emirates Stadium.

The Geordies have not had much to cheer about (on the domestic front) since the FA Cup win in 1955. We have had FA Cup final appearances against Liverpool, Arsenal and Man Utd ... but sadly we couldn't even put the ball in the back of the net once.

Alan Gowling scored in the League Cup final against Man City in 1976, but Geordie-born Dennis Tueart did a swivel turn to defy gravity and plant the ball past Mick Mahoney to take the trophy to Maine Road.

In our own little way, however, we have had success in Europe and have beaten the likes of Barcelona, Inter Milan, Juventus, Feyenoord, Rangers and PSV Eindhoven. 15 seasons playing the best Europe has had to offer, and in many cases frightening the life out of them.... and that is what this book is all about.

This is not meant to be just a history book. Yes, the facts and figure are here, but I try to put some meat on the bones and look at the matches with the view from the Leazes End.... and also from the 'away end' at some rather exotic places across the North Sea.

I have seen Newcastle play in 17 countries myself, and I've spoken to fans that travelled in the 1960's and 1970's, and I have used their experiences in an effort to give you a different perspective of the games.... hopefully in a way that has not been published before.

So please enter the world of Wyn Davies, Tino Asprilla, Alan Shearer, David Ginola ... and a man who will live in my memory forever as the epitome of Geordie grit and determination. Yes, the "kick them before they kick you" mentality that was the 1960s ... my schoolboy hero ... John McNamee.

I hope you enjoy the ride.

Kev Fletcher

THE START OF EUROPEAN COMPETITION

In April 1955 UEFA established the first European competition – the European Cup - for the champion clubs of UEFA-affiliated nations.

So who were the first British club to compete in it? And I bet if you ask anyone down the pub no-one would get the answer.

English league winners Chelsea knocked back the offer because Football League secretary Alan Hardaker said the competition was a "joke" and would not last because it would cause an enormous fixture pile-up in the English game.

But was there 'method' in Mr Hardaker's 'madness'? Because this was the man who five years later introduced his own brain-child … the League Cup … and that DID cause fixture problems. So much so, to prove him wrong, many of the top clubs chose to boycott the League Cup in favour of playing in Europe.

The first British club to compete in Europe was actually Scottish club Hibernian. The following season the English league was won by Manchester United, and the Football League again tried to step in and deny an English club entry to the European Cup. But manager Matt Busby defied Hardaker's wishes and Man Utd became the first English team to venture into Europe.

The Inter Cities Fairs Cup was introduced in 1955, but it was a bizarre competition that was not recognised by UEFA who, quite frankly, didn't want anything to do with it. The competition was dreamt up by Swiss pools supremo Ernst Thommen, Ottorino Barassi from Italy, and the English Football Association General Secretary Stanley Rous. As the name suggests, the competition was set up to promote international trade fairs, and didn't really have football as its core objective. Friendly games were regularly held between teams from cities holding trade fairs and it was from these games that the competition evolved. The first English team (and not a club at all) to enter the event when it finally became a 'competition' was 'London' – a collection of players from London clubs. Then came the equally bizarre rule that only one club from the same city could qualify to play … and Newcastle United would reap the rewards in 1968.

The third competition, the European Cup Winners Cup, was launched in 1960. The idea being that the participants would be the winners of the domestic cup competition in each UEFA-affiliated nation. However, in the case of 'double winners' – clubs that won both the league and the cup in the same season – the beaten finalists of the cup competition would take part.

FORMER TOON STARS IN EUROPEAN COMPETITION

Before Newcastle United qualified for Europe in 1968 there were a number of ex-Magpies who experienced the European stage – most notably Jackie Milburn, Ronnie Simpson and Ernie Taylor.

Jackie Milburn

JACKIE MILBURN

Although Newcastle's FA Cup Wembley triumph over Manchester City in 1955 was five years before the European Cup Winners Cup was formed, cup hero Jackie Milburn did get a taste of European football some years later, with Linfield.

In 1957 Milburn decided to leave St James' Park and he received an offer to join the Northern Ireland club as player-manager. This included a five-year contract, a £1,000 signing on fee, a large detached four-bedroom club house and a £1,300 salary. 'Wor Jackie' proved a great success and he scored over 100 goals in two seasons as the Belfast club recorded back-to-back titles. He played in the European Cup, scoring both goals for Linfield in a 1959 home tie against Gothenburg before a crowd of 41,000 at Windsor Park, his only goals in European football.

RONNIE SIMPSON

Ronnie Simpson spent seven years as Newcastle's regular goalkeeper, winning two FA Cup winner's medals and a Scotland 'B' cap, making 295 appearances for the club. But he was badly injured in May 1958 during Newcastle's tour of Romania and was put out of the game for almost two years. He only played three more games for the Magpies before making a move to Hibs in 1960.

Simpson answered a call from part-time Berwick Rangers, and went to Shieldfield Park to wind down his career. At the age of 34, however, and supposedly ready to retire, Celtic signed him as cover for John Fallon.... then came the chance of glory and he ended up on one of the greatest rollercoaster rides in football history.

In 1967 he helped the Hoops win every competition they entered, including a 'grand slam' of domestic honours ... AND the European Cup. The 'Lisbon Lions' defeated the mighty Inter Milan in Portugal to become the first British club to win Europe's greatest trophy, and they did it with eleven players all born within ten miles of Glasgow.

After the success in Lisbon, Simpson played for the Scotland national team, making his debut at the age of 36 in the famous 3-2 win over 1966 World Cup winners England at Wembley in 1967. He set a new record for being the oldest player to make his Scotland debut, going on to win five caps in total.

ERNIE TAYLOR

Newcastle United's "Tom Thumb" of the 1950's, Ernie Taylor, played a part in European history for Manchester United following the tragic Munich air disaster.

Although there was only one season (during his eight years at St James' Park) that he was officially seen as a first team regular at Newcastle, he is still highly regarded on Tyneside. The Sunderland-born inside-right was a major player in Newcastle's FA Cup run of 1951 when they beat Blackpool in the final. At only 5 ft 4", he was one of the shortest players in the game, but it was his cheeky back-heel at Wembley that set up one of Jackie Milburn's two cup final goals that year. After Blackpool's defeat, Stanley Matthews convinced his manager, Joe Smith, to sign him and the deal went through with a £25,000 transfer fee.

He was a member of Blackpool's famous FA Cup-winning side that beat Bolton Wanderers 4-3 in the "Matthews Cup Final". Then he signed for Manchester United two weeks after the Munich air disaster, as the Red Devils tried to patch up their ravaged team. As well as playing in the cup final of that year, he starred in the first leg of Man Utd's European Cup semi-final when they beat AC Milan 2-1, scoring one of the goals. He also played in the 2nd leg, when the Italian giants won 4-0 to qualify for the final.

GEORDIES AND MACKEMS

"Geordie" is a regional nickname for a person from Tyneside; "Mackem" is a person from Wearside; although that has not always been the case. When I was a kid the name "Geordie" was a term used for the whole of the north east of England, and "Mackem" was only introduced into north east vocabulary in the mid-1970's.

So how did the terms come about?

"Geordie" obviously derives from a familiar diminutive form of the name George, but there are two theories as to why it became associated with the city of Newcastle.

One explanation for the name is that local coal miners in the north east of England used "Geordie" safety lamps, designed by George Stephenson in 1815, rather than the "Davy lamps" designed by Humphry Davy which were used in other mining communities. Many ex-miners I know insist that this is the true reason, but history shows that the term has been used for 250 years…. so that rules out the lamp.

The other explanation is that it was established during the Jacobite Rebellion of 1745. The Jacobites declared that the natives of Newcastle were staunch supporters of the Hanoverian kings, in particular of George II during the 1745 rebellion. Allegedly, the people of Newcastle closed the city gates to the Jacobites, as they stood firm for King George II, and it was the Scots who came up with the name "Geordies".

"Mackem" is more straight-forward. It comes from the term "mak and tak" that was used by shipyard workers in the 19th century on the Tyne, to describe their Wearside counterparts. The Sunderland builders would make the ship to be fitted out by the Geordies, hence "they mackem and we tackem" ("make them" and "take them"). The two regions pronounced it in different accents. Tyneside people would say "mek and tek"; Wearside "mak and tak".

Although I remember the term being used amongst football fans in the early 1970s, it wasn't until the football fanzine culture of 1985 that the name appeared in print and took off nationwide.

CHAPTER ONE
INTER CITIES FAIRS CUP 1968/69

Joe Harvey

MANAGER: Joe Harvey

Joe Harvey had been an inspirational captain for Newcastle having signed for the club in October 1945, in a deal that saw Bradford City pick up £4,240. He led the team for eight years, longer than any other skipper at that time, and saw the club promoted and win two FA Cups. In June 1962 (after trying his luck as manager of Workington, then Barrow) he was offered the manager's job at St James' Park on a 12-month trial period. He impressed immediately and became full-time boss soon after.

United won promotion back to the top flight under his leadership in 1965, and had finished 15th, 20th and 10th before their European baptism of fire.

HOW NEWCASTLE UTD QUALIFIED:

The tail end of the 1967/8 season was a disaster for manager Joe Harvey's Newcastle, as they won only one of the last twelve games, dropping from fifth in the table (in March) to finally settle at tenth in May.

The last two games of the season saw a 6-0 humiliation at Old Trafford, as Matt Busby's side prepared for their European Cup final at Wembley against Eusabio's Benfica, then the other team from Manchester arrived at St James' Park knowing a win would give them the title. It was a straight fight for the league – Manchester United or Manchester City – and City ran out 4-3 winners on Tyneside to win the title for the first time since 1937.

However, that 4-3 Man City win over Newcastle; Man Utd's 4-1 European Cup triumph over Benfica; and West Bromwich Albion winning the FA Cup; all meant one thing ... Newcastle had qualified for Europe!

The Magpies finished tenth, having lost more games than they had won, as well as conceding 13 more goals than they had scored. But a whole host of strange results, and the most bizarre set of rules ever devised for a sporting competition, all worked in Newcastle's favour.

Nine clubs above them - and only six places given to English clubs - it took a Geordie with a wild imagination; a calculator without a battery; and a night down the Bigg Market supping a dozen bottles of Newky Broon to seriously expect European qualification. But by good luck ... or the grace of God ... it happened.

Man City were champions so took their place in the European Cup, and 8th placed West Brom were in the Cup Winners Cup, so that left four clubs for the Fairs Cup. But 2nd placed Man Utd had won the European Cup and were invited to try and retain it, leaving Liverpool, Everton, Chelsea and Spurs to qualify as the four. But the "only one club from each city" rules kicked in, so 5th placed Everton were knocked out of the race because Merseyside already had the Reds in the pot; and (7th) Spurs and (9th) Arsenal suffered at the hands of London rivals Chelsea. So the Geordie boys packed away their passports for an unforgettable journey.

Chairman Lord Westwood: "Well we're in it, and I think we are daft enough to WIN it!"

He couldn't possibly be right … could he?

September 11 1968 - NEWCASTLE UTD 4 FEYENOORD 0

McFaul, Craig, Clark, Gibb, McNamee, Burton, Scott, B Robson, Davies, Elliott, Allen.

Att: 46,348

Feyenoord had been crowned Dutch champions three times in six years, had reached the European Cup semi-finals, and they boasted ten internationals in their squad totalling 180 caps between them.

But Joe Harvey's boys were not in the mood to let a club's reputation ruin the carnival atmosphere, as 46,348 turned up at St James' Park hoping for a party. The question was – which Newcastle side would turn up? The league season was eight games old and the Magpies had only won one of those games.

MATCH REPORT: In the fourth minute Pop Robson set the pattern of the game by frightening the life out of the Feyenoord defence, as they struggled to get to grips with his lightning pace. Only desperate defending saved the situation on that occasion, but two minutes later he was at them again, setting up Jim Scott for Newcastle's first ever European goal. Wyn Davies found Geoff Allen out on the left, and the winger left big Van der Heide for dead before providing the perfect cross for Robson to beat goalkeeper Graafland to head to Scott to tap in.

Davies was the major threat, and the Dutchmen had two defenders on him, but it was the space allowed to Allen that turned the game. He was preferred to the experienced Jackie Sinclair, and he seized his chance, producing the greatest game of his short career.

In the 30th minute he went through the Dutch defence like a knife through butter, but Dave Elliott spurned the chance and shot wide.

Minutes later Allen rattled the bar, then it was Davies turn to test the woodwork. His drive came back off the post but Robson was on hand to make it 2-0.

The third came three minutes before half-time. Tommy Gibb hit a powerful drive that looked to be going wide, but it hit Dutch international Marinus Israel and squeezed inside the post.

Half-time: Newcastle Utd 3 Feyenoord 0

Gibb got the ball into the net in the 65th minute but the referee disallowed it, claiming the new signing from Partick Thistle had controlled the ball with his hand. But three minutes later Davies got the biggest cheer of the evening when he struck his first goal in eight months. Scott floated over a superb free-kick from the right touchline and Davies timed his jump to perfection to head home his tenth goal for Newcastle since his signing from Bolton Wanderers.

Joe Harvey, always a man of few words, had a smile as big as the Tyne Bridge at the final whistle. The only words reporters could get out of him were "They were great"!

Feyenoord coach **Ben Peeters**: "We were too slow in getting to the ball, and too slow in moving it. We lost 5-0 to Real Madrid a while ago and it took our players a year to get over that! It cannot happen again, definitely no. We have not got that long."

Just to show how bizarre this competition was, Leeds United played Ferencvaros this very same night ... in the 2nd leg of the FINAL of the previous season's competition. With the final scheduled so late, the organisers would not allow the winners to defend their trophy. That is just one of many reasons why EUFA, to this day, don't recognise the competition as ever being "official" and don't list the results as being part of European football history.

September 17 1968 - FEYENOORD 2 NEWCASTLE UTD 0

McFaul, Craig, Clark (Iley), Gibb, McNamee, Burton, Scott, B Robson, Davies, Elliott, Allen.

Att: 45,000

The return tie in Rotterdam the following week fitted into a very tight schedule for the Magpies. Following the 4-0 1st leg Fairs Cup win, they had to entertain West Brom at St James' Park and they suffered another league set-back, losing 3-2. Come October it was a dreadful run that progressed to one win in the first 12 games of the league season.

The Feijenoord Stadium was built in 1936 and received many architectural accolades at the time, but it had hardly been altered during the 32 years up to 1968. Some argued it was preservation of a great building, while many Dutch argued that it was neglect. The fans call the stadium 'De Kuip' (The Tub). The club was officially called Feijenoord in 1968, and changed to 'Feyenoord' in the early 1970s to ease the spelling for foreigners.

Rotterdam is a city of modern beauty, but it wasn't in 1968. It was still recovering from the German air attack that levelled the place on 14th May 1940.

An attack of such ferocity, the only building that was left standing in the city centre was the Laurenskerk church.

We saw the incredible Ossip Zadkine sculpture to recall the event of that night in 1940, "The Destroyed City" which stands as a symbol of Rotterdam. It is a man yelling and looking up at the sky with his arms lifted up and a hole where his heart should be.

MATCH REPORT: The Dutch found the pace their coach asked of them and they ran the show from the first minute to the last.

Backed by a home crowd of 45,000, they came close to scoring twice in the opening minutes but goalkeeper Iam McFaul was equal to their efforts.

But in the 26th minute defender Marinus Israel played a quick free-kick that set Swedish international Ove Kindvall on his way to the opening goal. The striker, tipped to become one of the best strikers in Europe, hardly had a kick at St James' Park, but was off the leash for this game. He was the major threat, and John McNamee and Ollie Burton did well to keep him at distance.

It was all 'hands to the pump' and, during this spell of desperate defending, United only tested goalkeeper Graafland twice.

Half-time: Feyenoord 1 Newcastle Utd 0

The Dutch swept back onto the attack at the start of the second-half and within nine minutes went two up. Full-back Van der Heide shot past McFaul from close range having been set up by Jensen.

Newcastle concentrated on preserving their two-goal cushion and seldom ventured beyond the halfway line. Henk Wery was fouled by Geoff Allen in the 61st minute and bottles were thrown onto the pitch. Wyn Davies went into the referee's book for a cynical tackle on Van der Heide and the home supporters again threw objects.

Several times Feyenoord came close to reducing the deficit. Frank Clark cleared off the line after a tremendous drive from Kindvall, who later saw two goal-bound shots saved by McFaul.

Later in the week Liverpool were knocked out by the toss of a coin after drawing with Spanish club Atletico Bilbao. Skipper **Ron Yates** had to choose between the red side or the blue of the plastic 'coin'. He picked red, saying afterwards: "I was hardly going to pick blue, was I?"

October 30 1968 - SPORTING LISBON 1 NEWCASTLE UTD 1

McFaul, Craig, Clark, Gibb, Winstanley, Burton, Scott, B Robson, Davies, Moncur, Foggon (Dyson).

Newcastle were drawn against Sporting Lisbon, Portugal's largest and arguably most popular club (although Benfica have since taken that mantle). The Newcastle players made the trip to Portugal following a 2-1 defeat by Liverpool the previous Saturday. Wyn Davies played in Portugal, despite the fact he had a broken finger, a split eyebrow, and a left arm he described as being "almost paralysed" after a kick on the biceps that he had picked up at Anfield.

The hotly fancied Sporting side had won the European Cup Winners Cup in 1964.

The ground, a massive concrete presence by the roadside, was situated close to Lisbon Airport. The Estadio Jose Alvalade Stadium must have been an impressive sight in the sun, but as it was only covered by a roof on one section of the ground, it was open to the elements on 80% of the building. The sudden torrential downpour before the match discouraged many potential fans, as no tickets were sold for the fixture, it was 'pay on the night'. Only 9,000 turned up for a stadium that held 49,000.

MATCH REPORT: Newcastle had a lucky escape in the sixth minute when full-back Celestino tried his luck from a distance and hit Iam McFaul's crossbar, with the Irish goalkeeper motionless.

Then ten minutes later a powerful shot from Lourenco was parried by McFaul, who managed to retrieve the ball as the Lisbon striker came charging in for a second bite of the cherry.

As well as the injuries to Davies, Bob Moncur suffered a broken nose, but it didn't stop him seeing out the entire 90 minutes. After 31 minutes Jim Scott boosted Newcastle's hopes of qualification for round three when he managed to get on the end of a teasing ball fed through by Pop Robson that was played across the face of the Sporting penalty area.

Half-time: Sporting Lisbon 0 Newcastle Utd 1

The home side continued to attack during the second-half, but Newcastle did well to hold out for so long. Sporting had beaten Manchester United 5-0 in this stadium, and, with time running out, it seemed the Magpies were set for a remarkable first victory on foreign soil in European competition.

Then with only 30 seconds of the match remaining, Sporting produced an all-out final assault and finally beat McFaul when Morrais scored from close range.

Newcastle returned home to Tyneside in jubilant mood, having demoralised the home side on their own patch, but they had to count the cost of their endeavour. Their immediate considerations were injuries to Davies, Scott, Moncur, and Alan Foggon. Geoff Allen missed the Lisbon trip with a knee injury he had picked up at Notts County's Meadow Lane. It was not thought to be serious at that time, but sadly he only played one more game for Newcastle (a home fixture against Sheffield Wednesday) when he limped off to be substituted. Soon afterwards he was forced to retire. He came through the junior ranks of the club, and his performance in the 4-0 win over Feyenoord will long be remembered. He only played 26 games for the Magpies.

November 20 1968 - NEWCASTLE UTD 1 SPORTING LISBON 0

McFaul, Craig, Clark, Gibb, Burton, Moncur, Scott, B Robson, Davies, Elliott, Dyson (Bennett).

Att: 53,747

In many respects Joe Harvey felt his team had done the hard work getting a draw away from home, and he was more than convinced that his Newcastle side would finish the job at St James' Park. Sporting had beaten Valencia 4-0 in the previous round at Estadio Jose Alvalade but only just managed to squeeze through after taking a 4-1 hammering in Spain.

MATCH REPORT: United came out of the blocks at a blistering pace that left the Sporting players shell-shocked.

Just like the first round tie with Feyenoord, Joe Harvey could not have wished for a better start from his Newcastle team, as a tremendous ninth-minute volley from Pop Robson sent the 53,000 Geordie fans wild with delight. The plan was for Keith Dyson to have roving commission and try to make a nuisance of himself wherever he could, and he did just that to set up the goal. He was badly obstructed as he tried to cut through from the left, winning a free-kick on the edge of the box. Tommy Gibb floated the ball high to Wyn Davies on the right, and he left his marker Manhica, rooted to the spot as he headed the ball for Robson to blast home.

It could have been an even worse start for the visitors, as Davies (just 20 seconds into the game) pulled the very best out of the inspired 21-year old Victor Damas, who somehow clawed away a piledriver. The goalkeeper kept Sporting in the game as his defence was run ragged by the pace of Robson and Dyson, and he kept the score down to 1-0 as the shots rained in from all angles.

In the last minute of the half Davies headed the ball narrowly over the bar and, seconds later, Jim Scott pulled his shot just wide of the post.

Half-time: Newcastle Utd 1 Sporting Lisbon 0

Despite all the pressure, Newcastle only managed to get the ball into the net one more time. On the hour mark, Davies beat the offside trap and headed past Damas, but the German referee ruled the Welsh international had climbed on the shoulders of one of the defenders.

After all of the excitement of the first half with Newcastle buzzing like a swarm of bees, the tempo dropped. The Sporting midfield gained more possession but the strikers never got the better of skipper Bobby Moncur and Ollie Burton in the heart of the Newcastle defence.

Although the visitors weaved some pretty patterns in the middle of the park with some impressive continental expression, the final ball was always lacking and Moncur was unbeatable on the night. Every ball pumped towards Iam McFaul's goal was dealt with before it even reached the Irishman and he said after the game: "I have never had an easier game in my life. They had the opportunities but I didn't have a shot to save all game".

Ollie Burton revealed later that he was lucky to see out the match: "I went over on my ankle in the kick-in before the match. I didn't say anything at the time, but I was lucky to get through the game."

Joe Harvey: "I thought Lisbon played a lot stronger and a lot harder here than they did three weeks ago. Yet the measure of their attacking strength could be summed up by the work of McFaul. He virtually had a night off".

Bobby Moncur: "I don't think it was an entertaining spectacle for the fans. On the other hand, we went out to get through to the next round and we achieved our objective."

Newcastle chairman **Lord Westwood**: "I'm not concerned about the performance. There is no such thing as a bad win".

January 1 1969 - REAL ZARAGOZA 3 NEWCASTLE UTD 2

McFaul, Craig, Clark, Gibb, Burton, Moncur, Dyson, B Robson, Davies, Scott, Foggon.

Att: 22,000

The Spanish outfit were experienced European campaigners, having won the Inter Cities Fairs Cup in 1964. Newcastle were the 11th British side they had faced in competition, and none of the other ten (including Everton, Leeds and Rangers) had managed a win at their Romareda Stadium. They were one of Spain's elite clubs having won the title - Copa del Rey – in 1964 and 1966.

The match was played on New Years Day 1969, and followed on from Newcastle's 2-1 defeat at Elland Road against Leeds United on Boxing Day.

The ground was not dissimilar to Sporting's Estadio Jose Alvalade in that it only had a roof over one section of the stadium.

The Geordie fans who travelled to Zaragoza (situated inland roughly halfway between Barcelona and Madrid) received a big shock if they expected to arrive in a sunny climate. The temperature was sub-zero, but 22,000 braved the cold to watch an amazing first half that produced four goals.

MATCH REPORT: Another early goal in this Magpie European jaunt, but it was the Spaniards who got off the mark in the sixth minute, following a corner. Centre-forward Miguel Angel Bustillo headed the ball towards the top corner but Iam McFaul could only push it out to Santos who scored from 15 yards.

Down but not out, Newcastle roared back and within a minute were back on level terms. They produced a dazzling four-man move which ended with Pop Robson netting from close range.

It was a rough and tumble affair and right-back David Craig damaged his right shoulder early in the game when he was brought down heavily by Irusqieta, the opposing left-back, but the Irish defender saw out the game.

Zaragoza, second from the bottom in La Liga, produced more fight than their league position suggested and put United under intense pressure. Bustillo beat the Newcastle defence to a lofted ball into the penalty area and headed past McFaul, but in the 32nd minute Davies produced a carbon copy and headed the Magpies level again.

Half-time: Real Zaragoza 2 Newcastle Utd 2

Newcastle, always dangerous in breakaway raids, sat a lot deeper in the second period and were caught napping when right-half Javier Planas headed, what proved to be, the winner. He glanced the ball home after winger Armandio Martin had beaten two defenders to put over the perfect cross.

Zaragoza brought on Violeta for Santos in a tactical substitution, and they closed out the game hoping to keep the score at 3-2. However, it almost backfired as United pushed for the equaliser in the last ten minutes. Wyn Davies produced a moment of magic to set up Robson with a chance to steal the headlines, but the Sunderland-born pocket dynamo missed from two yards.

January 15 1969 - NEWCASTLE UTD 2 REAL ZARAGOZA 1

McFaul, Craig (Guthrie), Clark, Gibb, Burton, Moncur, Dyson, B Robson, Davies, Scott, Foggon.

Att: 56,055

Zaragoza were having a difficult season, but some reporters suggested they were a more 'polished' side than Newcastle. However, it was the spirit of home side that proved the difference between the two teams. United didn't buckle as the visitors tried every trick in the book – not all of them legal – to get the better result. Santos, the skipper of the side, and Borras were booked for dangerous tackles, in a match that was not for the faint-hearted.

MATCH REPORT: Joe Harvey could not have wished for a better start as Pop Robson, two minutes into the game, produced the spectacular to send the crowd into raptures. Alan Foggon picked up the ball in midfield and slipped it straight to Robson, out on the right wing. Without breaking stride, he raced into the middle then struck a thunderous drive from 30 yards that left the goalkeeper rooted to the spot. It was Robson's 20th goal of the season, and the best by far.

The goal sparked some invention in the Zaragoza side that now needed to score to save the tie. Iam McFaul was soon called into action to make a courageous dive at Bustillo's feet following a fine through ball from Martin. And the Irish goalkeeper has delighted to see a Bustillo header flash over the top of the bar on 23 minutes.

But six minutes later Frank Clark, not known for his ventures into opposition territory, charged down the wing and won a corner. Robson crossed the ball and had the nervous goalkeeper in a flap. Nieves managed to punch it but he got no distance and Tommy Gibb charged through to react quicker than any defender and head in the goal that put United 4-3 up on aggregate.

Four minutes later Nieves collided with Foggon and he had to be carried off. The goalkeeper was replaced by Alarcia, and, not long after that, the tie was thrown into the balance when Santos scored. The striker made and scored the goal himself. He charged through midfield before playing a one-two with Bustillo, then brought the ball down, changed feet, and hammered the shot past McFaul.

Half-time: Newcastle Utd 2 Real Zaragoza 1

Davies was a massive threat to the Spanish side and he was hammered into the ground by Gonzales in the 60th minute, then things started to get very ugly. David Craig had been injured and replaced by Guthrie, and more than once the match threatened to boil over.

Gibb, having the game of his life, tested the reserve goalkeeper twice in a short period of time. Robson made a brilliant run in the 77th minute and tried his luck from 20 yards, and Davies had a bullet header miraculously saved by the 'keeper. It was frantic stuff, and still Newcastle kept roaring on looking for a third goal.

Two minutes from the end it looked as though Robson had made absolutely certain when from six yards he hammered in a shot from Gibb's free-kick, but somehow Alarcia managed to fall on it. Then some fans thought the referee had blown the final whistle and hundreds of young boys ran onto the pitch. It took police several minutes to get them off.

Although Harvey was proving an amazing success at handling continental tactics, his players were finding it a culture shock trying to get used to 'off the ball' incidents. Davies took a hammering all night from Santamaria and Borras and he left the field nursing a fair crop of bruises, including a black eye.

Another memorable night of European football at St James' Park as the Geordie crowd roared their heroes to victory and a place in the quarter finals for the Fairs Cup. They went into the last eight by virtue of scoring two away goals.

The result shocked a lot of people, particularly two high profile gentlemen at Elland Road – Jack Charlton and Don Revie – who had predicted a certain defeat for the Geordies.

Joe Harvey: "We started this competition as rank outsiders. No one gave us a chance, yet we have gone on and on. Give the lads every credit. It is a tremendous feat and this is a young side. Can we go further? We will give it a good try. We are learning all the time and we have a crowd right behind us whenever we step out at St James' Park. It all depends on the luck of the draw. Pop Robson gave us a tremendous start. I was on my feet when the ball crashed into the net. We did not allow them to get into the game. The second half was all ours. We could have got five!"

Cesar Rodrigues (Real Zaragoza manager): "I thought United played better in Spain than tonight, but the Robson goal is one of the best goals I have ever seen."

Pop Robson: "When I got the ball I saw a gap. I moved between the two defenders and I was surprised that no-one came to meet me. I just cracked the ball without aiming for any particular spot."

United made it into the quarter-finals to be joined by Glasgow Rangers, Atletico Bilbao, Leeds United, Vitoria Setubal, Göztepe A.Ş., SV Hamburg and Ujpest Dozsa.

March 12 1969 - NEWCASTLE UTD 5 VITORIA SETUBAL 1

McFaul, Craggs, Clark, Gibb, Burton, Moncur, B Robson, Horsfield (Sinclair), Davies, Scott, Foggon.

Att: 57,662

Another Portuguese club, this time a side Harvey admitted he knew nothing about. But they had knocked out Italian giants Fiorentina on their way to the quarter finals and, prior to that, had hammered French side Olympique Lyon 7-1 on aggregate.

MATCH REPORT: The snow fell from the heavens and we learnt afterwards that some of the Setubal players claimed they had never seen snow before. In blizzard conditions the Setubal ball-playing stars failed to find their footing and Newcastle brushed them aside as though they were of no consequence. This was not a football match – this was a massacre.

Two goals up at half-time, and another three in the second period, yet some reporters gave Setubal's veteran goalkeeper Vital 'Man of the Match', showing that it could have been even a whole lot worse than this shattering score-line suggested for the Portuguese.

Setubal started the game with the North Sea wind and snow on their backs, and to their credit, they tried to play one-touch football and got their rewards with two corners in quick succession. Nothing came of them, but there was 'intent' there, and they were going to show willing until someone got the better of them.

But Newcastle gradually started to step up their own pace, and one man started to dictate the play – Jim Scott. He was switched into the middle as a linkman to provide the ammunition for Pop Robson and Wyn Davies, and he gave a superlative display of incredible skill and accuracy of passes.

Vital made a great save from Robson on 13 minutes, but then United got the show on the road when they scored ten minutes later. Davies went deep into midfield to get the ball and made ground into the Setubal penalty area before finding the overlapping David Craggs. His cross was met by Alan Foggon, who headed past the diving goalkeeper.

In the 37th minute United went two up because of a mix up in the Setubal rearguard. Craggs put over a free-kick that Vital seemed comfortable with, but his own defender Carrico headed the ball out of his hands and straight into the path of Robson. The striker took little encouragement to thrash it home off a defender's legs.

Half-time: Newcastle Utd 2 Vitoria Setubal 0

In the 59th minute the Magpies got their third goal when Davies seemed to make a mess controlling a cross from Frank Clark. The ball skidded away from him, but he regained control and put the ball into the net as Vital dived at his feet. But the Portuguese players surrounded the Swedish referee and almost carried him across the pitch to a linesman who seemed to have flagged for offside. The referee eventually came out of the mob with his shirt collar half torn off, pointing to the centre-circle insisting the goal was going to stand.

Robson slammed in a fourth from close range but Setubal pulled it back to 4-1 with seven minutes remaining when Jose Maria beat Iam McFaul.

However, Tommy Gibb had the last word a minute from time with a crisp left-foot shot, following good work from Jackie Sinclair.

The Setubal manager **Fernando Vaz** conceded the tie, saying: "We are not in with a chance now. There are too many goals to pull back. God saved Newcastle! The conditions were all against us. As soon as I saw the pitch I knew we had no chance. My players could not feel any warmth in their arms, legs and feet.

"The referee was not good. He was not neutral. The third goal should have been disallowed. Davies was five metres offside. The linesman flagged and Davies said to one of my players that he was offside."

Joe Harvey calmly disagreed: "One game at a time. We are not in the semi-final yet. We don't want to be heroes out there and lose. The third goal was a good goal. The linesman pointed to the centre. The referee was manhandled by the players. He showed me scratches around his neck after the game."

March 26 1969 - VITORIA SETUBAL 3 NEWCASTLE UTD 1

McFaul, Craggs, Clark, Gibb, Burton (McNamee), Moncur, Sinclair, B Robson, Davies, Scott, Foggon.

Att: 34,000

Setubal is about 50km south of Lisbon on the west coast of Portugal, and there was a 34,000-capacity full house at the Estádio do Bonfim for the visit of the Tynesiders. The home side were going through their 'Golden Decade', having won the Portuguese cup twice and been losing finalists twice in a space of four consecutive years between 1965 and 1968. However, they weren't regarded as being part of the Portuguese 'Elite Three' (Porto, Sporting Lisbon and Benfica) simply because they had yet to win the league title.

MATCH REPORT: Joe Harvey said he didn't want Geordie heroes to go all out to attack, and he was happy to let Setubal have early possession. But United played a dangerous game because they didn't silence the crowd and Setubal grew in confidence. The Portuguese side made in-roads by forcing Newcastle to concede a succession of corners. The turning point could have been in the fourth minute when striker Jose Maria had a golden opportunity to score but he mistimed his shot with the goal at his mercy. That early goal, had he scored, could have changed the outcome.

Although the Toon boss set out his stall to defend, his players realised they needed an outlet to get the ball out of their own half. Harvey had enough forwards with pace to trouble the home side on the break, and Jim Scott did just that. But Vital made a spectacular save to rob the former Hibernians inside-right of the first goal of the match.

Just when it seemed Newcastle's defenders were handling the pace, the Portuguese side snatched the lead. Defenders were ball-watching on 26 minutes as Portuguese international Figueredo floated over a ball for Arcanjo to head home. It was a wake up call, suddenly Newcastle sprung to life and they were unlucky not to equalise in the 38th minute when Vital made a staggering save to take the ball off Pop Robson's toe. But minutes later Davies scored the goal (a header at the far post) that made the dressing room half-time talk a lot easier for the Newcastle gaffa.

Half-time: Vitoria Setubal 1 Newcastle Utd 1

Petita replaced the injured Cardosa and soon made his mark. On the hour he blazed home a 20-yard free-kick to give Setubal a glimmer of hope, and five minutes later Figueredo had the 34,000 crowd on their feet with the third headed goal of the match.

It set up a grandstand finish as Newcastle had to soak up the relentless pressure, leaving Jackie Sinclair the lone soldier on the half-way line looking for a counter attack. Davies played his part in defence, as did everyone else, and it was a frantic finale.

The last 15 minutes saw several angry clashes between players, but Bobby Moncur, John McNamee and Wyn Davies stood up to severe intimidation as the home side saw their dreams of qualification ebbing away.

No-one buckled, it was calm heads all round, and Newcastle got the result they deserved.

May 14 1969 - GLASGOW RANGERS 0 NEWCASTLE UTD 0

McFaul, Craig, Clark, Gibb, McNamee, Moncur, Scott (Sinclair), B Robson, Davies, Arentoft, Foggon.

Att: 75, 580

Rangers were, arguably, the strongest side left in the competition and they were the last team Joe Harvey wanted to be drawn against. However, the tie in Scotland was the one game in our European campaign that was assessable to the travelling fans – financially - with no need for boats or planes. 12,000 Geordies made the journey over the border.

This was 1969 and football violence was just starting to hit the newspapers. Manchester United fans were getting a growing reputation for trouble, and I had seen the odd rumble at St James' Park, although nothing major. Remember, the 60s was the decade when some north-east football fans would go to St James' Park one week and Roker Park the next (God forbid). I doubt it very much if it happens these days.

The English and Scots had long been uneasy bed-partners, anyway, and as for Glasgow – it was already a battleground for football fans. No derby in Europe is as ferocious as the Old Firm fixture, and football in Glasgow can simply be an excuse to mask the religious divide. Today both clubs insist religion plays no part anymore, but back in the 1960s Rangers had a strict policy of refusing to sign Catholics.

The English may have invented the game, but as far as football stadiums are concerned, the Scots refined it. While the majority of early English grounds were relatively small, by 1908 Glasgow boasted the three largest football grounds in the world – Hampden Park, Celtic Park and Ibrox. I have been to Ibrox scores of times and every visit is an occasion. Without trying to step on the toes of any religion, and Rangers fans probably won't thank me for saying it, but the place is the cathedral of all stadiums. You feel the tradition, the pride and the achievement the second you walk through the gates.

MATCH REPORT: May 14th 1969 was the day two players became Geordie legends - Iam McFaul for saving a penalty, and John McNamee for relegating Rangers star striker Colin Stein to mediocrity. Stein won nothing in the air; nothing on the ground; and he was reduced to being nothing more than a spectator as 'Big Bad John' ran the show. McNamee expected a hostile reception, having played for Celtic, and he got one. But he stoked the fires by saying "I will put Stein in my pocket", and he wasn't wrong. As well as McNamee's Celtic connection, Jackie Sinclair had scored five goals against Rangers in six games for Dunfermline, so the Gers knew all about the threat he posed. Jim Scott's brother, Alex, had starred for Rangers and Tommy Gibb had played for the "other" club in Glasgow – Partick Thistle, so there were many reasons for a 'difficult' confrontation.

It was an unforgettable experience for the visitors, and it could have been even better had Wyn Davies taken the chance that was presented to him early in the game when Sandy Jardine dropped a howler and let him head straight for goal. But he scuffed his shot and let the home side off the hook.

Pop Robson made a similar mistake minutes later when he went one-on-one with the goalkeeper. He made the snap decision to try and lob Neef but put the ball high and handsome into one of the stands.

Benny Arentoft had signed for Newcastle for £18,000 from Greenock Morton in February, and no disrespect to the man, because he was a fabulous player for Newcastle United, but I could never understand how he was allowed to play in the Fairs Cup because he had played against Chelsea in an earlier round.

There was a 'cup tied' rule in the European Cup, so either the law was different for the Fairs Cup, or no-one noticed and he slipped through the net.

Arentoft was a player who excelled in the 'marking' game. Give him a target and he would stick to it like glue, and Rangers skipper John Gregg didn't take kindly to the little Danish midfielder 'doing what he does best' on Ibrox soil and promptly upended him. Gregg was booked and it took the sting out of his game.

In the 35th minute McFaul clashed with Orjan Persson in what looked like a 50-50 challenge but the referee pointed to the spot as the Swede went down like only Swedes do, as though he had collided with a Tiger tank. The protests by Newcastle players were waved away and Andy Penman stepped up to do the deed, but McFaul read his shot perfectly, diving to his right to palm the ball away.

Half-time: Rangers 0 Newcastle Utd 0

The penalty save seemed to have knocked the stuffing out of the Rangers players and the second-half was bitty and never free-flowing. Personal battles built up and McNamee was spoken to by the referee for kicking Stein up a height – just for good measure – and Jackson and Robson had a bit of a spat later on. Davies suffered a broken nose, but that just seemed like a day at the office for the tough Welshman, and it happened often.

Henderson was the one Rangers player willing to have a go at the Newcastle defence but the first sign of danger saw Davies and Alan Foggon drop back to help Frank Clark to crowd him out and stifle the threat.

Penman and Jackson had efforts on goal but nothing that troubled McFaul, and Sinclair's introduction as substitute for Scott was probably too late in the game to have an effect.

Joe Harvey said: "We have done this part of the job, now it's up to us to finish it off".

Rangers boss **David White**: "It's only half-time in the tie. We are certainly not despondent about the return match. It should be an exciting match".

May 21 1969 - NEWCASTLE UTD 2 GLASGOW RANGERS 0

McFaul, Craig, Clark, Gibb, Burton, Moncur, Scott, B Robson, Davies, Arentoft, Sinclair.

Att: 59,303

The atmosphere around St James' Park, and in the city centre, was intimidating rather than being a football celebration. The Scots, to their credit, had welcomed the Geordies the previous week and both sets of supporters had mixed without major incident. But this day was contrary to anything I'd seen before. The tartan hordes literally took over the city, most carrying 'swally bags' of whisky and whatever alcohol they could get their hands on.

They called this "The Battle Of Britain" but it brought shame to Scottish football. Rangers fans invaded the pitch to try and get the game stopped, and we saw the most amazing scenes any of us had ever seen.

With only ten minutes to go, and shortly after the referee had broadcast to the fans that the players would leave the field should Rangers fans encroach the field of play, hundreds of Rangers fans ran from the Gallowgate End hurling bottles. They came on with the obvious intention of forcing the referee to abandon the game so that their club could have another chance of reaching the final. Police confronted them by the Main Stand and immediately more fans surged onto the pitch. All in all, over 100 fans were injured as Scottish supporters charged through the Newcastle streets after the game looking for trouble.

MATCH REPORT: The match took a long time to get into gear as both sides, knowing the price of failure, seemed petrified to go a goal behind. There were odd half-chances as Pop Robson saw his effort well saved by Neef and at the other end McKinnon stung McFaul's fingers.

But, like at Ibrox, it was another ill-tempered game that didn't live up to the occasion. Just before half-time Davies and McKinnon carried on from where they left off in the first leg and stood toe-to-toe trading punches. It escalated as more players joined in, and it quickly got worse when Rangers fans swarmed to the touchline to throw bottles at players wearing the black and white stripes. It was sickening, but even more concerning was the fact that there was no hint as to how it was going to end. There was fear that if Rangers scored they would charge the field, but even more worrying was the reaction if Newcastle scored.

Half-time: Newcastle Utd 0 Rangers 0

Finally, after 53 minutes someone created a goal-scoring opportunity … and took it! McKinnon gave the ball away and let Jim Scott cut in from a wide position. The Scottish international struck the ball beyond Neef and into the far corner of the net to put Newcastle ahead in the tie. The Geordies celebrated and some spilled onto the field, which had the police showing concern it may provoke another Rangers pitch invasion, but that didn't happen.

With 13 minutes remaining, Jackie Sinclair latched onto a Davies knock-down and thundered the ball into the net, and that was enough for the visiting fans. We saw scenes that defied belief.

For 17 minutes the police tried to restore order using dogs; announcements were made over the PA system for the Rangers fans to leave the pitch; and at one point Rangers officials even considered calling off the game and handing the tie to Newcastle.

The German goalkeeper, Neef, was one of the victims hit with a missile, and after the game there were calls for Rangers to be banned from European competition.

However, **John Lawrence** the Rangers chairman played it down: "I consider a small percentage of our supporters have brought disgrace to our club."

Joe Harvey only wanted to talk about the game: "The goals were tremendous. We had worked on this beforehand, for the wingers to cut inside the full-backs.

At half-time I told the lads to keep their heads. We have grown up in the competition. The youngsters have brought pride to Tyneside."

May 29 1969 - NEWCASTLE UTD 3 UJPEST DOZSA 0

McFaul, Craig, Clark, Gibb, Burton, Moncur, Scott, B Robson, Davies, Arentoft, Sinclair (Elliott).

Att: 59,234

Newcastle faced their first final since the 1955 Wembley FA Cup final against Manchester City, and once again Jack Charlton and Don Revie gave the Magpies "no chance". To be honest, it was welcome news, because the pair of them hadn't got a single prediction right all season. Ujpest Dozsa won both home and away against their beloved Leeds, 0-1 and 0-2, and they didn't predict that, either! So, understandably, they didn't believe Newcastle would do any better. So much so, Revie said: "Newcastle won't win even if they borrowed George Best and Bobby Charlton".

I take it Best and Charlton must have been on holiday sunning themselves on a foreign beach, because they didn't make it into the Newcastle team, and Joe Harvey happily went with the same side that beat Rangers.

MATCH REPORT: The Hungarians boasted a formidable strike-force of Antal Dunai and Ferenc Bene, but they were kept under lock and key by Newcastle's defence throughout the first leg. But, for the fist 45 minutes, it was Ujpest defender Solymosi who was probably the star of the show. Wyn Davies, Pop Robson, Benny Arentoft and Jim Scott always looked threatening, until they got into the box and the ball seemed to stick to the Hungarian sweeper like glue. He put in an inspired first-half, although Davies tried to unsettle him with a couple of knocks.

Robson tried an ambitious overhead kick that whistled over the bar, and the goalkeeper scrambled across his goal when he tried to plant a header inside the post. But five minutes before the break Ollie Burton's sloppy back-pass eluded McFaul for a split second and it seemed as though Bene was going to make up the ground to tap it into the net. However, thankfully, McFaul got there before the Hungarian international. Then a minute later McFaul made a magnificent save, clawing away a Solymosi thunderbolt free-kick that seemed destined for the top corner.

Half-time: Newcastle Utd 0 Ujpest Dosza 0

Newcastle regained control at the start of the second period and twice goalkeeper Szentmihalyi was forced to tip over efforts that threatened to catch him off his line, firstly from Tommy Gibb, then a 25-yard shot from Benny Arentoft.

But the breakthrough came courtesy of inspired skipper Bobby Moncur. Gibb chipped a free-kick into the penalty area and Davies took a touch before hitting a volley straight at Szentmihalyi. The goalkeeper didn't know much about it and it bounced back into play, ideally positioned for Moncur to strike it left-footed into the far corner of the net.

It was a bitter blow to the Ujpest players and they seemed rocked by it. In the 73rd minute they buckled again when Moncur went on an amazing charge through the middle of the park, and no-one was able to stop him. He used Arentoft for a wall-pass, then went into bulldozer mode. I'd swear he seemed to lose control at least twice, but then the ball appeared at his feet again, and when he could see the whites of Szentmihalyi's eyes he drove a screamer straight into the back of the net. St James' Park went mental!

Ujpest almost replied with a goal of their own but McFaul was equal to Dunai's effort. Then Jim Scott lit the touch-paper for Geordie delight with a goal seven minutes from time, carved out with Joe Harvey's classic tactic. Joe had it drilled into his wide men: "take on the full-back, cut inside and try a dig".

It was a great performance from the whole team, although Jackie Sinclair was probably the one exception. He had an off-day and was substituted by Dave Elliott.

After the game it was thought **Wyn Davies** had played with a broken cheek bone, but the towering striker played it down before being rushed to hospital for an X-ray ... "I'm going to play in the second leg regardless what the doctors tell me!"

Bob Moncur: "We will win the cup, I'm sure of that. If we don't win it now we never will! I have only scored in friendly matches for Newcastle, but I have been saving those two goals for a special occasion."

Joe Harvey: "We were too nervous in the first-half, too edgy. I think the lads were a little worried about the reputation of our opponents. In the second half they realise there was no Puskas in their ranks and we started to play."

It was chairman **Lord Westwood** who said: "We are just daft enough to win it" before the competition started, and he praised the Newcastle fans after the game, "they are the best fans in the world!"

June 11 1969 - UJPEST DOZSA 2 NEWCASTLE UTD 3

McFaul, Craig, Clark, Gibb, Burton, Moncur, Scott (Foggon), B Robson, Davies, Arentoft, Sinclair.

Att: 34,000

The Megyeri Uti Dozsa Stadion is situated in north Pest, as the river Danube splits the city into two districts - Buda and Pest. Although every club in the capital lives under the shadow of mighty Ferencvaros, Ujpest are actually Hungary's oldest club, being formed in 1885 – 14 years before their neighbours 'The Green Eagles'.

This was Ujpest's chance to even up the score, as Ferencvaros had an impressive Fairs Cup record of winning the competition in 1965 when they beat Juventus in the final, and losing the final in 1968 to Leeds United.

Dozsa Stadion was a very primitive structure in 1969. It held 34,000 and was a sell-out for the final, but was a completely open bowl. We thought Dozsa was the district the ground was situated in but apparently the club was named after a sixteenth-century noble called Gyorgy Dozsa who led a peasants revolt against the Turks.

MATCH REPORT: A date with destiny. June 11th – and on Joe Harvey's 51st birthday.

Has there ever been a club competition played so late in the season?

While the Newcastle players had two weeks kicking their heels waiting for this second leg, six of the Ujpest players (Szentmihalyi, Kaposzta, Zambo, Bene, Gorocs and Dunai) were in Dublin for a World Cup qualifier, and just arrived back in Budapest the day before this match. That must have gone in Newcastle's favour, because it was hardly ideal preparation for the Ujpest team.

If the Magpies thought this cup was in the bag, as Bob Moncur predicted, they were about to get the shock of their Fairs Cup lives. Ujpest went at them like a rabid dog and for 45 minutes it was almost total one-way traffic.

They pushed forward and got a corner after 30 seconds and that set the pattern of the play. Sinclair, who many felt would sit this one out after his poor performance in the first game, gave some welcome relief with a shot that went just wide, but then it was back to defending.

A break by Bene had Moncur pushed for pace, but the Toon skipper just managed to get a toe to the ball to get it back to Iam McFaul. Then seconds later Solymosi tried his luck from range and again McFaul was the saviour.

Robson had the chance to kill off the tie but he missed a sitter, with only the goalkeeper to beat.

McFaul pushed a Nosko shot onto the post, then minutes later Bene cut through the middle and finally got the break-though from close range.

United weathered the storm for the next 13 minutes, but conceded at the worst possible time just before the interval. Gorocs broke between two defenders and placed the ball past the advancing McFaul to put the tie back in the melting pot. It was a body blow of gigantic proportions and the Newcastle players headed to the tunnel shell-shocked.

Half-time: Ujpest Dosza 2 Newcastle Utd 0

Moncur looked for inspiration from the manager in the dressing room, but Joe Harvey was as stunned as the players and stood in silence. Moncur said to him: "If there is ever a time for a good half-time team talk, Joe ... NOW is that time!"

The players returned to the field and Newcastle pulled themselves together. They won a corner in the first minute of the restart and Sinclair placed his cross right into the heart of the Magyars' penalty area. 'Captain Fantastic' Moncur forced the ball over the line to make it 4-2 on aggregate, giving Ujpest a mountain to climb.

Five minutes later Sinclair started another killer move that ended up with Szentmihalyi picking the ball out of the back of his net. You never knew what you would get from the unpredictable former Leicester City left winger. He was a 'hot and cold' player that arrived at St James' Park with a massive price tag of £70,000, but didn't always deliver. But he had produced the goods against Rangers and he did the same here. He set up Scott with a snap-shot, and the ball bounced back kindly to Benny Arentoft, who hammered it home for the equaliser.

Scott limped off after 67 minutes and Alan Foggon brought his own kind of magic to the Hungarian stage. My granddad always insisted "Foggon runs as though he's carrying a bag of coals on his back", and in the 71st minute (just four minutes after his introduction) the 'coalman' went tearing through the middle in his own peculiar – but effective – fashion. He tore the Ujpest defence wide open and gave Szentmihalyi a piece of true Geordie thunder, a shot the goalkeeper couldn't hold. Pop Robson made sure it was a goal, but the ball was over the line before he got a touch.

Newcastle started to showboat, and the home fans started to slow-handclap their own players.

When the game finished and Moncur was presented with the cup, most of the home crowd had left the stadium. Lifting that trophy was a magical moment for the Newcastle skipper … but I don't think anyone realised at that time how long it would be before another player wearing the black and white stripes would lift silverware.

Joe Harvey: "The boys were just great. To fight back the way they did tonight is Newcastle! I was still convinced at half-time that we could win it. I told the boys that. I said all we needed was an early goal and Bobby Moncur went out and did it."

Liverpool manager, **Bill Shankly**, described Foggon's goal as "one of the best goals I have ever seen".

MAGPIES BRING THE CUP HOME!

As the Newcastle players walked down the stairs of the BAC 1-11 jet at Newcastle Airport, hundreds of fans perched on every available vantage point on the terminal buildings to give them a fabulous welcome home. When the Newcastle skipper lifted up the Fairs Cup the crowd went wild.

Some reporters suggested the occasion even outdid the reception Wor Jackie and the lads got when they brought the FA Cup back to Tyneside in 1951, 1952 and 1955, as the welcome stretched for nearly seven miles. Crowds lined the route as the team passed through small villages on the way to the city, escorted by two police cars. The convoy was completed by another coach carrying players' wives and press reporters.

Lorry loads of workmen caught up in the snarl of traffic, also stood and cheered as the team made their way to St James' Park. A banner saying: "Welcome Champions" was placed above the car park and each player got a great reception as they got off the coach.

An estimated 30,000 waited in the ground to see their heroes, and some had been there waiting for five hours.

Bobby Moncur spoke over the club PA system: "This is a great day in our sporting lives. We won the cup last night in Budapest, but it was a sorrow that we didn't win it at St James' Park for you".

The season started on August 3rd 1968 and finished on 11th June 1969 – 62 games in all - the longest in Newcastle United history.

CHAPTER TWO
INTER CITIES FAIRS CUP 1969/70

Bob Moncur

MANAGER: Joe Harvey

Joe Harvey went into the new campaign with only one major signing, the acquisition of Aberdeen wonder winger Jimmy Smith for £100,000. 'Jinky' became a crowd pleaser, with his arrogant style of play, but it has to be said he didn't win over the Geordie faithful immediately. He found the pace of the English game far faster than what he had experience to the Scottish league.

HOW NEWCASTLE UTD QUALIFIED:

Newcastle were voted into the 1969/70 Fairs Cup competition the day after their win in Budapest. The Fairs Cup Assembly met in the Hungarian capital and voted to keep the bizarre 'one city – one club' rule, and without it the Magpies would not have qualified for the competition – even though they were holders.

United finished ninth in the First Division in their glory season in Europe, and Everton (3rd), Chelsea (5th) and West Ham (8th) would have kept them out. Liverpool ruined Everton's European hopes, and Arsenal scuppered the dreams of Chelsea and West Ham.

The meeting was concrete proof that the members made up the rules as they went along, and it became obvious why UEFA didn't want anything to do with the Fairs Cup, or whatever name it went under.

After the two hour meeting the president, Sir Stanley Rous, announced that the competition would be known in future as the European Fairs Cup – not 'Inter Cities' – even though they decided to stick with the 'city' rule.

He also said that if the final proved a draw after extra time the teams would be declared joint winners. "When a team has played 12 games to get to the final it is somehow not right that they might lose on the toss of a coin." The rule, again, had UEFA in disbelief. The European Cup had a winner, even if it meant a replay.

Penalty shoot-outs were a thing for the future, and not seen as a fair way of deciding games.

Newcastle's proposal that the holders should be included automatically in the following year's competition was defeated by 17 votes to 9.

Rous also said there would be no action taken against Rangers for the crowd invasion at St James' Park in the semi-final, as it was an incident neither club could have predicted or prevented.

The draw for the first round of the 1969/70 competition was made and Newcastle were drawn against Dundee United.

September 15 1969 - DUNDEE UNITED 1 NEWCASTLE UTD 2

McFaul, Craggs, Clark, Gibb, Burton, Moncur, Robson, Dyson, Davies, Arentoft, Smith.

Att: 21,000

This tie was probably a bring-down for the Newcastle players hoping for a more 'foreign' trip, such as Barcelona or Juventus, who were also in the draw. But it was a simple trip up the east coast for the Geordie supporters.

Approaching Dundee by train is probably as impressive an arrival point as any you will find anywhere in Britain, but as one Dundee United fan put it: "Yeah, it's a great view when you arrive ... but it hides the biggest dump in Scotland!"

Tannadice isn't exactly Ibrox or Celtic Park, either, but the view from the Grampian End is nothing short of spectacular, with all Fife's Kingdom in view.

Dundee United's kit of tangerine was first used when the team played under the bizarre name of Dallas Tornado in the United Soccer Association competition of 1967 ... which they were invited to participate in after their first European excursion in the Fairs Cup when they knocked out Barcelona. After persuasion by the wife of manager Jerry Kerr, the colour was adopted as the club's own in 1969 to give Dundee United a brighter, more modern image.

MATCH REPORT: Glasgow-born winger Jimmy Smith fitted into the team for his debut at Tannadice at the expense of Jackie Sinclair, who was close to the end of his Newcastle career. Joe Harvey went for a 4-3-3 formation, but placed 'Jinky' in the middle of the park, in a position he was not used to and he struggled to get into gear. Joe Harvey was going through an experimental phase, trying to get Newcastle into the top bracket of English clubs to challenge Leeds, Everton and Liverpool. He went continental for a while, trying to bring in fancy ball-players into his midfield, but Smith couldn't get to grips with the flying boots, and the battles in the middle of the park. He showed the occasional classy touch but the fiery Scots (knowing what a threat he could be) were soon on his case.

As usual, this Anglo-Scottish contest was feisty at best, brutal at worst, and no quarter was given by either side. Tommy Gibb and Benny Arentoft made up the midfield trio and they were both tenacious competitors. But Newcastle's strength in this game was two-fold, the defensive qualities of the irrepressible

Bobby Moncur and the mighty 'Wyn The Leap' who was quite simply outstanding.

Almost 3,000 Geordies made the trip, and they were vocal throughout, although they had more to shout about than the home fans.

The game started quietly but burst into life in the 10th minute when Ollie Burton floated over a superb free-kick that picked out Davies. The Dundee United back-line found him unplayable all evening. His header flew past goalkeeper Donald Mackay but crashed against the face of the bar. It was a warning, but the home side simply couldn't do much about the Welshman, and 14 minutes later he rattled the bar again. David Craggs was the provider, and Davies again saw the woodwork keep the Dundee side in the game.

Just before the half-hour mark the game was held up for three minutes when some of the crowd at the Tannadice End boiled over onto the pitch and several spectators were either taken out by police or helped off by ambulancemen.

The game restarted and both Alec Read and Tommy Gibb missed chances, before Burton cleared a ball off the line and Davies had Mackay flapping at another header.

Half-time: Dundee United 0 Newcastle Utd 0

In the 58th minute Newcastle broke the deadlock. Gibb sent David Craggs charging down the right wing, and the former England Youth international crossed the ball perfectly for Davies to rise above three defenders to beat Mackay once again … but this time find the back of the net.

Six minutes later Pop Robson provided the high ball into the middle and Davies repeated the deed to put the Magpies two goals up.

The tie was slipping away from the home side and the match turned nasty as tempers started to fray. Mackay went off with a deep gash to the head as Gibb went charging into him like a steam train, and the goalkeeper was rushed to hospital for an X-ray. The Irish referee gave Gibb a lecture and the midfielder knew he was lucky to stay on the pitch.

In the 77th minute the Arabs pulled a goal back through Scott, but the action didn't stop there. In the closing minutes McFaul was knocked out by a horror tackle from Reid. But he recovered after a couple of minutes attention and played on.

October 1 1969 - NEWCASTLE UTD 1 DUNDEE UNITED 0

McFaul, Craig, Clark, Gibb, McNamee, Moncur, Robson, Dyson, Davies, Smith, Foggon (Arentoft).

Att: 37,470

The Arabs (the nickname evolved because they once played a game with a pitch full of sand in an attempt to beat the frosty weather) came down to Tyneside in force. The Magpies had won only one league game in nine, crashed out of the League Cup to lower opposition, and Joe Harvey's free-flowing tactics were being questioned.

Bob Moncur did not mince his words: "We are in a bad run and struggling to get out of it. We are having a bad time of it but we have the spirit to back us."

MATCH REPORT: From the start Newcastle didn't seem to have a system they were comfortable with and they looked like eleven individuals that had never seen each other before.

Dundee Utd were hardly world-beaters, but they seemed to have a formation and a purpose. Newcastle only kept them at bay in the early period because of luck, rather than good management.

The best chance fell to Reid three minutes from half-time. His shot beat Iam McFaul but the ball struck the post and Mitchell made a right mess of the follow up.

Half-time: Newcastle Utd 0 Dundee Utd 0

The start of the second-half saw much of the same. Mitchell produced a class header that looked goal-bound but McFaul pulled off the save of the match to keep it out. Then Reid went close with a powerful drive.

Moncur tried to raise his side as the 37,470 started to get restless. If things go wrong the Geordie crowd do tend to pick out a scape-goat. Gibb was their main target on this occasion, but the Scot hardly looked interested. Sadly, he was not the only one. Alan Foggon left the field in the 63rd minute as Harvey switched the play by bringing on Benny Arentoft, but the Dane was just as ineffective.

The last ten minutes saw the Scottish side start to tire and chances came thick and fast at the visitors end of the pitch. Gibb missed a sitter (to the disgust of the Leazes End that became even more vocal in their frustration) and Keith Dyson had two wasted opportunities before he finally put the supporters out of their misery with a goal. Smith played the ball to the right of the goal and Dyson found the right spot - third time lucky!

Bob Moncur: "Give them credit, Dundee United did well, but I could never see them score the goals to put us out. I've always praised the Newcastle fans but tonight the language was terrible. We could hear the chants (from the Leazes End) on the pitch and we were disgusted."

Joe Harvey: "We were below par again. At the moment we are playing with a lack of confidence. That is reflected in the goals we are missing. The chances are there but we are struggling to put the ball in the net."

November 18 1969 - FC PORTO 0 NEWCASTLE UTD 0

McFaul, Craig, Clark, Gibb, Burton, Moncur, Robson, Dyson, Davies, Arentoft, Guthrie (Scott).

Att: 25,000

Porto's ground - Estádio das Antas - was situated in the Antas district of north-east Oporto (the club has moved grounds since 1969), on a rise that was found to contain prehistoric graves. It was very modern for the time and had floodlights - unlike the Portuguese national stadium.

During this period they were an 'also-ran' side of Portuguese football, 9th in the league when Newcastle arrived, and struggling to find any consistency.

On the other hand, the Magpies had suddenly hit a rich vane of form in the league, winning three matches on the trot, including a moral-boosting 3-0 win over the Mackems.

MATCH REPORT: The match was played in freezing conditions and there were serious doubts about the inclusion of Bobby Moncur, who missed training and was sent to the hotel with a high temperature. But come kick-off time, the Toon skipper was in his usual place, ready to battle Porto … and the flu.

Nobrega tested Iam McFaul in the opening seconds, but Ron Guthrie sent a message of intent up at the other end, although his effort flew wide.

The first-half was too-and-fro stuff with most of the efforts coming from distance. Benny Arentoft came closest of anyone with a fine drive that shaved the bar.

Davies headed a corner on target, and it wasn't particularly difficult to save, but goalkeeper Rui flew through the air like a trapeze artist in typical Latin fashion. He was certainly good entertainment value.

Half-time: Porto 0 Newcastle Utd 0

Porto's tactic to surprise and unsettle the Newcastle defence was obviously not working, but they didn't seem to have a plan B. So the second-half was very much the same.

United were very cautious and didn't want to attack in numbers, but probably had the best chances early in the second period. Davies was brought down just outside the penalty area and Tommy Gibb found Arentoft with the free-kick. He shot straight at Rui, and then had another chance minutes later when the goalkeeper miss-timed his clearance kick and kicked the ball of the Dane's head. The rebound went goal-ward, but Rui was equal to it.

November 26 1969 - NEWCASTLE UTD 1 FC PORTO 0

McFaul, Craig, Clark, Gibb, Burton, Moncur, Scott, Robson, Davies, Arentoft, Foggon.

Att: 44,833

A 0-0 result away from home in a European tie is the most precarious 'advantage' any team can have. It gives you confidence because you seem to have done the hard work on foreign soil, but drop a goal at home and the balance suddenly switches dramatically.

MATCH REPORT: It was déjà vu – just like the Setubal fixture, Newcastle faced a Portuguese side on a snow-covered St James' Park pitch. But any hopes of hitting five goals (as they did against Vitoria Setubal) were soon extinguished when Porto started moving the ball around as though they were playing on a Portuguese beach.

The Portuguese were out to win – but not necessarily within the rules. In the first minute young Alan Foggon was stopped as soon as he set off out of the traps by a body-check, and it was remarkable Wyn Davies managed to keep his shirt on his back for 90 minutes – because half a dozen players seemed intent on swapping it before the final whistle.

The nerves were eased, to a certain extent, by a goal from 30-year old Jim Scott. We didn't know it at the time but it was to be his last goal in a black and white shirt. Benny Arentoft took time away from harrying the Porto forwards to set up Scott with a pass that was made in heaven. It cut through the defence like a knife through butter and the Scottish international read it perfectly and scored the goal from the corner of the six-yard box.

1-0 to the Geordies ... but still Porto only needed one goal to knock us out.

Half-time: Newcastle Utd 1 Porto 0

Newcastle should have had a penalty in the 62 minute when Scott struck the ball past goalkeeper Rui and Sucena blatantly handled on the goal-line, but the referee waved play on.

Davies was his usual self - probing, battling, and generally making a nuisance of himself in the opposing penalty area. Unfortunately the off-form Pop Robson (nor anyone else for that matter) was incapable of picking up on his good work.

Pavao raced in on McFaul's goal to hit a tremendous drive but the goalkeeper just managed to get a strong hand to it and smother it at the second attempt. That was the moment that ended Porto's hopes of progression to the next round. Not long after, Rui was taken from the field, injured in an attack in which Tommy Gibb should have made absolutely certain of winning the tie. Gibb shot wide from three yards out, but gave the goalkeeper a little souvenir from Geordieland in the follow-through. Rui was taken off on a stretcher and number eight Salim took over in goal.

Newcastle were paired with Southampton. Better the devil you know? **Joe Harvey** was not impressed: "European games are for trips to Europe."

The old warhorse obviously didn't see a trip to the south coast as much of an excursion.

December 17 1969 - NEWCASTLE UTD 0 SOUTHAMPTON 0

McFaul, Craig, Clark, Gibb, Burton, Moncur, Robson, Dyson, Davies, Arentoft, Scott (Foggon).

Att: 38,163

Joe Harvey had other things on his mind during the build up to this fixture with a transfer swap involving Sheffield Wednesday. The deal saw 'Magpie' Jackie Sinclair go to Hillsborough and 'Owl' David Ford move to St James' Park. Ford took a lot of convincing to sign for Newcastle, but he was involved in a serious car crash in which his fiancée was killed, and he was unsure about moving away from his family at Sheffield. Although Ford didn't actually play in this tie, many fans on the terraces didn't see the transfer as the answer to Harvey's striking dilemma because Ford had only scored one goal in his Sheffield Wednesday career.

The build up to this all-England tie was the prospect of the heavy-weight clash to frighten the life out of most boxers – Wyn Davies v former Newcastle defender John McGrath. Few Newcastle players have been more 'passionate' than Wyn and McGrath, and it was a case of 'light the touch-paper and stand well back'.

MATCH REPORT: The clash of the Titans DID happen, but the rest of the match had fans very disappointed. Davies and McGrath had a bit of a tussle in midfield in the 15th minute and some players claimed there was an ominous "crack" as a punch was thrown. McGrath stayed on his feet, but seconds later he ploughed into his own player, full-back Tony Byrne. Later McGrath was diagnosed as having a fractured cheekbone, although it was never clarified who gave him it, Davies or the accidental clash with Byrne.

In blizzard conditions, on a treacherous pitch, the Saints regrouped without McGrath, and took everything that Newcastle could throw at them.

Davies headed down for Dyson to try his luck in the first real attack of the game but goalkeeper Martin was equal to it. He was just as alert when Arentoft struck a pile-driver, and that was about the best we had to offer in a poor first-half.

Mike Channon frightened the Geordies when he seemed to hit the target two minutes from half-time, but his shot dipped over the bar.

With Pop Robson out of sorts and Keith Dyson playing a striking role he didn't particularly like, Joe Harvey was adding more grey hairs to this thatch.

Half-time: Newcastle Utd 0 Southampton 0

Southampton boss Ted Bates seemed to instil some self believe into his team during the half-time team talk and the Saints gave it a real go right from the restart. Welsh international Ron Davies had McFaul scrambling across his goaline with a decent header, then he set up Jenkins who wasted a great opportunity by blazing the ball high and wide.

The longer the game went on the better the Saints got and more rattled the Magpies became. Harvey needed changes but he surprisingly picked Jim Scott to be substituted, and he looked the most likely of the bunch to break the deadlock. He trooped off – never to play for Newcastle again. He signed for Crystal Palace in a deal worth £20,000. Alan Foggon came on but didn't give us anything we didn't have already.

The closest Newcastle came to a goal was a cross from David Craig that was headed against the post by Dyson.

Southampton had achieved two things that no foreign side had achieved to date – they stopped Newcastle from scoring at St James' Park – and stopped them from winning.

Perhaps Joe was right after all … "it was not a proper European game".

January 14 1970 - SOUTHAMPTON 1 NEWCASTLE UTD 1

McFaul, Craig, Clark, Gibb, McNamee, Moncur, Robson, Smith, Davies, Young (Guthrie), Ford.

Att: 25,182

This was the opposite to the Porto tie in that the Saints had their 0-0 draw – but all Newcastle needed was a goal to really upset the apple cart.

MATCH REPORT: Wyn Davies mis-kicked in front of goal in the second minute of this intriguing fixture at The Dell, but Southampton soon took control of the game and had the Newcastle defence back-peddling desperately for much of the first-half. Channon, Paine and Jenkins proved a lively trio, a little too hot to handle at times, as the Saints used Ron Davies much the same way as Newcastle used his Welsh striking partner Wyn Davies (no relation).

Even the unflappable Bobby Moncur was made to sweat. In the 16th minute Sydenham tried to get in a cross but the Toon skipper, trying to block the ball from reaching Ron Davies, saw it spin off his knee and head towards the top corner of the net. Only a desperate acrobatic save from Iam McFaul saved the day.

Three minutes later Ron Davies was the target man and he shot narrowly wide, and he did exactly the same a minute later as the Magpies struggled to cut out the service to him.

After 28 minutes Mike Channon headed in a pin-point Terry Paine free-kick. It was the least Southampton deserved as Newcastle failed to get in one seriously telling shot the entire 45 minutes.

Half-time: Southampton 1 Newcastle Utd 0

Only four minutes of the second half had passed before Wyn Davies produced the miss of the match. Gibb's low cross cut out the home team's defence to leave Davies the simplest of tap ins. But he lost his balance and appeared to tread on the ball, while new signing David Ford followed up and actually fell over it! It was a catalogue of errors and Southampton survived.

Ron Davies was less than an inch away from making it 2-0 in the 81st minute when he hit the underside of the bar, then Joe Harvey made his last throw of the dice by replacing David Young with Ron Guthrie. However, he had only been on the field 30 seconds when he was clattered to the ground by Ron Davies and for a moment it looked as though he would be stretchered off.

A fight broke out behind the Newcastle goal and McFall handed a missile to the referee that had been thrown at him, but luckily missed, and the atmosphere on (and off) the pitch got steadily worse.

Just six minutes remained and Newcastle got out of jail. The much-criticised 'Jinky' Jim Smith made his first start in five weeks after failing to impress following his big money summer signing, but he repaid a few coppers of the £100,000 fee by setting up Pop Robson for a stunning equaliser at a time the Saints fans were convinced they were heading for European glory. It came like a bolt out of the blue. Smith did the spade-work before crossing for Wyn Davies to head towards goal. Goalkeeper Martin punched it straight into the path of the on-rushing Robson and the ball ended up in the net.

On the final whistle several Southampton players jostled Gibb and he got embroiled in a fierce argument that escalated and Moncur had to drag him away. The home fans again started throwing missiles and a firework went off near Martin as he walked towards the tunnel.

Pop Robson was predictably overjoyed: "It was my first goal in Europe this season. How do I feel? What do you think?"

Joe Harvey: "We got the goal at the right time and we deserved it. I always believed we would score. People say we were lucky but how many times have Leeds got through in games like this?"

Bob Moncur: "They will have to kick the cup out of our hands to take it away from us".

QUARTER-FINALS:

RSC Anderlecht (Belgium) v Newcastle Utd

Hertha Berlin (W Germany) v Internazionale (Italy)

Dynamo Bacau (Romania) v Arsenal

Carl Zuis Jena (E Germany) v Ajax Amsterdam (Holland)

March 11 1970 - RSC ANDERLECHT 2 NEWCASTLE UTD 0

McFaul, Craggs, Guthrie, Gibb, McNamee (Burton), Moncur, Robson, Dyson, Davies, Smith (Elliott), Foggon.

Att: 30,000

There can be few better locations for a major football stadium than the Emile Versé Stadium that was situated in Astrid Park in the municipality of Anderlecht. However the ground has been totally rebuilt since this fixture in 1970 (and it now goes by the name Constant Vanden Stock Stadion).

Anderlecht were a highly competitive side and could boast five consecutive Belgian championships between 1964 and 1968.

MATCH REPORT: Although they didn't create much with their one-man strike force (Wyn Davies), for half an hour Newcastle looked to be comfortably containing the Belgian threat.

But the pride of Belgian football – Paul Van Himst – began to prise holes in the Newcastle rearguard, and once the dam was breached, McFaul faced the flood.

Jimmy Smith made an opportunity for himself and shot low and hard from eight yards but Trappeniers pulled off a superb save. However, the former Aberdeen winger fell badly and twisted his ankle, and struggled to get to half-time.

On 32 minutes Dutchman Jan Mulder set up Desanghere to open the scoring, and Newcastle were put under the cosh.

Half-time: Anderlecht 1 Newcastle Utd 0

Harvey hoped Smith could run off his injury and stuck with the Scot for the second-half.

The tough tackling from the Newcastle players didn't go down too well with the partisan home crowd, particularly a rather strong challenge by full-back John Craggs on Martens that left the Anderlecht defender in a heap. The referee booked the Newcastle player.

Puis made it 2-0 in the 62nd minute with a rocket free-kick from 25 yards and McFaul's goal spent the next half hour under siege. The Coleraine-born goalkeeper put in a fabulous performance as the shots rained on him, but he stood his ground.

Play was held up briefly while loudspeaker announcements asked the crowd to stop throwing fireworks on to the pitch.

Joe Harvey made a tactical switch, putting on Ollie Burton to try and add strength and height to support Davies up front. Sadly it made no impression in the final stages, and Anderlecht came very close to a third goal. Nordahl broke clear but McFaul charged out to make the save of the game and give his side a fighting chance in the second leg of this quarter final tie.

Joe Harvey: "We did not play as well as we could, but we are not disappointed. I still think we can do it at home."

March 18 1970 - NEWCASTLE UTD 3 RSC ANDERLECHT 1

McFaul, Craig, Clark (Young), Gibb, Burton, Moncur, Robson, Dyson, Davies, Guthrie, Foggon.

Att: 59,309

A crowd of 59,309 – even more than the attendance for the first leg of the Fairs Cup final against Ujpest Dosza – turned up at St James' Park to see the showdown of ALL showdowns. The Belgian side had a two goal advantage and Newcastle knew what was needed to stop their hard won trophy being snatched from their grasp.

MATCH REPORT: Newcastle threw down the gauntlet and Pop Robson's goal after only four minutes shook Anderlecht rigid. Kialunda, the towering Belgian defender, failed to clear Frank Clark's free kick any distance and sent it wayward across the penalty area. Robson nipped it to head it over the goalkeeper towards the goal-line. Foggon raced onto it to make sure and blast into the net, but the goal was given to Robson.

After 11 minutes Trappeniers punched away a Keith Dyson header and Robson came in to challenge the goalkeeper for the follow-up. The ball was there to be won, it was an honest challenge, but the referee booked Robson as everyone got caught up in the heat of the moment.

After 20 minutes Foggon picked up the ball from a throw-in and headed for the middle; he released Robson, who took a few steps before hitting an unstoppable shot into the top corner of the goal. Trappeniers didn't even sniff it!

Newcastle were level 2-2 and it was 'game on'!

But just when things were going so well Frank Clark, just back from injury, was carried off and sent to hospital for an X-ray on his leg. David Young took over at left-back and just before half-time Anderlecht started to regroup and look a dangerous side.

Half-time: Newcastle Utd 2 Anderlecht 0

Ten minutes into the second-half, Mulder out-paced the Newcastle defence but McFaul, the hero of the evening in Brussels, courageously dived at his feet to divert the ball for a corner.

Davies headed just wide from a free-kick as the home side took control again, and the crowd held their breathe as he lobbed the goalkeeper and the ball headed for the goal. But Heylens got back just in time to hammer it away.

It was amazing stuff, an atmosphere I will never forget. Foggon thrashed the ball goalwards and Trappeniers saved it, then at the other end (with only ten minutes left) Mulder drove a powerful shot that McFaul misread and the spinning ball bounced through his legs towards goal. Somehow he turned and lashed it way with his foot.

The seconds were ticking down, five minutes left, and Bobby Moncur produced another of his 'Captain Marvel' moments. He floated a free-kick from the left touchline to the near post and Trappeniers (for once) couldn't get near it. Dyson charged in and blasted the ball into the net – Newcastle Utd 3 Anderlecht 0.

St James' Park was bouncing with excitement, euphoria and relief. The impossible had been achieved.

But, sadly, someone should have told Anderlecht.

As they say in football circles: "You are never more vulnerable than when you have just scored".

Two minutes later Swede Tomas Nordahl and Van Himst broke away together. For the first time in the match the Newcastle defence was caught 'ball watching' and paid heavily for it. Van Himst played the ball to his left and Nordahl sent a screamer flying past McFaul.

It was a tragic end. The Newcastle players had given everything!

The final whistle was blown and Tommy Gibb collapsed on his back and gazed at the sky in disbelief.

The Fairs Cup dream was over.

Joe Harvey: "Well we may have gone out, but we have gone out like champions. The boys played some great stuff and I thought we were on our way again. I have never known a game like it – one minute we were through – next minute we were out. The man who scored the goal, Nordahl, scored with his left foot. The one he admits he only uses to stand on."

Arsenal won the Fairs Cup by beating Anderlecht in the final. The Belgians won 3-1 In Brussels; Arsenal won 3-0 at Highbury with goals from Eddie Kelly, John Radford and Jon Sammels.

CHAPTER THREE
INTER CITIES FAIRS CUP 1970/71

David Craig

MANAGER: Joe Harvey

Joe Harvey made changes to the squad in the summer, but nothing to break the bank, and certainly no big signing to get anyone excited. Stuart Barrowclough signed from Barnsley in a £33,000 deal, a 19-year old who only had nine league games on his CV, and was very much an unknown quantity. 24-year old Ian Mitchell came down from Scotland with a bigger reputation. He was signed from Dundee United for £50,000, was a Scotland Under-23 international (one cap), and was allegedly a left-winger with an eye for goal.

HOW NEWCASTLE UTD QUALIFIED:

Newcastle finished 7th in the First Division in the 1969/70 season behind Everton, Leeds United, Chelsea, Derby County, Liverpool and Coventry City. But once again the Magpies were extremely lucky to qualify for the Fairs Cup. Derby were banned from competing because of alleged irregularities in their books, and UEFA finally relented and allowed the holders of the Fairs Cup to defend their trophy, so Arsenal's inclusion left an extra place.

September 23 1970 - INTER MILAN 1 NEWCASTLE UTD 1

McFaul, Craig, Guthrie, Gibb, Burton, Moncur, Robson, Dyson, Davies, Arentoft, Young.

Att: 14,460

Newcastle didn't have the perfect start to their new European Fairs Cup campaign when they had problems with the aircraft that was due to fly them to Milan. It arrived at Newcastle Airport with a fuselage flap missing and the flight was delayed for hours as mechanics replaced it. But it was only noticed because the Dan-Air jet wouldn't start!

San Siro is the home of Inter and AC Milan – probably the most celebrated and successful ground-sharing arrangement in European football. The Milan clubs have co-existed since 1947.

The stadium is a fete of fabulous engineering, with its innovative ramp system (19 ramps in all) that makes it instantly recognisable. The ramps are access routes to the upper levels, as an addition to conventional stairways under the stands, and go around the stadium's outer walls.

Some fans call it 'Stadio dei Centomila', suggesting it holds 100,000, but the Italians love to exaggerate. The most it has ever held was 82,000.

Classed as Newcastle's coming-of-age game, facing the mighty Internazionale in the huge San Siro Stadium was a daunting prospect. But it was amazing how highly Heriberto Herrera rated Wyn Davies. The famous international coach said he "had plans for Davies", suggesting the Welshman was making quite a name for himself across Europe.

For some reason the Fairs Cup hadn't made much of a reputation for itself in Italy and most fans regarded it as a competition they could do without. The crowd of 14,460 was very disappointing for such a massive stadium, but it was larger than the attendance for the glamour tie of the Fairs Cup the previous season when they played Barcelona. An estimated 80,000 saw the first leg at the Nou Camp; only 10,000 turned up at the San Siro.

MATCH REPORT: The first half was an intriguing contrast of styles. Inter displayed some of their unquestioned skills but only sporadically, and although their one-touch play was impressive, it didn't get them any joy in the first half. Mazzola and Pellizaro were giants in the sport, and although they seemed potentially dangerous every time they had the ball, they never troubled Iam McFaul at all in the first 45 minutes.

Newcastle, on the other hand, kept it tight and simple and let the home team try and break them down. Then just when the Italians seemed to be getting a bit more adventurous, United hit them on the counter-attack. Pop Robson legged it clear but was taken out by an Inter defender on the edge of the box. The little inside-forward picked himself up and took the free-kick himself and produced a superb diagonal pass to pick out Davies. Whatever plan Heriberto Herrera had conjured up to stop the big striker, it didn't work, and Davies left the big name defenders stranded as he rose to head the ball into the net.

Half-time: Inter Milan 0 Newcastle Utd 1

I'm sure Moncur and his boys in the back-line braced themselves for a second-half onslaught, but it didn't happen until late in the game.

The plan was for the Milan players was to 'rough up' Davies (which they did) but rather than step up a gear, they went about their business in the usual patient Italian manner. Everything was at their own pace … the ethic being 'never panic'.

Striker Achilli struck the post with a powerful shot from distance in the 58th minute but it was an isolated threatening moment.

Everything the Italians did was built from the back and any attempt to pull the Newcastle players out of position failed. Harvey's side stayed disciplined through out the match and almost came away with an amazing result.

It was only in the last 20 minutes that the Italians started to push up the field and take chances, and suddenly McFaul was forced to work for his wage packet. He made three great saves but left-half Cella caught him out with five minutes left on the clock.

September 30 1970 - NEWCASTLE UTD 2 INTER MILAN 0

McFaul, Craig, Guthrie, Gibb, Burton, Moncur, Robson, Dyson, Davies, Arentoft, Young.

Att: 56,495

Nick Scurr of the Northern Echo gave a frank and candid description of this match: "In the face of the worst provocation and against the most ill-tempered and ill-behaved opponents it has been my misfortune to see – on any ground anywhere in over 25 years – Newcastle United reached the second round of the European Fairs Cup. Inter Milan gave the most disgusting display that has been seen on the St James' Park pitch."

Many went to the ground to see the Italian stars that had played against Brazil in the 1970 World Cup final (Facchetti, Burgnich, Mazzola and Boninsegna) but even though Newcastle United gave one of the best performances in the club's history, everyone came away disgusted at what they had just witnessed from arguably one of the greatest club sides in world football.

MATCH REPORT: As I said in the earlier report, Inter coach Heriberto Herrera said he had a "plan" for Wyn Davies, and it was blatantly obvious that "plan" was to see him carried off on a stretcher!

Central defender Facchetti was world famous, but his reputation went right down the pan (as far as the Geordies were concerned) for the most horrendous display of man-marking anyone in the crowd had ever seen, and I don't think I have seen anything like it since!

The Italians pulled everything out of the bag in this game. It started off a kicking match and gradually got worse. The turning point was on the half-hour mark when Newcastle scored. Frank Clark won a corner and Pop Robson crossed the ball close to the six-yard box. Vieri, the Italian goalkeeper, left his line and flapped at it but Moncur stole in unmarked and put the ball in the net. The 'keeper was livid. And less than a minute later he took out his frustration on Davies – who had already been kicked 'from pillar to post' by Facchetti. Davies stood by Vieri as he gathered the ball, but didn't touch the goalkeeper in any way, shape or form. Suddenly Vieri elbowed the Toon striker and the referee immediately gave an in-direct free-kick to Newcastle, even though it was a blatant penalty. The Inter players surrounded the referee and he went crashing to the ground, from what seemed like a punch from the goalkeeper. The Newcastle players walked away from the trouble as the police ran onto the pitch to break up a fracas between the Italians and the match officials. When the referee (Mr Minnoy) got to his feet he ordered off Vieri, but at first the player refused to leave the field of play.

There was confusion on the touchline and it seemed as though Inter were trying to sneak on a substitute to keep all eleven Milan players on the pitch. However, the referee spotted it and, in the end, they replaced number ten Achalli with reserve goalkeeper Borden.

Half-time: Newcastle Utd 1 Inter Milan 0

In the first minute of the second-half Tommy Gibb was sent crashing to the ground by Cella, and Corso punched David Young.

From a football point of view, Clark rattled the bar with a superb drive, and Moncur kept trying to push his players forward for a second goal.

Then came another two more moments of madness - Facchetti kneed Davies in the back and while the Welshman was writhing in agony on the ground, Bonninsegna punched Gibb in the face. Two incidents that would have seen both players sent off in any other game.

In the 70th minute Dyson sent a header crashing against the bar, then Davies followed up to head in the rebound to make it 2-0.

Two minutes from time Davies could have made it three when he headed a Robson free-kick past the substitute goalkeeper, but Cella cleared off the line.

Joe Harvey: "I am proud of my lads and the way they kept their heads, but I was very disappointed with Inter after we had such a fine game of football in Milan."

Bob Moncur: "If they won the fights … we won the match … and that is all that matters."

Heriberto Herrera: "I did not see the sending off. But my players say Vieri was pushed and collided with the referee."

October 21 1970 - NEWCASTLE UTD 2 PECSI DOZSA 0

McFaul, Craig, Guthrie, Gibb, Young, Moncur, Robson, Dyson, Davies, Smith, Ford.

Att: 50,550

MATCH REPORT: Like Inter Milan before them, the minnows of Hungary didn't know how to handle Wyn Davies, and he ran the show while Pop Robson had another off-night.

Jimmy Smith set up Moncur for a header in the 5th minute and the Toon skipper struck the bar, then three minutes later Robson had his best effort of the night when he shot from 25 yards and knocked the bulky Hungarian goalkeeper, Rapp, clean off his feet.

Then Pecsi had a couple of chances of their own, one from 35 yards that tried to catch Iam McFaul off his line, but he scrambled back and tipped the ball over the bar.

The first goal came just before the break when Davies soared high to head into the top corner of the net, but he suffered a bad cut to his head when he landed. He was taken off, but returned for the second-half.

Half-time: Newcastle Utd 1 Pecsi Dozsa 0

In the 58th minute Davies scored the second goal, this time from a David Ford corner, and it flew into the net off a defender's boot as he tried to clear off the line.

Everything constructive came from the brilliant Welshman, who again had Rapp struggling with a powerful header in the 62nd minute. And 11 minutes from time he thought he had collected the match ball with his first European hat-trick, and only his second ever hat-trick in Newcastle colours. He planted the ball into the net but the West German referee blew for offside. It would have been the first hat-trick since January 1967 when Newcastle beat Coventry City in the FA Cup 4-3.

The last ten minutes saw Newcastle rain a dozen shots at Rapp's goal, but the score remained 2-0.

November 4 1970 - PECSI DOZSA 2 NEWCASTLE UTD 0 (Pecsi win on pens)

McFaul, Craig, Guthrie, Gibb, McNamee, Moncur, Robson, Dyson (Mitchell), Davies, Young, Ford (Hindson)

Att: 25,000

Although Pecsi Dozsa had overtones of Ujpest Dozsa, the minnows were not from the Hungarian capital, but 125 miles south of Budapest close to the Yugoslav border. Or as one fan put it: "one hundred miles from anywhere!"

According to a newspaper at the time, Pecsi was officially a town "half the size of Newcastle, not dissimilar in character, having a university and mining community". In reality it was a place so remote and out of touch with the outside world it didn't have a hotel that could house all of the players. The squad had to split up, and some players had to share accommodation with press reporters.

Newcastle's new signing from Glentoran, Tommy Cassidy, missed out playing on the European stage because he had not been registered in time. He was substitute against Manchester United the previous Saturday but could not be considered for the game against Pecsi.

The match at the Stadium of Újmecsekalja was an afternoon kick-off and, such was the interest, it was shown live on Hungarian TV.

MATCH REPORT: Newcastle were warmly greeted by the Hungarian supporters, until the opening few minutes when the Magpies kept playing the ball back to Iam McFaul, and there were boos of derision for the negative play. Kinces was given the man-marking job on Wyn Davies and there were 'off the ball' antics that had the Welshman appealing to the referee.

Pecsi needed an early goal and it came on 18 minutes when Mate was extremely lucky to see his shot take an almighty deflection off a Newcastle defender and catch McFaul wrong-footed.

Davies tried a long shot that flew inches wide, but minutes later the Magpies had a major stroke of fortune when Bob Moncur was robbed in the penalty area and Mate missed a sitter.

Ronai was lectured by the Swiss referee for a terrible tackle on McFaul that left the goalkeeper hobbling, and it was obvious that Newcastle had to win a war - as well as the match. But despite all of the personal battles, with kicking and punching, that were going unchecked in every part of the pitch, Mate was booked for kicking the ball away.

Davies got free from his marker to get the very best out of Rapp on two occasions, then Pop Robson blasted hopelessly wide from a decent position. Rapp impressed the crowd by pulling a Ford corner out of the air one-handed, as he continued to get the better of everything thrown his way.

Davies was blatantly pushed in the back by Kinces, but the referee seemed reluctant to give a penalty because he didn't seem to want to upset the home support. He stopped, thought about it for a second, then let the play continue.

Half-time: Pecsi Dosza 1 Newcastle Utd 0

The crowd waved their purple and white banners and went ballistic when Ronai was sandwiched between two Newcastle defenders but the referee waved play to go on.

McFaul made a superb save from Toth as the home side pushed for a second goal, but the more they pushed up, the more vulnerable they were at the back. It took a desperate tackle to halt Keith Dyson from creating a shot at goal, and Davies had a stunning header cleared off the line by Konrad.

McFaul took a kick in the face and needed prolonged treatment before he was able to continue. And he was soon called into action to save from Ronai before Moncur made a last ditch tackle on the same player seconds later.

With just nine minutes to go, John McNamee tussled with Maurer on the left side of the penalty area and the referee pointed to the spot. Mate scored, much to the delight of the home supporters. The game ended 2-0, 2-2 on aggregate, and there was another 30 minutes of extra-time.

United had the best chance of the first 15 minutes when Davies headed a ball to Ford, but he failed to reach it to poke it into the net.

Ian Mitchell came on as substitute for his first (and last) taste of European action but, with chances missed at both ends, the tie had to be decided on penalties.

In truth, the penalties were a disaster for Newcastle. Konrad, Tuske and Dunai scored for the Hungarian side, while Robson, Mitchell and Gibb all missed.

Robson's hit the bar, Mitchell's was saved by the goalkeeper, and Gibb's shot hit the goalkeeper and bounced out after striking the post.

In a bizarre situation, the referee was informed AFTER the match that all ten penalties had to be taken, so Frank Clark and Iam McFaul went back out to take them while the rest of the players went in the bath. Both scored, making McFaul the first Newcastle goalkeeper to ever score in a competitive match. Pecsi missed one of their two, but Kinces scored the other.

Joe Harvey: "The field was a cow patch and the referee hadn't much of a clue. Talking about the penalites, we really lost this one when we were denied a clear penalty at St James' Park in the first leg when Tommy Gibb was brought down. However, it shouldn't have come to this. I told the players that all we needed was a single goal."

John McNamee: "I played the ball and not the man. All I did was put my foot in when the Hungarian player turned inside David Craig. As I turned the ball back to Iam McFaul, he threw himself over my right foot. The first goal was unfortunate, too, for the strong sunshine blinded me when the cross came over and I lost it. I volunteered to take a spot kick yet I was turned down even though some of the kickers were reluctant to shoulder the job. I scored ten out of 11 penalties in Scotland and I wasn't a bit nervous. I'm fed up at that decision."

Bob Moncur: "We didn't tell the boys beforehand merely because we didn't want the responsibility preying on their minds during the game and upsetting their natural play. What upset our plans were the two substitutions. It meant we had to think again. But anyone who blames our first three penalty kickers for our exit is looking for trouble."

Leeds won the competition by drawing 2-2 in Turin and 1-1 at home, to beat Juventus on the away-goals rule.

* Pesci Dozsa don't exist anymore. In 1973 four clubs - Pécsi Dózsa, Ércbányász SC, Helyipari SC and Pécsi Építők – disbanded to form Pécsi Mecsek FC.

CHAPTER FOUR
UEFA CUP 1977/78

Alan Gowling

MANAGER: Richard Dinnis

Richard Dinnis was Gordon Lee's number two during a strange period in Newcastle's history. Joe Harvey had resigned in 1975 after 13 years in the hot seat and the club directors made a short list of prospective managers, but many turned them down. Gordon Lee was well down on that list ... but he took the job.

Malcolm Macdonald hadn't even heard of the former Port Vale boss, and when he walked into his office for the first time he called him 'Lee Gordon'.

Lee was a controversial choice when he arrived at Tyneside - and a hated figure when he left. He walked out in a sensational manner in January 1977 to join Everton, and the Newcastle players insisted his assistant, Richard Dinnis (as an attempt at some sort of unity), should get the job.

It was a difficult situation because the directors knew the fans were unhappy at the appointment of Lee, and they believed there would be similar unrest if they made Dinnis the boss. After all, he was a qualified coach and PE instructor, and nothing more. He had no managerial experience at all. But the players 'revolt' of 1977 will long be remembered because the directors backed down and 'player power' won the battle. And the fans, although far from happy, gave Dinnis a chance.

HOW NEWCASTLE UTD QUALIFIED:

Gordon Lee (despite selling fans' favourites Terry Hibbitt and Malcolm Macdonald) left the club in a decent position. We had reached the League Cup final and were well placed in the league. Dinnis kept it ticking over very nicely and we finished fifth that season – behind Liverpool, Manchester City, Ipswich Town and Aston Villa. We qualified for the UEFA Cup – fairly and without dispute.

September 14 1977 - BOHEMIANS 0 NEWCASTLE UTD 0

Mahoney, D Craig, Kennedy, Cassidy, Bird, Nattrass, Barrowclough, Cannell, Burns, Callachan, T Craig.

Att: 25,000

Bohemian's Dalymount Park stadium is situated on Dublin's Northside at Phibsborough, and how it was allowed to host major international fixtures defied belief. The history of the place probably says it all, because it was originally common land with a large vegetable plot known as 'Pisser Dignam's Field' until it was taken over by Bohemian F.C. I'm sure Pisser was a decent enough chap, despite his name.

Affectionately known as 'Dalyer' by Bohemians fans, it was also historically the "home of Irish football" hosting Irish internationals. However, the ground was hardly developed from the 1940s, and when Newcastle arrived in 1977 it was like being transported back in time.

If there was an underlying current in fixtures between the English and the Scots in the 70s, a visit to Southern Ireland was going to be even more emotional. In the north - Belfast was a battle ground; in the south - Dublin was a tinder-box. To many in the Irish crowd, this was far more than a sporting event, and we had faced abuse right from the second we got off the ferry from Stranraer.

MATCH REPORT: New signing Ralph Callachan made his debut, after his transfer from Hearts, but it was a deal only Newcastle could have dreamt up. Manager Richard Dinnis was not involved and didn't even know of the player. It was a signing made by one of the club directors after he had been on holiday to Edinburgh and seen Callachan play.

Newcastle's plan at the start was to take the pace out of the game and take control of the midfield. Yet surprisingly, playing against £13-a-game Irish part-timers, it took some doing. But the hostile atmosphere played a major part in this game, and the Newcastle players were well aware that a riot could erupt at any time.

Full-backs David Craig and Alan Kennedy held it together at the back, keeping the unpredictable Gerry Ryan at arm's length, and Tommy Cassidy fully justified his recall.

The closest anyone came to a goal in the first-half was a spell when Micky Burns brought out a save from goalkeeper Smyth and, from the corner, Irving Nattrass's header was cleared off the line by the full-back.

The Geordies in the crowd gave the players a great reception as they left the field.

Half-time: Bohemians 0 Newcastle Utd 0

In the second period we saw the unacceptable side of European football when goalkeeper Mick Mahoney was felled by a bottle thrown from the crowd and the teams were taken off the field for 14 minutes. Missiles of all description were thrown onto the Dalymount Park pitch as Mahoney was receiving treatment. Tommy Craig ran to the Geordie fans and appealed with them not to retaliate. Half a building brick flew past Micky Burns' ear. Less than a dozen police were on duty and the Irish supporters threw bricks and sticks at the visiting fans. Police had to be brought in from three miles away.

But it was nothing that this place had not seen before, because the same had happened two years previously when the Republic played a Nations Cup tie against Turkey and the Turkish goalkeeper was knocked unconscious by a flying object. That said, how on earth did the organisers of this fixture (which was obviously high risk) expect ten policemen to handle a crowd of 25,000?

When the game re-started Bohemians had their one and only chance of the night, Ryan split the Newcastle defence with a neat ball and Turlough O'Connor's shot was superbly saved by Mahoney.

Stewart Barrowclough: "I was down by the corner flag when they started throwing missiles. A half brick flew past Mickey's ear and cut a huge divot out on the ground."

Irving Nattrass: "It was bad. I have never been as frightened in all my life."

Mick Mahoney: "I was bending down putting my gloves and cap in the net when I was hit on the head. I was not unconscious but I was dazed and I didn't know where I was."

Richard Dinnis: "We didn't know what was happening while we were locked in the dressing room. The noise above was deafening and Irish fans started throwing bricks at the window."

September 28 1977 - NEWCASTLE UTD 4 BOHEMIANS 0

Mahoney, D Craig, Kennedy, MacLean, McCaffery, Nattrass, Barrowclough, Callachan, Burns, Gowling, T Craig.

Att: 19,046

MATCH REPORT: Although Newcastle were never in danger of losing control in the first-half, they made a sloppy job of finishing off the Irish part-timers. And I'm sure Bohemians felt that there was hope the longer it went on. The Irishmen had ten men behind the ball at all times but Alan Gowling (who missed the first leg through injury) caught them out by converting a cut-back from Barrowclough on 27 minutes. Two minutes later, he came close with a header from a Tommy Craig corner but placed the ball wide.

Byrne was booked for a dangerous tackle on McLean, and Newcastle should have had a penalty when O'Brien handled in the penalty area.

Dinnis had said before the tie that the 37-year old Irish goalkeeper was the weak link in the side, and he wasn't far wrong. He looked uneasy in dealing with anything above head height and Gowling was always on hand to pick up anything he flapped at.

Half-time: Newcastle Utd 1 Bohemians 0

Tommy Craig made it two after 65 minutes. Gowling headed down a Barrowclough corner and Micky Burns tried a snap-shot at goal, but it came off a defender and Craig made no mistake from six yards. That was the end for the visitors and they collapsed under the strain of the growing pressure.

Gowling put the third away magnificently as he played a shot across Smyth into the far corner, and Craig made it 4-0 with a shot the goalkeeper didn't even see. Three goals in an amazing four minute spell.

Richard Dinnis: "David MacLean did well. He has good skill and can finish, but he tries to play the hard ball too much. I've told him to play it more simple and he'll get better results. Alan Kennedy was outstanding. He should be a regular choice for England."

October 19 1977 - BASTIA 2 NEWCASTLE UTD 1

Hardwick, Kelly, Nattrass, Cassidy, McCaffery, Nulty, Barrowclough, Cannell, Burns, Gowling, T Craig.

Att: 8,500

Although SC Bastia were the first French club Newcastle played in competition, the players had to fly to Corsica to play the tie at the small, but impressive, Stade Armand-Cesari.

Bastia, known as the Saint Tropez of Corsica, is a beautiful holiday resort on the north-east tip of the island. French since 1769, but it sits closer to Italy than France. The office language in Corsica is French, although there is a Corsican language called Corsu which is spoken amongst the locals in the villages. To the untrained ear, it sounds very much like Italian, and indeed if you do speak Italian, you may be able to make out snippets of conversation. Sadly – to the untrained ear – the locals couldn't understand Geordie.

MATCH REPORT: United put in an exhilarating first half performance and got the away goal that manager Richard Dinnis had called for. Prior to the game he said he would be happy with a 2-1 defeat, but for the first 45 minutes they looked the more likely team to get a win.

The game kicked off with the home supporters making it an occasion in a tight little ground with blaring klaxons and horns and a backdrop of scores of Corsican flags strung out all over the ground. However, unlike Dublin in the earlier round, the Corsican fans were intent on encouraging their team rather than trying to intimidate the opposition, and that made for a superb trip for the small band of Newcastle fans.

Tommy Craig and Tommy Cassidy were the driving forces in the early exchanges, and Steve Hardwick (playing only his fourth senior game following his move from Chesterfield) looked a class goalkeeper.

Paul Cannell scored after just seven minutes. He took his chance well as Alan Gowling back-headed an Irving Nattrass cross and Stu Barrowclough pulled the ball back for him to score from six yards with the goalkeeper at his feet.

The only two chances Bastia had in the first half were from French international Orlanducci, who managed to cut through the United defence and test Hardwick, and Lacuessa who blasted a 25-yard shot well wide.

The home goalkeeper, Weller, did well to use his legs to block a Gowling drive as half-time approached.

Half-time: Bastia 0 Newcastle Utd 1

The break took away none of the momentum from the match and within five minutes of the restart Bastia were level. Hardwick had just produced a superb save, and he did well again seconds later to push out a shot from Felix, but as he and Aiden McCaffrey scrambled in a bid to recover, Papi scrambled the ball over the line.

The one consolation for Newcastle - little had been seen of Dutch international Johnny Rep, the darling of the Bastia team. Nattrass stuck to him like glue. He was the Dutchman with the huge reputation but he did nothing in this game to enhance it.

Bastia made changes late in the game, replacing a defender with a striker, and with ten seconds left to play they provided the killer punch. Papi again did the damage, beating two Newcastle defenders before firing in a shot that Harwick almost saved. He got a hand to the ball but it squeezed agonisingly over the line.

Richard Dinnis: "I believe we can take care of them at St James' Park. There were several players who were obviously feeling the pace a bit towards the end, but how can you complain when they have given their absolute best? I thought they were out of this world in the first 45 minutes. We are at the half-time stage and we are still in a good position. People like Steve Hardwick and Peter Kelly deserve a special mention because they were considered to be stand-ins."

Tommy Cassidy: "I think Bastia are there for the taking now, but having said that, we should have taken them tonight after getting such a good start. We have heard such a lot about Johnny Rep and he is a good player on the ball, but apart from that we didn't see a lot of him, and that tells me we will be OK in the return leg."

* Stade Armand-Cesari is mostly known for the Furiani disaster, which took place on the 5th of May, 1992 when a terrace collapsed, killing 18 people and injuring more than 2,300 others.

It was a Coupe de France semi-final match against Olympique de Marseille, the Division 1 leader at the time. In order to receive more fans, the club board decided to create a temporary terrace at the section which could normally only contain 750 fans. The new capacity of the terrace was 10,000, but the whole structure collapsed, with supporters and journalists caught up in the wreckage.

November 2 1977 - NEWCASTLE UTD 1 BASTIA 3

Hardwick, Blackhall, Nattrass, Cassidy, McCaffery, Nulty (Bird), Barrowclough, Cannell (Hudson), Burns, Gowling, T Craig.

Att: 34,560

This was the like Paul Newman and Robert Redford's film 'The Sting' ... and Newcastle fell for it 'hook, line and sinker'.

Tommy Cassidy wasn't the only Toon player to suggest Johnny Rep was 'all fur coat and no knickers' (all flash and no product) and it was testimony to the Dutchman that he didn't reply to the jibes. What I found most remarkable was that the Bastia coach said: "We struggle to play away from Corsica and going to Newcastle is a difficult tie for us. I think Newcastle will go through to the next round."

That was it, all we had to do was turn up – job done! But ... let's take a reality check ... Newcastle had only won one of the last 12 league fixtures and were bottom of the league.

I was one of thousands of Toon fans who turned up hoping to see Rep demonstrate that he really was the genuine article and, on one hand, we were not disappointed. But perhaps he was a lot better than we anticipated, and Tommy Cassidy was certainly singing a different tune after the game.

It took Bastia nine minutes to end this contest ... and nine minutes for Rep to show the 34,560 crowd they were watching a truly world class individual.

MATCH REPORT: Three minutes gone and Jean Marie De Zerbi shot the visitors ahead after an unbelievable mazy run from Lacuestra.

Then we saw the full range of exciting skills from Rep that even seemed to have some of Richard Dinnis' players standing back to admire. The man was spellbinding. He played a one-two with French international Papi before blasting a left-foot shot off the body of shell-shocked Steve Hardwick and into the net. The Corsicans were 4-1 up on aggregate and coasting.

Newcastle's reply was to see Paul Cannell booked for kicking the Bastia goalkeeper in frustration, but they did get one of the four goals needed to progress when Alan Gowling headed in a Tommy Craig corner ten minutes before half-time.

Gowling started to cause a lot of problems in the Bastia penalty area just before the break and Gueston provided one way of stopping the former Manchester United striker by felling him in an off-the-ball incident.

Just before half-time Rep struck a superb first-time ball that set Papi on his merry way but he shot wide.

Half-time: Newcastle Utd 1 Bastia 2

Newcastle suffered another major blow after only seven minutes of the restart when Geoff Nulty was replaced by John Bird after suffering what appeared to be a recurrence of the pelvic trouble which had plagued him for months.

Gowling tested Weller at the far post, following a delightful cross from Craig, but the goalkeeper smothered it.

Then came the moment that became the 'talk of the toon' for years. Lacuestra spread the play with a good ball to Larios on the left wing. He knocked it square to Rep who set himself up for the most perfect strike most of us had ever seen. Malcolm Macdonald had struck a 25-yarder against Leicester City a couple of years earlier that took the breath away, but this goal was even better. It was a moment of magic that deserved to be appreciated, even though it was the death knell for our European hopes for 1997/8. I stood there and applauded … and I wasn't alone … 34,000 other Geordies did too!

With ten minutes remaining Cannell was replaced by 'Rocky' Hudson but Dinnis was grasping at straws in a game that we were never going to win, and any sort of purpose was replaced with desperation.

To the credit of the Newcastle fans, they gave Bastia and Rep a thunderous round of applause at the end. I don't think I've ever seen so many Geordies applaud a Newcastle defeat – before or since.

Richard Dinnis: "I will hold up my hands and say they gave us a soccer lesson. It was as simple as that. They weren't just better than us, they play a different game altogether. Not just us, I'm talking about the comparison with English football. The continentals are streets ahead in actual technique, but there are other things too. It would be worth spending some time over there watching how they work because while most managers accept they are better than us, I don't think many managers and coaches really know why. It's time we learned.

"We just don't produce the Johnny Rep's. When we come up with one you'll find he is the wrong sort of lad who will go off the rails. But Rep is a gentleman."

Johnny Rep: "A player cannot do anything without the ball. Here they gave me the ball – in Bastia they didn't. That was the difference."

At the end of the game there was a scramble to get Rep's shirt, but Irving Nattrass was the player who made the swap.

Geoff Nulty: "I am desperately disappointed especially after the way we played over in Bastia. They looked a different side – and so did we. Nothing is going right this season, for me or the team."

As for Dinnis, not only did he struggle with the Continental game, but he struggled with the English game too, and he was sacked soon after this fixture. He went to the States and joined Philadelphia Furies as a coach at the start of 1978 but he resigned five months later.

Bastia went on to reach the final, but PSV Eindhoven won 3-0 on aggregate.

CHAPTER FIVE
UEFA CUP 1994/95

Kevin Keegan

MANAGER: Kevin Keegan

In August 1982 Newcastle made one of the most sensational signings in their history when they coaxed 31-year old Kevin Keegan to leave Southampton and come to Tyneside. As a player he helped the club to promotion in his second season before he retired from football in 1984.

He moved into management at St James' Park on 5 February 1992, almost eight years after his final game as a player. Newcastle had been relegated from the top flight in 1989 and he joined the club following the dismissal of previous manager Ossie Ardiles. The club was struggling in the relegation zone ... heading towards the (old) Third Division.

But The Messiah returned, survival was achieved, and the following season (1992/3) Newcastle had an amazing 11–match winning start to the season and were promoted to the Premier League as Division One champions.

Keegan had conquered Europe three times with Liverpool; twice in the UEFA Cup and once in the European Cup. He also played in the European Cup final with SV Hamburg, but he confessed to opening night nerves as he prepared for his managerial debut in Europe: "We are inexperienced in European terms. We can't suddenly pretend we know it all."

HOW NEWCASTLE UTD QUALIFIED:

1993–94 was an enormous success for Newcastle as they finished third in the Premier League (behind Manchester United and Blackburn Rovers) and qualified for the UEFA Cup, bringing European football to the club for the first time in 16 years. Andy Cole was the Premier League's top scorer with 34 goals from 40 games, and he managed a club record total of 41 goals in all competitions.

Keegan then strengthened his side by signing Swiss World Cup defender Marc Hottiger, Belgium's defensive midfielder Philippe Albert, and Norwich City's quick winger Ruel Fox.

September 13 1994 - ROYAL ANTWERP 0 NEWCASTLE U 5

Srnicek, Hottiger, Beresford, Venison, Peacock, Albert, Lee, Beardsley (Watson), Cole (Jeffrey), Fox, Sellars.

Att 19,700

My lasting memory of this trip is of an old Belgian gentleman who stopped us outside of the stadium to say: "Where did you park your Spitfire, lads? You English are always welcome in this city. If it was not for the British you would be standing on German soil. Antwerp is more YOUR town than OURS!"

The Bosuil Stadium was arguably like something from the pre-war era ... only worse. Belgium's oldest club and its oldest stadium, and the place was a grim nightmare of neglect and shoddy construction – possibly the worst I had ever seen. The toilets were like World War II pillar-boxes, and the away end was concrete on a wooden scaffold that actually moved as the Toon fans danced and chanted. It brought back fears of Heysel (which was only 30 miles away), and I was amazed it passed UEFA regulations. I said before the game: "I'm not standing here, this structure is going to collapse", and we moved down the slope to the side terracing. Then ... as predicted ... one of the stairways collapsed when Newcastle scored the third goal but amazingly no-one was hurt. The Geordie fans in that section had to be moved.

I covered the disaster at Bastia (in the previous chapter) on a night when Newcastle were not the visitors, but so often I have stood/sat in foreign venues that have been nothing short of death traps! And this one was top of the list.

MATCH REPORT: It was amazing that, despite his time at Newcastle, Liverpool and Everton, this was Peter Beardsley's very first European game. The 33-year old missed out at Liverpool because of the ban imposed in the aftermath of the tragedy at the Heysel Stadium. He suffered a cheekbone fracture in Newcastle's opening Premiership match of the season at Leicester and had been wearing a mask for protection in training, but chose not to wear it at Antwerp's Bosuil Stadium.

Peter Beardsley: "I was a teenager when Newcastle were in the UEFA Cup the last time. It means a lot to me to play."

It took Newcastle less than a minute to open the scoring, when John Beresford crossed for Rob Lee to head it in from the edge of the box. But Antwerp were quick to respond with efforts from Kurt van Gompel and Francis Severeyns keeping Pavel Srnicek on his toes.

But Lee did it again in the 9th minute when he beat Andy Cole to Ruel Fox's cross to head in the second goal.

Five minutes before half-time Beardsley set up the third goal, feeding Fox on the right wing. His cross reached Cole at the far post, but the Nottingham-born striker was off balance and the chance went, so he squared to Scott Sellars who scored with a low drive.

Half-time: Royal Antwerp 0 Newcastle Utd 3

Five minutes into the second-half Swiss international Marc Hottiger crossed from the right and Lee was perfectly positioned at the far post to complete a PROPER hat-trick (all headers). Lee became the first ever Newcastle Utd player to score three goals in a match in a European competition.

Steve Watson completed the rout with an absolutely stunning goal. The substitute beat three defenders with a mesmerising run before beating Antwerp's 44-year old goalkeeper Ratko Svilar.

Kevin Keegan: "I certainly don't remember Liverpool ever playing like that away from Anfield. In all my years at Liverpool and at Hamburg, nothing like that happened."

Chairman **Sir John Hall**: "I was standing wondering if it's been a dream."

September 27 1994 - NEWCASTLE U 5 ROYAL ANTWERP 2

Srnicek, Hottiger, Beresford, Howey, Peacock, Albert, Lee (Watson), Beardsley (Clark), Cole, Fox, Sellars.

Att: 31,383

MATCH REPORT: There were 11 minutes on the clock when goalkeeper Yves Van der Straeten punched out a Ruel Fox corner, only for Robert Lee to send the ball back from the direction it first came and straight past the 'keeper from outside the penalty area. 1-0 to the Magpies.

When Andy Cole tapped in the second, after Fox again had done the hard work, it looked very much like 'here we go again – 5-0'. It was Cole's first strike in Europe, and Peter Beardsley equalled him ten minutes later from the penalty spot after Fox saw his run halted by Manuel Godfroid.

Five minutes before the break Cole got his second from ten yards when Beardsley found him with a superb pass.

4-0 at half-time and in no way did it flatter Newcastle because it could have been 6-0. Philippe Albert revelled in his new position of holding player in midfield, and he pushed forward at every opportunity. Twice he brought out the best in the goalkeeper from long range efforts.

Half-time: Newcastle Utd 4 Royal Antwerp 0

The second-half was a bit of an anti-climax and the Belgian fans started chanting, "Give us a goal!" and I don't think there were many amongst the 31,000 Geordies who begrudged Wim Keiekens' diving header that nestled in the back of the net.

Suddenly Antwerp got a shot of adrenaline and had the nerve to beat Pavel Srnicek again a minute later to make it 4-2. Once again, the 250 Belgians in the away end went bananas.

But Newcastle had to have the final word, and that was left to Cole to score and become the second Toon player to score a hat-trick in consecutive European games. It was Cole's seventh hat-trick of his short Newcastle career. (Hughie Gallacher holds the record of 14 between 1925 and 1930.)

Kevin Keegan: "It was one of the great European nights for me. After what happened in Heysel Stadium it was great to hear the banter between our fans and theirs – there was a lot of bridge building going on out there."

October 18 1994 - NEWCASTLE UTD 3 ATLETICO BILBAO 2

Srnicek, Hottiger, Beresford, Howey, Peacock, Albert, Clark, Beardsley, Cole, Fox, Sellars.

Att: 32,440

German referee Helmut Krug must have been colour-blind because he claimed Newcastle's black and white striped shirts clashed with the red and white stripes of Bilbao, so he insisted the Magpies forfeit their traditional colours. That may have been the case in the days of black and white TV … but come on!

MATCH REPORT: Bilbao started the game looking to stamp their authority on certain 'big name players' and assistant manager Arthur Cox was up and down like a Meer cat protesting about the over-zealous tackles. However, Darren Peacock manhandled Bilbao striker Ciganda in the penalty area and it looked a nailed on penalty, but the ref would have none of it.

Belgian Philippe Albert was once again a tower of strength in midfield, and it was his clever play that produced the first goal after ten minutes. Albert broke up a Spanish attack then Newcastle counter-attacked and Andy Cole flicked the ball over the Basque defence to create an opening for Ruel Fox. The winger beat Juan Jose Valencia with a low side-footed shot from eight yards out.

That settled the nerves and Cole blasted a shot a shot over the bar before we saw another carbon-copy penalty appeal in Pavel Srnicek's goal mouth. Ciganda again got the better of Peacock and the defender didn't exactly take the ball cleanly, but the referee again turned a blind eye.

In the 34th minute Cole split the Bilbao defence and Genaro Andrinua tripped him before he pulled the trigger, and the referee didn't get that one wrong. Peter Beardsley placed the ball to Valencia's right to double the lead, and 'Pedro' almost made it three just before half-time but his angle drive was parried by the goalkeeper.

Half-time: Newcastle Utd 2 Atletic Bilbao 0

Beardsley played at his vintage best in the second period, playing the skipper's role of conducting his orchestra from the heart of midfield. He produced three wonderful passes that cut open the Spanish defence, and one of them helped set up the third goal. In the 57th minute he found Fox who crossed for Cole to guide his header neatly past the advancing goalkeeper.

It was all going so well, until a 22-year old called Gonzalo Suances entered the battleground as a 70th minute substitute and changed the script. He had been on the field three minutes before setting up Ciganda to beat Srnicek from ten yards. Then with ten minutes remaining he met Ander Garitano's cross and headed into the Gallowgate End goal to bring delight to 800 Spanish supporters.

Despite the two late goals, the bookies still made Newcastle 6-1 joint-favourites to win the UEFA Cup.

Barry Venison: "Bilbao are very much mistaken if they think they've got this tie won. They're the team under pressure. They've got to score against us to win."

November 1 1994 - ATLETICO BILBAO 1 NEWCASTLE UTD 0

Srnicek, Hottiger, Beresford, Howey, Peacock, Albert, Lee, Beardsley, Watson, Fox (Jeffrey), Sellars (Clark).

Att: 47,000

The trip to Bilbao was unforgettable, as Spanish supporters bought drinks for Toon fans everywhere and the whole two days seemed like a massive celebration. Apparently the newspapers had been full of stories of how well the Geordies had wined and dined their counterparts before and after the game at St James' Park, and they did the same to us. What made it all the more bizarre was the fact that Atletico Bilbao was formed by Sunderland ship-builders who were working at the ship-yards in Bilbao in 1928. Just as Juventus wear black and white because of the Notts County connection; Bilbao wear red and white stripes because of the Mackems.

The two late goals Bilbao scored at Gallowgate always threatened to be costly, and with Newcastle robbed of Andy Cole, we didn't have a recognised striker. There was the option to use teenage Paul Brayson, but Keegan passed on it.

MATCH REPORT: Bilbao took control from the kick-off with Victor Alkiza and Ander Garitano bossing the midfield and Ciganda and Gonzalo Suances ready to punish any slip the backline happened to make. It was uneasy viewing because I couldn't seriously see how we were going to score. Newcastle didn't get into Bilbao's box in a threatening way until Lee headed over the bar on the half-hour mark.

Lee was our only real creative striker and he had another effort before the break when he was set through by Beardsley but he should have done better.

Half-time: Atletico Bilbao 0 Newcastle Utd 0

Lee tried again from 25 yards just after the break, but then came the moment we all dreaded - Ciganda found space in the Newcastle area. He was set up by his strike partner Alkiza and his low strike went under Steve Howey and Pavel Srnicek to give the home side the advantage on away goals.

Keegan replaced Fox with Mike Jefferey but the former Doncaster Rovers player was never comfortable in this sort of company. He was a lower-league player, nothing more.

Five minutes from time John Beresford up-ended Suances in the penalty area. Garitano's penalty hit the post and he blasted it into the net having taken two touches, and it was disallowed.

The home fans were happy enough and many handed us scarves as we left the San Mames Stadium.

Kevin Keegan: "I'm not sad. It was a great game and we have to give credit to Bilbao, they played well. I hope they win the cup so we can say we were beaten by the champions. Obviously we are disappointed, but that will last only a couple of days then it will be forgotten. Playing in Europe has been a good experience for my players."

Palma won the UEFA Cup that season, beating Juventus 2-1 on aggregate in an all-Italian final.

Party in Bilbao

CHAPTER SIX
UEFA CUP 1996/97

Pavel Srnicek

MANAGER: Kevin Keegan

Kevin Keegan ended the 1995/6 season having seen the Premiership title snatched from his grasp by Manchester United, after his side had been 12 points ahead in the table. We had the "I'd love it!" rant after the win at Elland Road, and there was a real bitterness growing between the two clubs. 1996/7 was going to be Keegan's 'make or break' season, and he put all of his eggs in one basket by making only one major signing - convincing Sir John Hall to pay a world record £15m for Geordie boy Alan Shearer.

HOW NEWCASTLE UTD QUALIFIED:

Although we finished as Premiership runners-up, the Champions League in those days was exclusively for champions, so we made our way into the UEFA Cup and a tie against Swedish semi-professional club Halmstads BK.

Newcastle looked a formidable side. Runners up in the Premiership, now with Alan Shearer, this was a serious European challenge, and the bookies took us very seriously.

However, the season didn't start off so well. Keegan proudly unveiled his new striker at Wembley in the Charity Shield, but Sir Alex brushed it off like 'water off a duck's back', and Manchester United trounced us 4-0. OK, it was only the Charity Shield – but it hurt.

September 10 1996 - NEWCASTLE UTD 4 HALMSTADS 0

Srnicek, Peacock, Watson, Howey, Asprilla, Clark, Lee, Shearer, Ferdinand, Ginola, Beardsley. (Subs: Albert, Gillespie, Barton)

Att: 28,124

Keegan opted for a three-man defence and an adventurous attacking formation and the Swedes didn't know what hit them. The move released Tino Asprilla and David Ginola to torment them down the flanks, and Keegan smiled: "It is similar to the old days with five forwards and two at the back. The only thing missing is a keeper with an outrageous hat and long woolly jumper."

MATCH REPORT: It didn't take long to for Newcastle to find the back of the net and the honour fell to Les Ferdinand, who bundled the ball past the Halmstads 'keeper after only six minutes, when David Ginola hooked the ball into the area.

Then after 26 minutes, just like 'Sir Les', Aspilla made his mark in history as a Newcastle European goal scorer. It was an absolute gem. Again it came from a Ginola cross, and the Frenchman was starting to get back in favour with the Toon faithful after trying to conjure up a move to Barcelona in the summer.

Half-time: Newcastle Utd 2 Halmstads 0

Philippe Albert got in on the act on six minutes into the second-half after a cross from … guess who?

Then Peter Beardsley scored his third European goal for the Magpies three minutes later. He picked up a short corner from Asprilla and looked to be going nowhere, crowded out by Swedish defenders, but he placed his shot in the only gap there could possibly have been to score.

Four goals and none of them to Shearer, but the 'GOALden Boy' didn't exactly set Europe alight when he played in Blackburn colours, scoring only twice in seven appearances. However, Tino should have given him a 'lamby' and squared to the Newcastle number nine late in the game. But he chose to blast the ball high and proud into the crowd. Shearer was not shy in telling the Colombian how he felt about it.

Halmstads almost put a slight damper on things when Vensson hit the post in the dying seconds.

Kevin Keegan: "I thought I would try something different and this sort of game gives you that chance. You've got to be brave to do it. If I wake up feeling adventurous for the second leg, I might play the same system again. I thought Asprilla was magnificent. In the last half hour, however, I didn't know what he was trying to do when he could have set up Shearer. He said to me after the game that it was all over by then. It was a great goal he scored – he's a great talent. And I thought that it was the best David Ginola has played for us for a long time. He made three of the goals with great crosses. And Peter Beardsley's goal was worth the entrance fee."

Tom Prahl, the Halmstad coach: "They remind me of the Liverpool of the 80s. We played as well as we can, but Newcastle are one of the top teams in Europe. They were like Liverpool in the way they passed, moved and never lost patience."

Pilippe Albert: "It was probably the easiest goal I have ever scored, but it was so important to me. It has been a very hard eight days. First I was dropped by my country and then by United, first at Sunderland and then against Spurs. It was not very nice. It's been a two-edged sword for me really. If I am not playing for United I cannot play for my country, and I want to play for both."

September 24 1996 - HALMSTADS 2 NEWCASTLE UTD 1

Srnicek, Beresford, Batty, Peacock, Barton, Albert, Lee, Gillespie, Shearer, Ferdinand, Asprilla. (Subs: Kitson, Clark).

Att: 7,847

We were based in Copenhagen for this trip, a different country but only a ferry ride over the water to Sweden and the coastal resort of Halmstads. Why Denmark? The beer was half the price to what we expected to pay in Sweden and we would have had to remortgage the house to spend three days there. Aston Villa fans were also staying in our hotel, with the same idea as ourselves, before heading to watch their UEFA Cup tie against Helsingborgs.

At the Örjans Vall stadium we, once again, had to risk life and limb on makeshift seating that was OK so long as you hung onto each other, didn't stand, and didn't move a muscle. Have you ever seen a Geordie crowd that sits and doesn't move?

The UEFA officials weren't too impressed either, because Halmstads were told (after this fixture) that their ground didn't meet the European demands for stadiums, and they were forced to play their future European games at Helsingborg or Göteborg.

MATCH REPORT: Kevin Keegan did threaten to go 'full steam ahead' with the same strike force that won the home leg 4-0, and sure enough, that was what we got. But it was not an impressive performance. It was simply a team defending a four goal lead. There was a lot of kicking going on, mainly on Keith Gillespie, and some of the Toon players decided not to get overly involved in the play.

Pavel Srnicek was forced into two early saves from striker Peter Voughts, and Alan Shearer missed a sitter at the other end, planting the ball the wrong side of the post with the goalkeeper beaten.

I think a few of the part-time Swedes wanted to make a name for themselves and Peter Lennartsson was obviously intent in 'sparking out' David Batty to prove he was a tough man or, more likely, get his nose broken. After one incident the referee pulled the Swede away from Batty for his own safety.

Any hopes of a Swedish miracle were ended two minutes before half-time. Gillespie passed to Ferdinand and there didn't seem much on, but he juggled the ball and hit it on the turn to volley his sixth goal in the last five games.

Half-time: Halmstads 0 Newcastle Utd 1

The second-half should have been a cruise, 5-0 up and coasting, but full marks to the Swedes for giving it a go. Srnicek was easily the busiest player on the field for the second-half, making saves from Voughts and Andersson twice.

In the 74th minute Arvidsson robbed Darren Peacock to slide home a consolation goal, but five minutes later Svensson scored a second via the underside of the bar.

Then came a bizarre period of 30 seconds when Hamstads played with 12 men! Svensson was taken off on a stretcher and substituted, but after treatment he decided to go back on to play.

Tom Prahl, the Halmstad coach: "It was great to get the win, and I think we deserved it. Newcastle are a great team and this is a very special result for us."

Philippe Albert: "Newcastle United have a brilliant team and quite naturally I want to be in it. I have had a good attitude."

October 15 1996 - FERENCVAROS 3 NEWCASTLE UTD 2

Srnicek, Watson, Beresford, Peacock, Batty, Albert, Lee, Gillespie, Shearer, Ferdinand, Beardsley. (Sub: Ginola).

Att: 18,000

We saw two sides to Budapest – and I don't mean each side of the Danube – Buda (north) and Pest (south). I mean the beautiful city and the friendly people... and then the football hooligans. The bars prior to the game were fabulous, and I cannot remember meeting such lovely people. But getting near the Üllői úti Stadion (it has been renamed since) was a frightening experience. I have never been in a bar when someone has walked in swinging a machete, and thrown it at a flag on the wall ... OUR flag ... but it happened here. We left seconds after. The flag is probably still pinned to the wall.

MATCH REPORT: Ferencvaros, the Manchester United of Hungarian football, provided a tough test in an intimidating atmosphere. Les Ferdinand was the target of the racist 'hate mob' and many waved white handkerchiefs whenever he touched the ball. It was nasty, but that was how the Hungarian's wanted it, as "Welcome To Hell!" banners were draped in front of the visitor's pen.

After 7 minutes Horvath chased a through ball from Romanian Miriuta but it seemed to beat him for pace ... or that was what John Beresford thought. The former Portsmouth full-back assumed Srnicek was coming for it and let it run, but the striker nipped in between the two Newcastle players and touched the ball into a gaping net. Beresford, in his frustration, made a high tackle seconds after the restart to end up in the referee's book and put more pressure on himself.

The night went from bad to worse in the 17th minute when the Magyars took advantage of more sloppy defending to double their lead. Ukranian Nichenko was given far too much space and he set up Horvath who headed against the post, then Lisztes followed up to score with ease.

2-0 down after 17 minutes and it was a time for BIG players. Step up Les Ferdinand and Alan Shearer, Newcastle's £21m strike-force.

'Sir Les' tried his luck from a Beardsley free-kick and went close, but minutes later (25th minute) Shearer used his strength to out-muscle Norbert Nagy and cross to the near post for Ferdinand to pull a goal back. Ten minutes later Shearer took a pass from David Batty and buried it with an amazing first touch.

2-2 and Rob Lee hit the post a minute later for what could have been a story book revival.

Half-time: Ferencvaros 2 Newcastle Utd 2

Lee shot wide and Ferdinand had a goal chalked off for offside, before (of all people) Beardsley set up Ferencvaros for the winner. Newcastle had actually stemmed an attack in the 57th minute and were progressing forward when the former England international played a back pass that went straight to Nichenko. With the defence as sixes-and-sevens, he squared for Lisztes to get his second.

Keegan took off Keith Gillespie and brought on David Ginola for fresh legs and the Hungarians were put under the cosh. Shearer thought he had scored the equaliser in the final minute but once again the flag went up.

October 29 1996 - NEWCASTLE UTD 4 FERENCVAROS 0

Srnicek, Batty, Albert, Lee, Peacock, Gillespie, Ferdinand, Ginola, Beardsley, Elliott, Asprilla.

Att: 35,740

On returning home from Budapest there was the minor matter of playing league leaders Manchester United at St James' Park, as Keegan set about getting revenge for the 4-0 drubbing at Wembley. Goals from Peacock, Ginola, Ferdinand, Shearer and Albert had the fans in raptures, but there was hardly a Man Utd fan left (to laugh at) when the final whistle blew.

MATCH REPORT: It was a warning to Ferencvaros, but Alan Shearer had picked up an injury at Filbert Street in the next game and Tino Asprilla was called upon to deputise. However, the Hungarians had their own troubles, two-goal Krisztian Lisztes was dropped after reports of a bust-up with manager Zoltan Varga.

The Magpies started brightly, Philippe Albert and Asprilla both firing wide.

Newcastle had the benefit of two away goals and only needed to score once to go through, but Peter Beardsley didn't help the cause when he missed a penalty. Tino broke for goal and Zoltan Jagodics fouled him from behind. 'Pedro' tried to place the penalty to the goalkeeper's left but he hit the outside of the post.

Although Ginola came close with a dipping drive (twice), Asprilla always looked the likeliest to score, buzzing around the penalty area like a manic bee. Three minutes before half-time he made the breakthrough, shooting home an Albert knock-down to put Newcastle 1-0 up.

Half-time: Newcastle Utd 1 Ferencvaros 0

Asprilla fed Ginola and the Frenchman crashed a left-foot shot against the bar. Never the 'brightest button in the box', Tino had turned up at training an hour early the day before this game when he failed to put his clock back (that was

Tuesday, the clocks went back on Sunday morning), but there was no doubting his expertise on the pitch. He made it 2-0, pouncing on a Darren Peacock header and the tie was beyond the visitors.

To cap it all off, we saw one of the greatest goals ever seen at St James' Park. Gillespie's corner was cleared away from the penalty area and Ginola teed himself up with his right foot and thundered a volley into the top corner with his left. Perfection – there was no other word for it.

Ferdinand capped off a remarkable evening with a goal in injury time.

November 19 1996 - METZ 1 NEWCASTLE UTD 1

Srnicek, Beresford, Batty, Albert, Lee, Gillespie, Ginola, Beardsley, Asprilla, Peacock, Barton. (Sub: Elliott).

Att: 23,000

The reporter from The Journal described Metz as being "a French version of Middlesbrough" so we expected to see a football ground stuck in the middle of an oil refinery. But the guy was wrong describing every place we visited watching Newcastle – without exception. Rather than a landscape of blast-furnaces (like the Boro), Metz had one chimney. It also has the very impressive Saint-Stephen cathedral, and there is nothing in Boro to come remotely close to such fine architecture. Metz is situated in north-east France, very close to the borders to Luxembourg and Germany, and some of our mates went to Luxembourg for the day.

I have to admit, this was one of the most un-friendliest places I have ever visited. I understand Geordies can be 'in your face' and brimming with exuberance, a little too much for some people's liking, but we were not made welcome anywhere we went in this city. We were shunned in hotels, bars, cafes and shops.

MATCH REPORT: The snow fell and there were serious doubts as to whether the game would go ahead. And of course, the French being French, they told a lot of Geordies "the game is off", when they knew full well it wasn't.

This is a game that I'm sure Pavel Srnicek will openly admit wasn't one of his better days. The Toon backline stood in disbelief as he made a hash of a clearance after only two minutes, playing the ball directly to Robert Pires. Metz scored but it was flagged because a pass was made to Amara in an offside position.

Newcastle grabbed the lead against the run of play after half an hour when Tino Asprilla went down under a challenge from goalkeeper Lionel Letizi. Peter Beardsley didn't let his missed penalty against Ferencvaros discourage him and he calmly sent the goalkeeper the wrong way.

Brazilian Isaias seemed to take exception to going a goal behind and confronted David Batty soon after the goal. The pair exchanged blows and both fell to the ground nursing facial injuries. Batty needed treatment and briefly left the pitch to get stitches inserted, while Isaias was booked.

Half-time: Metz 0 Newcastle Utd 1

It came as no real surprise when Metz levelled in the 67th minute because they looked increasingly menacing after the break and Newcastle (missing Ferdinand and Shearer) looked rather light-weight up front. Keith Gillespie and David Ginola didn't do the damage down the flanks we expected, and even when they did get clear, Asprilla was guarded by three defenders.

Traore capitalised when Srnicek charged out but failed to collect Lang's left-wing cross and, with Pav in no-man's-land, the Frenchman made his back-header count. Not pretty - but effective.

All eyes were on Metz winger **Robert Pires**, who was the player keeping Ginola out of the French international team at this time. Juventus had allegedly made a £5m offer for the 23-year old, but he said after this game: "I would like to play in England with Patrick Viera at Arsenal".

December 3 1996 - NEWCASTLE UTD 2 METZ 0

Srnicek, Batty, Albert, Lee, Gillespie, Shearer, Ginola, Beardsley, Elliott, Asprilla, Peacock. (Subs: Watson, Clark).

Att: 35,641

Controversial Colombian Tino Asprilla was at the centre of it all at St James' Park, having been hauled off at half-time in the Premiership game the previous Saturday for what Kevin Keegan described as "lack of effort". Newcastle lost 2-1 to Arsenal and Tino was read the riot act.

Metz coach Joel Muller dropped Brazilian midfielder Isaias, who had picked up a lot of bad press for his "attack" on David Batty in the first leg, and that toned the build-up down a touch. Muller only gave his side "a ten per cent chance of winning the tie".

MATCH REPORT: Metz started well, with Pavel Srnicek on his toes to stop Robert Pires and Jocelyn Blanchard opening the scoring. But stand-in goalkeeper Biancarelli wasn't happy having Alan Shearer niggling him at dead-ball kicks. Asprilla added to the goalkeeper's anguish when he won the ball from a high cross as the 'keeper flapped, but the ball flew wide of the post.

Four minutes before half-time Pires brought out the very best in Pav, and the Czech stopper made an amazing save.

Half-time: Newcastle Utd 0 Metz 0

Lee, Shearer and Ginola tested the water with shots that came close, and Frederic Arpinon blatantly handled in the penalty area but he must have been on the blind side of the referee because play was waved on.

Srnicek saved the day with an amazing stop on 77 minutes that turned the game.

There was a collective sigh of relief on 80 minutes when Gillespie crossed from the right and Darren Peacock set up Asprilla to stoop to head United ahead. Just when he had got back into Keegan's good books, what did he do? He took off his shirt and held it aloft on a corner flag that he had pulled out of the ground at the Gallowgate End, which brought a booking that ruled him out of the first leg of the quarter final. Keegan was furious!

Two minutes later Tino was back on a high as he scored a goal of pure genius. He tore through the Metz defence, rounded the goalkeeper, and blasted the ball into the far corner of the net.

Amazing scenes on and off the field, but he wasn't finished yet. He left the field two minutes from time ... on a stretcher ... due to a hamstring injury!

Kevin Keegan: "Pavel's save was crucial. For a long period we were as bad as we could be. If we play as badly again in the next round we will go out. I was going to take Tino off because he looked tired but I'm glad I didn't. The referee said he would take action against anyone who pulled his shirt over his head. When Tino put his shirt on the corner flag I could not believe it, and we knew we were in trouble".

David Ginola: "I think it's a bad situation and a bad decision when a player is booked for enjoying himself after scoring. People should remember that football is a show and a spectacle. Bringing a bit of fun into the celebrations is good for the fans. They enjoy it."

QUARTER FINALS:

Newcastle v Monaco

Anderlecht v Internazionale

Schalke 04 v Valencia

Tenerife v Brondby

March 4 1997 - NEWCASTLE UTD 0 MONACO 1

Hislop, Watson, Batty, Albert, Lee, Gillespie, Ginola, Elliott, Clark, Peacock, Barton.

Att: 36,215

Following an unbelievable 7-1 mauling of Spurs at St James' Park, then a 3-0 demolition of Leeds United ... Kevin Keegan quit Newcastle. After nearly five years of being in charge, in January 1997 the Messiah walked-the-walk, and the city of Newcastle was devastated. He blamed the reason on an issue behind the scenes, a flotation to transform the club into a plc. It was a move that was to raise massive funds but it required a long-term commitment from the manager, something Keegan was not willing to give. The relationship between Keegan and certain sections of the board (and advisors) deteriorated and the manager resigned.

The Newcastle directors didn't take long to appoint a new boss. Within days Kenny Dalglish was in the driving seat, and a home tie with Monaco was his Newcastle European debut.

The build up was not ideal, a shock home defeat to relegation-threatened Southampton was not exactly what the doctored ordered prior to a European quarter final. The result wouldn't have been so bad ... but we were rubbish.

MATCH REPORT: Dalglish's 46th birthday celebrations were interrupted when skipper Peter Beardsley was struck in the face by a ball during a training ground accident. Apparently it didn't ruin his looks but he was ruled out of the game due to concussion.

With Tino Asprilla banned because of his corner flag incident in the previous round, and both Les Ferdinand and Alan Shearer missing due to injury, Dalglish was left with limited striking options.

Acting captain Rob Lee was asked to fill the centre-forward position as Dalglish went for five in midfield, but despite his endeavour (and Ginola's lofted balls from midfield) it was a tough ask. He did put the ball in the net at one stage, but the whistle had blown and he was booked.

On show was French 'wonderkid' Thierry Henry, a target for Keegan before he flew the roost. He asked the directors to provide the money for him and they allegedly offered Monaco £100,000. That wouldn't by a pie and a Bovril in Monte Carlo.

Henry was a problem to Robbie Elliott throughout the first-half but Newcastle left the field fairly content to keep the score goalless.

Half-time: Newcastle Utd 0 Monaco 0

59 minutes and Ali Benarbia's brilliant long ball behind Philippe Albert set Monaco on the road to a priceless away goal. Elliott failed to track Henry and the young winger broke down the right before executing an amazing ball for Brazilian sensation Sonny Anderson to rifle home his 23rd goal of the season.

But Newcastle should have equalised ten minutes from time when Gillespie's angled shot was stopped by Fabien Barthez, and Albert thrashed at the ball and sent it flying over the crossbar into Row Z.

Gillespie saved the Magpies even more embarrassment by clearing off the line from Benarbia's glancing header.

Shaka Hislop had an X-ray on his finger: "When I made a save early on against Monaco my finger popped out of the socket and the physio had to pop it back in. I played on but I was in pain."

John Collins, Monaco's former Celtic midfielder: "Newcastle's strength is going wide and getting crosses in, but when they did there was nobody in the middle to take advantage."

March 18 1997 - MONACO 3 NEWCASTLE UTD 0

Hislop, Watson, Batty, Albert, Lee, Ginola, Beardsley, Elliott, Asprilla, Peacock, Barton. (Subs: Beresford, Gillespie, Clark).

Att: 18,500

Who would have thought it – the Toon Army in Monte Carlo! And I'm sure the sight of us Geordies frequenting the casinos lowered the tone a fraction, but the experience was something special.

I have visited some superb stadiums and hell-holes in my time following Newcastle United (and football in general to complete the '92 League Grounds') but nothing … and I mean NOTHING … comes close to the luxury of the Stade Louis II Stadium. No other football structure in the world packs so much into such a small space, so lavishly and with such ingenuity.

The lack of space is a major problem in this principality of only 480 acres, and a normal football ground would not fit in anywhere. Three hectares was cleared in this built up area and that had to accommodate a football stadium, a car park, offices, other sporting facilities and, most importantly, it had to be in harmony with it's environment from every angle of Monte Carlo.

You don't face turnstiles when you enter the building, you go through smoked glass doors as if you were going to a conference centre. Past shops, then up through the four storey 1750-capacity car park, up to an Olympic sized swimming pool complex seating 500, with adjacent bistro, and a multi-purpose sports hall accommodating up to 3,500 spectators. Then you come to the open-air stadium – on top of the car park – with its grass pitch laid on the concrete roof, with a 20,000 capacity.

But this is just scratching the surface. There is accommodation for players and office staff, AS Monaco's club HQ, three more pools, a gymnasium, shops and 9172 square metres of office space. All designed to withstand earthquakes.

MATCH REPORT: Due to the ban on advertising alcohol, Newcastle had to remove their Brown Ale logo from the shirts and they had 'Centre Parcs' strips designed specially for the game. The principality was celebrating 700 years of rule by the Grimaldi royal family and Princes Rainer and Albert were in attendance.

Dalglish's patched-up side had to win by a two goal margin to get through to the semi-final, or at least score two goals to get through on the away-goals rule. We hadn't won an away game by more than one goal in 17 months. Did we expect to win here? We are Geordies – we ALWAYS expect to win.

In the fifth minute Monaco skipper Franck Dumas misjudged Robbie Elliott's long punt forward and Tino Asprilla almost beat Barthez to the ball. So there was hope … for a while.

But Henry tested Hislop with a shot from the flank, and then Elliott almost put through his own goal.

A Ginola free-kick tested Barthez and Henry tried an amazing scissor-kick that flashed wide.

But the hopes of a shock result disappeared three minutes from half-time when striker Sylvian Legwinski profited from a double shambles as Steve Watson squandered possession and Peter Beardsley tried to make a tackle but only helped to set up the goal.

Half-time: Monaco 1 Newcastle Utd 0

Midfielder Ali Benarbia added the second five minutes into the second period. Sonny Andersson's shot was saved by Hislop, Henry followed up but Peacock blocked, and Benarbia pounced to score from close range.

The same player executed a stunning 25-yard free-kick on 68 minutes that flew into Hislop's right hand corner.

Dalglish didn't fly home with the team after the game, he flew to Turin to watch Juventus v Rosenborg in the Champions League allegedly to try to sign Alessandro Del Piero which, I'm afraid to say, didn't happen.

The competition was won by Schalke 04, who beat Internazionale on penalties in the final – as Germans tend to do.

Chester-Le-Street Toon fans in Monte Carlo

CHAPTER SEVEN
EUROPEAN CHAMPIONS LEAGUE
1997/98

Kenny Dalglish

MANAGER: Kenny Dalglish

The Newcastle board were bold, at a time when they had to be, because of the floatation. They needed a star manager, and Dalglish had won the title with two different clubs, and only Brian Clough had done that in modern times.

As a player Dalglish had won the European Cup with Liverpool on 3 occasions, in 1978, 1981 and 1984 and became player-manager of the Reds in 1985 following the Heysel Stadium Disaster. He brought the team a league and FA Cup double in his first year, and during his six-year tenure from 1985–1991, Liverpool won the league championship three times and the FA Cup twice.

He joined Blackburn Rovers in 1991 and, through Jack Walker's patronage, he turned the Second Division side into unlikely Premier League winners.

Dalglish joined Newcastle United on 14 January 1997, on a three and a half year contract, inheriting a squad of players reputed, by previous manager Kevin Keegan, to be "the best the club had ever had".

HOW NEWCASTLE UTD QUALIFIED:

In 1996/7 Newcastle United finished the season as runners-up to champions Manchester United for the second consecutive season, seven points adrift of the winners. UEFA, however, changed the rules to include the league runners-up in the Champions League, and at long last, with the Inter Cities Fairs Cup days behind us, we were "in with the big boys". Champions League here we come!

August 13 1997 - NEWCASTLE UTD 2 CROATIA ZAGREB 1

Given, Beresford, Batty, Lee, Asprilla, Pearce, Ketsbaia, Tomasson (Gillespie), Watson, Pistone, Albert (Howey).

Att: 34,465

Croatia Zagreb were really NK Dinamo Zagreb, the former Yugoslav club that won the Inter Cities Fairs Cup in 1967, but parading under a new political name. After the SFR Yugoslavia was dissolved, Dinamo took part in creating the Croatian Football League in 1992 and controversially changed its name to HAŠK Građanski, and then to Croatia Zagreb.

MATCH REPORT: Tino Asprilla squandered an early chance firing straight at Zagreb's keeper and skipper Dazen Ladic.

Steve Watson nearly created a goal for Asprilla in the eighth minute with a fine right wing cross but wing back John Beresford got in the South American's way.

Particularly impressive for the visitors was Silvio Maric (who became a Newcastle player a couple of seasons later), playing in a position just behind the Zagreb striker on the edge of the United penalty box.

The Toon Army went wild in the 21st minute when Beresford slid home from six yards after a great move involving Asprilla and Lee down the right. Asprilla played Lee into the box with a beautiful angled ball and, when he crossed, the Sheffield-born wing back had the simple task of side-footing home.

Maric began, and so nearly ended, a fine four-man move for the visitors on the half hour. But, after finding space, the midfielder headed over a Saric right wing cross.

Four minutes before the interval new signing from Dutch club Heerenveen Jon Dahl Tomasson was fouled by Mladinic on the edge of the Zagreb penalty area but Asprilla's free kick was blocked by the defensive wall.

Half-time: Newcastle Utd 1 Croatia Zagreb 0

Zagreb stunned the Toon Army with a 51st minute equaliser from Igor Cvitanovic who ran onto a Maric through ball and produced a clinical finish into the right hand corner.

Kenny Dalglish went for a change of formation eleven minutes after the break and brought on winger Keith Gillespie to replace the subdued Tomasson who looked well off the pace.

Albert injured his right thigh in the 64th minute and needed to go off for treatment. Although he returned he was eventually replaced by Steve Howey three minutes later.

The match started to get messy with Croatia happy to settle for a draw, but in the 75th minute Beresford, who had only scored two goals for Newcastle in five seasons, amazingly fired his second of the game.

Asprilla challenged Ladic for the ball and it broke free for Beresford who fired home from an acute angle.

August 27 1997 - CROATIA ZAGREB 2 NEWCASTLE UTD 2

Given, Barton, Beresford (Gillespie), Batty, Lee, Asprilla, Pearce (Howey), Tomasson (Ketsbaia), Watson, Pistone, Albert.

Att: 34,000

We found Zagreb (the capital of Croatia) a fascinating city, and like Bilbao, the fans who had visited Newcastle in the first leg were only too happy to mix with us in the bars. Newcastle United had issued everyone who bought a match ticket, two pages of 'where not to go and what not to do'. That went in the bin as soon as we arrived. We met the notorious 'Bad Blue Boys', the local football hooligans, on our way to the ground and they were wearing Chelsea and Millwall shirts. It was all for show, because these lads took care of us and showed us the sights of their lovely city.

The Stadion Maksimir is situated in the northeast part of the city, opposite the largest city park Maksimir.

MATCH REPORT: Tino Asprilla was in the bad books with Kenny Dalglish, following his non-arrival at St James' Park for the league fixture with Aston Villa.

Kenny Dalglish: "What happened on Saturday was unfortunate for Tino but it was just one of those things. But he's here now and I don't think an air traffic controller's strike will prevent him playing tonight."

The home side took control early on and, within 45 seconds, they could have levelled on aggregate. Silvio Maric was put through at inside right but fired straight at Shay Given.

United gradually came into the tie with their five-man midfield battling to try to create a chance for lone striker Tino Asprilla.

Cvitanovic missed a chance before Srdan Mladinic smashed a brilliant effort against the Newcastle woodwork in the 16th minute.

Newcastle suffered a blow on the half-hour when they lost England defender Stuart Pearce who was injured when making a brave block tackle on Maric. He was replaced by Steve Howey.

Three minutes on and Asprilla seemed to be in trouble when he elbowed Maric in the face, but the referee seemed to miss the incident.

Two minutes before half-time, Asprilla played in Tomasson and, as the Dane tried to round the keeper, defender Goran Juric up-ended him from behind.

Before Asprilla was able to coolly put away his penalty, Juric was shown the red card and Zagreb were down to 10 men with 47 minutes of the 90 remaining.

Half-time: Croatia Zagreb 0 Newcastle Utd 1

3-1 up on aggregate, United created a number of opportunities early on in the second-half for both Asprilla and Alessandro Pistone to kill off the home side, but they were squandered.

Then came the Croatian lifeline - Zagreb equalised in the 58th minute when a left-wing free kick by Cvitanovic was headed home by Simic from six yards at the far post.

Just when it looked as if Zagreb were heading out of the competition, with only 10 seconds remaining, Cvitanovic was fed by Maric and he slotted the ball home low to Given's left from an acute angle to leave the home crowd in raptures. 3-3 on aggregate.

The second period of extra-time saw both sides looking less and less likely to get that elusive winner and the tie seemed to be heading to penalties, then up popped Temuri Ketsbaia to put Newcastle into the Champions League group stage.

The Georgian international came off the bench to replace Jon Dahl Tomasson 12 minutes into extra-time, and he scored with less than 60 seconds of extra-time remaining. He beat keeper Drazen Ladic from 10 yards to start amazing pitch-side celebrations and in the enclosure housing the 450 Geordie fans.

John Beresford: "This is the happiest and certainly most emotional night of my Newcastle career. Losing out on the championship the season before last, hurt us all more than we'd ever admit. But today we can all stand proud. This is a great club and one built around every single fan who holds Newcastle close to their hearts. And those of us still here, spared a thought for those fans who suffered along with us when Man United pipped us.

"When the last minute goal went in I thought – here we go again. But this side has something special."

September 17 1997 - NEWCASTLE UTD 3 BARCELONA 2

Given, Barton, Beresford, Batty, Lee, Barnes (Ketsbaia), Asprilla, Tomasson (Peacock), Gillespie, Watson, Albert.

Att: 35,274

The Champions League … Barcelona come to Tyneside … Faustino Asprilla scores a hat-trick … let's be honest with ourselves, it doesn't get much better than that, does it?

Soon-to-depart chairman **Sir John Hall** had told us five years earlier: "The FA Cup and UEFA Cup are for losers, the Champions League is where we belong". He got his dream.

MATCH REPORT: Denmark international Jon Dahl Tomasson, brought in at the start of the season to stand in for Alan Shearer who suffered a horror injury in a pre-season friendly at Goodison Park, wasted two great opportunities within a six-minute spell.

Batty was booked for a late challenge, then in the 21st minute Asprilla earned a penalty after being up-ended by the visitors' stand-in keeper Hesp.

Tomasson played a superb inch-perfect ball to Asprilla, breaking from left to right in the penalty box. The keeper came out and although he appeared to make little contact, the Colombian went sprawling and Italian referee Pierluigi Collina signalled for a penalty.

Asprilla beat the keeper to his right.

Ivan De La Pena was booked for a foul on Robert Lee in the 29th minute before the home support exploded in delight in the 31st minute as Asprilla headed home a magnificent second goal.

Steve Watson played a quick free kick to overlapping Gillespie and after beating his marker Sergi, he produced a great cross which Asprilla headed home unmarked from eight yards.

While the Colombian was the hero, the whole side were all truly magnificent in this match, none more so than Gillespie. This was the Northern Ireland international's finest hour as he gave classy defender Sergi possibly the biggest roasting he had ever had.

Half-time: Newcastle Utd 2 Barcelona 0

Within seconds of the restart Rivaldo tested Shay Given (his first true save of the game), but within three minutes Asprilla completed his memorable hat-trick with the sweetest of headers - and Gillespie was again the architect. The Northern Ireland winger set off on a 70-yard run which left Sergi floundering. His right-foot cross was inch-perfect, and Asprilla leaped to head the ball home into the top corner before his customary celebratory somersault.

Enrique chested home a close-range effort in the 72nd minute after substitute Dugarry had forced a world-class save from Given. We thought it was nothing more than a consolation goal but then Rivaldo smashed a 20-yard effort against the United woodwork and Batty headed off the goal-line as the visitors took control.

Then Figo fired home from 20 yards through a crowded Newcastle defence and the final two minutes became a nail-biting affair.

There were amazing scenes when the referee sounded the final whistle, bring back memories of the fabulous Fairs Cup run in 1969.

On the same night Oasis were playing at the Newcastle Arena and were keeping the audience up to date with the score. But, the Gallaghers being the Gallaghers, they told the Geordie crowd Barcelona had equalised and the game had finished 3-3.

October 1 1997 - DYNAMO KIEV 2 NEWCASTLE UTD 2

Given, Barton, Beresford, Batty, Peacock, Lee (Ketsbaia), Barnes, Asprilla (Tomasson), Gillespie, Watson, Albert.

Att: 100,000

The Journal's travel co-ordinator was at it again, feeding us a load of junk about Kiev going through an "Indian summer", and many Toon fans turned up at Newcastle airport wearing Newcastle shirts and no coats. We were greeted at the other end by armed guards, pointing at their overcoats, suggesting in their own language that perhaps some of us were under-dressed. One fan replied: "We're Geordies, man, we divn't need coats, we're hard". This was the morning and the sun was out but, come 4pm, the reality kicked in ... we were in the Ukraine in October, not India in July! It was absolutely freezing, and Geordies bought bear-skin hats, overcoats, cardigans and bin-liners to keep warm.

Kiev, like our trip to Rotterdam, is like a new city – courtesy of the German's World War II 'scorched earth' policy. Nothing in this place was over 50 years old - it had literally been flattened. And of course there was the Chernobyl Nuclear Power Plant disaster on 26 April 1986 that was close to here. We were told not to eat fruit, vegetables or anything uncovered, and not to drink milk. This was 11 years after the event, so imagine what the country was like at the time.

The Republican Stadium (now called the Lobanovsky Dynamo Stadium) is in the heart of the city centre and is a major part of the community. It functions more like a public square. People meet there each day and school kids congregate there.

We were told how many of the Dynamo team were executed by a firing squad in the summer of 1942 for defeating an All-Star team from the German armed forces. Other players were arrested by the Gestapo, tortured and sent to the nearby labour camp at Siretz. The writer of the 1981 American film 'Escape to Victory' got the idea for his story from Dynamo Kiev.

The Kiev fans were absolutely fabulous with us. The most friendly, helpful, courteous, proud people I have ever met in my life.

MATCH REPORT: The home side caused problems from the start with their pace and ability to go past Warren Barton and John Beresford on either flank a little too easily.

Within four minutes disaster struck as Rebrov flashed a close range effort into the United net. The brilliant Belkevitch turned Steve Watson inside out before crossing into the six yard box. Given looked rooted to the spot as Rebrov fired home from six yards.

Asprilla was not put off by the close marking of Yuri Dmitrulin and looked lively as United hit back with some purpose and he should have equalised when finding himself free 15 yards out. He moved the ball on to his right foot but his final effort flew disappointingly straight at Shovkovsky.

Asprilla had to depart after catching his studs in the turf when taking a free kick and was replaced by Jon Dahl Tomasson after only 25 minutes, and the situation got a lot a lot worse when Shevchenko made it 2-0 with a deadly finish. United's defence had lost the ball 30 yards out and Belkevitch picked it up and fed Shevchenko who beat Given low to his right from 10 yards.

Half-time: Dynamo Kiev 2 Newcastle Utd 0

Lee, who struggled with an injury and looked decidedly out of sorts, failed to reappear after the half time interval and was replaced by Temuri Ketsbaia.

Ketsbaia always made a bigger impact on the game coming on as substitute, rather than being in the starting line-up, and he took the Magpies up another gear with his Red Bull-like enthusiasm and determination.

He pushed forward but his moves broke down because there was no cutting edge up front. Tino had gone off and Tomasson was looking less like Alan Shearer every game he played (this was October and he still hadn't opened his account in a black and white shirt).

Given flung himself to his left to palm away Veshtchuk's drive and keep Newcastle in the game, and finally Beresford gave the Magpies hope when he fired home his fourth goal of the season 12 minutes from time. Watson's long throw had been flicked on by John Barnes and the little left-back made it 2-1.

Then, out of the blue, the Ukrainian fans were stopped in mid-verse as Beresford salvaged a point for the Magpies with a speculative late strike which looped off Golovko's outstretched boot and crept inside Shovkovsky's right-hand post with the keeper having dived to his left.

An amazing finale.

Former Newcastle striker **Malcolm Macdonald:** "I think Waddington's must have given Kenny (Dalglish) a Monopoly 'get out of jail free' card. The normally reliable David Batty had a stinker. I think the game would have been different had Ketsbaia started. The whole pattern of the game changed when he came on and started to run at people."

October 22 1997 - PSV EINDHOVEN 1 NEWCASTLE UTD 0

Given, Barton (Albert), Beresford (Ketsbaia), Batty, Peacock, Howey, Lee, Rush, Tomasson, Gillespie, Watson.

Att: 29,200

Eindhoven is located in the province of North Brabant in the south of the Netherlands, and took over from Nottingham as the smallest city to have won the European Cup when they won the trophy in 1988. It is a lovely, quaint town similar to The Hague – but without the history. The problem we had with this trip was NUFC's insistence that ALL travelling fans had to go via the 'rip off' Travel Club. They handled excursions like a school trip, and took a wedge of money for the privilege. You were not allowed to socialise with the locals and they made sure alcohol did not touch your lips during the entire trip. Newcastle United announced that they would not sell match tickets to anyone making their own way to Holland, so we got on the internet and made our own plans. We offered ten tickets to Dutch supporters for the return game at St James' Park – in exchange for ten tickets at the Philips Stadium. And we were not alone, many others did it too. But the Evening Chronicle got wind of it and made a big deal of the story with the headline: "Touts put Toon fans in rival's territory".

The Dutch police got in on the act and I've never seen a police presence like it. They patrolled the train station and roads into Eindhoven – if you didn't have a ticket you were deported. We were based in Amsterdam for three days, and bluffed our way into Eindhoven with the help of some Dutch lads we met on the train.

MATCH REPORT: Eindhoven seized the early initiative and within three minutes Wim Jonk had fired wide after he had cut in from the left.

Newcastle were having great difficulty getting the ball out of their own half and all too often strikers Ian Rush (playing his one and only European game for Newcastle) and Jon Dahl Tomasson were left stranded upfield without any help from their midfield. Rush had arrived from Leeds, where he was so far down the pecking order he couldn't even make the reserve side, and many felt that the arrival of ex-Liverpool veterans Rush and John Barnes was a "jobs for the boys" exercise we could have done without.

PSV maintained their pressure and when Nilis was upended in the 31st minute by Darren Peacock the home side thought they had got a penalty but Italian referee Stefan Braschi gave a free kick inches outside of the United penalty box.

Nilis' free kick was curled around the wall only for Given to save comfortably with Lee completing the clearance.

Seven minutes before the break PSV took the lead when Jonk fired home to the right of the diving Given.

The move began 40 yards out when Nilis found De Bilde. He chested down and Jonk did the rest with a superb half volley.

Half-time: PSV Eindoven 1 Newcastle Utd 0

The key to any Newcastle fight-back was the pace of Keith Gillespie down the right, because he worried the home defence every time he had the ball. But the service to him was poor.

Romanian substitute Ovidiu Stinga foxed Howey, then he smashed in a fine effort which Given managed to block.

Second half substitute Temuri Ketsbaia had a great chance to become the hero for the Magpies in the 72nd minute but, after beating three defenders, blood must have rushed to his brain in a fit of excitement and he lifted his effort over the bar.

Newcastle lost and to make matters worse, Rob Lee and David Batty were booked and ruled themselves out of the tie between the two sides on Tyneside.

Darren Peacock: "They should have had a penalty. It was definitely inside the area when the ball struck my hand. We were kicking ourselves because the longer the game went on the more comfortable we felt."

After the game the Dutch police praised both sets of supporters: "There were no incidents involving Newcastle fans before, during or after the game. We made nine arrests, but that was an incident between PSV and Ajax fans on the outskirts of the city."

November 5 1997 - NEWCASTLE UTD 0 PSV EINDHOVEN 2

Given, Barton, Beresford, Barnes, Ketsbaia, Tomasson, Gillespie, Watson, Hamilton, Pistone, Albert.

Att: 35,214

We played host to ten PSV Eindhoven fans who kindly got us tickets for the Philips Stadium, and we organised for them to spend a couple of nights at Whitley Bay in a guest house … and they LOVED it. We remained friends for years, they came back to Newcastle several times, and I took my wife to Eindhoven for Millennium New Year to meet up with them again.

MATCH REPORT: After an opening 10 minutes dominated by PSV, Newcastle hit back with a stinging Keith Gillespie drive which curled a foot over Ronald Waterreus' crossbar.

United gradually came more into the tie but were still failing to give Gillespie any regular support, and just like at Monaco and Bilbao in previous seasons, due to injuries, we didn't have the fire power to make an impact.

Tomasson insisted prior to this game, "I am not a target man", after taking flak for some rather below average performances.

Pressure from Watson and Barton down the right forced a mistake from Ernest Faber in the 23rd minute. But Barton's shooting was well wide of the mark, showing United's desperation at shooting on sight rather than trying to conjure up anything constructive in the PSV penalty area.

The visitors took a deserved lead when Nilis nonchalantly slipped the ball under the advancing Given from 10 yards.

Half-time: Newcastle Utd 0 PSV Eindhoven 1

United's first shot on target finally arrived in the 48th minute when skipper John Barnes curled in a 22 yard free kick which Waterreus palmed over.

On 60 minutes Barnes carved out a chance for Watson, who was pushed up front to try to use his pace to cut through the PSV defence. It was a great effort, similar to his stunning goal at Anfield back in 1995 in the League Cup, but Waterreus did better than the Liverpool goalkeeper and palmed it over the bar.

Watson was only inches away from firing home a 69th minute equaliser. Albert allowed the ball to run on and the defender stroked a fine effort inches wide of the far post.

Albert climbed high inside a crowded PSV six yard box to head only inches past in the 76th minute.

But Newcastle could not force that elusive equaliser and, at the death, De Bilde hit a second for the Dutch side.

November 26 1997 - BARCELONA 1 NEWCASTLE UTD 0

Hislop, Beresford, Batty, Peacock (Pearce), Barnes, Ketsbaia, Tomasson, Watson, Hamilton, Albert (Hughes).

Att: 26,000

Newcastle lost any chance of qualifying for the knock-out stages of the Champions' League when they fell to a first half goal from Brazilian ace Giovanni, but the magnificent travelling army of 8,000 supporters made all the noise in a wet Nou Camp.

Just like our trips to Kiev, Ibrox, Bilbao, Rotterdam and Monaco, where the stadiums of those clubs were/are a statement of things far more significant than anything involving football, Nou Camp has an incredible history. Barcelona has long fought for independence and at one time, under fascist dictatorship from Madrid, the people could only speak their language of Catalan inside Nou Camp. In 1925, the crowd in the stadium jeered the national anthem in a spontaneous protest against Miguel Primo de Rivera's dictatorship. The ground was closed for six months as a reprisal. After the Civil War, the Catalan flag was banned and Barcelona had to remove the flag from its club shield.

MATCH REPORT: The pattern was set from the first minute when the home side could have taken the lead after Sonny Anderson crossed - only a fine clearance from Alessandro Pistone saved the day.

Home attackers Anderson and Rivaldo ploughed down the United right, a little too easily for Kenny Dalglish's liking, and the former Liverpool boss was very animated on the touch-line giving out instructions.

United keeper Shaka Hislop made a magnificent save from Celades in the 12th minute. Giovanni crossed for the left and the striker dummied past Pistone before firing in a low effort which Hislop, making his Champions' League debut, flung himself to his right to save.

John Barnes then smashed a superb 25-yard effort inches past Ruud Hesp's upright left hand, a brilliant effort from the former England international that brought the United fans to their feet.

Giovanni put the home side ahead in the 17th minute, however, when Guardiola split the United back four and the striker finished with some aplomb, chipping Hislop with ease.

Dragan Ciric should have made it two but Beresford got back to make a goal-saving tackle.

Darren Peacock injured his knee and was carried off, replaced by Stuart Pearce.

Ten minutes before the break, Tomasson hit the crossbar from 20 yards after a brilliant three-man move involving Beresford and Ketsbaia.

Half-time: Barcelona 1 Newcastle Utd 0

Philippe Albert was replaced at the interval by young Northern Ireland defender Aaron Hughes, who could always brag that he had made his Newcastle debut at the world famous Nou Camp.

There was a skirmish from (what seemed like) home supporters fighting between themselves behind the Barca goal, but it soon settled down when stewards got into the crowd.

Once again we didn't see the explosive pace and inspiration from Ketsbaia that he brought to the game when introduced as substitute. He was in the starting line-up and made little impact, despite plenty of effort.

Barca were hardly world-beaters on this performance, either, and frustrated their own fans with some woeful shooting in front of goal.

Five minutes from time Steve Watson had a great chance but he headed a couple of feet wide when he should have scored.

Bobby Robson: "The players Newcastle were missing were all attacking players. That's why they struggled. They were never going to make many chances here and I think they were happy not to lose by many. Newcastle had one or two little chances but Barcelona deserved to win. Don't forget we also had some important players out. We have a bigger and better squad in depth than Newcastle have. Barcelona only had their honour and reputation to play for."

December 10 1997 - NEWCASTLE UTD 2 DYNAMO KIEV 0

Hislop, Batty, Peacock, Lee, Barnes, Asprilla (Ketsbaia), Pearce, Gillespie, Watson, Pistone (Hughes), Albert.

Att: 33,694

MATCH REPORT: Newcastle started well, with Faustino Asprilla only inches away from converting Steve Watson's cross from the right, but within three minutes Serguei Rebrov missed a sitter when unmarked at the far post.

However, United took the lead in the 10th minute after a brilliant 40-yard run by Batty. He turned the ball back into the path of Barnes, who shot across Olexandr Shovkovski from 12 yards into the bottom corner.

Within 90 seconds Rob Lee miscued from 12 yards when the goal was wide open.

United went 2-0 ahead in the 21st minute when Stuart Pearce blasted a thunderbolt home from 25 yards for his first goal for the Magpies. Lee took a short free kick and placed it in the path of the former England skipper, who curled a superb left-footer into the near corner.

Just before the break Shaka Hislop made saves from Kalitvintsev and Rebrov.

Half-time: Newcastle Utd 2 Dynamo Kiev 0

A superb 51st minute move was ruined when Gillespie fluffed his cross with both Asprilla and Lee waiting unmarked in the middle, then six minutes later Watson headed wide.

The remainder of the half petered out to just about nothing. Kiev had qualified for the next round and were happy to see out time, while the Magpies had themselves a win but knew this would be their last match in the competition.

It was a richly deserved victory, with Batty and Barnes particularly impressive, and we can just look back at 'what might have been'. Kiev won the group – but we had taken four points off them.

Real Madrid beat Juventus 1-0 in the final at Ajax's Amsterdam Arena in the Netherlands.

Toon Fans party on in Eindhoven

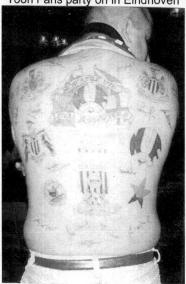

Doug's artwork

CHAPTER EIGHT
EUROPEAN CUP WINNERS CUP 1998/99

Ruud Gullit

MANAGER: Ruud Gullit

Amsterdam-born Ruud Gullit was, without doubt, one of the greatest players who had ever played the game. But so was Ossie Ardiles, and sadly he found it tough going at St James' Park in the hot seat. So perhaps we were fools to get too carried away with the promise of "Sexy Football". But get carried away we certainly did.

Gullit started his managerial career in the summer of 1996, when Glenn Hoddle left Chelsea to become manager of the England national team, and he was appointed as a player-manager. In his first season (1997) he guided Chelsea to an FA Cup triumph, the club's first major trophy in 26 years, and he became the first non-British manager to win a major trophy in this country.

The following season, with Chelsea in second place in the Premiership and proceeding to the quarter-finals in two cup competitions, he was sacked. Controversial Chelsea chairman Ken Bates famously said of Gullit - "I didn't like his arrogance - in fact I never liked him".

He joined Newcastle United in 1998 following the sacking of Kenny Dalglish, and the fans were singing: "We're gonna have sex on the pitch – come on everybody."

HOW NEWCASTLE UTD QUALIFIED:

United finished a lowly 13th in the Premiership just four points away from Bolton Wanderers, who were relegated. But Kenny Dalglish took the club on an amazing FA Cup journey, all the way to Wembley, where we were beaten by Arsenal. Under normal circumstances that would have been it, but with Newcastle's amazing record of getting into Europe by the back-door, it happened again. Arsenal won the double, and pipped Manchester United (by one point) to the Premiership, so the cup finalists gained a place.

This was the last year for the European Cup Winners Cup competition. UEFA struggled to get sponsors and the decision was taken to abolish the competition after the end of the 1998/99 tournament.

September 17 1998 - NEWCASTLE UTD 2 PARTIZAN BELGRADE 1

Given, Pearce, Charvet, Glass, Watson, Dabizas, Lee, Barnes, Speed, Shearer, Ketsbaia, Andersson. (Sub: Solano).

Att: 26,599

MATCH REPORT: In the third minute Robert Lee was forced to try his luck from distance with an 18-yard strike that Partizan goalkeeper Nikola Damjanac did well to save. Partizan's plan was to keep a high back-line – to keep the Magpies shooting from long range – and they caught Shearer offside three times within the first five minutes. But it was Russian roulette they were playing, because the GOALden Boy only needed to spring the trap once to make them pay.

However the visitors did enjoy one foray forward and Nikos Dabizas was forced to make a bicycle-kick clearance to deny Menad Bjekovic.

But just four minutes later Shearer struck.

Lee found Stuart Pearce in the centre of the Partizan half and the former England defender pushed forward before releasing a defence-splitting ball to the England captain. Shearer looked up once and placed the ball beyond Damjanac's left hand.

The visiting supporters reacted in bizarre fashion, turning their backs to the pitch and cheering.

Stephen Glass put over a free-kick and Gary Speed leapt above the Partizan defence but his header looped over the crossbar.

Half-time: Newcastle Utd 1 Partizan Belgrade 0

Eight minutes after the break, Stephen Glass jinked past Goran Trobok to get into the area, but Temuri Ketsbaia was denied by a last-gasp Partizan block after the former Aberdeen winger pulled the ball back to him.

The closest the visitors had come to scoring was when Steve Watson almost embarrassed himself with a sliced clearance in his own area which Given gratefully caught under his own crossbar.

Goran Obradovic was given a golden opportunity from 12 yards but his shot was so wild it ended up being a Newcastle throw-in!

But against the run of play Partizan equalised in the 69th minute. Bjekovic rushed into the area forcing Charvet into a rash challenge and Dutch referee Dick Jol had no hesitation in pointing to the spot.

Vuk Rasovic stepped up to send Given the wrong way with Partizan's first shot on target and a vital away goal.

But Newcastle were soon back in front when Dabizas sent a looping header over Damjanac from Glass' cross to restore the lead.

October 1 1998 - PARTIZAN BELGRADE 1 NEWCASTLE U 0

Given, Pearce, Batty, Speed, Ketsbaia, Charvet, Glass, Solano, Dabizas, Griffin, Shearer. (Sub: Albert).

Att: 26,000

A war was about to rage in Belgrade and getting to this match defied belief. We had to catch a train to Manchester, sleep in the airport, and catch an early morning flight to Hamburg; flight from Hamburg to Munich; then a business flight on a 20-seater flying box to Belgrade. When we landed the city was having an earthquake; we were told our hotel had been taken over by the army and we were put in a brothel; then I had an argument with a taxi driver (who added the equivalent of £30 to the bill for a two mile ride) and he pulled a gun out of the glove compartment and threatened to blow my head off!

The Partizan fans are nicknamed 'Grobari' - which in these parts means 'The Undertakers' – and they had attacked a small group of Toon fans with baseball bats in a bar. If you ever went to Millwall in the 1970s … times it by ten!

MATCH REPORT: It took all the combative talents of David Batty to prevent Newcastle's midfield from being swamped, and it was almost inevitable when the yellow card was shown to the former Leeds player in the 26th minute. He was quickly followed by Alan Shearer for dissent, which seemed a harsh decision, as all he did was shrug his shoulders at the referee.

Shay Given was called on to make saves from Nenad Djekovic and Dorde Tomic as the Yugoslavs gave early warning that they had the firepower to trouble the Geordie defence.

Djekovic climbed to head a cross against the Newcastle crossbar, but just before half time Temuri Ketsbaia squandered a gilt-edged opportunity, dragging his shot wide from 12 yards.

Half-time: Partizan Belgrade 0 Newcastle Utd 0

Partizan's relentless foraging sparked the incident which led to the winning goal. Sadly it was another penalty from Vuk Rasovic - the man who had slotted home the all-important away goal at St James' Park a fortnight ago. Laurent Charvet had given away the spot-kick needlessly on Tyneside, and this time it was Batty. The England midfielder tracked Partizan danger man Vladimir Ivic into the Newcastle penalty area in the 52nd minute and Batty, desperate to make the tackle before the lively striker got in the shot, tripped him up.

Rasovic slotted the ball easily passed the Newcastle keeper.

Newcastle had hung on through some desperate defending by the immaculate Nikos Dabizas, but that was the breakthrough that piled the pressure on Gullitt's side to score. They had to get a goal … or they were out.

Partizan could have added to their score several times but Newcastle still had their chances.

Gary Speed was the main culprit, missing his kick completely when put clean through by Shearer's pass.

The atmosphere was frantic, and the frenzied Partizan supporters hurled abuse - and their seats - over the metal barriers and over the heads of the armed police. The small pocket of Toon fans were in a compound with riot police in battle gear. Rather than defend us, the guys with the helmets and shields picked up the 'ammunition' that had been thrown at us (lighters, bolts, pieces of concrete, etc.) and handed it back to the Partizan fans to throw again!

The hostile atmosphere in the ground was in keeping with the tense situation in a country which was on the point of all-out war and the fans made constant chants against Tony Blair … as though we were bothered!

But the more worrying sound was a gun shot that went off as the home supporters starting fighting with each other. This was not football hooligans, this was all-out war between rival factions.

The team spirit from the Newcastle players, however, could not be faulted. They just lacked the cutting edge to break down the Partizan defence.

If only Charvet's shot, which was fumbled by keeper Damjanac and fell behind him, had landed on the right side of the goal-line we would have progressed in the competition … but the stadium would have become a bloodbath.

There were bizarre and frenzied celebrations at the end … as the home fans ripped out seats and tried to destroy the stadium. God only knows what would have happened if Newcastle had scored.

One fan said to me: "the stadium looks like a war zone". It didn't LOOK like a war zone … it WAS a war zone!

I'm not quite sure what planet **Ruud Gullitt** was on but he defended the Partizan supporters: "The atmosphere was no more intimidating than at St James' Park."

Lazio beat Mallorca 2-1 in the final played at Villa Park. They were not given the opportunity to defend their trophy the following season, nor were they allowed to keep the cup. Despite their protests, UEFA gave the cup to Barcelona, as they were the most successful club in the history of the competition.

Partizan Ultras

CHAPTER NINE
UEFA CUP 1999/2000

Bobby Robson

MANAGER: Bobby Robson

Bobby Robson had turned down the Magpies at least twice in the past, which didn't please his Newcastle-mad father, but we got him in the end. He became a legend at Ipswich Town and he progressed to manage the England World Cup team.

Before the 1990 World Cup, the FA told Robson that they would not renew his contract as England manager, so he moved on to the Netherlands to coach PSV Eindhoven. PSV won the Dutch league in both the 1990–91 and 1991–92 seasons.

Robson moved to Sporting Club de Portugal in July 1992, and he guided the club to a third place finish in his first season. Robson was sacked in December 1993, amazingly, with the club sitting at the top of the league table. Porto quickly hired Robson, with Jose Mourinho appointed as his assistant manager, and they went on to beat Sporting in the Portuguese Cup final. Then he won successive League titles in the 1994–95 and 1995–96 seasons.

Robson took over at Barcelona in July 1996. They won the Spanish Cup, Spanish Super Cup and European Cup Winners' Cup.

He returned to manage PSV on a short-term deal for the 1998–99 season, but following the resignation of Ruud Gullit at Newcastle United, Robson moved to St James' Park in September 1999.

HOW NEWCASTLE UTD QUALIFIED:

The 1998–99 FA Premier League season will be remembered as the one in which Manchester United won a unique treble of the league title, the FA Cup and the European Cup. And just like the previous season, we lost the FA Cup final but still qualified for Europe because our conquerors were 'double winners'.

The FA Cup apart, it was a difficult season for Newcastle, seeing Kenny Dalglish sacked early in the campaign and Ruud Gullit bring his "sexy football" to Gallowgate. We finished 13th.

September 16 1999 - CSKA SOFIA 0 NEWCASTLE UTD 2

Harper, Domi, Dabizas, Goma, Barton, Speed, Lee, Dyer, Solano (Hamilton), Shearer, Ferguson (Ketsbaia).

Att: 25,000

Like the visit to Budapest to play Ferencvaros, the people of Sofia couldn't have been more friendly ... until an hour before the game ... and the idiots suddenly came out of the woodwork.

The city is located in western Bulgaria, at the foot of Mount Vitosha, and still had it's 'old town' side, but was moving into the Western world very quickly. We were lucky enough to have a couple of students show us the sights for a couple of days.

The team's home stadium, Bulgarska Armia, is situated in the Borisova Gradina park, and it was a difficult journey getting from the city to the stadium without having some lout trying to strike out with a foot or a flag pole. They were a boisterous lot inside the ground, throwing lighters and assorted hardware, while waving banners showing various regiments of their "Ultras" gang - "City Boys", "Proud Ones", and "Ultra Separative Front".

The game, only Robson's second in charge, was a triumph of teamwork and commitment, and although there were a few anxious moments in a hostile atmosphere, they were rarely in any trouble.

It was only United's fourth away win in Europe, and it could not have come at a better time after an appalling start to the season which has seen them take just one point from a possible 21.

MATCH REPORT: Robson must have been well satisfied seeing his side dominate for long periods in the first-half and giving just as much as they took.

It was United who got in the first shot with five minutes gone when Shearer tested keeper Nenad Lukic from a tight angle.

But Sofia served notice of their own intentions on 12 minutes when Vladimir Mantchev was able to pull away from Barton at the far post and head just over from Roumen Hristov's cross.

Robson's gamble to risk Duncan Ferguson backfired with just 18 minutes gone. The tall Scot had been struggling from the kick-off and was forced to hobble off with Ketsbaia taking his place.

But Newcastle almost took the lead within a minute as Gary Speed met Solano's free-kick and powered in a header which Lukic did well to turn on to the bar at full stretch.

The woodwork came to Newcastle's rescue on 25 minutes when Goma could only half-clear Hristov's corner and skipper Milen Petkov blasted a first-time effort on to the crossbar with Steve Harper well beaten.

Half-time: CSKA Sofia 0 Newcastle Utd 0

United finally forced their way in front six minutes after the break after Kieron Dyer was brought down by Mrkic as the former Ipswich Town winger weaved his way towards goal. Solano only had one thing in mind as he stood over the free-kick, and Lukic barely moved as the little South American expertly curled his shot inside his right post.

The 200-strong band of travelling supporters celebrated in fitting style as they sensed a turning point in the season.

Despite all of their pressure, the Bulgarians were unable to create any serious chances and Dimitar Berbatov's wayward 63rd-minute shot was as close as they came to troubling Harper in the second half.

Solano and Dyer could have sealed the victory, but it was left to Georgian Ketsbaia to finish things off. He turned past Galin Ivanov and lifted a shot over Lukic to make it 2-0.

September 30 1999 - NEWCASTLE UTD 2 CSKA SOFIA 2

Harper, Barton, Marcelino, Goma, Domi, Dabizas, Solano, Lee (McClen), Speed, Maric (Robinson), Shearer (Glass). Att: 36,200

CSKA coach Dimitar Penev was deprived of the services of talented skipper Milen Petkov, who refused to travel because of a dispute over win bonuses, and he left midfielder Roumen Hristov (their best player a fortnight ago) on the bench.

MATCH REPORT: Newcastle's start was less than inspiring and Steve Harper was the busier of the two keepers in the early stages. The 'keeper rescued Alain Goma with just 10 minutes gone after striker Dimitar Berbatov played Dimitar Ivanov in behind the Frenchman, and Harper produced a great block to keep his side level.

Shearer went close but Spanish misfit, Marcelino, passed up a glorious opportunity six minutes later when keeper Nenad Lukic could only parry Dabizas' header, but he mis-kicked with the goal at his mercy.

United thought they had made the breakthrough seconds later when Gary Speed drove home, but hopes were dashed by the offside flag.

The Bulgarians took a shock first-half lead when Ivan Litera caught the Magpies defence napping, but the response was swift and devastating seven minutes later. Speed played Didier Domi into space and when he squared the ball, Shearer slid in to score his eighth goal in three games – having scored five goals against Sheffield Wednesday and two against Leeds.

Half-time: Newcastle Utd 1 CSKA Sofia 1

Maric (like Marcelino) had his critics and he squandered a fine chance to put Newcastle in front and silence the Boo Boys within a minute of the restart when he blasted high and wide from Shearer's brilliant knock-down. But it was either 'feast or famine' with the Croatian, and he produced a beautiful turn seconds later to leave Litera floundering before shooting just wide of the far post.

Maric was replaced by young Paul Robinson, and with two minutes remaining, the 20-year-old Robinson slid in at the far post to bundle it home.

But there was to be a twist in the tale as the Bulgarians claimed a share of the honours on the night when Simeonov headed home at the far post in injury time.

October 21 1999 - FC ZURICH 1 NEWCASTLE UTD 2

Harper, Barton, Dabizas, Hughes, Domi, Solano (McClen), Dyer (Serrant), Lee, Speed, Shearer, Maric (Robinson).

Att: 9,500

Zurich is the largest city in Switzerland and is located in the centre of the country at the north-western tip of Lake Zurich. The people could not have been nicer and the three days were an experience I will never forget. The Nelson pub was the least expensive in the city centre and the landlord gave us reduced rates, and when we left for home, each Geordie was presented with a commemorative 'Nelson' pint glass (which I still have at home).

The Letzigrun Stadium was arguably the friendliest foreign ground I think I have ever visited. The home fans thought it was hilarious when the Geordies sang: "You're just a town full of Germans!"

MATCH REPORT: The Magpies gave the ball away at depressingly regular intervals and didn't rise above the very ordinary Zurich side for some time. Indeed, they could have found themselves three down within 17 minutes as Frederic Chassot, Mikheil Kavelashvili and Cesar Sant'Anna were all guilty of bad misses.

The largely ineffective Maric was muscled off the ball as Speed put him through on goal. Then he messed up again when Solano shot straight at Pascolo, a shot he could not hold, but again Maric misjudged the loose ball.

Rob Lee had the last real chance of the half, smashing a 20-yard effort a couple of feet over the bar.

Half-time: FC Zurich 0 Newcastle Utd 0

Robson's half-time team-talk must have been stinging, because within six minutes of the restart his side took the lead. Maric took the ball on his chest and raced in on goal to beat Pascolo and claim his first goal for the club.

It was 2-0 nine minutes later, when Pascolo pushed Hughes' shot on to the bar and Shearer smashed home the rebound.

But Zurich gave themselves a lifeline with 68 minutes gone as Castillo cut in from the right and fired past Harper.

The United keeper was fortunate to escape his second red card within 10 days (he was sent off by referee Uriah Rennie for a foul on Andy Johnson at Birmingham) when he brought Bartlett down on the edge of the penalty area with 15 minutes remaining. But the referee cautioned him and awarded a free kick which came to nothing.

But United were rocking at the back, and the keeper saved from substitute Gauthier Akale and Bartlett (twice) in a matter of minutes.

The Swiss side came within an inch of an equaliser four minutes from time when Bartlett hit the bar.

November 4 1999 - NEWCASTLE UTD 3 FC ZURICH 1

Harper, Barton, Domi, Lee (McClen), Marcelino, Dabizas, Solano, Ferguson (Robinson), Shearer, Maric (Glass), Speed.

Att: 34,502

One of our friends (Tony Taylor) was an early bird and bought a cheap flight to Zurich as soon as the draw was made (as travel companies jump on the band wagon and double prices when they realise that there will be demand). But with Grasshoppers Zurich playing a European tie on the same evening, FC Zurich switched their games with Newcastle. So Tony ended up flying to Switzerland when we played them at St James' Park. But he was made very welcome at the Nelson pub where he, and our Swiss friends, watched the match on the big screen TV.

MATCH REPORT: Duncan Ferguson was handed his first start since September 16, after recovering from a hamstring injury, slotting in alongside Alan Shearer in attack. And the presence of the giant Scotsman had the Zurich backline in a right mess in the opening minutes. They knew the threat he posed but didn't know how to stop it. He set up a shooting opportunity for Nobby Solano with a neat flick after just three minutes gone, and he turned up in the penalty area two minutes later to get on the end of Barton's cross, but could not climb high enough to direct it onto goal.

Zurich hit back and Jamarauli squared the tie on 17 minutes. The striker turned up wide on the left to drive in a low cross towards Bartlett, but it slipped into the far corner with Harper and his defenders flat-footed.

Then the home side restored their aggregate league 12 minutes before the break after Shearer's free kick was tipped on to the bar by Pascolo but Silvio Maric followed up to head into the empty net.

Just before half-time Dabizas made a superb tackle to keep out Bartlett.

Half-time: Newcastle Utd 1 FC Zurich 1

United finally took the lead after Speed set Solano away, and although his shot was half-saved by Pascolo, Ferguson followed up to prod the ball home.

It was all over within three minutes when Speed rose unopposed to meet Solano's corner to make it 3-1.

Dabizas had three efforts on goal, but none beat the keeper.

Shearer went just wide with a header three minutes from time and drove a free kick wide in injury time.

November 25 1999 - AS ROMA 1 NEWCASTLE UTD 0

Harper, Barton, Charvet, Dabizas, Hughes, Pistone, Lee, Speed, Solano, Shearer, Ketsbaia (Robinson).

Att: 45,655

The 'Eternal City' and a clash with the mighty Associazione Sportiva Roma at their famous Stadio Olimpico, situated 3 kilometres due north of the Vatican at the foot of Monte Mario. I'm sure, being one of the most visited cities in the world (the Vatican receives 4.2 million tourists a year and the Colosseum gets 4 million), Rome needs no description from me.

In football terms, Roma is a club with many rivalries. First and foremost Lazio, the club who they share the Stadio Olimpico stadium with, but we were also told that Roma supporters allegedly don't like English fans. This is apparently because of their defeat to Liverpool in the 1984 European Cup Final at the Stadio Olimpico, and the subsequent violence outside the stadium which saw a number of Liverpool fans stabbed.

(* Since then, there have been further instances of some English supporters being attacked and stabbed in Rome, including Liverpool again, Middlesbrough, Manchester United and Arsenal supporters.)

We found them a bit "iffy" too, although there were no major incidents. Despite their so-called rivalry, Roma and Lazio fans followed us from bar to bar, constantly on mobile phones telling others where we were and trying to guess where we were heading. It gets you paranoid after a while, and we just kept on moving – they kept on following!

MATCH REPORT: Newcastle defended more than competently in the early stages, and Charvet in particular looked comfortable despite making just one appearance as a substitute all season.

In the early stages 20-year-old Aaron Hughes stuck manfully to the task of man-marking Roma legend Totti, although it was obvious he was going to be tested to the full.

It was Newcastle who were the first to create a genuine chance when Solano's corner was half-cleared, but the ball fell to Ketsbaia, who drove in a low skidding effort which was saved by keeper Francesco Antoniola at the second attempt.

Brazilian defender Zago gave Shearer a tough first-half, and eventually had his name taken on 25 minutes when he upended the England skipper ... not for the first time.

Warren Barton blocked Cafu's pile-driver with his arm, and the Roma players converged on the French referee, but no penalty was given.

Half-time: Roma 0 Newcastle Utd 0

Roma finally forced the breakthrough within five minutes of the restart when they were eventually awarded a penalty. Totti's ball over the top allowed Marco Delvecchio to charge into the box, and when Charvet slid in with a challenge, the referee pointed to the spot.

It was Totti who stepped up to drive his spot-kick low to Harper's right, but although the keeper got a hand to the ball, he could not keep the ball out of the bottom corner.

Totti started to get some freedom and that gave him the chance to cause all sorts of problems in front of Harper's goal. The Roma skipper was starting to pull the strings, and he was unfortunate not to increase his side's lead on 57 minutes when he let fly from 25 yards but saw his effort come back off the post.

Shearer earned his second booking in the competition for a foul on Zago as Newcastle become increasingly stretched, and Totti saw a 74th-minute effort slide just wide after he cut inside Hughes on the left.

To their credit, Newcastle pressed forward in search of an equaliser, and Lee went just wide with a curling effort 10 minutes from time.

December 9 1999 - NEWCASTLE UTD 0 AS ROMA 0

Harper, Dumas (Hughes), Charvet, Dabizas, Pistone, Dyer (Ferguson), Speed, Solano, Lee, Shearer, Ketsbaia (Glass).

Att: 35,739

Bobby Robson signalled his intention to take the game to the Italians by including Dyer in the starting line-up for his first action since undergoing surgery on a calf injury in October.

But striker Duncan Ferguson was kept in reserve on the bench, while Laurent Charvet came in for the ineligible Helder.

Serie A leaders Roma opted for two changes to the side which won the first leg, with Amedeo Mangone replacing Alessandro Rinaldi and Damiano Tomassi getting the nod over Eusebio Di Francesco.

MATCH REPORT: Both managers had vowed to adopt an attacking approach and the game did start that way. They were prepared to go end-to-end but soon the defences got on top.

Shearer and Dyer combined to set up Ketsbaia but Brazilian Zago intervened with a vital tackle as the Georgian shot.

But the Italians were, as expected, proving a threat on the break and Charvet had to time his tackle perfectly on Marco Delvecchio as the Italian took Zago's long pass on his chest and homed in on goal with 18 minutes gone.

Shearer drove a 25-yard free kick inches wide, and Ketsbaia should have put the Magpies in front on 31 minutes. Lee's powerful run set up the striker on the left side of the penalty area but keeper Antonioli was off his line quickly to block.

Steve Harper had to pull off a good reaction save to keep out Aldair's header, and the keeper was relieved to see the German referee wave play on as Delvecchio went down under his challenge.

Half-time: Newcastle Utd 0 Roma 0

Ketsbaia had a golden opportunity on 61 minutes after Shearer flicked on Charvet's cross. Dyer picked up the loose ball and fed it out to the Georgian on the edge of the box, but his shot was turned away by Antonioli.

Robson took a gamble and introduced the clearly unfit Ferguson with 17 minutes remaining. The Scot replaced Dyer and Stephen Glass came on for Ketsbaia in a last-ditch attempt to get back into the tie.

Ferguson's presence seemed to unsettle Antonioli, the goalkeeper, and he opted to punch away anything that came his way rather than suffer a challenge from the former Rangers striker.

The game erupted two minutes later when a scuffle broke out in the Roma penalty area with the visitors claiming that Ferguson had felled Zago with an elbow.

Newcastle piled forward as time ran out but it was the visitors who almost snatched it at the death, Totti chipping the ball just over the bar with Harper beaten and Delvecchio firing into the side-netting.

The final was held in Denmark at the Parken Stadium in Copenhagen. Galatasaray and Arsenal drew 0-0 but the Turks won the cup by winning the penalty shoot-out 4-1. Suker and Vieira missed for Arsenal.

CHAPTER TEN
INTERTOTO CUP 2001/02

Craig Bellamy

MANAGER: Bobby Robson

Bobby wanted some fire power up front following a poor 2001/2 season that had seen Carl Cort and Nobby Solano top goal-scorers with only six league goals each.

He signed Craig Bellamy, at the second time of asking. The Welsh international had snubbed an offer from Newcastle in order to join Coventry City the previous season, but he only scored six goals during the whole campaign and the Sky Blues were relegated. There was a clause in his contract allowing him to move on if they went down, and Robson took up the option.

Craig Bellamy: "Everyone who knows me says I'm not arrogant, but I am confident about my own ability. I won't be a quiet person and I'm sure Alan Shearer won't mind me shouting at him."

HOW NEWCASTLE UTD QUALIFIED:

This Intertoto campaign (2001/2) is not something Toon fans can brag about to the Mackems, because in this particular season, if league position is anything to go by, Newcastle should not have been in it … and Sunderland should!

Newcastle finished in the bottom half of the Premiership in 2000/01 (11th) while Sunderland finished 7th.

The back door was open once again to hopefully get us into the UEFA Cup, but it would take six games to get there. Most clubs snubbed the competition because it had a midi-July start that shortened the holidays of the players.

To make it possibly the most ridiculous competition in world sport, it didn't have one final - it had THREE! And there was no outright winner or a trophy.

July 14 2001 - S LOKEREN 0 NEWCASTLE UTD 4

Given, Barton, Elliott, Solano, Bassedas, Speed, Quinn, Bellamy, Hughes, Ameobi, Dabizas. (Subs: Lua Lua, McClen, S Caldwell).

Att: 3,500

The much maligned Intertoto Cup had its critics but England coach Sven-Goran Eriksson took the chance to fly to Belgium to watch the English-born players and was in the 3,500 crowd. Not that there were many Englanders in the starting line up - Warren Barton, Robbie Elliott, Wayne Quinn and Shola Ameobi (and none of them gained caps under Eriksson).

This competition started just seven weeks after the end of the previous season, but 600 Toon fans gave up their holidays to follow their beloved Newcastle United.

Lokeren is not the most liveliest of towns - in not the most liveliest of countries – so we were basically left to make our own entertainment in the local bars.

Lokeren's home record in European competition was rather impressive for such a small club. They had beaten Barcelona 2-1, FC Nantes 4-2, Real Sociedad 1-0 and held Dundee Utd 0-0 in previous seasons.

MATCH REPORT: Wayne Quinn turned in Craig Bellamy's 13th minute cross to give United the lead and the Belgians were never in the hunt after that. Quinn was a strange signing, considering he couldn't get into the first team squad at First Division (now the Championship) Sheffield United, yet Bobby paid £800,000 for him.

Shola Ameobi tricked 'keeper Daniel Zitka with a dazzling piece of footwork before scoring in the 24th minute, then showed his growing maturity with a contemptuous finish in the 39th minute after he held off a strong challenge on the edge of the area.

In between Ameobi's goals, Shay Given made a spectacular save to stop Arnar Gretarsson grabbing the Belgian headlines.

Half-time: Lokeren 0 Newcastle Utd 3

The second half was rather low key. Newcastle were happy to dictate the play without having to 'push the boat out' and exert much energy. After all, the players were still well short of match fitness.

Substitute Lomana Lua Lua finished off the scoring with a spectacular overhead kick four minutes from time.

It was more a good workout than a good performance, and the decision to take part in the competition seemed to be justified.

In the day of squad numbers, the chance to wear the famous number nine shirt falls to very few. But Ameobi took full advantage of Shearer's absence (and his shirt) to bag himself a brace.

Shola Ameobi: "The Intertoto is a great chance for me to learn about different football cultures and the way they play in other countries. There's so much competition amongst the strikers and I know Alan Shearer will be the first choice when he's fit – he can have his number nine shirt back."

Bobby Robson: "I didn't speak to Sven after the match but I think he will have been impressed by Shola's performance. He scored two marvellous goals and was a constant threat. He's certainly one for the future, he's going to be a good player. He linked up well with Craig Bellamy, and just think, we still have Alan Shearer and Carl Cort to come back".

July 21 2001 - NEWCASTLE UTD 1 S LOKEREN 0

Given, Barton, Elliott, Solano, Bassedas, Speed, Quinn, Bellamy, Hughes, Ameobi, Dabizas. (Subs: Bernard, McClen, Lua Lua).

Att: 29,021

Newcastle United set a new attendance record for the competition, beating it by almost 3,000 when 29,021 turned up at St James' Park for their first taste of the Intertoto Cup.

Full-back Robbie Elliott played in front of United's home fans for the first time since his return to St James' Park from Bolton.

MATCH REPORT: Bellamy had a fine opportunity to collect his first goal for the club with just nine minutes gone when Ameobi's clever touch left the Lokeren defence flat-footed, but keeper Mladen Dabanovic got the better of him.

For their part, the visitors were happy to throw men forward when they were in possession, with Okitankoyi Kimoto and Karim El Bodmossi looking dangerous on the run, but the United defence was able to deal with them well enough to leave keeper Shay Given without a genuine save to make.

Half-time: Newcastle Utd 0 Lokeren 0

The Belgians created their best chance of the game two minutes after the restart when Kimoto just failed to get a touch on Arnar Vidarsson's pile-driver.

Nobby Solano curled a free-kick just wide, but he turned provider on the hour when Bellamy turned his header into the net after Christian Bassedas had left Seyfo Soley for dead on the left.

Quinn sent a blistering left-foot drive inches wide, then nine minutes from time Mrzlecki used his hand to halt Dabizas' charge forward and picked up a second yellow card for his pains.

Arnar Gretarsson almost snatched a draw for his side at the death with a well-struck effort, but Given got down well to ensure a second consecutive clean sheet.

July 25 2001 - TSV 1860 MUNICH 2 NEWCASTLE UTD 3

Given, Barton, Elliott, Solano, Bassedas, Speed, Quinn, Bellamy, Hughes, Ameobi, Dabizas. (Subs: Bernard, Green, Lua Lua).

Att: 15,000

1860 share the Olympic Stadium with city rivals Bayern Munich, but they have little in common with their 'noisy' neighbours. Bayern have dominated Munich – and the Bundesliga – for decades, and are easily the biggest and richest club in the Fatherland.

For those interested in football stadia, I'm sure the 'Olymiastadion' is instantly recognisable. It really is beautiful, but in a German sort of way. Nothing is as it should be – but yet everything is in place.

MATCH REPORT: The visitors drew first blood after 10 minutes when Nobby Solano produced a fine solo goal. The Peruvian burst forward into the box, side-stepping the challenge of covering defender Vidar Riseth before expertly clipping the ball over the advancing Simon Jentsch into the corner of the net.

The Newcastle defence were guilty of ball watching as captain Thomas Hassler chipped into the path of Ned Zelic, but his fierce half-volley flew just wide of the post.

Newcastle looked the stronger side in the first half but just before the break they were nearly caught on the counter-attack as Shay Given saved Marcus Weissenberger's powerful shot.

Half-time: Munich 0 Newcastle Utd 1

After the restart 1860 came out with greater purpose and twice hit the bar within seconds.

Hassler drilled a free-kick against the crossbar before, from the rebound, Markus Schroth saw his header also cannon back off the woodwork.

Shola Ameobi's long clearance found Craig Bellamy in the home half and when he was bundled over on a charge into the area, Solano stepped up to fire home from the penalty spot in the 55th minute.

But within 90 seconds the German side had pulled a goal back as Hassler's clipped cross from the left was steered into the corner of Given's net by a spectacular overhead kick from former Bristol City player Paul Agostino.

Clearly buoyed by that strike, 1860 began to pile on the pressure and just 10 minutes later they were back on level terms.

The Newcastle defence failed to clear a cross and Filip Topolovic fired the ball off the underside of the bar and into the net.

But the rollercoaster tie still had one final twist and with seven minutes left, Solano blasted a Wayne Quinn cross back across the area, and Hughes stole in to head decisively past Jentsch.

August 1 2001 - NEWCASTLE UTD 3 TSV 1860 MUNICH 1

Given, Barton, Elliott, Solano, Lee, Speed, Quinn, Bellamy, Hughes, Ameobi, Dabizas. (Subs: Acuna, S Caldwell, Lua Lua).

Att: 36,635

Laurent Robert arrived at St James' Park and the £10million striker received a hero's welcome as he was presented to the fans before kick-off, and the Frenchman seemed taken aback by the reception. A new record Intertoto Cup crowd of 36,635 welcomed the former Paris St Germain winger to St James' Park.

MATCH REPORT: Only five minutes had passed when Shola Ameobi left defender Pfuderer for dead on the right and was unceremoniously felled. Solano, the hero of the first leg, drove his free-kick towards the near post and Speed arrived at pace to power a header past the helpless Simon Jentzsch.

It was all Newcastle as Solano, Ameobi and Craig Bellamy made life virtually impossible for the Germans.

Speed almost got on the end of another Solano cross and then flicked a header wide after a brilliant link-up between Solano, Bellamy and Ameobi.

But Munich finally managed to get a foothold in the game when they caught the Magpie defence napping three minutes before the break, to allow Borimirov to cross for Schroth to slot past Shay Given and make it 1-1 on the night.

Half-time: Newcastle Utd 1 Munich 1

Max volleyed over from an unmarked position seconds after the restart and Given had to tip the ball off Schroth's toe as Borimirov found space down the right.

Munich keeper Jentzsch had to kick away a weak shot from Wayne Quinn on 55 minutes.

Robson sent on Lua Lua and Acuna for Bellamy and Speed to try to change the flow of the game and within two minutes Lua Lua capitalised on a slip by Vidar Riseth to round Jentzsch and make it 2-1.

Munich defender Tyce handled inside the penalty area in the final minute and Solano stepped up to send the keeper the wrong way and score his third goal in the two-legged tie.

August 7 2001 - TROYES 0 NEWCASTLE UTD 0

Given, Barton, Elliott, Solano, Lee, Speed, Quinn, Bellamy, Hughes, Ameobi, Dabizas. (Subs: Bassedas, Lua Lua).

Att: 10,414

The club is officially called Espérance Sportive Troyes Aube Champagne, after it had to change its title in 2000 because of complaints that a French discount supermarket chain had claim to the same name.

Troyes is located in north-central France on the Seine river, about 95 miles south-east of Paris. Quaint and typically French, it has a quiet charm, but has nothing much to get the adrenaline rushing.

MATCH REPORT: Bobby Robson's side had to battle all the way against an impressive French outfit, who made light of the torrential rain which soaked the Stade de L'Aube pitch in the first leg of the Intertoto Cup final.

Newcastle arrived in France on the back of four straight victories in the competition but, from the off, wing-backs Gharib Amzine and Luciano Zavagno took the game by the scruff of the neck.

Things could have looked very black indeed for the Magpies with just seven minutes gone after they were torn apart twice in quick succession.

That they survived was down to the positioning of Given, who pulled off point-blank saves from first Gousse and then Ghazi.

The French side were irresistible in the early stages and, although Newcastle managed to restrict their opponents to a handful of long-range strikes, they were fortunate that Gousse just failed to connect with a Medhi Leroy cross and had Given to thank seconds before the break when he rushed from his line to deny Gousse once again.

Half-time: Troyes 0 Newcastle Utd 0

Troyes continued to dominate after the restart but largely without the clear openings they had forged before the break.

Gousse scuffed a shot harmlessly wide and it took a fine block from Robbie Elliott to deny Ghazi. But the visitors scrapped for every ball as they refused to let go of their UEFA Cup dream.

Bellamy and Ameobi kept making their runs, although they were too often isolated and found themselves battling against masses of blue shirts without getting any support from theNewcastle midfield.

Troyes could have snatched victory at the end as first Djukic took aim and then Saifi bore down on goal, but Dabizas blocked the first effort and then did enough to force the second wide.

August 21 2001 - NEWCASTLE UTD 4 TROYES 4

Given, Barton, Elliott, Solano, Lee, Speed, Quinn, Bellamy, Hughes, Ameobi, Dabizas. (Subs: Bernard, O'Brien, Lua Lua).

Att: 29,021

MATCH REPORT: Newcastle needed something early on to give them hope after their backs-against-the-wall performance in France, and it arrived within two minutes as they took the lead in superb style. Bellamy drew an early save from Tony Heurtebis, but the goalkeeper was picking the ball out of his net seconds later after being comprehensively beaten by Solano. Rob Lee's crunching tackle sent the ball rolling towards the Peruvian 25 yards out and he did not think twice before blasting his shot into the back of the net.

The French side had plenty of class in their ranks, however, and battered away at United's back-line.

Given, who dropped a clanger in the 1-1 draw at Chelsea the previous Sunday, could only palm Leroy's 35-yard screamer into his own net after it swerved viciously as it sped towards goal, and the home defence were rattled three minutes later when Gousse charged into the box and slotted easily past the goalkeeper.

Half-time: Newcastle Utd 1 Troyes 2

Robson attempted to reshuffle playing Warren Barton, Robbie Elliott and Nicos Dabizas in a backline of three, putting Hughes into midfield.

Troyes took a massive stride towards victory within 80 seconds of the restart when Barton gifted possession to Rothen and he fed Gousse, who saw his shot come back off the post for Boutal to fire home from close range.

The game and the tie seemed dead with 61 minutes gone after Boutal powered home a point-blank header from a Rothen cross to make it 1-4, but United gave themselves a glimmer of hope when Ameobi reduced the deficit within four minutes.

Robson responded with a triple substitution and saw his side edge further back into the game 21 minutes from time when Ameobi was hauled down by Meniri in the box and Speed stepped up to convert from the spot.

The visitors' goal led a charmed life as the clock ran down and the Magpies threw the kitchen sink at their opponents, and it took a miraculous late save from Heurtebis to prevent Dabizas levelling at the death.

But there was still time for further drama deep in injury time as Hughes turned Robbie Elliott's header past Heurtebis, although it was all a case of too little too late.

CHAPTER ELEVEN
EUROPEAN CHAMPIONS LEAGUE
2002/03

Kieron Dyer

MANAGER: Sir Bobby Robson

Bobby was soon to become "Sir Bobby". The honour was officially announced in the Queen's Birthday Honours in June 2002 and he was knighted on November 21st 2002. Robson joked about his age when the Prince of Wales told him he was thrilled to see he was still working in management and still enjoying it.

Sir Bobby said: "He said 'I hope it's not too taxing for you,' and 'Do take care'."

"And I said: "I'm doing exactly what I want to do. I'm happy doing it and I've got my health."

HOW NEWCASTLE UTD QUALIFIED:

Arsenal clinched the title on 8 May 2002 after a convincing win against Manchester United at Old Trafford, in the penultimate game of the season. This new attacking Arsenal side had won the FA Cup five days before and made history by accomplishing their third double; their second under the reign of Arsène Wenger.

Newcastle United qualified for the Champions League by finishing fourth.

August 14 2002 - ZELJEZNICAR 0 NEWCASTLE UTD 1

Given, Hughes, Dabizas, Bramble, Bernard (Quinn), Solano, Dyer, Jenas, Viana (Elliott), Shearer, Lua Lua (Ameobi).

Att: 35,000

FK Željezničar are based in Bosnia and Herzegovina, in the capital, Sarajevo. It was another incredible experience for the Toon travellers, visiting a place still recovering from the recent war. Sarajevo was shell-shocked, and I don't mean that flippantly. Belgrade was a hostile place when we visited it four years earlier, where the locals had no time for the English, but the people of Sarajevo couldn't do enough for us.

After an afternoon in the Manhattan Bar, we were taken to a pub I can only describe as being like a bullet-ridden Workingmen's Club (like Scotswood WMC on a good night), and they took us in the back room to show us their arsenal of guns. Unbelievable - we were handed an AK-47 semi-automatic rifle and asked if we wanted to go outside and fire it! We declined.

The match was switched to the Olympski Kosevo Stadium to cope with the large crowd and I would take a guess there were about 400 Toon fans. The view wasn't that good, as is usually the case when there is an athletics track, putting the pitch an extra 30 yards away from the supporters.

This was a qualifying fixture and Kieron Dyer fired Newcastle to within touching distance of the Champions League with a superbly taken goal. The 23-year-old played a flawless 56th-minute one-two with skipper Alan Shearer before lifting the ball over keeper Kenan Hagasic to give Newcastle a precious lead to take back to Tyneside.

MATCH REPORT: But for a couple of defensive slips, with French full-back Olivier Bernard guilty on more than one occasion, Newcastle were rarely in any trouble during a first half in which they could have taken control.

Dangerman Almir Gredic had the ball in the net with three minutes gone, but was well offside as he ran on to Adin Mulaosmanovic's through-ball.

Defender Sanel Jahic sent a header from a Mulaosmanovic free-kick high over Given's bar, but the Irishman did not have a save to make before the break, although it took an impeccably timed tackle from Dabizas to deny Gredic after front-man Guvo picked him out inside the box.

But in the main, it was the visitors who looked the more likely to score, and 19-year-old Jenas missed a glorious opportunity putting his header wide.

Half-time: Zeljeznicar 0 Newcastle Utd 0

Given had to be on his toes as Guvo turned smartly before firing in a left-foot drive which the Toon goalkeeper acrobatically turned away.

Lua Lua's pace was proving Newcastle's strongest hope of a break through, and Dyer capitalised to devastating effect. Lua Lua once again broke from halfway and committed defenders before finding Dyer, who played a perfect one-two with lynchpin Shearer and lifted the ball over the advancing Hagasic to send the small band of travelling supporters into raptures.

But the Bosnians hit back and within two minutes Gredic made the most of Bramble's momentary uncertainty to race in on goal and fire a low shot inches wide of Given's right post.

Lua Lua should have done better with 20 minutes remaining when Viana sent him clear, but with Dyer unmarked in front of goal, he tried to round the keeper and failed. He blazed over eight minutes later after getting the benefit of a dubious offside decision as the home side committed men to the search for an equaliser.

Ameobi almost made it 2-0 with two minutes remaining when he turned smartly just outside the penalty area and fired in a left-foot drive which clipped the relieved Hagasic's crossbar and dropped safe.

August 28 2002 - NEWCASTLE UTD 4 ZELJEZNICAR 0

Given, Hughes, Bramble, Dabizas (O'Brien), Bernard, Solano (Kerr), Dyer, Speed, Viana, Shearer, Lua Lua (Ameobi).

MATCH REPORT: Had it not been for two saves from Shay Given to deny Sanjin Radonja and Sead Seferovic, this tie could have had a very different look.

At long last we were starting to see the very best of Kieron Dyer and the England international tore brave Zeljeznicar to shreds. The buzzing midfielder was the architect of what proved to be a comprehensive victory over the Bosnians, who came and rolled up their sleeves but ultimately could not live with the Magpies.

The breakthrough finally arrived with 23 minutes gone when Nobby Solano exchanged passes with Shearer and slid the ball in to Dyer who, just as he had done in the first leg in Sarajevo, drew Hagasic before lifting the ball over him and into the unguarded net.

Newcastle's second goal arrived eight minutes before the break courtesy of an equally impressive finish.

Speed laid the ball into the path of Lua Lua, who needed a touch of luck to evade Haris Alihodzic's challenge, but the manner in which he dispatched it right-footed beyond Hagasic's despairing dive owed nothing to fortune.

Half-time: Newcastle United 2 Zeljeznicar 0

Hagasic pulled off a fine save to deny Shearer from distance then the England striker saw his pile-drive come back off the post.

Viana drilled a 67th-minute shot into Hagasic's chest but then, after Jahic had received his marching orders for a trip on Ameobi, went one better with 74 minutes gone when he barely broke stride as he ran on to Dyer's inch-perfect pass and blasted left-footed into the top corner.

Not to be outdone, Shearer got in on the act with 10 minutes remaining, beating the offside trap to reach another Dyer pass and fire past Hagasic.

The United skipper later hit the bar and had another goal ruled out for offside as United turned the screw.

September 18 2002 - DYNAMO KIEV 2 NEWCASTLE UTD 0

Given, Dabizas, O'Brien, Griffin, Hughes (Solano), Dyer, Speed, Viana, Bernard (Robert), Shearer (Ameobi), Bellamy.

Att: 42,500

Back to Kiev and the Olympic Stadium, and although the ground was only half full this time, it was 13 times the attendance for Kiev's league game the previous week. The Ukrainians notched up a record 8-0 victory over Vorskla Poltava played in front of just 3,200 spectators.

The 250 who had made the long trip from Tyneside were not taken in this time by any duff information provided by the 'Journal' travel reporter (if he still had his job). The Toon Army braved the rain, wind and plunging temperature, but were suitably dressed.

MATCH REPORT: Bobby Robson was happy enough with his side's share of the possession, but not with the way they used it. A Shearer header which failed to trouble keeper Vitalii Reva, and a deflected shot from Kieron Dyer, represented their best chances of the first-half.

But he will have been less than pleased with the way his side struggled to match the pace and movement of the Ukrainians.

It took them 16 minutes to find a way past Shay Given, although the Irishman was given little chance with Shatskikh's 25-yard pile-driver, unleashed without breaking stride as he met Leko's pass.

Bobby's defence had attracted more than it's fair share of criticism in recent times, with many questioning whether Andy O'Brien and Andy Griffin were good enough for Premiership or European glory. They struggled in Kiev and the backline was breached at regular intervals with Leko having a 30th-minute strike ruled out for offside, and Cernat curling a left-foot effort just inches wide of Given's post.

Half-time: Dynamo Kiev 1 Newcastle Utd 0

Robson shuffled his formation for the opening 23 minutes of the second half but things got little better.

Shatskikh had another strike chalked off for offside and both Nikos Dabizas and Olivier Bernard were the subject of penalty claims for hand-ball but escaped punishment.

Hugo Viana chanced his luck from distance with two shots, one better hit than the other, but with 62 minutes gone, Newcastle's task became even more difficult.

Cernat's intelligent pass put substitute Oleksandr Melashchenko into space inside the box, and although Given blocked his shot, Khatskevich was on hand to head home the loose ball.

Robert and Solano entered the fray with 22 minutes remaining, but United didn't improve.

As if the sting of defeat in the opening Champions' League game was not enough, Craig Bellamy was banned for head-butting Tiberui Ghioane.

Television picked up the incident in the closing stages of of the match, although the incident was missed by the referee.

This was not the only controversy - Laurent Robert was seen to clash with Sir Bobby Robson's assistant, John Carver, at the end of the game after appearing to refuse to acknowledge the travelling support.

September 24 2002 - NEWCASTLE UTD 0 FEYENOORD 1

Given, Griffin, Dabizas, O'Brien, Hughes, Solano, Dyer, Speed, Robert, Bellamy (Lua Lua), Shearer.

Att: 40,540

Newcastle United were taught a harsh lesson as Feyenoord returned to St James' Park to bring back long distant memories of our very first fixture in European competition.

MATCH REPORT: Robson, a student of Dutch football, knew exactly what to expect from last season's UEFA Cup winners, but he could not have anticipated that they would make their move so early in the game.

United had breezed through the early moments with Bellamy and Kieron Dyer looking particularly lively, but then the Dutchmen found their Achilles heel and brutally made them pay.

Andy Griffin failed to deal with Pierre van Hooijdonk's flick-on as he headed towards his own goal and Nikos Dabizas could only help the ball back to Pardo, who did not think twice before smashing an unstoppable volley past the stranded Given with just four minutes gone.

Thomas Buffel passed up an opportunity to make it 2-0, but it was keeper Edwin Zoetebier - ironically a former Sunderland goalkeeper - who was the hero as he produced a series of magnificent saves to deny Alan Shearer, Laurent Robert, Craig Bellamy and Gary Speed in a breathtaking individual display.

Half-time: Newcastle Utd 0 Feyenoord 1

Shearer mis-kicked as he met a Robert free-kick at the near post, and then Zoetebier got to the ball first as a Robert cross was heading straight for Shearer's forehead.

The keeper excelled himself again with 52 minutes gone when Bellamy slipped the ball to Shearer, who turned smartly but again could not get the better of the Dutchman.

Zoetebier was in the right place at the right time to turn away Solano's stooping header after the Peruvian had linked well with Bellamy and Robert, but it took a fine goal-line clearance from Shinji Ono to keep out a Shearer pile-driver from the resulting corner.

Feyenoord were seeing less and less of the ball, but Newcastle weren't hurting the Dutchmen when they were in possession.

Robert forced Zoetebier into a 74th-minute save with a dipping volley and Bellamy clipped the crossbar seconds before he was replaced by Lomana Lua Lua.

October 1 2002 - JUVENTUS 2 NEWCASTLE UTD 0

Given, Griffin (Lua Lua), O'Brien, Dabizas, Hughes, Solano (Viana), Jenas (Ameobi), Speed, Robert, Dyer, Shearer.

Att: 41,424

We did this trip the hard way because flight prices were extortionate as travel companies shot up the prices to exploit the fans knowing that there would be a massive demand (6,700 Newcastle fans travelled to Turin). In the end we did it our own way (as always) - car to London; flight from Heathrow to Milan; train to Turin.

The Italians imposed a "Booze Ban" on the Newcastle supporters and it ruined the day for many. They wouldn't serve us in the town centre, and when some Italians took Geordies to watering holes on the outskirts, the police followed and stopped us entering.

Unlike in Rome - and their anti-English support – the Juve fans were generally friendly.

Sir Bobby Robson returned to the Stadio Delle Alpi to be haunted by the ghost of the past as he sampled the bitter taste of cruel defeat for the second time in Turin.

Twelve years ago the then England boss saw his side denied a place in the World Cup final in a heart-breaking penalty shoot-out that left Gazza in tears in that memorable battle with Germany.

It could have been different for Robson this time, but for two moments of pure quality from superstar Alessandro Del Piero.

MATCH REPORT: The visitors started the brighter when Dyer's cross from the right saw Shearer's effort blocked by the diving Lilian Thuram.

Shearer squandered a better opportunity three minutes later when he pulled away from Thuram at the far post to meet Nolberto Solano's deep cross but mis-hit his volley.

A superb interception by Dabizas denied Di Vaio with 12 minutes gone but the Juve striker's evening came to an unpleasant end seconds later after he clashed heads with O'Brien and was stretchered off to a waiting ambulance at the side of the pitch.

His replacement David Trezeguet then forced a fine fingertip save from Given before ballooning a shot over the crossbar after Igor Tudor had flicked on Del Piero's corner.

With 22 minutes gone Del Piero picked up the ball wide on the left and cut inside to unleash a swerving 25-yard drive which evaded Given's athletic dive but cannoned back off the crossbar.

Against the run of play Newcastle were denied the opening goal in first half injury-time when Shearer's mis-kick from Dyer's cross fell perfectly for Robert to drive in a shot which Buffon parried at point-blank range.

Half-time: Juventus 0 Newcastle Utd 0

The home side emerged for the second half long before their opponents as Robson kept them waiting. If it was some sort of tactical ploy to frustrate the Italians, it didn't work. It was only a matter of time before Juve flexed their muscles once again.

Trezeguet tested Given twice before Dabizas fouled Del Piero inches outside the box, and got himself suspended for the return fixture. Del Piero picked himself up to smash an unstoppable 66th minute free-kick into the top corner.

Robert almost caught out Buffon with a blistering drive from all of 35 yards, but the ball sailed over the crossbar.

Robson made his last throw of the dice with 11 minutes remaining when he sent on strikers Shola Ameobi and Lua Lua in place of Griffin and Jenas, but Del Piero needed just two more minutes to wrap up victory.

Davids crossed from the left and Trezeguet dummied to allow his captain to drill a shot past Given and into the net to kill off Newcastle's hopes of a late comeback.

October 23 2002 - NEWCASTLE UTD 1 JUVENTUS 0

Harper, Griffin, Bramble, O'Brien, Hughes, Solano, Jenas, Speed, Robert (Viana), Shearer, Lua Lua (Ameobi).

Att: 48,370

United went into the game knowing that anything less than a victory would effectively end their faint hopes of a place in the second round and make even qualification for the UEFA Cup only a slim possibility, and that message had clearly been drummed home by the manager.

MATCH REPORT: If Juve demonstrated much of the class on show, Newcastle matched it with guts and determination.

Shearer thundered a 29th-minute header over the bar from a Solano corner and Frenchman Laurent Robert ran on to Speed's intelligent flick-on but directed his half-volley wide of Buffon's left post.

Di Vaio toe-poked a sixth-minute shot just wide and Steve Harper almost gifted Nedved the opening goal on 22 minutes when his casual pass towards Bramble was intercepted, but the Czech international shot horribly wide, and Harper redeemed himself moments later by blocking Di Vaio as he attempted to go round him on the edge of the box.

Del Piero went too high with a 25-yard free-kick nine minutes before the break, and Juventus probably went in at the break disappointed not to have been in front.

Half-time: Newcastle Utd 0 Juventus 0

United set out with more purpose and, but for Buffon, they could have had the points wrapped up long before the whistle.

The keeper saved bravely at the near post from Solano with 55 minutes gone and then produced a superb stop to keep out Shearer's blistering drive (on the hour). Buffon was the villain two minutes later, however, when Andy Griffin fired in a low shot across goal, and he scooped the ball into his own net to send the Geordie supporters into ecstasy.

Buffon redeemed himself with another magnificent save, this time from Solano's goal-bound pile-driver, and was in the right place at the right time to cling on to Robert's swerving a dipping 35-yard free-kick 14 minutes from time.

Substitute Gianluca Zambrotta had a chance to level a minute later but shot high over, and Marcelo Zayaleta shot against the bar.

Juve hammered away at the home side as time ran down, but there was to be no late heartache for Bobby Robson and his boys.

October 29 2002 - NEWCASTLE UTD 2 DYNAMO KIEV 1

Harper, Griffin, O'Brien (Bernard), Bramble (Dabizas), Hughes, Solano (Dyer), Speed, Jenas, Robert, Shearer, Ameobi.

Att: 40,185

MATCH REPORT: Sir Bobby Robson's side had come out on top in their 'must-win' clash with Juventus but this was another game with the same rules - they simply had to come away with the three points.

Although the visitors looked dangerous when in possession, Steve Harper did not have a single save to make before the break, with the mis-directed 36th-minute header from Shatskikh their only serious effort.

Newcastle tried to hold the fort in midfield and they handled Kiev's counter-attacks reasonably well, despite the loss of defender Titus Bramble with only 27 minutes gone.

Robert enjoyed plenty of possession down the left but too often couldn't make the cross count.

Shola Ameobi came agonisingly close to scoring the opener but his strike was literally an inch wide of the post.

Nikos Dabizas, on for Bramble, planted a diving header into the keeper's arms from a Robert free-kick but, try as they might, United could not find a way through the massed white shirts.

Half-time: Newcastle Utd 0 Dynamo Kiev 0

Kiev took full advantage when Newcastle players argued with the linesman on a dubious throw-in decision. Belkevich fed Peev to race away and slide in Shatskikh to beat Harper from close range.

United's response was to lay siege to the Dynamo goal, and the equaliser duly arrived within 11 minutes, Speed diving low to head Solano's corner home to restore parity.

But the visitors refused to lie down and Harper had to pull off a fine save to deny Shatskikh on 61 minutes with Andy Griffin just managing to deflect Jerko Leko's follow-up wide.

Newcastle continued to dominate and got their noses in front on 68 minutes when defender Andrii Husin dragged Shearer back as he tried to reach substitute Dabizas' cross. The United skipper sent Reva the wrong way from the penalty spot to give United the lead.

United weathered a late storm and could even have snatched a third goal in injury time when substitute Kieron Dyer forced a good save from Reva.

Juventus' 2-0 win over Feyenoord meant that United were off the bottom of the group, but they headed for Rotterdam knowing that even a victory would not take them through to the second round if Kiev defeated the Italians in the Ukraine.

November 13 2002 - FEYENOORD 2 NEWCASTLE UTD 3

Harper, Griffin, Bramble (Dabizas), O'Brien (Bernard), Hughes, Solano (Dyer), Jenas, Speed, Robert, Shearer, Ameobi.

Att: 45,000

Rotterdam was a changed city to the one the Geordies visited 34 year previous. In 1968 the city was starting a new beginning following the battering it took during World War II, but in 2002 the transformation was unbelievable. Some say Rotterdam now has an American feel about it – I just think it has its own unique character - and certainly nothing in Holland can compare with it.

During our trip to Eindhoven in 1997 we were based in Amsterdam and a group of Ajax fans got us tickets for their European tie with Italian club Udinese. There were three Newcastle United banners hanging by the side of the pitch, which I took to be Geordies taking in an extra game (like ourselves) on their way to Eindhoven. But our Dutch friend Imre told us they were Dutch banners because their bitter rivals Feyenoord "support Sunderland". I had never come across this before, and I certainly don't know of any Mackems who follow Feyenoord, but apparently the Rotterdam Ultras have a soft spot for the Mackems. Why? God only knows. But perhaps that could explain the hostile atmosphere towards the Geordies before, during and after this game in Rotterdam.

The local people of the city were fabulous and friendly, but as the game approached, the influx of Ultras into the city centre changed the atmosphere. They attacked pockets of Newcastle fans before the game but the major trouble happened at the end, when organised gangs tried to get the Geordies to break away from the police escort. It was really intimidating.

MATCH REPORT: Craig Bellamy's participation in the game had been the topic of much pre-match speculation, but it proved that the manager's decision to gamble on his fitness was absolutely correct, when he scored a minute into first-half injury time. He ran on to Shearer's flick-on and past defender Patrick Paauwe and prodded the ball past the stranded Patrick Lodewijks to send the travelling supporters in the crowd into raptures.

It was just reward for the Welshman, who had earlier passed up a similar opportunity after being sent clear by Kieron Dyer.

And it was difficult to argue that the visitors did not deserve their lead after a half during which they worked desperately hard to close down their opponents and suffered only a handful of real scares at the back.

With Gary Speed leading by example from central midfield, they worked extremely hard.

Bellamy's pace, allied to Dyer's darting runs and Shearer's power, had the Feyenoord defence worried at times, although skipper Paul Bosvelt, Lurling and Song Chong-Gug caused their own share of problems without ever really carving open Shay Given's defence.

Half-time: Feyenoord 0 Newcastle Utd 1

It got even better for United after the break when Dyer robbed Tomasz Rzasa on the edge of the Feyenoord box and crossed for Viana to calmly slot past Lodewijks to make it 2-0.

The joy on the terraces mounted further as news that Kiev's lead over Juventus had been overturned.

The Dutchmen, buoyed by the arrival of substitute Bombarda, launched a major assault. The super-sub made no such mistake on 65 minutes to slot home from Kalou's pass to reduce the deficit.

Bellamy sent Lodewijks full length to tip away a 70th-minute effort but, seconds later, his side's advantage was wiped out.

An error from Dyer allowed Lurling to take aim from close range, and with Given cruelly exposed, he volleyed home to set up a grandstand finish.

Bosvelt blasted just wide three minutes from time, but there was to be a dramatic twist at the death when Lodewijks could only parry Dyer's close-range effort and Bellamy smashed home the loose ball to spark mass celebrations.

Sir Bobby Robson's gamble on Craig Bellamy paid off, and that, coupled with Juventus' victory over Dynamo Kiev in the Ukraine was enough to cap an astonishing turn-around and propel Robson's men into the big time.

1 Juventus 13pts

2 Newcastle United 9

3 Dynamo Kiev 7

4 Feyenoord 5

Group A – **Newcastle United**, Internazionale, Bayer Leverkusen and Barcelona.

Group B – Valencia, Ajax, Arsenal, Roma.

Group C – AC Milan, Real Madrid, Lokomotiv Moscow, Borussia Dortmund.

Group D – Manchester United, Deportivo la Coruna, Juventus, Basel.

November 26 2002 - NEWCASTLE UTD 1 INTER MILAN 4

Given, Griffin, O'Brien, Hughes (S Caldwell), Dabizas, Solano, Dyer, Speed, Viana (Robert), Shearer, Bellamy.

Att: 50,108

Newcastle's hopes of snatching another famous Champion's League scalp were blown apart by Internazionale as Craig Bellamy's red mists descended once again. The volatile Welshman, who had already served a three-match ban for head-butting Dynamo Kiev's Tiberiu Ghioane, received his marching orders - and the certainty of another lengthy and costly suspension - just five minutes into the game for kicking out in retaliation at former Everton defender Marco Materazzi.

MATCH REPORT: The game was barely a minute old when Javier Zanetti slipped away from Aaron Hughes and sent in a cross which Crespo could not convert - but Morfeo did in emphatic style at the far post.

Bellamy's moment of madness came four minutes later when, after Materazzi roughed him up, he lost his cool and flicked out a boot, earning the inevitable red card.

The home fans were furious with referee Stephane Bre, but the striker's tears as he left the pitch stung all the more with the realisation that he had only himself to blame.

It would have been worse for Newcastle had Shearer not gone unpunished for a swinging elbow which saw Fabio Cannavaro fall to the deck as the players waited in the Inter area for a free-kick to be taken.

Nikos Dabizas might have levelled with a close-range 11th-minute header and Solano produced a superb diving save from Francesco Toldo with a dipping free-kick.

Almeyda made it 2-0 with a 25-yard rocket on 35 minutes, and then things got a whole lot worse when Crespo fired home at the near post from Okan's neat pass in injury time.

Half-time: Newcastle Utd 0 Inter Milan 3

Whatever Robson said during the half-time interval was irrelevant – the game was over.

Robert, who fractured his cheekbone just three weeks previous, replaced Hugo Viana at the break and his introduction injected fresh impetus into his side.

Kieron Dyer saw a close-range shot blocked by Giovanni Pasquale and Dabizas headed over from a Solano corner as United rallied.

Robert twice chanced his arm from distance as the home crowd raised their voices, and Alan Shearer went inches over the top with a bullet header from another Solano delivery.

And they got their reward with 18 minutes remaining when the Frenchman split the Milan defence with a perfect ball to Solano, who slipped his shot under Toldo to give Robson's side the faintest glimmer of hope.

Milan finally killed off United's mini-revival nine minutes from time when Stephane Dalmat combined with fellow substitute Recoba, who curled an exquisite shot past Shay Given to send the Italians delirious.

December 11 2002 - BARCELONA 3 NEWCASTLE UTD 1

Given, Griffin, O'Brien, Hughes, Bernard, Solano, Speed, Dyer, Robert, Ameobi, Lua Lua (Chopra).

Att: 45,100

Back in 1997 we went to Nou Camp with little or no chance of qualifying from the group stage of the Champions League, and Barca had already given up the ghost – they were already out. But this time the Catalan giants were very much alive, and Newcastle became Barcelona's record 10th consecutive Champion's League victims.

The 69-year old former Barca boss said he had walked into the stadium he knows so well with a lump in his throat. But Robson's boys had to make do with depleted support as the match was suspended for a day following horrific weather conditions. Not everyone could afford the luxury of a two night stay on the Mediterranean coast (like ourselves), because many had work the next day. We struck it lucky, but the majority had a wasted journey because they had flights to catch.

MATCH REPORT: Aaron Hughes, who was detailed to keep an eye on Dani, was left for dead when Xavi picked out his team-mate at the far post with seven minutes gone. Hughes was chasing shadows as the striker raced away from him and dispatched a well-placed volley past Given and into the far corner.

There may have been only around a quarter of the 4,200 Magpies supporters who initially made the trip to Catalonia inside the Nou Camp 24 hours after the game was initially expected to kick-off, but they were dancing, with 24 minutes gone, when Kieron Dyer rolled the ball into Ameobi's path. The Nigerian-born striker sent an inch-perfect shot inside Bonano's far post.

The superb Overmars warmed Given's hands with a 30-yard pile-driver and, inevitably, it was the Dutchman who put Barca ahead 10 minutes before the break. He mesmerised Griffin - once again - before squaring for Kluivert to finish.

Half-time: Barcelona 2 Newcastle Utd 1

The visitors returned after half-time determined to have a real go, with 21-year-old Ameobi leading the fight.

He powered a 52nd-minute header a foot wide from a Solano cross and then saw an even better effort hacked off the line by Riquelme as the travelling supporters dared to believe that the cause was not lost.

But just as their hopes were raised, they were torn apart when midfielder Motta got the slightest of touches on a Riquelme corner to deflect the ball over the line despite Dyer's best efforts on the far post.

Kluivert twice went desperately close, but Ameobi forced the best out of Bonano after surging through the heart of the Barca defence and letting fly.

Gary Speed powered a header wide from a Laurent Robert corner as the seconds ticked away to the final whistle.

We were kept behind after the game and a big beach ball was bounced around the away end with "Ole'" chants, until it went down to the next tier(we were on the top tier). A young lad climbed over a barrier to get the ball to the chant of "you're supposed to be in school" from thousands of Mags.

February 18 2003 - BAYER LEVERKUSEN 1 NEWCASTLE UTD 3

Given, Hughes, Bramble, O'Brien, Bernard, Jenas, Speed, Dyer, Robert, Lua Lua (Chopra), Ameobi (Cort).

Att: 22,500

We made the decision to base ourselves in nearby Cologne (ten miles away), after reading Leverkusen was definitely not the party capital of the northern Rhine region of Germany. It proved to be a wise choice. Cologne, on the other hand, is Germany's fourth biggest city and it has the extremely impressive Hohenzollern Bridge - which is like THREE Tyne Bridges riveted together – and that made the place home from home (in a weird sort of way).

The BayArena is a bit like Bolton's Reebok, far too fancy to be practical, with arches and curving steelwork that just doesn't fit in with German culture. But whoever decided upon heat lamps in the roof was onto a winner, because the evening was freezing.

MATCH REPORT: Bobby Robson, celebrating his 70th birthday, found the Germans in disarray after sacking their coach, Klaus Toppmoller, four days earlier.

Thomas Horster, promoted from the youth team after a run of five successive Bundesliga defeats cost Toppmoller his job, dropped eight of the players who had started the previous Saturday. But his masterplan was ripped apart inside 16 minutes.

The first blow was struck with barely five minutes on the clock when Lua Lua slipped through the German defence with almost embarrassing ease to gift Ameobi the simplest of chances to open the scoring.

It was 2-0 before the 1,100 United fans (who at one point serenaded Robson with a chorus of 'Happy Birthday') had regained their breath from the first goal. Ameobi robbed Thomas Kleine and shot past keeper Jorg Butt.

Bayer hit back on 26 minutes, however, when impressive Turkish international Yildiray Basturk set up Franca, who calmly lifted the ball over the advancing Shay Given to give his side a lifeline.

But, with 12 minutes of the first half still to play, Robert accepted the invitation to charge towards the penalty area before delivering an inch-perfect cross for Lua Lua to fire past Butt.

Half-time: Bayer Leverkusen 1 Newcastle Utd 3

Thomas Brdaric thought he had dragged the Germans back into a fighting finish with a 51st-minute header, but Newcastle were spared by an offside flag.

United went through a spell of being over-run, and it needed 33-year-old Speed's experience to take control in the middle of the field. The Welshman was up to the job, and marshalled his troops in expert fashion.

It took a good save from Given seven minutes from time to keep out Franca's close-range header, although Lua Lua really should have scored two minutes later after being sent clear by Kieron Dyer.

February 26 2003 - NEWCASTLE UTD 3 BAYER LEVERKUSEN 1

Given, Hughes, Bramble, S Caldwell, Bernard, Kerr (Viana), Speed, Dyer (Solano), Robert, Shearer (Lua Lua), Ameobi.

Att: 40,508

Alan Shearer kept Newcastle's hopes of reaching the Champions League quarter-finals alive with a quick-fire hat-trick to demolish Bayer Leverkusen. The 32-year-old, who had been forced to sit out the trips to Barcelona and

Leverkusen through suspension, took out his frustrations on the Germans on his return for his first United hat-trick since he claimed five goals in an 8-0 thrashing of Sheffield Wednesday.

MATCH REPORT: The returning skipper timed his run to perfection to meet a Gary Speed cross with a diving header which flew past the helpless Butt from point-blank range.

The keeper needed to produce a fine save to deny full-back Andy Griffin after a flowing attack down the Newcastle right, but the second goal arrived with 11 minutes gone. Ameobi's cross was tipped away by Butt but Shearer had the simplest of tasks to head into the empty net.

United were forced to endure an uncomfortable 10-minute period, and they were almost made to pay when Brazilian striker Franca went down under Given's challenge and Danish referee Claus Bo Larsen pointed to the spot. Neuville stepped up and aimed his shot low to Given's right, but the Irishman made a superb save.

Leverkusen paid for the miss 10 minutes before the break when Thomas Kleine tugged at Kieron Dyer's shirt and Shearer showed Neuville how to finish with a powerful shot into the roof of the net.

Half-time: Newcastle Utd 3 Bayer Leverkusen 0

Laurent Robert almost made it 4-0 with a free-kick from all of 40 yards which Butt had to turn away at full stretch.

But Newcastle surrendered their clean sheet when Babic and Basturk played a neat one-two outside the box before the former raced in to lift a clever shot over Given and reduce the deficit.

Kleine's 78th-minute header from a Simak corner had Given well beaten but it bounced back off the crossbar.

March 11 2003 - INTER MILAN 2 NEWCASTLE UTD 2

Given, Bernard, O'Brien (Hughes), Bramble, Griffin, Speed, Jenas, Robert (Viana), Solano (Lua Lua), Shearer, Bellamy.

Att: 53,459

Instead of flying direct to Milan, we flew to Venice and stayed a night there, then got the train across to Milan for the match. It still worked out cheaper, which just goes to show how much flight costs go up when a match is arranged. The Venice to Milan train journey was only something like £30 return, even though they are 150 miles apart.

Our second Italian trip of the season, and another "Booze Ban" by the Italian police. This one was probably worse than Turin because there were more police to try and keep us off the dreaded drink. So we bought tickets for the underground and set off into the unknown, picking some random destination five stops or so away from the city centre, and we were welcomed into a bar with help from some Inter fans.

San Siro, as I have reported earlier, is a marvellous stadium, but why was there only one entrance gate for Newcastle supporters? An estimated 12,000 Toon fans made the trip to Milan, so imagine Newcastle having one gate open for fans entering the Gallowgate End at St James' Park on a match day.

We were on the bottom tier, and during the whole game we were pelted with coins, lighters, bottles of piss and even a flare from the 'fans' above. As is life on the road following the Toon in Europe, the police did absolutely nothing to stop any of it. If any Mag asked for help or got agitated, they were either ignored or threatened with a baton. Nothing new, of course … we were getting used to being treat like animals.

MATCH REPORT: Titus Bramble had suffered a miserable first trip to the famous stadium with Ipswich Town when Christian Vieri plundered a hat-trick in a 4-1 win for the Italians the previous season. But after an early scare in which Emre cashed in on Andy O'Brien's error before shooting over, the United defence, and Bramble in particular, held firm.

Indeed, it was the visitors who enjoyed the better chances in the opening 45 minutes.

Nolberto Solano could count himself desperately unfortunate to see a fifth-minute volley come back off the crossbar before Francesco Toldo made a vital save.

Solano's intelligent pass allowed Bellamy to surge past the flat-footed Guly three minutes before the break.

He found Shearer exactly where he expected him to be to slot past the stranded Toldo from point-blank range.

Half-time: Inter Milan 0 Newcastle Utd 1

Just two minutes into the second half Inter silenced the Geordie hoardes when they levelled. Substitute Akinwunmi Martins found Sergio Conceicao down the right and his cross was headed home by the diving Vieri.

But two minutes later Toldo failed to claim Robert's swerving cross and Shearer kept his cool to steer home his second of the night.

O'Brien received lengthy treatment for a bloodied nose, and was eventually replaced by Aaron Hughes.

Defender Ivan Cordoba found space at the far post to meet Emre's free-kick with a pinpoint header to make it 2-2, and the battle for the points was back on.

Bellamy was booked for diving as he rounded Toldo, but it was Gary Speed who had a golden opportunity to restore his side's lead with 11 minutes remaining, only to head straight at the keeper.

March 19 2003 - NEWCASTLE UTD 0 BARCELONA 2

Given, Griffin, O'Brien, Bramble, Bernard, Solano (Ameobi 67), Dyer, Jenas, Robert (Viana 66), Shearer, Bellamy.

Att: 51,883

MATCH REPORT: We thought Barca, who had already comfortably qualified for the quarter-finals, might go through the motions and save themselves for the next game. Robson's men must have thought so too, as they went in search of a priceless victory.

Newcastle didn't take the chances they created before the break, however, and it ended up costing them the game. They had three glorious opportunities, all of them falling to striker Craig Bellamy, and he missed the lot of them.

The first two were created by skipper Shearer and, while the initial chance on three minutes was from a tight angle, he should have done better from the second two minutes later. Bellamy did little wrong when he was presented with the best of his first-half openings after Kieron Dyer slid in Shearer. He pulled the ball back for his strike partner to shoot from close range, only for goalkeeper Victor Valdes to turn his effort on to the post.

It was a blistering start from Newcastle, but they knew there would be a response from Barca.

With Xavi and the hugely impressive Juan Riquelme getting to grips with Dyer and Jermaine Jenas in the midfield, they kept possession well and began to threaten the United goal.

Fabio Rochemback should have opened the scoring after being put through by Xavi, and he forced a solid save from Shay Given with a well-struck left-foot shot from distance.

Half-time: Newcastle Utd 0 Barcelona 0

The Catalans returned after the break determined to get something out of the game.

Titus Bramble forced Gabri into a goal-line clearance with a clever flick from Robert's free-kick, but his side's hopes were dealt a killer blow on the hour. There seemed little danger as Bramble attempted to usher Gerard's long ball back to Given but, as the United duo stalled, Kluivert stuck out a foot to stab a shot into the net.

Bellamy was inches away from equalising seconds later when he lifted the ball over Valdes from Shearer's flick but saw his effort sail agonisingly wide.

Robson had thrown caution to the wind by throwing on Hugo Viana and Shola Ameobi in the search for a goal, but his plans were torn apart 16 minutes from time when Motta volleyed home Riquelme's free-kick from close range to make it 2-0.

It was heartbreak for Sir Bobby, as the club he took to European honours winning the Cup-Winners Cup dealt a fatal blow to his Newcastle dreams. The Magpies were surprise challengers for a quarter-final place in the company of 2002 Champion's League finalists Bayer Leverkusen and previous winners Barcelona and Internazionale ... but they put up a fight right to the end.

Obviously heartbroken, but the Geordie faithful put all of their disappointment to one side and gave

Shearer and his team a standing ovation as they trudged off the pitch on a night when experience and quality won the day.

As it happens, the result didn't matter because Inter won at Leverkusen 2-0.

1 FC Barcelona 16pts

2 Internazionale 11

3 Newcastle United   7

4 Bayer Leverkusen 0

The final was an all Italian affair played at Old Trafford, Inter and Juventus playing out a 0-0 draw. Inter won on penalties.

"If I should die, think only this of me:

That there's some corner of a foreign field

That is forever England"

The Soldier By Rupert Brooke

CHAPTER TWELVE
EUROPEAN CHAMPIONS LEAGUE
2003/04

Lauren Robert

MANAGER: Sir Bobby Robson

The 2003-4 campaign was a major season for the Newcastle manager. There were rumours that chairman Freddy Shepherd was getting impatient for silverware and, at 71-years of age, Sir Bobby was suffering from illness. From 1991 onwards he suffered recurrent medical problems with cancer.

HOW NEWCASTLE UTD QUALIFIED:

The 2002–03 FA Premier League was won by Manchester United - champions for the eighth time in eleven years – an achievement made all the more remarkable by virtue of defending champions Arsenal having led by eight points on March 2.

Despite actually doing slightly worse in terms of Premier League results, Bobby Robson's side managed to improve on their previous finish and achieved third place.

An administrative error by someone at St James' Park meant new signing Lee Bowyer had to serve a six-game ban from European competition. He was injured at the time so the person doing the paperwork (who was never named) decided not to register the former Leeds midfielder, and he was "not eligible to play" in their first six European games of the season.

August 13 2003 - PARTIZAN BELGRADE 0 NEWCASTLE UTD 1

Given, Griffin, Solano (Jenas), O'Brien, Dyer, Shearer, Bellamy, Speed, Woodgate, Robert (Ameobi), Bernard.

Att: 32,500

By no means as life-threatening as our earlier trip to Belgrade in 1998, but there were moments of frustration - like trying to get the match tickets off the Newcastle United officials who messed everyone about; and the expected 'hotel imprisonment' by armed guards that we had the last time. But at least no-one was hit with a baseball bat (as far as I am aware) and we didn't hear any gunshots in the JNA Stadium.

Around 100 of the travelling supporters spent the afternoon at the British Ambassador's city residence after initially being told they could not leave their hotel.

About 200 Magpies arrived in the stadium knowing exactly what to expect, and they were not to be disappointed as the home fans served up the traditional welcome. We were housed in the opposite end of the ground to where we were put in 1998 and all credit to the armed guards – they didn't return the missiles to the home fans to throw again, like they did five years earlier.

MATCH REPORT: Alan Shearer's birthday celebrations went with a swing as Newcastle picked up a priceless Champion's League qualifier victory.

Jonathan Woodgate had the sort of game which first won him England recognition, and his authority in the Toon backline was the main reason why Partizan had little to show for their share of the possession in the first half.

Indeed, it was not until the final minute of the first half that Given had a genuine save to make although, when it came, it was a vital one. The Irishman went full length to keep out Igor Duljaj's 20-yard drive. It came barely five minutes after the visitors had taken the lead.

Speed and Laurent Robert combined well on the left to create half a yard of space for the Frenchman, and although Shearer appeared to be dragged to the ground as he attempted to stab the ball past keeper Ivica Kralj, Solano followed up to slide a shot into the bottom corner.

Although Shearer and Craig Bellamy enjoyed few clear-cut openings, the Newcastle captain's aerial ability and the Welshman's pace were constant threats.

Half-time: Partizan 0 Newcastle Utd 1

Although Partizan returned with just as much vigour after the break, they rarely looked like hitting back until the death throes of the game.

Indeed, Given found himself a virtual spectator for much of the half, having to come to field a series of aimless crosses, but other than an early flurry during which Nikola Malbasa fired into the side-netting, never with any undue concern.

After struggling to mount a serious attack, the Serbs suddenly discovered a wave of form at the death, but Given kept his clean sheet. First he acrobatically turned away Nikola Malbasa's long-range effort in injury time and then somehow managed to block substitute Milan Stojanoski's point-blank shot seconds later, getting his slice of luck when Ilic headed the rebound wide.

Sir Bobby Robson: "I think Partizan are still very much in the game and I think it will be something similar in Newcastle. It was as we expected, not an easy match for us. It was always close - the difference between the two sides was minimal and Partizan in the last second missed a big opportunity.

"Maybe we were a little bit lucky, but it was also a very good save by the goalkeeper, and because we won 1-0, it gives us an advantage."

August 27 2003 - NEWCASTLE UTD 0 PARTIZAN BELGRADE 1 - (Lost on pens)

Given, Hughes, Woodgate, O'Brien, Bernard, Solano, Dyer, Speed, Viana, Ameobi, Shearer.

Att: 37,963

Newcastle's Champion's League dreams went up in smoke as Partizan Belgrade gate-crashed the party once again ... just as they did five years ago in the European Cup-Winners Cup.

Ivica Iliev cancelled out Nolberto Solano's first-leg while Jermaine Jenas passed up a golden opportunity to put us through.

MATCH REPORT: The match proved a landmark for Gary Speed, Nobby Solano and Shay Given, who all passed Rob Lee's club record of 27 appearances in Europe, but that was simply a sub-plot to a night which meant much more to United.

Sir Bobby Robson sent out his troops for the 200th time since he succeeded Ruud Gullit under no illusion that the game wouldn't be as tough as any of the previous 199.

Newcastle target Taribo West was given the task of keeping Shearer under lock and key and he just about got away with it. United enjoyed plenty of possession, but rarely managed to create any kind of opening.

Ameobi, deputising in attack for the injured Craig Bellamy, headed straight at keeper Kralj and then looped another effort just over 22 minutes later.

Shearer helped a 37th-minute Woodgate header over the bar and Igor Duljaj did superbly to block a Dyer effort two minutes later to frustrate the Magpies once again.

Half-time: Newcastle Utd 0 Partizan Belgrade 0

For their part, Partizan attacked swiftly on the counter, and within five minutes of the restart the United rearguard was completely undone. Albert Nadj's clever flick to Sasa Ilic set him away, and when he squared the ball for Iliev 10 yards out, he simply had to side-foot his shot into the empty net to level the aggregate score.

If Robson had told them during the break to sit back and control the play and see out the tie ... it all went pear-shaped after that. Newcastle's response was to panic, and they could quite easily have conceded on a number of occasions as they abandoned any resemblance of composure as the half wore on.

Ameobi wasted a golden opportunity to score when, instead of heading a Shearer cross towards goal, he took the ball on his chest and shot into the side-netting.

But Partizan sensed an opportunity, and they went close on 70 minutes when Iliev saw a long-range effort deflected past Given's right post and then Djordjevic headed wastefully over at the back post from the resulting corner.

Extra-time and the home side finally built up some impetus. Ameobi was just inches away from converting a 102nd-minute Robert cross and Jenas should have scored within moments of the start of the second period when he headed wide from Aaron Hughes' inch-perfect cross.

It all came down to penalties.

The only other penalty shoot-out that Newcastle had experienced in Europe was against Hungarian side Pecsi Dosza in 1970 … and they missed the first three spot kicks. It happened here too!

After Shearer, Kieron Dyer and Jonathan Woodgate had missed Newcastle's first three attempts, Shay Given saved from Nikola Malbasa and then saw Milan Stojanoski fire over.

Shola Ameobi, Lomana Lua Lua and Jermaine Jenas all converted, but when Aaron Hughes missed at 3-3, Milivoje Cirkovic calmly slotted home his side's seventh kick to clinch victory.

Partizan become the first ever side from Serbia to make the Champion's League group stages, while Newcastle had the consolation of a place in the UEFA Cup.

Sir Bobby Robson was not grateful for a second chance of European glory: "I don't think it's right that if you get knocked out of one competition you go into another as a result of failure. They are two separate competitions and should have two separate sets of clubs."

Jose Mourinho's Porto went on to win the competition, beating Manchester United along the way, and Monaco 3-0 in the final in Germany at the Arena AufSchalke, Gelsenkirchen.

UEFA CUP 2003/04

September 22 2003 - NEWCASTLE UTD 5 NAC BREDA 0

Given, Hughes, O'Brien, Bramble, Bernard (Viana), Jenas, Dyer (Ambrose), Speed, Robert, Shearer, Bellamy (Ameobi).

Att: 36,007

MATCH REPORT: Newcastle went into the game having failed to win any of the four home matches they had played this season and faced a Dutch team buoyed by a stunning 4-2 win over Ajax four days earlier.

United emerged in determined fashion, and with Kieron Dyer handed a probing role wide on the right side of midfield and Robert assisting Bellamy and Shearer, the signs were good.

The game was 31 minutes old when Shearer got up above Mark Schenning to flick Andy O'Brien's long ball into Bellamy's path, and he calmly drew out 'keeper Gabor Babos before deftly lobbing him for the opening goal.

Six minutes later, the Welshman scored again. Dyer surged clear from the halfway line to find Robert, who unselfishly squared for his team-mate to side-foot into the empty net.

But the Dutch side were not dead and buried as Shay Given had to pull off two fine saves to deny Johan Elmander and Tamas Peto as half-time approached.

St James' was a happy place when referee Nikolay Ivanov blew the whistle so United could regroup.

Half-time: Newcastle Utd 2 Breda 0

Bellamy came within inches of completing his hat-trick with less than two minutes of the second half gone when Schenning's attempted clearance hit Nebojsa Gudelj and dropped to the striker, but although he lifted his shot over Babos, the ball came back off the bar.

The third goal arrived a minute before the hour-mark, however, when Bramble timed his run to meet a Robert corner with a bullet header which gave the Breda keeper no chance.

From then on, it was really only a matter of how many United would win by, and Shearer passed up a glorious opportunity to make it 4-0 20 minutes from time when he got on the end of Robert's inviting cross but could not keep his shot down.

But the 'GOALden Boy' made amends within seven minutes when, after the Frenchman tapped a short free-kick to him, he took one touch before rifling a dipping shot into the bottom corner.

Robson withdrew Dyer to hand Darren Ambrose a home debut, and it was the former Ipswich Town midfielder who added the finishing touch a minute from time when he headed home another Robert cross.

October 15 2003 - NAC BREDA 0 NEWCASTLE UTD 1

Harper, Griffin, O'Brien, Bramble (S Caldwell), Bernard, Solano (Ambrose), Jenas, Viana, Robert, Dyer (Lua Lua), Ameobi.

Att: 15,564

Breda is a small town in southern Holland, but we flew to Amsterdam from Leeds-Bradford and spent two nights in the capital. Amsterdam is expensive but always enjoyable.

The infamous "Battle of Breda" is still a mystery to me because we were having a cracking time in one of the bars with Breda fans when it all kicked off.

87 Newcastle fans were locked up when the violence flared as running battles started a few hours before kick-off. Some of those arrested were just bystanders trying to get away from the trouble but they were rounded up by Dutch riot police. There was no indication that there was going to be trouble, and you can usually sense when something is brewing. We had Dutch 'runners' going to the square to see what was happening, then coming back to the pub (where we were having a brilliant time with Dutch fans) to keep us informed. They said it was Feyenoord and Chelsea supporters looking to fight Newcastle fans, and this Chelsea 'hooligan' thing has popped up often on our European travels. You go to Stamford Bridge, and there is no grievance between Chelsea and Newcastle, but for some reason the European hooligan culture sees Chelsea as their idols. It happened in Anderlecht at a pre-season friendly; Zagreb; Sofia; Belgrade; and Breda – foreign fans wearing Chelsea colours wanting to fight.

MATCH REPORT: United ran out at the 16,400-capacity MyCom Stadium knowing that their passage to the second round was a formality. Robson made six changes, choosing to rest Alan Shearer, Gary Speed and Shay Given, confident that the men who came in would do a good job. They did, to a degree, and I don't think anyone could blame them for coasting through a tie that didn't need the trimmings.

United threatened only fleetingly as lone striker Shola Ameobi hardly saw much of the ball. If anything, it was United's defence which underwent the sterner examination in the opening 45 minutes, and there wasn't much of that.

Steve Harper had to race from his line to prevent Johan Elmander reaching Marcel Koning's long ball in the game's first attack.

Hugo Viana forced a fine save from keeper Gabor Babos, then the game fell into slumber mode as Breda tried to break down a stubborn United defence, but rarely succeeded.

Harper had to rely on the woodwork three minutes before the break, however, when Koning met Nebojsa Gudelj's free-kick with a powerful header which came back off the upright.

Half-time: Breda 0 NewcastleUtd 0

If anything, the second half was even less eventful as the first. But Titus Bramble and Andy O'Brien almost gifted Elmander an opening within seconds of the restart and it was left to Jermaine Jenas to tidy up the mess after Harper's clearance had come back off the striker.

Ameobi sent a looping back-post header over the bar on 49 minutes, and Stefano Seedorf completely missed a sitter in front of goal.

Robson opted for a change 12 minutes from time when he sent on Darren Ambrose and Steve Caldwell in place of Nobby Solano and Bramble, but it was Dyer who almost broke the deadlock two minutes later when he collected Ameobi's pass but saw his shot blocked at close range by Coutinho.

Robert snatched victory with four minutes remaining when he ran on to Jenas' nicely weighted pass to beat the helpless Coutinho from close range. Sir Bobby celebrated his 100th win as Newcastle manager.

Sir Bobby Robson: "I hope the fans act with dignity and style and you should represent your country properly.

Steve Harper: "I was just happy it went well. If they had scored early it might have been a busy night but I only had a couple of saves to make. I enjoyed every minute of it."

November 6 2003 - FC BASEL 2 NEWCASTLE UTD 3

Given, Hughes, O'Brien, Bramble, Bernard, Solano (Ambrose), Jenas, Speed, Robert (Viana), Shearer, Ameobi.

Att: 30,000

Basel is located where the French and German borders meet, in the northwest of Switzerland on the river Rhine. Another picturesque city, and around 1,000 or so Geordie fans made the trip. We flew from Luton to Geneva, but struggled to get a hotel – they were either full or too expensive – and we ended up in a back-packer's hostel with a varied array of nationalities with poor hygiene. The place stunk!

FC Basel is known for having a big and loyal local following but, like our trip to Zurich, the Swiss fans kept themselves to themselves and were no trouble. FC Basel play their home games at the St. Jakob-Park which is nicknamed "Joggeli" by the fans. It is a modern stadium about the size of Boro's Riverside.

This was a side which beat Celtic, Spartak Moscow, Deportivo La Coruna and Juventus in the Champions League the previous season, and Robson knew it was going to be tough.

MATCH REPORT: Cantaluppi scored after 11 minutes gone when he latched onto a weak clearance by Jermaine Jenas and hammered an unstoppable drive past Shay Given.

Ameobi's perfectly weighted pass put Laurent Robert in on goal, and his early shot caught out 'keeper Zuberbuhler, who could only watch as the ball slipped inside his far post.

At the other end, Given was beaten for a second time four minutes later when Jenas was experiencing a horror opening spell. Chipperfield's shot clipped JJ's legs and evaded the keeper's grasp.

United desperately needed to slow the game down, but striker Marco Streller whistled another shot over and Bramble needed to get in a superb challenge to prevent Gimenez from converting Chipperfield's near-post cross on 33 minutes.

Newcastle started to show some resilience at long last, and they were rewarded eight minutes before the break when the home defence failed to clear a Robert corner and Bramble thumped home a half-volley to level.

Olivier Bernard went with inches of giving his side an unlikely lead, but Given needed the help of a post to keep out Gimenez's looping header.

Half-time: Basel 2 Newcastle Utd 2

Apparently, Robson laid down the law to his defenders during the interval and they succeeded in knocking Basel off their stride. The Swiss side struggled to handle the visitors for the opening 20 minutes of the second period, with Ameobi squandering a golden opportunity on 57 minutes after Robert picked him out unmarked in the middle.

Argentine striker Julio Hernan Rossi was introduced as substitute and that gave new impetus to the Swiss league leaders. He won a corner within seconds of his arrival and Solano had to clear a Murat Yakin header off the line.

On 75 minutes Solano had the time and space to pick out Ameobi on the edge of the penalty area, and he twisted and turned his way past the mesmerised Zwyssig before firing left-footed past Zuberbuhler.

November 27 2003 - NEWCASTLE UTD 1 FC BASEL 0

Given, Hughes, O'Brien, Bramble, Bernard, Dyer (Solano), Jenas, Speed, Robert (Ambrose), Shearer, Ameobi.

40,395

MATCH REPORT: Basel, like United, made the last 16 of the Champion's League the previous season, but when they fell behind with just 14 minutes gone, they never really looked like overturning United's 4-2 aggregate lead.

It was not the prettiest goal the St James' Park faithful had ever seen – a shot that went in off Smiljanic's boot as he tried to clear Robert's in-swinging corner – but they cheered as though it was. And the effect it had on the visitors was quite remarkable. Basel simply fell apart for the next half hour.

Goalkeeper Zuberbuhler did well to keep out Gary Speed's first-time effort on 25 minutes and blocked a blistering effort from Shearer three minutes later as his defence went AWOL.

Three times Robert cut through a ragged defence into the penalty area but failed to produce either a shot or a meaningful pass.

Having rode their luck at one end, the Swiss side were very unfortunate when Mario Cantaluppi went to ground under Shay Given's 26th-minute challenge and referee Knud Erik Fisker ruled that he had dived and booked him.

Half-time: Newcastle 1 Basel 0

Yakin took a free-kick 20 yards out and his curling shot left Given rooted to the spot but the ball clipped the outside of the post.

Argentinian Rossi had the ball in the net six minutes later, but from an offside position.

Basel continued to press without ever really threatening to hurt Newcastle, but was not until Jermaine Jenas missed the target on 71 minutes that Newcastle produced anything of note.

Robson withdrew Dyer and Robert with 11 minutes remaining to send on Nobby Solano and Darren Ambrose.

Speed flicked a header wide and Shearer blasted over the bar as the game came to a close, but the match had been in the bag for a long time.

Sir Bobby Robson: "Against Basel we gave a strong performance against a decent side. When we sent our scouts out to Basel they came back and told us we would have two difficult games and we have done well to get through."

Alan Shearer: "We had a scare when they had the appeal for the penalty. When I saw the ref go for the card I thought he was booking Shay and I assumed it was a penalty because I was quite a distance away."

February 26 2004 - VALERENGA 1 NEWCASTLE UTD 1

Given, O'Brien, Jenas, Bellamy, Speed, Ambrose (Dyer), Hughes, Bramble, Ameobi (Bridges), Bernard, Viana (Robert).

Att: 17,039

Valerenga play in the Norwegian capital at the Ulleval Stadium which they share with neighbours Lyn Oslo. But the weather was so bad that UEFA insisted the club propose a "reserve stadium" in the country just in case the fixture could not go ahead. Now that was a great proposal on paper, but what about the Geordie fans making arrangements to fly? Where do we fly to? As Oslo is about as south as you can get in Norway, what was the club supposed to do?

UEFA spokesman **Rob Faulkner:** "We have asked Valerenga to propose a reserve venue, as this is common practice with any club involved in our competitions and situated where weather conditions may pose a potential problem."

Valerenga replied: "The pitch is covered and fitted with under-soil heating. It should go ahead."

It was a bitterly cold night in Oslo, but the game did go ahead at Ulleval Stadium.

To damped Geordie sprits, however, there was trouble in the Newcastle camp.

Newcastle started without Alan Shearer, and there was a rumour circulating amongst reporters that **Sir Bobby** had told the 'GOALden Boy': "You are not the player you once were". **Shearer**'s reply about being dropped: "I am disappointed and angry, but that is the manager's decision. Of course I expect to play in the second leg, but I expected to play tonight, and it didn't happen."

MATCH REPORT: Robson took a gamble with his formation, leaving out Shearer, Kieron Dyer and Laurent Robert, and the Norwegians created the first chance with seven minutes gone when striker Freddy Dos Santos forced Shay Given to palm away his effort.

Titus Bramble and Andy O'Brien were largely untroubled through the first half, however, and Given was almost unemployed.

But David Brocken was impressive at the back for the home side, as the match took it's time to get beyond a defensive battle.

Goalkeeper Oyvind Bolthof had to kick away a 23rd-minute effort from Darren Ambrose as the visitors gradually increased their tempo, but Newcastle had to wait until six minutes before the interval before making the breakthrough.

Skipper for the night Gary Speed, who had earlier flashed a header wide, this time saw his effort cleared off the line by David Hanssen. But Hugo Viana crossed again and Bellamy volleyed into the bottom corner off the foot of the post.

Half-time: Valerenga 0 Newcastle Utd 1

Speed had whistled a volley over the bar but the home side found themselves back on level terms with 55 minutes gone after Normann climbed high above Aaron Hughes to head home a Brocken cross.

United could have fallen behind on the hour when Hanssen dragged a left-foot shot just wide.

It took another fine block by Bramble to keep out Edvardsen after Dos Santos had failed to get a clean strike on player-coach Rekdal's free-kick, and life was becoming increasingly uncomfortable for the visitors.

Robson opted for change 16 minutes from time when he replaced Shola Ameobi and Viana with Michael Bridges and Robert and the Frenchman used his first touch to drive in a long-range free-kick which was deflected away for a corner.

It was Given who found himself the busier goalkeeper in the closing stages, however, as he turned away an Ardian Gashi drive and claimed another effort from substitute Lars Ovrebo two minutes from time.

Sir Bobby Robson: "I don't think I am wrong in my decision – I don't think if Shearer was on the pitch Shearer would have stopped them (Valerenga) playing so well."

March 3 2004 - NEWCASTLE UTD 3 VALERENGA 1

Given, O'Brien, Woodgate, Bramble, Hughes, Bridges (Brittain), Jenas, Speed, Robert, Shearer, Bellamy (Ameobi).

Att: 38,531

136

Alan Shearer was back in the team but Newcastle were again a shadow of the side which had pushed for Premiership glory the previous seasons. They did just enough, however, to ensure their place in the fourth-round draw.

MATCH REPORT: Valerenga goalkeeper Oyvind Bolthof denied Shearer a ninth-minute opener with a fine reaction save, but then allowed a free-kick from the 33-year-old to squirm under him to hand Newcastle the lead.

Titus Bramble flashed a header just wide but Newcastle struggled to get to grips with the Norwegians in the middle of the park as David Hanssen, Jorgen Jalland and Ardian Gashi gave Gary Speed and Jermaine Jenas more troubles than they had anticipated.

Shay Given tipped a Gashi shot onto the bar then Hagen converted Rekdal's corner - despite the best efforts of Michael Bridges on the line.

Shay Given had to keep out another Gashi effort and a long-range free-kick from David Brocken as his side struggled to stem the tide in the closing minutes of the half, and it was boos rather than cheers which ushered the home side from the field at the break.

Half-time: Newcastle Utd 1 Valerenga 1

Bellamy struggled with a hamstring injury and had to be replaced by Shola Ameobi, but it was the switch that made the breakthrough almost instantly.

Picking up possession wide on the left, Ameobi cut inside Hagen and struck a rather tame right-foot shot which Bolthof made a right hash of and palmed into his own net.

It put Newcastle ahead in the tie but it was a very precarious lead, as the visitors weren't that much worse off. They knew that a single goal would be good enough to put them through on away goals, so Newcastle's work for the night was far from done.

The fans knew that the longer the game went on without a third Toon goal, the bigger the chance of a sucker punch from the Norwegians and less time to recover from it. Then with 16 minutes remaining Gashi cut inside Bramble and fired low towards goal, Jonathan Woodgate kicking his effort away before substitute Kjetil Waehler blasted the rebound high over.

Nineteen-year-old Martin Brittain was handed a debut as a replacement for Bridges.

After Berre went perilously close, Jenas sprang the offside trap with a minute remaining and squared for Ameobi to ease the nerves and score the third.

March 11 2004 - NEWCASTLE UTD 4 REAL MALLORCA 1

Given, Hughes, Bramble, O'Brien, Bernard, Dyer (Ambrose), Jenas, Speed, Robert, Shearer, Bellamy.

Att: 38,012

It was interesting to wonder how serious Mallorca boss Luis Aragones was taking the tie, as he made no fewer than nine changes to the side which lost 3-2 in La Liga at Barcelona the previous Sunday. He stuck with Alejandro Campano and Samuel Eto'o, but veteran defender Miguel Angel Nadal was put on the bench.

MATCH REPORT: The game was preceded by a minute's silence for the victims of the Madrid bombings.

Campano combined neatly with striker Correa down the right and sent in a cross which wrong-footed Bramble in the middle but Eto'o was unable to take advantage as he bundled his effort wide.

Jermaine Jenas set Newcastle moving in the right direction with a ball in to Robert, although the Frenchman wasted the chance with a lazy delivery.

Eto'o tested Shay Given with an audacious 22nd-minute volley with the outside of his right foot, then Bellamy went to ground appealing for a penalty after a clash with Cortes - more in hope than expectation.

Robert had Real's Argentine keeper Leo Franco scrambling in the 41st-minute when his free-kick from 25-yards was hammered just wide of his left post.

Half-time: Newcastle Utd 0 Mallorca 0

Eto'o was unfortunate to see a drive come back off the crossbar with Given beaten, but Correa followed up to head into the empty net and give his side the lead. It took the home fans by surprise because Newcastle were looking comfortable.

The match had taken time to get rolling but now it was time for the big name stars to start producing. They were booed off when they struggled to get to grips with Valerenga in the previous round, but the Geordie fans rose to the occasion and roared their heroes on.

In return Newcastle hit back after 68 minutes when Shearer flicked on Bramble's free-kick and Bellamy ran through to slot right-footed past Franco. The touch-paper was lit and United went on to record an incredible fight back.

Shearer was not to be denied, and when Robert drove the ball in, he charged unmarked to the near post to glance home his 20th goal of the season.

United forged further ahead after 74 minutes when Real conceded a free-kick 30 yards out and Robert crashed in a low shot which caught Franco flat-footed as it swerved into the back of the net.

The keeper did well to keep out another Robert pile-driver two minutes later as the Spaniards, who had no fewer than eight players booked, lost their cool and Moya was sent off for a second bookable offence.

To rub salt into the wound, Bramble volleyed Robert's free-kick from point-blank range into the back of the net to make it 4-1.

The Geordie fans had witnessed a classic.

March 25 2004 - REAL MALLORCA 0 NEWCASTLE UTD 3

Given, Bramble, O'Brien (Taylor), Woodgate, Bernard, Ambrose, Speed (Bellamy), Jenas, Robert (Viana), Shearer, Ameobi.

Att: 11,500

Yes ... only the Toon Army could fly to the sun-baked island of Majorca ... and get drenched! No sooner had we arrived at Palma when the heavens opened, and - Geordies being Geordies – most of the supporters had only packed a Toon shirt, a pair of shorts and a pair of sunglasses.

Fans took over several of the bars in Magaluf but the police kept a low presence and let them get on with it.

Around 3,000 Newcastle fans made it to the Son Moix stadium and one Geordie clambered onto the roof by the scoreboard, wearing a massive green sombrero, to do a dance ... cheered on by the visiting fans.

Craig Bellamy was involved in a bust-up with coach John Carver as the Magpies flew out to the Balearics on the Tuesday, and Newcastle spent the early part of the week trying to defuse the situation. But Robson signed a new one-year contract, to make happier headlines.

MATCH REPORT: Once again Mallorca coach Luis Aragones had major selections problems - what with a vital Primera Liga relegation battle at Murcia to come on the following Sunday. He again went with the reserves, virtually throwing away the tie.

Newcastle could have scored twice within the opening nine minutes as first Laurent Robert and then Jermaine Jenas tested replacement keeper Miki.

Arnold Bruggink, who played under Robson at PSV, produced a superb one-handed save from Given with a curling effort that almost crept inside the post, and suddenly Real started to taste blood.

Marcos started pulling the strings despite the best efforts of Jenas and Gary Speed to stifle him.

But with Jonathan Woodgate, Titus Bramble and Andy O'Brien defiant at the back and Given mopping up well behind them, United were containing the threat well.

Speed got in a fine block to deny Bruggink in front of goal, and then Toni Gonzalez pulled the rebound wide.

Half-time: Mallorca 0 Newcastle Utd 0

Within 37 seconds of the restart Shearer seized upon an error by Miki to finally break the deadlock. The keeper's scuffed clearance fell at the striker's feet 30 yards out and he took a controlling touch before thumping it into the net to spark mass celebrations among the 3,000 travelling fans.

But three times in quick succession Mallorca went close to levelling on the night.

Txomin Nagore and Jesus Perera both brought the best out of Given inside two minutes, although the latter wasted another good opportunity when he fired over from close range in between.

Robson sent on Hugo Viana and Bellamy for the closing minutes, and the pair combined to finally dump the home side out of the competition. Viana won a challenge on the edge of his own penalty area and the Welshman, who had been on the field for less than a minute, sprinted away before chipping a shot over Miki.

Shearer added a third at the death, tapping home from Olivier Bernard's inch-perfect cross to send the Geordies home in ecstasy.

QUARTER-FINALS:

Bordeaux v Valencia CF

Olympique Marseille v Internazionale

Celtic F.C.v Villarreal

PSV Eindhoven v Newcastle United

Sir Bobby Robson: "We weren't good in the first-half and at times our back four was all over the place. I'm pleased it's PSV. I'll look forward to going back there because they are a great club with a lot of great people and it was a happy time in my life when I worked there. I had a sneaking feeling Auxerre would beat them but PSV had a great result in the second leg."

Steven Taylor made his Newcastle debut nine minutes from time and came away with Samuel Eto'o's shirt: "I was fantastic for me to get on near the end and to get the shirt. He didn't ask me for mine, though. He obviously didn't know who I was! I was nervous at first but once I got my first touch I was fine. Obviously the game was won by the time I got on."

April 8 2004 - PSV EINDHOVEN 1 NEWCASTLE UTD 1

Given, Hughes, Bramble, Woodgate, Bernard, Ambrose, Jenas, Speed, Robert, Shearer (Ameobi), Bellamy.

Att: 35,000

Fans headed to Eindhoven on trains, boats and planes, with all 1,600 tickets on offer being snapped up – and many, like ourselves, being the guests of Dutch

140

friends. We stayed in Amsterdam once again, but others booked hotels in Utrecht, Dusselldorf, Antwerp and of course Eindhoven.

Proving that Breda was a 'one-off', there were no incidents to spoil the trip, and the bars in Eindhoven's Stationsplein and Stratumseind must have clocked up record takings. Best of all was the singing from both sets of supporters: "There's only one Bobby Robson!" followed by the Geordie classic "Shoes off if you love the Toon!"

Sir Bobby Robson: "My greatest experience football-wise was Barcelona. But it was a delightful time at PSV because the Dutch are so pro-British. I won two championships in my first two years at PSV and they really helped to promote my interests. They were great years of my life. It's a thrill to be back."

The Magpies knew that if they got through this tie they would face a semi-final clash with either Inter Milan or Marseille.

MATCH REPORT: PSV front two Kezman and Jan Vennegoor of Hesselink immediately set about the task of pressurising the Magpies' rearguard and with South Korean winger Park Ji-Sung ready to take on Olivier Bernard at every opportunity, it was going to be a long night.

Bramble survived an early penalty appeal as the red and white shirts poured forward, and United shot themselves in the foot twice within seconds. First Jonathan Woodgate mis-timed an aerial challenge with Vennegoor of Hesselink and and then Aaron Hughes failed to clear and the path to goal was open. Mateja Kezman took the time to settle himself before curling an unstoppable shot past Given from 20 yards and Newcastle were in big trouble 1-0 down.

Goalkeeper Ronald Waterreus was called upon to tip Gary Speed's long-range effort over the bar, then he made an excellent save from a Shearer header.

Bramble struck out at van der Schaaf, and the French referee missed it, but he penalised van der Schaaf for a trip on Bernard, and Jenas rose to head home Robert's free-kick for the equaliser.

Half-time: PSV Eindhoven 1 Newcastle Utd 1

Bouma powered in a bullet header from a 49th-minute corner which rebounded off the bar and had the home fans off their seats.

Hiddink's men went close again two minutes later when Given palmed away a de Jong cross and full-back Lee Young-Pyo dragged the rebound wide.

Ambrose created half a yard for himself on 63 minutes and drove a powerful shot into the side-netting.

Given was forced to block a 76th-minute Kezman shot with his chest as the striker cut in from the left.

United might have won it themselves with four minutes remaining when Bellamy's long-range effort was tipped over by Waterreus.

Alan Shearer: "We've got an away goal which could be vital to us, and we've got to make the most of it now. I think we we'd have settled for 1-1 before the game, but the tie is far from over. I still don't know who got our goal – Jermaine Jenas or Gary Speed – so I'm claiming it!"

QUARTER-FINALS:

Bordeaux 1 Valencia CF 2

Olympique Marseille 1 Internazionale 0

Celtic F.C.1 Villarreal 1

PSV Eindhoven 1 Newcastle United 1

Ladbrokes betting to win the UEFA Cup: Valencia 11/8; Newcastle 5/1; Villarreal 6/1; Internazionale 7/1; Celtic 7/1; Marseille 9/1; PSV 11/1; Bordeaux 22/1

April 14 2004 - NEWCASTLE UTD 2 PSV EINDHOVEN 1

Given, Hughes, Woodgate, Bramble (O'Brien), Bernard, Ambrose (Ameobi), Jenas, Speed, Robert (Viana), Shearer, Bellamy.

Att: 50,083

Gary Speed and Alan Shearer teamed up to fire Newcastle into the semi-finals of a European competition for the first time in 35 years on an agonisingly tense European night on Tyneside. The Magpies had not made the last four since they won the then Inter-Cities Fairs Cup in 1969.

MATCH REPORT: So often when Newcastle needed it most, it was skipper Shearer who came up with the goods, and (on the half-hour mark) it was the Toon skipper who headed the Magpies in front with his 26th goal of the season.

Both Aaron Hughes and Titus Bramble might have increased Newcastle's lead within minutes of the opening goal, although the Irishman could not control his diving header and his English counterpart wastefully failed to connect with an inviting Darren Ambrose cross.

However PSV, inspired by Johann Vogel and captain Mark van Bommel, put pressure on Jonathan Woodgate and the Newcastle defence.

Half-time: Newcastle Utd 1 PSV Eindhoven 0

Hiddink replaced the largely ineffectual Rommedahl with striker Jan Vennegoor of Hesselink at the break and his side were level within seven minutes.

Ambrose failed to clear a cross and, as Olivier Bernard attempted to control the ball on his chest, Park nipped in and was sent sprawling over the Frenchman's leg. Spanish referee Manuel Enrique Mejuto Gonzalez pointed to the spot to hand Kezman his chance of glory, and the Serbia and Montenegro international beat Given from the spot.

There was almost a repeat when there were appeals from the Dutch for a second penalty five minutes later when van Bommel went down over Bramble's outstretched leg. United were lucky that the referee waved for play to continue.

Bramble might have eased their nerves had he managed to direct Robert's 62nd-minute free-kick under the crossbar rather than over it and the home side were opened up again seconds later to allow Lee to test Given at his near post.

But as play switched rapidly from end to end Newcastle went ahead once again when Speed rose majestically to power a header from a 66th-minute Robert corner into the net and ease the tension.

It was one of those goals that eased the Toon to the winning line, but with the clause that meant a goal against would see them eliminated from the competition.

With just three minutes remaining, Given had to throw himself to his right to keep out Wilfred Bouma's curling free-kick, and then the same man crashed a long-range drive over the crossbar.

QUARTER-FINALS:

Valencia 2 CF Bordeaux 1

Internazionale 0 Olympique Marseille 1

Villarreal 2 Celtic F.C 0

Newcastle United 2 PSV Eindhoven 1

April 22 2004 - NEWCASTLE UTD 0 OLYMPIQUE MARSEILLE 0

Given, Hughes, O'Brien, Woodgate, Bernard, Ambrose, Viana, Speed, Robert, Ameobi (Bridges), Shearer.

Att: 52,004

MATCH REPORT: The visitors did not appear intimidated by the packed St James' Park with Camel Meriem immediately causing problems to Aaron Hughes and there was considerable relief when Didier Drogba, having climbed above Andy O'Brien to reach a cross, drifted a header across goal.

Shearer flicked a header across the penalty box and Ameobi shrugged off Abdoulaye Meite to set himself up for a fantastic opportunity but Fabien Barthez saved with his legs.

That save was matched by Shay Given, making his 300th career appearance, in the 25th minute when, not for the first time, Hugo Viana made a sloppy pass that was intercepted. Drogba's pace sent him scampering into the Newcastle area where he cut inside O'Brien and aimed for the corner only to see Given stretch out an arm to save.

Shearer's strength up front was impressive. He won a free-kick wide on the left, then timed his jump to meet Laurent Robert's penetrating ball across only to see his header glance wide.

As half-time approached Ameobi displayed some lovely footwork to get past Meite and Hemdani, but Barthez was smartly placed to snuff out his cross from the byline.

Half-time: Newcastle Utd 0 Marseille 0

Within seconds of the restart, only Woodgate's brilliance had prevented Marseille from taking the lead. Sylvain N'Diaye ghosted past Hughes and Drogba was poised to slide home his low centre only for Woodgate to take the ball off his toe.

A Shearer pile-driver almost caught out Barthez but he parried the ball to Gary Speed who spooned the rebound wide.

The match remained even with enterprising play from both sides. Drogba threatened when Speed became as careless as Viana with a stray pass, then Robert brought a good save out of Barthez with a long-distance direct free-kick.

Robert was the guilty man for allowing Ferreira to steal the ball and float a cross to Drogba who unleashed a fabulous left-foot volley that struck the inside of the post and bounced across the face of the goal.

There were nervous moments for the visitors when Speed and O'Brien were both denied in a penalty-box scramble.

The match ended amid high drama when Given stifled Drogba's effort at the near-post in injury time.

Marseille's manager **José Anigo**: "We had four real chances and they will have to be taken in Marseille. This was a fine result in a fantastic atmosphere. The return will be interesting."

May 6 2004 - OLYMPIQUE MARSEILLE 2 NEWCASTLE U 0

Given, Hughes, O'Brien, Bramble, Bernard, Ambrose, Viana (Bowyer), Speed, Robert, Ameobi, Shearer.

Att: 57,500

Another visit to France to continue my love affair with the adorable French – NOT! I wasn't too keen on them before this excursion, and the French Ultra's didn't disappoint.

In general, Marseille is a truly beautiful place - the second most populous city in France (after Paris). Located on the southeast coast, it is France's largest commercial port and the country's largest city on the Mediterranean coast.

Marseille is one of the main gateways into France, and this has attracted many immigrants and made the city a cosmopolitan melting pot. There are places tourists can go – and places to be avoided. I'd even go as far as to say there are places the FRENCH can go – and places they would rather stay clear of.

There is a Moroccan side to the city that is frightening - a genuine dirty, dingy, horrible, even evil side. Places the travel brochures fail to mention!

We had a good night before the match, but the day of the game the Geordies were made to feel most unwelcome. There was trouble before the game and even more after it. The underground was a hot spot for the French fans to ambush the visitors, and there were many incidents of trouble.

MATCH REPORT: Sadly, the band of 3,000 travelling Geordie supporters at the Stade Velodrome had their hopes dashed as they had to sit through the opening 45 minutes of an error-ridden display in which their side created little in attack, conceded possession in the middle of the field and were torn apart at the back.

Newcastle's chances rested on their ability to get the ball to skipper Shearer and strike-partner Ameobi in positions where they could hurt the Frenchmen. But instead they spent their time fighting fires, ... with a desperate lack of success.

It took Marseille just 18 minutes to forge their way in front as they turned defence into attack with breathtaking speed. They had a helping hand in the shape of 21-year-old Viana, who was the worst player on the field in the first leg of this semi-final, and again here in France. His failure to beat Meriem to a bouncing ball on halfway allowed the talented playmaker to slide Drogba into acres of space.

Aaron Hughes raced back manfully to try to hold the powerful striker up, but he was defeated by an audacious back-heel which left him in on goal, and he prodded the ball past Shay Given.

Thereafter, the Magpies were carved apart at regular intervals as Drogba and the excellent Steve Marlet made life intensely difficult for Titus Bramble and Andy O'Brien (whose 12th-minute booking for a clumsy foul on Meriem would have kept him out of the final anyway).

Marlet might have doubled his side's advantage had Drogba not over-hit a 27th-minute through-ball, and both the former and Ferreira chanced their arm from distance before the break, although Given was not unduly troubled by either.

United created only two openings of note ... Shearer finding himself denied by a solid block from Habib Beye and Laurent Robert (on another quiet night for the Frenchman) whistling an ambitious 35-yard free-kick over Fabien Barthez's crossbar.

Half-time: Marseille 1 Newcastle Utd 0

Newcastle sought a precious equaliser and twice went close within minutes when Robert's cross was flicked off Ameobi's head at the back post by the vigilant Abdoulaye Meite, and then the England Under-21 striker smashed a long-range effort just wide.

As Newcastle went for broke, Marseille looked ever more dangerous on the break.

But just when it looked as though Newcastle might get the goal that would change the tie and put them in the final, they handed Drogba the opportunity to enhance his blossoming reputation.

Substitute Laurent Batlles picked the striker out unmarked on the penalty spot from a free-kick and he swept the ball past the helpless Given to spark mass celebrations in the stands.

Drogba might have completed his hat-trick before being replaced at the end to a standing ovation, but Given's save was simply a cameo on a night when the plaudits went to the man destined for a fabulous career at Stamford Bridge.

Didier Drogba single-handedly ripped the heart out of Newcastle's UEFA Cup dream with a blistering display of finishing to book Marseille's place in the final.

There was anger from the Newcastle fans at the end – aimed at the board and Freddy Shepherd in particular – because this result hurt more than anyone could have imagined.

We were kept in the ground for over an hour and there was a 'welcoming party' of hundreds waiting outside. Getting away from the place was unbelievable, as the French turned on the police and a mass riot broke out.

Olivier Bernard: "The important thing is that we don't let it get to us. If anything – this will make us stronger and help us finish the season well. We want that fourth place, and we have three games to get it. We didn't deserve to get to the final because of the way we played. That's all there is to it. We know we were good enough to get there."

Steve Calwell: "I can't imagine Newcastle not being in Europe. This is a massive club which should be in Europe every year. Never mind the UEFA Cup – we should be in the Champion's League."

Marseille lost to Valencia 2-0 in the final in Sweden at Ullevi Stadium, Gothenburg.

Sir Bobby Robson (sacked August 2004)

Sir Bobby held the Newcastle post until 30 August 2004, when he was dismissed by Freddy Shepherd after only four games of the Premier League season: Boro (2-2); Spurs (0-1); Norwich (2-2); Aston Villa (2-4).

Apparently it was because of alleged "discontent in the dressing room".

Robson's dismissal followed publication of his 'disappointment' that only 5,000 fans stayed to see the traditional lap of honour made by the players at St James' Park at the end of the 2003/4 season.

His autobiography, entitled Bobby Robson: "Farewell but not Goodbye" was released in 2005. In the book, Robson was critical of Freddy Shepherd, claiming that (while manager) he was denied information regarding the players' contracts and transfer negotiations. He also criticised Shepherd and the club's deputy chairman Douglas Hall, for their focus on the first team and St James' Park, causing them to neglect less glamorous issues, such as the training ground, youth development and talent scouts.

CHAPTER THIRTEEN
UEFA CUP 2004/05

Graeme Souness

MANAGER: Graeme Souness

Graeme Souness was another of the Liverpool connection the Newcastle board of directors seemed obsessed with. He was the captain of the successful Liverpool team of the early 1980s and player-manager of Rangers in the late 1980s. He also played for Tottenham Hotspur, Middlesbrough and Sampdoria in a long career. He was manager of Rangers, Liverpool, Southampton, Benfica, Galatasaray and Blackburn Rovers before he joined Newcastle United.

Souness was appointed Rangers' first player-manager in April 1986.

Rangers record: 1986–87 they won the Championship and the League Cup. Two more Championships were to follow, this time in successive seasons (1988–89 and 1989–90), and a further two League Cup victories.

Liverpool record: The three years which followed were uneventful apart from a 2–0 victory in the 1992 FA Cup final over Second Division Sunderland.

He had major heart surgery in 1992.

He joined Galatasaray in Turkey and sparked a riot after placing a large Galatasaray flag into the centre circle of the pitch of arch rivals Fenerbahçe after his side had beaten them in the Turkish Cup final in April 1996.

Souness then returned to England to manage Southampton, but after one season he resigned, and went back to Italy to become the coach at Torino. He lasted just four months before being dismissed.

In 1997 Souness went to Benfica, but after two unsuccessful seasons he was sacked. But at Blackburn Rovers he got them promoted back to the Premier League in his first full season. During his four year spell he had a 2–1 League Cup victory over Tottenham Hotspur in 2002.

August 31st 2004 he become manager of Newcastle United.

HOW NEWCASTLE UTD QUALIFIED:

In 2003–04 Arsenal went through the season without a single defeat – only the second ever team to do so (the first was Preston North End in 1889 – 115 years earlier) and were crowned champions once more.

For the third season running, Sir Bobby Robson secured European qualification for Newcastle United, but it was a step backward as it was the UEFA Cup rather than the Champion's League, as had happened in the previous two campaigns. Their fifth-place finish was achieved despite bad runs at both the start and the end of the season, with the club failing to win their first six and their last five league games.

1 September 16 2004 - NEWCASTLE UTD 2 HAPOEL BNEI SAKHNIN 0

Given, Carr, Elliott, O'Brien, Hughes (Bernard), Dyer (Butt), Bowyer, Jenas, Robert, Ameobi (Milner), Kluivert.

Att: 30,221

MATCH REPORT: This was Graeme Souness' first game in charge – and he sparked some controversy by going with Sir Bobby Robson's summer signing from Barcelona, Patrick Kluivert – rather than Alan Shearer. The United skipper had found himself relegated to the bench for the final game of the reigns of both Ruud Gullit and Sir Bobby Robson, yet Souness launched his Toon career by naming the 34-year-old among the substitutes.

The Dutchman opened the scoring with just three minutes gone, however, firing home a left-footed effort from close range after great work from Lee Bowyer and Kieron Dyer. Then Kluivert did the trick once again four minutes before half-time, meeting a Robert corner with a powerful header that went in off the underside of the crossbar.

Zimbabwean keeper Energy Mumarbadoro made splendid saves from both Kluivert and Bowyer, but the work-rate and commitment of the Israeli side meant that, for long periods, the Magpies struggled to find the space they needed to open up their opponents.

Robert clearly had the beating of marker Ahmed Kasum, but the Frenchman should have made more of the opportunity.

Souness' men were guilty of squandering possession too often and struggled to break down a side that were clearly out of their depth.

Half-time: Newcastle Utd 2 Hapoel 0

United could have extended their lead with the second half barely a minute old after Kluivert turned elegantly away from his marker and fed Dyer, who in turn rolled the ball into Bowyer's path. The former Leeds United midfielder should have done better and Murambadoro was able to save comfortably.

Kluivert saw a long-range effort deflected wide by Basem Genaiem's lunge, but the fireworks were still to come when Nicky Butt, a 58th-minute replacement for Dyer, and Soan clashed in the middle of the pitch.

The former Manchester United man was given a straight red card for pushing Soan, who was himself yellow-carded for the second time.

Bowyer, who had adopted a robust approach from the off, went into the book for a foul on Olumide, sparking calls for calm from Souness on the sideline.

It took a last-ditch header from Avi Danan to deny Kluivert a hat-trick 12 minutes from time after substitute James Milner cut in and crossed from the right.

The United fans were not that happy with the performance, and many were not that impressed with the appointment of Souness to replace their hero Sir Bobby Robson. There was no rapturous welcome for the new boss, and the applause which greeted the final whistle was distinctly muted.

September 30 2004 - HAPOEL BNEI SAKHNIN 1 NEWCASTLE UTD 5

Given (Harper), Carr, Bernard, Hughes, O'Brien, Jenas, Bowyer, Robert (Ambrose), Bellamy, Kluivert (Milner), Shearer.

Att: 1,200

This Newcastle European adventure took Toon fans to places they'd never dreamt of visiting, and places where football played a bit-part in some religious, political and cultural divide ... and none more so than the trip to Sakhnin in Israel. Since when has Israel been part of Europe?

Sakhnin is situated in Israel's North District in the Lower Galilee, about 14 miles east of Acre, and was declared a city in 1995.

We knew several Sakhnin games had been plagued by hooliganism. Games against Beitar Jerusalem were particularly violent, due to the presence of Beitar's notoriously anti-Arab supporters, and Newcastle supporters didn't know what to expect on arrival.

During the Arab-Israeli war, Sakhnin surrendered to Israeli forces but was re-captured by Arab forces shortly afterwards. It finally fell without battle into Israeli hands but has remained a tinderbox for religious rebellion ever since.

The game took place against the backdrop of further bloodshed in Gaza to the south of Tel Aviv during the Jewish holiday of Succoth, making the Sakhnin side's Arab-Jew make-up all the more poignant.

MATCH REPORT: United kicked off at the 42,000-capacity Ramat Gan Stadium – with an attendance of 1,200 (the lowest ever for a Newcastle European fixture) - knowing that an early goal would all but settle the tie, and with Kluivert, Shearer and Bellamy all in the starting line-up, there was little doubting Souness' intentions.

The visitors did not have things all their own way, however, particularly in the first half. But the clinical finishing of two of Europe's most accomplished front-men - Alan Shearer and Patrick Kluivert - was more than enough to see them home.

Sakhnin, just as they had been at St James' Park a fortnight previous, were full of vim and vigour. But their physical approach was no match for Graeme

Souness' side, despite briefly getting themselves back on level terms on the night with Congalese striker Alain Masudi's 13th-minute strike.

It was Newcastle's fifth successive victory since Sir Bobby Robson's departure and ensured their place in the next round of the competition.

Only nine minutes had elapsed when Kluivert twice exchanged passes with Jermaine Jenas to split the home defence, and the Dutchman needed no second invitation to side-foot the ball past keeper Energy Murambadoro for the opener.

Shearer proved equally clinical seven minutes before the break when, after a flowing Newcastle move, Murambadoro spilled Lee Bowyer's shot from a tight angle and the former England captain slammed home the 350th league and cup goal of his career.

Kluivert scored four minutes later, sliding the ball expertly past Murambadoro after Laurent Robert had scythed his way through the Israeli rearguard.

Half-time: Hapoel 1 Newcastle Utd 3

Souness chose to give keeper Shay Given a rest when he replaced him with Steve Harper at half-time, and he had been on the pitch for only seven minutes when his side increased their lead.

Jenas' neat turn inside the box defeated Masudi, whose ill-timed tackle sent him sprawling to the ground and left Santiago with little option but to point to the penalty spot.

Shearer sent Murambadoro the wrong way and fired the ball into the keeper's bottom right corner to make it 4-1 on the night and 6-1 on aggregate.

Harper saved well from Kassom with five minutes remaining, but the home side's evening went from bad to worse when Murambadoro raced from his line to confront Bellamy and handled outside his box and received the inevitable red card.

Shearer took full advantage to blast home a superb left-foot drive in injury time and set the seal on a comprehensive victory.

Graeme Souness: "There were no bookings. They've not got involved in anything, and they should take credit for that. We have done everything right on the trip and it's been great. We had a proper hotel and the food and the training facilities have been excellent."

Patrick Kluivert: "I'm feeling very good and very happy. I've had a good start to my career with Newcastle United, but by no means am I finished. This is a very young Newcastle team and we have good possibilities in the future."

Alan Shearer: "It's a sign of my confidence when I'm shooting and scoring with my left foot."

October 21 2004 - PANIONIOS 0 NEWCASTLE UTD 1

Given, Carr, O'Brien, Elliott, Bernard, Milner (Ameobi), Jenas, Bowyer, Robert, Bellamy, Shearer.

Att: 8,000

A fiasco by Athens air traffic controllers caused major delays to flights carrying Toon fans to Greece, with some flights cancelled. Many fans were stuck at Heathrow Airport (although we were lucky because we flew from there a day earlier), and some arrived at Athens only to find their luggage (including match tickets) had not arrived.

It was a strange trip, in that Arsenal and Middlesbrough were playing in Athens a day before ourselves and all three sets of supporters were based in the same city. Thankfully it was Boro and not the Mackems. We got on well with them with an 'Englishman abroad' mentality, looking after each other. The Gunners were just as friendly. Although some Greek supporters allegedly have an attitude, Panionios fans were superb.

The club is based in the Athenian suburb of Nea Smyrni, and the ground is in the middle of a residential area.

MATCH REPORT: Craig Bellamy had to answer to his critics after apologising to Graeme Souness for a foul-mouthed outburst sparked by his substitution against Charlton at the weekend. **Bellamy:** "I was out of order for what I did and I want to apologise. I knew within 10 seconds what I did was wrong. In my view a player is substituted when he has been ineffective and I didn't feel I was ineffective. I know there is only so much the club and the fans can take and I know I have been to blame for what has happened in the past. There is no other club I want to play for."

The Magpies turned in a lacklustre display against distinctly ordinary opposition as Jermaine Jenas found support from his midfield colleagues Lee Bowyer, Laurent Robert and James Milner in depressingly short supply to leave Bellamy and strike partner Shearer woefully short of ammunition.

Panionios keeper Sorin Colceag was tested only twice in the first half, and on both occasions, proved equal to the task.

Frenchman Robert was the first to pull the trigger, atoning for a dreadful 28th-minute free-kick with a blistering follow-up which blazed through a crowded penalty area before being turned firmly away.

Jenas warmed Colceag's hands with an equally well-struck shot 10 minutes before the break, but the England international should have walked off at half-time with his name on the score-sheet.

Shay Given tipped a 23rd-minute drive from Mario Breska header around the post.

Defender Panagiotis Giannopoulos had two free headers but Given saved comfortably.

Half-time: Panionios 0 Newcastle Utd 0

Influential midfielder Martin Parodi wasted a good opportunity after 55 minutes when he smashed a 25-yard free-kick straight into Olivier Bernard but, in truth, the crowd got more enjoyment out of the arrival of a stray dog on the pitch a few minutes later.

Shearer forced a good save from Colceag with a powerful header, but Ameobi should have opened the scoring when he was presented with a free header at the far post but planted the ball wide.

Panionios' lack of adventure was not being well received by the home supporters, and their mood did not improve when the deadlock was finally broken three minutes from time when Ameobi was tripped by Grigoris Makos inside the box and Shearer did what he does best to snatch the points.

Craig Bellamy: "It was good to get the win. It was vital, as I would probably have got the blame if we hadn't. I was surprised at the way they played, they didn't come at us. They let us off the hook. The fans were great. The best thing about the Geordies – win or lose – they always have a great time."

Shay Given: "I was straight on the phone after the game. My wife is pregnant and I told her to hang on. Everything is OK. It's a huge thing in my life, I'm really excited".

November 4 2004 - NEWCASTLE UTD 2 DINAMO TBLISI 0

Given, Hughes, Elliott (Bramble), O'Brien, Bernard, Jenas, Bowyer (Ambrose), Robert, Kluivert, Shearer (Milner), Bellamy.

Att: 27,218

MATCH REPORT: Goalkeeper Shay Given had only one save of any real note to make, tipping over a dipping first-half effort from striker Levan Melkadze, as the visitors struggled to make an impact in attack.

It was just what Graeme Souness' men needed after meekly surrendering their 10-game unbeaten run at Bolton the previous Sunday.

Souness took no chances for a game his side were expected to win comfortably, naming his strongest available line-up. Newcastle were overwhelmingly dominant to the extent that it seemed only a matter of time before they opened the scoring. The fact that they did not do this until 38 minutes had elapsed, however, was a cause for concern.

Frenchman Laurent Robert wasted a glorious opportunity to open the scoring when his pace took him clear of the Dinamo rearguard to collect a Given clearance, although he shot wastefully wide with the goal at his mercy.

Instead, it was left to old campaigner Shearer to ease the growing tension on 38 minutes. Given's clearance was headed firmly infield by Robert from the right wing and Bellamy's dummy allowed Kluivert to steer the ball into the path of his captain. Shearer thumped a right-foot shot past the stranded Zurab Mamaladze to open the scoring.

Half-time: Newcastle Utd 1 Tblisi 0

The game was effectively over when Mamaladze and Nemsadze failed to clear a Robert corner and Bellamy thumped a volley into the yawning net to make it 2-0.

The tempo dropped as the home side switched to cruise control.

Shearer made way for James Milner with 72 minutes gone after seeing a close-range finish rightly chalked off for offside, and the newcomer almost made his mark within three minutes, crossing for Bellamy to shoot high over.

Kluivert and Robert both went close as the clock ran down and the Dutchman saw an injury-time effort kicked off the line by Jaba Kankava as the home side finished strongly.

November 25 2004 - SOCHAUX 0 NEWCASTLE UTD 4

Given, Bernard, Bramble, Hughes, Elliott, Bowyer (Dyer), Butt, Ambrose (Taylor), Milner (Robert), Ameobi, Bellamy.

Att: 15,173

Sochaux-Montbéliard was founded in 1928 by the Peugeot French car manufacturing company, and take away the motor company and Sochaux would have nothing. The place is situated close to the border with Switzerland on the far east of France and has a population of less than 5,000.

They play at the Stade Auguste Bonal in Montbéliard, in the region of Franche-Comté in eastern France. It is named after Auguste Bonal, the former sports director of the club, who, after refusing to cooperate with the Germans during World War II, was murdered.

Obviously being just a fraction of the size of Marseille, we didn't get the trouble we had experienced the previous season on French soil with this visit to Sochaux.

I flew to Geneva, Switzerland, for this game, originally planning to get a train to France, but met a couple of lads from County Durham on the plane who said they were meeting some other mates in Switzerland. They hired a minibus and drove to the game and there was a spare seat, so I bunked a lift with them. The most memorable thing about this trip though was that we nearly all died on the drive to the game. Passing through amazing mountain scenery, on some unbelievable hair-pin bends, we went round one such bend slightly over the line, and into to path of an articulated truck coming the other way. Bri (the driver) swerved, we missed the lorry by inches, but we skidded to a halt just inches away from a drop down a rock face that would have taken us five minutes to hit the bottom. Every one of us knew we were a fraction away from never making that or any other game ever again. We continued our journey for about half an hour - in total silence.

MATCH REPORT: Sochaux, who went into the game unbeaten in 11 matches in all competitions, impressed early on. Midfielder Romain Pitau tested goalkeeper Given with a fifth-minute shot which bounced awkwardly in front of him.

Bowyer once again let his passion get the better of him, and he earned himself his third European booking of the season (and a suspension) for an 11th-minute trip on Mathieu.

Newcastle first threatened in the 26th minute when Milner picked up possession wide on the left and squared for the fast-arriving Bellamy, but the Welshman blasted his left-footed shot well over the bar.

The breakthrough finally arrived after 29 minutes, Bowyer slamming a right-footed shot past goalkeeper Teddy Richert.

It should have been 2-0 within two minutes after Given found Bellamy and he hooked the ball across for Milner, but the teenager blasted his effort over from point-blank range.

Half-time: Sochaux 0 Newcastle Utd 1

Newcastle doubled their lead within 49 seconds of the restart, after full-back Olivier Bernard found space on the left and crossed into the box. The unmarked Ameobi slotted home at the far post. It was the England under-21 striker's 10th goal in Europe and put him level with Wyn Davies in second place in the club's all-time list - behind Shearer.

Newcastle found themselves up against it when the referee awarded a penalty for an apparent tug on Isabey's shirt - but Mathieu dragged his left foot shot wide of the post.

The home side committed men to the attack, and the visitors exploited the extra space to superb effect 14 minutes from time. Dyer broke from central midfield and allowed full-back Aaron Hughes to spring the offside trap and square for Bellamy to net.

The fight had gone out of the home side and their plight worsened in the final minute with Robert's inch-perfect free-kick.

Shay Given, who almost made a goal for James Milner: "If that one had gone in it probably would have been the best game I have ever played for Newcastle because, while I have saved a few in the past, I have never had an assist. Sochaux opened us up a little too easily and I was happy to keep them out, but I suppose we had a bit of luck when their defender missed the penalty. It was a great way to celebrate 300 games for the club, the games have flown by, even though it's taken me seven and half years to get them. This really is a fantastic club, and if you don't believe me, just look at the reception the fans gave us tonight."

December 16 2004 - NEWCASTLE UTD 1 SPORTING LISBON 1

Given, Taylor (Andrew O'Brien), Bramble, Elliott, Hughes, Milner, Ambrose, Jenas, Bernard, Bellamy (Guy), Ameobi.

Att: 28,017

MATCH REPORT: Newcastle, having lost to Sporting in a pre-season tournament, knew they faced a stern test. So it proved, as the visitors claimed more than their fair share of possession and passed the ball with style and adventure.

Sporting coach Jose Peseiro, who promised an attacking start, saw his side fall behind within five minutes of the kick-off.

Shola Ameobi rose well to meet Titus Bramble's deep free-kick and send the ball into the penalty area, where Bellamy pulled away from marker Roberto Beto to send a looping header over keeper Ricardo.

Sporting looked vulnerable at the back, particularly to the pace of Bellamy, and he really should have made it 2-0 with 24 minutes gone when he finally beat the offside trap to collect Steven Taylor's ball over the top, but shot straight at Ricardo's legs.

The Belgian referee rightly booked Bramble for a rugged challenge on striker Liedson, but ignored the Brazilian's shameful play-acting, and he had little choice but to show Ameobi a yellow card after he threw the ball away in disgust.

Aaron Hughes made a rash challenge on Martinho Paito and, from the resulting free-kick, Custodio powered a header past Given to level.

Half-time: Newcastle Utd 1 Sporting Lisbon 1

The work-rate of Bellamy and Ameobi put the Sporting defence under pressure as the second half got underway.

The visitors tried to claim a penalty, although with little conviction, after Liedson went down under Olivier Bernard's 65th-minute challenge, and the pressure mounted on the Magpies as the clock ran down.

Rochemback failed to test Given fully with a mis-hit free-kick 17 minutes from time after James Milner had felled him, but Souness soon moved to shore up the defence when he sent on Andy O'Brien for Taylor five minutes later.

Souness' problems deepened seconds later when Bellamy limped off injured to be replaced by teenager Lewis Guy.

The Magpies found themselves pinned back as the final whistle approached, but they had worked hard for their point and they deserved the draw.

February 17 2005 - HEERENVEEN 1 NEWCASTLE UTD 2

Given, Carr, Andrew O'Brien, Bramble, Faye, Babayaro (Hughes), Bowyer, Jenas, Kluivert, Ameobi (Robert), Shearer (Taylor).

Att: 19,500

Another trip to Amsterdam, then bus (provided by Newcastle United FC) to Heerenveen in the north of Holland.

A pleasant enough little town, and a great welcome from the Dutch fans, who took care of us all day. Their Abe Lenstra Stadion holds 26,800 (yet the population of Heerenveen is only 28,000) and is a little way out of town. There is a Sports Bar at the venue but it was strictly 'home supporters only', but our new Dutch friends got us inside.

The Dutch club only gave us 700 tickets and hundreds of ticketless Newcastle fans arrived on the morning of the game. Many had booked flights and accommodation expecting a decent allocation, and they had the choice to travel to try and get inside the ground, or lose the money. Most of the fans (like ourselves) were based in the Dutch capital because Heerenveen couldn't handle such an influx of tourists.

Although the fans were in high spirits, there was a lot of anti-Souness feeling about this tie. One win in five games, boring football, and many had still not forgotten Freddy Shepherd's decision to sack Sir Bobby Robson. Souness was not wanted by the vast majority of Toon supporters – and they were starting to voice an opinion.

Lee Bowyer returned to the scene of one of his biggest triumphs to fire Newcastle to victory over Heerenveen before getting himself sent off on an eventful evening.

The former Leeds midfielder, who scored twice against Partizan Belgrade at the Abe Lenstra Stadium in the 1999 UEFA Cup, backheeled an 82nd-minute winner past goalkeeper Brian Vandenbussche and then saw red for a second bookable offence as the Magpies scrapped their way to victory.

Graeme Souness recruited Jean-Alain Boumsong, Celestine Babayaro and Amdy Faye during the January transfer window but sent Craig Bellamy to Celtic on loan.

MATCH REPORT: The opening 45 minutes of this match served up a graphic illustration of just why there was so much doom and gloom on Tyneside this season.

It started reasonably well with Faye bossing the midfield battle and full-backs Babayaro and Stephen Carr exploiting the space on the wings. However, with the attacking trio of Shearer, Shola Ameobi and Dutchman Patrick Kluivert failing to trouble Vandenbussche once, the potential was always there for a slip.

A Titus Bramble slip on 24 minutes let in Jan Huntelaar to put the Dutch ahead.

It might have been worse for the Magpies within two minutes, had Huntelaar not directed a header straight at Given when it seemed easier to score.

Half-time: Heerenveen 1 Newcastle Utd 0

Bramble partially atoned for his first-half nightmare four minutes into the second-half when he slid in to dispossess Huntelaar with a superb tackle. The loose ball ran to Bruggink but he curled his shot just over the bar. The Toon fans were starting to lose their patience, singing for the introduction of Laurent Robert and against the Magpies' board of directors.

Robert arrived as a replacement for Ameobi, much to the delight of the Geordie faithful, but his first contribution was to deliver a free-kick from a promising position straight into Vandenbussche's arms.

But Souness had his skipper to thank for cooling the unrest in the camp. Kluivert laid off Robert's pass into Shearer's path and the 34-year-old blasted his 14th goal of the season and his 187th for the club past Vandenbussche to level.

The songs from the terraces immediately changed to "You're still England's number one", and if all was not well with the world, it was at least a little more pleasant.

But there was better to come for the visitors with eight minutes remaining when Robert and Kluivert combined to set up Carr to cross, and when he delivered the ball with pace, Bowyer cheekily back-heeled it past Vandenbussche to complete an unlikely comeback.

Bramble almost threw the lead away two minutes later when he gifted the ball to Mika Vayrynen, but Shay Given rescued him with an excellent save.

There was still time for Bowyer to get himself sent off for a second bookable offence after handling the ball, but the visitors held firm to boost their chances of reaching the last 16.

Lee Bowyer: "The ball bounced up and hit me on the hand but the referee thought it was deliberate, and there's not much I can do about it now. This obviously means I will miss the return with Heerenveen, and I won't be able to play against Chelsea in the league because I have picked up five bookings. These things happen."

February 24 2005 - NEWCASTLE UTD 2 HEERENVEEN 1

Given, Carr, Andrew O'Brien (Taylor), Bramble, Hughes, Dyer (Jenas), Faye, Butt, Robert, Ameobi, Shearer (Milner).

Att: 26,156

MATCH REPORT: Laurent Robert rewarded Souness for bringing him back into the team when he scored after just four minutes. He raced on to Shearer's perfect lay-off to fire in a cross which Michel Breuer could only help into the roof of his own net.

It was 2-0 when, after Said Bakkati had stopped the progress of Kieron Dyer 22 yards out, Robert touched the ball sideways - and Shearer hammered in a low drive which Brian Vandenbussche could not keep out.

Shola Ameobi tried to add his name to the score-sheet but was denied three times - twice by the goalkeeper, with a fine double save and from a powerful header, and once by the post.

It might have been different for the visitors had Given not managed to palm away leading scorer Huntelaar's eighth-minute strike, but there was only one team in it from then on.

Half-time: Newcastle Utd 2 Heerenveen 0

Dyer, who had missed the first leg with a viral infection, was replaced by Jermaine Jenas at the break.

Robert tested Vandenbussche with a 52nd-minute effort as the Dutch side put as many men behind the ball as possible but only invited pressure on themselves.

Shearer made way for youngster James Milner with 25 minutes remaining, and the former Leeds United star had a chance within two minutes of his arrival after getting in on the left - but he fired straight at Vandenbussche.

Then just as it seemed as the though to game was running down to an uneventful conclusion, Ameobi handled as he tried to clear a Ugur Yildirim corner. Referee Dejan Delevic pointed to the spot and Bruggink smashed the penalty past Given to give his side something to show for their efforts.

March 10 2005 - OLYMPIAKOS 1 NEWCASTLE UTD 3

Given, Carr, Andrew O'Brien, Bramble, Hughes, Dyer (Jenas), Butt, Faye (N'Zogbia), Robert (Milner), Shearer, Kluivert.

Att: 33,000

We enjoyed several pre-match drinks and played a few games of cards before the game in a bar right by the ground. What we didn't know was that the away end was at the opposite end of the stadium from the pub, and we left it until the last minute to go the game, which meant walking through the Olympiakos supporters -not the friendliest of fans. I'm not sure if it was luck, or us just not caring due to being under the influence of drink, but we walked through hundreds of them to the away end unscathed ... even though we held aloft a poster of Nikos Dabizas we found in a local newspaper!

The Georgios Karaiskakis Stadium is known for its powder-keg atmosphere ... and we were not disappointed as the 460 Toon fans were tucked into one corner and suffered the usual abuse and missiles. The organisation was a shambles as Toon fans tried to get into the ground and the club wouldn't open the away turnstiles, which had the riot police trying to keep supporters apart. It was nasty and worst of all ... expected! That's what you get in football backwaters like this – they treat you like vermin.

Kieron Dyer was getting treatment by the side of the pitch and missiles were thrown at him. Because of previous incidents, UEFA threatened to fine the club 1,000 euros for every flare thrown, and there were dozens of them!

We were kept in at the end but Greek fans threw everything but the kitchen sink at us as they left the ground, however, there were a number of riot police who shielded us from the missiles. They told us they were Panathanikos fans and "hated Olympiakos".

MATCH REPORT: The night saw the Greeks being allowed back into the Karaiskakis Stadium after a ban for bad behaviour.

The Greeks dominated the early exchanges, but their flow was interrupted on 13 minutes when a push on Kieron Dyer got Newcastle a penalty. Dyer ran on to Amdy Faye's through-ball and saw his shot saved by Antonios Nikopolidis, but Georgatos pushed him as he tried to head the rebound into the empty net. The referee pointed immediately to the spot and then, to the fury of the home crowd, produced a red card for the offence. Shearer had to wait for some time for calm to be restored before stepping up to smash the penalty high to the keeper's right for his 25th European goal for the club.

However, the home side were level within three minutes when O'Brien was judged to have brought down Stoltidis, and Djordjevic obliged from the spot to square it.

Newcastle restored their lead 11 minutes before the break when Robert was tripped by Gabriel Schürrer 22 yards out. The Frenchman took the kick himself and curled it into Nikopolidis' top right corner with the keeper rooted to the spot. He had done the same to Liverpool at St James' Park to win 1-0 the previous weekend.

Even with 10 men, Olympiakos continued to threaten for a period with Rivaldo pulling the strings, but that situation was to change.

Kostoulas, who had been booked for a 25th-minute foul on Dyer, felled Butt two minutes before the break as the visitors broke from deep inside their own half. Ibanez initially booked Schurrer, but after consulting one of his assistants, called over Kostoulas and sent him off, sparking angry scenes in the home stands.

Half-time: Olympiakos 1 Newcastle Utd 2

Souness decided to make a double substitution. Off went Robert and Dyer, two of the quickest men in his armoury, and on came Jermaine Jenas and James Milner.

Newcastle took a massive stride towards the last eight on 69 minutes when the impressive Butt played a fine ball out to Milner on the left and he carved his way through the home defence before squaring for Kluivert to guide home his 10th goal of the season.

Shearer went just wide with a 75th-minute free-kick and it took a last-ditch block by Aaron Hughes to deny Giovanni at the death.

Alan Shearer: "OK, they had two players sent off but we still had to go out and do a job, and that's what we did. We were not spectacular, but we did what we had to do. Whether it's our best ever result away from home, I don't know. There have been some great ones in the past."

16 March 16 2005 - NEWCASTLE UTD 4 OLYMPIAKOS 0

Given, Carr (Ramage), Taylor, Andrew O'Brien, Hughes, Jenas, Bowyer, Butt, Robert (N'Zogbia), Dyer (Milner), Shearer.

Att: 32,163

Alan Shearer edged closer to Jackie Milburn's club record of 200 goals as Newcastle brushed aside Olympiacos in their 100th European game to march into the UEFA Cup quarter-finals.

The 34-year-old scored two to take his tally for the Magpies to 191.

MATCH REPORT: Giovanni scored a Champions League winner for Barcelona against the Magpies back in 1997 and looked lively in the opening minutes, and skipper Predrag Djordjevic, who caused problems at the Karaiskakis Stadium, started impressively as they looked to inspire an unlikely fight-back.

Their hopes were ripped apart, however, when Laurent Robert's free-kick saw Dyer beat the offside trap and, dispensing with the formality of turning, back-heeled the ball audaciously past goalkeeper Antonios Nikopolidis to effectively kill off the tie.

Indeed, the game could have been over long before half-time as Shearer missed chances to get himself a hat-trick.

He missed the first by firing high over with his left foot after being played in by Jenas; failed to connect with Robert's quickly-taken 36th-minute free-kick for the second; and was desperately unlucky to see a diving header drop inches wide three minutes later.

With Nicky Butt having earlier hit the bar with a rasping drive and defender Steven Taylor heading wide at the far post, chances were going begging until the last minute of the first half.

Dyer cut inside past Spiros Vallas and squared for Shearer to smash the ball home off the legs of Georgios Anatolakis to make it 2-0.

Half-time: Newcastle Utd 2 Olympiacos 0

It took the Magpies just nine minutes to increase their lead further after the break when Nikopolidis was caught straying from his line. Bowyer did well to meet Robert's cross with a looping header and the `keeper had to hurriedly back-pedal to scoop the ball off his line, but Jenas followed up to square for Bowyer to score.

Souness took off Dyer and Robert to be replaced by James Milner and Charles N'Zogbia.

Pantelis Kafes fired harmlessly wide from a rare Greek attack, then Shearer scored with 21 minutes remaining. Jenas laid off a perfectly-weighted pass for the Newcastle skipper to round Nikopolidis and fire into the roof of the net.

Bowyer sent a glancing header just wide five minutes from time.

April 7 2005 - NEWCASTLE UTD 1 SPORTING LISBON 0

Given (Harper), Carr, Andrew O'Brien, Taylor, Hughes, Dyer (Bowyer), Jenas, Faye, Robert (Milner), Shearer, Ameobi.

Att: 36,753

MATCH REPORT: Souness warned the Newcastle fans that they would see Sporting enjoy plenty of the ball at St James', and he asked them to show patience if the visitors made life uncomfortable for the Magpies in the first half.

Andy O'Brien had put in a miserable individual display in the 3-0 mauling by Aston Villa the previous Saturday yet Souness stuck with him to marshal his defence that comprised Stephen Taylor, Aaron Hughes and Stephen Carr.

The pace of striker Liedson and the invention of midfielder Carlos Martins caused the home side problems before the break, but 'keeper Shay Given had only one real save to make, bundling a dipping Liedson shot around the post on 17 minutes.

The Portuguese outfit had beaten Middlesbrough in the last round, but Souness had noticed their defence didn't take too kindly to the ball being lofted high into the heart of the penalty area. In the 34th-minute Robert's free-kick did just that and Shearer came close as the visitors stood ball watching. Just three minutes more had elapsed when the Frenchman curled another free-kick into the box and Shearer met it unopposed to head sweetly past Ricardo.

Russian referee Yuri Baskakov left the pitch at half-time to a deafening chorus of boos from the Geordie fans after waving play to go on when Shola Ameobi had been tripped by Anderson Polga as he raced through on goal in injury time. It was as blatant a penalty as anyone had seen all season, but the vistors somehow got away with it.

Half-time: Newcastle Utd 1 Sporting Lisbon 0

Newcastle were dealt a blow at the break when Given failed to re-appear due to a hip problem, and Steve Harper took his place.

Sporting resumed in the same vein, looking dangerous without actually achieving anything.

Robert was clearly unhappy to be replaced by James Milner on 57 minutes and headed straight down the tunnel. He was to be joined within six minutes by the injured Dyer who was replaced Lee Bowyer. All eyes were on the former Leeds United midfielder as he embraced his team-mate before he ran on to the pitch. The team-mates had knocked 'seven bells' out of each other on the St James' Park pitch days before when United played against Villa.

Although Sporting only had fleeting moments of magic, there was still work to be done and Harper pulled off a fine one-handed save to deny Joao Moutinho on 62 minutes.

Bowyer picked up his usual booking, this time for a foul on Sa Pinto, then Shearer tested Ricardo with a low drive that didn't result to anything.

Bowyer could have sealed victory nine minutes from time, but fired over the bar after being played in by Taylor, and Ameobi wasted a later opportunity.

April 14 2005 - SPORTING LISBON 4 NEWCASTLE UTD 1

Given, Carr, Bramble (Andrew O'Brien), Taylor, Babayaro, Jenas (Milner), Faye, Bowyer, N'Zogbia, Dyer (Kluivert), Shearer.

Att: 45,000

Flight fares were doubled by the airline companies when they realised the game was on, so we went the cheapest way possible. Instead of flying direct to Lisbon, we flew from Liverpool to Madrid, hired a Nissan Micra and drove at 90mph all the way to the border with Portugal. We stopped the night there and carried on to Lisbon the day after. We saved money, but of course we had to do it all again back to Madrid after the game.

A day of destiny at the Jose Alvalade Stadium for 1,200 Toon fans, but there was bad feeling following Laurent Robert's amazing outburst and sorry performance against Spurs at the weekend. The Frenchman had hit out at Graeme Souness, saying "the team twelve months ago is better than the team now", suggesting that Souness had messed up in the transfer market. But it was the usual upheaval we have come to expect before a big game. That is the Newcastle tradition, shoot yourself in the foot!

On a good note, the Portuguese fans were absolutely fabulous, and just what we needed to restore some faith in humanity after the hell-hole of Athens.

MATCH REPORT: Jose Peseiro had predicted before the match that his side would score and Newcastle would not, while Souness would not be drawn into any fortune telling or tarot card reading.

Sporting did indeed score, a powerful header by Romanian striker Niculae breaching Shay Given's defences five minutes before half-time, and they would have done so again four minutes later had the Irishman not thrown out a hand to deflect away a rocket of a volley from Joao Moutinho.

Before that flurry of activity, however, emergency striker Dyer had put the Magpies ahead on the night and 2-0 on aggregate, running away from defender

Anderson Polga and cheekily slipping the ball through keeper Ricardo's legs to send the 1,200 or so travelling fans into raptures.

Newcastle might have extended their lead further - Lee Bowyer and Dyer both had good chances which went begging - but although the visitors threatened repeatedly on the break, they were vulnerable at the back.

Bramble rarely looked troubled in the first period and his 19-year-old partner Steven Taylor put in a performance far beyond his years.

Half-time: Sporting Lisbon 1 Newcastle Utd 1

Jenas failed to re-appear after the break and James Milner took his place wide on the right.

Sporting defender Rui Jorge drilled his effort over the bar with just Given to beat.

The Magpies were dealt a double blow, however, as the clock ticked towards the hour mark when both Bramble and Dyer limped off. Andy O'Brien and Patrick Kluivert took over.

Beto planted a 61st-minute header just wide but the home side were becoming increasingly desperate.

Kluivert should have done better when he was found in acres of space down the right, then O'Brien gave the ball away on the edge of the box to give Sporting the lead. Barbosa fired in a shot which Given could only parry and Sa Pinto tapped home the rebound to set up an agonising finale.

It got worse for Newcastle with 13 minutes remaining when defender Beto climbed high to power a header past Given from a Rochemback corner.

Souness' side couldn't reply with anything constructive and their fate was sealed in injury-time when Rochemback capitalised on an error by Stephen Carr to make it 4-1 on the night.

Alan Oliver (Chronicle reporter): "I hope that when Patrick Kluivert's £67,000 weekly wage packet drops on his mat, he has the decency to mark it 'return to sender'. He obviously doesn't know what it means to wear the shirt of Newcastle United judging from his pathetic effort last night."

Kieron Dyer: "We were cruising after my early goal. We had a game plan because we knew they would play a high line at the back and it seemed to be working a treat. But in the end it's all gone wrong. We did have the chances to finish them off but we didn't take them. I just hope we get into the FA Cup final by beating Manchester United."

Jermaine Jenas: We had the chances to kill them off and it's disappointing that we didn't take them and it's a bitter pill to swallow. Sunday's FA Cup semi-final with Manchester United is massive and it is important that we pick ourselves up. We have got to go into that game right mentally, and that is going to be hard, and we will see how tonight's defeat affects us."

Newcastle Utd lost to Manchester Utd 1-4 at Cardiff:

Given, Carr, Boumsong, Taylor, Babayaro (Andrew O'Brien 45), Milner (Kluivert 63), Faye (N'Zogbia 45), Butt, Robert, Ameobi, Shearer.

CSKA Moscow beat Sporting Lison 3-1in the UEFA Cup final at Estadio Jose Alvalade.

CHAPTER FOURTEEN INTERTOTO CUP
2005/06

Jermaine Jenas

MANAGER: Graeme Souness

Graeme Souness was finding Sir Bobby Robson a tough act to follow. Newcastle had done well in the UEFA Cup and reached the FA Cup semi-final in 2004/5, but their bottom half finish in the Premiership had many fans believing that the club was heading in the wrong direction.

Souness, much to Freddy Shepherd's annoyance, frowned at United's acceptance of an Intertoto Cup place and the Scot was happy to make his feelings known in public. That paved the way for an unhappy relationship between manager and the Newcastle United board. Shepherd was still trying desperately to rid himself of the 'Toongate' scandal (the 'News Of The World' exclusive) years after the event, but he was still as unpopular as ever.

The signing of Jean-Alain Boumsong from Rangers did Souness no favours. The tall central defender was struggling with the pace of the Premiership, but the manager continued to play him.

HOW NEWCASTLE UTD QUALIFIED:

Chelsea led the Premiership virtually all season long, and won the title.

We finished 14th, and once again qualified for Europe by the back door and the Intertoto Cup. There were six clubs above the Magpies (Manchester City, Tottenham Hotspur, Aston Villa, Charlton Athletic, Birmingham City and Fulham) with more right to qualify than Newcastle, but the Magpies once again seized their opportunity.

July 17 2005 - FC DUBNICA 1 NEWCASTLE UTD 3

Harper, Babayaro, Elliott, Boumsong, Taylor, Butt, Faye, Milner, N'Zogbia, Shearer, Chopra.

Att: 6,200

FC Dubnica play in the small Slovak town of Dubnica nad Váhom, and this was the biggest game in their 79-year history. Formerly of Czechoslovakia, they joined the Slovak league after the break up of the country.

Neither of Graeme Souness' new signings, Scott Parker and Emre, travelled, and neither did Stepen Carr, Titus Bramble or Shola Ameobi.

For the record books, this was Alan Shearer's first competitive appearance and first ever competitive goal in the month of July.

MATCH REPORT: Two goals in the opening seven minutes helped Newcastle to secure a battling first-leg advantage against Slovakian side Dubnica in the third round of the Intertoto Cup.

The departures of Patrick Kluivert and Craig Bellamy, and an injury to Shola Ameobi, had allowed 21-year-old striker Chopra a chance to impress manager Graeme Souness.

And the youngster wasted little time, latching onto an excellent pass from Milner before slotting past the advancing Dubnica goalkeeper Dusan Pernis.

Michael Chopra grabbed his first senior goal for the Magpies after just four minutes to give the under-strength visitors the ideal start, before Alan Shearer poached a second on the line three minutes later.

The hosts looked stunned by the early strike but soon found themselves two behind.

An awkward cross from the left by tricky winger Charles N'Zogbia caused confusion in the home defence, deflecting off centre-back Robert Novak and goal-wards - with Shearer waiting on the back post to double the lead.

Half-time: Dubnica 0 Newcastle Utd 2

To their credit, the hosts did not buckle under the early pressure and forced their way back into the game late in the first half.

The impressive Igor Drzik, excelling against a Magpies midfield without new signings Scott Parker or Emre Belezoglu, floated in a delicate cross from the right, allowing Lukas Tesak to crash home a header from close range.

The complexion of the game could have changed completely early in the second period but for a smart save by Newcastle keeper Steve Harper from a Marian Zimen rocket.

But when Milner made room and lifted a superb side-footed shot over the stranded Pernis from all of 35 yards in the 70th minute, a hard-fought win was secured.

Graeme Souness: "At 2-1 they were still in the game, so our third took the sting out of the match. It was hard for us in that heat, against a team full of youthful vigour. But it's a good day's work for us."

July 23 2005 - NEWCASTLE UTD 2 FC DUBNICA 0

Given, Carr, Babayaro, Boumsong, Taylor, Bowyer, Faye, Jenas (Chopra 46 [Brittain 57]), Milner, N'Zogbia, Shearer.

Att: 25,135

Alan Shearer postponed his retirement for one more year, but he was very unhappy that the club had not brought in a top striker to replace Craig Bellamy. Nicolas Anelka had been targeted all summer but he couldn't agree personal terms. And the former England skipper didn't seem very happy that he was involved in the Intertoto, either: "When I sat down with the chairman and the manager before I signed my contract, I knew I was not expected to play in every single game. That's physically impossible with what has gone on in the past (with injuries). With a bit of luck we will get more ammunition. Last season's defeat to Sporting Lisbon was the biggest disappointment of my career, by a million miles. The UEFA Cup will not be a distraction if the manager can get the players he wants."

MATCH REPORT: Boss Graeme Souness had not tried to hide his displeasure at having to use the maligned summer tournament in order to claim a lucrative UEFA Cup berth.

Bowyer made the first mark in a game distinctly lacking in urgency after Newcastle's comprehensive 3-1 success in the first match in Slovakia a week earlier.

The midfielder set up the lively Charles N'Zogbia on the left, whose cross was cleared from the Dubnica box by Robert Novak.

Jermaine Jenas blazed a right-foot shot over from the edge of the box before Bowyer set up Shearer with a 13th-minute chance. The veteran striker turned on a low through-ball in the box but could only stab his shot narrowly wide of keeper Dusan Pernis' right-hand post.

Milner was denied by a fine save from Pernis and Jenas' 25-yard free-kick hit the underside of the bar and bounced down only for Amdy Faye to head the rebound wide of his target.

Half-time: Newcastle Utd 0 Dubnica 0

Souness replaced Jenas at half-time with Michael Chopra, and before he had even touched the ball Chopra was involved in a collision with keeper Pernis which required him to exit the pitch on a stretcher. Although the youngster returned to the action he was forced to give up after another 15 minutes and was replaced by fellow substitute Martin Brittain.

Dubnica stole forward through Peter Kiska on the hour mark, finishing his run with a rising shot which the acrobatic Given did well to tip over the bar.

N'Zogbia finally fashioned an overdue chance for Newcastle after cutting in from the left and unleashing a cross-cum-shot which flashed across the face of goal.

Then Milner's cross was just missed by Bowyer in the box as the home side finally began to exert a bit of pressure.

Shearer's goal had an air of inevitability about it and the second came in an almost identical fashion. The Newcastle captain leapt highest to head home James Milner's 76th-minute corner, then Stephen Carr's final minute free-kick, to complete a welcome double in his second competitive match of the season.

Alan Shearer: "Deportivo are a massive club. They were in the semi-final of the Champions League two seasons ago. It will be a big test for us."

July 27 2005 - DEPORTIVO LA CORUNA 2 NEWCASTLE UTD 1

Given, Carr, Boumsong, Taylor, Babayaro, N'Zogbia, Bowyer, Butt, Faye, Milner (Chopra 71), Shearer.

Att: 16,000

La Coruña is situated right on the north-west tip of Spain, not too far away from Santiago de Compostela. I would describe it more as being a busy port than a tourist location, but they are trying to attract more visitors – and it does have two beaches Orzán and Riazor. It's hardly Benidorm, as it provides a distribution point for agricultural goods from the region and it has an oil refinery in A Coruña itself.

The Riazor Stadium is not on the scale of Barca or Real Madrid – but neither is the team – and it has a capacity of 34,600. The fans took exception to the Spanish all-seater rule when the stadium was refurbished in February 1998. Around 100 seats were stolen or thrown on the pitch during the match against Real Madrid (the first game all-seater), and 84 more against Alavés three days later.

MATCH REPORT: Early in the game James Milner felt the full force of a challenge from Aldo Duscher and later required stitches for a cut near the eye.

Deportivo were the more composed team throughout the first half but, being at home, that was expected.

Their first chance came after just two minutes when Pedro Munitis broke clear down the right and pulled the ball back towards goal but Jean-Alain Boumsong cleared.

Munitis exposed their weakness down the same flank to create the opening goal eight minutes later. Steven Taylor was caught flat-footed as Munitis broke into the box and squared for Ruben to side-foot home from six yards.

For a short spell it looked as if the Magpies might fold under the pressure as Ruben scuffed another shot in front of goal and Munitis fired straight at Shay Given.

They were almost caught out again just before the interval as the ubiquitous Munitis found space outside the area and sent another shot narrowly wide.

Half-time: Deportivo 1 Newcastle Utd 0

Newcastle finally started to show some attacking intent as the second half began and were instantly rewarded as they won a corner and claimed a superb 48th-minute equaliser through Bowyer. Stephen Carr's cross was cleared only as far as the edge of the area by Deportivo and the ball fell perfectly for Bowyer, who connected with a sweet left-foot volley that flew into the top corner.

Newcastle were back on level terms for just 10 minutes as Andrade ran unchallenged into the box from the halfway line and curled a superb finish past Given.

Ruben volleyed just wide with an acrobatic effort and Given needed to be alert to keep out a deflected Munitis cross.

Despite riding their luck on four occasions late on, Newcastle held on for a result their determination deserved.

Graeme Souness: "If we were truthful, we would probably have taken that score before kick-off. They had a load of internationals and you will see the difference when you look at the two benches. Theirs was packed with internationals while we were down to the bare bones. Deportivo are way ahead of us in terms of training and fitness. I thought Jean-Alain Boumsong was outstanding."

Alan Shearer: "The referee needs a new whistle after the number of free-kicks he gave. It's frustrating but that's European football. These teams go down at every opportunity and they used every trick in the book – and the referee fell for it."

August 3 2005 - NEWCASTLE UTD 1 DEPORTIVO LA CORUNA 2

Given, Carr, Elliott, Emre (Brittain 90), Boumsong, Shearer, Bowyer, Faye (Ameobi 53), Milner (N'Zogbia 72), Parker, Taylor

Att: 35,200

MATCH REPORT: Turkish midfielder Emre was presented with a shooting chance by Shearer but he screwed in a left-foot shot which Molina saved well.

Then Deportivo showed some adventure of there own. Munitis floated a free-kick over the crossbar and Ruben Castro was not far away with a diving header.

Shearer came agonisingly close to breaking the deadlock, meeting Milner's left-wing free-kick with a firm header which Molina kept out with a brilliant one-handed save.

The resulting corner saw Milner strike the ball home.

But Newcastle were guilty of giving Deportivo their lifeline with their first defensive mistake of the evening as Jean-Alain Boumsong's slow reaction let in Jorge Andrade to chip home an equaliser in the final minute of the first half.

Alan Shearer's challenge on visiting goalkeeper Jose Molina had sparked a mass melee which spilled over into an angry confrontation between the dugouts - and rumours of a tunnel bust-up at half-time.

Half-time: Newcastle Utd 1 Deportivo 1

As tempers started to fray Shearer and his captain counterpart Lionel Scaloni were brought together for a stern talking-to by referee Helmut Fleischer before the second half got underway.

Then two minutes into the second half Robbie Elliott obliged in hammering the final nail into Newcastle's continental coffin when he failed to spot Pedro Munitis, who tapped the ball past Shay Given and finished off when the ball ricocheted to him off the back-tracking Stephen Carr.

Shearer came close to getting the home side back on track three minutes later with a powerful low free-kick which Molina in goal did well to block.

But the revival didn't happen and Shearer exited Europe for the last time as his kamikaze Newcastle team-mates blew the chance to launch their skipper on one final bid for an elusive continental trophy.

The 34-year-old was due to retire at the end of the season, and what a sad way for him to bow out.

Steven Taylor

CHAPTER FIFTEEN
INTERTOTO CUP - 2006/07

Glenn Roeder

MANAGER: Glenn Roeder

In February 2006, Newcastle United parted company with Graeme Souness, and former Newcastle United defender Glenn Roeder took over – short term because he didn't have his coaching badges.

Roeder began his professional playing career at Leyton Orient, and played for Queens Park Rangers and Notts County before being transferred to Newcastle United in 1984, where he made 219 appearances during his five years at the club, scoring 19 goals.

He became player-manager at Gillingham; took over at Watford at the start of the 1993–94 season, but was sacked in February 1996.

He was assistant manager at Turf Moor; worked as a coach under Glenn Hoddle for the England national team; was assistant to Harry Redknapp at West Ham before taking over as manager after Redknapp's departure. In April 2003 he suffered a brain tumour and was replaced by Trevor Brooking for the final three games of the season and West Ham were relegated with a Premiership record number of 42 points.

After nearly two years out of the game, he returned to football in June 2005 when he was named youth-development manager of Newcastle United and in February 2006 he was appointed caretaker manager, with striker Alan Shearer as his assistant. The Premier League at first rejected Newcastle's request to make him full-time boss, but Freddy Shepherd got the backing of all 19 other Premiership club chairmen and they voted in favour of Roeder being allowed to gain the UEFA Pro Licence whilst in the job. Roeder was named as Newcastle's permanent manager on 16 May 2006, signing a two year contract with the club.

HOW NEWCASTLE UTD QUALIFIED:

Jose Mourinho's Chelsea retained the Premiership. Newcastle finished 7th and took up the invitation to play in the Intertoto Cup.

171

July 15 2006 - NEWCASTLE UTD 1 LILLESTROM 1

Given; Carr, Taylor, Bramble, Babayaro; Solano, Parker, Emre, N'Zogbia, Milner (Ameobi), Luque (O'Brien).

Att: 31,059

MATCH REPORT: Glenn Roeder had little option but to turn to Spanish misfit £9.5million signing Albert Luque and youngster James Milner, with Shola Ameobi struggling with a hip problem and gaps left by the retired Alan Shearer and the injured Michael Owen.

They found themselves on the back foot within 21 minutes, however, as the Norwegians put their superior match fitness to good use.

Koren's deflected shot gave the visitors a 21st-minute lead but Shay Given had already had to dash from his line to keep out the former Kaiserslautern front-man when he fired in a 12th-minute shot which almost crept in.

Babayaro cleared off the line and, apart from a 43rd-minute Emre free-kick which keeper Heinz Muller tipped away, there was little for the home crowd to shout about.

Half-time: Newcastle Utd 0 Lillestrom 1

On 50 minutes Luque, who had a poor first half, picked up possession just outside the box and skipped past Pal Steffen Andresen and Anders Rambekk before curling a pinpoint shot past Muller.

He might have added a second within two minutes but could not take Charles N'Zogbia's cross in his stride.

Scott Parker needed extensive treatment after being caught late by Occean, who was booked, but as he returned, Newcastle started to increase the pressure.

Emre had a half-chance and the Magpies did the most pressing, but the foot soldiers of the Toon Army were far from impressed with this performance, as well as a few others.

The general consensus was – if you don't enter the competition then fair enough – but if you DO enter, at least put a bit effort in!

Shay Given: "The game at Lillestrom is massive for us. Up there with the most important European games – such as the Champions League qualifiers. It's one of the carrots to attract the top players to the club, and the UEFA Cup could create a cash windfall."

July 22 2006 - LILLESTROM 0 NEWCASTLE UTD 3

Given, Carr, Taylor, Bramble, Babayaro (Moore), Solano, Parker, Emre, N'Zogbia (Pattison), Milner, Ameobi (Butt).

Att: 8,742

Lillestrøm Sportsklubb play in the city of Lillestrøm on the south-east of Norway, not too far away from Oslo. We flew to Oslo (where we were based) from Stansted, and travelled by train to the match. Oslo, like everywhere we have travelled in Scandinavia, is beautiful, cultured, friendly … and mega expensive. Oslo is listed in the 'Top Ten Most Expensive Cities' in the world along with the likes of Paris and Tokyo.

Lillestrøm's home ground is Åråsen Stadion, and following their 1-1 draw at St James' Park, the home fans were full of themselves and even displayed a banner "Who the hell are Newcastle?" – which I'm pleased to say was not seen again after half-time.

MATCH REPORT: Shola Ameobi was the only recognised out-and-out striker in the squad. Damien Duff was close to completing a reported £5 million move to St James' Park from Chelsea, but that was little consolation to the players in Oslo. They had to dig deep, and thankfully they delighted the fans who made the trip.

James Milner was the first to try his luck after just seconds of the start when he fired a shot wide from the edge of the box as Lillestrom failed to clear, and Emre drove a 30-yard free-kick into the wall six minutes later after a foul by Nolberto Solano.

The breakthrough came for Newcastle following another set-piece after 28 minutes.

Solano back-heeled on the edge of the box to Charles N'Zogbia who fired a shot goalwards. Lillestrom goalkeeper Otto Fredrikson managed to block the Frenchman's shot, but Ameobi followed up to give Newcastle the lead.

The Magpies doubled their lead in the 36th minute when Scott Parker rounded off a good run with a cross which was poked home by Ameobi to put the visitors in firm control.

Half-time: Lillestrom 0 Newcastle Utd 3

Lillestrom, captained by former Liverpool player Frode Kippe, had more of the possession in the second half but barely threatened Shay Given's goal.

Emre added a third in the final minute as he unleashed a curling shot into the top corner on an encouraging afternoon for Magpies boss Glenn Roeder.

There were boos after the first leg, but cheers greeted the final whistle in Norway.

Glenn Roeder: "It's all about credibility, and playing in Europe gives you that. Playing in the Champions League or UEFA Cup gives you a big profile."

Newcastle signed Damien Duff and **Shay Given** said: "I have been trying to sell the club to him, and Scott Parker has been on the phone to him too. It's a fantastic lift for everyone. It's one of the best signings we have made in a long time – I really believe that."

August 10 2006 - FK VENTSPILS 0 NEWCASTLE UTD 1

Given, Carr, Moore, Bramble, Babayaro (Ramage), Solano (Milner), Emre (N'Zogbia), Duff, Parker, Butt, Ameobi.

Att: 6,000

FK Ventspils are from Latvia, and the city is a port on the west coast of the county that faces Sweden across the Baltic Sea. Hardly big in itself, with a population about a fifth of Newcastle, but it is a major port for oil being moved out of Russia. The city's name literally means "Castle on the Venta" referring to the Venta River which flows into the Baltic.

The city was Russian until 1994 and, after independence, the Latvian government began a city-beautification process to make the place more attractive to tourists. But I ask you, being tucked away in a corner hard to find on an atlas, is this place really going to attract the jet-set from around the continent?

MATCH REPORT: Titus Bramble had one of his regular 'blackouts' in the Ventspils Olimpiskais Stadion that he became famous for during his time on Tyneside. He could put in a star-studded performance, as he did often, but there was always a moment of madness. And he could easily have been cast as the Magpies' villain after Igors Slesarcuks skated past him with just five minutes on the clock and forced an outstanding one-handed save from Shay Given.

Ten minutes later he was left rooted to the turf as Vladimirs Kolesnicenko rose between him and team-mate Celestine Babayaro to fire a 17th-minute header inches wide of the target.

Bramble's early blunders had the boss fuming, but the home side were fit and motivated, and we had to understand the Newcastle's players had just returned from holidays, and Ventspils boasted an unbeaten domestic record with more than three-quarters of their season gone.

Despite the debut of £5million man Damien Duff and a recall for Nicky Butt, the visitors looked slow and rusty. They had their own early chances to settle their nerves, with Emre's long-range effort almost deflected into his own net by Jean-Paul Ndjoumeck-Ndeki, and Scott Parker also having a shot knocked wide.

But after riding their luck a little, Newcastle's best chance of the half was a ball played across the face of goal by Duff, but none of the lurking front men got a touch.

Half-time: Ventspils 0 Newcastle Utd 0

Kaspars Gorkss missed the target with a long-range drive and Andreys Butriks flashed a header wide from Zangareev's right-wing cross.

Bramble may have been the sinner earlier in the game, but he was the saint at the death, as he was the unlikely hero with the goal that rescued the tie. It wouldn't make the second leg a formality ... but I'm sure the players had a happier flight home.

Shay Given: "I hurt my back when I was taking a goal kick just before half-time. There was a sharp muscular pain and it was touch-and-go whether I would make the second-half. This was a tough game. We didn't get at them and penetrate them the way we should have. But they didn't create much and I'm sure it will be a different game in the second-leg."

August 24 2006 - NEWCASTLE UTD 0 FK VENTSPILS 0

Harper, Carr, Taylor, Bramble, Babayaro, Duff, Parker, Emre, N'Zogbia, Luque, Milner.

30,498

Glenn Roeder paraded his new £10million signing Obafemi Martins on the pitch before kick-off to rapturous applause from the 30,498 St James' crowd. And I'm sure there was no disrespect to Roeder, but the home fans sung several choruses of "There's only one Bobby Robson" a day after the club's former manager underwent surgery to remove a brain tumour.

MATCH REPORT: James Milner came closest to breaking the deadlock with an 81st-minute free-kick which hit the bar, and that just about sums up what sort of game it was. But the Magpies started their season in the Intertoto Cup on July 15, and by hook-or-by-crook they achieved their first aim for the season. They went into the hat for the draw for the first round of the UEFA Cup in Monaco, and this game was probably forgotten about by the time the balls were shaken.

A combination of the woodwork, poor finishing and keeper Andris Vanins kept Ventspils in the game for the full 90 minutes. Although Roman Grigorchuk's men could not muster a single credible effort on goal, the game was always in the balance because Newcastle could not finish them off.

Martins settled into his seat to watch his new club book him a season of European football, and I'm sure Roeder was delighted that the ink was dry on the contract before the striker could change his mind.

Newcastle were utterly dominant before the break, and Steve Harper, starting his first game in more than a year, could have brought a deck chair, so uncomplicated was his first 45 minutes.

Emre fired in a long-range effort which Vanins fumbled around the post, and suddenly the pressure started to tell.

N'Zogbia and Milner both had shots saved in quick succession and Duff should have opened the scoring but drilled his effort high over the bar.

Half-time: Newcastle Utd 0 Ventspils 0

There were two ways of looking at it - the preservation of their clean sheet would be enough to see the Magpies through – but the visitors were well aware that a single goal was all they needed to stay in the tie. But they seemed remarkably reluctant to get it too early in case they poked a wasp's nest with a big stick.

Bramble almost broke the deadlock on 54 minutes when he curled a shot just over from 20 yards, and Duff provided an inviting cross two minutes later but was not up for it.

Emre tested Vanins once again on 59 minutes with a well-struck 30-yard effort, but the keeper was equal to the task and, as the half wore on, the Latvians started to adopt a more adventurous approach in the search for a goal.

Stephen Carr let fly from 30 yards and Luque, who had seen little of the ball where it mattered, had a chance when Milner picked him out unmarked at the far post, but he could not keep his header down.

Vanins tipped an N'Zogbia drive over 16 minutes from time as the Magpies queued up to take pot-shots at his goal, but he was helpless as Milner's free-kick bounced down off the crossbar and ran safe seven minutes later.

UEFA CUP 2006/07

September 14 2006 - LEVADIA TALINN 0 NEWCASTLE UTD 1

Given, Carr, Bramble (Milner), Moore, Ramage, Duff, Parker, Emre, N'Zogbia (Butt 73), Sibierski (Luque 80),Martins.

Att: 7,917

From Latvia to Estonia – and another club that makes you wonder what European football is all about these days. Since Europe has been dissected and cut up into minor nations, clubs like Levadia Talinn are allowed to parade on the European stage, playing in minor leagues but getting the nod from UEFA to compete against the best the continent has to offer. This club, for example, has only been formed since 1999, yet in the seven years leading up to the Newcastle Utd fixture they had already played in the Champions League and met such formidable clubs as Steaua Bucharest, Dinamo Tbilisi and FC Zurich. Yet their ground, the Kadriorg Stadium, only holds 4,700! The 8,300-

capacity Le Coq Arena, Estonia's national stadium and the home of city rivals FC Flora, was selected as the venue for the game.

The place is the most northern point of Estonia, over the water from Finland's capital Helsinki, and what stands out most in the flat landscape is the Estonia equivalent of the 'Twin Towers' that dominate the skyline. Like Latvia, it is ex-Russian, and although the people are trying to move away from their history, almost everything is still what you would expect the Soviet Union to be like. But, take nothing away from the people, they are very very friendly.

MATCH REPORT: The 200 or so travelling fans watched Antoine Sibierski score on his debut as Newcastle edged towards the group stage of the UEFA Cup.

The Frenchman powered home a 10th-minute header from Damien Duff's free-kick to give the Magpies the lead.

Levadia threatened when they went close through Marek Lemsalu and Konstantin Vassiljev minutes after Siberiski's goal.

Bramble, the villain in the previous Saturday's 2-1 home defeat by Fulham, proved the central character once again as the tide turned briefly. Striker Nikita Andreev caught the big defender late as they chased a ball into touch, and Roeder had little option but to replace him. James Milner lined up on the right, Peter Ramage moved from left-back into the middle and £5million winger Duff was asked to drop in at full-back.

Newcastle took time to readjust and began to look vulnerable.

Half-time: Levadia 0 Newcastle Utd 1

Martins went down under a 49th-minute Lemsalu challenge in the area, but referee Ingvarsson waved his appeals away.

Levadia might have been level within three minutes when, after Milner had given the ball away and Craig Moore had slipped, striker Vladimir Voskoboinikov cut in from the left and fired in a well-struck shot which Shay Given had to turn away.

Emre failed to clear the rebound and, in the process, presented possession to Konstantin Vassiljev, but he blasted his effort high over.

There was more trouble for the visitors on 59 minutes after Duff crudely blocked Andreev 20 yards out, but Nahk drilled his free-kick straight into the defensive wall.

Martins sliced wide after making space for himself, and Emre curled a long-range free-kick straight into Kotenko's arms, and there was a distinct lack of cutting edge. It got no better and Martins shot wide in injury-time.

Antoine Sibierski: "I know I was not the big name signing the fans expected on deadline day. While this was not technically my best game, I am pleased with the goal and the win. To get a goal in my first game is great. I knew a few days ago I would be playing, but I kept it to myself, as I wanted to prepare properly."

September 28 2006 - NEWCASTLE UTD 2 LEVADIA TALLIN 1

Harper, Carr, Bramble, Taylor, Ramage, Milner, Butt, Emre (Parker), N'Zogbia (Duff), Martins (Luque), Sibierski.

Att: 27,012

MATCH REPORT: Crowds at St James' Park were dipping alarmingly, and although Levadia Tallinn were a club many of us hadn't even heard of, I'm sure Newcastle Utd expected a bigger crowd than 27,000.

Performances had been excessively patchy, and this was no better.

Another lethargic opening 45 minutes by the Magpies had given the Estonians hope of clawing their way back into the tie.

Despite the best efforts of Emre, James Milner and Charles N'Zogbia, the home side created only two real chances during the opening 45 minutes, and both came from set-pieces.

Defender Steven Taylor saw his goal-bound shot blocked on 12 minutes, and then Emre forced keeper Artur Kotenko to make his only save of the half with a powerfully-struck free kick from a tight angle on 39 minutes.

Half-time: Newcastle Utd 0 Levadia Tallinn 0

Obafemi Martins headed home a 47th-minute Emre corner to claim his first goal at St James' Park, and then added a second three minutes later with a superb strike to see off the Estonian minnows.

First the 21-year-old Nigerian rose to glance a neat header past the helpless Kotenko from Emre's near-post corner on 47 minutes, and there was better to come three minutes later when, after Sibierski had headed the ball back, he smashed a left-foot drive past the keeper and in off the underside of the bar. He celebrated with his customary series of somersaults.

There were a few nervous moments when substitute Indrek Zelinski pulled a goal back with the help of an error from Steve Harper in the 65th minute, but Glenn Roeder's men saw the game out.

Nicky Butt might have wrapped up the victory on 67 minutes after cashing in on a mix-up between defender Tihhon Sisov and Kotenko, and Sibierski drilled a long-range effort wide with 18 minutes remaining. But Terry McDermott hugged Roeder on the final whistle for a job well done.

October 19 2006 - NEWCASTLE UTD 1 FENERBAHCE 0

Harper, Carr, Taylor, Ramage, Duff, Milner, Parker, Emre (Butt), N'Zogbia (Solano), Sibierski, Martins (Ameobi).

What a shame Graeme Souness missed out on this fixture. I'm sure he would have had the visiting Fenerbache supporters hanging off the Leazes End rafters giving abuse. He has a past history with this club, and Turks have long memories. As I wrote in an earlier chapter, Souness was manager of Galatasaray and enraged Istanbul rivals Fenerbahçe by planting a flag in the pitch during a Turkish Cup final. Could you imagine Sir Bobby doing that at the Bernabéu stadium (Real Madrid) when he was manager of Barcelona?

MATCH REPORT: Glenn Roeder targeted victories in both of United's home games, and hoped for some sort of result on the difficult trip to Palermo, knowing that another three would almost certainly see them through to the knockout stage.

Steve Harper passed a late fitness test with 18-year-old Dutchman Tim Krul waiting in the wings.

He took a series of calculated risks, however, asking winger Damien Duff to play at left-back, while Antoine Sibierski started in attack alongside Martins.

It became apparent very early on that Harper's mobility was restricted with Peter Ramage having to take his goalkicks, although he had only one real save to make from Mehmet Yozgatli's twice-deflected long-range shot in the opening 45 minutes.

In truth, opposite number Rustu was little more involved, collecting James Milner's 40th-minute volley with few problems.

Perhaps the best chance of the first half arrived in injury time when defender Steven Taylor met Emre's corner with a thunderous header at the near post but narrowly missed the target.

Half-time: Newcastle Utd 0 Fenerbahce 0

While the home side prospered down the wings, Fenerbahce were tidy in the middle of the field where Stephen Appiah and Tuncay Sanli ensured Brazilian Alex saw plenty of the ball.

But although the Turks played some attractive football, they rarely stretched the home defence and Harper, no doubt to his delight and that of his manager, remained largely untested.

Stephen Carr had to be on his toes on 50 minutes after Sanli, whose Champion's League hat-trick handed his side a famous victory over Manchester United two years ago, linked with Kezman.

Former Galatasaray midfielder Emre had picked up a knock before the break and was clearly struggling. His evening ended prematurely on 54 minutes as Nicky Butt was sent on in his place with the Turks growing in confidence.

Martins climbed high at the near post to meet N'Zogbia's best cross of the game and direct a downward header towards goal, where Rustu just managed to palm it away with an excellent save.

He was in action again five minutes later when, after he had linked well with Milner and Scott Parker, Martins fired in another effort.

The deadlock was finally broken with 11 minutes remaining when, after Taylor's effort had been blocked, Sibierski stabbed the loose ball past Rustu to claim a vital victory.

The visitors hammered away at the home defence as time ran down but, this time, there was to be no surrender.

November 2 2006 - PALERMO 0 NEWCASTLE UTD 1

Krul, Ramage, Moore, Bramble, Taylor, Solano (Carroll), Emre, N'Zogbia (Sibierski), Milner, Butt, Luque (Pattison).

Att:16,904

Palermo – the city - is noted for its rich history, culture and architecture. But Palermo – the football club (and its supporters) – had a reputation that we heard about as soon as the fixture was arranged. The city is on the northern coast of Sicily, just off the 'boot' of the Italian outline, and you won't find a more picturesque place in the Mediterranean Sea.

Some Italian clubs do have a reputation for trouble, as covered elsewhere in this book. But Palermo (as an Italian club playing in the Italian league) is a one-off because they not only have a problem with foreign invaders in football shirts from across Europe, but they also don't particularly like Italians either!

It's the Anglo-Scottish thing. I'm sure Juventus, Roma, Milan and Internazionale regard Palermo as cling-ons on the starboard bow, but Palermo have their Sicilian roots to defend.

We were told there would be trouble and, sure enough, the Mafia boys were after us. There was intimidation from the moment we arrived on the island to the moment we left.

West Ham had played Palermo before us and there had been reports of serious fighting and stabbings. That discouraged a lot of people from going to this game, plus the cost and logistics of getting there. I think there were only about 180 of us there in total, and it was an absolutely frightening place. There was tension everywhere we went all day. One of our mates (Peter) had got there the day before the game, and he and a couple of others went out for some drinks on the night. They were attacked and put behind the drinks bar for their own protection by the owner, who then called the police. The Ultras waited outside, but rather than give them a police escort back to the hotel, the cops flagged down a taxi. There were six of them and the police made the driver take five inside the car and put Peter in the boot!

The ground itself was like something out of the '80s with us walking through a metal caged tunnel to the away end. The obligatory 'Italian welcome' happened inside the ground, with them throwing coins, bottles and even an umbrella. But we were ok because of the segregation inside.

MATCH REPORT: Newcastle had only won one league game in nine and the pressure was on Roeder. Freddy Shepherd was reported to be looking at replacing him and one newspaper claimed Sven Goran Eriksson had been approached.

Newcastle had the help of a very special scout – French World Cup winner Patrick Viera. **Antoine Sibierski:** "I used to play with Patrick years ago and now he plays for Inter. He is a very good friend of my family. He has spoken to me about Palermo, and says they are a very well organised side. But from what he has told me, I am sure we can go there and get a result."

Steve Harper failed a medical and debutant goalkeeper Tim Krul kept Glenn Roeder's side in the game with several match-winning saves.

Palermo simply could not find a way past the Dutch giant and the handful of Newcastle fans were able to celebrate with calls of "we are top of the league" at the final whistle.

Luque earned a rare start in attack with Glenn Roeder having little option but to thrust the Spanish striker into the fray due to injuries and the unavailability of Giuseppe Rossi.

Luque was told to prove he deserved a regular place in his side - however it was James Milner (as always) who looked the more motivated. Shifting from the left-wing into a support role up front, the 20-year-old created the biggest threat for the Magpies.

Krul, the second youngest player to ever play in Europe for Newcastle, looked a little nervous and his kicking was particularly wayward with the home side's brightest player Franco Brienza almost capitalising on a poor clearance, only to fire over from 25 yards.

With Barzagli and Hernan Dellafiore both stood like statues in the middle, Luque stole in between the pair to head in Milner's left-wing cross and give Newcastle a lead they perhaps merited on the balance of play.

The goal was only the second Palermo had conceded at the Renzo Barbera in seven European games, and the other scorer back then was Georgian midfielder Temuri Ketsbaia who netted for Anorthosis Famagusta.

Half-time: Palermo 0 Newcastle Utd 1

Palermo camped in the Newcastle half for the second half.

It was backs-to-the-wall stuff for Roeder's men, but just as the Newcastle manager had predicted, it was time for heroes.

Palermo substitutes Giuseppe Biava and David Di Michele both failed to beat Krul as Brienza's left-wing free-kick seemed certain to produce the equaliser.

First, Krul dived low to tip Biava's stooping header to his left and then he got back onto his feet to block Di Michele's follow-up.

The Dutch shot-stopper then produced another top-drawer save to deny Andrea Carracciolo as Palermo increased the pressure.

But several wayward passes convinced the home fans it was not going to be their night and Newcastle were comfortably able to play out time.

Tim Krul: "It was an unbelievable debut to keep a clean sheet. My voice has gone, I was shouting so much. I was a little bit nervous but after a couple of minutes I knew I could do it."

Glenn Roeder: "Tim didn't surprise me. He is the best goalkeeper in his age group in Holland, but I thought his debut would be 18 months or two years away."

Steve Harper: "We are all 110% behind the manager. The reports are like water under the bridge to the players."

November 23 2006 - NEWCASTLE UTD 2 CELTA VIGO 1

Given, Solano, Bramble, Taylor, Ramage, Milner, Butt (Parker), Emre (Martins), N'Zogbia, Luque, Sibierski.

Att: 25,079

MATCH REPORT: Perhaps not surprisingly for a team which had a right-winger playing at right-back (Nobby Solano), a central defender at left-back (Peter Ramage) and no recognised striker on the pitch, the Magpies were disjointed and struggled for any kind of coherence.

Roeder had warned of Celta's counter-attacking style, and the visitors took the lead with just nine minutes gone. Steven Taylor headed a seemingly harmless Angel free-kick out of goalkeeper Shay Given's hands, and when the ball was recycled Canobbio skipped past Emre's weak challenge and curled a superb left-foot shot past the goalkeeper.

It was not until former Manchester United midfielder Butt began to stamp his authority on the game that the Magpies forced their way into it.

There were 36 minutes on the clock when James Milner picked up possession wide on the right and flighted a cross towards Sibierski at the far post, and he jumped unopposed to head firmly past Esteban.

Titus Bramble might have put the home side in front on the stroke of half-time, but he could not keep his header down from an Emre free-kick.

Half-time: Newcastle Utd 1 Celta Vigo 1

Newcastle returned knowing a draw would see them through.

But as time ran down, it was the home side who looked the more likely to snatch victory, substitute Obafemi Martins giving Charles N'Zogbia a run at goal and then seeing his own shot blocked 14 minutes from time.

Local hero Steven Taylor made sure his first Newcastle goal was a crucial one as he fired the Magpies into the knockout stages of the UEFA Cup. Taylor provided the decisive touch, thumping a header past the stranded Esteban from Luque's 86th-minute corner before sprinting the length of the St James' pitch in celebration.

The victory, coupled with Fenerbahce's 3-0 win over Palermo, meant that any result against Eintracht Frankfurt could only improve their finishing position in Group H with a maximum nine points already banked.

It also extended their unbeaten run in cup ties this particular season to 11 games.

November 30 2006 - EINTRACHT FRANKFURT 0
NEWCASTLE UTD 0

Given, Ramage, Bramble, Taylor, Solano, Emre, Milner, Butt, N'Zogbia, Sibierski, Luque (Martins).

Att: 47,000

You pay your money and take your chance at some of the countries we have visited. And although Frankfurt has an airport right in the heart of the city – we went for the cheaper option (Ryanair) - and I think they dropped us off somewhere between Siberia and Outer Mongolia, it was so far away!

Frankfurt reminds me of Rotterdam, so modern and full of excitement. You take people as you find them and the people in this city were fabulous to us. We mixed with the supporters and there was never a hint of trouble for the two days and nights we were there.

Geordies took over some of the pubs, but the locals didn't mind, and the police (although always on hand) kept a low profile.

The only down side was our cheap hotel. The Turk owner seemed terrified of us and put us in the cellar, away from the rest of the guests. When I say 'cellar', I genuinely mean it, along with the beer crates!

MATCH REPORT: Despite having already secured their place in the knockout stage, Newcastle headed for Germany determined to return in an unassailable position at the top of the group.

The Magpies had defended stoutly for the opening quarter of the game, but they eventually cracked with 25 minutes gone after Swiss international

Benjamin Huggel carved them open with a precise pass to Markus Weissenberger.

He looked up before delivering the perfect cross from the right for the unmarked Streit to head for goal, only for new skipper, Shay Given, to block with his legs before Titus Bramble and James Milner hustled the ball away.

Newcastle were hanging on and Bramble, who had endured several uncomfortable moments, came to the rescue with a vital 38th-minute challenge on Amanatidis as he prepared to shoot from point-blank range.

The visitors posed little threat as an attacking force, although Emre put a left-foot effort just wide on the stroke of half-time.

Half-time: Eintracht Frankfurt 0 Newcastle Utd 0

Friedhelm Funkel's side should have scored, and Amanatidis had some explaining to do. Just how he failed to head Takahara's 50th-minute cross past the stranded Given was a mystery, and Streit was unable to convert the loose ball as the Magpies escaped again.

It was to become something of a theme with Taylor having to block a Takahara effort before Streit sliced horribly wide from close range with the black and white shirts parting alarmingly once again.

Obafemi Martins, who had earlier replaced Albert Luque, worked hard to retrieve a long ball and cross from the right. Sibierski did well to get in a header, but although he beat keeper Markus Proll, defender Sotirios Kyrgiakos hacked it off the line.

Takahara glanced a header just wide 11 minutes from time, but Emre might have won it for the Magpies seconds later when he went one on one with Proll, but lost out.

Newcastlel headed into the last 32 of the UEFA Cup as Group H winners.

Steven Taylor: "I thought it was my best game for the club. The defence has done well in Europe and I think we have proved a point to many people. I have stud marks right down my leg, it was tough. We get criticised by people, some of whom should know better, but we've got to get on with it and take it on the chin."

Frankfurt coach **Freidhelm Funkel:** "If we had taken all of our chances we would have won 5-0. The fans booed us off and I don't blame them because it is our national responsibility to get through."

ZULTE WAREGEM

February 15 2007 - ZULTE-WAREGEM 1 NEWCASTLE UTD 3

Harper, Solano, Taylor, Bramble, Babayaro, Milner, Butt, Dyer, Duff, Martins (Luque), Sibierski.

Att: 8,015

We took the Eurostar train to Gent, then the train to Waregem which is in West Flanders. It's a small town full of students, and the Belgian fans very much kept out of the way all day. Bars were OK during the day but the nightlife after the game was poor. The transport service wasn't much good either – they took the trams off early and we had to walk miles back into town.

Another game we didn't get a ticket for because of the small allocation - which they decided to reduce even further before the game (for reasons no-one found out). We got tickets but many Toon fans didn't, and a couple of hundred watched the match in a bar in Ghent.

MATCH REPORT: Antoine Sibierski put his friendship with Frederic Dindeleux to the test as Newcastle went to the Jules Otten Stadium trying to shatter Zulte Waregem's UEFA Cup dreams.

The former Lille team-mates had known each other since the age of eight, and Dindeleux was Sibierski's best man at his wedding.

Zulte coach Francky Dury, a detective by trade, had admitted before the game that it would be a major shock if his side's first European adventure continued beyond their clash with Newcastle, saying: "If we had their reserves, we would be a top team in Belgium."

Opposite number Glenn Roeder nevertheless insisted that they would not take their unfashionable opponents lightly.

The Belgian Cup holders were neat and tidy in possession and nothing if not hard working, but they surrendered a series of chances to their opponents inside the opening 45 minutes which should have proved fatal.

That they survived to the break without conceding was simply a matter of poor finishing as the Magpies, without ever hitting their best form, failed to make the most of their opportunities.

Leading scorer Martins was the main culprit, firing hopelessly wide on 25 minutes after being played in by Kieron Dyer and then saw Merlier save his effort from point-blank range on the stroke of half-time.

James Milner and Duff had earlier missed the target after working themselves into promising shooting positions.

Zulte, who included four part-timers in their starting line-up, created little at the other end, although they had appeals for a 29th-minute penalty turned down by Genov after Tony Sergeant's effort struck Steven Taylor's hand.

Half-time: Zulte Waregem 0 Newcastle Utd 0

The deadlock was finally broken within 90 seconds of the re-start, although the Magpies needed a helping hand from their opponents to beat Merlier. Dyer drove the ball across goal, and Dindeleux deflected the ball into his own net.

Martins hit the outside of the post from a narrow angle and then blasted wide from distance as the Magpies stepped up a gear, and he finally got his reward on 59 minutes.

Duff's surging run into the box came to an end when he went down under Merlier's challenge, and the referee pointed to the spot.

Martins, who had handed spot-kick duties over to Solano after missing at Everton in December, took charge and sent the keeper the wrong way with his left foot for his 13th goal of the season.

But the game changed on 68 minutes when the home side grabbed a lifeline.

Midfielder D'Haene climbed to meet Loris Reina's free-kick and glance a header past Harper to give his side hope, and then forced Shay Given's deputy to tip a long-range pile-driver over the bar three minutes later.

But Sibierski restored order 14 minutes from time with a brilliant individual goal, mesmerising Dindeleux and Stefan Leleu before rounding Merlier to pass the ball into the empty net.

Damien Duff: "It was certainly a penalty, he took me down. No disrespect but they are a poor team and we should have finished off the tie. I've had a terrible season with injuries, I just want to get back to my peak."

February 22 2007 - NEWCASTLE UTD 1 ZULTE-WAREGEM 0

Harper, Taylor, Bramble, Babayaro (Huntington), Milner, Solano, Butt (Pattison), Dyer, Duff, Luque (Carroll), Martins.

Att: 30,083

MATCH REPORT: A crowd of 30,083 (including England boss Steve McClaren, who was checking out Kieron Dyer) expected more from the home side than they got. Although Glenn Roeder's men dominated for long periods, they never really looked like taking apart a team which included several semi-professionals.

While Newcastle started at a lively pace to put the Belgians under intense pressure, Steve Harper had only two saves to make all game.

Stijn Meert cleared Steven Taylor's thumping header off the line, and James Milner's blistering sixth-minute drive crept over the crossbar.

Bramble timed his 30th-minute tackle to perfection to dispossess striker Sebastien Siani after Meert had played him in, and Taylor had to be just as alert six minutes before the break after Stijn Minne picked out Wouter Vandendriessche's run into the box.

Half-time: Newcastle Utd 0 Zulte Waregem 0

Roeder's response was to switch Albert Luque to the left wing with Milner moving to the right, and Dyer joined Oba Martins in attack.

Celestine Babayaro, who was due to head to London for his brother Kennedy's funeral, did not re-appear after the break and was replaced by Paul Huntington.

Vandendriessche forced Harper into his first save of the game on 53 minutes with a curling shot from distance, and the keeper was happy to see Ludwin van Nieuwhuyze's skidding drive fly past his far post three minutes later.

Newcastle were labouring, and Roeder withdrew Butt and Luque for youngsters Matty Pattison and Andy Carroll in the search for fresh impetus.

But it was Duff who finally fashioned the opening goal on 68 minutes when he slid a pass into Martins' run, and the striker calmly lifted a shot over the advancing keeper.

March 8 2007 - NEWCASTLE UTD 4 AZ ALKMAAR 2

Given, Bramble, Taylor, Carr, Solano, Dyer, Parker, Butt, Duff (Emre), Sibierski (Milner), Martins.

Att: 28,452

Before the game Newcastle were awarded their first trophy in 37 years in the most bizarre presentation St James' Park had ever seen. Chairman Freddy Shepherd received a phone call from UEFA saying the club had won the Intertoto Cup and, like most supporters, he thought it was a hoax because he didn't believe such a trophy existed.

Freddy Shepherd: "I thought they were having me on and I put the phone down."

Although it was confirmed to be true, the club still played it down and decided a Newcastle season ticket holder should accept the award on the pitch, probably just in case it was a Jeremy Beadle moment.

Glenn Roeder: "We will be very happy to receive it. It would be disrespectful to consider it a lesser tournament, as some managers do."

Apparently Newcastle won the 'cup' (it was actually a rectangular plaque) as they were the last surviving Intertoto entrants.

The Toon supporter, and Newcastle skipper Scott Parker, collected the award before the game.

MATCH REPORT: Nine-and-a-half years prior to this game, AZ coach Louis van Gaal had travelled to St James' Park with his Barcelona all-stars and had seen them trail 3-0 in the Champion's League before fighting back to 3-2.

This time, he arrived confident of returning with a positive result, but admitting his side could not play a containing game.

Having scored three times in Istanbul to edge Fenerbahce out of the competition on away goals on a 5-5 aggregate, there was little doubt that they could cause problems going forward.

Here, however, the problems came at the other end as van Gaal again saw his defence breached three times inside 23 minutes.

AZ passed the ball superbly and their movement going forward repeatedly had the Magpies at full stretch, but they simply had no answer to Newcastle's attacking flair.

Defender Steinsson got the home side off to the perfect start when he turned Dyer's seventh-minute cross into his own net under pressure from Martins, after Damien Duff's outrageous backheel had caught AZ cold.

It was 2-0 with 20 minutes gone when Antoine Sibierski flicked Nicky Butt's pass into Dyer's path and he calmly lifted the ball over the advancing Waterman.

The home fans were still celebrating when Sibierski gave Martins the chance to run at defender Kew Jaliens, and he danced through the red shirts before blasting a right-footed shot into the bottom corner.

Van Gaal thought his shell-shocked side had grabbed a 31st-minute lifeline when former Rangers striker Arveladze headed home a Julian Jenner cross off the underside of the bar.

Martins was not done, however, and he restored the three-goal advantage within six minutes, swivelling to despatch Nolberto Solano's cross with a superbly-placed shot.

Half-time: Newcastle Utd 4 AZ Alkmaar 1

AZ picked up the pace swiftly after the restart and threatened in the 54th minute and it took a superb challenge by Titus Bramble to deny Koevermans.

Roeder replaced the tiring Sibierski with James Milner with 25 minutes remaining - before the visitors who gave themselves fresh hope in controversial circumstances with 17 minutes remaining.

Dembele drove a cross into Steven Taylor's arm and referee Busacca immediately pointed to the spot.

Given got down well to save the Belgian's spot-kick and Bramble prevented the taker converting the rebound - but the ball ricocheted to Koevermans, who gratefully blasted home.

Martins could have wrapped up a good night for the Magpies with eight minutes remaining when he burst in on goal, but shot straight at Waterman, before Scott Parker headed over from Emre's 85th-minute cross.

March 15 2007 - AZ ALKMAAR 2 NEWCASTLE UTD 0

Given, Solano, Bramble, Taylor, Huntington (N'Zogbia), Dyer, Butt, Parker, Duff (Emre),Sibierski, Martins.

Att: 16,401

Alkmaar is easy enough to get to, being in north Holland close to Bergen. Typically Dutch, with windmills, canals, and the place is most famous for its cheese market at the Waagplein. That didn't exactly fill us with excitement, but Alkmaar does have a great a nightlife scene which takes place in the pubs that are in front of the cheesemarket, as well as a red light district.

It wasn't as quiet as we imagined, however, and some fighting and running battles did take place in the town square before the game, with AZ supporters out to give us a rough time. Some arrests did occur, but (like at Breda) we saw it through the window of a bar. Those who wanted to fight – did – those who didn't want to fight – got the beers in.

MATCH REPORT: The Magpies arrived at the DSB Stadium knowing that a clean sheet would see them through, but that scenario went out of the window within 14 minutes when Shota Arveladze fired home from close range. Newcastle were still in the driving seat at 4-3 on aggregate, but Roeder once again fielded a makeshift defence - teenager Huntington came in at left-back, midfielder Nobby Solano played on the right, and Steven Taylor (who had passed a late fitness test on a calf injury) looked very uncomfortable in the centre.

Oba Martins and Antoine Sibierski were left to feed off scraps, because the midfield didn't get the ball forward often enough, with Alkmaar 'keeper Boy Waterman a spectator for much of the first half.

He had only one real scare when Parker whipped a right-foot shot inches over his bar on 15 minutes, but Sibierski's looping 41st-minute header was Newcastle's first effort on target.

Half-time: AZ Alkmaar 1 Newcastle Utd 0

Within two minutes of the restart the inexperienced Huntington was caught in no man's land by Demy de Zeeuw's intelligent pass inside him. Jenner raced away to cut the ball back into the middle and, although Solano got in a desperate block, Moussa Dembele latched on to the rebound only to fire high over.

The Magpies dropped ever deeper as they tried to protect Given's goal, but that simply invited pressure with Martins and Sibierski once again marooned.

Jenner forced Huntington to concede a corner and Danny Koevermans rose at the near post to head Martens' cross home 11 minutes after the restart.

Seconds later Koevermans just missed the target with an acrobatic overhead effort.

Roeder replaced the labouring Duff with Emre and his side might have regained their advantage when Parker latched on to Solano's pass, but fired straight at Waterman.

But with men committed to the search for a precious goal, the Magpies were looking increasingly vulnerable at the back and Given had to save from Jenner with 18 minutes remaining.

Newcastle's UEFA Cup dreams were torn to shreds as Scott Parker saw a late 'winner' disallowed. The former Chelsea midfielder briefly thought he had put the visitors 5-4 ahead on aggregate with three minutes remaining, only for French referee Bertrand Layec to blow for a foul in the build-up.

Emre, Sibieski, Duff and Martins refused to be interviewed after the game.

Kieron Dyer: "There's no excuses, we let ourselves down and everyone associated with the club. We twice had a three-goal lead in this tie and we have blown it again. It's like groundhog day – it always happens to us. Another season with nothing to play for. We have to get tougher mentally or we are going to get punished the way we always seem to do."

Nobby Solano: "We had to come here and concentrate and we didn't do that. The only way we can recover is by sticking together."

Nicky Butt: "We came here believing we would score and we didn't do that. In the end we didn't look like scoring at all and didn't play well. After the goal went in and was disallowed the referee turned to Kieron Dyer and said it was his foul, then he turned to me and said it was my foul. I don't know what happened."

Seville went on to win the UEFA Cup, beating Espanyol on penalties at Hampden Park, Glasgow.

Antoine Sibierski

APPEARANCES

Newcastle United have played 120 games in Europe and featured 142 players.

Pop Robson

INTER CITIES FAIRS CUP 1968/69

Allen 2, Arentoft 4, Bennett 0 (1), Burton 11, Clark 12, Craggs 3, Craig 9, Davies 12, Dyson 3 (1), Elliott 3, Foggon 6 (2), Gibb 12, Guthrie 0 (1), Horsefield 1, Iley 0 (1), McFaul 12, McNamee 3 (1), Moncur 10, B, Robson 12, Scott 12, Sinclair 4 (2), Winstanley 1

INTER CITIES FAIRS CUP 1969/70

Arentoft 4 (1), Burton 5 (1), Clark 7, Craggs 2, Craig 6, Davies 8, Dyson 6, Elliott 0 (1), Foggon 4 (1), Gibb 8, Guthrie 3 (2), McFaul 8, McNamee 3, Moncur 8, Robson 8, Scott 2 (1), Smith 4, Young 1 (1)

INTER CITIES FAIRS CUP 1970/71

Arentoft 2, Burton 2, Clark 4, Craig 4, Davies 4, Dyson 4, Ford 2, Gibb 4, Hindson 0 (1), McFaul 4, McNamee 1, Mitchell 0 (1), Moncur 4, Robson 4, Smith 1, Young 4

UEFA CUP 1977/78

Barrowclough 4, Bird 1 (1), Blackhall 1, Burns 4, Callachan 2, Cannell 3, D Craig 2, T Craig 4, Gowling 3, Hardwick 2, Hudson (0) 1, Kelly 1, Kennedy 2, MacLean 1, Mahoney 2, McCaffrey 3, Nattrass 4, Nulty 2

UEFA CUP 1994/95

Srnicek 4, Hottiger 4, Beresford 4, Venison 1, Peacock 4, Albert 4, Lee 3, Beardsley 4, Cole 3, Fox 4, Sellars 4, Howey 3, Clark 1 (2), Watson 1 (2), Jeffrey 0 (2)

UEFA CUP 1996/97

Srnicek 5, Peacock 8, Watson 4 (1), Howey 1, Asprilla 6, Clark 2 (3), Lee 8, Shearer 4, Ferdinand 4, Ginola 6 (1), Beardsley 6, Beresford 3 (1), Batty 7, Barton 4 (1), Albert 7 (1), Gillespie 6 (2), Elliott 4 (1), Hislop 2, Kitson 0 (1)

EUROPEAN CHAMPIONS LEAGUE 1997/98

Given 6, Beresford 7, Batty 7, Lee 6, Asprilla 5, Pearce 3 (1), Ketsbaia 3 (5), Tomasson 6 (1), Watson 8, Pistone 4, Albert 7 (1), Barton 5, Barnes 5, Gillespie 5 (2), Peacock 4 (1), Howey 1 (2), Rush 1, Hamilton 2, Hislop 2, Hughes 0 (2)

EUROPEAN CUP WINNERS CUP 1998/99

Given 2, Pearce 2, Charvet 2, Glass 2, Watson 1, Dabizas 2, Lee 1, Barnes 1, Speed 2, Shearer 2, Ketsbaia 2, Andersson 1, Batty 1, Solano 1 (1), Griffin 1, Albert 0 (1)

UEFA CUP 1999/2000

Harper 6, Domi 4, Dabizas 6, Goma 2, Barton 5, Speed 6, Lee 6, Dyer 3, Solano 6, Shearer 6, Ferguson 2 (1), Marcelino 2, Maric 3, Hughes 2 (1), Charvet 2, Pistone 2, Ketsbaia 2 (1), Dumas 1, Hamilton 0 (1), McClen 0 (3), Robinson 0 (4), Glass 0 (3), Serrant 0 (1)

INTER-TOTO CUP 2001/02

Given 6, Barton 6, Elliott 6, Solano 6, Bassedas 3, Speed 6, Quinn 6, Bellamy 6, Hughes 6, Ameobi 6, Dabizas 6, Lee 3, Lua Lua 0 (4), McClen 0 (2), S Caldwell 0 (2), Bernard 0 (2), Green 0 (1), Acuna 0 (1)

EUROPEAN CHAMPIONS LEAGUE 2002/03

Given 11, Hughes 12 (1), Dabizas 6 (2), Bramble 9, Bernard 8 (2), Solano 11 (2), Dyer 10 (2), Jenas 8, Viana 4 (5), Shearer 12 , Lua Lua 6 (4), Speed 12, O'Brien 11 (1), Griffin 10, Bellamy 5, Robert 10 (2), Harper 3, Ameobi 5 (6), S Caldwell 1 (1), Kerr 1 (1), Quinn 0 (1), Elliott 0 (1), Chopra 0 (2), Cort 0 (1)

EUROPEAN CHAMPIONS LEAGUE/ UEFA CUP 2003/04

Given 13, Griffin 2, Solano 4 (1), O'Brien 12 (1), Dyer 6 (1), Shearer 12, Bellamy 7 (1), Speed 13, Woodgate 7, Robert 12 (1), Bernard 13, Hughes 11, Viana 5 (4), Ameobi 7 (5), Bramble 11, Jenas 10 (1), Harper 1, Ambrose 6 (4), Bridges 1 (2), S Caldwell 0 (1), Lua Lua 0 (1), Brittain 0 (1), Taylor 0 (1), Bowyer (0) 1

UEFA CUP 2004/05

Given 12, Carr 9, Elliott 5, O'Brien 9 (2), Hughes 9 (1), Dyer 6 (1), Bowyer 8 (1), Jenas 4 (1), Robert 8 (2), Ameobi 6 (1), Kluivert 5 (1), Bernard 5 (1), Jenas 5 (1), Bellamy 4, Shearer 9, Milner 3 (8), Bramble 6 (1), Butt 4, Ambrose 2 (2), Taylor 4 (3), Faye 5, Babayaro 2, N'Zogbia 1 (2), Harper 0 (2), Guy 0 (1), Ramage (0) 1

INTERTOTO CUP 2005/06

Harper 1, Babayaro 3, Elliott 2, Boumsong 4, Taylor 4, Butt 2, Faye 4, Milner 1, N'Zogbia 3 (1), Shearer 4, Chopra 1 (2), Given 3, Carr 3, Bowyer 3, Jenas 1, Milner 3, Emre 1, Parker 1, Brittain 0 (2), Ameobi 0 (1)

INTERTOTO CUP/ UEFA CUP - 2006/07

Given 8, Carr 8, Taylor 12, Bramble 13, Babayaro 6, Solano 10 (1), Parker 8 (2), Emre 10 (2), N'Zogbia 9 (2), Milner 10 (3), Luque 6 (3), Ameobi 2 (2), Moore 3 (1), Duff 8 (1), Butt 9 (3), Harper 5, Ramage 6 (1), Sibierski 8 (1), Martins 7 (2), Krul 1, Dyer 4, Huntington 1 (1), O'Brien 0 (1), Pattison 0 (3), Carroll 0 (2)

MOST APPEARANCES – TOP 20

Shay Given

1 Shay Given 61

2 Alan Shearer 49

3 Aaron Hughes 44 (40 – substitute 4)

4 Nobby Solano 43 (38 – 5)

5 Shola Ameobi 41 (26 – 15)

6 Titus Bramble 40 (39 – 1)

7 Gary Speed 39

8 Andy O'Brien 36 (32 – 4)

9 Laurent Robert 35 (30 – 5)

10 Kieron Dyer 33 (29 – 4)

11 Olivier Bernard 31 (26 – 5)

12 Robert Lee 27

13 Jermaine Jenas 25 (23 – 2)

14 James Milner 25 (14 – 11)

15= Wyn Davies 25

15= Tommy Gibb 25

15= Iam McFaul 25

18 Frank Clark 23

19 Craig Bellamy 23 (22 – 1)

20 Steven Taylor 23 (20 – 3)

Nobby Solano

NEWCASTLE UNITED'S GOALSCORERS

Alan Shearer

30 goals Alan Shearer

12 Shola Ameobi

11 Craig Bellamy

10 Wyn Davies

9 Bryan 'Pop' Robson; Tino Asprilla

7 Nobby Solano

6 Laurent Robert; Oba Martins.

5 Jimmy Scott; Gary Speed; Patrick Kluivert; Kieron Dyer

4 Bobby Moncur; Robert Lee; Andy Cole; Peter Beardsley; Les Ferdinand; John Beresford; Lomanu Lua Lua; Lee Bowyer; Titus Bramble; Antoine Sibierski

3 Tommy Gibb; Alan Gowling.

2 Alan Foggon; Keith Dyson; Tommy Craig; Temuri Ketsbaia; Silvo Maric; Hugo Viana; James Milner; Albert Luque.

1 Jackie Sinclair; Bennie Arentoft; Duncan Ferguson; Wayne Quinn; Andy Griffin; Paul Cannel; Scott Sellars; Steve Watson; Ruel Fox; Aaron Hughes; Robbie Elliott; Philippe Albert; David Ginola; John Barnes; Stuart Pearce; Nikos Dabizas; Paul Robinson, Darren Ambrose, Jermaine Jenas; Michael Chopra; Charles N'Zogbia; Emre; Steven Taylor; Smiljanic (FC Basel, og); Dindeleux (Zulte, og); Steinsson (AZ Alkmaar, og).

Patrick Kluivert

INTER CITIES FAIRS CUP 1968/69

Sep 11 FEYENOORD - Holland (H) 4-0 (Davies, Gibb, B Robson, Scott)

Sep 17 FEYENOORD - Holland (A) 0-2

Oct 30 SPORTING LISBON - Portugal (A) 1-1 (Scott)

Nov 20 SPORTING LISBON - Portugal (H) 1-0 (B Robson)

Jan 1 REAL ZARAGOZA - Spain (A) 2-3 (Davies, B Robson)

Jan 15 REAL ZARAGOZA - Spain (H) 2-1 (Gibb, B Robson)

Mar 12 VITORIA SETUBAL - Portugal (H) 5-1 (Davies, Foggon, Gibb, B Robson 2)

Mar 26 VITORIA SETUBAL - Portugal (A) 1-3 (Davies)

May 14 GLASGOW RANGERS - Scotland (A) 0-0

May 21 GLASGOW RANGERS - Scotland (H) 2-0 (Scott, Sinclair)

May 29 UJPEST DOZSA - Hungary (H) 3-0 (Moncur 2, Scott)

Jun 11 UJPEST DOZSA - Hungary (A) 3-2 (Arentoft, Foggon, Moncur)

GOALS: B.Robson 6, Davies 4, Scott 4, Gibb 3, Moncur 3, Foggon 2, Sinclair 1, Arentoft 1

INTER CITIES FAIRS CUP 1969/70

Sep 15 DUNDEE UNITED - Scotland (A) 2-1 (Davies 2)

Oct 1 DUNDEE UNITED - Scotland (H) 1-0 (Dyson)

Nov 18 FC PORTO - Portugal (A) 0-0

Nov 26 FC PORTO - Portugal (H) 1-0 (Scott)

Dec 17 SOUTHAMPTON - England (H) 0-0

Jan 14 SOUTHAMPTON - England (A) 1-1 (Robson)

Mar 11 RSC ANDERLECHT - Belgium (A) 0-2

Mar 18 RSC ANDERLECHT - Belgium (H) 3-1 (Dyson, Robson 2)

GOALS: Robson 3, Davies 2, Dyson 2, Scott 1

INTER CITIES FAIRS CUP 1970/71

Sep 23 INTER MILAN - Italy (A) 1-1 (Davies)

Sep 30 INTER MILAN - Italy (H) 2-0 (Davies, Moncur)

Oct 21 PECSI DOZSA - Hungary (H) 2-0 (Davies 2)

Nov 4 PECSI DOZSA - Hungary (A) 0-2

GOALS: Davies 4, Moncur 1

UEFA CUP 1977/78

Sep 14 BOHEMIANS - Eire (A) 0-0

Sep 28 BOHEMIANS - Eire (H) 4-0 (T Craig 2, Gowling 2)

Oct 19 BASTIA - France (A) 1-2 (Cannell)

Nov 2 BASTIA - France (H) 1-3 (Gowling)

GOALS: T.Craig 2, Gowling 2, Cannell 1, Gowling 1

UEFA CUP 1994/95

Sep 13 ROYAL ANTWERP - Belgium (A) 5-0 (Lee 3, Sellars, Watson)

Sep 27 ROYAL ANTWERP - Belgium (H) 5-2 (Cole 3, Beardsley, Lee)

Oct 18 ATLETICO BILBAO - Spain (H) 3-2 (Cole, Beardsley, Fox)

Nov 1 ATLETICO BILBAO - Spain (A) 0-1

GOALS: Lee 4, Cole 4, Beardsley 2, Sellars 1, Watson 1, Fox 1

UEFA CUP 1996/97

Sep 10 HALMSTADS - Sweden (H) 4-0 (Beardsley, Asprilla, Ferdinand, Albert)

Sep 24 HALMSTADS - Sweden (A) 1-2 (Ferdinand)

Oct 15 FERENCVAROS - Hungary (A) 2-3 (Shearer, Ferdinand)

Oct 29 FERENCVAROS - Hungary (H) 4-0 (Asprilla 2, Ferdinand, Ginola)

Nov 19 METZ - France (A) 1-1 (Beardsley)

Dec 3 METZ - France (H) 2-0 (Asprilla 2)

Mar 4 MONACO - France (H) 0-1

Mar 18 MONACO - France (A) 0-3

GOALS: Aspilla 5, Ferdinand 4, Beardsley 2, Albert 1, Shearer 1, Ginola 1

EUROPEAN CHAMPIONS LEAGUE 1997/98

Aug 13 CROATIA ZAGREB - Croatia (H) 2-1 (Beresford 2)

Aug 27 CROATIA ZAGREB - Croatia (A) 2-2 (Asprilla, Ketsbaia)

Sep 17 BARCELONA - Spain (H) 3-2 (Asprilla 3)

Oct 1 DYNAMO KIEV - Ukraine (A) 2-2 (Beresford 2)

Oct 22 PSV EINDHOVEN - Holland (A) 0-1

Nov 5 PSV EINDHOVEN - Holland (H) 0-2

Nov 26 BARCELONA - Spain (A) 0-1

Dec 10 DYNAMO KIEV - Ukraine (H) 2-0 (Barnes, Pearce)

GOALS: Beresford 4, Asprilla 4, Ketsbaia 1, Barnes 1, Pearce 1

EUROPEAN CUP WINNERS CUP 1998/99

Sep 17 PARTIZAN BELGRADE - Yugoslavia (H) 2-1 (Shearer, Dabizas)

Oct 1 PARTIZAN BELGRADE - Yugoslavia 0-1

GOALS: Shearer 1, Dabizas 1

UEFA CUP 1999/2000

Sep 16 CSKA SOFIA - Bulgaria (A) 2-0 (Solano, Ketsbaia)

Sep 30 CSKA SOFIA - Bulgaria (H) 2-2 (Shearer, Robinson)

Oct 21 FC ZURICH - Switzerland (A) 2-1 (Maric, Shearer)

Nov 4 FC ZURICH - Switzerland (H) 3-1 (Maric, Ferguson, Speed)

Nov 25 AS ROMA - Italy (A) 0-1

Dec 9 AS ROMA - Italy (H) 0-0

GOALS: Shearer 2, Maric 2, Solano 1, Ketsbaia 1, Robinson 1, Ferguson 1, Speed 1

INTER-TOTO CUP 2001/02

Jul 14 S LOKEREN - Belgium (A) 4-0 (Quinn, Lua Lua, Ameobi 2)

Jul 21 S LOKEREN - Belgium (H) 1-0 (Bellamy)

Jul 25 TSV MUNICH - Germany (A) 3-2 (Solano 2, Hughes)

Aug 1 TSV MUNICH - Germany (H) 3-1 (Solano, Speed, Lua Lua)

Aug 7 TROYES - France (A) 0-0

Aug 21 TROYES - France (H) 4-4 (Elliott, Solano, Speed, Ameobi)

GOALS: Solano 4, Ameobi 3, Lua Lua 2, Speed 2, Quinn 1, Bellamy 1, Hughes 1, Elliott 1

EUROPEAN CHAMPIONS LEAGUE 2002/03

Aug 14 ZELJEZNICAR - Bosnia (A) 1-0 (Dyer)

Aug 28 ZELJEZNICAR - Bosnia (H) 4-0 (Dyer, Lua Lua, Viana, Shearer)

Sep 18 DYNAMO KIEV - Ukraine (A) 0-2

Sep 24 FEYENOORD - Holland (H) 0-1

Oct 1 JUVENTUS - Italy (A) 0-2

Oct 23 JUVENTUS - Italy (H) 1-0 (Griffin)

Oct 29 DYNAMO KIEV – Ukraine (H) 2-1 (Speed, Shearer pen)

 Nov 13 FEYENOORD - Holland (A) 3-2 (Bellamy 2, Viana)

Nov 26 INTER MILAN - Italy (H) 1-4 (Solano)

Dec 11 BARCELONA - Spain (A) 1-3 (Ameobi)

Feb 18 BAYER LEVERKUSEN - Germany (A) 3-1 (Ameobi 2, Lua Lua)

Feb 26 BAYER LEVERKUSEN - Germany (H) 3-1 (Shearer 3)

Mar 11 INTER MILAN - Italy (A) 2-2 (Shearer 2)

Mar 19 BARCELONA – Spain (H) 0-2

GOALS: Shearer 7, Ameobi 3, Dyer 2, Lua Lua 2, Viana 2, Bellamy 2, Griffin 1, Solano 1, Speed 1

EUROPEAN CHAMPIONS LEAGUE 2003/04

Aug 13 PARTIZAN BELGRADE - Serbia (A) 1-0 (Solano)

Aug 27 PARTIZAN BELGRADE - Serbia (H) 0-1 (Lost on pens)

UEFA CUP 2003/04

Sept 22 NAC BREDA (H) Holland 5-0 (Bellamy 2, Bramble, Shearer, Ambrose)

Oct 15 NAC BREDA (A) Holland 1-0 (Robert)

Nov 6 FC BASEL (A) Switzerland 3-2 (Robert, Bramble, Ameobi)

27 Nov FC BASEL (H) Switzerland 1-0 (Smiljanic og)

26 Feb VALERENGA (A) Norway 1-1 (Bellamy)

3 Mar VALERENGA (H) Norway 3-1 (Shearer, Ameobi 2)

11 Mar REAL MALLORCA (H) Spain 4-1 (Bellamy, Shearer, Robert, Bramble)

25 Mar REAL MALLORCA (A) Spain 3-0 (Shearer 2, Bellamy)

8 Apr PSV EINDHOVEN (A) Holland 1-1 (Jenas)

14 Apr PSV EINDHOVEN (H)Holland 2-1 (Shearer, Speed)

22 Apr OLYMPIQUE MARSEILLE (H)France 0-0

6 May OLYMPIQUE MARSEILLE (A)France 0-2

GOALS: Shearer 5, Bellamy 5, Bramble 3, Robert 3, Ameobi 3, Solano 1, Ambrose 1, Jenas 1, Speed 1, Similjanic og

UEFA CUP 2004/05

16 Sep HAPOEL BNEI SAKHNIN (H) Israel 2-0 (Kluivert 2)

30 Sep HAPOEL BNEI SAKHNIN (A) Israel 5-1 (Kluivert 2, Shearer 3)

21 Oct PANIONIOS (A) Greece 1-0 (Shearer pen)

4 Nov DINAMO TBLISI (H) Georgia 2-0 (Shearer, Bellamy)

25 Nov SOCHAUX (A) France 4-0 (Bowyer, Ameobi, Bellamy, Robert)

16 Dec SPORTING LISBON (H) Portugal 1-1 (Bellamy)

17 Feb HEERENVEEN (A) Holland 2-1 (Shearer, Bowyer)

24 Feb HEERENVEEN (H) Holland 2-1 (Robert, Shearer)

10 Mar OLYMPIAKOS (A) Greece 3-1 (Shearer, Robert, Kluivert)

16 Mar OLYMPIAKOS (H) Greece 4-0 (Dyer, Shearer 2, Bowyer)

7 Apr SPORTING LISBON (H) Portugal 1-0 (Shearer)

14 Apr SPORTING LISBON (A) Portugal1-4 (Dyer)

GOALS: Shearer 11, Kluivert 5, Bellamy 3, Bowyer 3, Robert 3, Dyer 2, Ameobi 1

INTERTOTO CUP 2005/06

17 Jul FC DUBNICA (A) 3-1 Slovakia (Chopra, N'Zogbia, Milner)

23 Jul FC DUBNICA (H) 2-0 Slovakia (Shearer 2)

27 Jul DEPORTIVO LA CORUNA (A) 1-2 Spain (Bowyer)

3 Aug DEPORTIVO LA CORUNA (H) 1-2 Spain (Milner)

GOALS: Milner 2, Shearer 2, Chopra 1, N'Zogbia 1, Bowyer 1

INTERTOTO CUP - 2006/07

15 Jul LILLESTROM 1-1 (H) Norway (Luque)

22 Jul LILLESTROM 3-0 (A) Norway (Ameobi 2, Emre)

10 Aug FK VENTSPILS (A) Latvia 1-0 (Bramble)

24 Aug FK VENTSPILS (H) Latvia 0-0

UEFA CUP 2006/07

14 Sep LEVADIA TALINN (A) Estonia 1-0 (Sibierski)

28 Sep LEVADIA TALLIN (H) Estonia 2-1 (Martins 2)

19 Oct FENERBAHCE (H) Turkey 1-0 (Sibierski)

2 Nov PALERMO (A) Italy 1-0 (Luque)

23 Nov CELTA VIGO (H) 2-1 Portugal (Sibierski, Taylor)

30 Nov EINTRACHT FRANKFURT (A) 0-0 Germany

15 Feb ZULTE-WAREGEM (A) Belgium 3-1 (Dindeleux og, Martins (P), Sibierski)

22 Feb ZULTE-WAREGEM (H) Belgium 1-0 (Martins)

8 Mar AZ ALKMAAR (H) Holland 4-2 (Steinsson og, Dyer, Martins 2)

15 Mar AZ ALKMAAR (A) Holland 0-2

GOALS: Martins 6, Sibierski 4, Luque 2, Ameobi 2, Emre 1, Bramble 1, Taylor 1, Dyer 1, Dindeleux og, Steinsson og,

Andy Cole

THANKS TO ...

A special thanks to ... Richie Everson and Julia Dixon for offering encouragement and helping me produce this book.

My thanks to the supporters who have given their accounts of their trips abroad:

Reggie James, Paul Marshall, Peter 'One Day We Will Be Free' Hodgson, Tony Taylor, Steve 'Hairy Arse' Taylor, Denis Taylor, Mark Thornton.

A MENTION FOR THE FOOT-SOLDIERS OF THE TOON ARMY ...

Paula Fletcher

Carole O'Connor

Michael Swan

Peter Hunter

Gavin Hunter

Mark Hunter

Spadger

Derek Graham

Alan Alderson

Peter Alderson

Robert Haugh

Chris Haugh

David Haugh

Alex Munro

Andrew Haugh

Liam Haugh

Ian Shanks

Ryan Barrass

Graham Firth

Claire Firth

Sam Firth

Jessica Firth

Ronnie Walpert

Michael Walpert

James Cunningham

Gordon Baxter

Dawn Marshall

Gavin Marshall

Rachel Taylor

Gordon Bone

Bob Taylor

Brian Russell

Jaq Richards

Vince Richards

Mark Thornton

Jeanette Bainbridge

Jim Lowery

Nigel Whitfield

Rob Patterson

Geoff Sober

Chris Sober

Steve Brown

Malcolm Brown

Dave Rowe

Norman Rides

Steve Walker
Dave Hardy

Sandy Barber

Mark Baston

Nicholas Baston

George Bland

Neville Blenkinsopp

Peter Blenkinsopp

Carl Boon

Lynn Bull

Andrew Burdis

Paul Cameron

Phil Cannell

Chris Craig

Graeme Donnelly

Kerry Foster

Ady Freemantle

Mel Freemantle

Tivadar "Tiv" Gaudenyi (Serb Mag)

Bill Gibbs

Mike Greaves

Tommy Henry

Marty Henry

Kai Henry

Bobby Henry

Chris Quinn

Irene Campbell

Julie Campbell

Lynn Campbell

Ratty Campbell

Beth King

Peter Hindmarsh

Stu Graham

Javier Julio

Jonathan Payne

Lyn Allman

Kevin Elmer

John Preddy

Robert Black

Hannah Black

Andrew Black

Gary Jackaman

Jonathan Easton

Anthony Cunningham

Mark Allman

Tom Allman

Alan Ashbridge

Lori Wilson Ashbridge

Chris Barber

Terry G (Breda)

Tony G (Breda)

Lyn Allman

Durham Pine Dave

Steve Humes

Margaret Humes

Sam Bainbridge

Stephen Bainbridge

Marion Bainbridge

Chris Gales

David Lawler

Rorrie Crocker

Ross Crocker

Paul Crocker

Andrew Kirkham Noosa Australia

Sue Scott

Supporters Club Vi

Colin Watson North Shields

Roland Watson Cullercoats

Andrew Bell

Jim Lowery

Kodi Smiles

Michael Payne

Brian "Chief" Abbot

Dave Jackson

Ryan James

Barry Keenan

Mark Keenan

Mike McCann

Keith Mason

Krista Mason

Gav Mills

June Payne

Michael Payne

Mike Rice

Dennis Ridley

Paul Ridley

"Spow"

"Sully"

Diane Thirlaway

Chris Turner

Steve Watson

Jay Welsh

James Welsh

Paige Welsh

Mick Whisson

Brian Wilkinson

Big Mac (Breda)

Richie (Breda)

Susan Wolfe

Anthony "Zoggs"

Mark "bobbyV"

Index

Nikos Dabizas

Shola Ameobi

Rob Lee

Brayson, 64

Brazil, 48

Bridges, 121, 134, 135, 136, 142, 191

Brittain, 135, 136, 166, 168, 191, 192

Brondby, 73

Brooking, 170

Budapest, 31, 33, 34, 50, 69, 70, 94

Bulgaria, 94, 197

Burns, 54, 55, 56, 57, 190

Burton, 15, 16, 17, 18, 19, 20, 21, 23, 24, 27, 29, 30, 35, 36, 38, 40, 43, 44, 46, 48, 190

Busby, 11, 14

Butt, 121, 122, 147, 152, 157, 158, 159, 163, 165, 167, 172, 173, 175, 177, 178, 179, 181, 182, 184, 185, 186, 187, 188, 189, 192

Callachan, 54, 55, 190

Cannell, 54, 56, 57, 58, 59, 190, 196, 201

Carl Zuis Jena, 42

Carr, 147, 148, 150, 155, 156, 157, 159, 160, 161, 162, 163, 165, 166, 167, 168, 169, 171, 172, 173, 174, 175, 177, 178, 179, 186, 192

Carroll, 179, 185, 186, 192

Carver, 112, 138

Celta Vigo, 182

Celtic, 12, 26, 35, 75, 132, 139, 141, 142, 156

Charlton, 22, 29, 150, 164

Charlton Athletic, 164

Charvet, 90, 91, 92, 98, 99, 100, 191

Chelsea, 11, 15, 27, 34, 46, 79, 89, 107, 131, 156, 164, 170, 172, 189

Chernobyl, 82

Chesterfield, 56

Chopra, 119, 120, 165, 166, 167, 191, 192, 194, 199

Clark, 15, 16, 17, 18, 19, 20, 21, 22, 23, 24, 26, 27, 29, 30, 35, 36, 38, 40, 41, 44, 48, 49, 52, 62, 63, 64, 66, 68, 72, 73, 75, 190, 191, 193

Clough, 77

Cole, 60, 61, 62, 63, 64, 190, 194, 196, 200

Cologne, 121

Copenhagen, 68, 100

Corsica, 56, 58

Cort, 101, 103, 120, 191

Coventry City, 46, 50, 101

Craggs, 23, 24, 35, 36, 43, 190

Craig, 15, 16, 18, 19, 20, 21, 22, 26, 27, 29, 30, 36, 38, 40, 41, 44, 46, 48, 49, 50, 52, 54, 55, 56, 57, 58, 101, 102, 103, 104, 105, 111, 112, 117, 118, 124, 127, 128, 138, 150, 151, 156, 165, 166, 176, 190, 193, 194, 196, 201

Greenock Morton, 27

Griffin, 91, 111, 112, 113, 114, 115, 116, 118, 119, 120, 122, 124, 126, 130, 191, 194, 198

Gullitt, 91, 92

Guthrie, 21, 22, 38, 41, 42, 43, 44, 46, 48, 49, 50, 190

Guy, 154, 155, 192

Hall, 62, 66, 80, 145

Halmstads, 66, 67, 68

Hamilton, 85, 86, 94, 191

Hardwick, 56, 57, 58, 190

Harper, 94, 95, 96, 97, 98, 99, 100, 114, 115, 116, 130, 131, 132, 148, 149, 160, 161, 165, 174, 175, 177, 178, 180, 181, 184, 185, 186, 191, 192

Harvey, 14, 15, 16, 19, 20, 21, 22, 23, 24, 25, 26, 27, 29, 30, 31, 32, 34, 35, 36, 37, 39, 40, 41, 42, 43, 45, 46, 48, 49, 52, 53

Hearts, 54

Heerenveen, 78, 155, 156, 157

Helsingborgs, 68

Helsinki, 176

Hertha Berlin, 42

Hindson, 50, 190

Hislop, 73, 74, 75, 76, 86, 87, 191

Hoddle, 89, 170

Holland, 42, 84, 116, 130, 155, 181, 188, 195, 197, 198, 199, 200

Horsefield, 190

Hottiger, 60, 61, 62, 63, 64, 190

Howey, 62, 63, 64, 65, 66, 77, 78, 79, 83, 84, 190, 191

Hudson, 57, 59, 190

Hughes, 86, 87, 96, 97, 98, 99, 102, 103, 104, 105, 106, 107, 108, 110, 111, 112, 113, 114, 115, 116, 118, 119, 120, 122, 123, 128, 129, 132, 133, 134, 135, 137, 139, 140, 141, 142, 143, 144, 147, 148, 151, 152, 153, 154, 155, 157, 159, 160, 191, 192, 194, 197, 198

Hungary, 31, 49, 195, 196

Huntington, 185, 186, 188, 192

Iley, 16, 190

Inter Milan, 10, 12, 47, 48, 49, 119, 123, 140

Ipswich Town, 53, 93, 95, 123, 130

Israel, 16, 17, 148, 199

Italy, 11, 42, 47, 56, 146, 196, 197, 198, 200

Jeffrey, 61, 64, 190

Jenas, 108, 109, 113, 114, 115, 116, 120, 122, 124, 126, 128, 129, 130, 131, 132, 133, 134, 135, 136, 137, 138, 139, 140, 141, 147, 148, 149, 150, 151, 154, 155, 157, 159, 160, 161, 162, 164, 166, 191, 192, 193, 194, 198, 199

Juventus, 10, 31, 35, 52, 64, 65, 72, 76, 88, 114, 115, 116, 117, 118, 125, 132, 179

Ramage, 159, 173, 175, 176, 177, 178, 179, 181, 182, 192

Rangers, 10, 12, 20, 23, 26, 27, 28, 29, 32, 35, 100, 146, 164, 187

Real Sociedad, 102

Real Zaragoza, 21, 22, 23

Redknapp, 170

Revie, 22, 29

Robert, 58, 62, 71, 72, 81, 90, 105, 111, 112, 113, 114, 115, 116, 118, 119, 120, 121, 122, 123, 124, 126, 127, 129, 130, 132, 133, 134, 135, 137, 138, 139, 140, 141, 142, 143, 144, 147, 148, 149, 150, 151, 152, 153, 155, 156, 157, 158, 159, 160, 161, 163, 165, 166, 191, 192, 194, 198, 199, 201

Robinson, 95, 96, 97, 98, 191, 194, 197

Robson, 15, 16, 18, 19, 20, 21, 22, 23, 24, 25, 26, 27, 28, 29, 30, 31, 32, 35, 36, 38, 39, 40, 41, 42, 43, 44, 46, 47, 48, 49, 50, 51, 87, 93, 94, 97, 99, 100, 101, 103, 105, 106, 107, 108, 111, 112, 113, 114, 115, 117, 119, 121, 124, 126, 128, 129, 130, 131, 132, 133, 134, 135, 138, 139, 140, 145, 146, 147, 148, 149, 155, 164, 174, 190, 194, 195, 196

Roeder, 170, 171, 172, 173, 174, 176, 177, 178, 180, 181, 184, 185, 186, 187, 188, 189

Romania, 12, 42

Rosenborg, 76

Rotterdam, 16, 17, 82, 86, 116, 117, 182

Royal Antwerp, 62

Rush, 83, 84, 191

Saint Tropez, 56

Sampdoria, 146

Sarajevo, 109, 110

Schalke 04, 73, 76

Scotland, 12, 26, 35, 46, 52, 195

Scott, 15, 16, 18, 19, 20, 21, 23, 24, 25, 26, 27, 28, 29, 30, 32, 36, 38, 39, 40, 41, 62, 165, 171, 172, 173, 174, 179, 187, 188, 189, 190, 194, 195, 196, 201

Sellars, 61, 62, 63, 64, 190, 194, 196

Serbia, 129, 141, 198

Serrant, 96, 191

Shankly, 32

Shearer, 10, 66, 67, 68, 69, 70, 72, 74, 80, 83, 90, 91, 92, 94, 95, 96, 97, 98, 99, 100, 101, 102, 103, 108, 109, 110, 111, 112, 113, 114, 115, 116, 117, 118, 119, 122, 123, 124, 125, 126, 127, 128, 129, 130, 131, 132, 133, 134, 135, 136, 137, 138, 139, 140, 141, 142, 143, 144, 147, 148, 149, 150, 151, 152, 153, 155, 156, 157, 158, 159, 160, 161, 163, 165, 166, 167, 168, 169, 170, 171, 191, 192, 194, 196, 197, 198, 199

Sheffield United, 102

Other Publications by this Author

"ARE YOU AFFILIATED?"

Dear friends, readers, bingo players and affiliated members ... this is my book "Are You Affiliated".

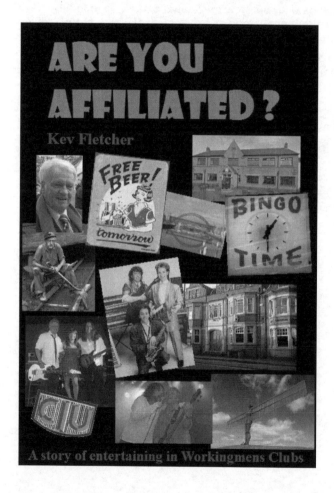

There are thousands of books out there recounting the struggles of the rich and famous, each telling a story of poverty to stardom, from rags to riches ... but don't be fooled ... because this is NOT one of them.

This is the north of England Workingmen's club circuit. The first rung on the ladder of dreams and aspirations, and if you have never visited a Workingmen's club before, I'm sure the 180-plus pages of "Are You Affiliated?" will be bloody confusing!

Realistically speaking, it is the alternative to stretch limos, drugs and lines of enthusiastic groupies. This is the real world. More like a knackered old transit van, a couple of pints of non-fizzy lager, and a kiss off an 'old slapper' who has slipped off the ball and chain, out for a night without the 'old fella'.

Sunday Sun: "As an in-demand musician, Kev Fletcher has done many 'turns' at the region's workingmen's clubs. Here he lifts the lid on his experiences ... his dealings with committee chairmen, performing to an empty club, finding out how to cheat at bingo ... and finally living out his dream performing on stage at a rock festival with a heavy metal band.

This book, which has a whiff of Peter Kay's Phoenix Nights, boasts a multitude of characters who have crossed Kev's path, from porn stars to petrol bombers. It's an affectionately wry look at a world now under threat.

STAR RATING: ***** (five out of five)

Available at £8.99 from:

www.Lulu.com

or

www.amazon.com

or from Kev himself (email): Kevnumad@fsmail.net

Knights C

Book 3

Fall
of the
Fatherland

D.N.J. Greaves

ORIGINAL WRITING

In Print ISBN 978-1-908477-12-5
ePub ISBN: 978-1-908477-24-8
Mobi ISBN: 978-1-908477-25-5

A cip catalogue for this book is available from the National Library.

Published by Original Writing Ltd., Dublin, 2011.

Printed by Clondalkin Group, Clonshaugh, Dublin 17

To Helen and Emma, and always with my love

About The Author

DESMOND GREAVES was born in Birmingham but spent the first five years of his life with his grandparents in Skerries, County Dublin. On returning to Birmingham he was educated at Holy Name School, then Grace Dieu Manor and Ratcliffe College in Leicestershire. He studied medicine at Birmingham University and worked as a general practitioner in Redditch.

Desmond was a Major in the Territorial Army, commissioned in the Royal Army Medical Corps (RAMC). He saw active service in the first Gulf War.

He lived in Staffordshire with his wife Helen and daughter Emma. Desmond died in December 2010, having spent three years researching and writing this trilogy of books.

USS Aurora, off Omaha Beach, Vierville, Normandy 1830 6/6/1944

General Omar Bradley, Commanding Officer, United States First Army, leaned against the railing located just aft of the bridge and focused his binoculars on the distant shore. A salvo from the 15-inch main guns shook the vessel, belching out huge clouds of black-grey smoke as the heavy calibre shells sped towards their targets, rousing him from his thoughts. He wore a worried frown. Today his characteristically friendly, although often shy and diffident manner, was absent. It was the evening of D-Day, the Allied invasion of France, and he was in command of the American landings. The day had been one of mixed success. The 4th Division had made a straightforward assault on the coastal defences at Utah beach, near the base of the Cotentin peninsula. That was about twenty miles away, not quite visible from where his flagship lay at anchor. The drive inland was proceeding rapidly enough and a quick link up would soon be achieved with the two airborne divisions, the 82nd and 101st. Their drops were for the most part on target, although he suspected that the cost, in terms of both disruption and casualties, was not insignificant. No, he was not worried so much about Utah. It was the invasion here at Omaha that greatly troubled him.

The landings started at 0630. The sea was rough, but the first waves went in on time. Troops from the 1st and 29th Divisions with engineer and armoured support hit the beaches according to schedule, but after that everything had gone wrong. The German defences were formidable, well-entrenched soldiers of good quality fighting from behind formidable fortifications. What few reports came back spoke of a murderous crossfire that swept across the open expanse of shoreline from the heights and bluffs above. It was extracting a terrible price in men and equipment. The amphibious tanks were knocked out, one by one. All bar one of the heavy 105mm howitzers planned to support the infantry were sunk before they could be landed, and the remaining gun that was put ashore was soon destroyed by German artillery. All that remained of the initial waves were isolated groups of frightened men, huddled behind whatever meagre cover they could find.

The Navy and Air Force had done what they could, but their ability to intervene was aggravated by the poor weather and reduced visibility. Low cloud hampered the aerial bombardment, which had swept over the beaches before the first wave had touched down. The bombers were forced to drop their loads blind, and Bradley reckoned that many of them had inadvertently left their intended targets untouched as a result. Dust and smoke from bombs and shells obscured much of the beach defences, making it equally difficult for the Navy to pin point accurately enemy casemates and guns.

The reality of the unfolding disaster was brought home to him by reports from the beach. A graphic illustration was also provided by aerial reconnaissance. A camera plane had flown directly over the beaches late that morning. The film was quickly rushed back to England, where photo intelligence assessed the results. By early afternoon a report was in his hands. It made disturbing reading. The casualty count was extremely high - the pictures taken had shown bodies stacked like cordwood along the beach, rows and rows of matchstick men lying on the shore or floating in the surf, the dead and dying. Bradley was prepared for heavy casualties in achieving his objectives, but the count shocked him. An estimate spoke of between five and seven thousand dead and wounded men, an extortionate amount to pay for such a miniscule amount of real estate. The future of the landings here hung in the balance.

But even as these depressing reports reached him, matters ashore began to look up. By early afternoon several groups of soldiers at different points along the landing zones had managed to fight their way up the slopes and bluffs and through the minefields and onto higher ground. There they had begun to attack the defences, rolling them up by outflanking them, their bravery and fury overpowering the defenders and inflicting heavy losses on them. Soon more and more men were able to get off the foreshore and advance inland and as they did so the enemy fire sweeping the beaches dramatically eased off. Several navy destroyers and even a cruiser almost ran aground in moving closer to the beaches. The risk was worth it. Their point blank fire had pulverized the remaining defences, particularly those concentrated around the beach exits and gullies between the bluffs. As a result, successive waves of men and equipment began to land without significant loss and were moving steadily inland to expand the precarious foothold.

The shoreline still looked angry, sullen in the glare of exploding tanks and burning landing craft. The USS Aurora shuddered as yet another volley of heavy shells sped from the thickly armoured turrets towards the shoreline. Bradley sighed to himself. He was pleased that the overall situation was improving, but he still had serious concerns. Would the beachhead be deep enough? Were there enough men and equipment ashore to protect it against the inevitable counterattack? Where was the German armoured reserve?

The answers to his questions were almost immediately forthcoming. The first message was from a regimental headquarters, the 115th Infantry. It was struggling to gain possession of the village of St Laurent, but had little to say about the presence of other units on its flanks. He could read between the lines of the report- it spoke of considerable confusion and disorganisation ashore. A quick glance at the tactical map revealed that they were less than a mile inland - nowhere near far enough. The second message was even more alarming.

A reconnaissance aircraft had spotted a column of German armour on the road just outside Bayeux, no more than eight or nine miles away. Where had they come from- was it 21st Panzer near Caen? If armour reached the coast at Omaha then the consequences could be fatal. The troops ashore had little in the way of anti-tank weapons or tanks to protect them. If Omaha was subsequently lost then the whole of the D-Day landings were at risk. A huge gap would separate the British beaches from the Americans at Utah, inviting the Germans to defeat the remaining landings in detail. He had to do something and that something needed to be done right now.

An ADC hurried up to where he stood, looking out towards the shore. 'Excuse me, General, but members of the Press Corps are here. They want to hear your opinion of today's events and take some photos. With your permission sir.'

Bradley turned around quickly. 'No way,' he said, gesturing angrily. 'There's no time. We have a crisis on our hands. I'll talk to them later. But no photos damn it!' That was the last thing he wanted. A wad of sticky plaster covered his nose. An unsightly blind boil had caused the tip to swell up and turn red, and he was embarrassed by his appearance. The public most definitely did not need to see it. 'Get me General Quesada at Ninth Tactical Air Command, immediately.' The boil was a minor blemish. He had far more important things to think about.

❊

Luc-sur-Mer, Normandy 2100 6/6/1944

Oberst Hermann von Oppeln-Bronikowski stood up in the turret of his command Mark IV Panzer and stared out at the scenes in front of him in wonder. The impeccably attired and normally suave and cool commander of Panzer Regiment 22 was quite stunned. He found it hard to believe the view on display. The Channel coast lay but a mile away, but this was not the source of his amazement. What staggered him was the numbers of Allied ships that lay at anchor on both sides of the narrow salient still open to German forces – it was a profoundly shocking sight. He knew that the Allies possessed a large combined fleet, but he had never expected to see so many vessels laid out before him. There were all types - from menacing battleships, bristling with guns and firing off salvo after salvo, to a multitude of small assault craft ferrying troops and equipment ashore, and everything in between- cargo ships, cruisers and destroyers, vessels carrying tanks - the list went on and on. The sheer scale of naval activity threatened to overwhelm his usual sangfroid. The Kriegsmarine and Luftwaffe were conspicuous by their absence. Where the hell were they? He gritted his teeth in frustration. They would never have a better chance to strike at such at such a richly concentrated target.

To his right he could see the landing area on the beaches near Ouistreham. That was busy enough, but over to his left the activity was even more intense. Enemy landings were visible from St Aubin-sur-Mer to La Rivière and even further west. How many enemy divisions were coming ashore? He estimated at least three in the sectors he could see, maybe more to the west, but how many were there altogether?

All told, it was an eventful, frustrating day. The madness had begun in the early hours. Divisional HQ received reports just after midnight about airborne landings on the right bank of the Orne – then nothing for several hours. In the grey dawn enemy bombers were out and about in unprecedented force, attacking anything that looked like a worthwhile target. As a result, communications were badly disrupted by the bombing. Later that morning news began to filter through of seaborne landings to the north of Caen and elsewhere, but the division remained paralysed. There were no orders from OKH. It seemed that nobody there could make up his mind what to do. Even worse, his division commander, General-Major Edgar Feuchtinger, had not exactly covered himself in glory. Nobody could find him in the early hours - the general was not in his quarters, and all telephone calls throughout the division net had drawn a blank. Some of the divisional HQ staff suspected he had been playing away from home with a stunning African beauty from one of Paris' racier nightclubs, but no one could be sure just where he was. Eventually, well after the news of enemy activity had circulated throughout the Normandy sector, Feuchtinger had turned up, looking more than a little sheepish. And as for senior command intervention in France, where was Rommel? Rumour control said that he was at home in Heerlingen for his wife's birthday, and that he was in the process of hurrying back to Normandy. All in all, it was a right cock-up. There was nobody on the spot to issue definitive orders.

Feuchtinger now found himself impaled on the horns of a dilemma. Did he really have to wait for OKH to get back in contact, or should he seize the initiative and make an all out attack now, as Rommel had suggested to him back in May? If so, was he to continue to attack the parachute drop zones across the River Orne, or bypass them entirely and charge straight ahead towards the coast where he would annihilate the beach landings north of Caen?

Even now he could not use all his strength. Nearly half of his division's sub-units were already placed under the control of other local commanders - two battalions of infantry, the anti-aircraft, assault gun and anti-tank battalions - a large proportion of his normal command. The assault gun and infantry battalions were fiercely engaged with the airborne landings at Ranville, just across the river on the east bank of the Orne. Did he have a strong enough case to change their orders and impose his will, especially without higher authority? It was like fighting with one hand tied behind your back. What should he do? If he took the risk of acting without OKH's permission, he might easily make the wrong choice and jeopardize the chances of successfully beating off the enemy. The threat of a court martial and a firing squad was at the back of his mind. These options were always available as punishment for those commanders who made a mess of things. All he could do was to wait. At long last the eagerly awaited OKH directive arrived, shortly before two o'clock. Feuchtinger was finally given the permission he needed to act decisively. The bulk of what was left of his division would attack north towards the enemy landings at Ouistreham, while continuing to contain and attack the airborne landings east of the river. Another smaller kampfgruppe would move towards Bayeux to help the 352nd, hard pressed by the Americans. Additional help would arrive from elsewhere to help him deal with the airborne landings, but until then his troops committed there would have to stay put.

But another complication soon followed. During the early afternoon, not long after Feuchtinger had issued his orders and his sub-units started to move, the Chief of Staff at the 352nd Division HQ rang up. His forces were dealing with the American landings and could manage on their own. Then four hours later he called back to revise his opinion, saying that the Americans were enlarging their beachhead and that his division urgently needed extra help. The kampfgruppe dispatched earlier towards Bayeux and Omaha had by this time almost returned to Caen, turned back by the first message. When the later report arrived the kampfgruppe then had to reverse course and head straight back to Bayeux. No sooner had it reached the outskirts of the town when it was caught in an intense bombing raid that destroyed it almost entirely. Only a few disorganized and scattered remnants were left, in no fit state to carry out a major attack.

Von Oppeln-Bronikowski's own command had concentrated the Panzer Regiment as ordered, although part of one battalion was already across the river and engaged at Ranville against the enemy paratroops. The remainder, under his direct command, eventually cleared the congestion caused by Allied bombing in Caen and headed north towards the beaches. A few tanks were lost to an enemy anti-tank ambush near Perriers but the rest had continued onwards, some forking left towards Douvres, the rest holding open the corridor to the rear as he drove on towards the sea. And here he was, smack in the middle of two landing areas. Reports from his rearward HQ told him that the British to his right had seized a corridor stretching from the coast to near Lébisey, just north of the city, while the Canadians on his left were advancing on a broad front to the west. A potential enveloping noose was being drawn around his neck.

But what could he do on his own? All he had left was less than a dozen Mark IVs and a few half-tracks crammed with infantry, hardly an overwhelming force, not enough in itself to make a decisive attack on his own. Still, it was better than nothing. Which way to go? The beachhead to his right appeared to be smaller, less formidable than the other. He looked at his map, considered contacting divisional HQ, then he thought the better of it. He would simply attack first and wait for permission later.

Oppeln-Bronikowski was about to give his orders when a distant droning noise distracted him. It was coming from the sea over to his right, in the direction of England. He raised his binoculars to his eyes and scanned the horizon - where was it? Suddenly he could see what appeared to be a large grey-green cloud rapidly approaching from the sea. On closer inspection he could make out individual aircraft - hundreds of them. The droning quickly became louder and louder. He could pick out transports, tugs and gliders, all surrounded by a wall of fighters weaving in and around the formation. Soon he no longer needed his binoculars. The noise was deafening. It was like a huge swarm of bees, relentlessly buzzing as they drew closer and closer. Puffs of black smoke began to appear among the formation as the aircraft crossed the coast- that must be the coastal anti-aircraft batteries opening up.

For one wild moment he thought they would have a field day. After all, they could hardly miss. The heavy transports and gliders were flying a straight, undeviating course, not bothering to take evasive action, chugging at a measured pace across the sky. But only one of them began to smoke, a great plume of fire belching from one of its wings. The reason soon became apparent. The escorting fighters had already swept down, almost to tree level, as they sought out the anti-aircraft guns and raked them with machine gun and cannon fire, smashing the batteries and suppressing their ability to wreak havoc in the skies. As the tugs passed across his field of vision the gliders were cast loose. They banked and then slipped downwards towards the ground, a heavy hissing of wood on air as they swooped gracefully down towards the fields on either side of the river and out of view.

The spectacle was incredible. There must be well over two hundred gliders landing only a few miles away. A multitude of parachutes filled the air, suspending tiny figures or heavier bundles of equipment as they slowly floated downwards. He could hear the cries of his men as they looked on in wonder and dismay. The airborne drop was directly in front of him and across the path of his intended attack. But what was the point? At least a brigade must have dropped directly ahead. However, he still had his orders.

At that moment his headphones began to crackle. It was divisional HQ. The order was simple enough, but hardly helped his feelings of disappointment and gloom. In view of the airborne landings that everybody had just witnessed, higher command had decided to pause while all the divisions' subunits could be reassembled for a concerted, decisive drive to the coast. The Panzer Regiment, complete with all its supporting units and all the division's infantry battalions, would be assembled just north of Caen for a night-time attack, or at the latest first thing in the morning.

He swore to himself. Bloody idiots! By then it would be far too late. Every single wasted minute gave the enemy more time to land extra forces and to reorganise for the battles ahead. He had no confidence in the division's ability to mount a coordinated attack at night. It had not trained enough for it, and God knows how long it would take to reorganize. What about petrol supplies? His tanks were not far off running on empty and needed urgent refuelling before a regrouping and subsequent attack could be considered, let alone mounted. To make matters worse, most of the division's fuel dumps had been hit hard by the Allied air forces during the day. With a sigh of exasperation he ordered what was left of his kampfgruppe to turn around and head back towards Caen.

Krankenhaus Hohenstein, near Höxter, Westphalia 1130
17/7/1944

Schellenberg's Mercedes drew up to the front door of the private hospital, located at the edge of a series of undulating, heavily forested hills that stretched away east towards the Harz mountain range. The air was warm, and the late morning sun glinted off the imposing façade of the long, low building set back into a wooded slope. The Krankenhaus Hohenstein was a famous clinic and sanatorium, well respected and recognized in the world of Neurology as one of the foremost centres in Head and Spinal injury rehabilitation, certainly in Germany, if not throughout the whole of Europe. Its reputation was second to none, and the accommodation was first class, better than many a five-star hotel. It was a place where many dreamed of being treated, but few could afford the bills. However, all that had changed since the onset of war. The clinic had been 'persuaded', by none other than the Reichsführer himself, to volunteer its services to the war effort and make some beds available to those suffering from serious neurological injuries.

Because of its relatively small size, only the few, the privileged and well connected could be treated here. This meant officers only and the more senior you were the more likely the chances of admission. Schellenberg had to pull a few strings to get his newly promoted Sturmbannführer admitted at very short notice. The hospital at Bremerhaven, where his patient was initially treated, was a fine institution in its own right. Unfortunately it had little experience of this type of injury, and was only too keen to get him out of its overcrowded wards. The clinic director at the Hohenstein had been quick to cooperate, particularly after he realized that the 'request' had come from the very top at RSHA. A judicious, if not slightly early, discharge was arranged to free up the necessary bed.

The purpose of his visit today was to inquire after the patient's health, and see if he was able to tolerate a few questions. Schellenberg recalled his previous telephone conversation with the clinic director. Professor Mobius had been encouraging, but also quite specific in his stipulations about care - on no account was his patient to be overtaxed with prolonged questioning. He had only just regained consciousness. The ultimate prognosis was still somewhat in doubt, and Mobius emphasized the need to keep stress to a minimum. Schellenberg had insisted on the best medical and nursing care, and Mobius naturally guaranteed that his patient would have it. Time and costs would be irrelevant in this case.

Hansen turned the engine off and leapt out of the car to open the rear door. As Schellenberg stepped out he was pleased to see that the director was waiting for him, assembled along with several members of his senior medical staff.

'Good morning, Brigadeführer. I hope you had a pleasant journey.' Clinic director and Professor Wolfgang Mobius smiled obsequiously and performed a slight bow in due deference to Schellenberg's rank. 'May I present the rest of my senior staff?'

Schellenberg seized the proffered handshake and Mobius introduced the senior medical and nursing team. It was rare to have such an eminent high-ranking officer to come to visit their clinic, especially at this stage of the war, and it was only appropriate to show the necessary enthusiasm and respect. When the obligatory introductions and courtesies had finished Schellenberg thanked the assembly briefly, telling them that the Reichsführer was very pleased with the clinic's work, and that they should be proud of their achievements. He turned to the director.

'Thank you, Herr Professor. Perhaps we can now discuss my patient. I need a full update since I last spoke to you on his admission, and in particular your impression on how long his recovery will take.'

Mobius led him inside the clinic and down a heavily carpeted corridor into the administration wing where his office was situated. The room was quite luxurious, with a glorious view out over the River Weser towards the nearby woods and hills. Schellenberg was offered a comfortable leather chair, while Mobius organised refreshments.

After coffee arrived Mobius sat down and began to summarise the salient medical points.

'As I understand it, from the records supplied by the St Joseph Krankenhaus in Bremerhaven, the patient suffered a blow to the side of his skull and cervical spine on the night of the fifth of June. The blow was sufficient to cause a prolonged state of unconsciousness. The coma was complicated by three other injuries. First, there was a closed fracture of the right radius and ulna-'

'I apologise for butting in, Herr Director, but as I'm not medically trained I'd be most grateful if you would translate the more complicated medical terms into everyday language.' Schellenberg softened his interruption with a smile.

'Of course, Brigadeführer,' Mobius beamed in return. Everything must be sweetness and light for such a distinguished guest. 'Thank you for reminding me. It's much too easy for doctors to rattle off a multitude of medical terms without realizing that they're not always that easily understandable. As I was saying, the right forearm was broken, but this was easily taken care of by manipulation and a plaster cast. What was far more worrying was his neurological state- his brain and spinal cord. X-rays taken at the time showed that he had a fractured- I beg your pardon- broken skull, presumably due to a heavy object striking him there. Examination over the next twenty-four hours suggested that a blood clot was building up around and under the damaged area, a significant complication. In view of the danger of further irreversible brain damage that could occur because of pressure from the expanding clot, he was operated on. The clot was removed- quite successfully according to the neurosurgeon's report. However, he still remained unconscious afterwards.

'The other problem was his spine - the cervical spine, that is, the neck.' Mobius got up and walked over to where an anatomical skeleton and spine were suspended from a display stand. He pointed to the areas under discussion. 'These are the areas of the skull and spine in question. As for his neck, initial examination revealed heavy bruising around the base. In addition, testing of his nervous system revealed a complete absence of reflexes one would normally expect to be present, even when unconscious. The physicians assessing him suspected serious damage to the spinal cord- a possible paralysis. Fortunately, X-rays taken of his neck did not show any evidence of fracture -- broken or dislocated bones.'

'Why 'fortunately', Herr Direktor?'

'Irreversible spinal paralysis is associated almost invariably with broken or displaced bones in the neck. As there was no evidence of this we could probably rule out a complete and permanent paralysis of all four limbs.'

'So what's his condition now?' Schellenberg was itching to know the latest situation, but managed to remain patient while the clinic director continued his discourse. .

'Well, there's good news.' Mobius smiled. 'As you know, he regained consciousness two days ago - but only for brief periods of time, an hour or two at most, but enough to suggest that the effects of his head injury are wearing off. I expect these periods of prolonged unconsciousness will become shorter.'

Schellenberg nodded. He would have visited earlier but urgent business in Berlin had kept him away. 'Is he able to stand up to some questioning?'

'Yes, as long as it's not too intense and overlong. We don't want to overtire him at this stage.'

'That's fine by me.'

'Excellent.' Mobius continued. 'As I've already hinted at, the other piece of good news is that we don't think he has any permanent damage from his neck injury. We suspect he suffered a hyper-extension injury to his neck.' He simulated the injury by moving his hands. 'The paralysis is temporary, caused by internal bruising. It's like a prolonged state of shock to the area. We think that the actual mechanism of the shock is a large blood clot that is pressing on his spinal cord. Eventually this will resolve and he should return to complete normality, given the correct care and rehabilitation'.

Schellenberg shifted in his seat. 'How long will this take?'

'It's hard to tell, Brigadeführer. Nine months, perhaps more, perhaps less. A lot depends on his mental state. If he's strong, and is not distracted by worry and stress, then it will be quicker. Also, you've got to remember that he will have to relearn to use all his muscles again. Most of these will have wasted away due to his enforced inactivity, so he'll have to work hard in physical therapy to rebuild them.'

'I presume you have experience of these sorts of injuries?'

'Yes. We've had several cases like this over the years. The outlook is good, but as I said, it will take time. Your patient is an exceedingly lucky man to have survived almost intact what appear to be very serious neurological injuries.'

Schellenberg stood up. 'Thank you, Herr Direktor. I would like to see him now.'

Mobius bowed again. 'Of course Brigadeführer. However, if I may be so bold as to reiterate, please do not overtire him. He is still in the early stages of recovery, and we do not want to add to his physical injuries.'

'Don't worry, Dr Mobius.' Schellenberg nodded in his direction. 'I will be guided by your advice, as always. And I have his best interests at heart, just as you do.'

Simon struggled to regain consciousness. It felt as if he was slowly ascending from a very great depth, a constant battle to float higher and higher through the veils of his mind. He could see sunlight ahead, a fierce yellow ball that rippled and shimmered in front of him. Gradually it grew closer, until at last he broke the surface, blinded by the sudden burst of light.

He opened his eyes. Blearily, he began to focus on his surroundings. He was in a room, lying on a bed with his head propped up. Everything was white- the walls, ceiling, sheets on the bed- a sterile, clinical environment. The only splash of colour came from the view outside the window- leafy green trees and the gentle curve of a river far off to the right.

The door to his room opened, and a nurse walked in, again dressed in white- a severely starched uniform and cap. The austere effect was offset by a shapely figure and pretty face. As soon as she noticed him awake she smiled, displaying a perfectly even set of white teeth.

'Good morning. How are you feeling?'

Simon groaned. It was always the same- surrounded by attractive nurses and completely unable to do anything about it.

'I've got a splitting headache and a dry throat,' he croaked. 'Otherwise, I can't feel a thing.' Suddenly he remembered the last time he awoke. An elderly, white-haired man had been poking and prodding him, not that he could feel any of it. The man had introduced himself as the director of the clinic, a cheerful, efficient doctor with a decidedly optimistic view of life, and Simon's progress in particular.

'Don't worry about it', the doctor had smiled when the subject of his paralysis had come up. 'I have no doubt that you will make a full recovery. It may take a bit of time, but we'll have you up and back on your feet. But you are going to have to be very patient and be cooperative. I'm sure you know this from the last time you were in hospital.' He had smiled and left him to the tender attentions of the nursing staff...

'I'll get you a drink and some tablets for the pain in just a moment.' The nurse was busy adjusting various things at the bottom of the bed that he could not quite see or feel. She lifted up the sheets, sniffed and looked concerned. 'We're going to need to turn you again. I'll be back in a moment.' A minute or two later she returned with two other nurses. Quickly, with almost military precision, they adjusted his body in the bed to lie in a slightly different position.

'That's better.' The other staff disappeared. 'We need to make sure you don't get any pressure sores from lying in one position for too long. Did you feel anything now as we moved you?'

'I'm not sure. Maybe some tingling in where I think my legs are...'

'Well, that's encouraging. I'll get those tablets now. By the way, you have a visitor, a general.' She smiled, arching her eyebrows and looked impressed. 'You must be quite important...'

❧

A few moments later Schellenberg entered the room. He turned towards the director who had followed him in, and said 'thank you, Herr Professor. I really must insist that I talk to him alone.' Mobius bowed and closed the door behind him. He walked over to where Simon lay on the bed, pulled up a chair, and made himself comfortable.

'I'm pleased to see you again, Sturmbannführer.' He smiled easily, not in the least embarrassed that his actions had indirectly led Simon to being wounded again. 'Well done in carrying out the mission. Sorry about your injuries. However, the good news is that the Direktor tells me you'll make a full recovery, although it may take some time before you're up and around again. By the way, congratulations on your promotion- it went through while you were in England. Are you well enough to answer a few questions?'

'Yes sir.' Simon croaked. 'After all, I'm not exactly in a hurry to go anywhere.'

'Good.' Schellenberg grinned. 'I see you haven't lost your sense of humour. Now we will get down to business. I need you to fill in some gaps in our knowledge about what happened in England. We were getting quite worried, particularly about the lack of radio transmission. Tell me what happened.'

Simon cast his mind back to the events in May. After a few moments pause, he gave a brief résumé of his insertion into England, and his stay at the safe house in Hanwell. 'The house was damaged in a bombing raid. Part of the roof fell in and hit the transmitter, damaging some valves and diodes. It took ages to source replacement parts, but Simms eventually found some on the black market and managed to repair it. There was no possibility of taking it anywhere else - too many questions would be asked.' Schellenberg nodded, but kept silent. He was eager for answers, but all in good time. 'Simms did not have a license for a radio transmitter, and we couldn't take the risk.' He took out a gold pen and pad from inside his jacket pockets, and began carefully making notes. The questions came thick and fast. 'Can you remember the date of the bombing raid?'

'It was about four or five nights after I parachuted in, the twelfth or thirteenth of May, I think.' He cleared his throat. "Could you pass me some more water? My throat's still very dry.'

'Of course I can.' Schellenberg obliged. Simon sipped the water through a feeding tube. After a few gulps to ease his dry throat, he continued.

He told him about the initial abortive rendezvous in Hyde Park, followed by the events of the Thursday two weeks later when 'Rothermere' turned up. All mention of MI6 interference was carefully omitted, as was the second safe house.

'So Rothermere was unable to give you any documents, any written information on the invasion site?'

'No. After he informed me that it was the Pas de Calais, he quickly became ill and slipped into a coma. He never regained consciousness. All he gave me was the area. I searched him, but I was unable to find anything.' Simon looked him straight in the eye, hoping that his barefaced lies and omissions would pass muster. Schellenberg sat thoughtfully, making no comment for a few minutes.

'Sir, I presume the signal got through?'

'Yes... Our experts recognised your transmission characteristics, just in case our friends in MI6 were trying to fool us.' He smiled, humourlessly. 'So they weren't involved in the mission at all, were they?'

'No sir. I was not aware of any enemy surveillance.'

'Hmmm.' Schellenberg looked thoughtful. 'So why did you not report in that same night?'

'Sir, the radio was still damaged. We couldn't get it to work for another four or five nights. Then I sent in the transmission and arranged for the U-boat rendezvous.'

'I see.' Schellenberg paused, and then carried on in the same mild manner. 'And now we cannot contact Simms at all. Do you have any explanation for that?'

'No sir. Unless he's been arrested or killed in a bombing raid.'

The latter was more of a possibility, now that Hitler had launched the V weapon rocket offensive, directed mainly at London. Simon's explanation was plausible, but perhaps just a little bit too convenient for comfort. However, there was little Schellenberg could do to check his agent's story at present, and there was no point in upsetting him and questioning his version of events - not yet, anyway.

'What about getting out? Did you have any difficulties with the U-boat rendezvous?'

'No sir. It was straightforward enough. I managed to get a train to North Wales. After that it was a bus journey and walking to the right beach, then the pre-arranged signal by torchlight. The U-boat sent in a shore party to pick me up in a dinghy, and then off we went back to Germany. There were a few hairy moments when we were attacked by enemy aerial patrols, but that was it until we reached Bremerhaven - just in time to get caught in a bombing raid.'

'Yes, that was most unfortunate,' Schellenberg agreed, 'but at least you're still alive, more than can be said for some of the U-boat crew.' He was aware that Simon was beginning to tire. Out of the corner of his eye he could see that Mobius was hovering outside, ready to interfere should his patient become exhausted.

'That's enough for now, I think. You're starting to look weary. I'll let you rest, and come back later this afternoon when you've had a sleep. Then we'll have another chat.'

'Yes sir. But before you go, please can you tell me what's happened in the meantime?' Simon pleaded. 'Nobody's told me anything.'

'All right - but I'll be brief. In the East the Russians have launched a series of very heavy attacks, their summer offensive. Our troops are holding, although we've been pushed back in a few areas'. It was much worse than that, but he did not want to depress Simon unnecessarily. 'In the South the Allies have taken Rome, but they're not making as much progress as they'd like. We should be able to stop them along the Appenines. In the West they landed in Normandy in reasonable strength. For the moment, Rommel is managing to contain them – just about. OKH feel that this is but a feint. They're convinced that the real landing will still occur in the Pas de Calais area. Why? Because all the intelligence reports, yours included, all indicate that this area is where the main invasion will occur. And again, according to the bulk of our intelligence, the Allies still have thirty or forty enemy divisions on their order of battle in England. There's another thing- we have yet to hear where the American general Patton is. OKH regard him as the foremost Allied general, far more aggressive and dangerous than Montgomery. They suspect he will lead the second invasion, in the Calais area, sometime soon. Maybe in the next week or two. So the Fifteenth Army and all its reserves are standing by, waiting for this new landing. None of its divisions have moved to Normandy.'

'What do you think, sir?'

Schellenberg shrugged noncommittally. 'Me, I don't know. I'm not a soldier, I'm a spy. I still suspect that all of what we're mixed up in, including yourself, is part of a huge deception operation, and with MI6 at the bottom of it. The 'Rothermere' report is genuine, as far as I can tell, in terms of the correct number of divisions the Allies have. I very much doubt that Patton has got another huge army or two in England ready to strike elsewhere.' He smiled ruefully. 'The trouble is, nobody else believes me.' He quickly glanced at the door. He could hear Mobius' voice outside.

'That's enough for now. I'll see you later today.' With that, he swept out of the room.

❁

Simon gratefully closed his eyes. The debriefing was tiring enough, and he was glad that Schellenberg did not ask any more questions. Did his boss suspect that Simon had lied? That was the one redeeming feature of operating on your own in enemy territory. It was highly unlikely that Schellenberg would be able to confirm or refute the details of his story. Who else would be able to contact to corroborate Simon's version of events? Not Simms. He was behind bars now, residing somewhere at His Majesty's leisure. For a very long time.

The fake firing squad was just another of one of Menzies' little perverse jokes, a trick to reinforce Simon's absolute dependence on the MI6 chief's largesse. That and the sleep deprivation period was only a minor foretaste of how rough things could get. Afterwards, over a healing gin back in the house, Menzies had given him a stark choice - work for MI6 as a double agent, or experience the real thing. All the guards were issued with blanks for the firing squad detail, but that could easily change. There were other inducements as well.

'We can quite easily arrange for the wrong information to be delivered into Himmler's hands. Provide certain facts about your father - and Canaris in particular - that could prove very damaging indeed. I think Himmler would take a rather dim view of the sort of revelations I have in mind.' Menzies murmured, then he waited for a few moments, all the while watching the younger man's face, ready to detect any weakness. 'There is also one final item that you may find just as persuasive, perhaps even more so.' His expression was remote, detached.

'What's that?'

'The suit you were wearing when you were apprehended. It has a label on the inside. It was from a tailor in Saville Row. I should know - I use the same one myself. After that, it was an easy matter to track down the former owner - or, in this case, his widow...' Menzies had left the rest unspoken, but the veiled threat was obvious. A look of dismay flitted across Simon's face for a brief moment, before he was able to compose his features. Once again, his life was being directed by others, and there was nothing he could do about it. He rapidly made up his mind.

'It seems that I have no option but to work for you,' Simon said resignedly. 'But this is a one-sided agreement. I think it only fair that in return for my services you give me an undertaking that you will leave that lady alone. The same applies to my father and Canaris. After all, I did cooperate voluntarily.'

The answer was abrupt, and chilling in its finality. 'We would have got that information out of you sooner or later. Nobody resists prolonged interrogation of that sort. You know that just as well as we do.' Menzies studied him, then paused for a while, as if he was struggling to make up his mind. 'Alright, I'll accept what you say. But bear in mind what I can do. I have no wish to compromise the work your father and Canaris have done. Nor do I wish to punish anyone, man or woman, without just cause.' He looked at Simon for a long time, then smiled. 'I think you're an honourable man. So am I, in spite of what you may think. Just remember who you're working for now.'

The arrangement was concluded. Simon would return to Germany. That evening they would travel back to Hanwell, arrest Simms, 'repair' the transmitter and use it to send the fake message back to Schellenberg, and arrange the return journey. It would all be under the closest of MI6 scrutiny of course. And on his return he would be contacted. Who that person or persons would be was not revealed, but the recognition passwords and phrases were drummed into him. Depending on his duties, at some stage in the future, he would be called on to pass on information that could be beneficial to the Allies. There might be other tasks, too, but again they were left unsaid.

Finally, before sleep took him, he wondered, as he had often done before, just how many agents did Menzies have inside Germany? Who were they, and at what level did they operate? He chuckled grimly to himself. After all, he was hardly in a fit state to pass information back to England, nor would he be able to for at least six months. Then a sudden anxiety gripped him—would Menzies keep his word? Would his MI6 agents be able to find out where he was, and report back his condition? There was nothing he could do about it, so why worry. With that his eyes became heavy and shortly afterwards the mantle of sleep washed over his senses.

The Wolfsschanze, Rastenburg forest, East Prussia 1305 20/7/1944

Oberst Graf Claus von Stauffenberg sat attentively in his car and watched while the Führer and the rest of his entourage walked out from the main bunker complex and along a path into a nearby wooden hut. He cursed his misfortune bitterly, but quietly and to himself. This was his fourth journey in the last few weeks to Hitler's field HQ. Each time he had travelled with a bomb hidden inside his private brief case. The other three visits had been aborted for a variety of reasons. Today would almost certainly be his last chance. If he did not act now, then the incipient military disasters that threatened to collapse both the Eastern and Western fronts would weaken any bargaining position that a new German government might gain.

The first piece of bad luck was that two of his intended targets were absent, busy elsewhere on duties of their own. The whole point of the assassination plot was to deprive Nazi Germany of all her top leadership at one stroke, seize control of the essential organs of government using units loyal to the plotters, and change the course of the war by negotiating a peace with the West. Where were Himmler and Goering? Both of them had their own private armies, but it was Himmler's SS that the plotters were most concerned about. The SS would be most likely to act the quickest in protecting their Führer in case of an emergency. Still, he grumbled to himself, if it had to be Hitler alone, then that hopefully should be enough. Stauffenberg had plenty of loyal fellow officers and government officials scattered across Europe who were opposed to the Nazis and longed to be rid of them. These men would act on the secret code signal to disarm and arrest supporters of the Führer. In addition, local Wehrmacht units would neutralize their SS counterparts in the field. The Gestapo would be hunted down and imprisoned, to await a suitable fate. That should be enough to win the day and change history.

However, the absence of Himmler and Goering was not the only thing that made him swear. Instead of the normal concrete bunker today's conference was being held inside a temporary, flimsier structure. If the bomb was to have exploded inside the usual conference room, then everybody at the scene would be dead - instantly, smashed to pulp by the reverberating shock waves reflected off the concrete walls. But for some unknown reason the Führer's bunker was undergoing repairs today and this hut would have to serve as a one-off change of venue. To make matters worse the day was hot, and the heat was amplified by the dark, oppressive woods that surrounded the complex. Someone had thrown open the windows to provide extra cooling and ventilation. Stauffenberg, with his trained soldier's eye, suspected that the combination of the wooden hut and open windows would diminish the effect of the blast, but there was nothing he could do about that. The trick would be to get the briefcase as close to Hitler as possible. The subsequent explosion should take care of every other detail.

He looked at his watch. Time ticked past slowly. He would give it another five minutes, more than enough for the conference to get going. Then he would slip quietly in, place his brief case as close as possible to where the Führer was speaking, and make a suitable exit. The fuse would give him a few minutes to make his excuses and get clear. His heart began to race; he trembled with excitement, the adrenaline surging through his body. The palm of his left hand became moist as he perspired, and not just from the early afternoon heat. He had seen more than his share of combat and although he was well used to the stress of battle the situation he was in now was tenser than anything he had ever experienced before. After all he was about to kill Hitler and most of the top generals at OKH - all in a single blow. Hopefully he would save his country from utter destruction and rid the world of a deranged menace at the same time. A few deep breaths would help to calm his nerves.

It was ten past one, his watch told him. It was time to arm the bomb, fused to explode in five minutes - giving enough time to get in and out. Stauffenberg made a rapid, furtive scan of the surrounding area. Good - nobody was watching. He lifted the brief case up in his left hand, bent forward and pulled the fuse pin out with his teeth. He would have used his right hand, but that was not possible. The explosion in Tunisia over a year ago had robbed him of his right arm, right eye and two fingers of his left hand. It had taken him nearly nine months to recover from his wounds, and he knew he would never again be judged fit enough to serve in the field. And if, for whatever reason, he would die today, then at least it would be for a worthy cause. Someday his wife and his four children might understand.

As soon as Stauffenberg armed the bomb he got out of his car and walked over to the wooden hut, entering through the open main door. The room was dominated by a large, chunky oak table, supported not by four legs but by a central thick block of wood. Stout beams ran off to each corner. Most of the participants had gathered on one side, the better able to see the maps that were spread out across the top, depicting the latest situation reports on critical sectors of the Eastern front. Even from where he stood he could make out the seriousness of the situation - large, thick red arrows denoted the latest advances made by the Soviets, casually brushing past the German dispositions, thinner marks depicted in blue. Hitler was speaking. The angry rash of enemy markings seemed to match the Führer's mood. He was evidently unimpressed with the defensive efforts made by all the forces in the East and made his feelings quite clear to all present, gesticulating and shouting in an impetuous, irritated manner.

Stauffenberg knew from past experience that this could go on for quite some time. Quietly he moved around the table and took up a position not far from the door. After a few minutes of listening to Hitler's harangue, he moved his briefcase off the table and onto the floor, pushing it as far as he could in the direction of the Führer.

Stauffenberg turned towards his neighbour. It was Brandt, deputy to the Chief of OKH's Operations Staff. 'Excuse me,' he whispered. 'I must go and use the telephone. Keep an eye on my brief case. There are secret papers inside.'

Brandt nodded. Stauffenberg quietly made his exit and walked away from the hut. He had gone no more than sixty metres when there was a sudden blast that almost knocked him off his feet. Looking back all that he could see of the hut was a dense cloud of smoke and dust. Debris flew all over the area, some of it landing near him. The destruction looked impressive. Nobody could possibly have survived that explosion. Without waiting to assess how successful the bomb had been, he turned away and hurried quickly back to his car. He needed to get back to Berlin and help set the revolt in motion. As he drove off nobody paid him the slightest attention. All the guards were running towards where the hut had been, still shrouded in smoke and dust. There was only the guard post at the gate four kilometers away to get through, and then he would be at the airfield. He hoped that Fellgiebel, Hitler's personal Signals Officer and the only conspirator on Hitler's personal staff, would perform his part of the job properly and send off the code word 'Valkyrie'- the signal that Hitler was dead. If so, by the time his plane reached Berlin the revolt would be in full swing and the Nazis would soon be history.

The Wolfsschanze 2100 21/7/1944

Hitler sat slumped in a comfortable leather sofa. He looked pale and tired. The events of the last two days were exhausting enough, but at least the revolt had been put down, and the Nazi domination of the Reich remained unchanged. All the leading conspirators, those that they knew about, were caught. Most of them, including von Stauffenberg, were dead. They had all been summarily executed by firing squads. Some of those who had ordered the immediate shootings were now being questioned themselves. Himmler had suspected that a certain number of killings were ordered just a little bit too quickly for his liking. The Reichsführer had been denied the opportunity to extract information under prolonged and heightened interrogation, as he liked to put it. Now the main task ahead was to root out all the conspirators' accomplices, no matter where they were- in the Wehrmacht, and at all levels of government. Nobody would get away. After all, Hitler was the embodiment of Nazi Germany. To strike at him was to strike at the state and all it stood for. It was an absolutely unforgivable crime, for which there could only be one penalty.

The euphoria at having survived the explosion had long since gone. What remained was a cold, implacable anger. Although the circle of leading conspirators was now known to be small, no one could be sure of how far the roots of the conspiracy had spread. He needed to take measures to ensure that absolute loyalty to the Nazi cause was the order of the day, at all levels of life throughout the Reich. He had already spoken to Goering and Goebbels. They were summoned to attend instantly. Both were given extensions to their already wide powers. Total obedience to the war effort must be the order of the day throughout every facet of life in the Reich- from this time on, and with no exceptions. And now Himmler, the most important of his top three aides, was sat in front of him awaiting his orders.

'Thank you for coming, Heinrich', he began wearily. 'I apologise for the delay in seeing you, but there have been so many matters to take care of since the events of yesterday. First, though, I want a report on what happened in Berlin, and your activities in the last twenty four hours.'

'Certainly Führer. But first let me congratulate you on your good fortune.'

Himmler hoped that he would strike the appropriately fervent note. 'I thank God that divine providence shielded you from the blast and foiled those malicious and irresponsible conspirators. It must be a sign from on high, considering how minor your injuries are.' A few bruises, grazes and cuts, nothing worse than that. And the tremor that had affected Hitler's left arm and leg over the last year seemed to have disappeared.

'Yes, thank you.' Hitler smiled wearily. He had heard this countless times

in the last day, most notably from Goering and Goebbels. They'd all said the same thing, almost parrot-fashion. It was proof, if any was needed, that God must surely be keeping an eye on the fortunes of the Reich. He was on *their* side; definitely against the godless Communists and the decadent West.

'Some of my forensic men have had the chance to sift through the remains of the conference room,' Himmler continued. 'It seems you were saved by three things. First, most of the blast was deflected and absorbed by that heavy oak table, and in particular the wooden beams that supported it. It was another example of fine Reich workmanship if I may say so Führer.' He smiled unctuously. 'And to consider that you were only standing six feet away from where the bomb went off...Also, the doors and windows were open in view of the heat. Finally, the walls of the building gave way under the force of the blast. All these factors led to your survival. I shudder to think about what would have happened had the conference taken place in the usual location.'

'Yes so do I.' Hitler grimaced, then softened his features. 'Your report, if you please.'

Himmler began by detailing a chronological record of events in Berlin and all the major European capitals in the last twenty-four hours and concluded with a summary of the main points. 'We have apprehended all the plotters that are known to us so far. They are either dead or undergoing further intensive interrogation at Prinz Albrecht Strasse as we speak. They will not resist our efforts, Führer.'

'Good. We must get to the bottom of this, and find out just how far this conspiracy has spread. In addition to your other duties as Reichsführer SS, Chief of Police and Minister of the Interior, I now appoint you as Commander-in-Chief of the Home Army. This will place you in charge of all interior military and police forces inside the Reich. With these powers, I want you to be utterly ruthless in exposing and bringing to trial all those who have any association, in any way, with the attempted assassination. Set up People's Courts to try their cases in public. They must be discredited and punished severely, as must their families. The law of *Sippenhaft* must apply. I know you will spare no effort in your customary zeal to hunt these traitors down.'

'Yes, my Führer.' Himmler beamed. This was excellent news. At one stroke he had become the second most powerful man in the Reich, far more powerful than those other two toadies, Goering and Goebbels. His personal power had now become awesome. And should anything happen to Hitler, well...

'I want you to concentrate particularly on the Wehrmacht,' Hitler continued, sitting up and raising his voice. 'The conspirators would not have been able to get far without significant involvement of senior Army figures with enough power to disarm SS police units and fighting formations. I have always suspected that some of our generals are not totally committed to our cause. This is now our chance to root them out, once and for all, in the way we National Socialists are accustomed to.'

Himmler nodded diligently. It was a feeling he had shared with his leader for some time. The Army had always regarded the Nazis as second rate, political upstarts and lower-class guttersnipes. That would change. He would no doubt enjoy wiping the condescending smiles off their snobbish, patrician faces and watch some of them spit blood and teeth out on the cellar floors in Prinz Albrecht Strasse. Himmler clearly understood the hidden reference in the last part of the Führer's instructions - he was referring to the Night of the Long Knives, Hitler's purge back in June 1934. Ernst Röhm and other senior members of his upstart SA organization had become too self-important and dangerous to be allowed to carry on existing. All of them were ruthlessly eliminated in a single night's orgy of extreme violence. A similar fate would apply now, no matter how senior these figures were, no matter how tenuous the link to the plotters. And if there weren't any links then so much the better. He had in mind a few individuals who could quite easily be arrested on the flimsiest of excuses...

Himmler was well aware how desperate their situation was. The war on the Eastern and Western fronts and in Italy was not going well. Drastic action needed to be taken to ensure the absolute loyalty of all those who defended the frontiers of the Reich and this was a heaven-sent opportunity to do so. From now on the Army would bow to the will of the Nazi Party. He also remembered his secret bio-weapons project. The V rockets had not proved to be the war winning weapons that Hitler had dreamed they would be - at least, not so far. But if his biological agents could be mounted inside them, then perhaps that might swing the balance in favour of Germany...

❖

Between Cintheaux and St Aignan de Cramesnil, Normandy 1225 8/8/1944

Hofheinz stared out at the view in front of him, slowly scanning the horizon. From where he sat in the turret of his Tiger he could clearly see the terrain spread out, as flat as a pancake in all directions. Over to his left, no more than a few hundred meters away, lay the Falaise to Caen highway, shielded by some trees. Up ahead in the distance he could see a few small buildings on the other side of the highway, the village of Gaumesnil. The dusty road ran straight as an arrow almost due north. To his right the gently rolling open farmland stretched out into the hazy distance, villages basking in the glorious sunshine of a late summer's day, cornfields ripe with grain. In the foreground several buildings clustered around a small farm that indicated where the tiny hamlet of Robertmesnil lay. It all looked so peaceful, a beautiful setting for a landscape by one of those French impressionists - he could never remember which one. But equally he knew that appearances could be very deceptive, especially with regard to hidden danger. To his north, that was where trouble lay. That was where the enemy positions were thought to be, but nobody was completely sure. There were some reports of Canadian armour beyond the road, over to the west, but he could see nothing from where his Tiger sat. The orchards and copses that surrounded the strung-out villages of Cramesnil and St Aignan de Cramesnil looked peaceful enough, devoid of any signs of the enemy, even after a careful, thorough examination of the area using his high-powered binoculars. If the reports were correct the area was only loosely held by Scottish infantry, with possibly a few tanks in support - nothing that would cause too much trouble for the Tigers of the 101st Schwere Panzer Abteilung, and their 12th SS Panzer comrades.

The unwelcome news they'd received during the night was that the British and Canadians had broken through the front line defences, roughly eight kilometers north of where his unit lay in reserve. They had decided to attack under the cover of darkness a most daring and unexpected event, something that the cautious and conservative British general Montgomery was not noted for doing. Despite the inherent difficulties of attacking in darkness it seemed to have worked brilliantly. The British had smashed southwards through the 89th Infantry Division's defences, leaving most of its sub-units in tatters. Not only had the division been overwhelmed by a powerful armoured attack, but it had also been devastated by a cataclysmic artillery barrage and heavy aerial bombardment. As a result the 89th had virtually ceased to exist as a fighting formation, with some of its survivors streaming to the rear in complete disarray. The unexpected nighttime attack had caused a panic in the German defences that blocked the route to Falaise, and beyond that, Paris.

The 101st, and with it what was left of the 12th SS Panzer Division, were positioned directly behind the 89th's front lines in case of just such an event. But all that had changed with the American attack further to the west. Two weeks ago Bradley's troops had burst their way through 7th Army's positions and driven southwest to reach the coast at Avranches. This was a critical development, threatening not just the whole of Brittany but also a sweeping encirclement towards Le Mans and into the rear of both German armies fighting in Normandy. If the front lines were not restored and the Americans stopped then it would mean the end of the defence of France and quite possibly the war itself. There would be nothing left between here and the western border of the Reich to stop the Allied advance. This was the reason why both units had received orders late yesterday evening to move west, in preparation for an attack to retake Avranches and cut off the Americans.

But Montgomery's overnight attack had taken everyone by surprise and threatened a catastrophic breakthrough of its own, away from the main threat in the west. Fifth Panzer Army had acted fast. The 101st and 12th SS were hastily turned around and forced to make a laborious and dangerous journey back to their previous positions. Other units further west would have to stop the Americans. Everyone hated travelling at night, but it was the only safe way. Sleep could wait for another time. Daylight movement along roads was a certain invitation to be hammered by the enemy air forces. The Luftwaffe, despite all of Goering's promises, was still nowhere to be seen.

It had taken them the remaining hours of the night and most of the morning to turn around and retrace their route back to where they had been based yesterday. Luckily the early morning haze had masked their movement and kept the enemy fighter-bombers away. Even so, several Tigers had overheated their engines and broken down. Most of those had to be dragged off to the battalion repair workshops, hidden in the woods just north of Potigny. The remainder, including his own Tiger, had just reached the forward positions of Sturmbannführer Waldmüller's 25th SS Panzergrenadier regiment, the advance guard of the 12th SS Panzer. The rest of the division was probably another half hour or more behind them, struggling north along cross-country routes and heavily camouflaged to avoid enemy air detection. The eight Tigers that were immediately available were now partly concealed behind a tall thick hedge, at best a temporary cover. As far as anyone knew there were very few, if any, friendly troops to their front. Nothing substantial was ahead of them except the enemy.

A heavy droning noise made him look up. Towards the north he could see an enemy fighter-bomber approaching, circling as it spied out the land. After a few minutes of this, it began to drop coloured flares close by. Suddenly his headphones crackled. It was the boyish voice of Michael Wittmann.

'Listen in, everybody. I've just been speaking to Oberführer Meyer.' Hofheinz's ears pricked up. *Christ! It must be really serious with Meyer up at the front line.* The irrepressible commander of the 12th SS was a highly decorated veteran who never shirked danger and who could always be found in the midst of a crisis, wherever it was located. He had an uncanny nose for trouble and could detect it no matter where it was.

'We're not going to wait for the rest of 12th SS to catch up - we're going to attack now,' Wittmann continued. 'I take it that everybody has just seen the flares dropped by that enemy plane?

Oberführer Meyer assures me that in a few minutes this area is going to subjected to heavy bombing. This is a standard Allied tactic which he's seen many times before. In his words, we need to get off our arses, move out of the bomb zone and attack now!' If they stayed where they were they could easily become targets for the bombers. Even a heavy tank like the Tiger could not withstand that sort of punishment.

'Dollinger will lead the way in right echelon formation, with Iriohn second and Kisters third. Höflinger, you take the Caen-Falaise road, and keep von Westernhagen on your left. The two of you will cover us from that direction. I'll be in the command Tiger just inside the line of advance. Heurich and Hofheinz will act as a reserve and bring up the rear.' He hesitated for a moment, and then continued. 'Everybody clear on our formation?'

He was answered by a series of clicks over the external circuit.

'Good....Keep an eye out on those woods over to our right. I'm betting that there might be some enemy dug in over there. Let's go. Panzers, march!'

The rumble of tank engines grew louder as they prepared to move off. Clouds of dust suddenly appeared, partially blocking the view forwards, as the treads ground their way over the dry terrain. Hofheinz shielded his eyes and waited for the seven Tigers in front of him to manoeuvre their way and smash through the cover of the tall hedge that shielded them from enemy eyes.

He was a little concerned about the command situation. Wittmann had only recently been nominated as a troop commander of the 101st, and while he was a brilliant and highly decorated officer with well over a hundred 'kills' in armoured warfare to his credit, he was still somewhat inexperienced in commanding larger formations. Hofheinz also knew that Wittmann was using Tiger number 007, a command tank, which carried more radio equipment and less ammunition, something that Wittmann disliked. The orders were decisive enough, but Hofheinz thought he could detect a hint of nervousness in his commander's voice, as if his leader was not quite entirely sure of what he should do in the current situation. His tactics might work in the broad expanses of Russia but this was Normandy, with plenty of close cover that could hide hostile anti-tank batteries and enemy tanks easily enough. Maybe it was the loneliness of command, but for some ill-defined reason Hofheinz could not help but feel a little uneasy about Wittmann's decision to advance so boldly into the unknown. Where was their infantry support?

The lead Tigers were now further away, advancing on a course alongside the main road. Heurich was over to his right. After a half a minute or so he gave the order to advance. Wiese, the driver, gunned the engine into life and the heavy tank ground forward with a jerk. As the Tigers left the cover of the hedgerow they had been sheltering behind an artillery barrage started to impact on the cornfields up ahead of them, up around the villages of Cramesnil and St Aignan. Almost by coincidence heavy guns to his rear began to open up, pounding the same area. The thunder of heavy explosions rent the air, mixed with the whistle and scream of shells as they arched over their advance. Smoke and dust rose in dense clouds, mixed with the burning corn. Hofheinz shrank lower into his commander's seat. He was safe enough inside his tank, but the same could not be said any scattered Panzergrenadiers lying up there, hidden in the wavy corn. *Poor bastards.* He hoped for their own sakes that they had dug in deeply enough.

As the Tiger moved forward Hofheinz spotted the two senior officers, Meyer and Waldmüller, hiding in a ditch near the side of the main road. Ignoring the danger Meyer stood up and waved cheerily as the Tigers passed by, a big grin on his face. Hofheinz found it impossible to make out the words of encouragement Meyer was shouting above the noise of the explosions, but he did not need to be a lip-reader to understand the sentiment behind the expression - *hit them fast and hit them hard, and don't piss about!* Meyer was the very personification of the old adage: positive action, today, not tomorrow or some other time.

Hofheinz fervently hoped that the enemy was unaware of what was about to smash into them.

The woods and orchards to his right slowly drew closer. They had gone no more than three hundred meters when Wittmann gave the order to button up, and engage some tanks he had spotted on the other side of the road. Hofheinz could not see what they were shooting at from where his tank sat at the rear of the formation, but he estimated the distance to be well over a thousand meters. A few explosions later and billows of smoke started to rise, but from where he was sitting he could not make out the targets. *Probably enemy Sherman tanks. They're no match for us at long range.* The lead Tigers set off again. Soon Wittmann was back on the command circuit. He reminded them to keep an eye out to the right, where he suspected the most danger would come from. No sooner had he said that when Wiese came through on the internal circuit.

'Sorry sir, but the motor's overheating again. We've got to stop and let her cool down - otherwise all you'll have is a fused block of metal instead of an engine.'

Hofheinz swore to himself, and slid lower down into the turret. He could smell burning. The ventilators were struggling to keep the air breathable inside the tank. He could just make out the temperature dial on the driver's bulkhead- the needle was deep into the red zone.

'All right, driver, stop the tank, but keep the engine ticking over. Let her cool down for a few minutes. Peters, help me get the engine covers up at the back- it might help.' Duly he reported in on the command circuit, and Wittmann clicked back in return. The 101st company commander was far too busy observing the battlefield in front of him to bother with a verbal reply.

Hofheinz and his gunner quickly exited the turret hatches and began to work on the back of the tank. As they started to raise the heavy steel covers up, the throbbing beat of aircraft engines grew louder and louder, distracting him from his task. Soon he could make out the massed formations flying directly his way, their silver fuselages flickering and glinting in the sunlight. The aerial armada flew straight on, directly over their positions and onwards, further towards the rear. A few bursts of black smoke burst among the formations, but the anti-aircraft fire was not enough to disturb or deflect the menace of their approach. Almost immediately clusters of tiny dots became visible beneath them, as a multitude of bombs sped earthwards. With a tremendous roar the ground shook as the bomb carpets opened up, dwarfing the effects of the artillery barrage. The view to the far south soon became almost completely obscured by massive pillars of smoke and spurts of flame. Dust rose in huge clouds. The sky turned black. Even from where he stood it was a terrifyingly impressive spectacle, awesome in its destructive power.

'Thank God we're not trying to live through that lot.' He breathed a sigh of relief, glancing over at Peters. The gunner was open-mouthed and wide-eyed in fear and awe as he gazed at the distant explosions. Hofheinz chuckled grimly. 'The only good news is that I think they've missed. If they were trying to smash our little grenadier friends from the 12th then they were at least a kilometer too far to the south.'

Peters slowly nodded, still in the grip of what he had just witnessed. Hofheinz had to nudge him to get his eyes off the view south and get him back on the job. As soon as they finished they jumped back into the tank and waited for the engine to begin cooling down to a manageable level. Hofheinz sat up in the turret and watched as the remaining six Tigers moved further and further away. Some of them had stopped again, briefly to engage a few more targets, but as before he could not make out the results. A quick glance at his watch told him it was 1240.

Suddenly he noticed a flash from his right, over from the orchards near St Aignan. Shortly afterwards there was another flash, and then several more. Up ahead the Tiger nearest to the woods began to burn. As soon as the others noticed this their turrets began to turn to the right and open fire.

It was impossible to tell the results of the return fire, but more and more flashes appeared along the dark margins of the trees. There were also rapid flashes to the front, from the village of Cramesnil. Soon a second Tiger, probably Kisters', began to burn. Dollinger's vehicle began to turn around in circles in the confusion of the melee. Hofheinz guessed it was either running gear damage or a smashed commander's periscope. Then suddenly, further off to the left from across the highway, more flashes lit up the afternoon as hidden guns fired on the Tigers from an unexpected direction. It was a trap! He grabbed his headset and clicked on the command circuit, desperate to try and get them out of there. 'This is Hofheinz. Get back! Fall back now! Enemy guns are firing on both sides of the road and directly to your front. You're heading straight into a lethal crossfire. Pull back! Pull back!'

It was too late. Wittmann's Tiger suddenly seemed to lurch to the left, and the turret jerked around to lie at an odd angle on the hull. Another explosion and Höflinger's tank sat burning on the Caen highway. The last two Tigers, those belonging to Heurich and von Westernhagen, had by this time turned about and were retreating back towards his position, their guns pointing directly over the stern of each tank and firing as they moved away from the ambush.

He sat there in shock, tears of rage and frustration in his eyes. Five precious Tigers destroyed in less than ten minutes. The heart of his unit had just been ripped out, and lay bleeding and blackened amongst the burning corn. Another explosion rent the air, momentarily distracting him. Out of the corner of his eye he spotted the turret from where Wittmann's Tiger lay smouldering. It span lazily through the air and landed with a heavy thud alongside the smoking hull.

The surviving Tigers were drawing closer. It was time to retreat. He clicked on the internal circuit. "Wiese, get us in gear. We're pulling back. Don't tell me about the engine,' he spoke quietly, through gritted teeth. 'Just try and coax her back a few hundred meters back to where we were before.'

The Tiger's engine started up with a groan. Hofheinz looked north back at where the five burning tanks lay, his vision blurred and misted over. The image would forever be printed indelibly on his mind. He doubted there would be many survivors - almost certainly none from Wittmann's tank, and the others would probably be much the same. As the tank began to move, he suddenly thought of Max Simon. Where was he now? It would grieve him deeply to know that so many troopers and NCO's he knew so well had found death in such an abrupt and brutal fashion. Yes, it was a fate all panzer men knew could happen. If any tank could be regarded as being indestructible, then it was the Tiger...But even so, the rapidity still shocked him to the core.

Hill 140 area, between Estrées-la-Campagne and Assy, 0805 9/8/1944

'Easy boys, let him get a little closer.' They were holed up at the edge of a spinney. Looking out to the northwest, a large village partly blocked the view back from where they had travelled overnight. The rest of the distant panorama was obscured, shimmering vaguely in the morning mist. The sun was over to the west, still climbing on its way up into the sky, a blurred ball of liquid fire.

The vehicle they were tracking was moving towards the east, bouncing its way along a rough track that crossed at right angles to where they lay hidden. It looked very similar to the one they had fired upon earlier that morning from a different position, but with little success. Perhaps this time if they let the vehicle come closer they would have a better chance of a kill.

'Looks like one of those armoured half-tracks they use for reconnaissance missions,' Second Lieutenant Dick Booth observed, tensely. The camouflaged vehicle was throwing up a huge cloud of dust. Normally such a lack of caution would almost certainly have signed its own death warrant, but the heavy golden haze had yet to burn off, and rocket-firing Typhoons of the RAF were yet to get airborne and range the battlefield. Booth placed his hand on the PIAT gunner's shoulder, as if to steady the man and keep him from pulling the trigger prematurely.

'Just a little more...Easy...Wait for my call,' he whispered in the man's ear. The mottled yellow-green enemy vehicle shifted slightly in its path, bringing it even closer to where the small band of Canadian infantry were lying in wait, hidden amongst the trees and undergrowth that bordered the small wood. At its nearest point it would pass no more than fifty yards away from where his men lay in wait. As yet there was no sign that they had been observed. The heavy machine gun, mounted directly above the driving compartment, was still tracking straight ahead. Booth could see three soldiers in the rear of the vehicle. One of them was manning the gun.

'The rest of you, aim for the gunner and his mates. Get your retaliation in first.'

Closer, closer...The men, most of them combat veterans, could be relied on to wait for the signal and keep their fire discipline. The Germans were almost within optimum firing range. Just another few seconds...

'Fire!' Private Fred Rousseau pulled the trigger. The rocket shell streaked away, swiftly looping up and down, and slammed into the enemy vehicle just in front of the armoured driving compartment. A loud bang shook the air, and a cloud of smoke and flame temporarily obscured the front from view. A fusillade of rifle and machine-gun fire swept the armoured sides and gun shield, ricocheting away into the skies, but enough bullets went home to ensure the gunner would never fire again. Booth leapt to his feet and stormed forward, pistol at the ready. A dozen infantrymen ran after him, loosing off a hail of shots as they neared the stricken motor.

There was no reply from the enemy. He ran up to where the armoured car lay smoking and burning. The driver slumped forwards, dead behind the wheel. The co-driver was only partly conscious, and sat tilted sideways towards the far side of the compartment. A bullet had creased the right side of his skull, and blood was running down his face, soaking his camouflage smock. A shout from the back of the vehicle distracted Booth. He hurried around to where the rest of his troopers stood. Two Germans lay dead on the floor of the rear-fighting compartment. A third was stretched out on the dusty track. He must have been thrown out by the force of the explosion, and lay holding his right arm gingerly. It was bent into an abnormal position.

'Sir, what shall we do with him?' Several of his men edged closer, weapons still cocked. It was not difficult to gauge the look on their drawn, unshaven features. One of them pulled out a bayonet and held it idly, a grim, sardonic smile on his face.

'Put that away, Wilkinson. You're frightening the life out of him.' Booth spoke lightly, but he was worried. His men were sometimes difficult to control, more so in the heat of battle and especially if they were up against the 12th SS. The man lying in the dust in front of him looked to be from that division, judging by the type of uniform he wore and the rank lapel on his camouflage jacket. The sewn-on cuff around the bottom of his left jacket sleeve provided the final clue. The words 'Hitler Jugend' could clearly be seen in white boldly scripted in a Gothic font.

A muttered growl came from some of the men standing further away. One of them shouted angrily. 'He's one of those murdering bastards from the SS. Remember what happened to the Winnipegs at Audrieu and the massacre at the Ardenne Abbey!' His outburst was rewarded by several cries of agreement from a few of the others. 'Let's do him now!' Some of the men moved closer still. The tension in the air was palpable.

'Knock it off. Now! That's an order. Ease springs!' Booth shouted. 'He's an officer, dammit, and standing orders state very clearly that all enemy officers, no matter what formation they come from, are held for further questioning. Do I make myself clear?' Booth glared angrily at them, and moved to place himself between the more rebellious of his men and the injured German. He still held his pistol in his right hand.

'Sar'nt Garièpy!

'Sir', the reply was instant..

'Get your men back to their positions, now. I'm taking this prisoner to the CO for further questioning. Get the MO to have a look at that wounded co-driver. In the meantime, take over in my absence and deploy the rest of the platoon for all round defence. Detail one of your men to accompany me and keep an eye on this German.'

'Yes sir.' Garièpy sprang to attention, an impassive look on his face, and started to boss the men back to their foxholes. At least he could rely on the platoon sergeant. Several loud clicks rang out as weapons were un-cocked and made safe. The group broke up slowly and began to march back to the edge of the copse but not without a few mutters and angry looks directed both at him and the prisoner.

Booth breathed a sigh of relief as he watched them depart. The men were still angry and confused. They were all exhausted before the start of yesterday's mission, and the subsequent night march had tired them out even more so. To make matters worse, nobody was exactly sure of their current position. They were supposed to be on Hill 195, but Booth wasn't so convinced. He was unable to orientate his map to the topographical features around him and the haze was not exactly helpful either, obscuring much of the surrounding terrain. Hopefully his commanding officer would be able to make more sense out of the mess they were in and find out their true location.

'Monk, cover him.' The soldier moved a few feet to one side to guarantee an unobstructed line of sight, and held his rifle at the ready. Booth leaned forward and offered his left hand to the German, who grasped it and pulled himself upright.

'Sprechen-zie Englisch?'

The German nodded, still shocked from the explosion that had destroyed the half-track. 'A little. Thank you.' He spoke with a marked accent. From the look on his face it was quite clear that he had understood most if not all of what had just happened.

Booth eyed him warily. 'Don't thank me yet. The day is still young. Follow me.'

Lieutenant-Colonel Donald Worthington, the commanding officer of 'Worthington Force', as his battle group had come to be known, was tired, irritated and above all frustrated, and all at the same time. The mystery of their current location had yet to be solved. Where exactly were they? None of the officers in his headquarters section had demonstrated conclusively, and to his complete satisfaction, the exact position on the map that his force occupied. This was not Hill 195. Somehow their overnight navigation had gone awry. What was just as worrying was the sound of tank motors coming from the valley beyond and below him. They were highly unlikely to be friendly. His force of Canadians had been spotted, and the enemy was on the move. That much was certain, but where was his follow-up support?

New orders had reached him just after midnight. Worthington's command, the 28th Canadian Armoured Regiment, otherwise known as the British Columbia Regiment, would be merged in with additional infantry and other armoured support from the Algonquins, a sister regiment of the same division. The plan called for this composite battle group to make a surprise attack through enemy lines under the cover of darkness. It was almost an exact repetition of the previous night's attacks, but on a much smaller scale. Once a breakthrough was achieved his force would head across country to take the commanding hill top position at Hill 195. This feature dominated the surrounding countryside, and was only six miles north of Falaise, the next big objective. By bursting through the enemy lines and seizing this vital height his superiors hoped to continue the momentum of their recent attacks. The German defences would be prised open and the route to the southeast would be unblocked. Other Allied forces, attacking at daybreak, would then break through to back him up. The Americans were rapidly approaching from the south, and if all went well then the two pincers would meet somewhere between Falaise and Argentan, and bag two German armies in the process.

But all had not gone well. The 'best laid plans of mice and men' echoed dimly in his mind. Navigating in the dark was tricky in the extreme, and enemy resistance had not made life any easier. Somewhere along the route Jack Carson, the officer in charge of B Squadron and leading the attack, must have taken a wrong turn. In the early light of dawn, the rising hill mass in front of him would have looked much like their planned objective. However, now that they were here, Worthington had a strong suspicion that they were nowhere near where they should have been. The local terrain simply did not match up to where he thought their presumed position was.

Half an hour ago, events out of his control had forced him to react and play his hand. In response to the enemy movement coming from the valley beyond, Worthington had sent three troops of Shermans to the small wood he could just see over the brow of the hill on which he stood. According to the map the

French had named it 'Les Trentes Acres', Thirty Acres Wood for some unknown reason, despite it being nowhere near that big in size. Maybe it was the size of the field it stood in. It lay five hundred meters to the southeast from where he now stood. Twelve tanks in all, the Shermans were to mount guard and cover the approaches from the area of the Laison valley, where the enemy reserve was thought to be hidden. They would form part of his forward defences, a trip wire in case the Germans mounted a sudden attack.

He stood in front of the prisoner, eyeing him carefully. An officer from the SS was a rare catch. What should he do with him? So far, the man had only given his name, rank and number, strictly in accordance with the Geneva Convention. That was all very well, but how often had the SS followed the dictates of decency and accepted behaviour on the battlefield? A colleague from the Régiment de la Chaudière had already told him about the murders of surrendering Canadian soldiers shortly after D-Day. He'd also heard of quite a few other stories that told much the same thing, all of them common knowledge, and all no doubt told from the Allied point of view. But he was old enough and wise enough to know that history was written by the victors, who were often quick to hide the excesses of their own side. Only a few weeks ago, after one too many beers, a tank commander from the 2nd Canadian Armoured Brigade had told him a rather different story. The Chaudières had exacted their own kind of revenge shortly after the murders were discovered.

The regiment had just taken Carpiquet village and the neighbouring airfield, not far from the western outskirts of Caen. Many of the German defenders, one of the battalions from the 12th SS, was caught in the attack and suffered heavy casualties. The enemy dead and dying lay strewn around the village and surrounding fields. By this stage of the battle some of the Chaudières were out of control, and almost impossible to discipline. Contrary to orders they slipped into the fields where the enemy lay and slit their throats, irrespective of whether they were still living or dead. A few SS soldiers were even scalped.

Afterwards, the only way order could be restored among the troops was by force, at the point of a gun. This horrific story made him realise that both sides were equally guilty, and in the heat of battle, neither side could claim the moral high ground. The Canadians could hardly hold their bloody hands up and proclaim their own innocence.

The officer in front of him looked just like one of his own men, bar the obvious difference in uniform. Injured, dirty, unshaven, battle-soiled and wary of his fate, he hardly looked the picture of Aryan supremacy. Even so, he stood his ground without flinching or cowering. Could the man be persuaded into a more cooperative frame of mind? Possibly. He must have realised by now that they were Canadians, and what their reputation was like on the battlefield. The thought of some hastily improvised intimidation crossed his mind, but he quickly rejected it -Worthington had no time for brutality, even in the midst of battle. Perhaps a different approach would be more productive.

He smiled and pulled his hip flask and unscrewed the cap. The SS officer looked amazed, unable to believe that an enemy would be so considerate and friendly in the midst of battle.

'Drink?'

Meitzel looked at him warily, took the flask in his good hand, cautiously sniffed the contents and took a small sip. He frowned a little as the strong liquid went down, spluttered slightly, and then wiped his lips with the sleeve of his battle smock.

'OK?' Worthington smiled again.

'Ja...Yes. Brandy?'

'Yes.'

'Very good. French?' Worthington nodded. 'Yes, much better than we have in Germany. Thank you...' Meitzel looked at the crown and star on Worthington's epaulette, clicked his heels and stood to attention, acknowledging his enemy's superior rank. Besides, a Heil Hitler salute would be quite inappropriate, considering the pain in his broken arm and the situation he was in.

Worthington responded with a salute of his own, reciprocating the gesture. He could see a few shocked looks from some of his head-quarter's staff nearby, but he ignored them. He needed help in establishing just where they were. Maybe the shock of capture, followed by unexpectedly decent treatment, would help loosen the German's tongue.

'Some more?'

Meitzel nodded gratefully, and took a decent sized slug out of the hip flask.

'Good'. Worthington took back the flask, and at the same time pulled his map out, thrusting it in front of the SS officer. 'Obersturmführer Meitzel, would you be so good as to show me your position on the map- the spot where your vehicle was hit. In return I guarantee that you will be treated well.'

What? Surely this enemy officer must be joking. Meitzel tried desperately to hide his astonishment that a senior enemy officer was asking him to confirm where his location was on the battlefield? This was ludicrous. Despite the pain in his arm he almost felt like laughing, but of course that would have been unwise. Meitzel was in a dangerous position, and there was no telling what the enemy would do. The Canadians had a fearsome reputation, well deserved from what he had heard. They shot prisoners, just as some men from own division had done. Did that apply to officers as well? Perhaps it would be better not to provoke them, and pretend to cooperate. From the sound of things it looked like his own side was not too far away, and he strongly suspected a new battle would break out shortly.

Earlier that morning Meitzel reported the location of this new enemy force that had established itself deep inside their own positions to his division commander. Meyer, as usual, was quick to appreciate the gravity of the altered situation. A rapid glance at the map confirmed just how dangerous this unexpected Canadian thrust was, and orders soon flew out thick and fast. Meyer then sent him back to observe the same area. He needed a more extensive reconnaissance of the enemy positions, and a better idea of how strong they were. Meitzel was in the process of carrying out his new orders when his armoured infantry carrier was knocked out. What could he do now? Cooperation with the enemy was out of the question, but perhaps he could add to their confusion.

He leaned forward and squinted at the map held in front of him. The enemy used a different type of map, and it took him a few moments to orientate himself. 'There', he pointed with a grubby finger to a spot several kilometres away from where he knew his true position had been, up until the encounter with the anti-tank rocket.

'Are you sure?' The Canadian officer looked at him quizzically, a look of suspicion on his face.

'I think so, sir. Ja...' Meitzel nodded his head quickly.

Worthington shook his head, trying to hide his disappointment and annoyance. That couldn't possibly be where they were now. Either this German was lying, or he was as much confused as the Canadians were. Worthington was about to call his adjutant over when suddenly an explosion rent the air. It came from the small wood where the out-posted Shermans lay. A thick column of black, oily smoke rose upwards, an unwelcome sight he'd seen far too many times before. *One of ours, Christ...* Another volley of shots rang out, and the noise of revving tank engines sounded much closer now. It was time to act.

'Searle', he shouted out.

'Sir!' The Forward Observation officer ran up.

'Get on the radio to division HQ. Request an urgent defensive fire mission...no cancel that, just ask them for a ranging shoot on our location. Give them our coordinates and add five hundred meters to avoid friendly fire.'

'Sir.' Searle ran off to the half-track that carried the communications link to division. Perhaps the fall of shot from the artillery fire mission would give him a better idea of their real position. He turned to his adjutant.

'Harry, get the men under cover quickly. Pass the word around. All tanks are to button up and await my further orders. Find out what's happening to Captain Hope's Shermans.'

'Yes sir.' The officer hurried off to obey. He turned to where the captive German stood.

'Lieutenant Booth, get this man out of my sight. Make sure he's under guard at all times. The MO can fix him up with a sling later on.'

Booth hurried to obey. Any second now shells would start landing, hopefully somewhere in the field beyond where the battle group was currently deployed. He preferred not to hang around and find out. Sometimes friendly fire could be a little too friendly.

Hofheinz glanced up at the sky. The beautiful August summer sky was marred by dense columns of smoke that rose interminably, blotting out much of the view forwards. *At least they're theirs, not ours.* The Canadian tanks around the small wood to his left front were all destroyed, victims of their lack of thick armour and inadequate main gun. 'Tommy Cookers,' his men called them, a grimly apt joke. The enemy Sherman tanks were well known for their tendency to 'brew up', even at very long range. He'd seen so many of them go up in flames, a roaring inferno of orange-red flame that usually immolated everyone inside, unless you were fortunate enough and quick enough to bale out in the few seconds before the tank exploded. He wondered how anybody could be persuaded to get into such a death trap in the first place, let alone go forward into battle and slug it out with the enemy. The enemy tank crews deserved his respect for such courage. They must have known how heavily the odds were stacked against them. The Tiger crews had a much greater chance of survival in battle – usually, but not always. Yesterday's irreplaceable losses were still fresh in his mind.

It was nearly half past two in the afternoon. His Tiger had just received a fresh load of 88mm shells and machine gun ammunition, not a full load but enough to keep them going for the next few hours. They were situated a few yards from the crest of the slope in front of them, effectively in a hull-down position so only the top of the turret and main gun presented a target to any enemy tanks. It was so easy to pick off the enemy vehicles, one by one. Although his tank had suffered three impacts they were all glancing shots, deflected away by the thick turret armour. None of them left any serious damage.

He could hear the sounds of battle further off to the north, but what was really going on was difficult to tell from where he was positioned. The smoke and haze made long-range observation very difficult. He suspected it was the battered remnants of Meyer's division blocking any relief attempts by the enemy to rescue their surrounded colleagues. Once that mission was accomplished then they could begin the final assault on the surrounded Canadians. One sharp, hard blow should be enough to finish them off.

Booth looked tired a he glanced at his watch. It was nearly seven o'clock, and evening shadows were beginning to fall slowly across the sky as the sun moved slowly down towards the horizon. The day had been a disaster. It had started so well, but now everything that could have gone wrong *had* gone wrong. The artillery barrage had roared in, but nowhere near their position. One of the headquarters staff spotted where the shells were landing. It was at least four miles away, somewhere over to the west. The haze made pinpointing the exact spot difficult, but the fact that it was so far away simply confirmed what they all suspected- the battle group was in the wrong location, miles off course.

Worse was to follow. Within half an hour, stragglers from the forward positioned Shermans struggled back through the waving cornfields. Most of them were burnt or smoke blackened, with a high proportion of them wounded. All twelve Shermans were knocked out. The last man in was their commander, Captain Hope. His right arm was missing. He was the only survivor from his tank. His unit had been attacked from both flanks. The enemy was using Tigers and Panthers, as well as infantry equipped with anti-tank weapons, and they could not be stopped.

It was soon obvious that the rest of them were more or less surrounded. Worthington drew up his forces into a wagon-wheel position, just like the beleaguered settlers in North America a hundred years ago. The Germans now played the part of the American Indians, but this time their weapons were far more effective than bows and arrows. As the day ran its inexorable course, more and more Shermans blew up. Under-gunned and poorly armoured, they were easy kills for the technically superior enemy weapons. Dense clouds of smoke billowed all over their position. To add to their misery, mortars were ranged in, showering lethal shell fragments that sliced cruelly through the air. By the early afternoon Worthington had given permission for some of the surviving vehicles to break out, and take with them the wounded. Somehow they had run the gauntlet of enemy fire and miraculously disappeared in a cloud of dust towards the north.

Shortly afterwards the RAF decided to pay a visit. The pilots mistook the presence of armoured vehicles so far behind the front lines as those belonging to the enemy. Swooping in low, the aircraft bombed and strafed the woods and fields, returning with rocket attacks against the remaining tanks and half-tracks. It was all the Canadians could do to release yellow smoke canisters and desperately warn them that their targets were friendly forces. Realising their error the pilots soon changed targets and began to hit the encircling enemy, much to the delight of the Canadian defenders, but with little obvious effect.

The situation was fast becoming out of control. Most of the remaining tanks were destroyed, and few other vehicles were capable of movement. Two enemy infantry attacks were beaten off in short

order, but now the end could not be far off. Ammunition was running out, and Booth had the additional responsibility of scavenging weapons for those knocked out tank crews that were still fit to fight.

A runner from headquarters' company sprinted along the shoulder-high hedgerow that ran up to the copse they were sheltering in, and jumped into his foxhole. He lay there for a moment, gasping for breath. It was Corporal Labatt.

'What's the news, corporal?'

'Not good sir,' Labatt gasped. 'SNAFU.' Situation normal, all fucked up. The man looked scared and despondent, but then they all probably looked much the same. A shout of 'incoming' made them duck. Another barrage of shells landed in the field to their right front, blasting earth and hot shards of steel far and wide.

'Division HQ thinks they've finally identified where we are. They sent two relief forces to break through towards where they think our position is- our own 4th Armoured Division and the Poles.

Trouble is, sir, they're both having a torrid time. The Krauts are not giving an inch, and it looks like we'll have to do the job ourselves.'

Booth swore silently to himself. 'What have we got left? Any tanks?'

'Three or four half-tracks, maybe, but it's hard to be sure if they're in working order. All the remaining Shermans were brewed up in that last attack- that's about it. There's worse, sir...'

'What is it?' A feeling of icy despair gripped his heart- as if anything else could go wrong.

'Sun Ray's down, sir. His dugout was hit by a mortar round. The MO dashed across over to him as soon as he could, but I don't think there was anything he could do.'

Booth felt a numbing shock settle over him. The last thing they needed was to lose their commanding officer. Worthington was a good man, an inspiring and dynamic leader. It was not his fault that they had been given a foolhardy mission, mounted at such short notice. The operation smacked of wishful thinking and unrealistic, inadequate planning. What was division HQ thinking of? The Germans were not yet finished off, and they were damn good soldiers.

'Who's in command now?'

'There's only Lieutenant Hudson left, and he doesn't know what to do.' Labatt's expression said it all. Hudson was a very new second lieutenant who had only just arrived in France, and could hardly be expected to take command and get them out of the mess they were in. 'All the other officers are dead or badly wounded. Sir, the MO can't make a military decision, but he thinks we should get the hell out of here before they wipe us out.'

'Sounds like the right thing to do. Get back over to him and tell him I concur. Tell Hudson to get everybody that can move over here pronto. We're going to break out on foot- anything else is too much of a give-away.'

'But what about the wounded?' The concern in Labatt's voice was urgent. If there were SS out there...

'Get the MO to assess who can be moved. The others will have to stay where they are and take their chances.' A thought flashed through Booth's tired brain. 'Hold on, I've got a better idea. We'll leave that captured SS officer in charge of them. He's been treated well enough today, and I think we should be able to persuade him to ensure their safety. Off you go.'

Labatt nodded. After a few seconds wait he shot off back in the direction from which he had just come, running hard in a crouched-over hunch to lower his profile. Booth ignored the lack of salute. Military courtesies could wait until they were safely behind their own lines. Anybody stupid enough to be saluted at on a battlefield was likely to be shot dead by the ever-wary snipers that kept a constant look out for enemy commanders. No officer he knew wore rank epaulettes on their shoulders, or swaggered about with maps and their reflective talc covers on display- too many had already paid the ultimate price.

Sadly, quite a few more had joined that list today - all because of an error of navigation, and an over-optimistic plan. Booth rolled over and surveyed what was left of his platoon. Probably less than a third would be able to move under their own steam.

He was confident that Meitzel would see sense and guarantee the Canadian wounded were treated well. After all, he had suffered the same murderous attacks and barrages as they had throughout the day, and doubtlessly wanted to survive, just the same as any other man. It was time to strike a deal.

Coudehard and the Mont Ormel area, Normandy 1145 20/8/1944

The time on Hofheinz's wristwatch told him it was nearly midday, but the dense clouds of heavy black smoke that obscured the sun made it look more like midnight. The choking, acrid fumes from explosions and burning vehicles were more in keeping with Dante's description of hell. And hell was happening here, in this normally beautiful and quiet part of the Norman countryside, a whirling inferno of shellfire and explosions that smashed trees, uprooted the ground and flung men and tanks around with callous disregard.

The Allies had caught them in a steel vice, the jaws of which were relentlessly closing with unceasing pressure. To the south, less than half a mile away, an American division was reported to be holding firm, the southern jaw of the pincer. To the north the British and Canadians were pressing hard from the direction of Falaise to meet up with the Americans. Up ahead he could hear the unceasing rattle of machine gun fire. Mortars and artillery were smashing the area where the remnants of his unit and others were huddled. The intermittent bark of tank guns mingled in with the storm of explosions- some of them probably Shermans, from what he could tell. Their escape route was blocked; a stopper inserted into the neck of the bottle to prevent any more units escaping the boiling cauldron that lay just behind him. Further back, what was left of two armies was trying to escape. There must be a way out, but which way would lead to safety? From where he crouched it was hard to tell.

All their Tigers were knocked out, save one or two that had been sent back to the factory at Kassel, for repairs beyond the remit of the field workshops. There were maybe twenty men from the 101st still with him but it was hard to tell at times, such was the confusion in the wooded valley. So many had already been hit by shell fragments, their wounds dressed with the few remaining bandages, or left to bleed freely. The more seriously injured remained where they lay, unable to move further. Nobody had the strength to carry them onwards. At times remnants and stragglers from other units had merged with his men, only to disappear later in their own efforts to find a breakout route. Everybody was exhausted, throats parched from thirst, their stomachs rumbling with hunger. The water had long since run out, and nobody had eaten or slept properly for two or three days. The men were dead on their feet, almost at the limit of human endurance.

Tiredly he pulled the large-scale map out from his hip pocket, and unfolded it with his grimy fingers, trying to orientate it in the direction of north and approximating his position. A gap in the trees lay just up ahead, and he crawled carefully through the long grass to the edge of the wood, staying in the shelter of a large oak. Almost directly in front of him a steep slope led up towards to a wooded ridgeline that lay along the crest of a series of hills. From the map and his own observation he estimated the height to be nearly a hundred meters, not a problem for typically young fit men, but much more of a serious obstacle for the wounded and exhausted. To his right the ridge twisted its way south towards the spot height at Mont Ormel. There the crest was shrouded in smoke, broken up by the intermittent flash of artillery shells exploding. The roar of approaching aircraft engines made him look up at the darkened skies. Through the smoke he could vaguely make out the shapes of about six aircraft. They swooped nearer, suddenly launching multiple volleys of rockets around the far end of the ridge. The tree line erupted in a series of thunderous detonations.

Over to his left the northern end of the ridge looked more inviting. However, beyond that lay an exposed slope nearly a kilometer away. The roar of battle from that direction was even louder than to his right. He thought he could hear the distinctive whip-crack of an 88mm gun firing, but it was hard to be sure. Maybe there was a counter-attack going on there, trying to open a hole for the encircled units to break out. Directly in front of him the slope up to the ridgeline was far too open. Anybody trying to go that way, even with the clouds of smoke billowing across the area, would soon be spotted. There were probably several hundred bodies there, torn and scattered over the pockmarked ground that bore silent testament to the murderous effects of Allied artillery fire. There were more trees and cover a little further up on the left. He checked the terrain again and swiftly made up his mind. Then he slid back the way he had come, soon rejoining the others who lay in a small hollow, sheltering as best they could from the hot, angry shrapnel that fizzed about between the trees.

'OK lads, I think I've found a way out,' he said brightly despite his dulling fatigue, hoping to galvanize some enthusiasm from his weary men. 'One more effort and we should be through.'

'Sir, what about Reisler?' It was Schmidt, who looked angry and frightened. His friend lay on the grass beside him. The surrounding area was stained red from where a shell fragment had sliced into his left side. His face was pale. Sweat ran down his forehead, soaking his black panzer jacket. His trousers were already sodden, but from a far more vital body fluid. Hofheinz knelt and examined him quickly, then turned and stood up.

'I'm sorry, Heinz,' he said quietly in Schmidt's ear. 'Looks to me as if he's beyond anybody's help now.' He put his arm around the younger man, whose eyes were filled with tears. 'At least he's had some morphine.' There were no more ampoules left. 'We can't take him with us - we'll kill him if we move him. The best thing to do is leave him here. He'll be far more comfortable and better off that way. And if the opposition find him, he'll have a much better chance with them than where we're going.'

Schmidt nodded, unable to speak. Hofheinz looked around at the rest of them, shouting above the noise of the artillery barrage. 'Right, follow me. We need to move quickly and get out of this shit hole. Nobody stops for nothing. Let's go.' With that, he bent low and plunged through the trees, heading north. The little group had gone no more than two hundred meters when they bumped into another, much larger group of soldiers. They were paratroops, distinctive by their unique helmets and camouflage smocks. They looked just as desperate and tired as Hofheinz's own men, their gaunt, unshaven faces sunken and sallow. Further off, he could hear tank engines running among the noise of the shell bursts.

One of their non-commissioned officers ran up. This band of brothers was one of the last remnants of the 3ʳᵈ Fallschirmjäger Division. Their commanding officer was further on ahead. He would soon give the order to advance up the ridge to the north and smash through the enemy who dominated the approaches. There was a rumour that the 2ⁿᵈ SS Panzer Corps was counterattacking from the other side of the ridge in a similar direction. Did they want to join in and break out that way? Hofheinz declined. The direction of their attack looked to be heading straight towards where the battle was at its most furious. Besides, his men were tankers, not infantry. They only had a few machine pistols and revolvers among them, and the rest were unarmed. Thanks for the offer, but they would go their own way.

They moved off again. This time Hofheinz turned right and led them directly up the slope, trying to move from tree to tree and staying undercover as much as possible. Behind him, his men struggled to follow. As they moved further away from the valley floor the shelling grew less intense, but the going became much harder. Bushes and thickets snagged their progress, and the slope seemed to rise almost vertically, at times making them crawl on their hands and knees as they scrambled their way upwards. Soon they reached a thick hedgerow, the boundary of a country lane that ran under the shadow of the ridge above. It barred their way. There was only one thing that they could do- force an opening in the hedge, crawl through the gap and sprint across to the other side, where they would have to repeat the same process all over again.

A sense of desperation overtook them. They ripped the base of the hedge apart with their bare hands, thrusting their way through, oblivious to the cuts and thorns that ripped into the flesh of their fingers and arms. Soon a wide enough hole was made. Hofheinz urged them through. One by one they forced their way through the hedge and sprinted across the lane to lie in a small ditch at the other side. He was the last to go. As he made his way through the gap the noise from the bombardment temporarily eased, enough for him to hear the *pfftt* of mortars firing from close by. He wriggled through and dashed across the lane, launching himself into a dive to land in the far side ditch, clattering into some of his men who already lay there. He was only just in time. Three explosions crashed into the area they had just come from, shredding the trees and hedgerow with lethal fragments and showering them with dust and stones where they lay.

'Quick,' he gasped, ignoring the groans and shouts from the men he'd landed on. 'We can't stay here. We've been spotted. Keep moving.' With a fury born of desperation they clawed their way through another hedge and struggled further up the slope, panting and sweating as they neared the top of the ridge. Several more explosions followed them, but once they had regained the cover of the trees, the shelling stopped. The enemy gunners had either run out of ammunition or found more lucrative targets to concentrate on.

Their pace slowed to a crawl as they reached the top of the slope. Hofheinz left them to recover while they sheltered in the lee. He crawled further ahead, up the last few metres and keeping to cover as much as he could. The summit of the ridge gradually came into view. He cautiously inched the last few meters forward to spy out the land. Thick cover surrounded him to his right and blocked out the view. Ignoring this he crawled over to his left, carefully pushing his way along a small hedge that bordered a heavily cultivated maize field. The air was clearer here, the views less obscured than those in the valley below. At the corner of the field the vista suddenly opened out in front of him. He was looking roughly north, his gaze running along the length of the wooded ridge towards the exposed area he had spotted earlier.

There was movement there. Five tanks were grinding their way slowly across the open pasture, their turrets slowly traversing from side to side as they searched for targets. Hofheinz pulled out his Zeiss binoculars, quickly adjusting the lenses until the tanks came into sharp focus. They were Shermans, possibly British or Canadian. No sooner had he identified them than the furthest one away lurched to the left and exploded in a sheet of flame. The flat crack of a cannon report followed almost immediately. It was a 75mm, almost certainly from a Panther, the sound of it ingrained permanently in his memory. The other Shermans began to fire wildly, unable to spot where the opening shot had come from. The Panther's cannon cracked again. In short succession it brewed up the four remaining Shermans, smoke and flames belching out as tiny figures, some of them on fire, scrambled out of the burning hulks and scuttled away to relative safety.

A noise to his right disturbed him. Barely thirty metres away two soldiers emerged from a foxhole, their helmets and uniforms unmistakably British. The explosions away to the north had caught their attention. One of them was screaming and shaking his fist at the destroyed tanks, or was it at the hidden assassin? Hofheinz listened to the shouts. It was hard to make out above the noise of battle, but he thought he recognised the language - was that Polish? Reports in the last week or two had suggested the presence of a Polish armoured division operating in their vicinity. Could this be the enemy unit that was blocking the exit from the pocket?

Carefully he reversed his tracks and hurried back to where his men lay resting. There was no point in trying to head further north and reach the area where counter-attack was coming from. Already they could hear the sound of explosions and firing from the direction of where the paratroops had indicated that they would attack from. His men were far too few and poorly armed to have any effect on the outcome of what was happening over there. It was best to use stealth and cover, and sneak through the enemy lines to safety. If they could find some more Tigers, then and only then they would be able to help out.

His men quickly crawled the last few meters, up over the ridge and into the cover afforded by the hedge that flanked the near side of the maize field. They kept close to the hedge, avoiding observation by using a shallow drainage ditch that led east, in the direction where safety lay. Soon they came to an open field. A few mortar shells burst in the area, but it was nothing compared to the hell of the wooded valley that now seemed so far away. A gap in a hedgerow at the far end led to another field that backed up onto yet another hedge. Stooping low, they dashed along the hedgerow until they could go no further. Beyond the next hedge was a small road that crossed their path, marked by spirals of smoke drifting lazily up into the air. The smell of death and destruction was suddenly much worse here. Hofheinz stood up and took a quick look over the hedge. The bloody remains of a transport column lay dead and dying along the road, stretched out as far as the eye could see. Men, horses and field wagons lay smashed and broken, the road matted in thick black stains where blood had soaked into the dust. It was an appalling, horrific sight, worse than most things he had seen in Russia. Suddenly, a squeal of tank tracks distracted him from the gory spectacle. It was coming from the left. A pair of Sherman tanks came into view, moving along the road and driving over the destroyed column, grinding to a pulp both living and dead.

He ducked back down, cursing the fate that made him helpless to stop the carnage on the road in front of him. None of them had any weapons that could take on a tank, let alone two of them. He doubted they could stay where they were, but where else could they go? The field they had just crossed was far too open to keep them hidden. If they tried to return the way they had come, the enemy would most likely spot them quickly enough, as soon as they drew level. A short burst of machine gun fire, and that would be that. There was nothing he could do except pray and hope that they would not be noticed. His men could see the look of horror and disgust on his face-they knew that the approaching sounds could only come from the enemy.

He was just about to give in to despair when the sound of a tank coming from the opposite direction broke into his thoughts. A quick glimpse of the silhouette revealed it to be a Panther. Before he could react the flat bark of its cannon rang out, rousing all of them from their dread. A tremendous explosion lifted the turret off the lead Sherman, flinging it sideways and into the opposite field. A belching inferno of orange and red flames shot out of the hull, casting a dense cloud of smoke across the road. The second Sherman fired almost instantaneously in return, disabling the Panther, ripping off its left main sprocket and shredding its nearside track into a mass of twisted steel. It drove on around the wreck of the first tank and began to close the distance between the two. The Sherman quickly reloaded as it moved forward. Another shot rang out, bouncing off the sloped armour of the Panther, the solid shell screeching away into the heavens. The Sherman drew closer and closer until barely thirty meters separated the two. At the last moment both tanks fired simultaneously. The Sherman slewed sideways into the ditch, smoking furiously, an armour-piercing shot smashing straight through the turret and out the far end. But the Panther was mortally stricken as well. Flames licked the edge of the turret ring. The commander's hatch was flung open, and a blackened and burnt body tumbled out onto the rear deck and rolled off backwards onto the road.

Hofheinz tore his eyes away. 'Move you bastards. Across the road now!' They struggled to clear the hedge and ran across the road and into the field beyond. Hofheinz hurried to the front of the Panther, but the heat from the flames kept him at bay. He recognised the tactical insignia of Das Reich, the 2nd SS Panzer Division. Moving back, he skirted around the rear of the tank. The body that lay in the road was as near death as made no difference. Flames licked the head and torso. The smell of burnt flesh was overpowering. It was all he could do to stagger away and fight back the nausea that threatened to overwhelm him.

Quickly he rejoined the rest of his men. They ran as fast as they could across the next field, keeping as close to the nearest hedgerow as possible. The distant sounds of battle on either side continued to ring out, but as far as he could tell they were through the advanced enemy positions. He kept them onwards in an easterly direction, avoiding open spaces and keeping to the cover of bushes and trees as much as he could. For the moment they seemed to have escaped. He was sure that there was a long road in front of them before they would reach any semblance of real safety.

Near Dyhernfürth, Silesia 0125 5/2/1945

The night was dark and still. Little disturbed the silence. Leutnant Karl Kruger scanned the horizon slowly, straining to make out any visible detail. He knew that up until recently this area had been the scene of heavy fighting. But tonight everything was unusually quiet. Even the enemy heavy guns had stopped firing, a rare event indeed, for which he was grateful. The Russians sure loved their artillery – Red God of War, as they called it. It was a fearsome sledgehammer of a weapon, a man-made typhoon that was capable of ripping up entire front lines, trenches, dugouts and anything else that stood in its way. He'd experienced it a few times, at Kirovograd and other places. Once was enough for it to indelibly grind its way into your consciousness, and deep into your worst nightmares. But now there was little to be heard, nothing but the hiss of the wind through the bare branches of the silver birch under which he stood. In front of him the Oder River calmly pursued its own business, oblivious to the wars of men. The turgid river meandered forth from the Sudeten hills on the old Czech - Polish border, somewhere behind where he stood, and onwards towards Breslau and the distant Baltic. The river was full from the recent sleet and rains that had blanketed the area. It made a miserable change from the snowfalls that had covered southern Poland and Silesia over the last two weeks. A few wisps of fog settled over the slowly moving waters and partially hid the far bank. That would be in their favour, obscuring vision and masking their purpose from watchful eyes.

The angry rasp of a machine gun suddenly broke the silence, but it was far off, probably a kilometre or two away to their left. *It was theirs not ours, from the sound of it.* In the distance, an orange flare arched into the sky, then slowly sank towards earth. A few desultory rifle shots followed, and all gradually became quiet and peaceful again. The next few minutes passed slowly - nothing else disturbed the silence. A quarter moon provided a small amount in the way of illumination, and a few scattered stars twinkled deep in the heavens. There was just enough light to get by. They would not use flares or anything else by way of additional illumination. That would merely alert the enemy to their presence.

The Soviet offensive in the middle of January had smashed through the thin German-held crust and flung the front line back, well inside the Reich's old borders. Warsaw, or rather what was left of it, had fallen very quickly. The front line was now along the Oder, both here in Silesia and near Berlin. At its closest point it was less than fifty kilometres from the capital, precious little in the way of breathing room. It was not quite so bad here, along the flanks of the breakthrough. The Russians had arrived only recently, and had not fully prepared their defences. Even so, tonight's work could well be tricky, full of uncertainties as to what exactly lay over on the far side of the river.

Kruger reviewed tonight's mission in his mind. His task was to destroy the chemical weapons factory that lay directly to his front, on the far side of the river. The plan also provided for a large covering force to screen him and his men from enemy interference. Maior Sassenheimer would be in charge, an experienced East front veteran. Sassenheimer's men were in position over to his left, just by the old railway bridge that spanned the Oder. They would cross over at the same time as his men, move into position and block any Russian reinforcements from interfering with his job. Kruger hoped that they had enough firepower to deal with any eventuality.

He looked at his watch. Sassenheimer would no doubt be doing the same almost a kilometre away along the river bank. 0130 – it was time to start moving. He slid out from behind the shelter of the tree trunk, and gave a low whistle. Immediately, a mass of men emerged from the ditch that ran parallel to the course of the river and began to move forward, dragging a score of canvas boats with them towards the water's edge. He ran towards the lead group, just in time to give them a hand to manoeuvre their boat down the muddy bank and into the slow-moving stream. The sound of a heavy splash broke the stillness.

'Quiet,' he hissed urgently. 'Keep the noise down'. Somebody had slipped on the greasy surface and fallen in. Hands quickly grabbed the unfortunate and hauled him into the nearest boat. As they moved across the river, Kruger looked back and across to where his reinforced platoon was. They had all managed to successfully launch their craft and were now paddling their way across. Some of the men were using rifle butts to help propel their way, in addition to the two men in the rear of each boat using paddles. *So far so good. Twenty boats, six men in each.* He looked to his front. The far bank was getting closer, still shrouded in mist. Nothing had disturbed their crossing – no gunfire or flares. The enemy was either not guarding this section of the river, or maybe getting their heads down and catching a few zeds. Or maybe they were holding their fire to the last possible minute, letting them get nice and close so they couldn't miss...He put those thoughts out of his mind. This was no time to start worrying.

His boat temporarily grounded on a mud bank, then shot forwards the last few meters. He climbed over the edge into the knee-deep water. All around him his platoon were doing the same, slipping and sliding through the muddy water as stealthily as they could towards the reeds and grass that lined the enemy side of the river. There was still nothing. If the enemy were here they would surely have opened fire by now. Cautiously he crept forward, levering himself up onto the far shore. Still nothing. Kruger turned and signalled to his recon team close behind him. They silently acknowledged his gesture, and began to move quickly ashore to reconnoitre the immediate area to their front. The rest of his men began to drag the boats onto the grassy bank, and prepare for all-round defence.

A few minutes later the recon team returned, suddenly materializing out of the gloom. A figure approached. It was Hans Meinert, their leader. 'Nothing here sir. No signs of the enemy at all,' he whispered in Kruger's ear. 'No trenches, wire, mines – not a sausage, as far as we can tell. Ivan here's all safely tucked up and in bed, nicely asleep.' Kruger could just make out his grin in the near darkness.

'Good.' Kruger nodded. He pulled out his map and crouched down, covering his head and arms with a poncho roll. He flicked on a pen torch, checked their presumed location against a large scale map of the area, checked distances and bearings against his field compass to be absolutely sure, and then emerged.

'OK, Hans,' he whispered back. 'We'll continue as already planned, no change. The factory and engineering complex are 1200 meters to our north. The town is further over to our left, along with the castle. The Russians are sure to be there, but we'll leave them well alone. Sassenheimer's lot should take care of them. Use your team to scout out the approaches in case they've posted additional protection in front of our objective. Remember, no noise – bayonets and entrenching tools only. We'll be right behind you.'

Meinert nodded and disappeared quickly into the darkness. Kruger could barely hear them move off. They were extremely stealthy. All of them had tied rags around their boots to deaden any sound. They had already checked their packs on the friendly side of the river – no give-away noises, no rattles from unsecured equipment, tell tales in the still night air could be heard. He turned to face the rest of his assembled men, split them into three teams as pre-arranged, and began to move forward. The next hour or so would be interesting.

Major Alexei Alexeyevich Rybalko surveyed the interior of the engineering works he had been detailed to investigate for the umpteenth time, and shook his head in anger and frustration. His small team had arrived here by jeep less than an hour ago. Front intelligence had previously identified this small industrial complex from aerial reconnaissance photos. It had all the hallmarks of something well worth a special investigation, and he had received orders to get himself down here as soon as the leading front line elements booted the Germans out and secured the area. This was a special mission. The 1st Ukrainian Front's NKVD coordinator, Lieutenant General Andropov himself, had stressed the importance of this task to him personally. His words still echoed in Rybalko's ears.

'This is the most important thing we've identified so far. As you know, we're looking for evidence of German technology we can use, especially in the area of rocketry and associated telemetry.' He waved a hand. 'I have little understanding of these areas, but this order has come from the very top, via the Academy of Scientists. Koba himself is said to be interested in this, so that should underline how important this is.' Rybalko nodded. 'Koba' was the *chekist* nickname for Josef Stalin, an old peasant name from Stalin's formative years in the Caucasus.

'So far we've captured very little in the way of German scientists and rocket technology, and we know they lead us in several important areas in this field of research,' Andropov continued. 'I am sure you will get to the bottom of this and provide detailed findings of what the Germans have been doing in this area. Rest assured that I will be personally grateful when you successfully complete this mission'.

Rybalko was not fooled for a moment, no matter how soft-spoken and outwardly pleasant Andropov was. The *chekist* threat was always there. Succeed, and your star will rise with mine, fail and you will feel my displeasure. He was under no illusions as to Andropov's real role –the NKVD officer was there to apply the muscle of the Soviet State, and to enforce rigorous subservience to the Party line. Anybody who did not perform to requirements would quickly find that life would be very much less pleasant than before. Even Konev, the Army Front Commander and a Marshal of the Soviet Union, was known to defer to Andropov on all but strictly military matters. And NKVD ruthlessness was well known. He knew about the Penal Battalions and what they endured. 'Need to clear an enemy minefield? No problem, we'll send in a Penal Battalion. Let them run through it, then round up the survivors and keep doing that until all the mines are exploded, or you run out of men. We'll send you another batch if you need any more.'

He'd seen for himself what went on in the rear areas after the Red Army had executed a 'liberation'. It was nothing he ever wanted to see again. Yes, the Germans were no angels themselves, from what he'd heard and observed in Byelorussia, but the relentless devastation and vicious brutality on both sides sickened him. But he was careful enough to keep his opinions to himself. All he was interested in was his chosen calling – the field of rocket ballistics. A careful subservience to the Party line was vital for personal survival. He liked to think of himself as just that - a born survivor. After all, the war was nearly over and the Soviet Union would need men like him for the future. A man with his experience and skills would do well in post-war Russia, and missions like this would not harm his reputation one little bit.

But this so-called important trip had turned out to be a complete waste of his time. Front Intelligence had messed it up again - there was no evidence here of any ballistic missile research or capability. This was a chemical warfare factory, and from the looks of things had been closed down several weeks ago. The Germans had fled, leaving all their paperwork and documents behind. There was nothing remotely useful, unless you counted the chemical weapons. He'd already ordered his team to remove every document for further analysis, and although chemical weapons were not his particular field, he doubted his masters would find anything particularly new. The Soviets already had a powerful arsenal of similar agents, but so far had declined to use them. With the war almost won, there was hardly any need...

He glanced at his watch. It was time to leave and get back to Front HQ in Krakau. Rybalko was not especially looking forward to reporting a lack of success to Andropov, but that was hardly his fault. If the Lieutenant General was going to be angry and disappointed, then that was his problem, and he should take it out on those desk-bound idiots who had screwed up in the first place.

'That's it,' he announced to all his men within earshot. 'Load everything that we can carry onto the transport. Then we'll get back to base.' His men rushed to complete their final few tasks, and then began to head towards the trucks. Rybalko wanted to get away as soon as possible. They had already spent enough time in this dreary place.

Good. We'll be out of here in a moment. It wasn't the proximity of the enemy that worried him, although he knew they were only just across the river. No. One of his team had been sent into the local town to act as liaison to the local Russian regimental commander, who was responsible for this area and the defense along the Oder. The man had come back wide-eyed and shaking. All the local civilians in the town were dead - brutally executed, shot, impaled on farm instruments, repeatedly raped until death – even the children...None of the troops there were sober. They were all Mongolian brutes, sky-high on vodka and captured brandy – most of them probably comatose by now. Rybalko shuddered. It was something he had no desire to see.

He took a last look around, turned off the light switch and walked out of the main office block towards the waiting transport. There was no sound from the courtyard where the trucks were parked. *Funny – they should have their engines turning over. Maybe the men are too busy loading up at the rear.* As he moved closer to investigate, a dark blur shot forward and, clamped a hand over his mouth, pinioning his body back and slamming him against the door. He felt a sharp prick in his neck.

'Careful, tovarisch,' a hard, no-nonsense voice said in passable Russian. 'Don't move. This knife could make an awful mess of your uniform, and you being an officer-type wouldn't like that one little bit. So do me a favour – no sudden moves, otherwise you might end up like some of your comrades here. Understand?' The knifepoint pushed in a little harder.

'Y...Yes'. Rybalko stammered, all the time aware of the stabbing pain in his neck. There was little he could do. In front of him all his men were lying on the floor. How many of them were still alive? He swore quietly to himself. Where were the troops guarding this area? If he ever got out of this alive, he would make sure the Mongolian colonel in charge would suffer a suitable punishment for what had happened here tonight.

❋

They were nearly home, almost back at the river. The operation had been a resounding success. The engineer specialists that accompanied Kruger and his men had managed to open most of the tanks that stored lethal chemicals and dump them into a nearby watercourse, one of the numerous streams and tributaries in the area that ultimately led to the Oder. It did not matter if the river became polluted downstream. The fish and local wildlife would die, but so what? The ecological damage would only be temporary, and Nature would ultimately remove the toxins and the river would recover. At least that's what he had been told, and that was what he chose to believe, even if he was not completely comfortable with the rationale. But he had his orders, and that would have to do. As for the rest of the factory, Kruger had made sure that enough explosives were planted to blow the whole area to hell and back, including anything that could possibly incriminate German research into chemical weapons.

There had been no opposition, not unless you counted the captured Russians caught in the act of looting the factory of its secrets. None of them came across as hardened soldiers. They were not front line troops, he judged, but looked more like rear echelon types. The captured officer appeared to be much more interesting, however. His shoulder lapels gave him away as belonging to the rocket artillery corps. Kruger had seen those before, and was well aware of their significance. Standing orders were quite explicit – any enemy officers, especially those of field rank and above, and in certain categories of specialty, were to be taken alive and transferred to the rear for immediate interrogation, if at all possible. This one fitted the bill. The rest, those who hadn't died resisting, were ordinary cannon fodder. They were almost certainly of no use, and would be destined to go straight to the nearest POW camp. Poor bastards. He had an idea of what sort of fate awaited them there.

He checked his watch and then scanned the vicinity. Still no reaction from the Russian defenses, but that would change as soon as the factory blew up. That was what Sassenheimer's troops were covering them for. His paratroopers had now reached the river's edge, herding the captive Russians in front. Meinert was keeping a close eye on their commanding officer – he was the prize catch, the icing on the cake of tonight's mission. Another quick glance at his watch...thirty seconds to go...'Everybody flat on the ground,' he hissed, throwing himself onto the wet Silesian earth. Shouts were repeated, some of them in Russian. Soon everyone lay flattened on the muddy landscape. Ka-boom. A thunderous explosion rocked the ground where they lay. Even though they were over a kilometre distant from the blast site, the detonation and shock blasts were extremely impressive. A volley of secondary detonations rent the air. *Probably some of the storage tanks going up as well. Those chemicals sure make damn good explosives.*

After what seemed like an age, but was probably less than thirty seconds, the light from the blasts subsided. Kruger could see several large fires raging where the factory had once been Their fuses had given them enough time to clear the immediate area, but not enough to get back across the river. That couldn't be helped, not with the general shortage of equipment and ammunition at this stage of the war. The Russians would soon show up, and it was definitely time to be gone. He stood up.

'Into the boats and back across now!' Immediately, his men began to move to the canvas craft and maneuver them back into the water. Another five minutes and they should be safe, back on the friendly side of the river. Another successful mission for the élite of the Fallschirmjäger.

❧

Between Höxter and Göttingen 1545 12/3/1945

The early spring sun cast a pale, lukewarm glow over the countryside, giving an artificial warmth to the villages and fields that in reality did not yet exist. Winter's icy grip was only slowly being relinquished, and the trees and fields still looked gaunt and lifeless. The heavy snowfalls had recently melted, transforming the sodden landscape into a mud bath. The war was yet to touch this area of the Reich, but even now, the roads were busy with refugee traffic, many of them innocents who were fleeing westwards from the Soviet onslaught in the East, but only a few eastwards from the approaching Americans and British.

They were speeding along in the back of Schellenberg's Mercedes, comfortably insulated from the frigid temperatures outside. A lot had happened since his admission to the Krankenhaus Hohenstein, and not just his almost complete recovery. The war had gone disastrously for Germany. Not long after Schellenberg's first visit the front in Normandy collapsed. As a result the Allies had scored a dramatic victory. Only shattered remnants of two once powerful armies escaped from the encirclement and destruction at Falaise and fled back to the borders of the Reich, hotly pursued by the enemy. But there, a miracle of improvisation turned the tide of fortune. Units were scraped together and rapidly reconstituted. The Westwall, the almost obsolete fortifications also known as the Siegfried Line, had played its part in anchoring the German defense. Together with the worsening Allied supply situation and the autumn mud and winter snows, the front was stabilized.

The ensuing breathing space had given Hitler the chance to create a strategic reserve for the first time in several years of hard defensive fighting. With this powerful force he hoped to repeat the events of May 1940. Then, German armies had driven through the difficult terrain of the Ardennes and bypassed the Maginot line to strike behind the French, British and Belgian armies. This unorthodox attack had taken the Allies by surprise, created widespread shock and confusion, and within a few weeks produced a resounding victory. Now, nearly five years later, a similar strategy would isolate and surround the British and Canadian armies in Belgium and Holland, destroy their supply lines and alter the course of the war in the West.

Instead of driving to the Channel coast as before, this time however the objective would be the port city of Antwerp. Attacking from a completely unexpected direction would throw the Allies into confusion, just like 1940 all over again. The winter weather would negate the overwhelming power of the enemy air forces and ensure another unlikely victory.

It was the last desperate throw of the dice. The odds were heavily against success, but Hitler had decided to risk all anyway and chance his arm once more. It was either that or wait for the inevitable. However, this time the result was a failure. The Allies were far stronger now than they were in 1940 and much better led and equipped. The furthest advance had barely reached halfway to Antwerp before it was stopped and smashed. The strategic reserve, that precious commodity that had taken months to carefully build up, was squandered in a few weeks of heavy fighting. And at this stage of the war there could be no hope of ever recreating it.

The soft leather seats in the rear of the Mercedes squeaked and rustled as he tried to get into a more comfortable position. Eight months of rehabilitation had seemed never ending, a constant struggle to keep his spirits up as his body began the painstakingly slow process of recovery. He would never forget the euphoria at the first sign that his nervous system was recovering-the sensation of pins and needles and muscle twitching in his neck and chest. Arms and legs had taken much longer, and then there was the exhausting and relentless physical therapy, first in a wheelchair and then shakily on his wasted legs. The nurses and physical therapists were wonderful- supportive, cheering him up when he became despondent about his slow progress, and chivvying him along to try even harder than before.

Things were much better now. He still felt weak and wobbly on his feet, and his muscles were still some way off regaining their full bulk, but he had now reached the stage where he could support himself and get around without too much difficulty. As every day went past his muscles grew stronger, and he felt more in control. Mobius had pronounced his almost complete satisfaction with Simon's recovery. There were only a couple of areas that were still not quite as the Professor wished. Fine motor control and sensation in his hands and feet were not quite fully back to normal, and there was a question mark as to whether they ever would be.

'I don't think you've quite got the manual dexterity required to become an eye surgeon,' Mobius had chuckled, and then lowered his voice, making sure it did not carry. 'But then, who knows for sure? The war won't last much longer, and I suspect you'll be looking for new employment soon.'

So now, here he was, sitting in the back seat of Schellenberg's comfortable limousine as they sped along towards destinations unknown. The glass partition between them and Hansen, the driver, was raised, sealing them off, almost like an enveloping cocoon. The general had visited him twice over the intervening months, whenever his duties and commitments allowed, but talked little about events that were happening outside. Simon suspected that his progress was being closely monitored by phone calls to Mobius, and no sooner had the Professor pronounced his final discharge date than Schellenberg had turned up to whisk him away. The Brigadeführer had been his usual polite and affable self, but had said little else since. Simon felt it was time to probe deeper.

'What's the latest situation, sir? I've only had hearsay to go on, plus a few out of date copies of the Volkischer Beobächter.'

'Not good, I'm afraid.' Schellenberg roused himself from his thoughts and turned to face his fellow officer. He looked grim. 'The Russians are only forty miles from Berlin, not a comforting thought. We've managed to stop them short of the capital. Hitler's health has not been the best, not since the abortive Bomb plot last July. I presume you've heard of that?' Simon nodded. 'It's all been hushed up, but I suspect he may have had a minor stroke caused by the after-effects of the explosion. The Führer was simply unable to cope with the workload. Elsewhere in the East, things are not quite so bad. 'I'm more worried about the West, though. Since the failure of the Wacht am Rhein attack, everything's gone pear-shaped.' Schellenberg was referring to the codeword for the Ardennes counter-offensive. 'The Allied armies are in the process of clearing the entire area west of the Rhine. Yesterday there were a few unconfirmed reports that American troops have already reached the river at Obercassel and are trying to cross over. All the bridges are prepared for demolition, but even if they're all destroyed that won't stop them. Sooner or later, their armies will cross over. Once they do that then the war will be finished. There's very little left of our armies on this side of the river to stop them from what I can tell.'

'So what are you doing now?'

'Not a great deal. Routine paperwork mainly. There's still some call for military intelligence reports, but you don't need a crystal ball to see how heavily the odds are stacked up against Germany now. Berlin is heavily damaged. A lot of the buildings in the centre are lying in ruins. Even RSHA has not escaped the destruction. Most of the top floor is out of action. The Reichsführer is working less and less in the capital, thanks to the relentless bombing.' A quick smile crossed his features. 'Don't worry we're not heading back there today. I keep my promises.'

Simon recalled Schellenberg's words the night that Brandt died. The memory of those events was still disturbing and unpleasant. He shivered involuntarily.

Schellenberg was watching him closely. 'There are still some things that we need to discuss, now that you've recovered. Mobius has sent me his final report on your progress. He says that you are still not fit for combat duties, which is actually very convenient for what I have in mind. What do you think about becoming a combat instructor in Panzer tactics? That should be ideal for a man still not yet fully recovered.'

'I don't know, sir.' The suddenness of Schellenberg's proposal had taken him by surprise. 'I've never thought of that before.'

'Well, I think you're admirably qualified. Your combat record speaks for itself. Himmler set up a new SS Panzer school near Sondershausen at the beginning of the year. There's a place on the instructing staff there for a man of your ability. That's where we're heading today, and not the Wehrmacht's armoured warfare school at Paderborn. It's all arranged.'

'What about the failure of my visit to England?' It was something that had been at the back of Simon's thoughts while he recovered, and still worried him. Would Himmler still hold a grudge? He would not tolerate failure, unless there was an acceptable reason to explain it away.

'Relax, Sturmbannführer.' Schellenberg drawled, waving a gloved hand in the air. 'The mission failed, and, naturally, he was displeased. But that's small beer now. There have been many things to occupy his mind since then. I managed to persuade him that the lack of results was in no way due to your efforts, which were commendable, hence your promotion. Rather, the absence of success was due to a combination of bad luck and unfortunate timing.'

'But what about the invasion- correct me if I'm wrong, sir, but the Allies only landed in Normandy and not the Pas de Calais as well. Isn't that so?'

'Yes. You're right. It was a gigantic bluff all along. The Allies kept us guessing until it was far too late to do anything about it. After that, the armies in Normandy were destroyed. The 15th Army in the Calais area was swept up in the retreat. MI6 was at the bottom of it, I'm certain of that. From what we can now piece together, Rothermere's first report was quite genuine. The intelligence we have on the enemy order of battle fits in with that. So who knows why Rothermere told you what he did? Maybe he was unaware of MI6's deception plan, and that it fooled him as well. As you say, he told you that it was the Calais area, but MI6 could have easily planted disinformation like that for him to access- once they'd realized about the leak of his first report. On the other hand, maybe he had a last minute change of heart, and the stress of it all was too great for him. Alternatively, he could have been working for MI6 all along, but that's most unlikely. I very much doubt if they would have risked letting him expose the true details of Allied strength.'

Simon kept silent. Had Schellenberg accepted his side of the events in London, or did the master spy still have any reservations? It was difficult to be sure- it was best to keep quiet and no longer mention the subject. The good news was that Himmler appeared to be no longer interested in him. Hopefully the same would apply to his father. The only worrying thing was that he had not heard from him for several months.

'I have another job for you while you're working at Sondershausen. There's a secret weapons facility nearby in the Nordhausen area. Security is tight, but there's nothing like a combat veteran to give the place a once over and assess the measures that are already in place and see if they can be improved. That is your task. But there's something more that I wish you to talk to you about.'

Simon looked at his superior officer. He could sense that Schellenberg was in two minds about how to proceed next. He decided to wait him out in silence.

'Very well, then…' Schellenberg looked him squarely in the eye. 'Do you remember when we first met at RSHA? I sensed at the time that you mistrusted me, and who could blame you for that? As an SS general I was asking for you to tell me your innermost thoughts. Apart from giving me some realistic advice about the state of the Eastern Front- and quite rightly so- you toed the party line and gave little away. But I suspected all along that your true feelings were at variance with what you told me. I thought you were sick of war and the senseless bloodshed. With the death of your wife, and what you'd seen in Poland, all of these things would be enough to make any man question just what he stood for…

He lowered his voice to a whisper. 'I know you and your father were close to Canaris. You know that the admiral and I formed an alliance. It is a loose one admittedly. I doubt he ever really trusted me. Am I right?'

Simon gave a tiny nod, but kept his silence.

Schellenberg sighed, somewhat bitterly. 'It is as I suspected. But realistically, I could not hope for more. I'm sure the admiral said that I would always look after my own interests first, and that everything else was secondary. I used to think that way too, but that's changed, for a variety of reasons. Despite whom I work for, and the things I know about and have witnessed, I still like to think of myself as a man of honour and integrity.' He laughed, in a self-deprecating manner, and then suddenly grew serious. 'Yes, even me. So I'm going to be honest with you...' He paused, keeping his voice low and all the while holding Simon's gaze.

'I gave my word to Canaris. I also gave my word to you. And I've kept both. It's not been easy- such is the way of things these days. Remember Brandt?' He waited for a few moments to let the impact of his words to sink in. 'Of course, how could you ever forget? You kept a promise then, so in return I'm being honest with you. Despite what you may think, I always have been.'

Schellenberg paused, watching him closely. 'Max, I'm as sure as I can be that your version of events of the operation in England is not entirely accurate. I can't as yet tell you how I know, and I doubt if you would believe me anyway. Yet here we are- and *now is the winter of our discontent*.'

Simon froze, as if in a dream. The words shocked him to the core. That was the exact recognition phrase Menzies had drummed into him in Hermitage House, all those months ago. And to cap it all, Schellenberg had just whispered it in English. He stared open-mouthed at the general, not quite believing what he had just heard.

Schellenberg affected a casual smile, watching the look of astonishment flit over Simon's face. 'So perhaps now you see where I'm coming from. Maybe you will trust me somewhat better from now on. You're going to need to. What happened in England is now ancient history and no longer matters. What concerns me now is our immediate future. The next few months are going to be quite dramatic. We're all going to need friends we can trust, implicitly, and with no questions asked. There won't be enough time to be polite and check alibis. It will be very much shoot first and ask questions later.

'The other, more important reason for sending you to Sondershausen and Nordhausen is this- the secret weapon establishment there is run directly on instructions from the Reichsführer. Few of the details have leaked out, but I've learned through various sources that biological weapons are being produced secretly and illegally. I know that this is directly against the Führer's wishes, but that's not the sort of thing to challenge Himmler with, not if you wish to stay alive.' He continued to keep his voice low. 'So, while your overt mission is to check the security there, your covert role will be to report to me on what's really going on, and how close they are to finishing these weapons. You'll report back to me by any means you can. Understood?'

Simon nodded.

'It's very much like before, back at RSHA.' Schellenberg carried on. 'I can't be seen at Nordhausen itself, not without a very good reason, which at the moment I don't have. You, on the other hand, will have every excuse to snoop around and pry everywhere and anywhere, without question or comment. There's also some other news.'

'What's that, sir?'

'An acquaintance of yours is there already, an old friend. I won't spoil the surprise by telling you who he is yet. Wait and see. Are you happy to go ahead and do this?'

Once again, Simon found it hard to see a way he could refuse. His brain worked furiously. Was Schellenberg really in contact with MI6? The man had not specifically said so, but how else could he know that password? It was inconceivable that Schellenberg had let slip that famous opening Shakespearean line entirely innocently. But this was still a highly dangerous situation, one without any guarantees. Who would be believed if push came to shove and all this secrecy was exposed- a major or a general? Just as before, he was entirely dependent on Schellenberg's protection. The answer was clear to him. Simon would have no choice but to comply with this latest 'request'. But maybe another deal could be struck.

'Before I answer your question, you haven't told me about my father. Or Canaris. And I haven't heard from either of them for quite few months. Sir, what's going on?' Simon's tone sharpened, his voice rising. 'You said you were a man of your word. Prove it.'

'Quiet. Keep your voice down,' the general muttered, glancing towards the front of the car. He no longer looked casual. A grim look dominated his features. 'I trust Hansen in most things, but I trust nobody with any of this.' A note of sorrow crept into his voice. 'I have kept my word, believe me. Otherwise, Himmler would have had them both executed by now. You remember the Bomb plot last July?' Simon nodded but he was afraid of what was about to be revealed. 'It failed. Hitler wanted to lash out at all those in the conspiracy, and anyone else associated with a lack of suitable National Socialist fervour. So he appointed Himmler as commander of the Home Army. As well as being the Reich's chief police officer and Minister of the Interior, Himmler now has total authority over virtually all aspects of life in the Reich, and a large amount of control over the Army as well.

'Most of the conspirators were from the Home Army, or scattered throughout regional government. Both organizations were brutally purged, an orgy of torture and death. The same happened throughout the rest of the country. Mock trials, the usual travesty of justice aided and abetted by crazed and crooked lawyers in the pay of the Party. Anybody who was even remotely not fully committed to the Nazi cause was seized. As far as I know, possibly five thousand or so have already been strung up, or hung on meat hooks to die horribly. A similar number is currently languishing in concentration camps, and subject to the usual degradation and ill-treatment. Are you aware of the concept of *Sippenhaft*?'

Simon shook his head.

'It means that the same, or a similar fate, is visited on the relatives of all those accused. Nobody can plead ignorance. A lot of innocent women and children are in labour camps, or dead. As for your father, I'm not sure what happened - perhaps someone implicated him while under interrogation. I don't know the details.' Schellenberg shrugged ruefully. 'I've done what I can, but he's now in Flossenberg concentration camp.' Simon's heart sank. 'What? Dear God! How is he?' 'He's surviving. I have a contact there on the camp staff that keeps an eye on him and ensures he's reasonably well treated. That's all one can ask for and do in a place like that.' 'How long has he been there?' 'Since November last year. He's done well to stay alive. A bit of weight loss, but little else to worry about.' 'For Christ's sake, why didn't you tell me that before?' Simon said accusingly. 'Because you were still recovering, and I didn't want to jeopardize your progress. Besides, there was nothing you could have done, lying half-paralysed in a hospital bed. The knowledge of your father's predicament would have driven you mad. Now you're much better able to help, should the need arise. After all, Sondershausen is only a few hours' drive from Flossenberg.' 'What do you mean by that?' 'Work it out for yourself,' Schellenberg said, a touch of exasperation entering his voice. 'If you've listened to what I've been saying, then surely you must know that the war will soon be over. I think we have a duty to ensure that we try to keep alive all of those who are dear to us, who can help to rebuild our shattered country. Your mother and sister are safe and out of the way. Your father will need your help. If the country begins to fall apart, as I think it will soon, then you may need to act quickly and get him out of there before it's too late.' 'And the Admiral? You haven't mentioned him.' 'No. As luck would have it, Canaris too is in Flossenberg, for much the same reason - a lack of suitable Nazi fervour. Even with your father's previous exoneration, the fact that he had once been under suspicion was probably enough to earn him a ticket to a concentration camp. As for the admiral, well, we both know that Himmler has hated him for quite a few years. The failure of the bomb plot was the perfect opportunity to settle old scores and put Canaris behind bars. The only reason I can think of that Canaris is still alive is that Himmler is still afraid the old man has some hidden, incriminating evidence tucked away somewhere. A sort of ace-in-the-hole should the worst happen. My concern about this is that when the country does begin to break up Himmler will take his revenge no matter what evidence Canaris has.

'The Reichsführer's becoming more and more desperate. I know for a fact he is trying to arrange peace negotiations behind the Führer's back. Himmler has been in contact with the Swedish embassy in Berlin, something that he's been very careful to keep hidden. And at the same time he's developing these bio-weapons at Nordhausen - a desperate, despairing gamble if ever there was one.'

He fell silent. 'So, what do you think?' Suddenly, the roar of aircraft engines intruded, rapidly followed by the hammer of cannon fire. Hansen swerved the car just in time. A double row of dirt puffs streaked along the length of the road, barely missing the Mercedes. In front of them a small truck suddenly burst into flames. Traffic and people scattered wildly. Several dirty looking bundles that once were living human beings lay scattered along the road like carelessly strewn dolls in a child's bedroom.

Schellenberg urgently lowered the partition glass. 'Quick, Hansen. For Christ's sake get us off the road and under cover.' But his driver was already in motion. Gunning the engine hard, he shot the Mercedes up the road. Schellenberg anxiously cranked the side window down, trying to track the circling aircraft. A squat grey-green shape was climbing back into the heavens, the beat of its engine receding as it flew further away. Then it began to turn, looping over viciously and angling down for another strafing run.

A village lay up ahead and beyond that a small wood. Hansen drove like a man possessed, hurling the car around a variety of moving and stationary objects in the road with the skill of a skier negotiating a slalom course flat out. The village drew closer and closer until suddenly they reached the outskirts. 'Turn right at the next junction,' shouted Schellenberg. They could hear the roar of the plane approaching as it swooped down and flew nearer.

Hansen jumped on the brake pedal, both feet jammed hard down on it to gain maximum pedal pressure, then hurled the car right and ramming a racing gear change through the 'box. The Mercedes shot around the bend just in time. A barrage of shells slammed into the wall of a nearby house as the fighter rocketed past, smashing clouds of plaster and brick dust into the street. The car sped up the lane and then violently turned left, heading towards the wood. Less than a minute later, they were safe and hidden from view by the mass of conifer branches above them.

'That was close!' Schellenberg sank back in his seat with a sigh of relief. He looked over at Simon and smiled shakily. 'You've probably experienced that before.'

'Not in the back of a Mercedes with leather seats,' Simon said dryly.

'Speak for yourself, but that's the first time for me.' He wiped his brow with an immaculate handkerchief. The departing fighter roared away overhead, searching for a new target.

They waited for another five minutes before gingerly venturing out of the wood. There was no sound to be heard, except the swaying of branches in the chilly wind. Over to the left, in the direction of where the attack had first started, several columns of smoke drifted lazily upwards in the late afternoon gloom.

'We should be able to get going without further harassment, sir.' It was Hansen, speaking from the driver's seat. 'I doubt there's enough visibility for any further attacks.'

Cautiously they resumed their journey. Dusk was rapidly approaching, the setting sun casting a bleary red haze as it settled below the rim of clouds in the west. The car twisted and wound its way across the undulating landscape. Less than half an hour later they were nearing the outskirts of the university town of Göttingen. Only a few scattered lights twinkled, soon to be turned off by the imminent black out regulations.

In the meantime Simon was given plenty of time to consider the lack of options open to him. Although there was little chance of him being ordered to return to active duty, at this late stage of the war anything was possible. Schellenberg had told him that even ten and twelve year-old boys from the Hitler Youth were being given rudimentary training in how to knock out enemy tanks, using Panzerfausten and homemade Molotov cocktails. Elderly men were given rifles and a helmet, and were then forcibly inducted into the *Volkssturm*, the German equivalent of the Home Guard. Desperate measures indeed. Simon knew full well the naked, terrifying fear that gripped even the most experienced of soldiers when facing up to a massed tank charge by T-34s. *Those old men and kids wouldn't last five seconds.*

'Tell me more about what's going on at Nordhausen,' he asked, as the car left Göttingen behind them.

'I've told you most of what I know already,' Schellenberg said. 'The underground factories in the Nordhausen area already produce the V1 and V2 rockets. Other areas produce jet engines. A special sealed off area is involved in biological research and development.'

'How close are they to completing their work?'

'It's nearly finished, as far as I know. What worries me is this - if Himmler authorizes deployment then millions more will die., including frontline soldiers and innocent civilians on both sides. It will be the last ride of the Valkyries and the Four Horsemen of the Apocalypse all rolled up into one- you know how much Hitler and Himmler love Wagner and Norse mythology. I've heard the Führer say it himself- 'we shall not capitulate- no, never! We may be destroyed, but if we are, we shall drag a world with us - a world in flames!' It is total madness.' Schellenberg shook his head in despair. 'There's little doubt that he's lost all sense and reason. Hitler's already authorised Speer to destroy anything of value, no matter what, throughout Germany. The Reichsführer could easily go the same way. There must be a way of preventing Himmler using these deadly weapons for his own ends.'

'So in return for working for you again...?' Simon let the rest of his sentence unfinished, waiting for Schellenberg's reply. 'I promise to do whatever I can to keep your father and Canaris alive.' 'You'll have to do better than that, Brigadeführer,' Simon snorted derisively. 'I'm beginning to feel very much like a minor pawn in a much bigger game of strategic chess - not much use and therefore quite disposable.' 'You're not disposable.' Schellenberg for once was in deadly earnest. 'And if you know your chess, sometimes a pawn can be the most powerful piece on the board - in the right situation and at the right time. I'll do everything I can to protect them. I have access to most of the Reichsführer's personal files. If I get to hear that he's decided to eliminate your father and Canaris, I'll warn you. A resourceful soldier such as you should be able to manage the rest. But it means you must always be contactable at short notice. A code word should suffice- how about 'Brandt'? If you hear that from me, then you'll know what you must do. I may even come myself.'

Simon thought for a moment then turned to Schellenberg. This time the arrangement would be on a more even footing. 'Alright I accept. But if I need extra resources, then you'll help, no matter what, even if it requires your personal intervention.'

'No matter what...' Schellenberg offered his hand, and Simon took it.

Mittelbau-Dora camp, Nordhausen, central Germany 1500 14/3/1945

Sturmbannführer Richard Baer wore a worried frown. As far as he could see, the future did not appear to hold anything worth looking forward to. His previously unshaken faith in the dream of National Socialism dominating the world had taken a series of bad knocks over the last ten months, more so recently. The Reich was beginning to crumble, both in the East and in the West, and as every day went by the end appeared to be getting closer and closer. Painfully, he cast his mind back to recent events, the ones that had affected him personally. It was only a month ago that the Soviets had quickly smashed their way through the German front lines in southern Poland and seized the Auschwitz area with all its factories, mines and workshops. That was disastrous enough in itself, but worse still, the camp had fallen into their hands almost completely intact. Only a few demolitions in the most incriminating areas were hastily completed before the Red Army marched in. The crematoria and some of the processing centres were demolished, but everything else was left untouched. Those inmates fit to walk were brutally marched off to the West. Most of the rest were shot where they lay. There simply had not been enough time to do anything more.

As a result, the Reichsführer had been most displeased. Once again, his explicit orders to erase all evidence of Entlösung had not been fully carried out. Baer was summarily recalled to Berlin to face a very difficult interview. Himmler was suitably scathing. Why was this area not destroyed completely? Baer had offered a list of reasonable excuses, only to see them rejected one by one by a frigidly uncompromising Reichsführer. There *had* been enough time, and all demolitions *should* have been completed as soon as the Soviets showed any possibility of breaking through the regional defences. The fact that nobody in the Wehrmacht had bothered to inform Baer until it was much too late was utterly irrelevant. *He* should have acted sooner.

Baer was then abruptly dismissed and left to kick his heels around what was left of Berlin before his fate was decided. It was not long in coming. A few anxiety-filled days later, one of Himmler's assistants delivered his punishment. The letter from Himmler was short and to the point- immediate demotion in rank by one grade, and a new posting to a camp in the Thüringen area. It could have been a lot worse. Baer was expecting a one-way ticket to some front line SS unit, where life expectancy could be counted in minutes rather than days. Perhaps the Reichsführer had taken Baer's exceptional performance during his time as Auschwitz camp commandant into consideration before passing final judgment...

So here he was, stuck in yet another facility that reeked of death and despair. However, compared to the scale of racial cleansing that had gone on in Auschwitz, Mittelbau-Dora was small beer indeed. His former camp had exterminated at least a million Jews and other sub-humans while he was in charge, something that he was still very proud of. Auschwitz was a dedicated killing machine that had made a significant contribution to the racial purity of the Reich, a strictly controlled operation that ran smoothly and almost entirely without any operational hiccups. The only conceivable blot on its performance was that ridiculous incident with the misdirected troop train, but that had been easily corrected. The beauty of it all was that there was very little evidence of the scale of the killing, bar the stench that covered the surrounding area. Eventually, even he had got used to that. It was all so neatly and tidily controlled, an operation that was virtually invisible in its efficiency. It appealed to his Germanic sense of order and discipline.

But here, things were very much more disorganized. The whole area of the camp and surrounding operations was a mess, a testament to inefficiency, sloppy planning and disorder. It affronted his sensitivities as a meticulously well-organised administrator. There were dead bodies lying all over the place, ignored where they dropped, and left to rot where they lay. Nobody seemed to be remotely concerned about keeping the camps functioning in an orderly manner. As long as enough workers were provided to take care of immediate labour requirements, then that was all that mattered. In the two weeks since he had taken over from the previous commander he had struggled to install some form of order into the camp's operations, but so far with little success. The previous commandant, Obersturmbannführer Otto Förschner, had left him a monumental mess, and with minimal resources to sort it out.

The area around the small city of Nordhausen was a mass of secondary camps dominated by the main labour camp at Dora itself. On his arrival he had visited all the outlying camps under his command. There were nearly forty of them. All of them mimicked Dora in their disorganization and chaotic conditions. Their single priority was to provide slave labour for the Mittelwerk rocket factory complex. This was located underground, below the Kohnstein hill region that formed the southern boundary of the Harz Mountains. His visit to the Kohnstein complex, part of the usual 'getting to know you rigmarole', had been short and not very productive. Security was tight. He'd met the SS officer in charge of the facility, a veteran of the Eastern front.

The rockets assembled at Mittelwerk were vital to the war effort, that much he knew. They powered the V1 and V2 Vengeance weapons that were already wreaking havoc among the enemy rear areas. Jet engines were also manufactured at the Kohnstein factory. There were rumours of other secret weapons as well, but security was tight and few details were forthcoming.

Obersturmbannführer Hartmann was decidedly unfriendly and very abrupt. It was quite apparent that the man had little time for him, and resented any interruption to his busy schedule. The message was clear - keep supplying the workers, and take care of all other business. We're much too busy here to be concerned with any minor difficulties you may have outside. Don't waste our time and bother us with trivia - speak to RSHA if you have any problems. And that was that.

Still, at least he had wide latitude in his own area of command. He'd made some inroads into cleaning the camps up. There were no crematoria facilities, so many of the bodies were buried in huge, open graves or in ditches that bordered roads and tracks. Those who were no longer fit to work and about to die were railed off to Buchenwald, where they could die in a more dedicated extermination facility. However, these were comparatively few in number compared to those who simply expired on the spot, in the middle of a job. This problem was compounded hugely by a lack of food. The current camp population was approximately eight thousand, but food deliveries were barely enough to keep a quarter of that total alive, even on minimal rations. One of his staff had calculated that probably two hundred inmates a day were dying of the combined effects of heavy labour and severe malnutrition. On top of that were those who were beaten to death for attempted sabotage, or summarily executed for the most trivial of offences. That was something he was quite unconcerned about. After all, most of the inmates were captured Russians or Polish and French Jews, none of whom had any right to a long, happy life. As long as fresh supplies of workers were delivered by train every day to keep topping up the numbers, then all would be well, and he would sleep easy.

But he needed to bear in mind the example of Auschwitz. Who knows how long it would be before the heart of the Reich would be torn open by the Allied advance? He had no wish to be captured by a vengeful enemy and be associated with command of a death camp, so this was another good reason to clear up the mess and bury the evidence.

And what of his own future? The war would soon be over, and it was already apparent that those who could were making plans for their own escape. He was certain that most of the top SS command were busy buying their way out, with faked Swiss or Spanish passports, and the right contacts in the right places. He had heard a very quiet rumour that Hans Frank had already disappeared, and was lying low in preparation for the best time to flee Europe and head elsewhere, to where he could not be caught. But Baer had no wish to do that. Germany was his home, and besides he did not have access to the kind of sources that would give him that level of protection. Perhaps his brother Erich would be sympathetic. The man worked in the Reich Forestry service, up near the Danish border not far from Hamburg. Erich would have enough influence to find him a job and hide him from further investigation. Baer had a small collection of diamonds, a highly illegal source of income from a series of shady deals carried out in the last few weeks before Auschwitz was lost to the Soviets, when he had finally decided that his own safety was more important than the future of National Socialism. They would no doubt be useful in helping him to disappear from view...

His thoughts were interrupted by a knock on his office door.

'Enter.'

It was Keller, his adjutant.

'Sir, your three o'clock appointment is here.'

'Thank you. Give me a minute, then send him in.'

Baer looked at his schedule for today. There was a Sturmbannführer Simon to see him, sent over from Sondershausen at the request of RSHA. Simon? Surely it was not the same officer on that strange day in Poland last year? The rank was different, but a promotion could have quite easily occurred in the intervening months. What was the purpose of his visit? RSHA had not given a reason. He would soon find out.

The door opened, and an officer in field grey walked in, not without some difficulty. Baer stood up, taking in the newcomer's appearance. Yes, it was the same man but he was different, slimmer, almost a pale shadow of the man he had met last May. The face was thinner, more lined than before, and there was a touch of grey at the sideburns. He returned the Nazi salute and gestured to a chair. The other man sat down. The relief to be off his legs was quite apparent.

'Sturmbannführer Simon, a pleasure to meet you again.' Baer watched him carefully while the newcomer gradually adjusted himself into a more comfortable position. 'May I offer you some refreshment? It's some time since we last met. I hope my behaviour did not cause any offence at the time, but you must surely have understood the, ah, delicate position we both found ourselves in.'

'Yes, of course, *Sturmbannführer* Baer. Thank you, perhaps a glass of water later.' The emphasis on Baer's demoted rank was not unmissed. 'Thank you for seeing me at such short notice. As you probably know, this visit is at RSHA's request.' Simon had already decided to play a straight bat and ignore any references to their previous meeting, although he would never forget it. That Baer was in command here, the same Baer as on that fateful day in Auschwitz, had come as quite a surprise. Perhaps this was the same surprise that Schellenberg hinted at. And now, for whatever reason, they were at the same rank.

'Yes, although they have not told me the reason. Perhaps you could explain.' Privately, Baer was more than a little worried. Perhaps Himmler had sent him to check up on conditions here, to snoop on him behind his back and report clandestinely.

'I have been ordered to perform an overall security assessment of the facilities here at the Nordhausen-Dora complex, and all other local operations. I require access to all your facilities at a moment's notice, at any time.' Simon slowly extracted a letter from his jacket pocket and slid it across the desk. Baer picked it up and studied it for a moment. The letter was straightforward enough, and signed by a Brigadeführer. There appeared to be no obvious hidden motive, as far as he could see, but relying on its face value could well be dangerous. He decided to dig a little deeper.

'I can see no problem with that,' he acquiesced, the picture of cooperation. 'Tell me, Max, if I may be so bold, how far will your survey extend? I'm most anxious to ensure that all is as it should be, particularly if higher command becomes involved more directly in the running of these camps. By the way, please call me Richard.' Baer was keen to keep his personal concerns under control and appear nonchalant, but he was unable to hide the hint of anxiety that crept into his voice.

Simon smiled briefly. It was obvious that Baer was on some sort of hook. Why not enjoy letting him hang there, the picture of uncertainty. He was in no rush to help him out. 'I'm afraid I can't really say, Richard. This is on a need to know basis only. My orders explicitly prevent me from revealing anything else.'

Baer was still the picture of affability, despite a sinking feeling in his stomach. 'Of course, Max. Naturally, I understand your position.' He smiled, desperately trying to keep his anxiety hidden. 'Out of interest, are you going to report about the internal conditions here?'

This last question was the give-away. 'I couldn't possibly comment, Richard. You know how it is. It all depends on whether this affects security. But I can promise you one thing - that is you'll be the first to be informed.' Max left him dangling there. The exact interpretation of that last comment would keep Baer on his toes. That was all he needed to know for the moment. If this slimy bastard was under pressure from the top then so much the better. He would not lose any sleep about it.

Baer smiled again, all the time struggling to maintain his composure. It was quite obvious that Simon would go no further.

'Thank you, Max. I'll bear that in mind. Please see my adjutant on the way out. He'll arrange all the necessary documentation and inform the various facilities you wish to see. Is there anything else I can help you with?'

'No thanks.' Simon slowly levered himself up out of the chair. It was only at this stage that Baer took in the Oak Leaves cluster above the Knight's Cross. 'Congratulations on your promotion and decorations Max if I may again be so bold,. It looks to me as if you're recovering from more wounds again, same as last time?'

'Yes, thanks - something like that.' Simon slipped on his field cap and retrieved the letter from the desk. 'Thank you for your cooperation. I'm sure RSHA will be suitably, ah, grateful.' With that, he saluted, turned and walked out of the office.

Baer watched the door close and sat down again. His face fell. How much did Simon know about his recent demotion and disgrace? Was he working directly under orders from Himmler himself? It was hard to tell. He didn't recognize the name or signature on the letter, but it appeared to be genuine. Was it worth risking a discrete enquiry back to RSHA? Probably not, considering the present cloud he was under. Besides, there was really no one there at the moment that he could trust well enough to ask the necessary questions.

There was nothing more he could do but to play a waiting game, keep his eyes open, and make sure he did not leave himself open to further criticism and censure. And if the going became too rough, then a set of forged papers and civilian clothes would be his best bet if he needed to make a sudden escape north...

Kohnstein factory complex, Nordhausen area 1000
15/3/1945

Simon levered himself out of the passenger seat of the Kubelwagen and stood by the camouflage-painted vehicle, his breath condensing in the frosty air. It was a clear day, rare for this time of year in the Harz. The ground was frozen hard, and clumps of snow and ice lay scattered across the area that lay just outside the factory entrance. The air was crisp and cold. Overhead the sky was ice blue, a picture-perfect panorama broken only by a few shreds of cotton wool clouds high up. He shivered. The journey over from Sondershausen had taken nearly an hour, just about long enough for the primitive heating system in the Kubelwagen to make a half-decent attempt to warm its occupants up and provide some protection from the subzero temperatures outside.

Today's duties were clearly established in his mental diary. First, a trip to the underground secret weapons establishment at Kohnstein, followed by a return to the SS Panzer school at Sondershausen to begin a series of tactical discussions and field training exercises for the next course of recruits and officer cadets. The last two days had been spent getting to know the area, and understanding the remit of his new posting. Yesterday's visit to see Baer was an obligatory formality, but useful enough in its own way. Nearly all the relevant documentation he needed was either ready for collection or shortly would be. However, today's visit here would be far more important.

This was the secret base for biological weapons synthesis. Rocket production here was just as vital, especially the newer types he had heard hints about. These weapons needed to be delivered accurately and at a suitable range. Most of the technical problems associated with the mobile launchers had been overcome, emphasizing that this underground factory would be the only place where sabotage would be completely effective. Once the rockets were ready it would be a simple matter to scatter them far and wide on their mobile launchers and launch this biological offensive. If production of either could be temporarily delayed then there might be a chance to disrupt Himmler's plans sufficiently and save countless lives. And if Schellenberg was correct then the Allies would be here soon, maybe in six to eight weeks at the latest, if not sooner. In the meantime he would have to find some way of halting further progress. But first he would need a lot more information.

The guards positioned at the final checkpoint were minutely inspecting his paperwork, just the same as the half dozen or so other security roadblocks they had already negotiated on their way over from Sondershausen. After a few minutes one of them walked back to the main sentry building, probably to check that the necessary clearance had been granted in advance. Although he was naturally on edge and tense, Simon was relatively unconcerned. Like all the other checks this should be merely routine, the sort of scrutiny one would expect at a maximum-security installation. His credentials should stand up to any inspection. Schellenberg guaranteed to have taken care of all the necessary details.

He took his time to survey his surroundings. The factory entrance was cut abruptly into the side of a large, steep hill, itself covered in a mass of tangled pine trees that marched away into the middle distance on all sides. When closed the outside of the massive doors had been painted to look like a normal hillside. Between them a double rail track led straight into the mouth of the tunnel entrance, alongside a minor road and a muddy path that bore the marks of regular heavy foot traffic. The road was deeply rutted and broken up, although in these frigid temperatures the ground around it was sufficiently hard enough for driving over, even with heavy trucks. The main road from Nordhausen that led on north towards Herzberg and Northeim turned west over five hundred meters away, leaving only the much smaller route that led up to the gates.

It was clear from his tactical inspection of the area that every effort had been made to keep the factory's activity concealed from Allied air reconnaissance. Heavy camouflage netting was strung between surrounding trees to cover the transportation routes into the factory. He could just make out a couple of camouflaged cooling stacks and radiator vents positioned halfway up the hillside. Both of them were expertly disguised to look like natural features. The railway lines were the most obvious potential give-away from the air, but someone had taken great pains to minimise the chances of aerial recognition. In addition to the netting the tracks were heavily disguised at ground level all the way from the nearest rail junction, and covered with large mobile covers that were easy to move back into place once a train passed by. External buildings were kept to an absolute minimum. Anything that vaguely resembled a man-made structure or vehicle was draped in disruptive pattern netting and located between clumps of trees.

He quickly realised that everything that came in or out of the factory moved under cover. Even with the protection from aerial reconnaissance, this would mainly occur at night, unless the daytime cloud cover was low and thick. Simon judged it unlikely that the Allies would ever spot this place from up above. The undulating cluster of densely wooded hills that surrounded the area would make them think that there could be nothing here worth bombing, nothing that looked like a military installation or heavy factory.

The guard was coming back.

'All clear, sir. Only essential vehicles are allowed inside, so please get your driver to park over there in the trees.' The guard pointed to a covered area over to the right. 'The CO's expecting you. One of his staff will meet you inside.'

Simon returned the salute. Shortly afterwards the Kubelwagen was driven away to be parked. As he turned towards the hillside several tired and emaciated looking men in shabby civilian attire and carrying heavy brushes emerged from the tunnel entrance. They were double marched from the main gate to where the Kubelwagen had driven up. It was soon clear that their job was to cover up any evidence of activity that could be seen from the air. The guards gestured harshly and the men sprang into action, working vigorously to brush away all evidence of vehicular activity.

He was met just inside the gates by a young, slim, blond Untersturmführer who quickly introduced himself and led the way inside the darkened entrance. As soon as Simon entered the tunnel his ears were almost overwhelmed by deafening noise. The cacophony came from several mobile diesel-powered generators that stood lengthways along the corridor. The racket was unbelievably loud, but mercifully did not last long. After a hundred meters progress an intersecting tunnel opened up on both sides, and his guide took a right turn. The noise suddenly dropped to a far more manageable level, much to his relief.

'Sorry about that bit, sir. That's the worst - the rest of the underground area is much easier on the ears.'

'Thank God for that,' Simon grunted. 'I'd go mad if I had to work down there for any length of time without ear protection.'

'I know what you mean, sir.' The man gave a cheery smile and winked. 'Quite a few of the prisoners who work there do. We ship 'em back to Buchenwald where they're taken care of, if you know what I mean.'

Simon looked momentarily puzzled.

The Untersturmführer laughed callously, sensing Simon's lack of comprehension. 'They're all Jews, sir. The usual *Untermenschen* scum along with a few Russians and Frenchies thrown in for good measure. Ah, here we are. This is the Administration section. The CO's office is at the far end. Follow me please.'

He led Simon into the office area. Almost immediately he noted that the air temperature was much more pleasant than the cold air in the dank tunnels. They passed through a wide open-plan area of desks and filing cabinets, populated by uniformed men and women, each busy with their own tasks. At the far end a partitioned area was sealed off from the main administration. The Untersturmführer led him into a short corridor. At the far end he knocked on a solid steel grey door.

'Sir, the CO will see you now'.

Simon walked into the brightly lit room, and glanced down at the officer seated behind the large desk. He was busy reading a large report held in front of his face. As he lowered it Simon gaped in surprise, before quickly recovering and offering the obligatory salute.

It was Harald Hartmann.

❄

Broadway Buildings, London 1100 15/3/1945

'Is everything OK Charlie?' Menzies asked. He was in a very good mood. Such was his general demeanour these days. The war was going extremely well, MI6's star was in the ascendancy, and at long last the end was in sight. He was already planning and thinking about the next set of tasks, specifically those against the Soviet Union. While the Russians might still be allies for the moment, he was under no illusions as to who the next enemy was going to be. Once Nazi Germany was destroyed and peace had broken out in Europe again, then the Russians would become enemy number one. His natural anti -Communist tendencies, carefully curbed during the wartime period to satisfy his political masters, would almost certainly be allowed a fuller expression - as long as Churchill won the post-war election, that is. It was no secret that the current PM distrusted Stalin, and was utterly convinced that the Soviet Union wished to dominate Europe, politically and militarily, for many years to come.

'Yes, Chief', Monkton replied. 'The weather forecast is reasonable- partly clear skies over central Germany tonight, although there's a cold front from the east approaching that might move in tomorrow. The RAF anticipates a straightforward insertion over the target area. Luftwaffe defences around the Harz area are minimal and what's left of their night fighter force is going to be busy elsewhere- what with the Russians bombing Berlin into more rubble, and the Americans and our air forces flattening everything else.'

'Excellent. What about our man Steele?'

'He's all taken care of, Chief. Mission, briefings, equipment - the works just like his previous trips to the Fatherland. Nothing's been left to chance. We're all ready to go. He flies out from RAF Northolt at midnight.'

'Is there any more information from our source in Berlin?'

Monkton shook his head. 'No - nothing as yet. And no joy with our aerial surveys either. The RAF has sent several daytime reconnaissance missions to the area, but hasn't been able to get any decent photos. Either the area is covered by thick cloud cover or on the few occasions where the skies are clear they are unable to pinpoint the location. Jerry must have an excellent camouflage operation in progress.'

'Hmmm.' Menzies sat back in his chair, and lapsed into thought while his deputy made his excuses and left the room. Nothing had changed appreciably in the last few weeks. The information coming from Germany had not altered in any way, and there were no new developments.

He cast his mind back towards the beginning of the year, and his surprise secret trip to Spain. The contact had come in December, through a roundabout neutral channel. An unknown senior German officer had wished to meet up, entirely off the record, and propose a deal. Menzies was initially sceptical. He suspected that it was probably some disaffected Nazi who'd had enough of Hitler's rabble, a man with an eye to the future and most likely the main chance. He had a good idea of how the meeting would unfold. A deal would be proposed, almost certainly involving some form of immunity from prosecution once the war was over. In exchange Menzies would be offered some supposedly priceless information, something that would possibly alter the course of the war.

At first, he had almost dismissed the whole idea as some sort of desperate ploy. What could this German possibly have that the Allies did not know about, now that the war was nearly won? The last German offensive in the West, the Battle of the Bulge, was in its final despairing throes. Once the Allies fully recovered, they would resume their general offensive and Germany would be overrun. That would be that, the end of six years' slaughter. What else could happen?

In the end, despite his rather jaundiced point of view, he had decided to go. There might just be something worthwhile for him to hear. One should never look a gift horse in the mouth, or so the old saying went. Menzies was also well aware that, even at this late stage of the war, the Allies did not have a complete understanding of everything that was going on inside the German High Command and Hitler's mind. The recent surprise German attack in Belgium was a case in point. It had fooled everybody, all the way up to the top. Even SHAEF's senior intelligence staff, and Kenneth Strong in particular, had absolutely no inkling of what the Germans had in store for them when the attack came in. It was contrary to all their expectations and assessments. They'd all assumed that Nazi Germany was nearly finished.

Besides, the Britain in winter was a miserable place to be. He quite fancied a few days break in the sun of southern Spain. Now that most of the occupied territories in Europe were liberated, MI6's normally hectic pace of work had slowed down to a far more reasonable and steadier rhythm, and a few days' absence from his normal routine would not be catastrophic. Monkton was quite capable of running the show while he was away.

He was glad he had gone. His German counterpart, whoever he was, had chosen the venue and the terms of the meeting, from which he could not be dissuaded - a shady restaurant in the harbour area at Cadiz. The British were given carte blanche to inspect the rendezvous and ensure that they were satisfied with the security arrangements. A secluded table with a view of the harbour was chosen. Menzies would arrive first and take the chair facing the sea. The German would then arrive by car, alone, and take the opposite seat. No photographs or records would be taken by either side, to ensure security and anonymity. The German was obviously paranoid that his position could be compromised if news of the meeting was leaked to the wrong people.

Unsurprisingly his bodyguards and MI6 minders in Spain were not happy with the arrangements. What if the German pulled out a gun or a snatch team whisked him away before help could arrive? Menzies had dismissed their concerns. There was a certain thrill to be had from working in the field again, out on your own with just your wits to survive on - something that had been duly submerged in all his years of office work at MI6's HQ. He was looking forward to the challenge. Besides there was a safety net in place, just in case the worst should happen. The area would be discretely cordoned off and subject to careful scrutiny by Colonel Cruz and a team of his Spanish heavies, just to ensure fair play and prevent dirty tricks by either side. The day in January was cool but clear. The bright sun in the cloudless blue sky provided some warmth even at that time of the year. A blustery wind swept across the city and out to sea, but from where he sat, he was safely sheltered from most of the elements. The harbour view from the restaurant terrace was quite superb. Much of the busy port area was away to his left and out of direct view. To his front he could see a flotilla of yachts close up against their moorings, while a constant stream of trawlers and smaller boats headed in through the breakwaters, fresh from their early morning trips to the fishing grounds further out to sea, gulls wheeling and flapping overhead. The medieval walls, ramparts and fortifications of the port area dominated the scene. Beyond them endless ranks of white horses foamed and marched out towards the darker blue of the deep ocean, whipped up by the stiff offshore breeze.

But, as edifying as it was, he was not there to admire the view. A little after 1230 a black Mercedes pulled up outside the restaurant and a heavily wrapped up man of medium height got out. He wore a dark hat and overcoat, with the collar turned up. The car pulled away, and the stranger made his way over to where Menzies was seated. All the tables nearby were empty. Beyond that, Ruiz's men occupied the remaining seats and studiously scrutinised their menus.

The man sat down. Menzies studied his appearance carefully, trying to commit every feature of his opponent's face to memory. It looked vaguely familiar, but he could not immediately place it. The youthful face was slim, dominated by a heavy moustache, but Menzies concentrated on the eyes. Moustaches could be faked, but the look in a man's eyes often held a clue as to his real identity. Before he left for Spain he'd studied the photographs on file of all the leading Nazis, but this man's face did not immediately stand out in his mind. MI6 had a reasonably complete collection of photos on all the top officials inside Germany, but there were some notable gaps.

This man must be one of those. No matter. He waited for the German to open the conversation.

'Thank you for agreeing to attend this meeting, Colonel Menzies.' The stranger smiled affably, his eyes twinkling with amusement. He spoke excellent if slightly accented English. 'I'm so glad you managed to persuade your colleagues here in Spain to agree to the terms of this meeting. It looks like Colonel Cruz has done his usual thorough job.'

'Yes,' Menzies replied coolly, 'so it seems.' An awkward silence followed for a few moments. Menzies then decided to take up the challenge. 'I may be interested to hear what you have to tell me, but please don't waste my time. As for whatever you want in exchange, I can't give you any assurances. This is purely a preliminary meeting, with nothing on offer. From the point of view of MI6 your safety here is guaranteed - for the moment. That's the only guarantee I can give you. We have followed your stipulations precisely.'

'Good'. The German smiled again, ignoring Menzies' somewhat abrupt manner. 'I know. Thank you for your cooperation. The same guarantee applies from my side. I'm sure you can summon a team of agents to your assistance at the drop of a hat. So can I, but I sincerely hope that neither action will be necessary. And so let's get down to business.' The stranger looked at him intently, his casual manner gone in an instant. 'This will *not* be a waste of your time. I rather think that you will be most interested in what I have to tell you.'

'Ah. Some information then. And in exchange?'

'You probably think you know what I'm looking for, but you may well be mistaken. Not money, or false passports or a new identity. I could organize these myself, if I wanted to - if I wished to run and hide, that is.'

'I see,' countered Menzies, knowingly. 'Then it must be immunity from prosecution. Could it be perhaps that you have secrets that you wish to conceal, secrets that would be better off hidden from the light of day?'

'No', the German replied, firmly. 'I don't have any dirty laundry, as your American friends would say. Just the usual military intelligence secrets - I'm in the same line of work as you. I have a clear conscience, as clear as any man can have in the circumstances I find myself in. You may find it hard to believe, but decency and integrity are not entirely absent for some of us in Germany.' He sighed. 'But let's be realistic for a moment - within six months, the Reich will be no more. You, the British, your American allies and the Russians will see to that. I have no illusions as to what life under Russian occupation will be like. Also, I'm well aware that the victors always write the history - at least, their version of it. People in my organization will be labelled as criminals and mass murderers, and given short shrift. I doubt that justice will be entirely fair and unbiased - it usually isn't, in my experience. So I would like to alter the scales to weigh a little in my favour.'

So he's a Nazi, one of the SS undoubtedly. 'I'm not sure that could be arranged.' Menzies grunted, his expression entirely non-committal. This was very much along the lines he had suspected. The man in front of him was most likely to be involved in some of the more brutal aspects of Nazi Germany, and wished to wriggle off the hook. His sense of justice began to rebel at the thought of making a deal, but at the same time he was pragmatic enough to realize that sometimes such compromises needed to be made, no matter how distasteful the individual circumstances might be. 'All I can say is that I will listen to what you have to say. If what you tell me is worth my time here and if it checks out, then we *may* have an understanding as long as my superiors agree. That's all I can say at present.'

'Agreed.' The German nodded, equably. 'I would say exactly the same if I was in your position. But I somehow think that what I tell you will be considered as priceless - possibly the most important thing you've ever heard. It will be even better than Rothermere's report in May.'

Menzies face must have betrayed him for an instant, for the German briefly chuckled. 'I see that's not exactly news to you. Then tell me what you think of this.'

The information that followed was breathtaking. It concerned a top-secret underground weapons facility in the Harz

Mountains in central Germany, heavily guarded with limited access and stringent security. It was in the process of producing deadly biological weapons that would be delivered by rocket. The overall plan was a deadly aerial offensive - a combination of short-range tactical weapons for the battlefield and centres of communication and supply behind the front lines, combined with longer-range missiles targeted against large cities in the rear. Menzies was immediately aware of how dangerous this could be. Already a rain of V2 rockets had pounded London and Antwerp over the last few months, and their permanent elimination was a top Allied priority. But so far, almost no progress had been made in that direction. Nobody knew exactly where the rockets were being constructed. The other alarming fact was that these missiles could be launched from anywhere, and at very short notice. Aerial reconnaissance had identified that the rockets used mobile launchers that could launch from a forest clearing, a patch of woodland or any similar secluded and hidden location. It would be a chance in a million for an Allied aircraft to pinpoint the launch and destroy the missile on the ground. And once the rockets were airborne, they could not be shot down - unlike the V1s, they were far too fast and flew much too high to be tracked and caught.

That was bad enough, but this revelation sounded much worse. Apparently, some of the newer rockets would have a much greater range than the already formidable V2s. There were hints that one of them was called 'Amerika', and that New York and Washington were likely targets.

Menzies was shocked beyond the capacity for words. The effects of such an attack would be devastating - widespread illness and death among the advancing armies, not to mention the disastrous effect on civilian populations throughout Europe and even America. It could quite easily change the course of the war.

'I thought you might be interested,' the German said quietly. 'I think you would agree that the use of such weapons would be a disaster for humanity. I, for one, would not wish to see this happen, nor would my saner compatriots. Too many have already died. But Himmler is different. He's like a mad dog. He cannot be reasoned with and when these weapons are ready he may be crazy enough and desperate enough, to use them.'

Menzies sat in silence for a few minutes, thinking about the consequences of such an onslaught. 'Of course, we would retaliate with our own weapons, or launch a pre-emptive strike. We have stockpiles of similar biological agents.'

'Yes, I know that, but are you desperate and ready enough to use them first?' The German paused and let the question hang in the air. 'I very much doubt it. The Allies are seen as having the moral high ground, infinitely so compared to the Nazis and the Third Reich. And because you are so close to winning, why would you want to use such weapons anyway? Germany is nothing more than a huge heap of rubble. All your bombers are doing now is simply convulsing the same devastation every time they drop a new load of bombs. No - I can't see you stooping to such a level, unless Germany used them first. And if you did, what gain would you achieve? My country is in ruins. As for Himmler and the Nazis, they have nothing left to lose.'

Silence stretched between them. The stranger's logic was irrefutable, but Menzies was not about to accept his point of view quite so easily. He wanted corroboration. 'How do I know this is not a complete fabrication on your part? We've heard nothing about this through our own sources.'

The German looked back at him evenly. 'I understand your concern and doubt, Herr Menzies. Believe me, I would not risk my life to bring you this information without a very good reason. And as for you, can you afford to ignore me and take such a risk?'

'What about proof? Location, production schedules, specifications and so on - I'll need documentation to add weight to what you've told me.'

The German pulled out an envelope from inside his inner coat pocket, deftly concealed it in his serviette, and surreptitiously slid it across the table. 'I apologize for the rather cloak and dagger approach, as you English are prone to say, but you never know who's watching. These are copies of the few documents that exist. Getting access to them has not been easy. Himmler has been extremely careful to keep knowledge of this operation as restricted as possible, and I've yet to find out the factory's exact location. It's well known that Hitler is against the use of such weapons, for fear of Allied retaliation. But his health has not been the best of late, and I have no doubt that Himmler would take over in a flash should anything happen to his beloved Führer. That's all I have at present. More may follow. As for when the weapons will be ready, I'm not sure, but if I were you I wouldn't waste time. I suggest you take this back to London and consult with your superiors immediately. Then we can discuss the terms of our agreement.'

They had agreed to meet again within the next month. Before the German slipped away, Menzies asked one final question.

'In all this time, you haven't told me who you are.'

'No...there's no need for the moment.' His opponent grinned for a moment. 'Though I'm sure you have a few ideas. It's best that my identity remains unknown at present, for my own protection. I'm not ready to trust your side completely, not yet. You never know when somebody's tongue might slip, and I don't want you to hold the threat of exposing my identity over my head. That's why I don't want any photographs. But I need to know whether I can trust you. And as I'm sure you know, in our line of work trust is not easily established. Perhaps when we meet again, things will be a little easier, although a lot of that will depend on what your masters say. I look forward to our next conversation.' With that, he smiled again, pulled the brim of his hat down to cover his face, turned and hurried off. Almost as soon as he reached the restaurant exit, another dark car appeared almost out of nowhere and whisked him away.

The news had produced a furore in London and Washington. Yes, the Allies had their own chemical and biological weapons. But they had nothing as lethal as what this report claimed the Germans had, and nothing approaching the means of targeted delivery. The enemy was acknowledged to have an overwhelming lead in rocket technology, far beyond the fledgling progress the Allies had made in this field. His German contact in Spain had been right. The use of such weapons by the Allies would be considered only as a last resort. The political realities of the world situation had dictated that. So what could they do to stop the threat?

He remembered the urgent trip to Washington, and his summons before the Combined Joint Chiefs of Staff meeting at the Pentagon. It was the most high-level meeting he had ever been to, full of the most senior Allied commanders. The Americans were especially worried. This was the first time since the surprise Japanese attack at Hawaii that they had ever needed to seriously consider the possibility of an attack on their home soil. The knowledge that Nazi Germany could reach out across the expanse of the Atlantic and target American cities shook them profoundly, even if some of them were more than a little sceptical.

The conference buzzed along throughout a long day at an unprecedented level of intensity. Many options were discussed at length, but all of them bar one were ruled out as impractical and ineffective. Bombing would probably not produce the desired result. Neither the British nor the Americans had bombs that would penetrate deep enough underground to destroy such a target. They might be able to block the entrance and bury the area temporarily, but without the pinpoint location of where this factory was the chances of success were remote.

Another option that was considered was sending in an American airborne division to seize the area and destroy the factory. However, again this would probably not be a viable mission, not until the precise location of the factory had been identified. Moreover, much of the Harz mountain region was known to be unsuitable for airborne landings. The area was full of woods, hills and steep valleys. Parachute and glider landings in this type of terrain were considered highly risky. The resulting disruption and heavy losses would seriously compromise the success of a mission, and the survivors would most likely be easy meat for any local German garrisons. The example of what had happened to the British at Arnhem only a few months ago was still fresh in everyone's mind.

Something else was briefly discussed. One of the American generals present made an oblique reference to something called the Manhattan Project. Menzies was instantly on high alert. He could not fail to notice the sudden hush in the conversation, and the widespread look of puzzlement on most of those present. But the moment was fleeting. George Marshall, the most senior American general present, had simply glared at his colleague who had been so indiscrete as to bring the subject up, and announced that it would not be ready for at least six months- far too late to help them in their current predicament.

In the end, there was only really one way to do it - sabotage from inside the factory, before the weapons were finished and the rockets sent on their mobile launchers to wreak havoc from wherever their launch sites were. A dedicated German-speaking team of saboteurs would have to be sent in, but from where would they be found, and how would they get past the heavy security? Menzies' suggestion that MI6 would be the best organization to take care of the job was eagerly accepted. The Americans had few assets available, and all were fully occupied with the latest enemy developments in Belgium and France. Besides, MI6 had several agents in Germany who might be able to help out, and get inside the factory without arousing suspicion.

So the responsibility for the mission passed over to him. And now here he was, ready to insert another agent into Germany, and hopefully start the ball rolling to neutralize yet another Nazi threat. A further secret meeting in Spain had produced a little more information, but still no exact confirmation as to the factory's location. In exchange, he had promised that the German's case would be looked on favourably at the war's end. His opponent appeared satisfied, as if he suspected that Menzies' pledge was all he could hope for. The German also provided details of how he could be contacted in Berlin, with various recognition codes. In addition, there was the possibility of him getting someone inside the factory. One of his own agents was making excellent progress in recovering from his wounds, and would soon be sent to work at the underground complex. The

German smiled enigmatically. Perhaps the name of this agent might be familiar?

It was. The man facing him had to be Schellenberg. Who else could find out such secret information, and be of sufficient trust to be able to make secret trips abroad at this stage of the war? He had never been photographed by MI6, or by anyone else for all Menzies knew. The man courted anonymity. The German had merely smiled in response to Menzies' obvious question, and declined to comment. 'When I need your help I'll know how to get in touch' was all that he said. The important thing was to remember where Max Simon could be contacted, and how he might be used to help abort Himmler's deranged plan. The deal was then concluded, and the German disappeared again as quickly as he had arrived.

Steele's cover was good enough. His credentials should be impeccable, and he could easily pass for an SS officer. He'd spent most of the last three years inside Germany, and could move about without restriction. Steele would link up with Simon and a plan would be devised, most likely with the help of this senior officer from Berlin. Part of the load he carried tonight was a new form of plastic explosive that was disguised as bars of chocolate, but was most definitely not for internal consumption. All it needed was the appropriate fuse, a timer, and placement in the right areas. The ensuing devastation should take care of everything else.

❋

Kohnstein factory complex 1130

'So what do you think, Max? Impressive, isn't it?' They had just finished the tour of the underground factory, and were back in Hartmann's office. A secretary had been sent off to organize coffee. In the meantime the factory commandant gratefully slumped back into his leather-backed swivel chair, glad to ease the weight off the stump of his left leg. It was clear that the amputation still gave him trouble from time to time. 'Yes Harald, it's very impressive indeed. It's quite a facility you have here.' Simon smiled outwardly, but inside he was less certain. His old friend greeted him warmly enough, and after a few opening comments and a brief catch-up on what had happened to them since they last met, whisked him out on a guided tour of the facility. But something between them was different from the last time they'd met, something that Simon was at first unable to put a finger on. The subsequent tour soon confirmed his fears.

The factory was indeed remarkable. Based on a pre-war underground chalk quarry, it consisted of two very large main tunnels, both linked by a multitude of smaller cross-connecting passageways and smaller tunnels leading to workshops, storage areas and other assembly halls. The main tunnels bored back under the Kohnstein hill mass for nearly two kilometres in length. Over twenty rockets were in the final stages of assembly, all mounted on flat-bed rail carriages and waiting to be railed out to their launch areas when completed. He counted at least as many more, in various states of assembly. All of them were surrounded by teams of bustling workers, watched carefully by supervisors and the occasional white-coated scientist type. The pace of work appeared to be chaotic, but after a time a pattern of activity became obvious to any careful onlooker. There was method in the frenzied madness, and a fearful precision and discipline in the way the workers laboured, but that in itself was unremarkable. What concerned him far more were the conditions they worked in.

They wore the same pyjama-striped uniform that he had first seen at Auschwitz-Birkenau. Most of them looked Jewish, although there was a sprinkling of Slavic faces amongst them- probably Russian prisoners of war, Simon guessed. All of them were emaciated, no doubt existing on starvation rations. They looked dirty, weary and depressed, and stank to high heaven, but none of them dared to slacken on the job or take a rest break.

Discipline was ferocious and brutal. There were guards scattered everywhere throughout the workshop and rocket assembly areas, all of them carrying Schmeissers or whips and truncheons. He had already witnessed the occasional kick and savage lashing from a few of them, directed at some poor unfortunate who was judged not to be putting in the required amount of effort. At one point in the tour several workers collapsed under the weight of a rocket motor component they were attempting to move into position that had slipped out of its restraining harness. Two of them were pinned to the concrete floor under the massive load. Their colleagues rushed to their help. As they did so they were mercilessly beaten as they struggled to lift the crushing weight off them, but by the time the two could be freed their screams of agony had gurgled into silence. They were far beyond any help. The guard in charge pistol-whipped several of the rescuers, then forced them to drag the two bodies away from the production area. A large crimson smear stretched back behind them, marking the trail of death and mutilation.

What shocked him most was his friend's seeming acceptance of the casual brutality that was evident here, directly under his command. Hartmann had merely ordered the mess cleaned up, and encouraged the guards to be even more vigilant in punishing slackers. A worrying thought crept into Simon's mind, something he was reluctant to entertain, but the nagging doubt would not go away. Had Hartmann become a different person to the one he thought he knew? What the hell was he doing in charge of this slave labour factory? What had happened to his desire to do something about the thugs that ran the perversion that was Nazi Germany? It was nearly a year since he had last seen his friend at that field hospital in Poland, and Simon was more than a little surprised and dismayed at the apparent change in Hartmann's attitude.

Hartmann had swiftly guided him away from the scene, carrying on as if nothing had happened. The tour led deeper into the mountain, past the Junkers jet engine assembly line and the rocket fuel and explosive store areas, eventually ending at a heavily guarded and sealed entrance. Hartmann's explanation was brief and to the point. 'Nobody's allowed in here except by a special pass, authorised and controlled by the Reichsführer himself. That includes both of us. I don't know what goes on in here, nor do I wish to, and if you take my advice, nor should you.' With that, Hartmann had led him back to his office.

Hartmann ceased rubbing the area below his left knee, and pointed to a chair. 'Sit down Max, it makes me uncomfortable seeing you standing there like a spare prick at a wedding. Besides, you don't look that steady on your feet.' He gave him a hard look. 'Something's on your mind, I know it. You look as if you've swallowed a toad.'

Simon eased himself down into a chair, and sat looking at his friend. 'Sorry, sir, but I just can't reconcile the fact that you're working here.'

'A pleasant surprise, eh?' Hartmann frowned. 'Are you just referring to the coincidence that brings us together again? Or is it just fate, if that's what it is?'

'Neither sir. It's just that I never thought I'd see the day when I'd find you working in a place like this. It's a far cry from the front line.'

'Yes, so it is. But you better get used to it - quick.' Another hard look crossed Hartmann's face. 'Remember this - I'm still your boss whenever you're here, still two ranks above you, despite your promotion, so you'd better mind your manners and clear anything you plan with me - in advance. Got it?'

Simon nodded quickly. 'Yes sir.'

'That's better.' Hartmann's face suddenly broke out into a big grin. 'Just testing, Max - it's still the same Harald Hartmann you knew from before, eh? For Christ's sake, stop calling me sir, and stop looking so bloody serious!' He laughed. But Simon still felt uncomfortable. Somewhere along the line something was different. What was it? Was he under some form of duress? 'Harald, I don't understand it. How can you work here? It's just like...' He stopped himself just in time. He was about to blurt out 'Auschwitz', but that would have been unwise. He was still under oath to keep his mouth shut.

'Just like what?'

'Sorry, Harald, but I'm under orders not to say any more. I can't talk about it, not even to you.'

'I see. That's OK - perhaps I don't want to hear it anyway.' Hartmann shifted in his seat. The smile left his face. He looked somewhat awkward and apologetic. 'Look, Max- I'm not trying to justify this place or why I'm here. Last summer I was ordered to report here, once my rehabilitation was complete.' He tapped his wooden leg. 'Direct orders from the Reichsführer himself, and no questions asked. God knows why they picked me, of all people, but I had no choice. I was expecting a desk job at the divisional depot, or something similar. Instead, I get this shitty little job as camp commandant. I'm under strict orders here - rocket production is top priority, and everything else, *everything else*, is secondary and utterly unimportant as far as RSHA goes. That includes the workforce. I don't like it one little bit, but there's bugger all I can do about it.'

'You could give the workforce more food, and treat them better.'

Hartmann shrugged resignedly. 'I tried that, shortly after I arrived. However, it changed little, and the Reichsführer soon put a stop to any humanitarian measures I took. Himmler keeps a very close eye on what we do here. He has informers all over the place. The guard's pay rigorous attention to detail, and the reduced rations state keeps the prisoners very much on their toes, even if they suffer as a result. The Reichsführer introduced this strict regime towards the end of last year. Since then the amount of sabotage has dropped to virtually zero, and production has reached record levels. But all the time I'm under pressure here to produce results, and keep production at increasingly higher quotas, and if I fail my head's on the chopping block. I don't like the way things are run here, but all I can do is look the other way, as I'm sure you noticed. The prisoners here are, according to RSHA, quite expendable, and my orders give me precious little room for maneuver. '

'But they're starving!'

'I know.' Hartmann looked unhappy. 'Like I said, there's nothing I can do about it. You've got to remember that it's not much better for ordinary civilians living in the Nordhausen area outside. Food is scarce everywhere at this stage of the war.'

'Precisely - at this stage of the war.' Simon had yet to get over the shock that his friend was in charge here, and he was still angry. 'You said it. Do you have any real idea what's happening outside?'

'No. I rarely get the chance to leave the factory. Most of the staff are quartered here and sleep underground. So how *is* our splendid war going?'

'I reckon we have no more than two or at the most three months left, if what I hear is true.' Max looked at him, leaned forward in his seat and dropped his voice to a whisper.

'The Russians are not far from Berlin, and the Americans are on the Rhine, if not already beyond. This place is going to be over-run soon. Do you want to get caught in command? I don't think the Allies will look kindly on this sort of operation, or anybody associated with it.'

'But what can I do?' Hartmann grunted in exasperation. 'I can't just disappear on my own, not in my position. Where would I go? And what about Elke and the girls?'

'They'll be alright. From what I'm told, the country's about to break up anyway, and you'll have as much a chance as any.'

Hartmann snorted in derision. 'Will they? Max, that's easy for you to say, but I don't think I can take that sort of chance with their lives. I wouldn't put it past them to keep Elke and the house under observation, just to keep me sweet. They're all I care about now. Besides, I'm watched much too closely. So will you be for that matter, especially whenever you visit here.'

He raised his voice. 'By the way, I haven't forgotten that letter confirming your appointment, after Ohlendorff was reassigned elsewhere. Who is this Schellenberg character anyway? I've never heard of him before. He must have some clout to get you assigned to both here and the Panzer Training School at Sondershausen. I need to-'.

There was a knock on the door and in walked Hartmann's secretary with a tray bearing two mugs of coffee. Despite the rather severe uniform and military hairstyle, there was no doubt that this woman was a stunner.

'Thank you, Barbara.' She smiled pleasantly, turned and left the room. Simon noted that Hartmann's gaze lingered lasciviously on the shapely profile as the door closed. Hartmann winked and said, 'see what I mean? Very pretty but just a little *too* willing, even if you disregard my legendary charm. I'm sure she reports secretly to Prinz Albrecht Strasse. As I was saying, who is this Schellenberg?'

'He's in charge of Military Intelligence. I work for him now. He arranged my transfer here to keep an eye on things.'

'Well, Max, much as it's good to see you again, there's very little for you to do here. Ohlendorff took care of virtually all aspects of security. So tell me the real reason why you're here.'

Simon paused for a moment. So far their conversation had not touched on anything too incriminating, but now they were moving onto much more dangerous ground. 'It might be a better idea to discuss this outside,' he said in a low voice, looking warily around the room as if the walls had ears.

'That's fine by me. I need some fresh air, anyway. Finish your coffee, and let's move.'

In a few minutes both of them emerged from the main tunnel entrance, wrapped up warmly against the chill. The guards stationed at the factory entrance hurried up to salute, but Hartmann peremptorily waved them off and led the way into the trees. By now the sun was even higher in the pale sky, but the day was still blue with cold. After a few minutes Hartmann reached a small clearing in the pines.

'I think we'll be safe enough here. You better tell me what's on your mind.'

Simon hesitated for a few moments. He would need Hartmann's help if any sabotage was going to take place inside the factory. There was little else he could do but hope that his trust would not be misplaced. Another worry flashed across his brain. Was Hartmann under some form of duress he could not talk about? It would be worth finding out. Maybe Schellenberg could help?

Quickly he related all the information that Schellenberg passed on to him, watching as the shock and realization spread across his friend's face. 'That heavily guarded entrance at the far end of Tunnel B must be where they're doing the work on all those secret biological weapons. I'm not surprised that entrance is strictly controlled and only open to those who really need to be there. Is there any way you can get me a pass?'

Hartmann shook his head, evidently stunned at the news. 'No. As I said, they're all strictly controlled. Nobody gets in there unless there's an overwhelming requirement to do so. Ohlendorff made that an absolute priority. Maybe you might get in there because you're the new security adviser, but probably no more than once. Any more than that and you'd most likely need authorization, almost certainly from Himmler himself.'

'Alright, point taken, but will you help me?' Simon looked at his friend searchingly, scanning for the slightest sign of hesitation, or even worse. 'I seem to remember a speech of yours at that hospital, something about putting an end to all the madness we've had to go through over the last six years, something about getting even with those corrupt bastards at the top. Do you still feel the same way?'

'Yes, I do.' Hartmann returned his look steadily, then sighed and looked away. After a while he continued in a soft, low voice. 'I remember what I said, though maybe a lot of it was hot air said in the heat of the moment... Perhaps there was some delayed shock from losing this leg.' He stood silent for several minutes, gazing at the endless ranks of trees that stretched away into the distance. 'But if I help, then the timing has got to be absolutely accurate. If you want to destroy these rockets and their lethal payload, and coincidentally save millions, then the best time would be to strike just before they're ready to be railed out- before they leave the factory. The big question is, when will the weapons be ready, and if so will Himmler decide to use them?'

'I don't think we can afford to wait for him to make up his mind. You've got to find out and let me know.'

'I'll do what I can. How are you going to destroy them?'

'I haven't worked that one out yet,' Simon said. 'But I'm sure I'll think of something.'

Near Schernberg, Thüringen area, Germany, 0715 16/3/1945

It was freezing - brass monkey weather. Steele cursed to himself. He shivered repeatedly in the early morning cold. The temperature must be well below zero, he reckoned. He was standing inside the edge of a snow-covered wood, a few yards from a minor road that led north from Schernberg towards Sondershausen. The last few hours had been spent tramping his way along paths through the forests and across open fields, generally heading east until he could get a better idea of where he was. The light broadened only gradually as the early morning sun arose, somewhere above the heavily laden clouds. The landscape was a frozen whiteout of snow that merged into the horizon, with barely discernible difference between earth and sky. The tiny villages he passed through all looked much the same, with very little sign of activity at this ungodly hour - Kleinberndten, Grossberndten, Immenrode, the signs said, but they were of little help in determining his exact position. It was only when he reached Schernberg that the road signs became a little more informative.

The night had not gone exactly as planned, and he was only just getting his bearings. The flight from Northolt in the C-47 transport was cancelled at the last moment, apparently due to irreparable engine problems. Shortly afterwards a car whisked him away to RAF Lakenheath, just inside the Suffolk border, a two hour drive from West London. There a Lancaster bomber was almost ready to go. It was due to take part in a night raid on the Rostock area earlier that night but some minor technical faults had delayed its final readiness, and the rest of the squadron had taken off hours earlier. The bombs had been unloaded and the crew was passing the time, waiting for their new payload.

So there he was, bundled up in a freezing cold recess just aft of the bomb bay, his parachute strapped on his back, waiting for take-off. The flight lieutenant behind the controls briefly welcomed him, pointing out a spot where he could stow himself and his kitbag and not get in the way. The RAF officer looked as if he had only just left school. But the eyes told a different story. Steele had seen that look many times before - an almost robotic stare into the middle distance, fixed on some undetermined point - a look that had seen too many friends and colleagues die, too many planes shot down. The rest of the crew was much the same. They barely acknowledged him.. Perhaps they were under orders to look the other way and not take too much of an interest in their special cargo, whatever the reason for their altered mission was tonight. He sensed a degree of resentment. Perhaps they were angry and disappointed, when earlier on it looked as if they'd have a night off and not risk yet another brush with death. The end of the war was in sight, yet here they were, risking their necks yet again, on what they called 'company business', a relatively polite term that denoted working for the British Government. A brief conference with the navigator confirmed the altered flight plan and destination. Then with a thunderous roar the engines started sequentially and they were off.

The noise was deafening, even with earplugs. The cold was even worse. Steele was wearing a parachute smock and trousers over his uniform, as well as gloves, boots and an SS field service cap, but he was still chilled to the bone. The mission brief, and all the necessary contact information and plan of action, were clear in his mind. He was not particularly tired, but as an old pro he was used to getting his head down at the slightest opportunity. After all, you never knew when the next suitable occasion for sleep might arise, so make the most of any slack time immediately. Eventually, despite the noise and the cold, he managed to drift off...

He was rudely awakened by a hand pummelling his shoulder. It was one of the gunners. Suddenly the Lancaster pitched to the right, followed immediately by a burst of machine gun fire from up near the main cockpit.

'Enemy night-fighter below us!' Someone shouted urgently. The gunner ran off towards the front of the aircraft. At that moment there was an ugly tearing and spitting sound as a burst of heavy cannon-fire crashed through the right wing and into the central fuselage. There was an instant scream, followed by a roaring sound. Steele quickly staggered to his feet, braced himself as the Lancaster lurched to the left, and then slowly righted himself. He was about to go forward and try to find out exactly where they were, but the navigator beat him to it. He had staggered back to where Steele lay. He was clutching his right shoulder. Blood was welling through his fingers.

'Quick!' He gasped, his face screwed up in pain. 'We're over the area, a little west of where you needed to go but-'.

Another long burst of machine gun fire roared out, interrupting them.

'What about-'Steele never finished the sentence.

'No time for that,' the man shouted desperately. 'We've lost an engine, maybe two, and any moment now that night-fighter will come back on another pass. Jump!'

The bomb-bay doors were opening, the increased roar and turbulence buffeting and filling the Lancaster with a wall of sound. Steele simply turned around, braced himself for a moment, then jumped down through the open bay into the swirling darkness below, his kit bag following him. An instant later he pulled the ripcord and was suddenly jerked upwards as the parachute deployed. He caught a last glimpse of the stricken bomber as it flew away, a mass of flame engulfing the right wing. A dark shadow zoomed around him as he fell. Another angry burst of cannon fire shot up towards the Lancaster, the tracer flashing in the night sky, and then they were gone.

Steele glanced below. Clouds were looming up fast. Through a rent in the canopy he saw the terrain beneath him- a mixture of heavily forested, undulating ground and open fields, all shrouded in white. Nothing was instantly recognizable. A minute or two later he made an unremarkable landing at the edge of a wood, the deep snow cushioning the impact. It took but a few minutes to hide his parachute and smock, and rescue his greatcoat from the kit bag. The map, printed on the inside of his silk scarf, would be next to useless until he could orientate himself. He took a compass bearing, and determined the most promising axis of advance.

That was some time ago. He looked at his watch - it was just after a quarter past seven. It had taken him nearly three hours of slipping and sliding to reach his present location. There was as yet little activity in the villages and farms he had passed by. The heavy snowfall had seen to that. *Bloody typical. The Crabs got the weather forecast wrong again, and so much for the optimistic assessment that all the Luftwaffe night-fighter boys would be elsewhere.* He hoped the bomber crew had managed to make their way home, but the odds were heavily against it.

The steady thump of an approaching horse and cart along the snow-covered road broke into his thoughts. One of the local farmers was off into town, no doubt having risen much earlier and sorted out the daily chores on his smallholding. A few sacks were loaded in the back. The farmer was old, in his sixties, Steele guessed, his weathered features unshaven, an unlit pipe clamped firmly between his teeth. A heavy overcoat, not dissimilar to what the rank and file wore for warmth in the winter, was draped over his shoulders.

'Morning,' he grunted, eyeing him cautiously, as the horse and cart reached the spot where Steele stood. 'Need a lift? I'm off to Sondershausen.'

'Yes. Thanks, grandfather.' Steele smiled easily. A lift would be very useful. 'That's where I need to get to.'

'Well, throw your kitbag in the back.' The farmer jerked a thumb over his shoulder. 'It'll be safe enough there. I'm taking a few sacks of turnips and apples to market – see what I can get for them. Not much food around here at the moment.' He settled in his seat as Steele threw his kitbag into the rear and climbed up beside him. A brief shake of the reins, and they were off.

The old man was curious at first. How had Steele got there, and where was he off to? Where was he posted, and how was the war going? Steele had a cover story ready. It rolled off his tongue easily. He had just been discharged from hospital, and was visiting his family for two days leave. Now he needed to get to the new SS Armoured Warfare School in Sondershausen. He'd managed to get a lift in a farm truck up to here. The School was only a few kilometres away but he was still recovering from his wounds and the doctors had told him that any long distance walking was out of the question for now. The farmer seemed to be reasonably satisfied with that.

'I couldn't help but notice the cuff on your sleeve'. He took the pipe out of his mouth and pointed at Steele's left arm. 'Totenkopf, eh?' When did you join them?'

'The year before last. Spent most of the time on the Eastern front.' The cuff with the Gothic script in white embroidery was clearly visible, identifying him as a member of one of the most battle hardened divisions in the German army, and with probably the most fearsome reputation. But Steele needed to be careful. He was determined to not give away too much detail. It would be easy enough to spin out a yarn, but you just never knew how much trouble you could get yourself into, especially if the opposition was alert and informed. A little knowledge could be quite dangerous.

'So you weren't at Demyansk, then?'

'No. That was before my time.' *Best not to give too much away.*

The farmer shrugged. 'Sorry to enquire. The reason I ask is that my eldest son was in your division. Went to Russia in '41. They brought him back in the summer of '42. He'd lost a leg to a mine. But that was not all he lost...' The old man's voice thickened, as if he was struggling for words. 'He wasn't the same man anymore. For the last two years he's sat in his room, virtually every day, barely moving, just staring at the wall. God knows what else happened to him there. He never talks about it. And he can't bear winter any more. The snow drives him mad...' The old man slumped on his seat. Steele could clearly see that the man was close to tears.

Poor old bastard. Steele had heard plenty of horror stories throughout his clandestine travels inside the Reich. The Eastern front was nothing if not a nightmare. But this sort of story was nothing unusual. At least the man had his son back. There were so many other families who were far less fortunate.

'I'm sorry, old man,' Steele commiserated. The farmer grunted, cleared his throat, and made a show of adjusting the reins. The rest of the journey passed in silence. They had passed through the wooded Hainleite hills, and the town soon hove into view. The Panzer school was clearly visible off to the left – a new concrete monstrosity on the edge of the town, markedly different to the other, older buildings that lay nearby. The farmer stopped just outside the gated entrance. Steele climbed into the back, hefted his kitbag off the cart and stepped down onto the road.

'Thanks for the lift.' The farmer nodded brusquely, shook the reins and moved off.

Steele picked up his kitbag, slung it on his right shoulder and walked up to the sentry checkpoint on duty at the main gate. The guard saluted as soon as he approached, examined Steele's documents and checked his name against what appeared to be a list on his clipboard.

'One moment sir. Please wait here.' The guard turned and moved off towards the guardhouse. The three other guards eyed him watchfully, calmly waiting the unfolding of events, their weapons close by. None of them spoke a word.

Steele did his best to look unconcerned. He was an old hand at moving around Germany. His forged paperwork was in perfect order and had never failed him, even under the closest of scrutiny. This time his documents identified him as SS Untersturmführer Karl Akkermann, transferred from the 3rd SS Panzer Division 'Totenkopf' for specialist armoured warfare training, courtesy of RSHA. The SS uniform was enough to open most doors and sail through routine paperwork and documentation checks. Even the Gestapo rarely bothered him, seeing that he wore the uniform of the Führer's Praetorian Guard. But something was bothering him, a vague sense of unease. Something felt different this time. Menzies had assured him that his German contact had arranged his arrival at the armoured warfare school, and there would be no problems. Steele, in his latest disguise, would be expected. Maybe it was his imagination, but perhaps the guards were trying just a little bit too much to look casual and bored. And what exactly was the other guard checking?

Steele weighed up his options. He carried a Walther PPK in a shoulder holster under his left arm. A smaller Beretta was fitted to a leg holster, an extremely snug fit inside his right boot. His SS dagger was in his kitbag. The remaining guards he could easily dispose of, but that would blow his cover. Besides it was a fair hike to the nearest cover. The wooded hills were nearly a kilometer away, and the parade square just beyond the gates was filling up with troops and armoured vehicles. The odds for a successful escape did not look good at all. Perhaps it would be better to wait and see what would happen in the next few minutes. His pulse began to quicken, his eyes taking in all the details of his immediate environment. Casually he undid his greatcoat, ready to free up his weapon. At least he would be ready if the worst came to happen...

The guard was returning, this time with what appeared to be a couple of senior officers and two other armed soldiers. They soon reached the checkpoint. One of the officers walked up to him. Steele tensed, springing slightly onto the balls of his feet, at the same time keeping a wary eye on the others.

'Untersturmführer Akkerman?' The officer gazed at him impassively.

'Yes sir.' Steele saluted, his right arm ready to slide inside his greatcoat and whip out the PPK in an instant.

'Good. We've been expecting you. Come with me. There is something I need to ask you.'

Flossenberg concentration camp, Bavaria, 0830 16/3/1945

They never turned the light off. The naked bulb constantly threw its stark light out, a harsh glare like a powerful searchlight that lit up every corner of the room and made sleep difficult, if not at times impossible. It was just one of their little tricks to make life as uncomfortable and unbearable as possible. But he could cope with that. Even the constant hunger was not so bad. Since his arrival he had gradually become used to the starvation diet. After a few months he reckoned that his stomach had shrunk so much that the minimal servings of whatever the disgusting mess that passed for food here would just about enable him to survive. He estimated that his weight had dropped by about ten kilograms, quite a significant loss for a man of such a small frame, but he was still here, tired, weak, with a constant racking cough that never got better, but surviving nonetheless.

The intense cold was probably the worst of all the things that he had to put up with. His cell was tiny, windowless apart from a barred grille set high on the rear wall, unheated and more like a freezer compartment than a room. Sheets of frozen condensation and black mould lined the walls. The damp air made his breathing more difficult and aggravated his chest infection. The only comfort was that the low temperatures kept the smell down from the latrine bucket placed a feet away from where he lay on the bone-chilling floor.

He had managed to come to terms with his predicament, and although the outlook was poor he had not given into abject depression and demoralization. What worried him were the fate of his fellow conspirators and the lack of news from the outside world. There was almost no chance of finding out how the war was going, and whether the Allies were yet inside Germany's borders. The last thing he'd heard was that the front in France had collapsed and that the Russians were in Poland, but little else since then. The guards here seemed to be just as much in the dark as the prisoners, from what he could piece together from their conversations. He knew in his heart that the Nazis were nearly finished, but would they resort to some desperate last-minute madness, a sort of Wagnerian *Gotterdamerung* that would engulf the country and turn it into some form of hell on earth? It was quite possible- the last perverted act of vengeance from desperate, insane men. At least he knew that his family was safe. The girls were hidden away, protected and hopefully beyond reach. Erika had been spirited into Switzerland as soon as the failed assassination attempt became news. Sadly, there was little chance for him to follow her. Since Max Simon's visit the watch on his house had intensified almost to the point of house arrest. Besides, he knew that one day Himmler would catch up with him. He could face that with a degree of equanimity knowing that his loved ones were safe and beyond the Reichsführer's clutches.

What about his accomplices - and their plot to kill Hitler? It had been a lot worse for his fellow conspirators and others arrested after the 20th of July. So many friends were being brutally tortured and executed, all as slowly as possible to maximize the agony. The method the Gestapo favoured most was an agonisingly slow death by hanging, usually with piano wire. At first Himmler's lackeys had not come for him. It was only several weeks later that he was finally arrested, as a so-called 'enemy of the state'. Shortly afterwards he made his first, and probably last, acquaintance with the less savoury parts of 8 Prinz Albrecht Strasse, the basement and torture cellars. Even Himmler himself had turned up in person to watch his interrogators begin. They had started by delivering a few well-aimed blows to the more vulnerable and tender parts of his anatomy. The method that followed was a Gestapo favourite – whips soaked in water, something they called 'Kashumbo'. However, for reasons not made entirely clear to him at the time, the interrogators avoided carrying out too rigorous a session, leaving his face unmarked, thus guaranteeing that at least he would be presentable in front of a public trial.

But no charges were ever made. Himmler had merely contented himself by watching with icy, gloating amusement. After that they left him alone. He spent a few weeks in solitary confinement, bound hand and foot in chains, on a diet of bread and water. Then one day his guards marched in, quite unexpectedly. After a few cursory blows he was roughly cleaned up, handcuffed and escorted to a transport detail that took him out of Berlin. Only later did he find out that the destination was Flossenberg, a hellhole reserved for special 'guests' of the Reich, set deep in the pine forests of the Sudetenland, up in the hills near the former Czech border.

So here he was, finally cornered, but it could have been much worse. All in all the experience of being the Führer's guest at one of his infamous concentration camps was less severe than he thought it would be. It was just as well for him that the camp staff appeared to be complacent and more than a little lazy- after all, it was quite a cushy assignment for them. Physical punishments were relatively minor- just the occasional kick during a bout of floor scrubbing while his guards mocked him and occasionally spat at the diminutive figure working away on his hands and knees. They seemed to take a vast amount of pleasure in watching an admiral of the Reich scrubbing and polishing away, just like a menial house servant.

So why had they gone relatively easy on him? Was it the Führer's personal intervention, making sure that an old loyal servant was not abused *too* much? That was unlikely - usually a trip here was part of a one-way ticket. The only special dispensations handed out in a place like this were particularly nasty punishments and beatings. So why hadn't they strung him up? Was Himmler still scared about the dossier Canaris had hidden away? That was more difficult to answer. The interrogation sessions here were child's play to what he had really expected. Yes, there were the usual thugs and bullies present among the concentration camp staff, but he had played the simple senile old fool and up until now it had worked. Nobody had yet managed to break down his resistance, and he could cope with the physical abuse. Perhaps Himmler was merely toying with him, like a kitten with a captive field vole learning just how far it could go with its prey before delivering the final killing bite.

He had been able to communicate with the others imprisoned in this cellblock. Shortly after his arrival he'd begun by tapping the walls to the cells on either side to try to communicate with whoever else was being held in captivity. Soon he had discovered that the man to his left was Nils Lunding, the former head of Danish Military intelligence. To his right it was none other than Hans von Oster, his former deputy at the Abwehr headquarters in Bendlerstrasse, and the man behind the bomb plot when Hitler flew to Smolensk in September 1943. Gradually he managed to piece together a picture of the other prominent residents of this fine establishment- quite a few senior Army officers were present, including his old friend Manfred Simon, Judge Advocate General Carl Sack and a few priests and theologians. All of them shared one thing in common- resistance in one form or another against the tyranny of the Nazi state, sufficient enough to displease the Reichsführer.

Canaris was about to turn over and ease himself into a less uncomfortable position on the floor when he heard the sound of marching boots rapidly approaching. A key turned in the lock and the door swung wide open. Two guards stood there, looking at him with a mixture of loathing and contempt. The more senior roared at him.

'On your feet Herr Admiral Shitface!' A well-aimed blow from his boot caught Canaris in the side. The older man grunted in pain, and then eased himself up as quickly as he could to stand in front of them. The throb in his side made him gasp for breath He wondered if a rib was broken.

'About time!' The same guard laughed harshly and then reached forward to lift up his head and cuff him hard across his face. 'Special surprise for Prisoner 106 today. Somebody's come from Berlin to persuade you to be a bit more cooperative. They've got something for you, something you'll *really* enjoy. I hope you like special treats, oh yes. This one will make you hot with excitement!'

The other guard guffawed with laughter, and then quickly moved behind him and pinioned both his arms together into a steely grip. Handcuffs were jammed roughly over his wrists, and a kick propelled him out of the cell into the adjoining corridor. He slammed up against the far wall. Just then the sound of a prolonged, terrible scream, almost sub-human in its agony, rent the air.

'Looks like they're warming up for the main attraction,' observed the second guard, with a grin. 'You're next.' With that, they pushed him further up the corridor towards a distant room with an open door. A disgusting smell of burning flesh met him.

❀

Sondershausen area, Germany 1230 21/3/45

Simon steadied the binoculars in his hands, adjusted the manual focusing ring, and rested his arms on the parapet of the wooden observation tower. Even now, his arms ached and grew tired after too much exertion. The cold air was enough to make your eyes water. He blinked rapidly to clear his vision, and carefully studied the low hills and woods in the distance. He could just make out half a dozen well-camouflaged tanks hidden along the edge of a small wood. Other 'friendly' forces were scattered elsewhere nearby, equally well hidden and lying in wait.

'Everything's in position, Sturmbannführer'. It was Hauptmann Enseling, standing beside him. Simon grunted in acknowledgement. 'Thanks, Willy. That's the last I can see of all the dispositions from Blue Force. Red Force should show up anytime now. And stop calling me by my rank, for God's sake. I'm Max when there's nobody else around – remember?' He softened his voice with a smile.

'Sorry sir – I mean, Max'.

'That's better. Fellow officers don't insist on strict observance of military etiquette, unless it's absolutely necessary - especially if they come from the same unit. Got it?'

'Yes, Max.'

'Good. Then let's see how your tactics work. I want to see how von Manteuffel won his battles. Better start warning your lot now.'

Enseling picked up his headset, and began issuing orders. He job was to direct the deployment of Blue Force, which was made up of a new group of officer cadets and NCO's. Some of them were combat veterans promoted through the ranks, others were novices in the art of command and control. Enseling had set them up exactly along the lines of the Battle of Targul Frumos the previous April, down on the Russian-Rumanian border. There, the elite GrossDeutschland Panzer division had managed to halt the Soviet drive on the oil fields at Ploesti, and in the process destroy over four hundred enemy tanks.

The division commander at the time, von Manteuffel, had made clever use of the terrain, and with excellent camouflage had lured the best part of several Soviet tank corps forward to their doom. He achieved this stunning victory with a depleted panzer regiment, less than forty tanks in all. The rest of the division was similarly under strength, but their defence was first class.

Willy Enseling had served in GD's Panzerjäger battalion in charge of an assault gun troop, and had personally accounted for nine T-34s in the battle. His recent transfer to the SS Panzer School was exactly along the same lines as Simon. Himmler's Panzer school needed experienced instructors, and few could be spared from the desperate defence of the Reich. And just like Simon, Enseling was still recovering from battle wounds and as yet not officially considered fit for combat duties. A formal draft ordering him into the Waffen SS was expected any day now. The two of them had got on well from the start.

'Here comes Red Force'. Simon had already spotted a mass of vehicles moving across the snowy landscape no more than three kilometres away. They had reached the crest of a low ridge of hills between two woods, and some of them were working their way forward into the area where Blue Force was hidden. The roar of engines was becoming increasingly louder in the cold air. Red Force consisted of a similar number of inexperienced officer cadets, but to even things up, the Panzer School Commandant had told Simon that he was sending an experienced officer to control them for this exercise, a new Untersturmführer who had only arrived at the school late yesterday evening. Perhaps this new officer would give Red Force a better chance, or perhaps not. Enseling looked like he knew a thing or two about armoured warfare. Simon was impressed with the way he had positioned his forces, and how he was setting the trap lying in wait for Red Force. Willy's voice rang out with crisp instructions. All that the 'enemy' had to do now was move a few hundred meters further forward, directly into the killing zone.

Suddenly Red Force halted, the majority of its tanks keeping back in the cover of hull-down positions on the ridgeline. From the leading edge a few APCs and tanks moved forward and began to spread out across the down-slope, simulating the activities of an enemy reconnaissance battalion.

Simon smiled to himself. *Someone up there has spotted a trap. Instead of charging forward recklessly into a killing zone, they've sent a few expendables to lure out the unwary and spring the trap. Good. The next few minutes should be illuminating.*

The APCs spread out, easing themselves nearer to where Blue Force lay in wait. It all depended on how good their camouflage was, and who would keep cool under pressure. No real shots would be fired, but there were plenty of observers scattered around to keep score and determine who had achieved tactical surprise, who were the victors and who were the losers. Afterwards the 'battle' would be relived, using models and a sand table to demonstrate the correct solution.

The reconnaissance APCs moved nearer and nearer and then suddenly stopped, reversed and roared back up the slope. At that same moment, several Blue Force tanks moved from the edge of one the small copses and took up firing positions. Flat barks echoed across the landscape as the defenders fired on the escaping recon team. A confused fight began to take place, with answering fire from Red Force tanks along the ridgeline. Simon was dimly aware that Enseling was roaring into his microphone. More and more tank motors revved into life. A rapid redeployment of Red Force tanks was taking place, many of them disappearing from view behind the crest of the hill. He thought he knew which way they were going.

Enseling was studying his map, and barking out fresh instructions to his ambush teams. He looked across at Simon, who caught his glance and smiled, looking pointedly at his wristwatch. Willy began to redouble his efforts. The exercise would no doubt finish shortly, and his trap was not working as planned. Somehow somebody up there on Red Force had realised the danger his tanks were in, and had pulled back just in time.

The remaining minutes passed by quickly. Firing on the ridgeline and forward slope had ceased. Suddenly tank engines could be heard on both sides of the distant ridgeline and two groups of tanks suddenly roared into view, arcing around the edge of the woods towards where the original Blue Force ambush teams had lain in wait. Several of them halted as the others advanced, and began firing.

'Bugger!' Enseling roared, looking frustrated. Whoever was in charge of Red Force knew how to smell a trap, and was quick enough to react and turn the tables on the enemy. Just then a yellow flare shot up into the grey skies. He dropped his headphones in disgust.

'End of exercise.' He swore several times. 'Damn and blast! That was some

canny bastard over there. The Russians never use recon – they simply send their tanks forward and keep going until they hit trouble. By all rights Red Force should have walked straight into that trap.'

Simon could barely stop from laughing. He walked over to Enseling and put an arm around his shoulder. 'Not to worry, dear boy, these things happen,' he said, soothingly. 'Besides, Red Force could be British or American, and not necessarily Ivan and his friends. Different armies use different tactics. Let's find out who was in charge of Red Force – he'll be able to tell you what went wrong.'

A few minutes later, a procession of vehicles began to pass by. Most of them had red splotches on their armour, some had blue. All of them had seen better days and were no longer fit for battlefield service. Some of them were enemy tanks – a few T-34s, some M4 Shermans, and even a couple of antiquated French Renault light tanks. Several Kubelwagens belonging to exercise control brought up the rear and kept an eye on the procession. One of them detached itself and sped across the snow towards the observation tower.

'Ah, here comes the Red Force commander'. Simon watched closely as a bulky figure in a hooded winter camouflage combat uniform stiffly climbed out of the passenger seat and limped slowly towards the wooden hut. There was something about him that looked vaguely familiar. As the figure moved closer he stopped and pulled back the hood, revealing an officer's side cap and a large grin.

'Sturmbannführer, I beg to report that whoever commanded Blue Force owes me several drinks and needs a good kick up the arse!'

It was none other than Charlie Hofheinz.

❀

'Charlie, you smooth talking bastard...Its great to see you again!' Simon was amazed and delighted. This was a complete surprise, utterly unexpected but nonetheless very welcome indeed. Simon grinned broadly and stepped forward, giving his friend a quick hug. "Well, look at you...now an officer, maybe even a gentleman to boot, although I find that hard to believe.' He turned to wink at Enseling, who was watching them both with interest. 'What's happened to you since we last met?

I'll bet you have more than a few stories you can tell me, eh?'

'Yes Sturmbannführer.' Hofheinz grinned. 'One or two, perhaps. I -'

'No more formality, please Charlie,' Simon interrupted. 'From now on call me Max unless we're in company, just as it used to be. By the way, this is Willy Enseling, fresh from hospital and my old friends in GrossDeutschland, about to be transferred into the SS just like I was.'

Enseling leaned forward and shook Hofheinz's hand. 'Glad to meet you, Charley. Congratulations - looks like you know more than a thing or two about handling armoured warfare. Was that your own trick, or is it something Ivan has recently introduced?'

Hofheinz grinned back. 'Thanks. A bit of both, really. The Russians have finally begun to equip their tank and mechanised corps with reconnaissance battalions, much along the lines of what we used to do in the panzer divisions, until we began to run short of men and vehicles. They're still getting the hang of it. The British and Americans are much better at it than they are, but I doubt Ivan will take long to catch up.'

'Where did you learn that?' Simon asked him.

'Oh, you know - Normandy, Belgium, Hungary, all the usual places these days we seem to find ourselves in, and with all the usual suspects in tow ...' The smile faded from Hofheinz's face, replaced almost immediately by a hard, far-away stare. Simon was immediately aware that some of these memories were perhaps not the best. A quick change of subject was called for.

'We'll talk about that later, over a few beers' he quickly interjected. 'Right now I could do with getting back to some warmth, with a bit of lunch thrown in as well. Willy, you don't mind if I drive back with Charlie? We've got a lot of catching up to do.'

'No, Max. No problem at all,' Enseling replied, instantly in tune with Simon's request.

'I'll catch up with you later, after the afternoon classroom exercises'. Simon turned to his old friend. 'Come on, man, let's go.' He put his arm around his friend's shoulders. 'I've got a lot to talk to you about.'

Der Rot Löwe, Kaisersallee, Sondershausen 1700

They were sitting in a private booth in a small bar, the Rot Löwe, situated just off the main road that led out towards where the new Panzer School was located. The afternoon classes were finished for the day and the students had been dismissed for the evening - a rare opportunity to catch up on reading, equipment and weapons maintenance, as well as a hundred other things they needed to keep abreast of. Even sleep, the most precious of commodities.

The bar was quiet. Only a few stools were occupied. Beer supplies had been somewhat disrupted of late, thanks to the dislocation on the roads by enemy air forces that ranged almost unopposed across the length of breadth of the Reich. The surrounding buildings and hills of the densely forested Hainleite range close by were fading into the gathering gloom of the early evening, dim blurs and shadows as the light failed. Only a few outside lights were visible. The blackout would come into force in the next half hour, and the bar shutters would be closed and curtains drawn, strictly in accordance with the regulations.

They kept their voices low. You never knew who was listening, who might report on conversations that might be interpreted as unpatriotic, or even treasonous. It barely mattered at this stage of the war what uniform you wore. Anyone was fair game. Stories of SD security squads, roaming the rear areas in search of suitable candidates *pour encourager les aûtres*, as the French would put it, were commonplace. Summary trials took place at the drop of a hat for those judged not to be contributing one hundred percent to the Reich in its desperate time of need. Invariably they were immediately followed by swift dispensation of 'justice', usually in the form of a quick lynching – bullets were too scarce and precious to waste on these shirkers.

Hofheinz had spent the last hour or so talking about what had happened to Simon's former unit in France, Belgium and Hungary. It was not easy listening. There were only a few survivors left from over four hundred men who had made up the battalion numbers. It was Russia all over again, only worse.

The normally cheerful Hofheinz was scathing in his contempt for the way the war was being run. That was nothing new, but Simon was quite shocked by the bitter change he noted in his friend.

'You didn't miss a great deal when they took you away from us and put you on that new assignment,' Hofheinz was saying, quietly. 'We had a couple of months' quiet to form the new Heavy Panzer battalion, and then the Allies landed. If you thought things were bad in Russia, Max, they were infinitely worse in Normandy. Nothing could move in daylight, unless it was a very cloudy day or raining. The Luftwaffe was nowhere to be seen, and the enemy air force ruled the skies. Their artillery was the worst I've ever come across and considering what we experienced on the Eastern Front that's saying something.' He related the stories of St Aignan de Cramesnil and the escape from the Falaise pocket. 'We lost virtually everything. Tanks, equipment, even the shirts off our backs for those few lucky enough to get away. We had to swim across the Seine – there was only one bridge still available, and we were nowhere near it. All the rest were already destroyed by the Allies.'

He shook his head sadly, and then carried on. 'The Ardennes was almost as bad. We were part of Sixth SS Panzer Army. Our task was to break through the weak enemy defences and race for the bridges across the Meuse, with Antwerp as the next stop. What happened? Another fucking fine mess. Some idiot directed our attack onto the strongest American positions, along the Elsenborn Ridge.' He snorted scathingly. 'Guess who that was?' He looked around carefully and lowered his voice. 'Fucking Grofarz, who else. He'd decided that, because we were SS and therefore ideologically pure and trustworthy, we would be bound to smash the enemy and secure victory. What a stupid tosser!'

Hofheinz laughed grimly. 'I got that little gem straight from Dietrich himself.' Hofheinz was referring to the army commander, SS Obergruppenführer Josef Dietrich, a former street tough and bruiser from the earliest days of the fledgling Nazi Party in Munich, but promoted well above any military prowess he may have had to the exalted position of army commander. 'Old Sepp came to see us for himself, on one of the rare days that he was sober. He may not be much of a soldier but by God he's a realist, and he's got precious little time for any arse-licking Führer crazed idiot these days. I overheard him talking about the disaster in France to some senior officers from a Wehrmacht parachute - infantry division who were questioning some of the less comprehensible decisions from on high. The gist of what he said was this – 'there is no option but to follow orders blindly and to the letter. Even I, a senior SS officer cannot change this, not unless I want to put myself straight in front of a firing squad! I know what we've all been through is madness, but we have no choice in these matters'. What do you think of that?'

Simon was not that surprised. 'I've heard this sort of thing before. Gille, Viking's commander when we were trying to break through to them at Korsun, said much the same thing. I met him, you know, not long after we said goodbye at Breslau.'

'Gille?'

'No the Führer.'

'What? You mean, Grofarz himself?' Hofheinz was incredulous.

'Yes. He presented me with these'. Simon pointed to the Oak Leaves that glittered above his Knight's Cross.

Hofheinz gave a low whistle. 'So what was he like?'

'Well, it was only a brief presentation, a handshake, a few words of congratulation and then off he went.' Simon cast his mind back almost a year. 'He didn't strike me as being a great orator with a powerful, charismatic presence. He just looked old, tired and rather worn out.'

'So – no words of wisdom then, no stirring exhortation to *carry on the fight against the brutal enemy, the barbarous Bolshevik hordes...*'

Simon grinned briefly at Hofheinz's mimicry of the Führer in full cry. One or two heads at the bar turned around.

'Not really – and keep your bloody voice down. There may be one or two here tonight who may take exception to any piss taking.' Hofheinz looked suitably chastened, but only for a moment. 'Well, I suppose it's all that responsibility on his shoulders, running the war, you know – all that strain...'

'More like a guilty conscience, if you ask me. Remember what we saw on the way back from Poland?' His words had an instant, sobering effect. Simon left the rest unsaid. There was no need to say anything else. The memory of the horrors of Auschwitz was still there.

After a few moments of silence, Hofheinz carried on.

'Hungary was almost as bad as Normandy. It doesn't matter anymore if we knock out ten, twenty or even more enemy tanks for each one of ours lost. Ivan will always find more to replace them and slowly grind us down. Another bloodbath, another failed offensive', he sighed. This time the mission was to liberate the surrounded forces trapped inside Budapest and get them out of the mess that the deteriorating situation in Hungary had become. 'When virtually all our tanks were destroyed, and most of our men dead or in hospital, we get a message from OKH, from the Führer himself. Apparently, he's displeased at our latest efforts, and has decided that we are not worthy to bear his name anymore. Would you believe it?' Hofheinz's voice rose. 'Hitler ordered every member of what was left of the Leibstandarte, and anybody else in Sixth SS Panzer Army who wore them, to remove the honorary cuff with the Leibstandarte SS Adolf Hitler script from their sleeves.' He shook his head in bemusement. 'Dietrich was absolutely speechless with anger. It just so happened that he was visiting our unit to congratulate us on our latest defensive effort when the message came through - just one of those strange little coincidences that happen from time to time. I don't think I've ever seen anybody quite so pissed off as he was that day. Sepp was shaking and quivering with rage. Can you imagine it? After all the shit we'd gone through, all the battles, the dead, wounded, maimed and scarred for life, all the madness... we then receive this? Is that the sort of thanks we deserve for all our efforts over the last six years?'

Hofheinz continued. 'It should have been a day to remember. I'd already heard that I was well overdue for some sort of recognition, some sort of reward that recognised our recent battles. Dietrich simply strode up, looked at me, and offered me a choice – either a battlefield commission right there on the spot, or a cast-iron recommendation for the Knight's Cross. Another bit of tinsel to add to those already in my collection...' Hofheinz chuckled bitterly and pointed at the medals across his chest – the Iron Cross first and second class, and all the rest – wound badges, tank destruction and close combat clasps and so on. This was the paraphernalia of some of the more seasoned veterans, by this stage of the war; those that were still left alive. 'No disrespect intended to those that already have it, of course.' He winked at Simon.

'Then he said this – 'I should go for the promotion if I was you, Charlie. All of this' – he pointed to all his numerous decorations –'all of this is just a pile of worthless junk. Besides, the pay's much better as a junior officer'. I took his advice, and a few minutes later I was no longer an Oberscharführer but a brand new Untersturmführer with what was left of the battalion to command. All the other senior officers were either dead or hospitalized. Later on that day, we heard from division HQ that Dietrich had sent a latrine bucket full of medals and Leibstandarte arm cuffs by special delivery for the particular attention of Grofarz himself.' He paused and winked at Simon. 'I'm not absolutely certain if they cleaned out the bucket before putting them in there. Dietrich doesn't mess around.'

Hofheinz laughed mirthlessly. 'My time in command didn't last long. It was typical fucking sod's law. Less than twenty four hours later I was lucky enough to get this...' He pointed to his left thigh. 'A Russian machine-gun bullet smashed the femur, so the docs told me. I spent eight weeks in some out of the way clinic in Bavaria, then a transfer here as an officer instructor. Still, it's better than being in Hungary at the moment – or should I say Austria. I've heard that Ivan has managed to break through towards the west and nearly reach the outskirts of Vienna. I wonder what the former Austrian house-painter himself has to say about that piece of good news.'

He broke off, leaned forward for his drink and swallowed. Simon looked at him closely as he drank. It seemed as if his friend had reached the same level of war weariness and contempt for those in command as he, and doubtless quite a few others, had. But there was something else there as well – a hard bitterness that he had never seen before in his friend, something that had changed him over the course of the last ten months.

During their conversation his mind had started to explore a few possibilities, some courses of action that would soon be most likely needed. His last words with Schellenberg were still fresh in his mind. Even so, he knew he had to be careful in what he said and how he said it. What he was going to propose was clearly treason. Charlie was a good mate, but Simon was still a little unsure as to where his inner loyalties lay, even now.

'You haven't said a great deal about yourself, Max'. Hofheinz looked at him. 'I've done most of the talking. What happened after you were ordered to Berlin? Anything you can tell me about?'

'Yes, but only a few details, Charlie.' Simon shrugged apologetically. 'A lot of it I can't tell you about...military intelligence secrets, all that sort of thing. I've been sworn to secrecy, and you probably wouldn't believe me if I could tell you everything, anyway. But here goes. I'll tell you what I can.' With that, he launched into a shortened version of the events in Berlin and the mission abroad. He left out all references to Canaris, Patricia, the real reason for his mission and his 'turning' by MI6. There was simply no reason for Hofheinz to know, and the last thing he wanted his friend to hear about was Simon's involvement in successfully duping German Intelligence into believing that the Normandy landings were only a sideshow, and not the real thing. Too many of their friends had failed to come back from France. In a way, he still felt dirty about betraying his own side. Yes, 'betraying' – there was no other way to describe it. It was a bitter pill to swallow, and even despite what he had seen and heard of Auschwitz and other places, the fact that he had finally turned against his own country still haunted him at night, when sleep was hard to come by. Maybe time would ease his sense of guilt.

Hofheinz hid his surprise well. Only a few raised eyebrows expressed his silent amazement at what had happened to Simon.

'So you see, Charlie, things have been more than a little interesting for me as well, but in a rather different way to what I was expecting when I left you and headed off to Berlin. As I said, the mission they sent me on was ultimately a failure, and I was very lucky to get back alive. Even so, nine months' recovery in a special clinic was not quite what I thought I'd be letting myself in for. I'm still a bit stunned by your arrival today. I never thought we'd meet up again.' He laughed. 'One of the nicer surprises I've had recently, I must say. I wonder if some guardian angel has our best interests at heart.' *Was it indeed coincidence, or was it more than just mere luck. Schellenberg? How would he know who Charlie was...?*

Their glasses were nearly empty. Simon made his mind up. Now would be as good as any time to ask his friend to consider what he had in mind. A tentative plan was forming in his mind. Several options and permutations were falling into place. The only major uncertainty left was the British. How would MI6 get in contact? What did Menzies have up his sleeve? Somebody should have been in touch by now...

One thing at a time. There was little point in worrying too much – perhaps things would become clearer soon. But he would not broach what was on his mind to his friend here – it was far too open a place for that sort of discussion.

'Finish your drink, man. There's something I need to talk to you about...outside, not in here. I have a special favour to ask. Interested?'

Hofheinz nodded. He picked up his glass and swiftly emptied the contents down his throat. 'Lead on, boss. I'm all ears'.

SS Field HQ, Mittenwalde 25/3/45 1130

The early spring sunshine shone fitfully through the gloomy wrack of dark clouds that hung over the city. The view from the top of the hill Schellenberg was standing on was quite panoramic. He could make out the low hills and woods that skirted Lake Havel to the west, almost as far away as Potsdam. From there his gaze swept right, across the centre of the city and further over to the flat plain and dense forests that stretched east towards Seelow. The Oder River lay beyond. That's where the Russians were, less than fifty kilometres away – far too close for any comfort. The city looked to be peaceful, but the appearance was deceptive. Large areas of the city were a mass of rubble, ruin heaped upon ruin

The Red Air Force had yet to make its appearance today, probably as a result of the heavy rain and low clouds that had settled over Berlin and across to the east during the night and early morning. He tried to imagine the chaos going on at the enemy air-fields in Poland. The majority were muddy grass strips, useless in the rain. There would be little in the way of air missions from there today. As for the western Allies, the Americans and British had largely given up their relentless bombing of the capital. There wasn't much point these days, with so little left to target and the Russians now so close.

The new field headquarters was situated in a wood a few hundred meters south of the trig point he was standing on, carefully concealed beneath a mass of camouflage netting. OKH's main headquarters was nearby, only a couple of kilometres away at Zossen. SS Technicians had already tapped into the Army's communication apparatus, giving them reasonably secure telephone connection to what remained of the Reich. The radio transmitters were hidden further away, in a remote spot, theoretically a secure distance from where the main HQ lay. The enemy had directed quite a few bombing missions to destroy these transmitters, but so far they had only achieved limited results. Repair crews managed to mend the damage almost as quickly as it occurred, and the current aerial threat seemed to be quite limited. The Soviets as yet appeared not to have mastered the technique of precision pinpoint bombing.

Mind you, all that would be for nothing when the long awaited, war-ending ground offensive came in. The Army's Military Intelligence department, using what little was still available from Luftwaffe aerial reconnaissance, was of the firm opinion that the Soviets would start their final attack in the next two or three weeks, no more than that. The SS had concurred. Both reports had ended up on the Fuhrer's desk. Unfortunately, and as was always the case at this stage of the war, the contents of both had to be suitably toned down. Nobody dared tell the Führer the real picture, if only to avoid provoking him into one of his well-known incandescent rages. *These damn reports cannot be accurate! How can the Russians still have so many men, even after all the millions we've killed.* He could just imagine Hitler standing there, ranting and raging, screaming at the top of his lungs while the generals looked on, powerless to do anything. He'd seen it so many times before. It was perfectly clear to him that the man was deranged. Hitler had simply lost touch with reality.

He knew from his own analysis of the German defences that lay along the Oder that they might slow the Russians down for a few days, but the issue would never be in real doubt. He smiled grimly to himself. Germany was almost out for the count. The Allies had recently crossed the Rhine in overwhelming strength and were quickly closing in from the west. The knock-out blow from the east would be just as swift. The Russian offensive would be short, brutal, and implacably final.

There was little more that he could do, now that they were all so close to the abyss. In theory Hitler still required the occasional intelligence assessment from him, but they were rarely asked for these days. Anybody with half a brain could see that the writing was on the wall. Himmler still went in to see him from time to time, mainly to provide some moral support and reassurance that all would turn out for the best, but his visits often went unheeded and probably even un-noticed. The atmosphere inside the Fuhrer bunker, hidden deep under the ruins of the Reich Chancellery, was becoming increasingly bizarre. It was almost like a travelling circus. There were all sorts of charlatans and other equally shady characters from all across the Party, all eager for a last brief interview with the Fuhrer before the final victory of the Third Reich. Or at least that's what Josef Goebbels, Reich Minister for Information and Propaganda, kept on proclaiming. The Russians would be defeated on the Oder, he announced to all and sundry and the western Allies would soon fall out amongst themselves. This would lead to a miraculous and unexpected victory that would soon change the course of the war. Clearly Goebbels was just as mad as the rest of them. Martin Bormann was still running the show. A loathsome, odious thug, the *eminence grise* who ran Hitler's day to day affairs remained with his Führer, weaving his own internecine plots and spinning webs of deceit like a particularly dangerous spider. You were never quite certain where you fitted in with his plans. Schellenberg couldn't stand the man.

No, he would no longer miss his trips into the city and the Fuhrer bunker. The sight of beautiful Berlin lying in ruins was far too depressing, no matter how quickly and tidily the rubble was cleared away. There was no need to return to the infamous building where he used to operate from. Number eight Prinz Albrecht Strasse was no longer fit to work in. Bomb damage had destroyed most of it. Only the prisoner cellars in Columbia House at the rear were still habitable, if that was the right word for them. He was secretly pleased. It was a huge relief not to return there, especially at night. He'd heard enough screams of agony to last him many lifetimes over.

The spring winds whistled through the bare branches of the silver birches that crowned the hill he was standing on. Schellenberg shivered involuntarily. His thoughts were interrupted by a small convoy of cars that suddenly appeared along the road from Rangsdorf, less than a few kilometres away. *That must be Himmler, back from his latest visit to the inmates at the asylum.* Schellenberg turned quickly on his heels and strode towards his waiting car. Hansen was sitting behind the wheel.

'Back to the compound, Hansen, and don't hang about. That was the Reichsführer's entourage, and I expect he'll want to see me very shortly.' Schellenberg got in. Hansen started up the engine, and rapidly drove off towards the security checkpoint. It lay just inside the border of the wood.

Himmler arrived a few minutes later. His car was waved through quickly, and within moments he was deposited outside his personal tent, a minute's walk from the main complex that housed all the communications equipment. Schellenberg was waiting for him.

'Good morning, Reichsführer. How was your trip?'

Himmler emerged from the rear seat, grimaced sourly, and walked quickly inside. Schellenberg followed him in. A quick glance dismissed the guards to a safe distance away, well out of earshot.

'A waste of time, as usual', Himmler grunted moodily. 'I simply cannot get through to him. The Führer refuses to listen to reality. He keeps on thinking that some last-minute miracle is going to save Germany. The enemy will fragment, their alliances will break down, and the Third Reich will go on to a glorious future.' He sat down grumpily and snarled. 'He seems to be entirely under the influence of that rat-faced little shit Goebbels. Our glorious minister for propaganda keeps on boring us about the similarities of our current predicament with that of Frederick the Great during the Seven Years War. The Americans, British and those Soviet snakes will fall out, just like the Austrians and Russians did back in the 18th Century. Can you believe it?'

Schellenberg managed to look suitably worried and deferential. 'I'm sorry to hear that, Reichsführer. Is there anything that can be done?'

'No...not directly. Not if the Führer carries on like this.' He glanced around furtively, making sure that nobody was within earshot, and lowered his voice. 'However, I think it may finally be time to do something about the mess we're in. I've been thinking about this for some time. What do you think, Brigadeführer? What's your real opinion? You must surely realise that the war is at an end. Miracles are no longer a possibility...or are they?'

Schellenberg knew he was being put on the spot. Now, more than ever, a false step, a slip, could be fatal, especially for a senior officer in Hitler's elite. Absolute unquestioning loyalty was the order of the day, and the slightest hesitation could easily sign a death warrant. But was now the time when Himmler at last began to open up and reveal his innermost secrets? This could be a rare opportunity to find out what really made the Reichsführer tick. He chose his words carefully.

'I admit that things look grim, Reichsführer. The military situation is critical, especially since the western Allies crossed the Rhine. General-feldmarschall Model's army in the Ruhr may well be in danger of being cut off and encircled if the Americans and British keep on advancing, as reports would suggest. Our Intelligence assessments indicate that the Soviets will attack us very soon, and with overwhelming strength.' He shrugged apologetically. 'I do not wish to appear to be pessimistic, but it's hard to see a miraculous turn-around in our present situation'.

Himmler smiled, a rare event that did little to soften his persona. 'Walther, I agree. That's the obvious conclusion anybody with a rational mind would draw. But you needn't worry. I'm not trying to test your loyalty. I know that you're trying to follow your National Socialist duty and not appear to be defeatist.' He pointed to a chair across from where he was sitting. 'Relax. Have a seat.' He waited while Schellenberg sat down, and then continued. 'We've known each other for a long time. Your service has always been exemplary, and you have been a shining example to all in the Party who hold dear our ideals and goals.' He smiled again, as coldly as before. 'Considering our current circumstances I think we can talk frankly between ourselves and not be too concerned about any apparent deviation from the Führer's wishes. Don't you agree?'

'Absolutely. As you wish Reichsführer'. Schellenberg smiled back in return, all the while still aware that he was on very dangerous ground. His pulse quickened. *What did Himmler really have in mind?* He decided to wait him out.

Himmler drummed his fingers on the table, all the while watching his subordinate carefully. 'Very well then...I'm going to let you into a few secrets, things I've kept hidden in the last year or so...things that could prove dangerous for all concerned should they be whispered in the wrong ears.' He paused, eyeing Schellenberg narrowly. 'Do I take it that what I am about to tell you is utterly confidential and must not be told to anyone else... *no matter who?*'

Schellenberg nodded dutifully. 'Yes Reichsführer. You have my word as a loyal officer in the SS.' He breathed heavily. There was no point mentioning his blood oath to the Führer. That no longer seemed to be appropriate.

His promise appeared to satisfy Himmler. The leader of the SS leaned closer.

'I think we have now reached the stage where we must consider every option Germany still has available, whether the Führer approves it or not. As far as I can see, there are several choices that are available to us. We can fight on, and almost certainly be overwhelmed from both East and West. Being overrun by the West is the better option, as I'm sure you would agree. I would rather not live to see the day when the Russians hoist their flag over the Reichstag and conquer Berlin. It takes little imagination to work out just what sort of future Stalin has in mind for us.' Indeed. They both knew what had happened under the joys of Soviet occupation. The horror stories from the overrunning of East Prussia and Pomerania were known to many. An orgy of rape, murder and brutal occupation had been visited on those unfortunate German civilians still living there – those who had been unable to flee in time...

'As I said, being overwhelmed by the British and Americans without Soviet interference would be the least unpleasant. But I cannot see any chance that Germany's enemies will fight amongst themselves and disintegrate at the last moment. They are much too near to total victory to do this.' He paused, again carefully searching Schellenberg's face for any reaction. 'So let's explore some other possibilities. Why not try to do a deal with America and Britain? It's not altogether out of the question, from what I can see. We could form an alliance, right at the death, so to speak.' Himmler grew animated. 'Our combined forces could match up against the communist hordes from the East. After all, what's going to happen if we are conquered? A Europe split down the middle – on one side, the Americans, with their British and French lapdogs... on the other, Stalin, and his allies from Eastern Europe.' He pursed his lips. 'That's a recipe for future world conflict, if ever there was one. Surely Churchill and Roosevelt must realise this? That is why I have been in contact with the Swedish embassy. I have sent a message to the Prime Minister and President exploring this possibility. The Führer would almost certainly not approve, but I feel this is a road we must explore. What do you think?'

News of Himmler's illicit visits to the Swedish embassy was indeed known to Schellenberg, but it would not be wise to reveal this secret information, not just yet.

'I agree, Reichsführer. It is a possibility worth exploring. But sir, do you really think this has a chance? I know the Western Allies distrust Communism, as do we all, but could this happen at such a late stage?' Privately, Schellenberg was extremely doubtful. A hidden source deep within the former Abwehr had hinted that this was something Canaris, that sly old fox, had already discussed with MI6 and the OSS several years ago – an anti-Hitler plot that would destroy the top Nazi hierarchy and leave Germany free to fight the Russians. Nothing had ever come of it then, and it was even less likely to be successful now.

'I don't know, but the chance is worth pursuing, especially in our current predicament. However, I have added a small inducement to help concentrate their minds.' Himmler watched Schellenberg's face like a hawk. 'I have threatened them with a war-winning weapon of destruction that should command their attention - the ability to unleash biological weapons that could destroy Britain and America.'

Schellenberg pretended to be amazed, if not suitably mystified. It was vital that Himmler did not suspect for one moment that he had prior knowledge of such a development. 'What...? But Reichsführer, surely that is against the Führer's wishes. He has a horror of such weapons. He once told me that the consequences to Germany if we used those sort of weapons first would be catastrophic. '

'Yes,' agreed Himmler, 'that is what he said to me, too. At the time I think he was referring to the poison gas shells used in the trenches in the Great War. He was there, and knows what it's like to experience such an attack. But he did not mention biological weapons, only chemical ones'. Himmler smiled slyly. 'There is a subtle, but nonetheless important distinction. I realise the use of these weapons is not without risk, but I believe we have the element of surprise. Our intelligence assessment of enemy capabilities leads me to believe we have outstripped them in this field of research, just like our jet aircraft and our V1 and V2 rockets.'

'But Reichsführer, how can you say surprise if you've given them this warning? And why should they believe you?'

'Simple, Walther, very simple.' Himmler grunted. 'I have given them a deadline. If we do not receive a suitable reply from them by midnight on April 12th, then I will give the order to commence our rocket offensive. This deadline will not give them enough time to mobilize their own stocks and attempt to pre-empt us. Besides, I am sure that they have no idea where our production facility is and even if they did, it would be impossible to attack from the air. This is completely different to Peenemünde, when they tried to destroy our rocket research base and all our best engineers and scientists.' Two years ago RAF bombers, using information passed onto them by Polish Resistance, had severely derailed missile development by almost a year. Although that factory was heavily protected it was still relatively easy to bomb. The Harz mountain base would be a far more difficult, if not impossible target by comparison.

Himmler continued. 'As to why they should believe us, well...I am arranging to give them a little demonstration.' A grim look of satisfaction washed over his features. 'We will target Birmingham. It's a good choice, easy enough to target and essential to the British war effort. Otherwise, it's unremarkable – factories, workers' housing, little of historical or sentimental importance, nothing for them to get too upset about. We will only use a small to medium dose, nothing like the full load should we need to launch in anger, but enough to demonstrate to them our reach and capability. That will happen in the next day or two. That may not in itself be sufficiently persuasive, so we will also target New York...'

'What?' Schellenberg hoped his astonishment was sufficient to be convincing. 'Good God...We can reach America...?'

'Yes' Himmler smirked exultantly. 'Von Braun, our leading rocket expert, is confident that we have developed missiles that are capable of crossing the Atlantic. Their production is only days away – another fine example of German technology! This is, of course, top secret – not a word of this must be mentioned to anyone. But we can do it, so he assures me.'

'But is there enough time left? Won't it take time for an epidemic to develop and spread?'

'Yes, but that's not so important. The British will know where the rocket will land. Their air defences cannot stop it – our rockets fly too fast and too high to be intercepted. It will only take a few days for them to discover that we are serious. Once they realise that they are powerless to stop us, then we will convene a meeting on neutral territory to call a halt to their advance, and conclude an alliance, *on our terms...*'

Himmler sat back in his chair, a look of triumph and utter certainty on his face. Schellenberg did his best to appear enthusiastic, but inside he was worried. *Christ, he is truly mad...Does he really think the West will stop now? This will only galvanise them into even more determined action to seek out this menace and destroy it once and for all. I've got to act now...*

'Reichsführer, this is absolutely brilliant...wonderful news,' Schellenberg gushed enthusiastically, 'the best thing I've heard in a long time. This is all down to your forward thinking and vision. How can I be of service?'

'Thank you, Walther', Himmler waved a hand, basking in the reflected glory of his brilliance. 'The first steps are already in motion. I want you to read this file.' He pulled a key from out of his pocket, unlocked a desk drawer, took out a thick folder and dropped it on the desk top. 'Familiarise yourself with these details. I want your thoughts and observations. Look for any weaknesses in the plan, let me have any options you recommend and appropriate solutions.'

'At once Reichsführer. I'll get on to it straight away.' Schellenberg got up from his seat, braced to attention, and then turned to leave.

'Good.' Himmler paused for a moment. 'Walther, there is one more thing.' Schellenberg turned back. 'You remember all those traitorous bastards we have incarcerated at Flossenberg – Canaris, and all those other subversives? I think I have at long last convinced the Führer that now would be a good time to deal with them, once and for all. If I can get his final approval then he will order their executions by the end of the first week in April.' An evil smile slid over his features. 'It will all be quite legal, and covered by the appropriate documentation. I think it would be an excellent idea to get rid of them at the same time, purge ourselves of this scum while at the same time concluding a deal with the West...or wiping the British and Americans off the face of the earth. Liaise with Amt II. I want to be sure that there are no problems when I present the Führer with their death warrants. See to it'.

SS Panzer School, Sondershausen 26/3/45 2100

'I'm sorry I haven't been able to report to you earlier, sir.' SS Untersturmführer Karl Akkerman, aka John Steele, stood in front of him. He had arrived in Simon's room a few minutes ago, and quickly established his real identity and what his mission was – all in code words that Simon remembered from his incarceration and 'conversion' in England. Their conversation was thoroughly disguised, just in case there were any inadvertent eavesdroppers listening in. Evening lectures were over for the day, and the armoured warfare school was settling down for the night. Dinner had finished half an hour ago – poor fare, admittedly, but what was on offer was almost certainly better than what many in the area would eat that night, what with the disruption in transportation and the almost non-existent resupply situation.

'Explain yourself,' Simon spoke curtly.

'As soon as I arrived here – it must be ten days ago now – the CO immediately sent me off to Kassel, to the Tiger production factory there. He wanted someone to supervise the repair of a batch of Tigers that had recently been delivered there, grab them at the first opportunity before anyone else did, and bring them back here. I-'

'I thought you had specific orders to report here under my command', Simon interrupted.

'So did I, sir. But I was picked up as soon as I got to the gates.' His voice sank to a whisper. 'I thought my cover was blown. The guards at the gate were spending far too long checking my paperwork. Then the CO suddenly turned up, and I thought for a moment that I'd been rumbled. But no – he needed some dogsbody to get to Kassel ASAP. All his other officers were busy, up to their eyeballs with instruction duties and other tasks, that sort of thing. My transfer to the school was unexpected. It seems that it caught him unawares, a last minute request from Personnel at RSHA, with a glowing recommendation and personal file. So off I went - I was given absolutely no choice.'

'But why did it take so long?' Simon kept his voice equally low. He was still annoyed about the delay in communication. 'Our mutual friend was supposed to have been in contact some time ago.' There could be no mention of anything English, a name or anything else that could be incriminating. He'd checked the room for bugs several times, but it was still best to take every precaution.

'Repairs took longer than expected,' Steele continued. 'We managed to get our hands on three battle-scarred Tigers - Mark VIE's. Sir, it was a real problem getting them back. There was no possibility of moving them by train. Allied fighter bombers always seem to be around, shooting up anything that moves. We've had to travel mainly by night, and the buggers kept on breaking down every few miles. A complete pain in the arse, if ever there was one...'

'Anyway, here I am, sir. I'm now at your complete disposal, subject to the CO wishes, naturally.' Steele grinned slyly. 'Our mutual friend has also asked me to give you your birthday present.' Steele winked, and then slipped off the small field rucksack that was slung over his right shoulder. 'Some chocolate, and some fancy pencils for you to draw with. It seems he knows about your love of landscape sketching and confectionery.' Steele winked again. 'He's a very generous benefactor, if I may say so, sir.'

Simon stood up and walked slowly over to where Steele was standing. He opened the top of the rucksack. Inside were what appeared to be several bars of chocolate, and a selection of coloured pencils.

Steele stood close and whispered in his ear. 'The chocolate is military grade plastic explosive, courtesy of our Czech Resistance friends. It doesn't look much, but these bars pack one hell of a punch. More than enough for a controlled explosion in a confined space - perhaps somewhere underground?' He left the rest unsaid. 'The pencils are pencil fuses, funnily enough. If you look carefully at the markings on the end, it tells you how long each one is set for. Simply insert the fuse into the plastic, activate it with a twist, make your escape...then boom. There's also this'. He fished a long cylindrical steel object out of his great-coat pocket. 'This may come in handy'.

It was a silencer. Simon turned towards him. 'Thank you, Untersturmführer', he said in a louder voice. 'Please pass on my heartfelt thanks. This is most generous, an excellent present.' He would need to conceal them carefully later. 'In the meantime I have another task for you. Please read these instructions.'

He handed Steele a piece of paper. On it was a hand written message and an address. Steele read it slowly, and looked up. His face was a picture of mounting indignation mixed with curiosity. Simon pursed his hand to his lips to indicate silence, and leaned closer.

'A change of orders. Things have moved on since your mission started, 'he whispered. 'This has been approved by my boss, and also, by the way, by yours as well. Or should I say, 'ours'.' Simon continued. 'You will leave first thing in the morning. Your mission here is successfully concluded.' He pointed at the rucksack. 'I have what I need to complete this part of the operation. And believe me, you cannot help. There is no chance of you being able to get to the intended destination of my 'present'. Security is far too tight, and you would have no reason for being there. It's a one-man job, and I will do it. There will be no further discussion about this.'

Steele was about to open his mouth, but Simon cut him off. 'This part of the operation' Simon whispered, pointing to the piece of paper 'is in many ways just as vital and important. Your boss expects full cooperation. I need to know if you can do this. Can you?'

Steele nodded. 'Yes sir. This will not be a problem'. He still looked indignant. 'I hope you know what you're doing.

'I do. Memorise that address, and then give me back that piece of paper'. In a louder voice, he carried on. 'Good. Thank you again, Untersturmführer. You may go now. I will see you in the morning before you leave.'

Steele saluted, and then left the room. Simon picked the paper up and fed it into the small fire that burned in the grate.

Almost immediately it curled up, the edges blackening, and then it burst into flame.

Schellenberg's message had got through to him this morning. There were certain things he needed to do, but the question was- how? The timescale was going to be tight. At the least, Steele could help him take care of one problem. But the most pressing problems still remained, and their deadline was rapidly approaching.

SHAEF Headquarters, Versailles, Paris 0900 27/3/1945

Menzies paced around the ornate anteroom like a restless tiger. He had been up since 0600. A hurried breakfast in the hotel he was staying in, and then a rapid dash through the suburbs of Paris before the early morning traffic slowed everything down to a crawl. At least the city looked to be in fine shape. There was little damage visible to its famous facades. The liberation of the city the previous August had been a brief, almost bloodless affair. The German commander, von Choltitz, had pulled out the vast majority of his troops in the city before the Allies arrived, ignoring Hitler's order to blow all the bridges across the Seine and destroy the most famous historical landmarks in the city. It was just as well for him that he had managed to get himself captured. The consequences of returning to Germany after directly disobeying a Führer directive hardly bore thinking about.

SHAEF's HQ was located in the pleasant suburb of Versailles. Most of it was concentrated in and around the magnificent Trianon Palace, once the home of the French regal dynasty. Security was tight, far greater than it needed to be, in his opinion. This level of scrutiny was unprecedented, even now when victory was close at hand. Menzies had to pass through six separate checkpoints before entering the Trianon, let alone getting close to the holy of holies where Eisenhower's offices were. It was all just a little bit over the top, he thought, laughing quietly to himself. The Germans were finished. The front line was deep inside the Reich, and Berlin was there for the taking. Menzies shook his head in wonder. Just how some of these rear echelon types considered themselves to be military men was a mystery to him.

Rumour had it that all this increased security was a legacy of the Battle of the Bulge. When the Germans attacked unexpectedly, the shock of their assault was compounded by stories of German commando infiltration deep behind the front lines. These enemy troops were said to be deliberately disguised in Allied uniforms, and their mission was to spread widespread panic and confusion in Allied rear areas. In the first few days of the German offensive they succeeded beyond Hitler's wildest expectations, causing an immense amount of disruption and disarray. Somewhere the story got around that part of their mission was to head towards Paris, assassinate the Supreme Commander himself and all his top brass. As a result, Eisenhower was so locked down that he couldn't even visit the bathroom without an armed guard in attendance!

Needless to say there were no assassination attempts. Almost all the commando units were rounded up quickly, once the Allies had got over their shock at the surprise German counterattack. None of them had got anywhere near Paris. Most of them were given a summary trial, lined up against the nearest wall and shot. Being caught out behind the lines wearing an enemy uniform was strictly against the Geneva Convention, and there could only be one sentence. The threat was long gone, although judging by the number of armed guards and checkpoints, you'd think it was only yesterday, and not nearly five months later...

He reviewed the events of the last twenty-four hours in his mind. The message from Germany had come through early yesterday morning, quite unexpectedly. The result was feverish activity at MI6, and then an urgent trip across London to RAF Bomber Command HQ at High Wycombe, in Buckinghamshire. At last they had a location for the underground factory, even if it was a ten kilometre square grid reference in central Germany, somewhere to the north of the town of Nordhausen.

Menzies had spent most of rest of the day there, kicking his heels while events unfolded. Even after he had convinced 'Bomber' Harris and the rest of the senior RAF command staff about the threat they all faced, it would still take time to mount a bombing offensive, let alone perform all the necessary preliminary operations. Orders had to go out to the nearest available aerial reconnaissance unit, in this case the 834th Tactical Surveillance Wing at Mons in Belgium. The Spitfires and Mosquitos based there would have to be urgently diverted from whatever tasks were planned for that day, refuelled and readied for the new mission, and their pilots briefed with all the intelligence needed for their new destination. All this would take time. Even then, there was always the weather to contend with. It might be a clear spring day at Mons, with barely a cloud in the sky and no adverse weather to deal with, but the story over central Germany might be another matter entirely. Two flights of Spitfires equipped with belly-mounted cameras managed to over-fly the area before darkness set in. The initial results were disappointing. Even though there were no Luftwaffe fighters out and about, and there was a complete absence of anti-aircraft defences to trouble them on their way in, little was immediately apparent. The area was partly obscured by cloud, and the limited detail they could photograph was a mass of undulating and heavily wooded hills, with only a few minor roads and a rail line. The results of the initial photographic survey were sent by teleprinter to Bomber Command HQ for further, more detailed analysis. The photos themselves would be flown over the next day.

At least Harris was sympathetic to the urgency of the situation, perhaps a better reaction than Menzies had expected. After all, Harris was known to be a prickly customer who rarely tolerated outside interference in his private domain, and who needed a great deal of convincing before changing his mind about how the RAF was to be used. But he remained quite adamant in his views. Yes, they needed to hit this area hard and soon, but without further corroborative information as to exactly where this factory was located it would not be possible to go ahead, not until better results were obtained. He had the lives of his bomber crews to consider and although there was a pleasing absence of flak in the area this did not mean that it did not exist. Maybe it was merely keeping quiet, waiting for a more worthwhile target to turn up. The Germans had pulled many a trick like this in the past, and their flak defences were often formidable. Besides, they did not have enough heavy bombs to cover the entire area. No more than thirty Tallboys, super heavy bombs that were capable of penetrating underground structures, were available from current stocks. That would be nowhere near enough to cover such a large area. No, there would be little point in proceeding unless more detailed targeting information became available. Several reconnaissance flights would cover the area tomorrow and in the next few days, until the revealing tell-tales showed up. Until then the bombing mission was on hold. Menzies was disappointed and irritated, but it was also perfectly obvious to him that nothing further could be done at present. At least, not from the RAF's point of view. He had already detailed Monckton to pass on this latest information to SHAEF HQ in Paris. Perhaps if he went there himself, appealed directly to the Supreme Commander, there might be a way to send ground forces into the area, and maybe involve the United States Army Air Force as well. Even Harris might bow to the Supreme Commander's wishes.

This was the reasoning behind his quick dash to Paris, late yesterday evening. It was widely known that the German defenses along the Rhine were in a state of collapse. Both Hodges' First US Army and Patton's Third were across the river, driving east towards the centre of Germany and what used to be Czechoslovakia, as well as in a southeasterly direction towards Munich and the Austrian border. Perhaps an armoured division or two could be diverted towards Nordhausen. Maybe the town was already in the sights of the advancing US forces heading into the area.

The door to the inner offices opened, and a tall, immaculately attired major with a trim moustache stepped into the room.

'Colonel Menzies?'

'Yes.' The MI6 chief stopped his pacing.

'Sir, if you will follow me. The Supreme Commander will see you now.' Menzies nodded, and followed the officer through the door.

They passed through an outer suite of offices, where men and women in a variety of uniforms were engaged – answering phones, typewriting, updating maps and a myriad of other duties. The place was a hive of activity, and the offices seemed to go on forever. It always puzzled Menzies just what all these people were doing. Yes, running seven allied armies was quite a task, but most of the direct administration went on at each army's own HQ. This was the tier of administration above that level, some of it no doubt very necessary, but he suspected a lot of it was bloated beyond control. Somebody had once told him that there was enough staff at SHAEF HQ to form a regular infantry division, well over ten thousand men and women! The mind boggled. Did they really need that number of people to run the show? The old adage about too many cooks ran through his mind.

Eventually they reached the inner offices of the Supreme Commander. One final document check, and yet another unnecessary briefcase and body search and then he was through. At last he had finally reached his destination. The door was opened and he walked through into a large conference room. Eisenhower was sitting at the far end of the main table, deep in conference with three other senior officers. Menzies recognised Major General Kenneth Strong, head of Military Intelligence, as well as Lieutenant General Walter Bedell-Smith, Eisenhower's Chief of Staff, and the second most powerful man in the Allied senior command, sitting on either side of the Supreme Commander. There was a smattering of other senior officers spread around the table, a few of whom he recognised from previous visits to SHAEF.

Eisenhower looked up, recognising Menzies in an instant. The MI6 chief saluted smartly, standing to attention. 'Ah, Stuart, 'Eisenhower drawled in his well known Texan twang, a broad smile across his face. 'Good to see you again. Have a seat. I hear you have some interesting information for us.' He gestured towards an unoccupied place at the far end of the table. Menzies sat down, sliding his briefcase onto the surface of the well-polished table. Although he was no expert, it looked old and very expensive. Possibly Louis 16th. The room was dominated by a huge ornate mirror, edged in gold filigree, and a large fireplace with an impressive mantelpiece. A carriage clock quickly chimed that it was nine o'clock.

The Supreme Commander glanced quickly at his fellow officers seated next to him, and then continued. 'Before you start, I'd like your opinion on another rather pressing matter.'

He cleared his throat. 'Kenneth here,' Eisenhower nodded to his left, 'is very concerned that in our current strategy we are not focusing on a potentially very serious problem. As you can see from this map,' he pointed briefly to the latest situation map displayed on a large stand behind him, 'events are moving quickly. Hodges is moving north and east to link up with Simpson's Ninth Army and pocket all the remaining German forces in the Ruhr. Patton is beginning to drive south and east towards Austria, in conjunction with Patch's Seventh and the French First Army.' He pointed to the area north of the Ruhr. 'Monty is almost ready to drive northeast towards Hamburg and the Baltic coast at Lubeck...All in all, a highly satisfactory state of affairs. The Russians will attack soon, cross the Oder and take Berlin - probably in the next few weeks. We'll meet up with them along the Elbe, as previously agreed.'

'But what's not so clear is what the top Nazis are doing. Their western front lines are crumbling almost everywhere, but they don't seem to be reacting to this unfolding catastrophe. The only thing we have is this – we've received some information from a variety of sources that Hitler and his cronies are going to flee from the capital soon. We think they're going to debunk south into the Austrian Alps and set up some sort of impenetrable Alpine fortress. Kenneth is very concerned that this is a real possibility, and that we may have a prolonged fight on our hands in very difficult terrain before we finally eliminate them all. That's why Patton has been ordered to head for Austria as soon as he shakes himself loose from the German lines along the Würz and Main rivers. His main task is to cut all the land routes into the Austrian Alps and prevent the Nazis making a last stand there. Do you have any information to back this theory up?'

Menzies was completely taken aback by this unexpected news. Nothing along these lines had reached his ears. He'd not heard of any suicidal defence plans, not unless you counted Berlin. As far as he knew, Hitler and all the top Nazis were still in the capital, and had no intentions of going elsewhere. That was where the heart of Nazism, and all that it stood for, lay.

Eisenhower's concern was all very well, but wasn't the news about the location of the rocket factory and bio-weapon base just a little more important than anything about some desperate last-ditch shootout? Possibly not, he thought, looking at all the serious faces around him. He was aware that he had few real friends here, and possibly some enemies he might not be aware of. Perhaps he should proceed carefully.

'No sir,' he said, careful to keep his voice neutral. 'I've heard nothing of this as yet. May I ask about the basis of your suspicions?'

Eisenhower turned towards Strong. 'Over to you, Kenneth.'

'We've received various bits of information,' Strong began, looking immediately uncomfortable under Menzies' penetrating and at least to his eyes, mildly sardonic stare. 'Harrumphh...' He cleared his voice and began again. 'We know that what's left of the Sixth SS Panzer Army is defending eastern Austria from the Russians. So why should Hitler's elite be down there, rather than defending Berlin? It doesn't make sense. From what little our Soviet allies tell us, it would appear that the German defences along the Oder are second rate by comparison, so it would be more logical for Hitler to use his best forces around where he will fight it out to the last – Austria. That's where he comes from, along with many of his cronies in the upper echelons of the Nazi Party.'

Menzies grunted to himself sceptically. Just when was the last time Hitler did anything logical? And why should he start now? This all sounded rather vague.

'Do you have anything else, anything more substantial, Kenneth?' Menzies asked.

'We've captured a few documents that refer to an Alpine redoubt,' Strong continued, casting a quick glare in Menzies' direction. 'Moreover, some of the SS prisoners we've captured recently have referred to this in their interrogation. In addition, quite a few villages and towns we've taken recently have been difficult to subdue once our forces have moved on to their next objectives. There seems to be a growing resistance among the teenagers in the population. They call themselves Werewolves, fanatical young Nazis armed with grenades and Molotov cocktails. Most of them fight to the death, but the few we've taken alive also refer to what I've already mentioned.'

Eisenhower interjected. 'Admittedly, it's not much, but Kenneth here thinks it's something that we can't afford to ignore, even now.'

Yes. Menzies could see the logic in that. But it was all rather flimsy. Granted, a large swathe of central Germany had yet to be captured, but the enemy looked to be finished. The knock-out blow of the war was about to be delivered. The defences in the west were surrendering in ever- increasing numbers, the captured German troops well aware that the war was almost over and glad to surrender to the western Allies... anybody but the Russians. But when had Strong ever been right about anything? It was only four months ago that he was proclaiming that the war would be over by Christmas, and that the enemy was out for the count. Only a few days later the Germans counterattacked in great strength in the Ardennes.

'I can understand your concern, sir,' Menzies began, addressing Eisenhower directly and deliberately ignoring Strong. Menzies knew he had to be careful in expressing his doubts. Here he was in the highest echelons of Allied power, and while it was usually a wise move to act as some sort of Devil's advocate, it was also necessary to do it respectfully and not needlessly antagonize the powerful figures that were seated around the table. 'Sometimes it can be very difficult to be sure what the enemy's intentions are, but I have no evidence, not even a hint, of anything like this taking place. I have some sources inside the enemy camp, but none of them has mentioned anything remotely resembling this.' He shrugged his shoulders. 'There is always the possibility that this may be a hoax...'

He left the rest unsaid. Strong was not exactly a friend. He thought back to some of their previous meetings. The impression that he had gained over the last two years was that Strong had an over- active imagination, coupled with an unhealthy dose of wishful thinking. SHAEF's chief intelligence officer would mould his hypothesis first, and then fit the facts in to support his theory afterwards, rather than looking at it the other way round. But the man was highly placed, and had Eisenhower's ear. That counted for a lot. .

'Nothing at all?' Eisenhower pressed him.

'Absolutely not, sir. Has the OSS turned anything up?'

'No,' Eisenhower sighed. 'Our boys have drawn a blank, much the same as you and MI6'.

'I see.' *Enough of this nonsense.* 'Sir, may I turn to the information I've received in the last twenty four hours?'

Eisenhower waved a hand and leaned back in his chair. What Menzies told him soon made him sit up and pay very close attention. The MI6 chief summarised the latest developments, and gave a brief description of his journey to Spain in January.

'I received a message from the Joint Chiefs of Staff about this,' Eisenhower interrupted, still looking somewhat sceptical, 'but I must confess that I found the whole idea a little far-fetched. Yes, we know about their rockets, but biological warfare? Are you sure?'

'I'm afraid so, sir.' Menzies continued. 'The facts are there. I must admit that I felt the same way at first, but soon realised that we cannot afford to take this sort of threat casually. The potential for disaster is too great.' With that, he launched into the latest news, and the imminent threat to Birmingham, and possibly New York.

Utter silence dominated the meeting. The faces around the table were a mixture of incredulity and shock. Then everyone began to talk at once.

'Silence!' Bedell-Smith roared, speaking for the first time. The hubbub quickly ceased. He turned to his boss. 'Birmingham? I can well believe that. These V2s can hit London without a problem. But New York? How the hell can the Nazis have developed a weapon that can cross the Atlantic? I find that very hard to swallow.'

Several voices joined in, expressing similar sentiments of doubt and amazement. Eisenhower abstained from the frenzied discussion, all the while quietly watching Menzies face. After a minute or two he raised a hand for silence. 'Do you believe all this, Stuart?'

'It's hard to say, sir,' Menzies shrugged his shoulders. 'I know it sounds very far-fetched, and I still find it hard to believe. But our scientists say that technically it's possible. With the right type of fuel, and appropriate modifications to their rockets, if they can reach Birmingham then they can reach anywhere, possibly even the United States. As to these biological weapons, who knows? But theoretically, all this *is* possible.'

This time Bedell-Smith did not need to demand quiet. The silence was profound. The shocking implications of the news Menzies had brought were not difficult to work out. After a prolonged pause, it was Eisenhower who spoke first. 'Gentlemen, let's review our options. What about our air forces?'

Menzies brought him up to date with the RAF's reconnaissance mission, and it's essentially inconclusive results. Eisenhower, however, saw no problem with this. He would instantly order the Eighth and Ninth Tactical Air forces to carpet bomb the entire area, as soon as it could be arranged. But Bedell-Smith voiced his concerns almost immediately.

'It may not be quite that simple, sir,' he said diplomatically. 'All our planes are being used as tactical support for the ground forces. Their commanders may make it difficult for us if we suddenly decide to switch them away to something much less obvious and profitable.' Nobody there was in much doubt as to what he had left unsaid, what needed to be read between the lines. The Allied air commanders were notorious for their independence and bloody-mindedness. There was a very good chance that they would only cooperate if it suited them. 'Besides, I doubt if we would have enough immediately available planes with the correct armament to destroy an underground factory, or sufficiently bomb the area around the clock.'

'What do you think?' Eisenhower looked back at the MI6 Chief.

'I think General Bedell-Smith has raised some valid points, sir,' Menzies acknowledged, with a gracious nod in Bedell-Smith's direction. 'The Joint Chiefs of Staff were similarly concerned at the meeting I went to in Washington. We can try bombing, but I don't think we can necessarily rely on it alone. There a quite a few technical difficulties that are not immediately apparent – do we have the correct type of bombs to penetrate underground, and enough of them to do the job? We've narrowed the location of the factory down to a few square kilometres, but is that sufficiently precise? If not, what about our ground forces and airborne troops? I know the area is not ideal for a para-drop, but could this be done, if all else fails?'

Nobody spoke for a moment. Eisenhower steepled his hands under his chin, looked thoughtful and then turned to the map. 'I don't think using the Allied Airborne Army is the answer, 'he said, after a long pause. 'The US 82nd and 101st Airborne divisions are advancing as ground infantry units with the rest of our front line forces, and they're tied up in heavy fighting. The British 6th and American 17th Airborne are still involved in Monty's Rhine crossings, and what's left of the British 1st Airborne division is recovering back in England from the setback at Arnhem last September. We have the 13th US Airborne in reserve, but it's still undergoing jump training, and is not considered combat ready as yet. Besides, it usually takes at least several days, if not a week or two, to plan and mount such an operation, concentrate all the available aircraft, gliders, and get the whole thing off the ground. It doesn't look like we've got this time available. When did you say the Germans would start launching?'

'In the next day or two, sir. If we don't cooperate with the Nazis after these warning shots, then their main rocket offensive will start in the first or second week of April.'

Eisenhower thought for a few more minutes, and then made up his mind. A grim, purposeful look set over his normally genial features. 'Okay, I know we've got limited options, but we're not gonna give those Kraut bastards an inch on this,' he barked determinedly. He turned to his Chief of Staff. 'Walter, get all the Allied air commanders over here today, without fail. I don't care what they're doing and who they're doing it with. I'm going to read the riot act to them this last time, and by God they'll do what I tell them!' He thumped the table. 'Pinky!' He roared. The diminutive figure of General H.R. Bull shot up. 'Sir!'

'Get me Brad on the line immediately!' Eisenhower was referring to Omar Bradley, now commander of the 15ᵗʰ Army Group. 'I need the latest up-to-date information on where Courtney Hodges' 1ˢᵗ US Army units are.' He stood up, strode over to the map and studied it for a few minutes, measuring distances with his fingers. 'They're closest to Nordhausen. It looks to me as if Courtney has got enough assets to hand. Let's see what they can do.' He paused for a moment. 'One last thing – get me General Brereton at 1ˢᵗ Allied Airborne Army HQ. Let's see if he can put a scratch airborne operation into motion. We've got to use every possible source to knock this factory out.'

The meeting began to break up. The rest of those in attendance prepared to leave. Before they started to file out, Menzies stood up and looked towards Eisenhower. 'Sir, if I may...'

'Go ahead, Stuart.'

'Thank you sir,' Menzies inclined his head in acknowledgement, and turned to face everyone in the room. 'Gentleman, I beg to remind you that everything that has been discussed today, and in particular my report, is kept top secret. It must not be discussed beyond the confines of this room. It is vital that no word gets back to the enemy that we have a source at the top level over there.' He smiled apologetically. 'Please do not feel insulted. I realise that you are aware, as well as I am, that anything spoken in here is classified and on a need-to-know basis only. However, this new information goes beyond the normal security concerns, and I cannot begin to stress just how important this is. Thank you.'

There were a few surprised, even indignant faces, but no one commented, at least not in the presence of the Supreme Commander. Soon the room emptied, leaving Eisenhower, Bedell-Smith, Strong and Menzies alone. Eisenhower turned towards him and smiled. 'Thanks, Stuart. You handled that well, very diplomatically, especially considering just how many

egos were sitting around this table up until a few moments ago.'
He grinned wryly. 'Present company excluded, naturally'.

'No problem, sir,' Menzies smiled in return. 'Thank you for
acting decisively. We may just be able to head this off and avert
a catastrophe.'

'I hope so.' Eisenhower's smile faded. 'But there's one thing,
at the very least, in all this that you've not explained – your
German contact. Who is he? Can you trust him? And do you
have anyone inside Germany who can possibly help us out?'

'Exactly,' Strong echoed, somewhat aggressively. 'We've
taken everything you've told us on faith alone. Where's the
proof?' Bedell-Smith nodded in agreement.

Menzies knew this was coming, sooner or later. There was
no way to avoid it.

'I'm sorry, sir,' he said apologetically, addressing Eisenhower
alone. 'All I can say is that my source is at the very top of German
Military Intelligence. Part of the deal is to protect his identity at
all costs. He's given me sufficient reason to believe that all this
is true, and at considerable risk to himself. I'm sure I'll be able
to reveal him soon – the war will end shortly, no matter what
happens. And yes – I do have assets working inside Germany.
Two of them are well positioned to help us out. That's all I can
say for now.'

Eisenhower chuckled. He had expected little else, but it was
worth a try. 'Of course - I understand. Just as long as you're
sure you're doing the right thing.'

Menzies nodded in return, placed his papers inside his
briefcase, saluted and left the room. *Christ, I bloody well hope
so.*

❀

Kohnstein factory complex, Harz Mountains 1645 29/3/45

The light was fading rapidly as Hartmann looked out from the concealed main factory entrance that lay beneath the hill mass that housed the rocket factory complex. The blast doors were almost closed, leaving just a small gap for him to peer out. He stood in their shelter behind the left-hand door, peering out as the daylight faded. Dusk was approaching, and the trees and slopes of the surrounding hills were quickly slipping into deep shade. The bombing had been going on all day, a wartime phenomenon that had never concerned them before. There didn't seem to be any pattern to it, but the fact that the Allies seemed to have found them was disturbing nonetheless. You could feel the explosions sometimes, especially the nearer hits. The earth would tremble and occasionally shake. A few of the tunnels had reported minor cascades of dust, and there were one or two instances of chalk landslides from walls and ceilings, but nothing serious, nothing too structural. The factory would go on functioning, even if the fresh air supply was not as good as it had been before the bombers arrived. Some of the air vents must have taken direct hits, but he was not too concerned about that. Much more worrying to him was the state of communications with the outside world, and the re-supply situation.

They'd lost the ability to reach Berlin, or anywhere else for that matter. Since the bombing started he had not been able to get out a clear message. All telephone links were severed shortly after 0900, and less than an hour later the radio transmission also went down, never to return. The enemy bombers must have hit the two radio transmitters disguised as pine trees on top of the Kohnstein. That was serious in itself, but what also worried him was the fact that several supply loads had failed to turn up by rail. Sure, he had enough slave labour to last him for a few more days, but little in the way of food and water had reached them. Still more important was the delivery of rocket components. The last shipment had reached the factory at 0200, but several more should have arrived throughout the day. The weather was still excellent for resupply purposes, a dense mixture of heavy cloud and rain. It should be safe enough to permit rail movement by day. He reckoned that the enemy was bombing blind, relying on their radar to consistently hit their targets. That was just as well, but it could be worse. If the weather cleared up, then the Allies' efforts could dramatically improve, and seriously interfere with current operations.

Hartmann knew he had to do something. In desperation he'd sent a four man reconnaissance team out to find out how bad the effect of the bombing was. Part of their mission was to check the camouflaged rail lines down as far as the bend in the main road, and the area where they joined the main line from Nordhausen to Northeim. That was nearly two hours ago. They should have reported back in by now, but maybe conditions out there were worse than he realised. Still, he needed to get some idea of the damage to the area, and what sort of shape the road and railways were in. And Berlin would want to know what was going on, why he had been unable to contact them...

He was about to turn away when he caught sight of movement to his right. It looked like two men, struggling to make progress, running and crawling through the undergrowth. They were getting closer, no more than a hundred metres away. He was just about to call out when suddenly the sound of aircraft engines somewhere above the clouds reverberated through the trees. Several screaming whistles revealed that a clutch of bombs was falling earthward. In a flash four explosions rent the air, followed by a series of concussive blast waves that slammed through the trees, crashing up against the blast doors and flattening the surrounding area. Hartmann had just enough warning to jump quickly back into cover before the shock waves hit. The sudden rise in air pressure lifted him off his feet and forced him backwards, popping his ears and thumping him into the side of the main tunnel. Then mercifully the compression waves were gone. He gasped and struggled to his knees, his back aching where he had hit the tunnel wall. Some of the guards around him were groaning. One of them held his arm at a strange angle, another clasped his head. Blood was oozing out of a cut on his face. Two more lay still on the tunnel floor

Hartmann managed to stand up, somewhat shakily. There was a buzzing noise in his ears, and spots swam in front of his eyes. He swallowed. At the same time something clicked inside his head, and then his hearing improved. He suddenly found that he was better able to focus on his surroundings. Ignoring the scene of confusion behind him, he stumbled forwards to the gap in the doors and looked out. It was like a scene from Dante's inferno. Fires were raging throughout the woods, especially where the camouflaged railway had been. One of its tracks was curled up, pointing at an odd angle to the sky. The rest of the detail was difficult to make out, mainly due to the clouds of smoke and failing light. Hartmann was about to turn away when blurred movement over to the left caught his eye, and a man in a dirty, charred uniform stumbled into view.

'Quick, over here!' He shouted. The figure caught sight of him, and staggered his way over to the blast doors. It was Förster, the NCO in charge of the reconnaissance detail he'd sent out earlier. Hartmann caught him as he stumbled and fell. There was blood on his face, and a dark wet patch along his back.

'I beg to report, sir...' The NCO gasped, as Hartmann laid him gently down on the floor of the tunnel entrance, cradling the younger man's head. '...The railway's gone, smashed up in the bombing.' He began to make gurgling noises in his throat, his chest heaved, and a gush of dark red blood welled out of the corner of his mouth. Hartmann fished a handkerchief out of his pocket and wiped the bloody mess away, but at the same time noticed that Förster's lips were starting to turn blue. He was getting more short of breath now, his chest labouring heavily. Something from Hartmann's first aid training echoed dimly in his mind, something about how to treat a casualty with a chest injury. There wasn't much time, he realised. He had to act immediately. Quickly he grabbed Förster by the shoulders and, ignoring the NCO's groans, levered him up into a sitting position. The bloody patch along his back was spreading, but almost instantly at least Förster's breathing began to become less laboured. Hartmann then leaned him over onto the injured, wet area, hoping that his emergency measures would give the man more time.

He turned to the other guards, most of whom were in various stages of recovery. 'Quick, get me a doctor over here, now!' One of the guards hurried off to find the resident medical factory officer. He turned back to check the NCO again. Förster was looking marginally better, but for how long?

'Heinz, Is there anything else you can tell me?'

'Yes, Standartenführer...' Förster paused to catch his breath, gasping for air. 'Road's heavily cratered...so is the railway.' He stopped for a moment, then resumed. 'Felder and Pfannenstiel were killed just after we reached the road...A bomb blew them to pieces...They were only fifty meters from where I was standing. Poor bastards...never had a chance...Where's Stumme?'

'I don't know, 'Hartmann lied. Stumme was most likely a victim of the last bomb load. 'Were you able to check the transmitters?'

A shake of the head. '...No...couldn't get near...too many bombs...'

Försters' eyes closed, and his head slumped down onto his chest. Hartmann immediately felt for a pulse. It was still there, weak and thready, not a good sign. But there was nothing else he could do here. He had no equipment or specialist first aid training. Förster would have to take his chances until medical help arrived.

Carefully he stood up, grasping the wall for support. The ache in his amputated leg reminded him that he was not quite as mobile as he used to be, but he had more urgent considerations on his mind. Berlin needed to know what was happening, and that there was going to be a change of plan. The first rocket should have launched earlier today, according to his instructions, and the second soon after. But that was clearly impossible now, thanks to the enemy bombers. Did Berlin realise that the secret was out, that it now seemed likely that the Allies had located the position of the factory? How could he get in contact? The nearest place with reliable communications was Nordhausen, but it might equally be under attack. One thing he knew for sure – there was little chance of launching anything until the skies were less unfriendly, and railway movement was now out of the question. At least he had enough road launchers to get the rockets away from the factory and in the air, if the roads were negotiable. Maybe he would get a chance tonight. The enemy air forces always seemed to take a break in the evenings, tea-time or whatever the British called it. Then at least he could fulfill his duty. He hoped it would be enough to make sure that Erika and the girls would be safe.

❀

Rybalko knew he couldn't take much more of this. The long hours of intense physical labour, the appalling rations, the random beatings - all were beginning to take their toll. He'd only been here a few weeks, but it felt almost like a lifetime. He'd lost count of the numbers of fellow workers, Slavs, Jews and others who had succumbed to the harsh regime in the short time since he arrived. But the Germans couldn't care less – worker's welfare was the least of their concerns. Fresh batches of prisoners would turn up every few days to replace those that couldn't last the pace, and the back-breaking grind carried on remorselessly. It was a wonder to him that he'd managed to last even this long. His weight had dropped substantially, possibly ten or even fifteen kilograms since his capture, he estimated, and he was more tired than he could ever have imagined a human being could be. Conditions were poor - there was no daylight, just the constant glare of underground lights and the noise of a factory at work. You were lucky to find a spare cot to rest on. Usually it was just a space on the dirty floor. First come first served was the overall principle. The occasional fist fight and scuffle were necessary to claim a prized spot, but most of them now were too hungry and tired to bother – just get your head down, anything to get away from brutally hard labour and a lashing from the guards.

They'd not treated him too badly at first, not after his capture at the end of January. There were several interrogations by local

Wehrmacht officers, none of them too unpleasant – all they wanted to know were details of the latest deployments of Red Army rocket artillery units, and some idea of when and where the next round of attacks would take place. The occasional blow, nothing too painful - Rybalko could cope with that. He'd given them a few insignificant details, nothing of any great importance. After all, he was only a middle grade officer, not privy to the major operational movements and planning that went on at Front HQ. It seemed to be enough to satisfy them, at least for the moment. But after the first few weeks things became less civilized

The Germans wanted to know more. His interrogators knew that he belonged to the Rocket Artillery Corps. Maybe he could tell them about the latest advances in Soviet rocket science. The Soviets had started it all off several years ago with the invention of the Katyusha, the truck-mounted rocket launcher. Little Kate, as they called her, was a devastating weapon, well capable of saturating any battlefield with multiple rocket salvos. Although small she packed a punch well beyond her size. It had come as a nasty shock to the German Army. Sure enough, the Wehrmacht quickly followed suit, copying the idea and developing its own rocket artillery. But surely if the Russians had taken the lead in this field, then by now they must have moved on to bigger, more powerful delivery systems – bigger rockets, longer ranges, more deadly payloads?

He was transferred further to the rear, for more thorough and intensive interrogation. That's where the real nastiness began. Rybalko would never forget his sessions with a couple of Gestapo thugs dressed up in leather coats. He'd heard enough about their sort to realise that he was now in the company of hardened professionals, as compared to the relative amateurs who had worked on him previously. He knew from the moment he saw them that he was in real trouble. They had just as fearsome a reputation as the experts on his side, the specialists who worked in the NKVD cellars. Their activities were something best not discussed in public, but that didn't stop the whispers and stories. Those were the boys who really knew how to extract a confession. There was nothing a victim wouldn't say to stop the relentless pain and bring a merciful release to the unending agony. You'd swear that your own mother was the devil herself just to please the interrogators. And the Gestapo were every bit as skilled as their opposite numbers in the Lubyanka, and wherever else the NKVD found a need to be.

There was another man with them, smartly dressed in civilian attire, cool, detached, and quite impervious to his protestations that he simply did not know the answers to what his interrogators were looking for. This man was the picture of calm, studied deliberation, several steps above the more physical side of things. He took detailed notes, made reasoned suggestions and comments, and with a nod or a flick of the hand brought on the different phases of coercion. Nothing was too distasteful for him. The beatings were expertly applied, almost like a scientific experiment – the right lever in the right place at the right time. The process would unlock his tongue, and liberate all that knowledge and memories behind the protective wall he had built to shield them. It was all done dispassionately. There were no shouts or raised voices – if anything, it was conducted in an almost friendly, reasonable way.

Spare yourself the pain, they said. *Nobody can resist it. Every man has a breaking point, and sooner or later we'll get to yours, so why make it difficult on yourself?* They left his face and fingers alone, as well as his genitalia, something he was grateful for later, though at the time it terrified him that they were reserving these areas for the next round of persuasion. No, it was his kidneys, legs and feet that took the brunt of their displeasure. Each session was preceded by a pep-talk, a little exposé into what type of pain lay ahead. Their favourite was something they called 'bastinado', a relentless assault on the soles of his feet. Nobody, they assured him, could take that sort of agony for long.

And ultimately they were proven right. He told them all he knew. It did not matter that he fainted several times during each session. A bucket of icy-cold water soon brought him around again. Finally, they must have decided that they had achieved all they could, short of beating him to death. His defences were laid low and they had picked him clean, the way a pack of vultures do to a decomposing carcass.

And a few days later – or was it a week? - all in solitary confinement, still unable to walk much and passing blood in his urine, they loaded him on the back of a lorry and dumped him at a place called Buchenwald. He'd heard about some of the death camps the advancing Soviets had come across as they liberated large parts of eastern Poland during the previous summer. Although this place was not a dedicated extermination facility it still reeked of the horror of what the Nazis had perpetrated elsewhere. The degradation and torture was less immediate, more gradual, but just as brutal in the long run. And from there he had graduated here – literally, out of the fire and into the frying pan. There was no explanation for the transfer. Perhaps it would be a long, slow grilling.

The clock on the main tunnel wall told him it was 2015. He'd been working since 0600, with two fifteen minute breaks to wolf down the disgusting mess they called food. A few sips of oily water, and then back to work. His shift was due to finish at 2330, another few hours of back breaking work to go, but he no longer thought about it. Something was different today, something had changed. The guards were on edge, more so than usual. They appeared fretful, even nervous at times. What was happening outside? They could all feel the occasional tremors in the tunnels that shook them from time to time. Sometimes the lights flickered, and on several occasions showers of dust and chalk cascaded from the tunnel roof in which they were working. Someone, maybe one of the French prisoners who was working on his detail, had whispered that it was the Allies bombing, that liberation could not be far off. It was just possible, he told himself – could it be that the Red Army had broken through the Oder line and was streaming into the central Germany? Or could it be the British and Americans, advancing from the West? Either way, the fact that the guards were paying more attention to the disturbances outside than what was immediately in front of them might give him a chance.

Take the rocket in front of him – he had never seen anything
so big, so technically complicated. The motor housing Rybalko
had been detailed to work on all day was fascinating, the degree
of sophistication well beyond anything he'd ever seen before.
He knew the Red Army Rocket Corps had secretly performed
experiments with large scale rockets at the testing grounds near
Lipetsk, but that was nothing compared to the scale of what
lay stretched along the main tunnel in front of him. It was
huge, maybe thirty meters or more from needle tip point to the
stabilizer fins at the rear on which it stood, presumably, before
launching. It was bigger than the others he had seen before,
but why? For some reason the fuselage panels on this one were
painted in alternate black and white quarters, although most of
the others he had previously seen at the factory were covered in a
matt olive green paint. And now all the access panels were now
closed, bar one section near the nose. What was its purpose?
The Germans appeared not to have packed what looked him to
be the weapons area with high explosive, or anything else so
far. And what was its range? He could only guess, but from
the size of the fuel tanks, and the special steel containers that
housed the propellant, he estimated a distance of maybe two
thousand kilometers, possibly more – enough to reach easily
England, perhaps, or maybe even Moscow itself.

The thought made him shudder. Rita his wife and his son
Oleg, who was now no more than nine months old, lived there
with his elderly father. Their house was located in the suburb
of Zdhanov, only a few kilometers from the city centre. Was
the Kremlin and the top Soviet leadership a target for whatever
diabolical weapon the Nazis had in mind? Would the rest of
Moscow also suffer a similar fate? A conventional warhead,
filled with even the most destructive explosive, would only
damage a relatively small area, not even enough to significantly
harm the Kremlin citadel. The Germans would need to launch
multiple missiles to achieve that scale of destruction. But did
the Nazis have something more ambitious, more widespread
in mind, a weapon that was much more insidious and lethal.

Perhaps it was some sort of special poison, a deadly toxin, or maybe even a plague?

'You!' The shout disrupted his thoughts. A guard was pointing at him. 'Get up to the control section.' He pointed to where a couple of white-coated figures were working. 'They need some help. On the double!'

He nodded subserviently and hurried as fast as he could towards the top of the rocket. One of the other workers took over the task he was working on. Rybalko soon reached the area where the two German technicians were working. Rybalko's German was not fluent, but from the way their conversation was being conducted it was clear to him that the two scientists were having a considerable difference of opinion about something. One of them turned to him angrily.

'Hold this,' he ordered, glaring at him. The German pointed to a large spring-loaded compartment door deep inside the housing. 'Keep this open. I'll be back in a moment. Hans, keep an eye on him!' The other scientist nodded

The first German turned and walked quickly away towards the nearest workshop area, leaving the two of them alone. The other German shrugged his shoulders and carried on working on a complicated series of dials, at the same time glancing at a flip chart in front of him. It was clear that he was setting some parameters of some sort, possibly targeting information. Rybalko squinted out of the corner of his eyes, trying to look at the chart that lay upside down from where he was looking. The figures looked like latitude and longitude information, and the technician was loading them into the destination data. He took a closer look at the area just behind the compartment door he was holding up. Yes – those were gyroscopes. He'd recognise their type anywhere. Even if they were a far cry from the primitive ones the Russians used for guidance on the battlefield, they still looked familiar. If he could just alter one of the settings when nobody was looking, then maybe that might just be enough to throw the rocket off course and sabotage its mission.

The second technician was finished. He checked his adjustments one last time, then put away his tools with a look of satisfaction. His job was over. Something made Rybalko look up, back along the length of the missile. The first German was returning, followed by two workers gingerly carrying a large steel cylinder. It looked heavy, with a complex series of fins and baffles running along each side. Both the German and the guards following the group wore face masks, but none were available for their prisoners. As they drew closer, Rybalko could make out 'GEFAHR' written in large black stencils along the side of the cylinder, and an image of a skull and crossbones next to the script. *Danger!* The warning signs told him all he needed to know. This was the weapon, possibly some sort of toxin. He needed to act now. There would not be any further opportunity.

A heavy tremor suddenly rocked the tunnel. The lights flickered for a moment and then went out. Immediately there were cries and shouts. Somebody ordered 'quick, the emergency generators!' There was confusion all around. Rybalko seized his opportunity. He slid his right hand back to where he knew the automatic gyroscope controls were, felt the series of circular cogs and levers, selected one, and moved it forward two notches. That should work, he hoped. The rocket would deviate off course just enough to miss its intended destination. Anything more than that and someone would notice. His hand slid back to its former position.

A low-pitched groan announced the start up of an emergency generator in the darkness beyond him, and a few moments later the lights suddenly came back on again. Everyone was standing in the same position as before, more or less. The first technician immediately started forward, reached the open section near the rocket's tip and quickly checked the area he had been working in. Rybalko began to sweat profusely, his heart hammering unhealthily under his ribs. *If he discovers anything different, then I'm a dead man.* He held his breath, awaiting the inevitable furious outburst, then the beating, or more probably a bullet on the spot. But nothing happened. The German stood up, grunted, then beckoned the two workers carrying the steel cylinder forwards. Under his strict supervision they carefully slid the steel cylinder into its housing. A final series of checks and adjustments, and then he pronounced himself satisfied. 'Everything OK with you, Hans?' He asked his colleague. The other technician nodded casually. He'd finished his work some time ago, and there was no point in performing yet another check. 'That's it. *Raus!*' He shooed all of them away, including Rybalko. The remaining work at the rear of the rocket took a few more minutes, followed by a final series of inspections and checks. A whistle blew, and all the workers were herded off to their next tasks. As Rybalko was marched away he allowed himself a small sigh of relief. He hoped that what little he had been able to achieve would be enough to make a difference somewhere.

Somewhere over the Nordhausen area 2230

Wing Commander Mike Richardson gazed out at the dark terrain that lay below him. He was flying at just over six thousand feet in a loose figure of eight pattern that covered the area north of Nordhausen. The twenty five square kilometer area he was responsible for was largely made up of densely wooded hills and valleys, and he needed to stay at this height to avoid getting too close to some of the higher peaks. There was very little to see in the darkness. The moon was hidden by a heavy veil of cloud that intermittently covered most of the area. Some of the more distinguished land features were just visible, but most of the rest of the area was pitch black. The occasional patch of burning woodland, no doubt sparked off by the earlier bombing runs, lit up the dark backdrop.

This particular Mosquito was a particularly specialized type of night reconnaissance fighter-bomber. Everything about it was matt black, purposely painted to blend into the night skies over enemy occupied territory. The engine cowlings on each wing were ducted into specially concealed apertures to make spotting their characteristic exhaust signatures much harder. Cockpit instruments were shielded to reduce glare and help pilot eyesight to adapt to the reduced light energy available during night missions. Everything about it spoke of its clandestine nature, sneaking inside the Reich's borders to drop an agent, paradrop in supplies, or pick up a secret radio transmission.

Tonight's mission was a tough one. It was just as well that his navigator, Flight Lieutenant Milo O'Brien, was one of the best he'd ever flown with. Richardson was very glad that O'Brien was there, helping to keep the aircraft orbiting over a defined area and on the watch for any missile launches. It was a tricky job, relying on a lot of cross-checking and dead reckoning to keep them on course and avoid straying beyond their allocated patrol zone. He knew that other Mosquitos were performing a similar job further out. They were flying a similar series of orbits to cover the region outside his central area, where the underground rocket factory was presumed to be.

They'd been up here for the last hour or so, helping to keep an eye on the area until Bomber Command reached the area. The Lancaster heavy bombers were due to arrive at midnight. B-17s and Liberators from the Eighth and Ninth USAAF had given the area a pasting during the day, but apparently with little effect for all their efforts. Later on, after the Yanks had gone home, RAF photo-reconnaissance had shown up, eager to assess the extent of the damage. But they were unable to reveal little more than yesterday's results. The cloud cover was still a nuisance, and the photos revealed very little useful information beyond what was already known. Maybe things would be better tomorrow. A high pressure front was said to be moving towards central Germany, according to the meteorological experts. He reminded himself that no man was a master of weather patterns. Weather forecasting was still too unpredictable a science, and not subject to the desires and wishes of men.

Time stretched past slowly. O'Brien stirred in the co-pilot's seat, scratched his side and shifted into a more comfortable position.

'Anything to see, Mike?'

'No. Not a damn thing'. Richardson's eyes flicked over his instrument panel for the umpteenth time. Everything was OK, all the dials looked to be satisfactory and working normally.

'What exactly are we looking for?'

'I'm not sure, Milo.' Richardson performed another instrument check, and then smoothly banked the aircraft into a sweeping turn. 'Something like a huge exhaust flash, a large flare of light as the rocket's engines ignite and shoot it up into the skies. I've never seen one before. Very few pilots have. The boffins say these V2s are so quick they're up and gone before you can react.'

O'Brien nodded, looked back at his knee pad and timer, and glanced out of the left canopy Perspex. 'Something like that, perhaps?'

Richardson followed his gaze.

'Bloody hell, yes! Mark that spot!' In an instant, he banked over the Mosquito into a steep dive, angling the nose of the aircraft towards the distant glow in the trees. Several jets of bright light splashed off the ground in the distance, surrounded by a mounting pall of smoke. Suddenly the lights began to lift, moving above the tree line. A dark shape could just be seen, rising swifter and swifter towards the heavens.

'It's launching!' O'Brien yelled. Richardson slammed the throttles as far forward as he could until they hit their stops. If he could accelerate fast enough, then they might be able to get into cannon range and have a chance of shooting the missile down. The Mosquito bucked and trembled as the aircraft raced forward on an interception course. Richardson adjusted the aircraft's flight controls and tried to adjust his path to where he estimated the rocket and Mosquito would reach their best closing position. But he had never seen a V2 launch before and the speed of the thing was beyond his reckoning - even when it was moving at its slowest speed, at launch time. It arced upwards, cleaving its way towards the base of the nearest cloud.

He slid his thumb over the firing button, but in his heart knew that they were too far away to be effective. A stream of tracer shot away from the nose if the Mosquito, but the missile had now disappeared. Richardson swore softly. If they'd had a few more seconds warning they might have interfered with the launch, perhaps winged the missile or even destroyed it. There was little point in trying to pursue it now – the rocket was too damned fast. It was time to break radio silence and report in.

'Milo, get on to squadron HQ and report what we've just seen. Give them the location, as near as you can estimate it.' There was nothing else they could do but hang around until their mission time was over. Had they just identified the position of the factory, or did the Germans have the capability, as RAF intelligence hinted, to launch their rockets with ground mobile units? He knew that tonight and for the foreseeable future they'd have to cover all eventualities.

❀

Nordhausen area 2300

The military policeman at the road block was deferential but adamant. 'Sorry sir, but there's no way through tonight. It's far too dangerous. Security's screwed down tight. This area's been hit hard all day by enemy bombers, and Luftwaffe Area Defense HQ has advised that more are on the way very shortly.'

'But I'm under orders to get through to the Kohnstein', Simon protested irritably. He had already established his credentials. 'By order of the Reichsführer SS himself!' He waved a piece of paper in the direction of the Feldwebel in charge.

'That may well be the case, sir.' The sergeant shrugged his shoulders. He was not particularly bothered by the SS officer in front of him. He had to deal with all types, SS as well as Wehrmacht, and they were all treated just the same, no matter who they were. Not unless Himmler turned up in person, and that would be highly unlikely. After all, he had his orders to follow, and they came first. 'However, I've got mine. And my orders state that all traffic is to be halted and moved off the roads until further notice. So please pull over into the shelter of those trees over there. You'll have to wait until I receive further instructions.' He pointed to a dark mass of woodland on the other side of the road.

Simon ground his teeth in frustration. Schellenberg had managed to get a message through to him earlier. Two rockets were being launched tonight, the first in Himmler's biological assault on the West. Was there any way he could get into the underground factory, plant the explosives and disrupt their launch? The message gave him precious little time to act, and God knows how he would bluff his way in with a rucksack containing pencils and chocolate - but he had to try. However, the enemy bombing had cancelled all that. He was only five or six kilometers away, but the factory might as well have been on the dark side of the moon. There were very few roads north of Nordhausen, and the others he'd already tried were either impassable by bomb damage or blocked by military police.

'OK. I get the message,' he muttered grumpily. 'Thanks anyway.' The Feldwebel nodded, keeping a watchful eye on Simon all the same. *Probably making sure I don't do something unexpected.* Simon was aware that there were at least three others positioned around the roadblock, all of them with Schmeissers held loosely but easily capable of being brought to bear in an instant. There was nothing he could do but accede to the 'request'. He turned the engine over, and slowly moved the Kubelwagen across the road to where another MP was indicating for him to park.

There were no other vehicles under the trees. He got out simply to stretch his legs. They still felt somewhat wobbly. The night air was cold and crisp. Most of the recent snow had melted, but a few patches remained in the deep shadows of the wood. Simon could make out the sounds of maybe two or three aircraft circling the area, but they were invisible in the night skies.

A few minutes later there was a muted rumble of an approaching convoy from further down the road, in the direction he had intended to take. From the sound of it several large vehicles were approaching, slit headlamps dimly lighting their way in the dark. They were obviously expected - the MPs quickly raised the barrier as the convoy drew closer. With a grinding of gears the vehicles continued on, barely slowing as they passed the roadblock. On the back of a large transporter lay a long shape, draped in camouflage netting and tarpaulins. It looked huge, nearly thirty meters long and bigger than those he'd seen inside the factory. Could that be the one Schellenberg hinted at, the one destined for America?

A few more minutes passed by. The roar of the vehicles drew further off. The Feldwebel in charge walked over to him.

'I'm afraid you'll have to take your chances with us tonight, sir.' Simon could just make out the smile in the gloom. 'Local air defense have just reported in. They've confirmed that a large force of enemy bombers is heading this way, and as a result all road traffic has been shut down until further notice. At least we've managed to get the two convoys through.'

'So that was the second?'

'Yes sir.' He hesitated for a moment. 'I shouldn't really talk about it, but seeing as you're from the factory I'm sure it will be OK. They sent the first out about half an hour ago.'

'I presume that the large load on board that transporter was another rocket?'

'Yes sir. They launched the first one just over the brow of the hill behind us – one hell of a sight. We might just get a view of the second.' The MP grinned. 'That'll certainly give our British and American friends something to think about.'

Simon nodded. He had little to say, and soon the Feldwebel drifted back into the shelter of a patch of birches where the rest of his detail stood huddled together. The next half hour passed slowly. The muted droning of aircraft flying above the clouds echoed through the woods, the only thing that disturbed the sound of the wind whistling through the trees. It could have been worse - at least it wasn't raining, not yet. But there might be a different, more lethal kind of rain to contend with later.

He was roused from his thoughts by the sudden roar of engines, away to his left. It was probably one or two kilometers away, but the dark made it impossible to estimate precisely. The noise rapidly grew louder, quickly followed by a burst of glaring light that lit up the surrounding area.

'That's it, number two!' The military policeman was by his side, pointing wildly towards where the cacophony was coming from. 'Any second now, and...'

He was interrupted by another blast. Suddenly something was moving in the trees, a large object with a fierce red-white jet of flame shooting out from its base. As it cleared the tree tops Simon caught sight of the rocket as it struggled upwards against the force of gravity towards the dark skies. It began to rise, slowly at first, then progressively quicker and quicker as it accelerated away from the ground and reached for the heavens above. The noise was immense, a thunderous din that drowned out all other sounds. A few seconds later and it was gone, vanishing quickly into the clouds. Nothing was left behind, only a diminishing rumble as the missile sped further away towards its final destination.

But the rumble did not entirely go away. Soon Simon was able to make out noise of a different type, the mounting roar of aircraft engines moving in from the northwest, from the direction of Belgium or maybe even England. A heavy throbbing began to fill the air, dense and malevolent. It grew louder and louder. Soon they could hear the high pitched whistle of falling bombs.

'Best get under cover, sir. We've made a little shelter over here.' The MP pointed to a dark shadow under the trees. 'Won't save us from a direct hit, but I think we'll stand a good chance of coming out unscathed. Follow me.'

Little Aston, Staffordshire, England 2320

John Roberts peered out from the shelter of his porch and gazed up at the night sky. It was a lovely night, cold but clear and the stars twinkled far away in the heavens. The black-out was still in force, even at this late stage of the war - a good thing, as far as he was concerned. It meant that his eyes would quickly adjust to the dark, and he could experience the natural unspoiled quietness of the countryside at night. He loved to slip out late in the evening and stretch his legs whenever he could, whenever his gout was not playing him up. A short, brisk walk before bedtime always helped to settle him down for the night, that and a small shot of rum – strictly for medicinal purposes only, of course.

There was nobody else at home. His wife, Edith, had sadly passed away the previous year from a bout of pneumonia. She'd had a good innings – after all, seventy eight was a good age and the end was mercifully quick. There was little Dr Wall could do. Somehow the good doctor had managed to get hold of some drugs to help her, some of these new fangled antibiotics that were very hard to come by, but by the time they arrived it was all too late. His son, a senior lieutenant commander in the Royal Navy, was able to make the funeral, but he was back in London now, hard at work in the Admiralty. His only real friend was Redford, a black Labrador who accompanied him wherever he went, even slept on the end of his bed. All the rest of his elderly mates were either dead or living in old people's homes, something that saddened him greatly. He had vowed to himself that he would never end up in one of those awful places and as far as he was able, he would look after himself - until Old Nick himself finally paid him a visit.

He stepped slowly out into the front garden, circled the small cottage and headed for the gate that led from his garden into the fields beyond. A low whistle and Redford suddenly appeared from behind the bushes that flanked the pond close by the back fence. The latch lifted easily and the gate swung noiselessly outwards, and they were off, following a well-trodden path across the ploughed and furrowed landscape. A hedge lay over to his right, well lit up by the light of the full moon. It marked the boundary of Forge Lane. Behind him the village, strung out along the main road that ran from Sutton Coldfield to Walsall, was quiet. There was virtually no traffic at this time of the night, another good thing. He was not a fan of the internal combustion engine, even though it made a lot of sense in being able to get around and travel. He much preferred the old times when he was a lad, back in the days of Queen Victoria, and how the countryside was then, before the rapid spread of urbanization and the noise and pollution that went with it.

A copse of dark trees loomed up ahead. Suddenly Redford began to bark for no obvious reason. Maybe it was a badger or a fox? 'Quiet, boy!' He grumbled. There was no point in upsetting the neighbours. Bill Jarvis' farm was only a short distance away, and the last thing he wanted was to get *his* dogs barking and growling this late at night. Their racket would be enough to wake the dead. 'Shhh!'

Redford whined and crouched down with his tail between his legs, looking up at the sky. Richards followed his gaze. Something was arcing down towards the earth, rapidly closing the distance with an ear-splitting shriek. A blinding flash of light, quickly followed by the blast of a large explosion suddenly erupted from just over the crest of the low hill in front of him. Even from where he was, maybe a third of a mile away, the impact and compression wave was enough to rock him backwards.

'Good God,' he muttered to himself. What the hell was that? A bomb, or maybe one of those new rockets the Germans were desperately flinging around? He read the reports in the *Telegraph* about how the Nazis were using them to bombard London and Antwerp, but here? What could be of importance in this part of the world? Did they have rockets that could travel as far as this part of England?

He quickly made his mind up and turned back towards his house. The Air Raid people would need to know about this as soon as possible. So would the Fire Brigade and Police. The bomb was right where Jarvis had his farm and where some his workers had cottages. Although the farmer was sometimes a miserable old bastard, the least he could do was help. As he hurried back over the field he did not notice a cloud of vapour rise and slowly appear over the brow of the hill.

❀

The Skies over Nordhausen 2345

This time the RAF had better luck. A Mosquito on patrol duty caught a glimpse of the rocket launch through a gap in the clouds and the pilot brought the aircraft over onto a direct intercept course. The crew was able to track the slower, heavier missile as it reached the cloud layer, and squeezed off a burst of cannon fire just before the rocket accelerated away and out of range. A chance in a million, or maybe even worse odds than that, but it was the closest anybody got that night to hitting let alone downing a rocket. Two shells clipped a rudder on one of the tail fins. There was no visual telltale of what had happened, no explosion or flying debris, and as the rocket shot away the pilot cursed his luck, unaware of what he had achieved. The damage was relatively minor, not enough to spin the rocket out of control or deviate it sufficiently to miss a target at short ranges, but it would still prove critical to the success of the mission. The shells caused just enough deformation over the steering surfaces to disrupt airflow and create a small amount of additional drag. Unknown to the pilot, the missile's target was Manhattan in downtown New York, a distance of nearly four thousand miles. And at that range the damage could make all the difference in the world.

Off Long Island, New York 1815 Eastern Standard Time

Captain Jack Bridges was beginning to feel tired. It had been a long day, endlessly flying anti-submarine patrol circuits. The loop he was allocated to patrol stretched from the Ambrose Channel that marked the entrance into the Hudson River, up along the length of Long Island, past Block Island, Martha's Vineyard, Nantucket Island and out into Massachusetts Bay. Then he would turn back again, retracing his path as far as South Amboy before repeating the pattern. There was little to see to keep him focused on the job, just the familiar shoreline and the usual navigation points. The crew was equally tired - tired and bored. The last time a U-Boat had ventured anywhere near his patrol route had been months ago, as far as he knew. No, there were simply too many watchful eyes out there, too many aerial patrols and anti-submarine nets to risk, and the Navy had the area sewn up tight. The Brooklyn docks might be a highly tempting target, with all the convoys and troop ships that regularly left the harbour for England, but the dangers for U-Boat commanders were too great. It was better to chance your arm further out in the expanses of the North Atlantic, he reckoned, than risk a decision closer in.

The four-engined PB4Y-1 Liberator's engines droned on, throttled right back for maximum endurance, never missing a beat. They were flying almost due west, heading back towards Newark and home. Visibility was excellent, just as it had been all day, not a cloud in the sky. But now the sun was sinking quickly into the west, and it was high time to go home. Over across the starboard wing he could just make out the southern coastline of Long Island. Jones Beach State Park receded to his right as the Liberator flew on, with Long Beach swiftly coming into view. A few lights were on, but little else showed at this point of the island's expanse. The sea was calm, with only a few lines of breakers close to the shore. In a few minutes he would begin his final navigation checks, but that was just for form's sake, rather than any specific flying need. He knew the area like the back of his hand, and the approach would be as routine as ever. His co-pilot, Bill Kowalski, was browsing through a flight manual for entertainment. Bridges gave him a quick nudge. 'Time to earn your greenbacks, Bill. Take over the controls. I'm going to do a crew check and grab a coffee. Want one?' 'No thank you sir,' Kowalski smiled and put the manual down. 'If I have any more to drink I'll burst. It'll be good to get home soon.' Kowalski scanned the instruments, then leaned forward to hold his joystick. 'Okay, sir, the controls are mine.' 'Acknowledged. Hold the fort. I'll be back in a few minutes.'

Bridges slipped his throat mike off, slid out of his seat and clambered back to where his navigator was hidden away, behind the bulkhead that separated the cockpit from the rest of the aircraft. He slid around where Hanks, the top gunner, was manning the dorsal machine gun.

'Everybody OK?' He shouted.

A chorus of 'yessirs' greeted him. He braced himself and sat down by the navigator, a recently promoted Lieutenant by the name of Harry Bell. He was just out of flying school.

'How are you doing, Harry?' Bridges smiled at him. Bell was very young.

'Fine, sir. I-'

Suddenly the Liberator pitched violently up and down and then slammed to the left, almost as if a giant hand had picked the aircraft up and tossed it aside. The impact threw Bridges across into the navigator, squeezing them together into the confined space. Bridges' head collided with the bulkhead, temporarily disabling him with a sharp blow to his skull. He saw stars for a moment, and the pain was like a blinding sheet of white light that seared across his vision. And then it was gone as quickly as it had arrived, leaving in its wake a pounding throb.

The Liberator had veered violently to the left and was now in a dive. Dimly he was aware that the engines were roaring at full speed. Kowalski must have instinctively reacted, driving the throttles forward and losing height to try to regain control.

He needed to get back to the cockpit now, find out what had happened and report in.

With Bell's hel, he managed to disentangle himself, turn around and make his way back towards the front of the aircraft. Something warm was trickling down the side of his face but he ignored it, struggling forward to grab a handhold and lever himself into his flying seat. Kowalski had both hands on the control stick, his feet kicking hard to force the rudder over and straighten the Liberator. A quick glance at the altimeter told him they were passing three thousand feet rapidly, and the ocean began to fill the view forward. The air-frame creaked and groaned as the plane struggled to straighten. He leaned forward, grabbed his control stick and pulled back with all the strength he could muster, grunting with the effort. Slowly the plane began to pitch up and the altimeter needle slowed its crazy descent. They finally leveled out at three hundred feet. Kowalski slumped forward in relief, sweat pouring off his face.

'Christ, that was close!' He muttered.

Bridges had the controls. A rapid check of the instruments revealed nothing out of order. He glanced at his co-pilot. 'What the hell was that? Bill, did you see anything?'

Kowalski looked up, his face white. 'I'm not sure. I think something flashed across the canopy ...It must have created the shock wave that threw us right out of our normal flight path.' He drew a deep breath and wiped the sweat off his forehead. 'Whatever it was, it was sure moving at one hell of a speed...'

Bridges felt the back of his head. His fingers came away red, sticky with a congealing ooze. He must have cut his scalp when the aircraft span out of control. 'Bill, you did well to keep us from spinning out of control.' He slipped his throat mike back on to speak to the rest of the crew. 'Report in. Anybody seen what just gave us a couple of heart-attacks?'

'Sir!' It was Becker, the rear gunner. 'Behind us...there's a big impact in the sea, about a thousand yards off the shoreline. I can see some wreckage there as well, sir.'

'OK. Bill, get on to the airfield. Have the Navy to check out the area.' He checked his instruments, especially the fuel gauges. 'We'll do a single pass over the crash site before heading back to base.' That was more than enough excitement for one day. Bridges let out a long, heartfelt sigh of relief. He no longer felt in need of another cup of coffee to keep him awake.

❀

Downing Street, London 1930 1/4/45

The car turned off Horse Guards Road and pulled up to the barrier, the early evening sunlight glinting off the bonnet. Menzies leaned forward and spoke to the driver. 'Thanks Ted. Wait for me here, please.' He opened the passenger door and slid out of the Alvis. It was only a short walk from MI6's headquarters along Birdcage Walk, but it would be more appropriate to arrive composed and calm, as befitting the occasion. After all, it wasn't every day of the week that the Prime Minister himself wanted to see you and he wanted to look his best. The chauffeur was all part of the occasion.

Two policemen were manning the road block in front of him that stopped further access to the government buildings that lay beyond. Menzies flashed his pass at them. The one in plain clothes carefully studied his paperwork, issued him with a temporary pass and nodded curtly. 'This way sir'. Menzies followed him up the passage that led between the Foreign Office and Treasury buildings, and then left through an alley, shielded by high grey walls and on into a small courtyard. The policeman knocked at a door set into the wall. It opened silently to reveal a small, immaculately maintained garden backing up to the rear of an imposing Georgian house. 'Walk up the path to the back door, sir.' He indicated politely. 'They're expecting you.'

Menzies nodded as the policeman turned away and walked back to his post. The rear door closed again, revealing a uniformed officer wearing a shoulder holster. There was another at the back door, who checked his papers again, pressed a buzzer and let him into the large kitchen. The sound of hurried footsteps could be heard rapidly approaching. The door flew open, and a short, distinguished looking man in a grey pinstripe suit hurried up to him and grasped him by the hand.

'Stuart, thank God you're here!' It was Sir John Colville, the PM's private secretary and personal assistant.

'I came as quick as I could, Sir John', Menzies smiled, returning Colville's handshake. 'How is the old boy?'

'Don't ask.' Colville groaned, putting his hand on his forehead and shaking his head in dismay. 'It's been one of those days I'd rather forget. Winston's had a tough day in the House of Commons, thanks to Attlee and all those Labour lefties in the Cabinet. They've been demanding all sorts of social reform once the war's over, and threatening to withdraw support if something's not done *now* to ease the plight of the lower classes.' He sighed. 'They don't seem to realise that the war's still not finished. One thing at a time.' He groaned again. 'As for the Japs, well…I don't know. They're still fighting tooth and nail, and Winston is worried about Burma and what's going on in China. He sees Reds everywhere. You know what he's like.'

Menzies nodded. Not that he disapproved of the Prime Minister's intolerance of Communists, but he knew that Winston was tired, very tired. So were they all. The last six years had been a grueling slog, from the desperate days of the fall of France and the Battle of Britain until now. And even though they were winning, there were still so many unknowns to face up to and decide the best course of action. The Nazis were down and nearly out, but they could still cause tremendous damage even in their present state. That was why he was here.

'The final straw was your report late this afternoon,' Colville continued, looking more anxious than ever. 'At first I thought it was April Fool's Day, somebody with a poor sense of humour having us on. But I know you don't tolerate fools gladly, and the summaries from Lockhart at the JIC have confirmed our worst fears. I don't suppose there's anything you can tell me before you go in?' Colville looked anxious, surprisingly so for so senior a figure in the PM's office.

'Sorry, Sir John, you know the drill. Mum's the word for now, but I'm sure Winston will enlighten you soon enough.'

'Yes, yes, I understand, Stuart.' Colville wrung his hands, the picture of worry. 'You see, it's just that I have a sister who lives just outside Lichfield. Too close for comfort, I think.'

Menzies could say little.

'Well…' Colville swallowed and cleared his throat, keen to change the subject and avoid further embarrassment. 'I see you've come prepared.' He glanced at the leather slip case tucked under Menzies' left arm. 'The PM wants to hear about the latest developments immediately. He's spoken to Eisenhower in Paris not so long ago, and the air's been thick with telegrams from Washington. Looks like there's been some untoward activity over there as well.'

'Indeed?' Menzies raised an eyebrow. Despite the secret intelligence emanating from Germany, he still found it hard to believe that the Germans could reach across the Atlantic and strike at America. It was just so far away. *Did the Nazis have such a superior technological lead that they could really do this? And if so, what else could they do?*

They walked back into the main part of the house. Colville led the way upstairs, past the portraits of previous holders of the keys to 10 Downing Street and into a small anteroom on the first floor. "I should tell you that the CIGS is in with him,' Colville said quietly before knocking on the ornate wooden door that led into the Prime Minister's private conference room and study.

There was a muffled grunt followed by a bellowed 'enter'. Menzies slipped through into the room. The Prime Minister was dressed in his usual black waistcoat and suit, and sat slumped in a large leather recliner chair that faced away from the windows. In front of him was a large desk stacked high with files and paperwork. He looked exhausted and tense. The dark rings that circled around his eyes were silent testimony to the late nights, poor sleep and stress of his job. Across from him sat Field Marshall Sir Alan Brooke, Chief of the Imperial General Staff. The CIGS favoured him with a small smile of welcome, but he looked almost as tired as his political leader. Menzies stood to attention and saluted.

'At ease, Colonel,' the PM gruffly ordered and gestured to a chair opposite him. Menzies sat down and waited for the Prime Minister to speak.

'Ahem.' Churchill cleared his throat and looked wearily at the head of MI6. 'Thank you for coming, Colonel. I received your report two hours ago. Field Marshall Brooke has just brought me up to date with developments in Germany. I want to hear your opinion, so please give me a summary of the events of the last few days.'

Menzies began by summarizing the intelligence he had received from Germany about the bio-weapon offensive, the rocket factory, and the latest developments. 'These weapons were launched on the night of the 29th. Two rockets, as far as we know. One targeted for Birmingham, the other possibly New York, but as yet I have not received any information regarding the latter. One of our Mosquitos witnessed the first launch, another possibly winged the rocket at the second but there was no visual evidence of damage. That was over the Harz area. We know the Germans are still firing other V2s from occupied Holland towards Antwerp and London, but to reach Birmingham and elsewhere from the Nordhausen area suggests these have much greater range than the normal V2 rockets.'

'What about Birmingham?' The PM leaned forward in his chair.

'There's been some more news since my report was sent, Prime Minister,' Menzies said. 'The preliminary bacteriological analyses have yet to bear fruit, but I spoke to a Professor Davies from the Pathology Department at Birmingham University Medical School. He's had some experience in the field of unusual foreign diseases, and he's quite convinced that we're dealing with something nasty, possibly Bubonic Plague, and maybe other diseases as well. The area's been cordoned off and quarantined. Luckily for us, the missile must have somehow strayed off course and landed in a relatively unpopulated area. It would have been much worse if it had landed in the centre of the city.'

Churchill sank back into his chair, looking a little less anxious. 'Yes, but what about casualties?'

'Only six so far, sir, and three of them we reckon were from the impact. As for how many others, it's hard to say. The warning from Germany helped us to concentrate local resources, and the emergency services have done a fine job. I think we can contain any spread into the surrounding areas, from what the medical men tell me.'

The Prime Minister breathed a sigh of relief, and then got up and strode over to the large-scale map that was pinned on the far wall of the study. 'Thank God for small mercies. It would be a disaster if this spread.' He studied the map carefully. 'There must be at least five hundred thousand people living in Birmingham and the surrounding areas.' Churchill thought for a few moments, and then turned back to face Menzies, a determined look on his face. 'We've got to keep a lid on what's happened. I've already spoken to the Press and slapped a D Notice on this. The last thing we need is a wild panic about all sorts of nasty infectious diseases flying around the country. We're just about to achieve a hard won and costly victory, and we certainly do not need something like this....What about security at your end?'

'All taken care of sir. David Petrie from MI5 has cooked up a cover story, and the Staffordshire police are none the wiser. The local press have been warned off, and Davies and his medical teams are sworn to secrecy – I invoked the Official Secrets Act when I was up there. They've all signed. I think *that* end of the operation is reasonably secure.'

'Good, good...' Churchill sat down again. 'So what's your opinion about Himmler's threat?'

'The same as before Prime Minister. At first I didn't believe any of this, but my contact in Germany has made me aware of certain truths that were undeniable. He supplied this information. We know that the Nazis are desperate, and it would seem that they would try anything to derail the course of the war. Naturally all of this is still hard to believe, especially the possibly of Nazi rockets reaching America, but we now know they can reach Birmingham. As for the other, well who knows where that's ended up...'

'I have news for you, Colonel.' Brooke interjected, speaking for the first time. He casually brushed an invisible speck off his immaculate uniform. 'It would seem that the Americans have had a lucky escape. A rocket crashed into the sea just off New

York, an hour or two after the second launch in Germany. It must have been one of their longer-range efforts, the one your source hinted at. The good news is that, as it landed in the sea, there appears to have been no human casualties.'

'What?' Menzies was temporarily amazed. 'You mean they actually managed to fly one across the Atlantic? Good God!'

'Yes. Rather worrying, isn't it?' He smiled wryly. Brooke was not known for an overt sense of humour, but he was the master of the dry, understated comment. 'The Prime Minister received notification from them today. One gets the impression that our American cousins too scarcely believed just how far these rockets can travel, but now they're taking the threat very seriously indeed. Anyway, the upshot is that they're driving hard for the Nordhausen area. The First US army is leading the charge.'

'And what about the bombing? Sir, have we had any positive results?'

'Nothing as yet. Air Chief Marshall Harris was here earlier, but neither the RAF nor the American Air Force has achieved any measurable results, as far as we can tell.'

'So you see our concern, Colonel Menzies.' Churchill's eyes bored into him, pressing him intensely. 'It would seem that Himmler is intent on carrying out these murderous tactics, as we have just seen.' He almost spat the words out. 'Do you have any further information? Is there anything else you can do? Can your source in Germany help stop these rockets, before this deadline your report mentions?'

Menzies thought hard. Even now he was reluctant to discuss certain events and reveal identities, for fear of an inadvertent leak. It went against all his training to disclose operational details – the old 'need to know' basis of intelligence sharing, even in the presence of such senior and powerful men.

'Yes. I believe he can,' he said slowly. 'We have an agent who has access to the factory, and he has a supply of explosives. He now has a definite deadline in which to act before Himmler's threat to launch a general offensive. The message has gone out today. But he's only one man. If I may say so, sir, it would be wise to have other options - just in case he fails.'

'Hmmm. Naturally, I agree, but finding those options is not that easy.' The Prime Minister paused. 'I hope you're not suggesting we actually *negotiate* with Himmler?' The tone in Churchill's voice was that of disbelief, with more than a suggestion of menace behind it.

'Good Lord, no, Prime Minister.' Menzies was suitably aghast.

Churchill fixed him with a steely gaze, puffed up his cheeks and sat up in his chair. 'Just so that there's no confusion on this issue, I wish to make it quite clear that there will be no real negotiation with Himmler or any other Nazi thugs,' he said in a hard, no-nonsense voice, slamming the table to emphasise his words. 'That is something I am absolutely determined to uphold. As a nation we have suffered far too much to be held at gunpoint by a murderous criminal. If necessary we may have to suffer a little more to see that Hitler and his cronies, and all that they stand for, are destroyed once and for all. Do we all speak as one on this?'

Both Menzies and Brooke nodded their heads in agreement.

'But it might be worth trying to play him for time, if it's at all possible', Menzies persisted.

The Prime Minister appeared to be marginally more mollified, but still gave Menzies a distinctly baleful look.

'I'll bear that in mind. If necessary I can make contact via by the Foreign Office - get a message through using the Swedish Ambassador in Berlin.' He paused for a moment, still clearly uncomfortable with such a ploy. 'Field Marshall Brooke was briefing me just before you arrived. The Americans are putting together a scratch airborne force, but it's taking time and this option might not be the answer we're looking for. What about their ground forces?' Churchill turned towards Brooke.

'The good news is that the Americans have linked up with our forces to encircle the Ruhr Industrial Area. Intelligence estimates that we've trapped an army group there, maybe a quarter of a million or more. That should clear the way for the drive to Berlin.' Brooke shrugged. 'As for Hodges' Fist Army, they're pushing as hard as they can, but SHAEF estimates it will take them another week to drive past Kassel and reach the Nordhausen area.'

'That's just about the same time as Himmler's ultimatum.' There was a lull in the discussion as the news sank in. Nobody spoke for a few minutes. In the hall the grandfather clock chimed the half past the hour mark. It was the Prime Minister who finally broke the silence.

'Well, Colonel, the next step is up to you... and the Americans. Keep me informed – in person. You have access to me twenty-four hours a day. Speak to my secretary – he'll sort out the arrangements with my staff.' Churchill waved a hand.

Brooke nodded briefly in his direction. Menzies realised he was being dismissed. He got up, saluted smartly and left the room. As he left, the weight of expectation settled heavily on his shoulders, and he grimaced inwardly. *No pressure then. Oh no - none at all.*

SS Field HQ, Mittenwalde 1345 7 /4/45

Himmler's Mercedes staff car rolled up to a halt outside the main operations tent. His ADC leaped out and hurried to open the rear passenger door while the Reichsführer emerged from the backseat.

'Get me Brigadeführer Schellenberg. I need to see him immediately.'

'*Zu befehl*! At once, Reichsführer.' The officer snapped to attention, saluted, and hurried off. Himmler walked over to his tent, threw his briefcase on the table, slipped off his leather coat and sat down. A few moments later, Schellenberg arrived. He stood outside the tent flaps and coughed discretely.

'Reichsführer, you wished to see me.'

'Ah...yes, Walther, come in. Close the tent flap and sit down.' Himmler pointed to a chair.

'Thank you sir.' Schellenberg took a seat. 'How was your trip?'

Himmler had just returned from another visit to the Führer's underground HQ in the centre of Berlin. The Reichsführer made a face, a combination of weariness, disgust and exasperation.

'The usual pig's ear of a mess, with the usual charlatans, flunkeys and yes-men all vying for the Führer's attention.' Himmler slumped in his chair. 'Nothing's changed. Thanks to that stupid idiot Goebbels, the Führer still thinks we're all going to be saved by some sort of divine miracle!' He laughed bitterly, snapping his fingers. 'Fat chance!'

Schellenberg shrugged sympathetically. 'Sir, did you manage to achieve anything at all?'

'I gave him your latest report, not that it did much good.' Himmler grunted, then sat up in his chair. 'I crosschecked the contents with that spineless cretin Keitel before delivering it to him. The two reports are broadly in agreement. The Americans and British have cut off Model's Army Group in the Ruhr – another Stalingrad, I'm afraid. The British are now well on the way to Hamburg and cutting off our remaining troops in Denmark – but that won't be much of a loss. There's only a couple of reserve divisions there, anyway. The Americans are being temporarily held up along the River Main, but it won't be long before they get to the Kassel area and beyond.' He looked meaningfully at Schellenberg. 'Nordhausen is not that much further, so we've only a few days left.'

'And in the East?' It was not really a question. Schellenberg already knew the answer.

'Pfft!' Himmler's usually emotionless face was for once animated. 'The Führer still insists the Russians are near the end of their strength! Ha! The man is delusional. They've managed to force us back all the way from Stalingrad and the gates of Moscow all the way to the Oder. What's to stop them now?' Himmler was almost shouting. 'He insists on sending our best troops to Austria to save Vienna from the Russians, while all the time the chief danger is here, in front of Berlin. And even then, there's precious little in the Harz and along the Elbe to stop the Western Allies overrunning us from that direction. Madness! Utter madness!'

Himmler slammed his fist on the table, two bright red spots on his cheeks high-lighting the anger he felt. Schellenberg could see that his boss was clearly very angry, a rare show of emotion on normally so expressionless a visage. He waited a few moments to let his superior cool down.

'Sir, when did Keitel estimate that the Russians would attack?'

Himmler's mind was elsewhere. For a moment he gaped uncomprehendingly, and then returned to the present. 'Eh? Oh, probably no more than ten days or so. Aerial intelligence suggests that the Red Army is making its final preparations... repairing rail lines, stocking up ammunition dumps, the usual deception operations. He estimates the attack date as anything from the 15th to 18th. Do you have anything new from Zossen?'

'No, Reichsführer. I spoke to Oberst General Reinhard Gehlen this morning. He's my counterpart over there. We both agree that Stalin will set his forces off around these dates. I would not be surprised if he has already reached an agreement with Churchill and Roosevelt – the Russians will take Berlin, and the Western Allies will meet up with them halfway across the Reich. I estimate somewhere along the Elbe.'

'In that case there's not much time to lose, then.' Himmler stood up and paced around the inside of the tent, arms clasped behind his back, deep in thought. After a few moments he stopped pacing and walked over to his desk, opened his briefcase, pulled out some papers and handed them to Schellenberg.

'Today's trip was not entirely in vain,' he grunted. 'The Führer has finally approved my request to deal once and for all with certain undesirable elements within the Reich.' A small smile of triumph lit up his pasty features. 'See for yourself.'

Schellenberg leafed through the paperwork, with a growing sense of dismay. The names were all familiar to him – Oberst-General Hans Oster, Judge Advocate General Carl Sack, the Reverend Dietrich Bonhoeffer, Dr Theodor Strünck, Hauptmann Ludwig Gehre – all suspected if not proven of treason against the Reich. Most of them were known to have been involved to some degree in the Bomb Plot of the previous July, or linked with other anti-Nazi activity. But it was the last two names that that made him feel sick to the core – Oberst Mannfred Simon and Admiral Wilhelm Canaris.

'At last,' Himmler exulted, looking extremely satisfied with himself. 'I'm finally going to settle some old scores, especially with that slippery old bastard, Canaris. He's going to get the fate he deserves, once and for all.' In his gloating triumph, Himmler failed to notice the look of regret on Schellenberg's face. With barely a glance at his subordinate he resumed his pacing up and down, all the while his mind feverish with plans and deadlines.

'Walther, here's what we are going to do,' he continued, oblivious to his subordinate's anguish. ''I want you to arrange for two legally qualified officers from Amt II to go down to Flossenberg in the next day or two, along with these death warrants. They will arrange the legalities, and make sure that all paperwork is in order. I will alert the camp commandant myself. I wish him to be very clear as to how these executions will be carried out.' Schellenberg shifted in his chair, trying to hide the shudder of revulsion he felt. He had some idea of what Himmler had in mind. He'd seen the newsreel of the executions after the Bomb Plot. It had not made pleasant viewing.

'As for Nordhausen, I want you to go down there and personally make sure that all is ready. In the meantime I will continue to pursue a diplomatic solution here in Berlin, via the Swedish embassy. But if it all falls through then the rockets will fly in the early hours of April 12th. After that there may still be room for a settlement before the Reich is conquered. You will then fly to Stockholm and continue the diplomatic pressure from there, especially with the Russians. Make sure that Hartmann has planned for the next batch of rockets to go eastwards. That should focus Stalin's mind wonderfully. There should be just enough time to stop him launching the final Russian offensive.'

What? Enough time? He's completely flipped. The timescale is far too tight. I'm going to have to move really quick on this... And I've got to do something about Canaris and Simon...

'Walther?' Himmler had stopped pacing, and was looking closely at Schellenberg. 'Did you get all that?' The Reichsführer had a suspicious look on his face.

'...Yes sir.' Schellenberg forced his mind back to the present. 'My apologies, Reichsführer. I was just thinking about how I'm going to plan the logistical side of this. Leave it to me.'

'Good.' Himmler appeared momentarily mollified. 'Make sure that you get things organised immediately. I want twice-daily situation reports, at the very least. Let me know the names of the two officers you will be sending to Flossenberg. They must have impeccable credentials and be completely trustworthy. There will be no mistakes or failures this time. This is our last chance to save the Reich. See to it.'

❈

Flossenberg Concentration Camp 1630 7/4/45

He lay against the damp wall, shivering, barely conscious. His body was a mass of burns, cuts and bruises, but they were nothing compared to his face. He could not focus properly on his surroundings, and his head felt as if it was stuffed with red-hot needles. His nose bled profusely, probably from the last barrage of blows those thugs had inflicted on him. Gingerly he traced the outline with his least painful finger. Halfway down from his forehead the profile was bent to the left, markedly deviated from the normal direction. Some of his remaining teeth felt loose, but his tongue was swollen and felt different, and he was not entirely sure that what it told him was indeed reality. None of that was of any great consequence, he reckoned. The dental plate he'd worn for years had disappeared some time ago, and he couldn't remember when they'd last fed him. Was it yesterday or the day before? His mind feverishly tried to count off the last few days, but there was nothing to break up the endless hours of solitary confinement, nothing apart from his recent beating. He desperately wanted to close his eyes, but something warned him that if he surrendered to blessed unconsciousness, he might not wake up again...

So the buggers have broken my nose this time. They finally seem to have lost their patience, or is it something else...? Maybe they've decided to get me after all this time. Has Himmler finally received permission to do what he's always wanted to do? He tried to laugh but it was too painful.

This time Canaris had sensed a difference. Nobody held back. They were no longer fooled by him playacting the old imbecile. The sadists were out to inflict as much pain as they could without killing him on the spot. He had to admire their devilish ingenuity, even if their loyalties were somewhat misplaced. They knew exactly where to hit to cause the maximum pain without pushing him too far. But there was one thing he was reasonably sure of – the end must be near. His starved body could not take much more of this. There was only one thing left to do, one final duty.

He began to tap as best he could on the damp wall surface. Each knock brought a gasp of pain, but at least it kept him awake. His knuckles were quite badly bruised, but he ignored the agony. It was important that he send his last message out. He needed to know that somehow, someday his wife would learn of his fate, and what was last in his mind. Hopefully they would spare Nils Lunding, the Danish Colonel who was incarcerated on this side of his cell. He doubted he had the strength to crawl over to the other side. And if his head was on the chopping block, then so was Hans Oster's. The Nazis would never let either of them go.

He ceased tapping. He could just make out Lunding transmitting a reply. 'How are you?' Lunding tapped on the wall. 'Not good' went Canaris' reply. 'Badly mishandled. Nose broken at last interrogation. My time is up. Was not a traitor. Did my duty as a German. If you survive, please tell my wife…'

Flossenberg area 0730 8/4/45

The early morning view was dominated by masses of heavy, dark fir woods that stretched as far as the eye could see. They wrapped the Erzgebirge, the range of hills that formed this part of the old border between the Reich and what used to be Czechoslovakia, in a thick dark green blanket that clung to the folds in the land in an all-embracing grasp. The mists that had descended during the night and slowed their journey from Nordhausen to not much more than a crawl were gradually beginning to lift. Up above he caught the occasional glimpse of a patch of blue. It promised to be a fine day, probably by late mid-morning, but there were far more important things on his mind.

The Kubelwagen was parked behind a small, dense grove of trees, just off the winding forest road that led up to the camp area itself. Hofheinz was struggling to jack up the front nearside. A puncture had gradually deflated the tyre, probably a few kilometers ago lower down the road up towards Flossenberg village and the infinitely more notorious concentration camp of the same name. It must have been a piece of sharp stone, or maybe something else, maybe one of the many potholes on the road that they had struggled to avoid in the poor light. The delay, as much as he found it irritating, was unavoidable. Their plan was based on speed and precision. If they had any hope of carrying it out successfully, then everything must work like clockwork, with no room for error, least of all silly problems with transport.

Simon looked at his watch – it was just after 0730. Five minutes to loosen the wheel nuts, then take the spare from the rear and replace the damaged wheel and tyre. His map told him that the gates of the camp were only a minute or two away by car, hidden from his view by the dark outline of a hill. They still had plenty of time. The two SS officers from Amt II were not due to arrive until 1000, at least according to the schedule that Schellenberg had told him last night.

'How's it going, Charlie?'

'Bit of a bastard...' Hofheinz grunted in reply, breathing heavily. There was a brief screech of metal on metal. 'There... you sodding little bugger', he panted, holding up a rusty wheel bolt so that Simon could see the cause of the delay. 'This was the one that was causing all the problem. Some sloppy arse of a mechanic hasn't been doing his maintenance checks properly, but that's what we have to work with these days.' He grinned, despite his tiredness. 'Don't worry. The rest should be a piece of cake. Only two more to go...'

'Need a hand?'

'No, Max. You keep an eye out on the road, just in case some awkward sod decides to drive up and investigate. I can manage the rest...' Hofheinz bent down to apply his not inconsiderable brawn to the next reluctant bolt.

Simon moved over to the belt of trees, looking up and down the rutted, muddy forest track that ran away into the near distance. There was nothing to see or hear, not even birdsong. The silence was all-enclosing. Hofheinz's grunts and muttered curses were clearly heard from where he remained hidden in the trees. He'd never been to this part of the Reich before, but in his experience the woods should be teeming with wildlife, and especially birds. Was it the same sort of silence he witnessed when that train was accidentally diverted into Auschwitz? He shuddered. His father and Canaris were close, and he hoped to God they were still alive. No doubt the rockets back at the underground factory were important, but his first mission, as far as he saw it, was to save his father and the old admiral. Once that was achieved, then he could concentrate on derailing Himmler's madness and saving Germany from ruinous destruction...

He cast his mind back to the events of yesterday and the increasing anxiety of the last few days. Communications from the Panzer school to Berlin had become increasingly difficult if not damn near impossible, with only intermittent contact available at odd, unpredictable times - and then for only a few minutes at best. It was hardly surprising. Large sections of the country were now in enemy hands, and the rest was being bombed mercilessly, even now. The telephone systems were only functioning at a fraction of their capacity and the enemy dominated radio transmissions with its own, flooding large sections of the airwaves with coded signals and deliberate jamming. It was almost impossible to get through to anybody, let alone wherever RSHA was now. Despite this, Simon had expected Schellenberg to be in contact earlier in the week, but as each day passed there was nothing. What was he to do? Time was running out, and nobody was entirely certain how close the Allies were. He'd already formed a tentative plan in his mind, but that very much depended on any last minute information the Brigadeführer might be able to give him.

Then yesterday evening everything changed. The SS General arrived unannounced at the Panzer school in the early evening, as darkness closed in. Simon met him on the barracks square, a few meters away from his staff car. He clearly looked harassed. Once they were alone and out of earshot he briefed Simon at top speed.

'I apologise for not being in contact before, but...well, everything's in a complete mess. Communications have been badly interrupted by the enemy. It's no longer safe to drive in daylight.' Schellenberg wiped a sheen of sweat from his forehead. 'We had a couple of very close shaves on the way down, similar to that little episode we had in the Harz last month. Listen carefully. There's a lot to take in, and I haven't much time.'

With that he launched into a rapid update on events in Berlin, and what he thought was happening elsewhere. 'Himmler has ordered me to come down here and check that the Kohnstein complex is ready to fire the rockets. He knows time is pressing, and the Allies are not far away. The Russians will attack Berlin in the next ten days, and if he's going to act it will be imminent. I'm to fly to Stockholm tomorrow and directly negotiate with the Western Allied representatives...but I think it will be a complete waste of time. How are things at the factory?'

'That's hard to say, sir. The area is being heavily bombed, and it's too dangerous to get near to at present. But as far as I know, it's still working satisfactorily.'

'Good...or rather, bad. I was hoping that a lucky bomb might have finished off our work for us. I'm supposed to give it a final tour of inspection before I fly to Sweden.'

Simon shrugged. 'That's up to you, sir, but I wouldn't recommend it. The roads are too dangerous'.

'But what about you?' Schellenberg looked concerned. 'Can you get in? Will you be able to derail the planned launch? I presume you have the necessary equipment?'

Simon nodded. 'Yes, I have what I need. As for getting in, they can't bomb it twenty four hours a day. I'm sure I'll find a way.'

'I hope so. But I want you to move quickly. There's little time to waste. And there's something else you're going to have to do. Tonight.'

Simon thought he knew the answer to this. 'Flossenberg?'

'Yes.' Schellenberg looked grim. 'Himmler has finally received permission to do away with those he really hates. Among them are your father and Canaris, naturally. Hitler has signed the paperwork and apparently everything has been taken care of. There are two legally qualified SS officers in RSHA that have been appointed to check all the paperwork, then drive down from Berlin and oversee the executions. They were supposed to leave yesterday, but a few last minute obstacles have delayed their departure. I had a hand in those.' He sighed. 'It was the best I could do. As far as I know they are scheduled to arrive at 0900 tomorrow morning, and the sentences will be carried out shortly afterwards.'

He looked unhappy. For the first time that Simon could recall, Schellenberg looked almost guilty. 'I'm sorry I could not have done more,' the general said,' but it's the best I can do under these circumstances. You have about twelve hours to come up with a plan, get in there, rescue them and get out again before the party from Berlin arrives.'

'That's precious little notice,' Simon snorted in exasperation. 'Christ, how the hell am I going to be able to do this? I'm going to need people I can trust, trucks, weapons, ammunition, a plan of the camp...if I 'm going to break in there and batter my way out by force, and hopefully without getting everyone killed in the process.'

'I know. I've given this some thought on the way down. I don't think force is the best way to accomplish this. Before I left I managed to come up with something that should help, something much better than your own private army.' Schellenberg pulled an envelope from an inside pocket of his leather great-coat. 'Read what this says.'

Simon slipped two folded sheets of foolscap from inside the envelope. Both letters were printed on embossed paper, with the watermark and headings of Himmler's personal office at RSHA. Each specifically named him, Sturmbannfuhrer Max Simon. The first letter granted him unlimited powers within any area of Reich internal security, and in particular to remove the two named prisoners from custody for the purposes of 'special treatment'. It was dated today, the 7th of April, and superceded any prior orders from that office. The second letter required any and everybody to assist the bearer in any activity deemed necessary for the Reich's final victory, no matter what the price. It was a carte blanche get out of jail card, if ever there was one.

'The first letter should get you in, without any questions asked. Using this you should be able to get Canaris and your father out before the lawyers from RSHA arrive. The second letter you may find useful, should someone doubt your authority. My recommendation would be to take only those you can trust, and to get in and out as quickly as possible before the alarm goes up. You'll need to move quickly.'

Simon nodded. Suddenly a plan was falling quickly into place. 'How did you manage to get hold of these?'

Schellenberg grinned for the first time. 'I still have a few resources that the Reichsführer does not know about.' He tapped his nose. 'You may not appreciate it, but the signature is a particularly fine piece of forgery. Not by my fair hand, but somebody I know. Getting access to Himmler's locked drawers was a bit more difficult, but nothing is impossible if you are sufficiently determined...'

The Brigadeführer turned to leave. 'If what you say is true about the bombing, then I'd best leave now. It's dangerous enough driving at night, but I have to be at Oranienburg airfield early tomorrow for the flight to Stockholm, and it's a long drive.' He offered his hand. 'I'm afraid this is goodbye, Max. I'm glad to have known you, and I wish you well, especially in what you need to do in the next twenty four hours.'

Simon shook his hand. Schellenberg continued. 'It always seems that I'm giving you difficult, if not impossible missions to carry out. This is the last time, I think. It seems unlikely we'll meet again. Good luck. '

'Thank you. What will you do?'

'Probably seek internment from the Swedes, once my diplomacy fails, as it's bound to do. I can't see the Allies chucking in the towel at this stage of the war, no matter what Himmler may throw at them. Besides, my fiancé is already there. I got her out a few weeks ago.'

Simon nodded. 'There's one thing you never told me – why do all this in the first place? Why risk everything, especially for a man in your position? It must have been very dangerous.'

'Danger? Yes, sometimes,' Schellenberg nodded. 'But a general can't always hide behind his rank and let others get their hands dirty. I would like to be able to look in the mirror and recognize myself staring back, and not someone who didn't have the guts to do something about all this we're caught up in... Besides, the only person I ever spoke to, about how I really felt about the war and the way our country was going, was the Admiral himself. And I don't think he ever quite believed me.' Schellenberg chuckled deprecatingly for a moment and then grew serious again. 'No, I'm no hero. I've done what I can. If there's anyone who deserves that title then it's Canaris and others like him.' He sighed heavily, and was silent for a few moments. 'I used to know a couple of girls quite a few years back. Anna and Margareta. They were identical twins, bewitching, enchantingly beautiful, vivacious, all the best things a woman can be. I never was entirely sure which one was which – they used to dress identically. It was all part of their little game. The only time you could ever be entirely sure was when you undressed them – Anna had a small mole on her left breast. And I loved them both…then the day came when they were taken away in those trains that went East and never returned.' He stood quietly for a few minutes, his face in shadow. 'They were gone before I realised, before I could do anything about it, but that's no excuse. Could I have saved them?' He shrugged in the darkness. 'Probably not. But in the end I did nothing to stop it…' A hint of disgust crept into his voice. 'Maybe that's the real reason, a bad conscience. It's something I can never forget.'

The image of the woman and her children in the line that led to the gas chamber at Auschwitz suddenly flashed into Simon's memory. No, there was nothing he could have done at the time, but that didn't make the memory less real, less painful. Maybe it was the same for Schellenberg.

Hofheinz's grunt brought back to the present. 'All done. The spare's on.'

Simon turned away from the road and moved back to where the Kubelwagen stood, now back on four wheels. He took a deep breath. 'OK, Charlie, let's get this over with.'

❦

Barby, Magdeburg 0745

The derelict gästhaus stood at the corner of an intersection. Steele had left his shelter in a bombed-out house before the sun had come up, and was now sheltering behind a large oak that stood in the grounds of what used to be a small hotel. In the early morning light, the suburb appeared almost completely normal – a few pedestrians, the usual signs of life, nothing too much out of the ordinary. Only the fogged up windows of the Volkswagen parked across the street indicated the presence of any unusual activity.

From where he stood there was a clear view in all directions. There were no other watchers, as far as he could tell. But it might not be too long before the day shift turned up, perhaps with reinforcements. Two he could handle – beyond that, things might get more complicated. It was a risk he was unwilling to take. He looked at his watch. OK - now was the time. The girls would be up and getting ready for school. The occupants of the car would probably still be bleary and tired from a cold and uncomfortable night. He knew just how they felt. He'd spent many a night on similar stake-outs, and the one thing he had never succeeded in doing was getting a decent few hours' kip in a car. Far too uncomfortable, even with the seats reclined as far as back as they could go.

A blustery wind ruffled the bare branches of the tree above him. He shivered involuntarily, despite the heavy overcoat. Steele briefly cast his mind back to the events of the last few days. The briefing in Berlin had been routine. His contact had supplied him with an address, new rank badges and paperwork to go with it, hair dye to help match his looks to the photo on the ID card - enough to get through any documentation check. It had worked well – nobody had dared to question an SS Standartenführer on the numerous checkpoints he had passed through on the way here. The photo was barely looked at. Just a respectful 'Heil Hitler' and he was on his way. This was the final stage, the tricky bit. He had been warned there might be surveillance, but he could take care of that. As long as there weren't too many of them...

He straightened his cap, slid out from the cover of the tree and walked up to the intersection, glancing casually at the parked car. No movement as yet. He crossed over, walked a few more meters and then turned right and up the garden path towards the front door. Thankfully this one had been spared from the horrors of the bombing campaign against the Reich. The garden was neat and tidy and the house looked well-cared for, at least from the outside.

He knocked on the front door and waited. Somebody had rubbed clear part of the Volkswagen's windscreen, but he still could not make out how many were inside. The door opened. An attractive blonde in her early forties looked out at him.

'Yes? Who are you?' There was a hint of fear behind the green eyes.

'I'm sorry to bother you at such an early hour, ma'am. My name is Standartenführer Akkermann. I'm from RSHA. It's about your husband. May I come in?'

'Oh my god...What's happened? Is he alright?'

'Yes, ma'am. He's fine.' Steele put on his best, most reassuring smile. 'There's nothing to worry about. But I need to speak to you urgently – inside, as quick as you can.' His voice dropped. 'We're being watched.'

'Of course...' Her eyes flickered over his shoulder, across the street. 'Come in.'

There was a small porch that led into a hallway. She led the way through into an open-plan lounge, with a dining area at the far end. He could hear the sound of light footsteps racing around upstairs. She turned to face him, a mingled look of anxiety and query on her face, but he gave her no chance.

'Quick – there's not much time.' He slipped forward to stand behind the drawn curtains, careful not to move them. A glance out told him all he needed to know. The doors of the Volkswagen were opening. He turned back to her. 'OK. Here's what you need to do – go upstairs immediately and pack, and

don't hang about. Same goes for the children. A small suitcase each – no more. You know you're being watched?'
'Ye – yes,' she quavered. 'Who are they?'
'Gestapo, or some Sicherheitsdienst goons. It doesn't matter which. How long have they been watching you?'
She gasped. 'I'm not sure - months, I think. There's always somebody who keeps watching the house, following me around. The Kriminalpolizei say it's nothing to do with them, and told me to stop asking questions – for my own good. Why are they here? We've done nothing wrong. '
'I'm sure. But it's not you they're really after – it's your husband.' He took another quick glance. Two bulky figures in hats and leather trench coats were approaching from across the street. 'You have to move now,' he grated urgently. 'I'm a friend. Believe me - this house is no longer safe for you and your daughters. I'm here to get you to a place of safety. Besides, it won't be long before the Russians get here, and you really don't want that experience.' She suddenly looked very frightened. Her husband must have told her about the Eastern Front. 'Leave it to me. I'll deal with these thugs. Now go!'
She nodded, suddenly turned and fled upstairs, just in time. A few moments later and there was a heavy knock on the front door. Steele took a deep breath, walked back to the porch and opened the front door. 'Akkermann' was now consigned to the rubbish bin, at least for the moment. The new disguise and false papers would just have to do. He opened the door.
'Good morning, gentlemen. May I help you?'
'Kohl, 'stapo.' The shorter one grunted out of the slash that was his mouth. There was a quick flash of some form of ID. 'Are you Hartmann?'
'Standartenführer Hartmann, if you don't mind. Come in'. Steele led the way into the lounge. No guns were visible as yet. He turned to face them. 'What can I do for you?'
'What are you doing here? You're supposed to be at the factory in Nordhausen. Gone AWOL, have we?' He smirked nastily.

Steele smiled back, without a care in the world. 'No, gentlemen. A loyal officer of the Reich would never desert his post. Especially now in our time of greatest need. Naturally, I have permission from the Reichsführer himself.' His left hand eased slowly towards the lapel of his open greatcoat. 'May I?'

The taller Gestapo man's hand slid towards his coat pocket. 'Nice and slowly, Hartmann. No sudden moves .'

Steele kept smiling. He slowly pulled out his papers and handed them over. The other two watched him very carefully. 'My ID, and something else you may find interesting'.

The smaller one checked his documents carefully for a few minutes, and then passed them over to his colleague. 'See what I see, Hans? What do you think?'

The taller one examined them minutely, and then grinned. 'Yes, they're good...Very good. Even the photo's a good match.' He looked back at Steele. 'Almost. But you're not Hartmann'. His voice took on a hard edge. 'Who are you and where do you come from?'

Steele was beginning to tire of all this. 'My name's unimportant, but you may have heard of these – MI6 and London?'

The smile disappeared from the taller man's face. Both men momentarily froze. He dropped his right hand towards his pocket, but he was too late. A muffled *phut* erupted from Steele's greatcoat. A red hole blossomed in the Gestapo man's throat, pitching him backwards onto the floor. The smaller man twisted into action, arcing around to face Steele. Both guns roared simultaneously. Steele winced as something hot burned across his left side. The shorter man fell backwards onto a settee, twitched a few times, and then gazed up at the ceiling with unseeing eyes.

He moved across to where the taller man lay choking on the floor, his hands clutching at his neck. The carpet was sodden with red ooze. Blood was welling out between his fingers in great gobs, flooding his mouth as he gasped and strained for air. Steele leant down painfully and spoke in his ear. 'How did you know the papers were fake?' But the Gestapo man was beyond caring. His eyes began to roll up in his ashen face, and his hands fell away. A few more spurts of blood, and then nothing.

Footsteps raced down the stairs. Steele rifled the dead men's pockets, extracting car keys and wallets. He stood up, as quickly as the pain in his side allowed him to, and moved to close the door behind him.

You don't want to go in there.' Frau Hartmann and her two daughters looked at him in a mixture of shock and horror.

'Who are you?'

He winced again. The pain in his side was a damned nuisance, but he had suffered worse. 'As I said, a friend. I'm here to get you away to safety. You can't stay here now, especially with what's just happened.' He could feel blood trickling down his left side.' I could do with some hot water, a bandage and some strapping, if you've got any...'

'Yes, of course... ' She rushed past him into the kitchen. He grinned at the two girls in their school uniforms and pigtails. No more than nine or ten. They looked at him with scared, suspicious eyes.

Hartmann returned with a bowl of water, a towel and box full of dressings. He emptied the contents onto the small table in the hall, slid his coat off and opened his tunic. The left side of his vest was caked in blood. Quickly he lifted it up and off. A collective gasp came from Hartmann and her daughters. The skin over the left side of his ribcage was gouged and torn open along the track where the bullet had creased him. It looked much worse than it felt.

'Here, let me help you. I've done this before.' She soaked some dressings in water, and began to clean up the wound . He took a deep breath in – painful, but not the searing agony of a broken rib. Another inch and it could have been much worse.

'Thanks.' He grabbed a large dressing and pressed hard against the wound track. Some surgical tape held it in place. 'Looks like you've done this before.' He smiled at her.

'Yes. Once or twice. I've had some nurse training at the local hospital.' She still looked scared. 'What are we going to do now?'

'Leave, and quickly. I don't know if these two thugs are due to be relieved soon, but I'd rather not take the chance and wait to find out.' He buttoned up his jacket, slipped the greatcoat back on and fished out the Volkswagen's keys. 'We'll use their car as for as long we can. After that we may have to walk. We're heading west -how well do you know the side roads around here?'

'Reasonably well. Are you sure you're fit to drive?'

Steele grinned. 'I'll have to be. But you may need to help out.' He turned to look at the girls. You haven't yet introduced me...'

'Katrina and Hannelore.' She pointed at her daughters. 'This is...'

'Call me Johann.' It was close enough. Steele moved to where they stood uncertainly at the bottom of the stairs. 'No school today, girls.' He smiled. 'We're going on a little car journey to the countryside, and later on we'll go to see your father. OK?' They nodded, still wary of this stranger.

'Good. Let's go. We've quite a drive ahead of us.' With that he led the way out of the house and across the road to where the car was parked.

❋

Flossenberg Camp, 0815

'So, Sturmbannführer Simon, this is from the Reichsführer himself?'

Max Simon nodded. He was standing in the camp commandant's office, a well-furnished room with a good view of the camp and the rolling hills and forest that surrounded it. Seated across the desk from him was a tall officer in the field-grey uniform of an SS Obersturmbannführer, one rank above Simon. He had introduced himself as Max Koegel, a hard, spare-looking man with a thin, mean face and piercing glance. A scar ran a jagged course along his left cheek. Koegel looked more like someone you might have the misfortune to bump into in a dark alley by the docks rather than a ranking senior SS officer. He studied the document again, and then looked back up at Simon.

'I'm a little puzzled. Here you are, waving this piece of paper that bears the seal of the Reichsführer's office, and his own signature to boot. And I'm supposed to obey without question anyone bearing this letter? Is that it?' Another hard, searching glance.

'Yes, Obersturmbannführer. I have been ordered to remove two of your prisoners for further interrogation purposes. The names are listed there.'

'So you say. But why? They have already been interrogated here, at length. And most persuasively, I might add.' Koegel sat up in his leather chair and looked suspiciously at Simon. 'I cannot see why this is suddenly so important. What will further 'special' interrogation reveal?'

'I'm sorry, sir. I cannot answer that question as I do not know the full story behind the Reichsführer's decision.' Simon was worried. This was not going as smoothly as he had hoped. He decided to exert a little pressure. 'However, with all due respect, sir, I don't think the Reichsführer would look too kindly on anyone going against his wishes.'

'Aha!' Koegel smiled at him, but only his mouth smiled. Nothing reached his eyes. The effect was more like a grimace. 'So now you tell me that I should simply mind my own business and follow everything Berlin sends me without question?'

Simon shrugged his shoulders. 'Sir, I can only pass the message on and obey my orders.'

'Of course.' Koegel shrugged, glancing at his watch. 'We must all obey orders, even when at times they make no sense.' He paused for a moment, and then reached for the buzzer on his desk and pressed it. 'But a little checking never did any harm.' A few moments later there was a knock on the door to the commandant's office. It opened, and a young blond Untersturmführer marched in, came to a halt and braced to attention. Koegel barked at him.

'Fritsch, get on the phone to Berlin now. I need to speak to somebody senior at once – preferably the Reichsführer himself, if he's available, or Obergruppenführer Kaltenbrunner. As quick as you can.'

The adjutant saluted and raced out of the room. Koegel gazed out of the window for a few minutes, taking in the view of the low hills of the Sudetenwald beyond. The occasional shout echoed up from the quarry, no doubt where an SS guard was berating one of the slave labourers, or worse...

'I would not normally question your word as an SS officer, and for that you have my apologies.' Koegel resumed. The words were spat out, almost distastefully. 'But, as you must surely realize, these are difficult times...'

'Yes sir. Indeed they are'.

'The funny thing is, Sturmbannführer Simon, that I have already had a visitation from two senior officers from RSHA. There are on a mission directly authorized by the Reichsführer, just like you appear to be. It seems that he wants to be finally rid of some troublesome individuals that are guests of ours.' Koegel was watching him very carefully now. 'These officers arrived here earlier this morning, somewhat ahead of schedule, I may add. Funnily enough, two of the men on their list have the same names as the two you're interested in.' Simon's heart lurched. He tried not to show any reaction, but inside he was sick with worry. Was he too late? Had the executions already been carried out?

Koegel smiled again. There was something in Simon's reaction that had caught his eye. 'Bad news, perhaps?' He paused. 'It's perhaps a coincidence that one of the prisoners has the same surname as you, eh?'

'That may well be, Obersturmbannführer. But that's entirely coincidental. No relation whatsoever.' He was beginning to sweat freely under the camp commandant's close scrutiny. But there was one last thing he could try. 'I don't know if you're aware of this, sir, but there's something else you should consider.'

'And what would that be?'

'The Americans will soon be here.' The change in Koegel's self-assured pose was dramatic. .

'What?' Suddenly he looked alarmed and shocked. 'What kind of treasonable, defeatist talk is this?'

'Nothing of the sort, sir.' Simon needed to press his luck as far as it would go. 'You may not be aware of this, but the Americans have crossed the Rhine and the Main Rivers and are now rapidly moving east. The Panzer school where I've just come from is preparing for all round defence, even as we speak. I would have arrived here earlier, but we had to take several detours to avoid contact with enemy reconnaissance units.' None of this was true, but it couldn't be long before the Americans penetrated the area - no more than a day or two. Simon was banking on the fact that Koegel would be unaware of this, being stuck in an out-of-the-way camp with little contact with the outside world. RSHA was a long way away...

'You're sure about this?'

'Yes, Obersturmbannführer. I'm not exaggerating. I received my orders from RSHA yesterday evening. They were in no doubt as to the deteriorating situation.' He paused, weighing up the odds. 'This probably explains why the Reichsführer issued these orders to me. I would imagine that they supersede any instructions these officers have recently received. It appears that the situation has changed rapidly. Do you really want to risk going against his wishes?'

Koegel looked worried for the first time.

'No. Perhaps...'

It was time for the trump card, the killer blow. 'There is one more thing you should consider, sir.' He struck home. 'I don't think the Americans will look kindly on anybody found in charge of a camp – a camp like this.'

Simon let the words sink in. The man in front of him was obviously not a real soldier, just some rear echelon thug in a uniform. He doubted that Koegel would have any real courage in a tight spot. There was a flicker of fear in Koegel's eyes. *Good.*

Just then there was a knock on the door. 'Yes?'

Fritsch entered and saluted, addressing Koegel. 'I'm sorry sir, but we can't get through to Berlin. All the telephone lines are down. The radio is unable to pick up anything – nothing but static.'

Koegel appeared distracted, his mind elsewhere. After a while he finally spoke. 'I see. Keep trying', he said mechanically, then stood up and addressed Simon. 'We'd better go and see how they're getting on - if it's not too late,' he muttered. 'Follow me.'

❈

They were in a small courtyard at one end of the camp, not far from the main gate. The sight that greeted him almost made Simon stagger with shock and disgust, but even so he could not look away. The diminutive, emaciated figure above him swung idly in the cold breeze. The naked body was emaciated and badly bruised, but it was the angle of the head and blackened face that told him he was too late. The admiral had been viciously strung up from a meat hook that was crudely attached to a gallows. There were several other bodies stacked in a heap nearby – all lifeless, some of them horribly mutilated and disfigured.

One of the guards marched up to Koegel and saluted smartly. 'Just a few more, sir, and then we've finished. I-'

Koegel cut him off. 'Is that Canaris?' He pointed at the suspended body.

'Yes sir.' The guard had a brutal , rough face. 'The old bastard took some time to die, probably the longest of all of them so far.' He grinned. 'But we made sure it was nice and slow. Took over an hour for him to croak – just as the orders said to.' The guard seemed pleased that he had obeyed his instructions to the letter.

'Who's left?' There was a new-found urgency in Koegel's question.

'That fairy Bonhoeffer. Also, Canaris' mate, Simon. We're just about to get them, Obersturmbannführer.'

Koegel turned to Simon. 'Well, it appears that you're too late for one of them. But at least we can save your namesake.' He shrugged. 'Sorry. You'll have to tell the Reichsführer that the mistake was unavoidable, thanks to these conflicting orders. But you can't have Bonhoeffer. He's ours, and besides his name is not one of the two on *your* list.'

Simon forced himself to look away from the scene of death. He felt sick to his soul. All the old Admiral's courage and integrity had not been able to save him from this grisly end. A feeling of rage and helplessness almost consumed him, but he knew that his mission was still not over.He steeled himself to keep his voice normal.

'I hope, Obersturmbannführer, that for your sake Himmler will take a reasonable view on this. But I doubt it. He does not like to be disappointed, no matter what the reason. You'd better show me where you have Oberst Simon locked up. I hope he is in a reasonable state.'

'We'll soon find out. Reichel – '.

The guard braced to attention. 'Sir.'

'Tell those two gentlemen over there from RSHA that we'll be back in a moment with the last of them.' Koegel pointed to the far corner of the execution yard where the two stood. 'Then send one of your men over to me. We'll be at the cell block. Understood?'

'*Zu befehl*, Obersturmbannführer!' He saluted and hurried off.

❁

The cell block was a dirty grey concrete pile that oozed a vile mixture of sweat, terror and pain. The smell was awful, as if a million rotting corpses were stacked inside its walls. The young Sturmmann that Reichel had sent led the way. All the usual guards were back in the courtyard, enjoying the agonies of the prisoners they had guarded up until now. The door to the last cell along the ground floor was unlocked and opened. Slumped in the far corner was what was left of a man who had once been powerfully built, but was now a shadow of his former self – skeletal, bruised, matted in filth, and clothed in the usual zebra-striped garb common to all those who had displeased the masters of the Reich. Simon's heart sank at the pitiful remnants of his father, but thank God he was still alive – the head moved, one of his eyes slowly opened and focused on the new arrivals.

'On your feet, scum!' The young soldier stepped forward and aimed a vicious kick at the legs stretched out on the dirty floor. It was the last time he would inflict any more pain. Simon's bullet caught him across his spine, lifted him up for a moment, and then slammed him into the far wall. The silenced pistol made very little sound in the confines of the cell.

Koegel turned towards him, a look of surprise and shock across his features. The Luger was pointing at the centre of his chest.

'You heartless piece of shit!' Simon stepped forward and kicked him hard in the stomach. All the pent-up rage and disgust had made him see red. The commandant jack-knifed almost in two, slumping to his knees and gasping in pain, his hands clutching at the area where the boot had slammed into him. Slowly, very slowly he began to straighten up, climbing centimeter by centimeter from the pit of pain that threatened to drown him.

Simon risked a quick look at his father. The sight tore at his heart. His nose was broken, and the left side of his face was matted with dried blood. The right eye was closed up, and there was a mass of purple bruising around the jaw and neck. Beyond that, there was little to see apart from blood-stained hands and feet. Could he walk?

Koegel finally stood straight, his breathing still labored. A look of vicious hatred flashed across his face. 'You'll hang for this, Simon,' he gasped. 'You traitorous scum...'

Max stepped forward and thrust the muzzle of the pistol hard under Koegel's chin. The pressure rammed his head back. At the same time he deftly relieved Koegel of his pistol. 'Maybe, but not just yet. In the meantime, you're going to help me get this man up and out of here, just like that bastard Himmler wants. So if you want to live a pain-free existence, you'd better start cooperating – right now. Otherwise, it's a bullet in both knee-caps and no cock and balls for starters. That *would* be a lot of fun, don't you think?' He pressed the gun in much harder. 'Your choice.'

Koegel gasped in pain. 'Yes...OK, I'll do what you say. Just take that gun off me.'

Simon stepped back, all the while keeping the pistol trained on the commandant. 'Get on with it. Be as gentle with him as if he was your father. Move'.

❈

Almost there. They were nearing the Kubelwagen, parked just inside the main gates of the camp. He'd left Hofheinz in charge of the vehicle and in reserve, just in case there was trouble. The aim of the exercise had been to get in and out as fast as possible, bluffing his way past camp security using the power of the forged document. His father was half-dragged, half carried by a very reluctant Koegel, with Simon's pistol dug into the small of the SS officer's back - as a gentle reminder.

'Stop here'. Simon halted them at the corner of the last blockhouse, at the intersection of one of the main paths that traversed the camp. He risked a quick look to his right – nothing but endless rows of low-roofed buildings that housed the inmates. Far off, a few prisoners were being marched away, probably towards the quarry. To his left, about a hundred meters away were the camp gates, heavily protected by barbed wire. They were closed, unsurprisingly. Two or three guards stood close by the guard post on the other side. Above them a sentry in a watch-tower with a machine-gun looked out over the entrance. The gun pointed inwards, in their direction. Beyond them he could make out Hofheinz leaning idly against the side of the Kubelwagen. He was casually smoking a roll-up. The exit road stretched away to his left, swiftly disappearing behind a thick clump of trees. He could just make out the camp administration buildings away to the right – barracks, offices, living quarters and the commandant's offices. There was nobody else in view.

He turned back to Koegel and his father. 'Not far to go. You'd better make sure the guards let us out without a problem – no funny tricks.' He waved the pistol in front of the commandant. 'Remember – any false moves, anything at all...' He let the words hang in the cool air.

Koegel nodded, swallowing nervously.

'Let's go'.

They turned the corner. The gates slowly drew closer. One of the guards spotted them almost immediately. He shouted to the other two. His two comrades rushed to the gates, lifted up the heavy wooden latch, and swung them open. As they neared them, the first guard dashed forward, stopped in front of his CO, and saluted.

'Sir, may I...'

Koegel stopped in his tracks. 'Not now, Heinrici. I'm helping this officer with this prisoner. He is under orders to deliver this man to the Reichsführer.'

'But sir...' The guard looked puzzled. Simon cut him off. 'Obey your commanding officer! Get that vehicle over here now.' He pointed to where the Kubelwagen stood. 'Understand?'

'*Zu befehl*!' The guard snapped to attention, then dashed off to where Hofheinz stood. In less than a minute the kubelwagen roared up to them in a cloud of dust. Hofheinz jumped out, saluted the commandant, and eased Mannfred Simon off him and in to the back of the vehicle.

'Thanks, Charlie.' Simon turned to Koegel. 'OK. You're coming with us – just to make sure we get out of here alive.' He pointed to the front passenger seat. 'Get in there. Charlie will drive. I'll be sitting just behind you to keep you sweet. Get it?' Koegel nodded through gritted teeth.

Hofheinz drove slowly towards the gates. The other guards looked at them as they approached. The guard commander had disappeared into the guardhouse. Above them Simon could see the machine gunner watching them curiously. They reached the gates. Beyond them was a single red and white striped pole that hung suspended across the road. The stopped a few meters away from it. One of the guards raced up to lift up the barrier. At the same time the guard commander rushed up again.

'Sir, I cannot let you out!' The guard commander pushed his comrade away from the barrier pole. It slammed back down into its housing. 'I've checked with your office. We've received a message from RSHA. The camp has been placed under an immediate curfew – nobody in or out, regardless of rank!'

'That's alright, Heinrici.' The guard looked even more puzzled. Koegel continued. 'This officer has written authorization from the Reichsführer himself. It supercedes any other orders...'

'Sir, that's not my name...You know me – Rottenführer Kempf.' Simon tensed. The pistol eased away from Koegel's back. Something was definitely wrong here. He looked back at Koegel's face and saw the camp commandant desperately contorting his features, arching them back towards where Simon sat behind him. Kempf opened his mouth, and then quickly reached for his side holster, whipping the flap open and grabbing his pistol. His right arm was a blur of motion. At the same time Koegel threw himself backwards, trying to twist around and grab Simon's right arm.

He was too late. The gun went off in Simon's hand. Koegel slumped forward in his seat. Simon swung the PPK around. His shot lifted Kempf off his feet, slamming him backwards and away. The second guard was just in the process of slipping his rifle off his shoulder when Simon turned and put two rounds in him. He could hardly miss. The man was no more than a meter away.

'Quick, Charlie – let's get out of here!' Hofheinz needed no urging. He slammed the pedal to the floor. The kubelwagen raced away. There was a splinter of wood as the vehicle smashed through the barrier pole. Behind them there was a shout. Simon turned to look back. The remaining guard was pointing a Schmeisser at them.

'Get down!' A volley of shots reached out at them, but they were accelerating and too far away to be within the lethal range of a machine pistol. But that wasn't all that Simon was worried about.

They had almost reached the bend and the copse of trees when a high-pitched rasp opened up, as if someone was tearing a calico sheet in two. Simon knew that sound from long experience. It was the sound of an MG 42 firing, a weapon that had saved him in many desperate situations – and one of the last things he ever wanted to face. Thank God it had been pointing inwards, towards the camp. Otherwise they would never have made it this far.

The man behind the gun must have been out of practice, or the gun sights out of kilter. That in itself was nothing unusual. After all the concentration camp wasn't in the front line against the Red Army. The first burst missed them by a few meters. The gun was aiming low and off to the right, but the necessary correction would take but an instant. The second burst caught them just as they reached cover, clipping the rear and side of the kubelwagen. The windscreen disappeared in a hail of smashed glass. Several heavy blows thumped against the bodywork – and then they were gone. The tree cover had saved them. Another prolonged burst followed them but it was too late. They were safe, for the moment. There would be a pursuit, no doubt, but they could lose them easily. There were many forest trails that led down into the valley and the main roads going north and west.

Simon glanced quickly at his father. Mannfred was still slumped in the right rear seat. He looked greyer than before, but otherwise appeared just the same as when he was rescued. Hofheinz drove the vehicle as fast as he dared, skidding around bends and accelerating as hard as possible down the few straights. After two minutes of this they came to a crossroads deep in the fir trees.

'Turn right'.

Hofheinz drove along this road for another few minutes, and as then road began to plunge downhill, pulled off into the cover of cutting. He gently braked the Kubelwagen to a halt.

'Why are we stopping, Charlie?

'Engine's getting too hot. And there's a funny vibration from the rear.'

Hofheinz got out to check the rear of the Kubelwagen, and then moved around to the front to lift up the bonnet.. Simon glanced at Koegel, but instantly knew that he was beyond any form of help. *Well, the bastard had had a quick release, more than could be said for many of his victims.* Simon's only regret was that Koegel died far too easily. The rage inside him, the brutal treatment of his father and the agony of Canaris' death, was still there. There was simply no justice in this world...

He pushed Koegel's body out of the front of the car. It fell onto the forest floor in an untidy heap. Simon lifted the seat forward and got out. As he moved towards the front, Hofheinz stepped out from the cover of the bonnet. A Luger was in his right hand. It was aimed squarely at Simon.

It was a moment before he could take it in. 'What?' He couldn't believe his eyes. This must surely be some kind of perverted joke. Not Charlie, his long-time friend and confidante. Surely not? But the gun spoke volumes, and it was pointed directly at him.

'Sorry, Max, but I can't allow you to go any further. Drop that pistol, and get your hands in the air - slowly.' There was nothing Max could do except comply. The pistol was as steady as a rock. 'What you've just done is high treason – treason against the Reich and everything I believe in. That's enough to hang you.' Hofheinz was deadly serious. Gone was the normal Charlie. Now something fanatical looked out at him, someone he didn't recognise. Simon was dumbstruck for a few moments, and then finally found his voice.

'Come on, Charlie. This is a poor time to be playing games. We've got to get out of here, and fast. They'll be sending out patrols to hunt us down.'

'Not us. Just you.' Hofheinz's face broke into a broad grin. 'The joke's on you, Max and you've been blissfully unaware of it for the last two years - ever since you joined the Leibstandarte. Do you think you could just stroll in and join the club, without someone keeping an eye on you?' He laughed scornfully, but the muzzle of the pistol never wavered. 'All transfers in from the Wehrmacht are watched carefully. But even though you passed the test and turned out to be a good soldier, we always watched you. And then came that funny mission - England, wasn't it? I'm told that you were out of contact for a bit and then returned home, the mission a failure – apparently. Well, the Reichsführer wasn't so sure. He never really trusted you. He suspected MI6 all along, but he had no real proof and nothing to hang on you. Now he does.'

'What? You're in contact with Himmler?'

'Yes – of course. What took you so long to work that out?' He laughed again. 'He visited me while I was recovering from that Russian bullet. In that nice Bavarian clinic I told you about. Himmler arranged my transfer to the Panzer school. The plan was simple – get back into your confidence, and be there should anything funny start to happen. I was to keep in close contact. Couldn't follow you everywhere, could I? But don't worry - the Reichsführer prides himself in covering all bases. And now you've given him an excuse to interrogate you at length.' He smirked nastily. 'I will have the responsibility of getting all the answers out of you – like who set you up to come here and rescue that doddering old admiral, and your treacherous father. The Reichsführer is *very* interested in finding out who has been helping you. And I'm sure the guards at Flossenberg will take a keen interest in making you talk – especially seeing as you've murdered their commander and a few of their mates.'

Simon still couldn't quite believe it. The Jekyll and Hide change in his former friend stunned him. He had been played like a fool. All the time he thought he had confided in a friend, someone privy to most of his inner thoughts. But all he had succeeded in doing was clutching a viper to his breast. The man in front of him had become unrecognizable.

'I thought you were a friend, someone who couldn't stand the pomposity and stupidity of the Nazis. And all the stories you told me about your experiences since we parted. Just after Auschwitz, wasn't it? And what about those Jews? Even you were shook up after what we'd all seen there.'

'Yes. Not very pleasant, wasn't it?' Hofheinz laughed. 'But who cares about a bunch of stinking Jews? Not me. They all deserve to go up in smoke. Somebody else can do that job. And all those stories about France and Hungary? Yes, they're true. But the war's not over yet. And I'm sure that Himmler has a few tricks up his sleeve that will give us final victory, even at this late stage. Now get back in. You can drive us back to Flossenberg.'

He was mad. There could be no other explanation. Simon watched as Hofheinz moved away from him, keeping well out of striking range.

'Drop the bonnet and get behind the wheel'. Hofheinz waved the pistol at him and motioned him into action. As he got in the driver's seat Hofhinz slid in beside him. Suddenly he felt a sharp pain in his right side. Hofheinz had dug his pistol deep into his ribs.

'Just make sure you drive us back to the camp, and no funny stuff. Let's go.'

Simon started the engine. The kubelwagen was turned around in no time, and he began to head back towards the crossroads. He took a quick look back at his father. The older man appeared even greyer than before. His eyes were closed, and there was a deathly pallor to him.

'For Christ' sake, Charlie, let me stop and look at my old man. He's looking terrible.'

Hofheinz glanced quickly at the rear seat. The pressure of the pistol eased for a moment. Mannfred Simon indeed looked very ill. But what the hell did he care?

He turned back. 'Forget it. Just keep your eyes on the road. And if he dies on the way back it'll be a small mercy, compared to what's going to happen-'.

There was a loud crack. The centre of Hofheinz's chest suddenly erupted in a shower of blood and bone, thumping him forward and into the dashboard. He was dead in an instant. Simon slammed on the brakes. The kubelwagen skidded to a halt. He jumped out, tore the dead man out of his seat and climbed into the back. His father lay weakly across the rear seats. A red stain was slowly growing around his right side. It could only have been from that second MG42 burst. A pistol lay in his open hand - probably Koegel's. It must have slipped out of Simon's pocket. The man was barely conscious.

'...Sorry I couldn't help earlier...'

'Father...' Simon's voice choked. So near, yet so far. The older man was near death and there was damn all he could do.

'...tell mother and Kirsten that I never stopped loving them... nor you...'

The light in his eyes gradually faded away. Not so long ago there had been four living men in the car. Now only one of them remained alive.

❖

Near Niedersachswerfen, Nordhausen area 1330

Colonel Charles 'Chuck' Horner, commanding officer of
the United States Army 517th Independent Parachute Infantry
Battalion, stood on a small hillock and gazed around at the
empty farm landscape in front of him. To his north lay the
undulating hills of the Harz, less than a mile away. Over to
his right lay the small town of Niedersachswerfen, peaceful
in the spring sunshine. Behind him and to the east was more
farmland, and beyond that some low wooded ridges. No sign
of the enemy – as yet.

He surveyed the scene in front of him with considerable
satisfaction, although he was careful not to show it. All around
him his battalion had made a perfect drop, smack dab on the
correct drop zones. The last transports were departing, and
as they did so the rest of his battalion floated down, directly
on target. To the uninitiated the unfolding scene looked like
organised chaos, but he knew better. Almost all the parachutes
were folded away. Men were racing to open weapons canisters.
The rest were deployed in an all-round defensive posture,
waiting for the order to advance.

The pathfinders had gone in on time, and the USAAF
Transport Command had done a fine job in getting them there
- with no cock ups. So far it had been a milk run. Even Nature
had played its part – cool, clear blue skies, light winds, no more
than 5mph – nothing that would cause any real difficulties. And
there had been no flak, thank God. The Luftwaffe was yet again
conspicuous by its absence. High above him two squadrons of
Thunderbolts circled the drop zones, weaving complex vapour
trails across the sky - all eager for the slightest sign of trouble.
No – there was no real threat from above. The hard part would
be when they moved north towards the Harz – the hills were so
close he could almost touch them from where he stood. Who
knows what they would find there?

The fact that he had back-up coming was some comfort,
although he knew from bitter experience that nothing ever went
according to plan. The briefing, a rush job from some senior G2

officer at SHAEF, stated that there should be little opposition in the area. Most likely they might run into units of the local *Volkssturm* – old men and young boys, maybe armed with a few rifles and Molotov cocktails, but nothing worse than that. There were few, if any, surviving Wehrmacht units in the area – the rest were either bottled up in the Ruhr pocket, or busy stemming the advance of the US 1st Army. The word from the top was that the advancing spearheads of the 3rd Armoured and 104th Infantry Divisions were only a day or two away – worst case scenario. Most likely they would show up tomorrow – motorized infantry, backed up by heavy weapons and tanks. Enough muscle to deal with anything – in theory. That was all very well, but he would only count on them when he could see them for real.

But there was one thing he knew he could immediately rely on, a real comfort if things started to go pear-shaped - there was another friendly parachute battalion in the area. This one was a composite force from the remnants of the British 1st Airborne Division, the Red Devils who had endured the agony of Arnhem last September. Barely a third of the division had escaped that disaster, but those who had returned to Britain were still ready and willing to fight, and had jumped at the chance of one final hurrah before the war ended. They were damn good soldiers – he'd seen them in action in Sicily at the Primosole bridge back in '43, when he had been attached to them as a liaison officer. They would give it their all, just as he knew that his own boys would.

The plan was pretty simple. The British would drop in the open area just west of the village of Werna, about five kilometers to the north-west, and then sweep east. His boys would advance to the north, keeping Niedersachswerfen to their right. Their joint target was an area just beyond the railway line that cut across this area. The briefing had told him that the objective was some sort of underground factory producing V2 rockets. Its precise location was still in doubt – photo reconnaissance was still unable to pinpoint the entrance. They'd already tried saturation bombing by the strategic air-forces, with little apparent success. SHAEF had called off the bombers a few hours ago, and now it was down to the Airborne. Get in on the ground and neutralize the target, no matter the cost. The mission was deemed to be of vital importance. The rockets were a deadly menace, and the factory needed to be shut down permanently.

The two battalions could not land any closer, due to the rolling and wooded nature of the terrain in the area where the factory was thought to be. So it was going to be a fighting advance, hopefully with little to oppose them. Their biggest obstacle would probably be the terrain itself – the area inside this part of the Harz would almost certainly have been torn up and pulverized by the bombers. Well, that was something they'd just have to take in there stride.

'Excuse me sir.' It was 2nd Lieutenant Clarke, from his HQ section. Beside him was a signaller with a field radio. 'Just made contact with the British. Their 2ic says they've landed without any appreciable problems. A few Krauts took a few pot shots at them as they came in, but they didn't last long. Their CO's waiting for the all clear from us to advance.'

'Good. Tell them we're all fine and dandy.' Horner glanced at his watch. 'ETD 1335. Radio contact and position check every fifteen minutes.'

'Yes sir.'

'Then scoot around to the company commanders, with my compliments. A and B companies will advance on a bearing of 015 degrees in echelon. We'll follow with C company as reserve. Company D will clear out Niedersachswerfen, and then move north as our right flank guard. Companies to move out in two minutes.'

Clarke saluted and dashed off. The rest of Horner's HQ section, dug in nearby, rose and followed him as he began to move north. They had a few hours left before it would begin to get dark. With a bit of luck that should be enough.

❀

Kohnstein factory complex, 1350

Simon wiped the sweat off his brow as he walked up the last slope to the hidden entrance at the foot of the hill. He'd had to leave the Kubelwagen about five hundred meters away - the bombing had made it impossible to get any closer. The terrain was all smashed up, as if a giant had plucked up the landscape, given it thorough shake up, and flung it down haphazardly. Hundreds of trees, most of them stripped of their branches and splintered into fragments, lay scattered all over the area. Enormous craters, each piled up one on top of another, had made the going more like an assault course than a gentle uphill stroll. But it wasn't the exercise that had made him hot and out of breath. The road up from Niedersachswerfen had been far more dangerous.

He'd heard the rumbling thunder of the enemy transports as he drove along the road from Nordhausen. Simon pulled over in the village to watch them as they came in from the west. In next to no time the skies were filled with a myriad of parachutes floating down, no more than a few hundred meters away. Dozens of fighters swooped and circled above them, looking for the slightest sign of enemy activity below. The houses in the village could only be temporary shelter at best. Sooner or later he would be spotted, and he desperately needed to reach the factory before he was cut off. There was no time to lose. In an instant he gunned the Kubelwagen up the road that led north. But as soon as he emerged from the cover of village, he knew that the game was up. Simon barely reached the cover of the nearest trees when death was suddenly upon him. At least four enemy fighters swept down, each one blasting away in turn along the general direction in which he was driving. Volley after volley of cannon shells slammed blindly into the trees all around him as the Kubelwagen raced away. Luckily the road had a good tarmac surface and there was no dust to give his position away, but even so it was still almost too close to call. Several times shells smashed into the road, missing him by a whisker. One of them hit the Kubelwagen somewhere behind him, but he was oblivious to the damage. In a flash he recognised the spot where the road bent around to the left, where the disguised rail tracks lay with camouflaged route up to the factory. The engine groaned as he dropped down three gears, pulled the wheel hard over to the right and flung the vehicle off the road.

Almost immediately the engine quit without warning, but it made little difference – the massive craters and torn up ground to his front stopped him in his tracks. He jumped out and dived behind the cover of the nearest trees, just as the last fighter screamed overhead. Another burst of cannon-fire, and then the air was suddenly clean again.

There was a strong guard under cover at the gates to the factory, watching him warily as he approached. One of them saluted him and rushed forward.

'Sir – are you OK?'

'Yes. I'll live,' he grunted. His hands were shaking, but this was no time to muck about. 'Where's the guard commander? I need to speak to him urgently.'

'Sir, I'll get him immediately.' The guard dashed off. He reappeared shortly with an officer in tow – the same young blond Untersturmführer who had met him on his first visit. He barely looked nineteen. The junior officer saluted politely.

'Sturmbannführer Simon. Glad to see you again, sir. What can I do for you?'

Simon pulled the second letter out from inside his jacket. 'Read this'.

The SS officer scanned the letter, his eyes widening at the signature on the bottom. Suddenly he snapped to attention. 'What are your orders, Sturmbannführer?'

'I'm taking command of this facility, with immediate effect.' The Officer gaped. 'There's an enemy parachute force no more than an hour or two away, almost certainly heading in this direction. I need you to get as many guards out from the factory, with as many heavy weapons that you can lay your hands on. Get them dug in well beyond the road down there.' He pointed back, in the general direction of the main road from Nordhausen.

The officer looked worried. 'But sir, what about security inside the factory? I can't just -'

'I don't give a damn about what you can or can't do Untersturmführer,' Simon snapped. 'This is an emergency, and this letter gives me absolute power over *anybody anywhere*. I could put a bullet in your head right now, and no one would ever question my right to do so. So you'd better make your mind up quickly, or it'll be the last thing you ever do.' He began to un-holster his pistol. The SS man swallowed nervously.

'Yes sir – forgive me. I was only concerned about the prisoners and the security situation inside. We're understaffed as it is –'.

'I'll take responsibility for that. In the meantime, your orders are clear. Leave a minimal guard – all the rest out here – immediately.' The Untersturmführer braced to attention, one eye still warily on Simon's pistol. 'Any of you have any combat experience?' Max scanned the rest of the guards.

'Yes sir.' A tough-looking Oberscharführer stepped forward from the rest. 'A couple of years in Russia with Das Reich.'

'Good.' Simon smiled briefly, and turned back to the officer. 'This man will give you all the advice you need. Use him well. In the meantime, get cracking. Where's your CO?'

'In his office, sir. Shall I send someone to inform him of this latest threat?'

'No. Leave that to me. I've got to see him about another matter - something equally urgent. You have your orders.'

The Untersturmführer saluted again, barked out a few commands and then raced inside. The others, led by the Eastern Front veteran, began to march away towards the south. In a moment he was on his own.

Here we go. He plunged inside.

✡

Rybalko sat in the corner of the fuel storage area deep in tunnel B, shivering. Although the air inside the cave was warm and close he still felt cold throughout, right down to his bones.

He'd managed to wolf down some food of sorts in the morning, but the cough had come on in the last few hours and he knew that he was coming down with something he would find hard to resist in his weakened state – some sort of nasty bug. . His muscles ached all over, and he could feel a sore throat starting – a raw, burning sensation at the back of his mouth. He prayed to God – his god, not some socialist substitute but to the Orthodox faith his family had worshipped for generations. *Please don't let me get ill.* The one thing that frightened him above all else was pneumonia. The most recent outbreak in the underground factory had been a month ago, or was it more than that? It was difficult to keep track of the days inside this hell-hole.

The Germans were absolutely paranoid about health, and the last thing they wanted was an outbreak of infective disease among the emaciated workers. Not because they were concerned about the workers – no. They were far more concerned about themselves. Most of them had taken to wearing facemasks when dealing with the inmates, but that was only a start. The guards had 'cured' the last outbreak by taking those found suffering outside and shooting them. Typical German efficiency. But the bombing had interrupted fresh supplies of slave workers, so much so that conditions were now strangely better – very few beatings and no summary executions. Maybe the end of the war was near. Or maybe the guards were worried about what would happen to them if the factory was liberated and they were caught red-handed. He knew what the 'specialists' in the Red Army would do – it would take an awful long time, and be extremely unpleasant. Rybalko knew that he would lose precious little sleep over that – these bastards deserved everything coming to him.

But now the guards were nowhere to be seen. That's why he'd risked sitting down. In the last few minutes someone or something had drawn them away, an unheard of event. The only sign of authority was a lone SS officer, wearing a field grey uniform with an unbuttoned great coat over the top. He was walking past the last batch of rockets, into the fuel storage area and almost directly at him - calmly, utterly sure of himself.

Rybalko scrambled achingly to his feet. Two of his fellow workers lay on the floor beside him. They were too spent to move, but they followed the approach of the SS man with fear and dread in their sunken eyes. Anybody lying down on the job was normally shot out of hand.

But the man simply ignored them, walked past and beckoned him to follow. Suddenly, Rybalko realized with a shock that the newcomer was not wearing a facemask. Nor did he look familiar. He knew virtually all the factory senior personnel by sight, but this one was new. The officer moved to a far corner of the chamber, next to where the banks of liquid oxygen tanks were located. He had no choice but to follow. The stranger turned to him.

'Where do you come from – France, Russia? Can you understand me?' The officer's voice was urgent, demanding.

Rybalko nodded, amazed that he was being addressed this way. Normally communication was performed by a combination of grunts, kicks and punches. His German was reasonable. 'From Russia, sir. Yes, I can speak German a little, but I beg you - please speak slowly.'

His enemy smiled. 'Good. I need you to do me a favour. If you help me you'll be doing something that will benefit all humanity – your own people, as well as the rest of Europe – maybe even the entire world. The war will soon be over, but what I have to do must be done now. Believe me, this is no trick. Do you know what's being produced here?'

Rybalko nodded. 'Long range rockets.'

'Yes, but that's not the worst of it. They're going to be loaded with lethal biological weapons. The targets will be all across Europe. Even America and Moscow. I've got to stop them. Will you help?'

The face was insistent, the eyes bored into him. Rybalko coughed a little. The uniform told him that this man was his enemy, but there was something else about him, an indefinable air that made him think twice. Even so, the man was still an opponent- dangerous, unpredictable, and in absolute command.

Simon sensed the doubt.in the man's eyes. He pulled his pistol out, reversed it and handed it to the Russian. Rybalko almost dropped it in amazement.

'Ignore the SS rank. I'm a friend. The pistol is in case a guard comes. It's fully loaded. I take it you know how to use it?'

Rybalko nodded.

'Good. There's a silencer fitted on the end, so it'll keep the noise down. I'll need a few minutes. OK?

'What are you going to do?'

'Blow this place up. The oxygen cylinders will add to the blast. Next door is the sealed area where they're preparing those bio-weapons that will obliterate most of Europe. Are you with me?'

'I don't understand' Rybalko was still stunned. 'Who are you?'

'That's not important right now – maybe later. Please – will you help me?'

'Yes.' The pistol in his hand was quite real. It was beginning to make sense. But who was this man? A foreign agent? 'But how will we get out? The explosion will kill us all.'

Simon patted his pockets. 'Don't worry. The fuse will give us about an hour – more than enough time to get everybody who can move outside. Now keep watch.' With that he turned away and walked to the nearest tank. Rybalko found he was walking over to the vault entrance, as if he was in a dream. He positioned himself just inside the doors. Every now and again he'd look back at where the German was at work. It looked as if he was moulding a wad of brown matter around the base of two oxygen tanks.

It took Simon but a few minutes to slip the pads of plastic explosive from inside his greatcoat and attach them to the tank undersides. That was easy enough. But when he slipped out the pencil fuses from their case, he gasped in dismay. Most of them were cracked open and appeared to be quite useless. They must have been thrown about so much inside the Kubelwagen during that last wild ride, dodging those enemy fighters. *Don't panic,* he told himself. *Check them carefully.* He forced himself to stay calm as he examined them one by one. Mercifully he could salvage just two of them – but each had no more than a fifteen minute delay setting. He swore to himself. The margin would be very fine – would it be enough for him to get everyone out to safety in time? There was no real choice. Carefully he slid the fuses into the plastic, made sure they had a tight fit, and then twisted the caps. *All done.* His watch said 1408. It was high time to get out of there, but there was the last part of his mission to complete.

Rybalko watched him as he hurried back to where the Russian had propped himself up against the frame of the steel doors.

'OK. The good news is that this place will blow up. The bad news is that we only have fifteen minutes.' *Sod's bloody law.* He smiled ruefully. 'Not much I can do about that. Thanks for your help. Keep that gun out of sight – you may need to use it. Now get going, and take as many of your fellow workers as you can. If anyone asks what you're doing tell them that Sturmbannführer Simon, the new camp commandant, has ordered that all camp personnel must assemble outside – now. On pain of immediate death if my orders are not obeyed.'

He pulled the second letter from out of his inner jacket pocket. 'Give them this. It has Himmler's signature and stamp on it. That should be sufficient to convince anyone.'

'But what about those two?' Rybalko pointed at the two workers lying on the floor. I can't just leave them there.'

'I'm sorry. You haven't got a choice. I doubt you'll have enough time to everyone out. Do what you can. As for those who can't walk, well...' Simon's voice trailed off. There was nothing else he could say.

'And you?'

'There's one last thing left to do. See you outside.'

❀

The factory administration suite and office area was still manned by the time he got there, but there were far less staff present than at his last visit. A few of them glanced up at him as he passed by, but nobody dared to interrupt an officer of field rank as he made his way towards the inner sanctum. It was only when he reached the inner sanctum that trouble began. The statuesque Barbara looked up in alarm as he entered the outer office without knocking, and dashed forward to intercept him just before he reached the inner door.

'I'm sorry, Sturmbannführer,' she said in a loud voice, blocking his path and spreading her arms wide. 'I'm afraid you can't go in there just now. The CO is in conference and cannot be disturbed. He has some very important guests.'

He could hear the sounds of grunting and a series of heavy thuds coming from beyond the partition door.

'Sounds like a strange conference to me,' he muttered. Simon pushed her hard and away to his right. She stumbled, catching one of her heels on the office carpet. Ignoring her, he thrust the door open. The view almost stopped him in his tracks. Hartmann was seated in front of him, slumped in his leather chair and stripped to the waist. Two thickset men in shirt sleeves were bending over him, taking it in turn. Each held a black leather truncheon, smeared in blood. Hartmann was almost unrecognizable, his face bloody and swollen. An irregular mass of heavy welts and blotches covered his chest and sides. The man was barely conscious. Simon started forward, but something froze him in his tracks. The muzzle of a pistol ground into his neck.

'Well, well, well...Look what the cat's dragged in.'

It was his old 'mate' from the Liebstandarte – Egon Sammler.

The two thugs pinned his arms back in a flash. One of them wrenched his right arm and wrist back and upwards, almost as far as his left shoulder blade. The pain was almost unbearable.

Sammler sat in front of him, idly toying with a Luger. The pistol never strayed too far away from the centre of Simon's chest.

'So,' Sammler began, after a long pause. A very satisfied smirk was writ large across his bloated features. 'What a delightful, *truly* delightful coincidence. Here we were, trying to track down the famous Max Simon, and getting nowhere with this poor oaf Hartmann, when who should barge in the front door but the very man we were sent to look for.' He laughed uproariously. 'Excellent.' He clapped his hands in glee. 'The Reichsführer's going to love this!'

He leaned forward and suddenly flicked a boot in Simon's direction. The blow caught him hard in the solar plexus. It would have bent him in two but for the tender administrations of the men on either side. Each of them held him in a vice-like grip as he fought the waves of nausea and gasped for breath. The pain and retching rolled over him like an inexorable wave. Only slowly did he start to recover.

Sammler laughed again, relishing the pain he had inflicted. He flicked his little finger of his left hand up, and one of the thugs slammed a karate blow hard into his left kidney. A blinding sheet of pain arced up his back and into his neck. It felt like the top of his head was lifting off. Dimly he became aware of Sammler's right hand. The finger flicked up again, and the blow that followed almost blacked him out this time. Finally they let him fall to the floor where he lay like a dead man for a few minutes, before he was dragged up by his hair and roughly slammed onto a seat. Hartmann was ignored. His friend lay in a heap behind his desk, groaning. The two Gestapo men took up flanking positions.

Sammler leaned forward, but still well out of range. 'That's for starters. I have a good memory, you little shit. Remember that day in Auschwitz? You broke my nose, made me look stupid in front of my CO. Now it's pay-back time, and you owe me.'

The pain was still almost unbearable, but Simon slowly forced his head up degree by degree to meet Sammler's gaze. He was greeted by a shower of saliva.

'Not got much to say for such a self-important arse-licker, have you? Well, let me fill you in on some things that may have escaped your attention.' Sammler puffed himself up. 'The Reichsführer feels that the operation here could be run better, especially in the next few days when the great rocket offensive begins. Recent production has been most unsatisfactory. Also, factory discipline needs to be improved; it's been far too lax of late. That's why I've been appointed as commandant, effective as of today. My new rank is Standartenführer. How do you like that?' He sneered. 'Now you'll take your orders from me, in what little time there's left for you. As for this lump of shit' – he pointed at the inert form of Hartmann – 'he's finished ancient history - just like you.'

'Why are you bothering to tell me about all this?' It was such an effort to speak.

'Why?' He laughed again. 'I want you to go to your grave knowing that all your little plans have been uncovered.' Sammler was enjoying his speech. 'We know everything. It's a little late now, but at last we're getting to grips with all those closet traitors, flushing them out and giving them what they deserve. We should never have taken anybody into the SS who wasn't committed to the Nationalist Socialist ideal from the beginning – certainly not those Luftwaffe morons after Kharkhov, and rejects from the Wehrmacht like the two of you. And how have you repaid us with that trust?' Sammler spat at him again. 'The Reichsführer has recently become concerned about the activities of one of his most trusted aides, someone at RSHA. He told *me* that there has been some very suspicious goings on -unauthorised contacts with the enemy, and so on. He's not absolutely sure of this traitor's identity, but at this stage of the war he can afford to take a few liberties with evidence. And he's now convinced that somewhere at the bottom of it all is your dirty face.'

'How so?'

'Come on, Simon, don't be a dummy,' Sammler scoffed airily. 'Even a tosser like you can't be that stupid. Someone at Flossenberg got a communication off to RSHA this morning.

You're a wanted man. Killing a camp commandant and a loyal SS officer are fairly serious offences. Mix in high treason, and that's an automatic one-way trip to a meat hook, with a little entertainment thrown in before you go. We've been checking - any known contact you've made recently is being taken in for questioning. That's why we've been having this extended chat with your friend here, thanks to the loyal staff at the factory. We know that the two of you go way back, to your days in the Wehrmacht.' Sammler grinned again. This was all highly enjoyable. 'Shame about your father, isn't it. But he's met the same fate as that shriveled up old cunt Canaris. Like I said before, we're finally dealing with the Reich's riff-raff, once and for all. And now it's your turn.' He raised the Luger.

How much time was left?. 'I wouldn't do that just yet, old boy.' Simon was looking at death again. This time it amazed him how calm he felt.

'Oh, and why not?' Sammler knew he held all the cards. There was nothing to stop him. Total victory lay in his grasp.

'The enemy is almost here. I saw them land a parachute force on my way here from Flossenberg. They're no more than an hour away, at the latest.'

The pistol wavered in Sammler's grasp. For the first time doubt showed on his face, as well as a tinge of fear. But not for long.

'Bollocks.' Sammler stepped closer and slapped him hard across the face. 'You're just trying to buy more time. But just in case you're telling the truth – Muller!'

'Yes sir.' The man on his left took his eyes off Simon and turned towards his leader.

'Nip outside and find out if any of this is true. Gerhardt can help me deal with this little shit here.'

Muller grabbed his coat and exited the office quickly. Sammler watched him go then turned back. 'I think we'll start off with your joints,' he began casually, enjoying himself immensely. 'Where would you like it? Knees, elbows and wrists in that order? Or shall we vary it, just to keep you guessing? And don't worry I've got plenty of ammunition.' He made a show of patting his jacket pockets. 'Any last requests? Anything you'd like me to pass on to a loved one? I'd like to -'.

The sound was deafening in the small room. A red hole blossomed in Sammler's forehead. The far wall was smattered in a hideous pattern of blood and brains. Sammler's body pitched backwards and onto the floor.

Gerhardt gaped at the body of his commander lying spread-eagled on the floor in amazement – and for a split second too long. The gun boomed again, then once more. Simon twisted around in his chair. The swollen, distorted face of his friend winked up at him, spitting out a mouthful of bloody saliva.

'That bastard liked the sound of his own voice a little too much, I think…' Hartmann grinned then groaned in pain. 'For Christ's sake, man – help me up.'

Simon ignored his aching body and rushed over to help him. He had just enough time to help Hartmann upright and into his seat when there was a sudden commotion outside, followed by a fusillade of shots. Then the door was flung open, and Barbara staggered in, her hair disheveled, a bright red stain on the left side of her uniform. She had a PPK in her right hand. The muzzle started to move upwards.

Hartmann's pistol boomed out once more. His former secretary was thrown backwards, hitting the floor with a sodden thump, and then there was silence.

Simon took a quick look outside. Barbara's office was deserted. Nothing moved in the administration suite outside. On the floor lay Muller, a pool of blood oozing from his side. A few meters away lay the gaunt zebra-striped uniform of a camp inmate. The right arm was outstretched, grasping at the silenced pistol that Simon had given him only a few minutes before. It seemed like days ago now.

Well, whoever he was, he'd always owe him a huge debt of gratitude. He must have followed him here, just in case…

There was no time to lose. Simon limped back as fast as he could and helped Hartmann up on his feet.

'… never really trusted her, you know. That's why I kept a pistol taped to the underside of my desk - just in case there was trouble.' Hartmann grimaced.

'Can you walk?'

'Yes…just about,' His friend gasped. 'What's all this hurry?'

'This factory's about to go up big time, and we've got to get out of here before we go up with it.' Simon eased his friend's arm over his shoulder and got him moving. They staggered out, moving slowly towards the exit. He glanced at his watch. 1420. The factory gates were no more than three minutes away at a brisk walk, but Simon knew they'd never make it at this speed. His friend was moving far too slowly. Just then he spotted a trolley by the outer door of the suite. Someone had probably been using it to load files and distribute them wherever they were needed. He lost no time.

Hartmann was bundled onto it in a flash, despite his protests. Simon swung the trolley around, out through the doorway and into Tunnel A, and pushed it as fast as he could. They careered down the tunnel, dodging mounds of equipment and sections of rockets awaiting assembly. Simon ignored the pain in his sides. His lungs were beginning to burn but that would be nothing if they were caught in side when the plastic explosive went off. The concussion and shock wave would smear their bodies flat in an instant, like jam spread thinly on a piece of bread.

The mouth of the tunnel grew nearer. A great mass of figures in pyjama suits was blocking the way. They were pushing forward, trying to get out, but something was stopping them. Suddenly there were shouts, followed by a few blasts of automatic weapons, and then silence.

With almost the last of his strength Simon pulled the trolley to a halt. He grabbed the pistol from Hartmann's hand, fired two shots into the ceiling and pressed forward. The crowd parted instantaneously, like Moses commanding the Red Sea.

A squad of guards was outside the main doors, facing inwards and blocking the exit, their weapons leveled at the mob. Half a dozen slave labourers lay on the ground, covered in blood, dying if not already dead. Simon pushed the trolley in front of him and halted in front of the guards. The sound of battle was near, only a kilometer away. The SS men gaped at him in amazement.

'There's no time to lose! The factory's going to blow up any second now. Enemy agents have planted a bomb. They nearly killed the CO.' He pointed at Hartmann's bloodied and bruised body.

'What about this lot?' One of them pointed at the inmates. 'We're under orders to shoot them all in case of sabotage.'

Hartmann sat up and croaked. 'New orders, Ludwig. I'm still your commanding officer - now get your men out of here on the double, and go help your comrades. You heard the Sturmbannführer. There's a -'.

A deep *boom* rumbled behind them, followed almost instantaneously by several more explosions. The ground shook. 'Run!' Simon screamed, pushing his friend away and to one side of the entrance.

A roaring blast shook the side of the hill, followed by an enormous shock wave that slammed forwards and outwards, scattering both guards and prisoners like leaves in a storm. The pressure lifted the two of them off their feet, threw them forward, and then thumped them into the ground.

A huge eruption of dirt and dust roared out of the tunnel entrance. High above them a black cloud poured high into the skies. The hillside was covered in smashed trees and debris where the explosions had blown upwards, toppling the camouflaged ventilation stacks and air vents and scattering them far and wide. The ground heaved again as several more blasts issued from deep inside the hill, and then all was quiet. Even the sounds of fighting had stopped – for the moment.

Simon rolled over and turned to where his friend lay. One eye opened and looked at him. The battered face twisted into a tired grin. 'That was cutting it a bit *too* bloody fine, if you ask me...What did you do? Get the wrong fuse? Or were you too busy lying down on the job again?'

'I'll tell you later. As for lying down on the job- '. Simon glanced around. Most of the inmates were beginning to stir. Others lay unmoving, still concussed – or possibly worse. There was nothing he could do for them now. A few guards were groggily getting to their feet and staggering off, following the rail tracks away south. 'Come on. Right now, we've got to get out of here.'

He rose wearily to his feet, every muscle in his body protesting. In a moment he helped Hartmann up on his feet, and propping each other up they limped away, ignoring the scenes around them. Simon led them west, and slightly north – well away from what was left of the factory. The going was slow. Several times they had to stop and pick an easier way, or scramble slowly over felled trees and around large craters. The sounds of gunfire slowly eased off behind them. After about an hour and a half they reached the edge of the tree line.

'I need a break,' Hartmann gasped. Simon helped him sit down, easing him against the shelter of a large oak. It was getting cooler. He slipped off his greatcoat and wrapped it around his friend's bruised chest and shoulders.

'Thanks...You got here just in time. That bastard from RSHA took me by surprise. Barbara was in on it, no doubt – stupid bitch. She must have been communicating with Berlin all the time.' Hartmann paused to get his breath. 'They were trying to find out about you – where you'd been, who you were communicating with...I think they must have drawn a blank at the Panzer school and then tried here. Nice work with that bomb. Where did you plant it?'

'In the fuel stores, next to the Bio-weapon labs. Bit of a stupid place to store such dangerous chemicals, don't you think?' Simon grinned. It was just as well. There would be little if anything left inside from an explosion in such a confined space.'

Hartmann grunted. 'Nothing to do with me. That little shit Ohlendorff wanted to make sure that anything explosive was hidden deep in the hillside – just in case the Allies got lucky, found out the factory's location and slipped a bomb inside. Highly unlikely, a chance in a million – but not worth the risk.' He stretched his aching arms. 'Well, at least your timing was spot on. Another day or two and then all the bio-weapon warheads would have been ready to fly. I still can't believe that Himmler would have been mad enough, and desperate enough, to use them.'

'Well, at least my boss was convinced. That's why he sent me here.'

'So, who is he – that Schellenberg character, the one who signed the orders confirming your appointment?'

'Yes. A man with a conscience, unlike so many who fought for Germany. I was never really sure of where his loyalties lay, but he came good in the end. Almost as brave as Admiral Canaris, the real brains behind the fight against Hitler.' Simon paused for a moment. 'I think Canaris will rest easy now.'

'What happened at Flossenberg?'

Simon looked away. In all the excitement he'd almost forgotten the pain. 'I was too late,' he said quietly. 'Canaris was already dead. My father died during the breakout.'

Hartmann was silent for a few minutes. He bowed his head. 'I'm sorry, Max. You've lost so much...Your wife, now your father. I hope those Nazi bastards get everything they deserve.'

'They will, Harald. I'm sure of that. And here's something to help cheer you up – Elke and the girls should be safe. I sent an agent to get them away from Magdeburg and bring them west. His instructions are to surrender them into Allied custody. They'll be safe there – hopefully you should see them soon.'

Hartmann breathed a huge sigh of relief. 'Thank you, my friend. I've been worried about their safety for some time. I long suspected that Himmler kept watch on them, as leverage – to make sure I did my job the way he wanted it done. How did you know?'

'My boss again. Somehow he got to know about how factory security was organized. That included keeping an eye on the men in charge, - a veiled threat against their families would keep them sweet. He passed the details on to me. My *other* boss helped out as well.'

'Other boss? I don't understand.'

Simon smiled. 'I've been working for British Counter-intelligence for some time now.'

Hartmann's jaw dropped – and not without some discomfort. He looked bewildered. 'I don't understand...'

'I'll tell you all in due course. Right now, we have other things to worry about. Look over there.' Simon pointed to the fields beyond the trees. A skirmish line of troops was moving closer, in their direction. 'They're either American or British, I think. They should be here in five minutes or so. I think we'd better move away from the tree line so that they can see we're alone.'

His friend instantly looked worried. 'And what happens when they find out I was commandant of that factory? They'll shoot me out of hand.'

'I don't think so, Harald. I have a favour or two that the head of MI6 owes me. I'll testify on your behalf. The war's over for us.' He grinned. 'Come on, let's go and meet our new friends.'

He hoisted Hartmann up to his feet. Together they moved slowly towards the open fields.

❖

Postscript

Much of this novel is based on historical fact. The action at Korsun, the diverted train into Auschwitz, Canaris' actions against the Nazis, Kurt Gerstein's testimony, the death of Michael Wittman, the plot against Hitler, the rocket factory at Nordhausen, to name but a few – all of these are documented historical fact, and are well-known to students of military history. Equally so are the divisions amongst the Allies, the personalities and foibles of their senior political and military figures, and the bitter controversies that shaped Allied strategy from 1942 to the end of the war. Both the Germans and Japanese, as well as the Soviet Union, experimented in bacteriological warfare, as did the Allies. The only known use of these agents was during the German offensive in Southern Russia in the summer of 1942.

The German lead in rocketry, far in advance of anything the British and Americans had achieved, was the basis of the post-war race between Russia and America that led to Neil Armstrong setting down on the surface of the Moon in July 1969. The Germans had plans for further development of the V2 rocket program that *did* include a long distance ballistic missile, code-named 'Amerika'. It never flew, as far as we know.

Naturally, the main characters in this story are fictional, with the exception of the historical figures of Menzies, Schellenberg and Canaris, amongst many others. The purpose of this novel was to try my hand at writing a book, and, perhaps along the way, help bring back to the minds of my readers (if I am lucky enough to have this novel published) remembrance of the sacrifices and heroism of our predecessors, who fought for freedom and shaped the world we live in today.

Someone once said that if we do not learn the lessons that history has taught us, then we are bound to repeat the mistakes of our forefathers. I would like to add to that the sure fact that the victors always write the history. These days we hear far too little about those who detested the evils of Nazism in Germany. Men like Admiral Canaris have not received the accolades and widespread recognition that they are overwhelmingly due. It is to the memory of men and women like him that this novel is dedicated.

The Sea Glass Beach

TINA PRITCHARD

This book is dedicated to the mothers and children who entered and exited through the portals of Sean Ross Abbey and similar Irish Institutions.

Not all were survivors.

"Your battles inspired me - not the obvious material battles but those that were fought and won behind your forehead."

James Joyce

Prologue

S oon it would all be over and the worry and upset would disappear. The child would be gone to a new home and life would return to normal. By re-doubling her efforts and working hard, the goals and ambitions she had before could still be accomplished. There would be no cloying attachment, no romantic imaginings. It had been unfortunate. A mistake, that was all. Everyone was allowed one big mistake in their lives and already plans were in place to deal with the problem. Others who found themselves in the same predicament weren't so fortunate. Without family to support you, it was a dire situation. As long as she did what was expected, it would be as though it had never happened.

As the child flexed, she could see the curved outline of miniature feet and feel the insistent kicks against the tight drum of her swollen belly. '*Hush now,*' she would murmur, '*you can't run your way out of there.*'

If she sang a particular song, the child quietened, soothed by the ebb and flow of the ancient rhythms.

'*A Róisín ná bíodh brón ort fé'r éirigh dhuit.*'

'Little Rose, have no sorrow for all that hath behapped thee.'

A fierce protectiveness grew within her as each month

passed and with it came a growing realisation. This child, nourished in flesh and bone, was linked to her not only by blood, but by love.

It was a girl, perfect in every way, with hair the colour of a raven's wing and a mouth the delicate blush pink of a rosebud. It was customary for the nuns to give children born at the Home a religious name, but it was not for them to decide. It was her child and she was keeping her. *'Roisin Dubh,'* she whispered, 'yo*u are my little dark rose and I will love you and keep you safe for as long as I live. This is my promise to you'*.

Chapter One

Theresa often thought what a privilege it was to have such a precious creature entrusted into her care. She was proud of her girl. The joy she felt at her progress more than made up for the dark days of doubt and uncertainty. Roisin's enthusiasm was infectious. She rushed headlong into each new experience as though it was a great adventure. Theresa could hardly keep up with her. At nine months old she was up, wobbling on her feet and soon after she was walking, or more accurately running. Before she was two she was speaking in sentences and by three years old she was reading books on her own. She revelled in learning new words and phrases and her thirst for knowledge seemed unquenchable.

She was tall for her age and long-limbed. A child at one with nature, she loved to kick off her shoes and run barefoot. A joyous free spirit, she wanted to be outside in the fresh air, whatever the weather. Theresa encouraged her independence, proud of her exuberance, and zest for life. The joy the girl found in even the simplest of things made her heart soar.

On a day she overheard the local gossips refer to Roisin as 'odd' she was wounded to her core. Not wanting to give them anything else to talk about, she took extra care to show she was a capable mother. She brushed her daughter's thick glossy hair into submission, only to look on in exasperation as it escaped in waving tendrils around her delicate features. Each morning she made sure Roisin left for school as neat as a new pin, but it was a losing battle. By lunchtime her neatly ironed school clothes hung loose and shapeless. Exasperated, her teachers became weary of reminding Roisin to straighten her tie and waist sash and place her feet back into the black patent shoes she discarded beneath her desk.

When Theresa found the letter from the convent, crumpled at the bottom of Roisin's school satchel, her heart slowed, then skipped a beat. Smoothing the envelope, she paused, then took a deep breath before opening it. The sheet of snow-white paper had the school crest displayed in the top corner. The contents she knew would have been typed by the secretary, but the signature at the bottom was unmistakable. It was the spidery scrawl of the school Principal, Sister Agnes Sophia. Not a request, this was a summons. Theresa was to attend a meeting, two days hence, to discuss Roisin's educational future at the school.

Theresa had no idea what those words meant, but felt the familiar sense of unease associated with any contact from the school. She couldn't deny the nuns had helped her a great deal after Roisin's birth. That is once they had realised she was not going to change her mind about the adoption, despite the pressure they exerted on her to do so. They conceded, knowing Theresa would tackle the exacting task of bringing up a child on her own with dedication and fortitude. This they gleaned from their own snobbery and judgemental attitudes. Theresa, they concluded, was a 'good girl' who had been hapless. She was a sinner of course, but a better class of one, even if she was headstrong.

Discussing it amongst themselves, they considered it a great shame they hadn't been able to change her mind. The child would have been an excellent candidate for adoption, especially as the father was an architect. Ultimately, they had to concede defeat in the matter. Theresa was adamant she was keeping the child and they grudgingly accepted her decision, even though the loss of a few hundred pounds was galling. They had already lined up an American actress who was willing to pay extra money to adopt a child from what was considered a 'good background'.

'We have a supervisory job for you in the laundry with a small stipend attached,' Sister Philomena told her. 'The child will stay in the nursery and you will visit at specified times during the day for feeding.'

Having recovered from a long and difficult labour, Theresa had few choices available to her. She took on the role willingly, glad of the small wage they offered for her services. This along with her food and lodgings and a nursery place for Roisin was a boon in those difficult, early days.

The women in her charge came from all over the country. Often poor and casualties of a failed relationship, many were little more than children themselves. A few were petty thieves or victims of rape or incest. Those suffering from mental illness garnered no sympathy. If you got yourself pregnant it was your own fault. Rarely was the man involved singled out for blame, even if he had beaten the woman senseless. It was invariably the woman and not the man who suffered most in the fallout from such unions. In the eyes of the nuns they were branded 'fallen women with loose morals'. Some of the sisters could be harsh disciplinarians, selecting the most vulnerable to punish for even the most minor wrongdoing. Theresa's protestations were ignored. She swallowed her anger, in no position to challenge the bullying. What she could do was offer soothing words and a cup of tea and a chocolate biscuit in her little room next to the laundry.

It was a harsh regime. The hours were long in the sweltering humidity of the laundry and the work was exhausting. With few options available to the women, there was at least the security of having a roof over your head and food on the table. The small minority who chose to run away, invariably found life outside even more difficult. Soon they returned, exhausted and chastened, grateful to be accepted back into the fold.

For those who had come from a life of chaos, the routine was beneficial, with Theresa providing a calm and reassuring presence. For many it was the first time in their lives they had a degree of structure and stability. The nuns considered Theresa trustworthy and she was mostly left to her own devices, managing the workload and the books with minimal supervision.

When she told them she was leaving, the nuns were surprised and sorry to see her go. Surprised because they couldn't imagine Thersa finding a better arrangement and sorry because they knew how difficult it would be to replace her. The skills she had acquired from working in the laundry were going to be put to good use. She wanted to be at home as much as possible with Roisin and setting up her own sewing and laundry business seemed the obvious answer. When a tiny cottage on the outskirts of the town became available to rent, she and Roisin moved in. Once Roisin had started school, the nuns took it upon themselves to source a small educational endowment to help with uniforms and school books. It was a great help and Theresa was grateful to them for their support.

When she was under their care, the nuns made sure Theresa brought her child up in the Catholic faith. At first, she felt under obligation to comply, dependent as she was on their generosity. Over the years, as she observed at close quarters the stranglehold the church exerted on women and their lives, her faith waned and she and Roisin stopped going to church. Could this be the reason Sister Agnes wanted to see her now? Or was it that Roisin had been seeking answers to awkward questions again and had upset one of her teachers? *That was probably it*, Theresa told herself, *they would be making a mountain out of a molehill as usual.*

Keeping her increasing dissatisfaction with the church from her daughter hadn't been easy. The girl was intelligent and soon came to her own conclusions on religion. Theresa had always tried to answer Roisin's questions honestly. Her teachers, on the other hand, had much less patience when Roisin quizzed them about weightier issues. Unaccustomed to having their authority challenged by a child they saw as 'difficult', they made it known there was no room for an enquiring mind. One ageing nun lost patience and took a bamboo cane to Roisin's knuckles. She retired soon afterwards following Theresa's indignant complaint to Sister Agnes.

In place of a rap across the knuckles, the nuns resorted to mockery to silence Roisin. 'Well now, we have an expert here on God and science. Perhaps she should be taking the class,' Sister Mary Clare said, her mouth twisted in scorn.

Behind her back, the other pupils sniggered into their hands.

'My mammy says she's a heathen,' one of the younger girls announced in the playground one day. 'Heathen, heathen,' the chant went up, until one of the kinder nuns overheard and put a stop to it.

This nun came to regret her intervention when Roisin sought a satisfactory explanation as to the origin and meaning of the word 'heathen'. She never really cared what others thought or said about her, even when she was called a 'bastard' for not having a father like the other girls. She shrugged off their jibes and they soon lost interest. They were 'silly eejits', Roisin concluded. As for her, all she wanted to do was learn new things and have her questions answered. There was nothing wrong with that, was there?

A brisk wind at her back propelled Theresa along the main road leading to the convent. It was a gloomy day with the threat of rain and her apprehension grew with every step she took. She felt impatient at the summons.

She had a busy few days ahead of her and time was precious. There was mending to do and a pile of shirts, immaculately clean and starched, were ready for an iron. In addition, two more wash loads awaited her attention. She was in no mood to hear any gripes about Roisin's behaviour. Hopefully, she would only have to endure a lecture. A promise on her part to have a word with Roisin would be the end of it she hoped, for a while at least.

At the entrance to the large, imposing building she stood for a few moments composing herself, before climbing the worn, stone steps. The brown varnished door, peeling in places, was still giving off the oily, baked-on odour she remembered so well. Pressing the circular, brass bell, she waited for the housekeeper to let her in. Mrs Donovan, in her seventies and small and plump with red-veined cheeks, hadn't aged at all. She still looked the same as when she had answered the door to Theresa almost sixteen years ago. Theresa had stood on the exact same spot, heavily pregnant and quaking in her boots at the thought of what was to come. Mrs Donovan's hair was scraped back into a tight bun, just as it had been on that cool, late summer's day. Her style of dress hadn't changed much either. Black serge with an immaculate white, lace collar.

Once Theresa had stepped into the sunless hallway, still painted a bilious shade of pea-green, Mrs Donovan led her to one of the wooden chairs lined up outside Sister Agnes's office.

'And how are you keeping Theresa? Grand, grand, I'm glad to hear it.' Mrs Donovan had bustled away before Theresa had time to utter a reply. 'Sister will summon you when she's ready,' she called back over her shoulder as she disappeared into the gloom at the end of the long corridor.

Theresa had made an effort to appear presentable for the meeting. She had swept her hair up into a French pleat, and was wearing what her mother always referred to as a 'costume'. A slim fitting, worsted suit with a hip length jacket and over the knee skirt. Under the jacket she wore a crisp, white blouse and on her feet were her sensible black, lace-up shoes. Nerves were getting the better of her as she waited, conscious of the spindles of the chair digging into the small of her back. To distract herself she examined her reddened fingers. Having her hands constantly in water had taken its toll. They had coarsened and were the hands of a washerwoman, when once they had been smooth and unblemished.

Biting her lip, she struggled to hold back the tears as the memories came flooding back. It occurred to her how different her life could have been. So many what if's...! At that moment, interrupting her reverie, the heavy wood-panelled door opened with a creak and Sister Agnes beckoned her into her office with a wave of her hand.

'Come, come.'

Sister Agnes must have been close to eighty. Tall and bony, she stooped slightly as she made her way to her chair. This was situated behind a walnut desk, buffed to a lustrous gleam. Theresa could smell the lavender polish Mrs Donovan used to banish any particles of dust having the temerity to land on a surface within her sight.

Sister Agnes, wearing her black habit and a starched white bib, billowing out from under her chin, winced as she lowered herself onto the seat. Her look, as always, was stern and her figure imposing.

The room was dim, despite the open slats of the wooden blinds. Dust motes danced in the solitary shaft of sunlight piercing the gloom. Positioned in front of the high window overlooking the gardens, a circular table held a vase of rust-coloured chrysanthemums. Theresa could smell their earthy scent as she made her way to the waiting chair, her shoes squeaking on the highly polished floor. The chair, positioned in front of the desk, was a close, if somewhat unsteadier cousin to the one in the corridor. As she sat down, it moved alarmingly beneath her and she felt a sudden urge to stand up and flee. Instead, she fixed her gaze on the wall to the rear of the room lined with dog-eared, leather-bound books and Catholic periodicals. With her mouth dry and her breathing shallow, she waited for Sister Agnes to speak.

'Theresa, it's good to see you looking so well.'

Sister Agnes was peering at her intently and Theresa held her breath in expectation. She knew it was not her health the nun had brought her here to talk about. On the desk in front of the old nun, lay a sheaf of papers. As she spoke, Sister Agnes shuffled them, scanning their contents for reference.

'I'm not going to beat about the bush Theresa. The fact of the matter is, there is some concern with regard to Roisin's progress in school. I have spoken to Sister Mary Clare and Father Kelly, and they concur. Roisin is a bright and knowledgeable girl, but she spends too little time studying the subjects necessary to obtain a good education. I'm afraid she is too bold and forthright in her views and whilst I'm confident there is no real wickedness in her, she is a bad influence, especially on the younger ones.'

So far so predictable, Theresa thought, as Sister Agnes repositioned herself and adjusted a small cushion at her back.

Clearing her throat, the nun continued. 'They think it's hilarious, some of the things she comes out with. She challenges Father Kelly on religious teachings and Catechism and argues with Sister Mary Clare on scientific explanations. Can you believe it?'

Theresa could. Keeping her counsel, she looked over Sister Agnes' shoulder. Through a gap in the shutters she could see a crocodile of women, all dressed in identical brown dresses and white pinafores. They were crossing the path bisecting the greensward of undulating lawn. Surreptitiously she pulled back her sleeve and glanced down at her watch.

It's lunchtime, she thought and to her surprise felt a sharp pang of nostalgia. She realised although Roisin was always her main focus, she missed the bustle of the laundry and the companionship it offered.

Sister Agnes was still droning on. Theresa felt her temples start to throb and turned her attention back to what was being said. Pasting on a fake smile, she hoped it was an appropriate response.

'I also have to mention the running,' Sister Agnes was saying, sighing in exasperation, 'which again is a source of great amusement to the other scholars. If running was a subject that would get her an education and a career, I would be all for it. However it isn't, and the sight of Roisin in her bare feet, sprinting around the school grounds at lunchtime, is unsettling and disruptive. She is a credit to you in many ways Theresa, but I'm afraid she lacks focus and is too much of a free spirit.'

Pausing for breath, Sister Agnes licked her top lip where a beading of sweat had formed. 'After careful consideration, we have reached a decision. Roisin cannot continue to attend this school after her birthday in October.'

Theresa was conscious the pounding in her head was intensifying. She knew she was expected to respond, but her brain was racing and she couldn't rein in her thoughts. Was Sister Agnes really telling her that Roisin, the brightest in her class, was going to be prevented from continuing with her education? Why and how, had the powers-that-be come to such a decision? Roisin was an exceptional scholar and had always achieved top marks in all subjects. Excelling in Geography and Science subjects, her knowledge of the natural world was way beyond her years. It didn't make sense.

As she struggled to comprehend what was being said, the heat rose in her face. She knew if she tried to stand her legs would not support her.

How on earth could they have reached the conclusion there was no place at the school for her passionate, gifted daughter? Roisin loved studying, even the subjects she had less interest in. All this had nothing to do with Roisin's ability, Theresa surmised. This was their way of trying to control her. To subdue her spirit and crush the bones of her. The dishonesty of it all made Theresa's head spin.

An irritating buzz refused to clear with a shake of her head. There it was again. The sound she realised was emanating from Sister Agnes's lips. As the meaning of the words crystallised, Theresa felt the acid burn of bile rise in her throat.

'As I know you so well, I have managed to pull some strings,' Sister Agnes was saying, looking as though poised to pull a rabbit out of a hat. 'You'll be pleased to hear there is a place at the laundry for Roisin. She can start at the end of October. Now, isn't that good news? The discipline will be good for her and if we can get her familiar with the paperwork, she can earn a little money to help you out too.'

Theresa felt a flare of anger and her cheeks flushed red. *Had this woman any concept of what she was saying? Did she know her daughter at all?*

It seemed, with little forethought, she was ready to deprive her child of the opportunities an education would afford her. It was a ridiculous proposition. Everyone knew how much Roisin hated being confined. Putting her to work in the laundry would be akin to keeping a wild bird in a cage.

Over my dead body Theresa thought, outraged by the idea. *They want to sap the life and spirit out of her and I am not having it. Whatever the consequences.*

She stood, knees knocking and pushed back the chair. It made a sharp scraping sound against the wooden boards. Theresa didn't care. Her legs felt insubstantial, as though turned to jelly, but inside her anger had become white-hot.

Head held high, she paused to take a deep breath. 'I

can't and won't agree to your offer,' Theresa said, holding back tears of rage, 'but I do ask one thing of you. I don't want it mentioned by anyone at the school. I should be the one to tell her when I feel the time is right.'

Her composure regained, she strode from the room, down the corridor and out through the front door, slamming it with such force behind her, the windows rattled.

If Theresa had chanced to look back, she would have gained some satisfaction from seeing Sister Agnes' demeanour.

The nun, having observed Theresa's indignant retreat, had pushed back her own chair and was attempting to stand. Her knuckles, gnarled with age, were gripping the edge of her desk. She appeared diminished and unsecured, as though steadying herself in a gale. On her wizened face was a look of complete bewilderment. Theresa had always been so respectful and compliant. What on earth was she thinking, stomping out in such high dudgeon?

As far as Sister Agnes was concerned, the recommendations were in everyone's interest, including Roisin's. Theresa should be grateful. It was a sorry state of affairs when someone in her position could afford to turn her nose up at such a well-thought out offer. The notion her proposal, rejected in such a cavalier manner, might have far-reaching consequences escaped Sister Agnes completely.

She wasn't to know she would be the catalyst for momentous change.

Had she had one iota of awareness of her role in altering the course of direction of not one, but two lives, she likely would have remained untroubled. It would be out of her hands and in the remit of the Lord. *What will be will be,* as she was so fond of saying, ad nauseam.

Chapter Two

For Roisin, life continued at school as usual. She knew nothing of the heartbreak suffered by her mother and the imminent end to her schooling. Today was just like any other and as always it was a relief to escape the confines of the classroom. She ran barefoot from where the bus dropped her at the top of the lane, her shoes wedged into her satchel. The cottage she called home was a whitewashed one story building with a turf roof and a brick chimney stack. There were only two rooms. One she shared with her mother was the bedroom. The other, their living room, also served as a kitchen. Above the gleaming, cast-iron range, hung a slatted wooden rail with a pulley. Here the laundry was put to dry when the weather was inclement.

To the rear of the cottage in a tiny patch of garden, was an outhouse covered by a rusty, corrugated roof that let in the rain. This housed the earth closet. It still gave Roisin nightmares if she had to use it at night. You always had to take a lighted candle with you so you could see to remove the snails before you sat down to do your business. There was always a slimy trail, criss-crossing the wooden surface surrounding the open drop-hole.

It was in the outhouse Theresa did all the laundry, using a dolly tub and a washboard to scrub everything clean. The washing was then fed through the rollers of a mangle, left behind by the previous occupant of the cottage. Roisin loved to drop the little blue Reckitt's blocks, encased in muslin, into the hot, soapy water. She would watch as the clean washing emerged as if by magic, from the murky depths of the sudsy water.

Dropping her satchel to the ground, Roisin shooed away a couple of inquisitive chickens, then paused to look in through the half-open window. She was about to shout her customary '*Yoo hoo*' when she caught sight of her mother, who was folding piles of freshly dried laundry. Roisin felt a pang of guilt at how exhausted she looked. Theresa worked so hard to feed and clothe them and keep a roof over their heads and all she contributed was an extra burden of worry. She vowed she would try harder to keep out of trouble. Roisin knew she had a habit of annoying some of her teachers.

Maybe I should stop questioning so much of what I'm told, she said to herself. *Perhaps I'll get a little job to help bring in some extra money?* She considered the options and decided that a paper round would fit in best with her school hours.

A change in the weather meant there had been showers all day and drying had to take place indoors. Today the cottage was even steamier than usual.

Roisin longed to be outside, breathing in the clear air. Before she could escape, she had her homework to do.

She would then help her mother wrap the clean laundry in brown paper, ready for delivery the next morning. Only when her chores were completed was she free to go.

Summer was already in retreat and the days were growing shorter. The leaves were starting to turn golden along their edges and the hedgerows, now laden with berries and fruits, had become a larder for the birds. Darting in and out of the branches, their beaks were full with their end of day forage. Roisin loved the changing seasons, but autumn, the season of her birth, was her favourite. Taking a deep breath, she inhaled the musky odour of vegetation mingled with the faint woodiness of burning peat.

Wriggling her bare toes in anticipation, she flexed each of them in turn before rising up onto the balls of her feet. If she happened to run past you, you would think you had witnessed an apparition. Her feet barely made contact with the ground and her hair, loosened from the weight of its single, heavy plait, streamed like a black waterfall behind her. Running was as natural to her as breathing. Her body felt light and insubstantial as she flew over the rutted path taking her in the direction of the woods. Her destination was Molly's Glade, a magical place avoided by the most superstitious who believed it haunted. Myths and legends abounded in this rural community, but the fate of Molly was a true, but sorry tale. Young and pregnant she was spurned by her lover. In despair, she committed a mortal sin. Taking her own life by hanging herself from an ancient oak tree.

Roisin ran, untroubled by the possibility of ghosts. Rustling through the canopy of overhanging trees, the night air sighed, caressing her face. She was like a woodland creature, her senses attuned to the slightest movement. Beneath her feet was a mysterious world; a sponge-like carpet of decaying material. Layer upon layer of dead leaves, bark and twigs had been laid down over millennia. It fascinated her to think of an underground community, beavering away in the peaty, crumb-like humus, busily rejuvenating and nourishing the earth.

The trees, weighted with their end of year abundance, drooped to enfold her. High above, the sky darkened and a red-tinged moon reached its zenith as she approached the stream, fed by the Slieve Mish mountain range. With the arrival of winter rains, it would turn into a cauldron of swirling, frothing water, burying the moss-covered stepping stones. With no crossing point, the stream was impassable until the water levels receded.

The water level this evening was low as it bubbled over the ancient boulders. From her nature books Roisin knew these rocks were periglacial deposits, left behind after the ice age over 10,000 years ago. The glacial sheets had incised the landscape and carved out the deep, U-shaped valleys so characteristic of the area. Once they retreated, the deposits trapped in the ice were released, including the rocks left lying on the stream bed.

Pausing to rest on the grassy bank, she dipped a foot into the icy, crystal-clear water. High in the branches of a solitary Scots pine, she heard the churr of a nightjar, the rare, ghostly sound rising and falling in the air and echoing through the trees. As the water trickled over her toes, she remembered her mother's warnings. Theresa was forever telling her she had one pair of feet and they had to last her a lifetime. Being barefoot, she warned, meant possible injury from sharp stones, discarded broken bottles or pieces of metal. With her feet cut to ribbons there would be no more running. '*Then what would you do, Macushla*?' she would say.

Occupying Roisin's thoughts this evening were less mundane matters. She was looking forward to the time of bounty soon to come. Then she would arrive home with her pockets full of nature's gifts. These would be placed on her night stand: alder cones, ash keys, beech nuts, polished conkers and acorns that turned from bright green to brown before separating from their cupules. Toys were of little interest. Her playthings were the treasures provided by the natural world.

As the days grew shorter, Theresa would draw the curtains and light the oil lamp. Sitting together at the scrubbed table, Roisin would study the colour plates in her book of native trees and birds as her mother caught up with her sewing. She was aware she was different, having never encountered anyone who liked the same things as her. The girls at school weren't disagreeable, but they did treat her as a novelty. They thought her amusing, especially when she got up the noses of the teachers or Father Kelly. She didn't really mind being the centre of attention, as long as it was on her terms. She had little in common with the other girls and it wasn't of real concern to her. She preferred to observe and listen.

The girls seemed exotic, like the brightly coloured birds in her encyclopaedia. Most had reached puberty and unlike Roisin, had sprouted breasts seemingly overnight. Much of their time, in the playground they spent huddled together, their conversations about boys they had encountered, or the music they were listening to on the radio, and most importantly of all, what was the height of fashion.

The chattering she overheard involving boys was intriguing and Roisin would have liked to know more. She thought about asking her mother, but decided against it. Theresa was open-minded and no prude, but what the girls talked about Roisin kept to herself. She sensed her mother would be shocked and concerned.

Roisin had heard enough to know that the topic of boys, and what they were capable of, seemed frequently to lead to trouble further down the line.

Chapter Three

As the weeks passed, Theresa felt she was on borrowed time. It was with increasing anxiety she debated what course of action she should take. Roisin needed to be told she wouldn't be returning to school after her birthday, but what then? Finishing her chores early, she found herself at a loose end and to distract herself she took the bus into the town. It was Friday morning and Waterbridge was bustling with shoppers. She was the last passenger to alight and with a cheery nod and a '*Bye for now*' in her direction, the driver got up to shut the door before turning the vehicle around in preparation for the return journey.

The sun was struggling to give out any warmth and a slight breeze tinged with cold signalled the change from one season to another. Theresa shivered, wishing she had brought an overcoat as protection against the chill. People around her were busying themselves with their daily chores and the grocery store, once owned by her parents, had a steady stream of customers. She guessed at their purchases; anything from cooked ham or rashers of bacon, loose tea or sugar, freshly baked soda bread or delicious cakes delivered earlier by the baker.

The cold was getting into her bones and her feet were starting to go numb. She had a few items of shopping to collect before she had to return to tackle the stack of sewing waiting for her. Money was always tight and Roisin needed a new winter coat. Watching the pennies, Theresa contented herself with window shopping. Pausing at the material shop window, she wondered if there was anyone who could lend her a sewing machine? She could then buy a few yards of wool fabric and have a go at making the coat herself. It wasn't something she had tackled before, but she was a skilled sewer. If she bought a pattern and the fabric it would save her a small fortune.

The bus was not due for another ten minutes and she decided she would surprise Roisin with some ham for her tea. An extra sixpence found in the lining of her purse meant she could buy a cream cake and a quarter of her favourite sweets as a treat.

She crossed the road and was about to go into the store when out of the corner of her eye she saw a familiar figure coming out of the offices of Brown and Fitzpatrick, Solicitors. Her heart lurched at the sight. It was Greg Brown. He was carrying a bit of extra weight, but it was unmistakably him. He had the same shock of black hair, although a pair of spectacles perched across his broad nose made him look older and more distinguished.

Even though it was too far away for her to see his eyes, Theresa knew they were the same smoky grey colour as her daughter's. Not wanting to be seen, she lowered her head and dashed into the shop. Her response to the friendly banter from Mr and Mrs Hennessey, the new owners, was uncharacteristically curt. With shaking fingers, she handed over the money for her purchases, managing a flustered '*See ya* ', and clutching her packages to her chest, she stepped out of the shop.

With Greg rarely visiting from his home in England, either by luck or good judgement, she had seen him only a handful of times over the years, and then it was at a distance. It suited her not to have any involvement with him. As far as Theresa was concerned, he and his family had made it very clear where they stood. She and Roisin were of no consequence to them. Even Mr Brown the elder barely acknowledged her in passing, and then only to exchange a cursory nod. He never once enquired after his granddaughter. Following the death of his wife, he became withdrawn and seemed a sad and lonely figure.

To her annoyance she saw Greg was still very much in evidence. He was standing on the street corner and looking down the road, as though waiting for someone.

Retreating back to the safety of the shop doorway, Theresa found herself in a state of turmoil. So many of the emotions she had thought long buried were now resurfacing and she felt what? Angry? Sad? Intrigued? A madcap possibility occurred to her. What if she approached him? Spoke to him?

Hello Greg, how are you? Would you like to hear how your daughter is getting on? After all, it's been almost sixteen years. At least there would be some sense of gratification in watching him squirm.

The opportunity was snatched from her with the

appearance of a woman. She was waving to him and calling his name. From her accent, Theresa guessed she was English. She was wearing a striped Breton top and Capri pants which seemed unsuitable for the current weather conditions. At her neck was a knotted scarf. Her hair, too bright to be naturally blonde, was cropped into the gamine style favoured by Audrey Hepburn. Tanned and healthy looking and with the confident air of someone used to being adored and getting their own way, Theresa imagined she must be an actress.

A passing delivery boy stared hard at the woman and almost collided with another shopper. Theresa knew it wouldn't just be the men who would be showing an interest. The female population of the small town would be impressed by this exotic creature, envious of her 'style'. The look was one only seen on the cinema screen or on magazine covers unless you had money or generous relatives in England or America kind enough to send you parcels of fashionable clothing. Looking down at her own outfit, plain and dowdy in comparison, she blinked back rare tears of self pity.

The bus arrived and she knew she would have to catch it or wait for another half hour. Head down, she scooted across the road and boarded. Taking a seat giving her a good view of the pair, it was plain to see from their closeness they weren't just friends. She watched the woman stand on tiptoe to enable Greg to bend down to kiss the tip of her nose. Placing her arm in his, they walked back down the road together, before turning into a side street. *She probably has a car,* Theresa thought, as the bus pulled away with a jolt.

The whole episode had upset Theresa, although if asked, she would have been unable to say why.

Deep in thought, she walked down the lane leading to her home. Above her the trees formed a canopy, sheltering her from the brisk wind. For a moment she paused, listening to the rustle of leaves and the pure lilting trill of birdsong. Like Roisin, the natural world and the changing seasons delighted and entranced her, but with her daughter there was an intangible difference. It was as though Roisin had an enhanced level of awareness, intimately connecting her to the earth.

In contravention of any weather forecast, the girl could read the changing weather patterns. Observing the movements of animals, she knew the location of their hides. Captivated, she watched badgers and foxes at play in the woods, the animals seeming unconcerned by her presence. She was able to identify birds by sight and was fascinated by their migratory patterns, attuned to the restless excitement signalling their approaching departure.

My girl is not wild, she is not odd, she is exceptional and really quite remarkable, Theresa told herself. Still, she couldn't help but worry.

A rich seam of history and heritage contributed to who her daughter was. What she was at a loss to explain was why Roisin was so unlike other children, almost otherworldly, as some of the more superstitious in the town tried to claim. Theresa had laughed off the incident when an old widow woman, her head covered with a black shawl, peered into Roisin's pram. '*Siofra, Siofra,*' she cried, her quavering voice eliciting a wail of fear.

It's just superstitious nonsense, Theresa had thought at the time. Folk tales abounded in Ireland, some telling of Siofra, or changeling children left by the fairies in exchange for a human child. Theresa knew there was often a grain of truth at the core of these ancient stories. They served in earlier times to explain and make sense of a world that could be cruel and capricious. She didn't believe in mystical events, but was at a loss to interpret her child's seeming close affinity with the natural world. Any concerns she had she kept to herself. Roisin was different and loved being outside, where was the harm in that?

However hard she tried, she couldn't stop herself worrying, Her child was poised at the cusp of adulthood. In an uncertain future what would be the fate of her unconventional girl? She knew better than anyone how restrictive the state, the church and even her own community could be. Her fear was Roisin would be stifled and oppressed, or worse, treated as a misfit. Given the opportunity, they would mould her to suit their own restricting conventions. How could she protect her from their influence as she got older? This was a question Theresa had asked of herself on many occasions without ever seeming to find an answer. The meeting with Sister Agnes had only served to reinforce her concerns.

The idea came to her in an instant, as if borne on the autumn air. Stopping dead in her tracks, she clutched at her chest, a sharp pain in the area of her heart causing her to cry out in distress. She almost abandoned the idea before it came to fruition, as doubt and indecision vied with maternal instinct. What she was contemplating felt more like a betrayal than a solution. As she walked, she considered every possible scenario and found them all wanting. What other choice did she have?

By the time she reached home, she had formulated a plan. It was not one that gave her any consolation. Instead, she felt as though she had been fed through the wringer, emerging the other side flat and drained of emotion. It was a relief her work occupied her for the rest of the day. By the time Roisin arrived home from school, all was as it should be. Order was restored and the table, as always, was laid in readiness for their evening meal.

Chapter Four

F ull of chatter and pleased by the sight of the delicacies set out on the table, it didn't take Roisin long to realise something was amiss. Pale and preoccupied, Theresa looked as though she had been crying. Roisin felt a fluttering in her stomach. Was she ill or had she heard bad news?

'Are you all right Mammy? Do you have a headache? Is your back hurting?'

Wrapping her arms around Theresa's waist, she rested her head on her shoulder. What was troubling her? Her mother was always so strong and Roisin felt a prickle of fear.

'We'll have our meal first and then you need to do your homework,' Theresa said, her tone brisk and businesslike. 'After you check the chickens you can go for your run. When you come back I have something I want to show you.'

Intrigued, Roisin sat at the table and ate the ham and bread set out in front of her. She polished off the cake with a glass of milk and placed the sweets in a small bowl. Taking one, she savoured the syrupy, caramel sweetness whilst writing the essay she had been set for homework. Now and then she glanced over at her mother sitting opposite, trying to gauge her mood.

Roisin could not shake off an underlying feeling of unease. She was glad when she could put her books and pencils away and escape into the deepening twilight. The hens didn't appreciate being disturbed in their roost, but a search revealed half a dozen eggs, breakfast for the next few days.

Invigorated by her evening run, by the time she returned Roisin had convinced herself she was worrying unnecessarily. The old witch Sister Agnes had probably complained about her again. No doubt whatever the problem was, it would soon get resolved. Her mother would give her a talking-to and dole out a minor punishment. At worst, she might have to go and apologise to Sister Agnes and her teachers.

The doubts began to creep back in when she saw her mother was not attending to her usual pile of sewing. Instead, she was seated at the table, surrounded by a number of books and with a large atlas spread out in front of her.

'What are you reading Mammy? Can we look together?'

'Sit here next to me,' Theresa said, pulling a chair alongside her. 'Do you remember me telling you all about your Aunt Peggy? She was working as a nurse in England when she met a Canadian soldier, your Uncle Joe. When they married, they moved to the outskirts of a town called Halifax, over in Canada.'

Roisin nodded. She remembered how romantic their

story sounded and she liked it when her mother read her excerpts from Peggy's letters about the farm and the animals she and Joe kept. She wished she had paid more attention though, as she had a feeling whatever was brewing had something to do with her Aunt Peggy and Uncle Joe.

Theresa was pointing to a place on the map of Canada. It didn't appear in any way interesting to Roisin. It was just a small, irregular clump of land sticking out into the North Atlantic Ocean. It looked as though it had broken off from the main landmass and didn't even belong to the country at all.

'It's a really beautiful place called Nova Scotia,' Theresa said, picking up one of the travel books. 'I've been reading more about it. There are acres and acres of pine forests, and wild animals you can only imagine. Bears and wolves and turtles with shells the size of dinner plates. And, you don't have to go far to find sandy beaches and clear, blue seas.'

Turning the pages, she pointed out the pictures of wildlife and the white-painted clapboard houses with picket fences, surrounded by lush, green pastures.

Knowing she had caught her daughter's attention she held herself still, careful not to betray her own anxiety. Choosing her words carefully, she spoke of Peggy and Joe's home, so familiar to her from the descriptions in letters from her cousin.

Although Peggy was a few years older than her, the two of them were like sisters. Peggy's departure to England to train as a nurse was a wrench and Theresa felt bereft without her.

In the early days, Peggy came home at least twice a year. Once she and Joe had moved to Canada, contact was by letter. Peggy did send frequent parcels containing beautifully hand-sewn and knitted items of clothing for Roisin, but for Theresa these only served to emphasise the distance between them. With no close family around her and with little time and opportunity to make friends, Theresa missed her cousin terribly.

Peggy and Joe had chosen to distance themselves from the family drama surrounding Roisin's birth. They had tentatively put forward the possibility of adopting Roisin, but seeing how determined Theresa was to keep her child, they wholeheartedly supported her in her decision. Although they were now separated by thousands of miles, to Theresa, Peggy and Joe were family, the people she trusted most in the world.

'Roisin, you know you are my precious girl and I have loved and cared for you since you were born?' Theresa sang out the words in a voice she often used to make Roisin laugh. As she did so, she felt the familiar tightening in her chest returning. She thought back to the promise she made when she first held her child. The vow she made then was to keep her safe.

Swallowing hard, she blinked back hot tears. Roisin wasn't smiling. She kept her head down as though engrossed in the book in front of her. She felt confused by the undercurrent of sadness filling the room and unsure how to react.

'Look at me girl.'

The sharpness of her mother's tone startled Roisin. She didn't mind being told off when she deserved it, but this was different and she was finding it all overwhelming. What was her mammy going to tell her that was so important?

For once in her life she was mute, and any questions she might have had were dust in her throat.

'The truth of the matter is,' her mother said, keeping her eyes firmly fixed on a grease spot on the table in front of her, 'the time has come for you to make your own way in the world. You're almost sixteen and your prospects here in Waterbridge are limited.'

'But, I'm going to be doing my Leaving Certificate. I can't go anywhere until I've done that Mammy.'

Theresa didn't answer. From the set of her mother's shoulders Roisin could tell her mind was made up and there was no point in pleading with her.

The tiny flicker of hope she had been nursing began to fade as the reality of the situation crystallised. Her mother was sending her to live with her Aunt Peggy and Uncle Joe in Canada, it was obvious. In that moment she felt the world as she knew it start to tilt on its axis.

'I have given this a great deal of thought and it's for the best,' Theresa said. 'The winters are very harsh and Peggy has developed arthritis. She can't work on the farm any more. You'll be a great help to them'

At the sight of her daughter's face, crumpled and close to tears, Theresa felt like a Judas.

She reached for Roisin's hands and held them in her own. 'Just think how wonderful it will be to have all that space. You can be outside as much as you want and you will love looking after the animals.'

Roisin knew her mother had not come to such a decision

lightly. There must be a good reason if she felt the need to send her away. It would all become clear, she felt sure. It just wasn't the right time to ask.

'Will you come and see me there Mammy?' The trembling in Roisin's voice was the only indication of her emotional state.

Theresa knew if she tried to speak her resolve would crumble. Swallowing hard, she stood and moved to the back of Roisin's chair. Placing her arms around the girl's shoulders, she rested her head against hers, inhaling the scent of peat smoke and the earthy odour of outdoors.

'We'll see…,' was all she could utter.

With a heavy heart Theresa walked to the side of the fireplace and took down a red, leather- covered box from its place on a shelf. She reached inside and carefully drew out a pen, a sheet of fine writing paper the colour of a bird's egg and an envelope cross hatched with dark blue and red along its edge. In the top right hand corner of the envelope was the winged symbol enclosing the words 'Par Avion'. She held the pen in her hand for a few moments before returning it, along with the paper and envelope, to the box

'*It's the right thing to do. Tomorrow I will write the letter.*'

One of the books on the shelf had fallen sideways. As she reached to put it back, it fell open to reveal a page, well-thumbed from years of use.

She gave a little gasp as she realised it had opened at her favourite poem. She and Greg had read W.B. Yeats during the short time they were together. Later, as she and Roisin snuggled up in bed during the long, dark, winter nights, Theresa had encouraged her daughter to read it aloud. Even as a young child, Roisin was fascinated by the rhythm and cadence of the language and charmed by the poet's descriptions of nature.

Mouthing the familiar words, Theresa suddenly felt a sense of calm as though a weight had lifted from her shoulders.

'Look what I've found Roisin Dubh. Come, let's read it again together.'

Great Powers of falling wave and wind and windy fire,
With your harmonious choir
Encircle her I love and sing her into peace,
That my old care may cease;
Unfold your flaming wings and cover out of sight
The nets of day and night.
Dim powers of drowsy thought, let her no longer be
Like the pale cup of the sea,
When winds have gathered and sun and moon
burned dim
Above its cloudy rim;
But let a gentle silence wrought with music flow
Whither her footsteps go.

Chapter Five

It was early December and a bitterly cold day when Roisin left her home and everything she knew and held dear. Her mother was going to accompany her as far as Kent station in Cork City. From there she would take the train to the port of Cobh, where so many emigrants had set sail before her, each holding fast to the promise of a better life.

Now as they stepped from the bus in the bustling city centre, the hour and a half before the train departed, stretched ahead of them.

Theresa had arranged delivery of Roisin's trunk from Waterbridge to the train station where it would be loaded onto the train's luggage compartment. It would then be unloaded at Cobh and taken to the ship by porters. Roisin placed the docket for her trunk with her train and boat tickets and tucked them inside the leather valise containing her hand luggage.

Knowing the parting would be painful for both of them, Theresa had planned a farewell treat.

'We have time to walk into town for a cup of tea and

some cake, Roisin. It's a little cafe called The Copper Kettle. You will love it.'

From Glanmire Road they crossed St Patrick's bridge over the River Lee and cut through to Oliver Plunkett Street. Turning into Pembroke Street, they found the tea rooms located in a tall, thin building above a chemist shop. The rickety stairs led up to what had originally been an attic with sloping floors and beamed ceilings. Hanging on large hooks were items of copper ware, including the kettles from which the business got its name. The smell of coffee and fresh baking was enticing and in the hearth a fire glowed. The room was warm and inviting after the chill of the December air.

They were shown to their table by a cheerful girl in a black dress and white pinafore. Soon they had a large pot of tea and a plate of warm scones with butter and jam in front of them.

'You're very quiet Roisin. Are you not enjoying yourself?'

Roisin knew she had to put on a brave front for her mother, but felt shaky and a bit sick. The enclosed space, at first cosy and inviting, was now starting to close in on her.

She longed for the open fields and the woods surrounding her home. The scones she would normally have loved, felt dry and stuck in her throat. She took a long swig of tea and swallowed hard. Tears weren't far off, but she didn't want to show how upset she was. Deep down she knew her mother was acting in her best interest, but she was full of trepidation.

Wiping her eyes on the sleeve of her cardigan when her

mother wasn't looking, she sniffed deeply and forced a smile.

'I'm grand, Mammy. Do you mind if we get some fresh air?'

After paying the bill, they collected Roisin's valise and put on their hats and coats before climbing back down the precipitous stairs. Stepping out into the street, the pavements were slick after a shower of rain. Deep puddles had collected at the sides of the road and a delivery boy on a bicycle rode past, cursing as he swerved to avoid a large pool of water.

Roisin inhaled deeply. There was a strange smell in the air. It was rising up from the wet pavements and was quite unpleasant. She wrinkled her nose in disgust. A man in an overcoat and flat cap squeezed past and he gave off a strange odour too; a mixture of old, unwashed clothes and wet wool. A wave of longing for home overcame her. The country air was not always pure, but was far more pleasing than these rank, acidic odours assailing her sensitive nostrils.

Theresa linked her arm through Roisin's and steered her down the road. 'We have time to call at the Post Office. I need to get some more writing paper and stamps.'

Making their way back to Oliver Plunkett Street, Theresa wished she had worn her Macintosh as the rain had now settled into a steady drizzle. She remembered she had a see-through plastic mac in her bag and gave it to Roisin to put over her good wool coat. Despite herself, Roisin smiled as she pulled the hood over the red beret knitted by her mother. The mac grazed the top of her lace-up ankle boots and she felt glad she was unlikely to encounter anyone she knew. The girls at school would have had a good old laugh if they could see what she looked like.

The Post Office was quiet and they were in and out in no time. On emerging they were treated to a loud 'Echoooo' from the local newspaper seller. It made them both jump, then dissolve into giggles as he gave a cheeky wink in their direction.

'Now I can write to you and bring you up to date with all the news.'

Theresa was trying to remain cheerful but Roisin knew her mother was putting on as much of an act as she was. Checking her watch, Theresa noted they had about half an hour before the train for Cobh departed. Calling into a newsagent she decided against buying a newspaper knowing it would get soaked by the rain. Instead she allowed Roisin to choose a bag of toffees and some chocolate bars. The woman behind the counter placed the items in a brown paper bag and gave Theresa her change.

'Tis desperate this rain, but wonderful weather for ducks,' the woman chuckled.

Yes, desperate is the right word, Roisin thought. *If only you knew*!

The walk to the station took them a little over ten minutes. When they arrived, the train was already alongside the platform.

Roisin, usually so robust and good humoured, felt an unfamiliar sensation in the pit of her stomach. The nausea and dizziness were returning. She realised what she was feeling was apprehension and a growing sense of dread. It was only the start of the journey, but she felt she was losing the last, tangible connection to the mother she loved so dearly. Her roots were embedded in the soil of her homeland, and it was as though she was being wrenched away from everything she held dear.

Within her rose an irresistible urge to run away. To cast off her boots and find a field smelling of earth and green grass. Being accosted by the horrible odours rising up from the hard, city pavements was not a memory to offer her comfort on the long journey ahead.

For her mother's sake she remained compliant, allowing Theresa to remove the mac, give it a shake and roll it up before putting it back into her own bag. She was now fussing over her as she had done when Roisin was a small child, pinching her cheeks to bring back the colour and straightening her coat and hat to make her look presentable. There was little conversation. They were both too upset.

The guard bustled down the platform carrying a flag. Theresa knew the train was minutes away from leaving and choked back the lump forming at the back of her throat. Busying herself was a distraction. She made sure Roisin had her purse and all her paperwork in an accessible place in her bag.

All too soon it was time to leave. She needed to go if she was to make the last bus. After hugging her tightly, Theresa opened the carriage door and steered her daughter up the step and onto the train. Full of anxiety, she walked down the platform checking to make sure Roisin had found her seat. She had booked her one next to a window and just as the whistle blew to signal departure, she caught sight of her and her heart lurched.

It took all of Theresa's resolve not to scramble aboard the train. How easy it would be to take her back to their home and pick up where they had left off as if nothing had happened.

Roisin was still wearing the red and navy plaid coat her mother had made for her and the jaunty, red beret with its pompom.

She didn't look in the least bit cheery though. Her face pressed against the window was white and pinched. She seemed very young and vulnerable. Theresa placed her hand on the glass and Roisin did the same from the other side.

'I *love you, my Macushla,*' she mouthed, but Roisin's eyes were downcast.

It was perhaps just as well, for as the train pulled away the last image of her mother would have been of her bent over as if in pain, her body convulsed with wracking sobs.

The train made its way out of the city encircled in a cloud of sulphurous steam. Soon it cleared the urban outskirts, and gathering speed, it raced along through open countryside. The great expanse of water where the channels of the River Lee merged into the tidal estuaries of Cork harbour, glinted in the emerging sunlight.

There were five other people in the carriage, three men and two women. The men, all wearing tweed flat caps and rough jackets and trousers, seemed to know each other. There was a great deal of back slapping and noisy joshing. Her mother would have called their rowdiness *lairy behaviour* and Roisin was sure she smelt alcohol on the breath of one who stumbled and landed on the floor in front of her.

The woman sitting to her right was engrossed in a magazine and paid no heed to the ruckus. Conscious her mother would not want her to stare, Roisin observed the woman from the corner of her eye. She was wearing a small pillbox hat and was swathed in a loose fitting fur coat. A faint musky animal odour mingling with the scent of cologne caused a shiver to run up Roisin's spine. She knew from her books the best way to keep warm in very cold countries was to wear animal skins or fur. Still, she couldn't help feeling sad at the thought the sleek, brown coat had once covered a beautiful, living creature.

She glanced away and noticed the woman sitting opposite was looking in her direction with a faint smile hovering on her lips. Roisin felt as though she had been caught out, and feeling embarrassed, dropped her gaze.

'Are you going home to Cobh or travelling on?' The woman asked. Her voice was light with an accent Roisin found hard to place.

Roisin cleared her throat. 'I'm er, leaving on the boat bound for Halifax in Canada. I have relatives there and I'll be staying with them.' Her tongue felt thick in her mouth. She was conscious her voice probably sounded rougher than normal.

'Well that's a fair old journey for a young girl.'

Roisin felt she should explain and blurted out a shortened version of her story, adding, 'I'm not that young. I'm sixteen and quite grown up really.'

The woman raised her delicate eyebrows and her smile widened.

'Well young lady, Canada is a country of great opportunity. I should know. I was born in Toronto.'

Ah, Roisin thought, *she's Canadian, not Irish.*

As if reading Roisin's thoughts the woman spoke again.

'I came to Cork as a Governess ten years ago when I was only nineteen. The children are grown up now and the family doesn't really need me, so I am returning back home to pick up my studies. I am going to train to be a teacher.'

She went on to say that once she was back in Canada she would take the train from Halifax to Toronto and was excited to be seeing her family again. Sensing Roisin's apprehension, she attempted to reassure her. 'Don't worry, you will soon settle. At least you are going to stay with relatives. When I arrived in Ireland, I didn't know anyone, but I soon found my way around and made new friends.'

Friends weren't really what Roisin was interested in, but she thanked the woman and smiled wanly.

Turning to look out of the window, she saw the train was passing over the Slatty viaduct. Soon after, and with a hiss of steam and the clanging of brakes, they came to a halt at tiny Fota station where a few of the passengers alighted and one or two locals got on. After passing through Carrigaloe and Rushbrook it wasn't long before, with a high, piping whistle, the train pulled into the maritime town of Cobh.

By the time she had collected her valise from the overhead rack, the carriage had cleared. The platform was crowded and the assembled throng began to make her feel uneasy again.

She had never seen so many people crowded together. Remembering her mother's instructions, she took her ticket and luggage docket and walked from the train to the ticket office at the end of the platform. A queue had formed and the clerk seemed to be getting increasingly irritable with the excitable passengers clamouring for his attention.

Roisin reached the counter and handed over her paperwork, hands shaking with nerves. The clerk's attitude softened when he saw how young she was. Stamping her docket, he handed it back to her.

'Now, don't you worry at all Miss. Your trunk will be loaded onto the ship and will be there for you when you disembark at Halifax.'

His gruff voice with its strong Cork accent felt oddly comforting. Roisin thanked him politely, grateful for any display of kindness. Despite this, the encounter left her feeling even more homesick and very lost and alone.

Chapter Six

The RMS Mercinia, with its vast black hull and distinctive red and black funnel, loomed above a quayside teeming with porters, passengers and those who had come to wave off their loved ones. Local women, most of them widows wearing black shawls, carried willow baskets containing hand-made lace or bunches of lucky heather. Peddling their wares, they cried out in singsong voices. *'Will ye look at the quality of the workmanship Missus.'* or *'A bunch of lucky heather to keep ye safe on yer voyage Sir.'*

The ship was due to set sail at five o'clock and Roisin decided she would board around half an hour beforehand. As it was not long after three, she had plenty of time. A short walk in the opposite direction brought her to the edge of the town. There were plenty of people milling around and to avoid them she walked along the seafront until she found a quiet spot on a bench facing the sea. Brightly painted fishing boats bobbed in the harbour and seagulls dipped and squawked overhead. If she looked across the expanse of choppy water, she could see the outline of Spike Island. From her books Roisin knew the island was dominated by the star-shaped Fort Mitchel, used at times for defence and then as a penal institution. To her right was the wonderfully named Haulbowline Island, a naval base and home to the world's first yacht club founded in 1720.

With the earlier rain clearing, a watery sun was falling fast, sinking down through the cloud banks hovering above the horizon, like an elderly aunt re-arranging her skirts.

An icy wind whipped in off the sea and Roisin knew it would snow in the next hour. She shivered, but not with cold. Behind her she thought she heard whispering. When she turned there was no one in sight. Cobh had witnessed so much sadness over the centuries of its existence it was no wonder she was feeling the weight of its unhappiness. For many hundreds of years, so many had departed to avoid terrible famines or to seek employment and a better life. Men, women and children had said goodbye to their homeland and their loved ones, knowing they would never return. Roisin wondered if she too would ever set foot on Irish soil again.

Her musings turned to the passengers who set sail from the town on the 11th April 1912 when Cobh was still named Queenstown. Filled with excitement they had boarded the largest, fastest and most luxurious ocean liner of the time, the RMS Titanic. The vessel was set to continue on her maiden voyage to New York. Nobody could have anticipated that four days later the ship, deemed unsinkable, would lie at the bottom of the Atlantic Ocean with the loss of 1,500 lives.

Four booming reverberations from the bells of St Colman's Cathedral echoed around the harbour. It was time to go.

Realising she hadn't eaten since the tea and scones at The Copper Kettle, Roisin opened her valise and took out one of the bars of chocolate purchased on their walk to the station. She broke off a square and popped it in her mouth. It made her think of her mother. Chocolate was a rare treat and they had often played a game to see how long they could make a square last.

Theresa would be back at home by now. Roisin pictured her sitting by the fire with her sewing. She would be trying to get as much done before the fading light made it too difficult to see. The memory made her want to cry, but Roisin knew she had to pull herself together and make her way to the waiting ship.

The weather was starting to change. Thick, grey clouds began rolling in off the sea and Roisin could only just make out the spire of the gothic style cathedral high on the hill above the town. Lights were beginning to come on in the staggered rows of terraced houses climbing the hillside. They were a striking sight in daylight, with their walls painted a palette of distinctive pastel shades of blue, pink, green and terracotta. At this time of day they looked ghostly in the fading light.

It took only a few minutes to reach the quayside. There were porters everywhere, expertly manipulating their wooden barrows stacked with luggage through the milling crowd and then into the hold of the ship. Roisin hoped her trunk containing her clothes, books and mementoes would make it in one piece to Halifax. She really couldn't bear the thought of being somewhere new and strange without her most precious reminders of home.

She joined an exuberant line of people waiting to mount the gangway just as the first, downy flakes of snow began to fall.

~

With her papers checked and found to be in order, Roisin made her way onboard without a backward glance. Inside it was a free for all, with passengers jostling with each other in a search for their cabins. Hers was down a steep flight of stairs and along a narrow corridor. It was a compact space with bunk beds on one side and desk and chair pushed up against the opposite wall. In one corner there was an open wardrobe in which coats and hand luggage could be stored. The lower part held a small chest with four drawers. She was pleased to see there was a tiny washbasin with a mirror and overhead light. It meant she could at least brush her teeth and wash her face without having to trudge down to the public bathrooms.

A glance through the porthole revealed only a blanket of darkness. Not even the tiniest glimmer of light shone through to help her distinguish sky from sea. She knew she would be sharing the cabin and couldn't help but feel concerned. The idea of occupying the small space with a stranger made her feel anxious. She consoled herself with the thought at least it was warm and adequate for the five day voyage.

After hanging up her coat, she took her toilet bag and hairbrush from her valise. Placing her few items of clothing in the top drawer of the chest of drawers, she left the other drawers free for her cabin mate. Rinsing her hands and face in the basin, she caught a glimpse of herself in the mirror. How pale and disordered she looked, her hair escaping in untidy strands from her plait. She had practised plaiting her hair under instruction from her mother, but her arms felt tired and heavy from carrying her bag. For now she would settle for running a brush through it before tying it back with a ribbon. If she was to brave going to the dining room later for dinner, she wanted to make sure she was at least clean and well presented.

Sitting on the lower bunk, she could feel the low, thrumming vibration of the engines beneath her feet. Preoccupied with thoughts of home she lost track of time, until a long blast on the ship's horn heralded the Mercinia's departure. There would be tearful goodbyes and a carillon of bells from the cathedral as the mooring ropes were cast off. It was a mournful thought and enough to keep Roisin in the cabin anticipating the arrival of her room-mate.

She didn't have long to wait. Above the hum of voices in the corridor came a trill of laughter from someone outside the door. Roisin jumped to her feet as a woman burst into the cabin, followed by a uniformed porter carrying a small suitcase and bag.

'Oh God, I'm so sorry. I didn't think. I should have knocked before barging in,' the woman said when she saw Roisin.

After placing the woman's bags on top of the desk, the young man was rewarded with a few coppers and a conspiratorial wink.

'Thanks a million. You're a love doing that for me.'

The poor fellow exited the cabin backwards, blushing to the roots of his bright red hair.

The woman wasted no time in introducing herself. 'I'm Geraldine, but everyone calls me Ger. What's your name and how old are you? You look very young?'

Taken aback by the forthrightness, Roisin managed to stammer out her name and age.

'That's a pretty name, but if you don't mind I'm going to call you Ro. It sounds so much more grown-up. Jeez you have lovely hair. I'll show you how to style it so you look older.'

She patted her own blonde curls, swept up from the sides and held in place with bobby pins. Her lips were a pinky red and she was wearing a subtle shade of blue shadow on her eyelids, a perfect match for her powder-blue duster coat. As she busied herself unpacking, which involved hanging up her dresses and jamming expensive items of clothing haphazardly into the drawers, Ger asked Roisin to tell her about herself.

It's such an Irish thing, Roisin thought, tucking herself out of the way on the bottom bunk. *The need to find out every last thing about a person, even one you have only just met.*

She proceeded to tell Ger about why she was going to Canada, pleased she managed it without tears. She didn't want to be seen as a cry baby.

'Well,' Ger said gently, 'you are a very plucky young woman I must say. I don't think I would have had the courage to go on such a big adventure when I was your age.'

Unpacking complete, Ger sat down alongside Roisin.

'Here's a question for you.' she said matter of factly. 'You have to guess why I'm here and what I do for a living.' She tilted her head to the side waiting for a reply.

'I'm not good at guessing really, but are you a fashion model?'

The expensive clothes, the perfume and lotions and potions coming out of Ger's bags seemed to suggest not only that she took good care of herself, but she wasn't short of money.

Throwing back her head, Ger laughed out loud. 'That's a good one. I like it. A model. Oh Lordy. No, you silly goose, I'm a singer. They call me The Celtic Colleen and I've been invited to do a short tour of Nova Scotia. Irish and Scottish music is very popular there.'

Introductions over and with order restored in the cabin, Roisin took her book on the wildlife of Canada and climbed up the wooden ladder to the top bunk. Ger was adamant it should be she who should have the lower bunk. At some point and without a shadow of doubt she told Roisin, she would be *as sick as a dog* and didn't want to be hurling over Roisin if she were in the bed below her. The scramble to the top was worth it to avoid the possibility, Roisin decided. She didn't relish the idea of being vomited on from on high.

Dinner was being served at seven and it was agreed they would meet in the dining room just before. Ger took herself off in search of the smoking lounge leaving Roisin alone to gather her thoughts.

The warmth of the cabin and the low rumble of the engines was soothing. Exhausted after such a long and tiring day, Roisin felt her eyes droop and was soon lulled into a deep sleep. She dreamed she was flying over rolling hills with the patchwork fields and acres of lush, green woodlands of home spread out beneath her.

Waking with a start, it dawned on her the ship must now be well clear of the harbour and out in the channel. With the Celtic Sea behind them, they were cresting rolling, white tipped waves. Ahead lay two and a half thousand miles of deep, North Atlantic ocean. It was a daunting, even frightening prospect.

Roisin lay for a few minutes, the bed cover pulled up to her chin. She was waiting for the wild beating of her heart to slow and return to normal. Up until now, the day had felt almost unreal, as though it was happening to someone else. Now it hit her with a force that made her gasp. It *was* really happening. There would be no turning back.

Chapter Seven

By five o'clock, approximately the same time as her daughter was boarding the ship for departure, Theresa was back in Waterbridge. There had been an outdoor market that morning and a road sweeper was shovelling the leftover vegetable debris into his handcart. She was at a loss as to what to do with herself. She didn't want to return home just yet, even though she was worn out and full of apprehension.

Her walk took her past the Waterbridge Hotel. Lights were on in the windows and she stepped inside out of the biting wind. There was no-one seated in the lounge area, but a young man behind the bar was washing and drying glasses in preparation for the evening.

'You look perished,' he said. 'Have a seat there in front of the fire. What can I get you?'

'I suppose it's a bit too early for a port and lemon?' Theresa felt desperately in need of a shot of alcohol to warm her and settle her anxiety.

'No, it's fine. We'll just pretend you're a guest,' he said, holding up a glass to inspect it in the light. 'I think

I remember you. Did you come for a meal with your daughter a while back?'

'I did, it was her sixteenth birthday.'

'Lovely looking girl. Beautiful black hair if I remember rightly.'

Theresa nodded and reached into her bag. Taking out a handkerchief she wiped her eyes and blew her nose. The port and lemon duly arrived and the barman, sensing she wanted to be alone, went back to the bar leaving her to finish her drink in peace.

She had twenty minutes to spare before it was time to catch the last bus home. Although she didn't feel hungry, she knew she should eat something. On a whim she went to see if the Hennessey's shop was still open. Her stomach was starting to rumble and she thought she could manage to eat some crackers and cheese before bed. To her relief the lights were still on and Theresa pushed open the door and waited for someone to appear. The couple came through from the back room of the shop. They were in the process of getting ready to close, but greeted Theresa warmly.

'Will you take a cup of tea with us before your bus? It's bitter out there and you look frozen.'

Sarah Hennessey had heard on the town grapevine Roisin was leaving for Canada and could see Theresa was upset.

'Have you got back from seeing her off?' she said.

The question was asked sympathetically, but it was too much for Theresa. She tried to gulp back the tears, but they poured down her cheeks.

Sarah, clucking around her like a mother hen, led her to

a chair, afraid she was in danger of slumping to the floor.

'John, will you put the 'Closed' sign on the door and wipe the counter down before we get another customer calling in?' she said to her husband, 'I'll get the kettle on and make some hot, sweet tea. Theresa is staying with us tonight.'

She held her hand up as Theresa started to protest, 'No arguments now. You need some hot food and a warm bed. If you want to talk we will listen. If you prefer to be by yourself, we have a nice guest room already made up and you can just take yourself off to bed with a nightcap. Things will look better in the morning. They always do.'

The bed was comfortable and Sarah put in two hot water bottles to air the sheets. The couple couldn't have been more welcoming or understanding. They assured Theresa, given the circumstances, she had made the right choice for Roisin's future. They let her talk until she was too weary to continue.

Now, as she lay in the dark in the Hennessey's back bedroom, sleep eluded her. Her abiding hope for her daughter was she was safe and not too troubled. She had no prayers to offer up, just the words of the poem they had read together on that fateful day when she made the decision to send Roisin away. *Encircle her I love and sing her into peace.* The words were still on her lips when at last her eyes grew heavy and she sank into a troubled and fitful sleep.

Returning to the cottage the following morning, she wasn't prepared for how bare and unloved it looked. She lit a fire to cheer the place up and went to change out of what she had been wearing the previous day.

Looking around the bedroom she had shared with Roisin, she noticed how tidy it was, now she had the room to herself. The suit she had worn for her meeting with Sister Agnes was still hanging up on the outside of the wardrobe. She thought back to all those years ago when it had first been purchased for her.

She had passed her Leaving Certificate with honours and was resigned to spending the summer working in the shop with her parents. On Wednesdays she scoured the job pages in the local paper and was starting to think a career in shop-work was going to be her only option when an advert caught her eye. Brown and Fitzpatrick, a firm of local solicitors, were looking for a trainee. It was general office work to start with, but what caught Theresa's eye were the words, *opportunities will be available for further training for the right candidate. Ideal,* she had thought. *A wage packet and free training. What could be better?*

Her mother had taken her into the city to buy something suitable in preparation for the interview. She had been pleased to have Theresa's help in the shop during the holidays, especially when the books were brought up to date in record time. The dove grey suit was her reward, and although it was expensive, it gave Theresa a professional air. To go with the suit, Theresa was allowed to select a jaunty scarf with a nautical theme in pale blue and grey to complete the look. Although she only had one pair of good shoes, she was confident she looked both well turned out and competent.

The job turned out to be a great success and everyone at Brown and Fitzpatrick were pleased with her progress.

They even agreed to pay for a course for her to learn shorthand and typing. Once she was proficient in these skills, they told her, she would be taken on permanently and given a pay rise. Squeezed into a little cubby-hole adjacent to the main office, Theresa was overseen by Patrick Connolly, the barrister's clerk, a dishevelled man in his fifties who smelled of mints and pipe smoke.

The work was straightforward, mostly consisting of filing and preparing letters. She was a quick learner and Mr Connolly spotted her potential. When he wasn't busy, he asked her to join him in his office where he instructed her in some of the more complex aspects of articles of law.

'Sure, you'll be after my job. I'll have to watch my back,' he joked.

When Greg Brown dropped into the office she liked him immediately. He also seemed interested in her, chatting away as she practised her typing. He was home for the Christmas recess and when his father caught him flirting with her, he scolded him in mock seriousness.

'Have you nothing better to do than distract my staff, Gregory?'

Greg had taken her to a coffee bar in the next town and then invited her for a meal at his parents' house. Set back from the road on the outskirts of the town, it was a large, imposing Georgian residence. He was studying architecture and showed her the fanlight above the front door, a beautiful thistle and rose design, and went on to point out the striking geometric tiles adorning the entrance hall floor. A lesson in Georgian architecture went over her head, but he didn't seem to mind.

His parents were Anglo Irish and although the house was in need of repair and the furnishings were faded and shabby, it was clear the family were not short of money.

She would return in the spring under very different circumstances, this time accompanied by her parents. The maid who answered the door had looked at Theresa knowingly, eyeing her up and down before escorting them to the drawing room. It was an unseasonably cold spring day and she shivered, despite the late sun streaming through the tall sash window overlooking the gardens. Beyond a paved terrace, a profusion of scarlet tulips and acid yellow daffodils edged a sloping lawn.

With her parents on either side of her, Theresa waited, balling her handkerchief in damp hands. Nerves were making her stomach churn and bile rise into the back of her throat.

'Greg will be a little late. His train is delayed,' Mrs Brown said coolly. This time there was no show of hospitality, not even the offer of a cup of tea to wet Theresa's parched lips.

Mrs Brown wore a pale pink, wool sweater and navy skirt. The pearl necklace against her throat made her look classy and elegant. Theresa could see she was thinner than when she last visited. She looked tired and the dark circles beneath her eyes were an indicator of what was to come. In less than five years Eleanor Brown would be dead. All the money in the world could not prevent her from succumbing to the rare form of kidney cancer that would claim her life.

Greg's arrival, fifteen uncomfortable minutes later, signalled a start to proceedings. Watching him stride into the room it occurred to Theresa just how privileged and spoiled he was. She waited to see if she felt any rush of emotion. They had been close, in love even. It was what had got her into this awful mess. The bombshell of the pregnancy brought out an aspect of Greg Theresa hadn't previously noticed. His fear for his own future manifested as anger and he manhandled her and threw spiteful comments at her before turning his back and walking away. It was a show of weakness Theresa could not countenance. From that moment, any love for him dissipated and she lost all respect for him.

Greg had bent to kiss his mother's cheek, then remained behind her chair waiting for her to speak. His father contributed little to the conversation. Instead he sat on an overstuffed chair on the other side of the room, a dour look on his face.

'I think we are all in agreement as to what is going to happen over the next few months,' Mrs Brown said, coughing delicately. 'Greg, as we have said, will continue with his studies. As for you Theresa, you will have the child and when the time comes you will sign it over for adoption.'

A wave of sickness caused Theresa to search in a pocket of her jacket to retrieve a spare handkerchief. She held it to her mouth, hoping she wasn't going to show herself up by vomiting all over the Chinese silk rug. She watched as Eleanor Brown rummaged in her expensive handbag before pulling out a cheque book. Tearing off a cheque, she reached across and handed it to Theresa.

'This will cover your expenses and your loss of salary during the pregnancy. We do not think it appropriate you return to the practice afterwards. The money is a generous sum and will tide you over until you find alternative work.'

Theresa had felt irritated, but couldn't bring herself to protest. She was too weary. Her parents, who sat stiffly on the upright chairs either side of her throughout, looked straight ahead. They were far too much in awe of the Browns and their money to make any comment. She was being paid off, that was obvious, but her aching head and overwhelming sense of fatigue meant she couldn't sum up the energy to argue. She wanted to forget the last few months and not think about what lay ahead. All she wished for was to climb into bed and feel the cool sheets against her face. If only there was a way of blocking everything out. It would be wonderful if she could fall asleep and wake refreshed, ready to start again, the slate wiped clean.

It had all been so long ago, yet still she remembered the sense of panic and the feeling of rejection and isolation. It had felt as though choices about her life were being made to suit everyone else, not her. She had been vulnerable and resigned to the plans being put in place. That is until Roisin was born.

Her decision to keep her child meant sacrifices and these would not just affect her. She was going to be a mother and that came with responsibilities. It had been a hard fought battle from the start, especially with everyone turning against her. She had drawn upon reserves she didn't know she had. It had been an ongoing struggle, but she had worked hard to provide for the two of them. *Overall she hadn't done a bad job of it, had she?*

The money she had been given by Greg's family she couldn't bear to touch. Instead she had saved it and it was this, her nest egg, she had used to pay for Roisn's passage to Canada.

Now, the struggle she was having was with her own conscience. Had it been the right thing to do, sending Roisin away from everything she knew, even if it was done with the best of intentions? It would be unbearable if it turned out to be a disaster and Roisin was unhappy in Canada. It hurt her deeply to consider the possibility Roisin might resent her, or worse, grow to hate her.

She sat down on Roisin's bed and ran her fingers over the coverlet. A stray hair clip left behind in the haste of packing, caught her eye. She tucked it into her pocket and picking up Roisin's pillow, she sank her face into its downy softness. It smelled of her daughter, a mixture of ivory soap and shampoo.

Theresa couldn't cry anymore. Instead, she lay with her head buried in the pillow, surrounded by a silence that threatened to engulf her.

Chapter Eight

Passing the smoking lounge on her way to the dining room, Roisin caught sight of Ger. She was seated at a table and surrounded by a number of men in attendance. One in particular, tall, dark haired and well dressed, seemed especially attentive. He was leaning in to light her cigarette with exaggerated diligence. She was about to move on when Ger noticed her.

'Ro, come over here and meet these interesting people.' Ger, enveloped in a cloud of cigarette smoke, was waving her over.

Roisin would have preferred to carry on to the dining room, but felt it rude to ignore the summons. Making her way shyly towards the group, she couldn't help but notice she was being appraised by some of Ger's admirers. It was a new sensation. She felt a tingling inside. She had never been in the company of men who looked at her in that way before.

'Sit here with me,' Ger said, wafting smoke away with her hand. 'I shouldn't smoke, I know. It's terrible for my voice, but it's my one guilty pleasure.'

'Sing for us do. We'd love to hear one of your ballads,' the tall man implored, while a murmur of assent came from the group assembled around her.

'All right, just one. It's time for dinner and we are both starving, aren't we Ro?'

Ger stood and the tall man retrieved her cardigan which was slipping off her shoulders. Handing him the stub of her cigarette, she cleared her throat and moved across the room to a space lit by a single spotlight. Then, with a tilt of her head and a lowering of her lashes, Ger had the eyes of every man in the room focused on her.

Roisin watched transfixed as the clearest, purest notes of the song '*The Last Rose of Summer*' echoed around the room. When Ger reached the closing verse, it seemed the sweetest and most poignant of all:

So soon may I follow,
When friendships decay,
And from Love's shining circle
The gems drop away.
When true hearts lie withered,
And fond ones are flown,
Oh! who would inhabit
This bleak world alone?

As Ger held the final note, there was complete silence in the room followed by a collective sigh. Looking around Roisin saw many in the room were crying. This outpouring of emotion was followed by an explosion of whoops and claps.

Never had Roisin seen such a response to a song. She

felt proud and honoured Ger wanted her company, even if it was only for the duration of the voyage.

As they left the room with a breathless Roisin following in her wake, Ger raised her arm to wave to her adoring audience as though she owned the room.

The dining room was crowded and they took their places at a table already occupied by a middle aged man and his wife. With pleasantries exchanged, Ger and Roisin gave a waiter in a white coat their orders.

The first course of soup soon arrived and was demolished with relish. They were both ravenous. They polished off their respective main courses; fish for Ger, chicken for Roisin, then tucked into a delicious apple tart and cream, followed by coffee.

Feeling very grown up, Roisin knew her mother would have been proud of the way she conducted herself during dinner. For her birthday, Theresa had taken her out for a special meal at the big hotel in Waterbridge. Before the food arrived, her mother instructed her in the use of cutlery and linen napkins which Roisin was now grateful for. She didn't want to show herself up in front of this very sophisticated older woman.

How long ago that evening seemed. The time had flown by, taken up with hectic preparations for the trip to Canada. Following the excitement of her birthday, there was the whirl of sorting out her passport, organising the tickets, selecting appropriate clothing, the decisions as to what should go in her trunk, the fond goodbyes, and the heavy, pressing state of imminence. Now here she was, feeling gauche and unsure, yet at the same time, immersed in new experiences that were interesting and stimulating.

For the first time in many weeks, she was experiencing a growing feeling things weren't so bad after all.

'You all right there Ro? You looked as though you were drifting off for a minute,' Ger said, giving her a gentle shake.

Roisin noticed both Ger and the couple at the table were looking at her quizzically and realised she must have been daydreaming.

'Let's go for a little walk shall we? Stretch our legs before retiring?' Ger suggested.

With a polite 'good evening' to the couple, they set off in search of the covered promenade deck. They passed the smoking lounge crowded with people, and the writing room with only a small number in attendance, some of whom were reading newspapers. Roisin noticed the woman she had spoken to on the train was seated at a table and engrossed in writing a letter.

It was chilly on deck despite the area being enclosed and Ger had soon had enough and was keen to get back inside in the warmth. She left Roisin standing at the rail, looking out over the vast expanse of water, crowned with jagged white breakers. With the arrival of a number of after-dinner strollers, Roisin took the staircase to the smaller upper deck, pleased to see it was empty of passengers. It was open to the elements and with the wind and droplets of salt water whipping her hair and face, she felt as though she could breathe once again.

The spell was broken when a passing crew member spotted her and called out to her. 'The wind is getting up, young 'un. Better to be inside than out here when it starts blowing a gale.'

Back inside, Roisin suspected her appearance was very much like that of a drowned rat. She was pleased she didn't encounter anyone on the way back to the cabin.

Placing a towel around her head like a turban to help dry her hair, she made her way to the bathroom down the corridor to give herself a good wash. Here the sinks were more capacious than the one in the cabin. *Perhaps I will have a bath tomorrow*, she thought as she looked at the cubicles containing gleaming white tubs and shiny brass taps.

There was no sign of Ger and feeling tired she got into the flower-sprigged nightie made by her mother. Pulling the curtains across the porthole darkened the cabin, although a thin strip of light still shone under the door. Clambering up the ladder, she drew the set of curtains around her bed. Once tucked up in bed, it made her feel as though she was in a cosy nest. The small bulkhead light overhead was enough to read by, but within a short time her eyes grew heavy and sleep beckoned. She was dimly aware of Ger's return some time later, but fell back immediately into a deep and dreamless slumber.

Waking to the sound of movement and chatter from outside, it took a few minutes for Roisin to work out where she was. Her cabin mate was lying on her back, breathing softly below her. Not wanting to wake her, she made her way down the ladder as quietly as she could. Pulling on her day clothes wasn't easy in the cramped space and she disturbed Ger, who stirred and stretched her arms upwards.

'What on earth is the time?' Ger said, with a loud yawn. She reached across to get her watch off the desk.

'Holy Moly, it's after nine. We should go and get breakfast. Pull back the curtains Ro, and let's have a look at the watery world outside.'

An expanse of gunmetal grey was all that was visible through the porthole, with sea and sky seeming to merge. Occasionally a wave slapped against the glass as the ship dipped into a wide trough of ocean.

Ger looked a little off-colour but was in good spirits and eager for a morning cup of tea at the very least. Once dressed and with her hair brushed and her make-up applied, she linked arms with Roisin and the two made their way upstairs to the dining room where there was a wide selection of breakfast items to choose from. Ger explained to Roisin what was listed as oatmeal, was in fact porridge and they each had a bowl with a round of toast and a pot of tea.

'You know Ro, this is all very well, but one day I will be travelling the world first class, dripping in furs and jewels.'

This didn't sound at all pleasant to Roisin. She remembered the woman on the train with the fur coat and shuddered. Anyway, this might not be first class, but to Roisin, it all felt very luxurious in comparison to what she was used to. She thought it best not to comment and nodded her head instead.

'I have an agent back home and he has arranged bookings for me all over Canada and America,' Ger continued. 'I'm going places young Ro, and it's the greatest feeling in the world. You see, I'm twenty-seven years old and I've never hankered after the same things as other girls of my age. I've no wish to be tied down with a husband and children. I want to have my own career, make my own money and travel the world.'

Pausing for breath, Ger looked intently at Roisin, who was struggling with a fish bone from the mackerel she had ordered, unwisely it appeared. She slipped it onto the side of her plate hoping Ger hadn't noticed.

'Now you take my advice young lady,' Ger was saying, waving elegantly polished fingertips in the air. 'There's something special about you, I can tell. You just need to find what you love doing best and put your heart and soul into it and you will be a great success. You mark my words.'

'Special' was not a word Roisin would have used about herself. She was different to other girls her age, even a bit odd if others were to be believed. It had never occurred to her that there was anything about her that was exceptional. Her life up until now had been pre-planned and she had little say in decisions made on her behalf. It was interesting to be told she could choose her own destiny and perhaps even accomplish something in her own right.

Ger was good company and a refreshing influence, but a sudden wave of homesickness overcame her. It took her by surprise as she had felt she was adjusting to her new situation. Roisin realised she wasn't quite as grown up as she had thought, as just then she wanted her mother.

I know. I'll write her a letter and post it from here. The mail would take the best part of a week to arrive from Halifax, but she wanted to tell Theresa about all the details of life on the ship while they were still fresh in her mind.

Leaving Ger sitting on a steamer chair on the promenade deck, Roisin returned to the cabin to retrieve writing paper and envelopes from her bag.

The writing room was now empty and Roisin found a table tucked away in a corner. Never the tidiest of girls in other matters, she prided herself on her neat handwriting. Once her thoughts were organised, she found it easy to fill pages of white lined paper with everything that had happened to her so far.

She wrote until her arm ached, knowing her mother would relish every small detail. An hour or two passed and she was stiff from sitting. It was time for her to stretch her legs. The letter was unfinished, but she intended updating it before their arrival in Halifax.

There was no sign of Ger, but people were milling about in the vaulted entrance hall. Some were already making their way to the dining room for lunch. Wanting to keep her letter safe, Roisin took the stairs down to the cabin to return it to her bag. Turning into the corridor she could hear raised voices and noticed two figures outside the cabin. One was the tall man from the smoking room and the other was Ger. The man had her pinned against the wall, his arm against her neck.

Noticing Roisin, the man lessened his grip and Ger pulled away, rubbing the base of her throat. In contrast to her usual determined manner, she was visibly shaken and it was apparent the interaction had unnerved her. Reaching for Roisin's arm, the two watched as the man sauntered away as though he hadn't a care in the world. With trembling hands Ger pushed open the cabin door and shut it firmly behind them

'We need to keep our distance from that fella. He has a very nasty temper.'

'Do you think we ought to tell someone?' Roisin asked, a worried expression on her face.

'No,' Ger said, 'but we'll stay out of his way and keep the door locked at all times. If he tries anything again, I will go straight to the Captain and report him.'

Chapter Nine

There was no further sighting of the man and the rest of the day passed without incident. After a light lunch, Ger took herself off to read the newspapers and Roisin went to finish her letter to her mother. She didn't mention the incident outside their cabin. She asked instead if Theresa had ever heard of 'The Celtic Colleen' and described the scene where Ger had sung so beautifully. Sealing the letter, she addressed it and took it to the main desk where she paid threepence for the postage before popping it into the post box.

Writing had given her a headache. Stepping out onto the deck she could see a heavy swell developing. Turning her face into the wind, she experienced the faint electrical charge in the air that invariably preceded a storm. She had read the weather forecast written on a board adjacent to the menu outside the dining room. Heavy sleet and high winds approaching 22 knots were expected. It would be a rough ride until they passed through the squall.

Poor Ger won't like this at all, she mused, as she headed back down to the cabin. Sure enough, after unlocking the door, she found Ger lying on her bunk with a damp flannel on her forehead and a bowl next to her on the floor.

'Is there anything I can get you? They have barley sugar in the shop. That's always good for sickness.'

Ger rolled her head and clutched the flannel. 'I will be glad of it, but not now. I'm going to try and sleep for a while. Could you bring the barley sugar back after dinner? I don't think I'll feel like having anything to eat for a while.'

With that, she vomited noisily into the bowl and sank back onto her pillow with her hand over her eyes.

Turning off the overhead light, Roisin lit the desk lamp and collected the bowl, which she took to the washroom toilet to empty. She returned it to the floor next to Ger then gently lifted the flannel, rinsed it in cold water in the sink and returned it to Ger's brow, all without waking her. The next hour she spent reading before getting herself ready for the evening meal. As Ger stirred in her sleep, Roisin reminded her she was leaving and to lock the door behind her.

Making her way up the stairs, Roisin felt the boat pitching and rolling. Struggling to keep her balance, she made slow progress, gripping the brass rail to steady herself. The hardy few who were making their way to the dining room seemed unsure and looked as though they might change their minds about consuming any food. She saw the man they had shared the dinner table with the previous evening looking a little green around the gills. There was no sign of his wife and Roisin enquired after her health.

'I have a feeling it will be a while before she gets up out

of her bed,' he said, before suddenly standing stock-still and bringing a pudgy hand to his mouth.

'Er sorry, I must go,' he cried out in a muffled voice before hurrying away.

Roisin watched his retreating back with a bemused look before continuing on her way. The shop was still open and she selected two sticks of barley sugar and two postcards with images of the Mercinia in all her splendour. A small silver-coloured model of a ship's bell on a shelf caught her eye. Although her mother had told her to be careful with her money, she wanted to arrive in Halifax with a gift for Peggy and Joe.

The friendly shop assistant carefully wrapped the bell in tissue paper. Placing it in a gift bag, she tucked the cards and barley sugar in alongside.

'Don't forget to change your currency before we dock in Canada. If you go to the main desk they will do it for you.'

'Yes, thanks for reminding me. I'll do it now.'

The ship was still heaving alarmingly and with a purse full of Canadian dollars and loose cents, Roisin took her purchases and went to check on Ger before dinner. A very drowsy, wan-faced figure opened the door and then sank back onto her bunk, pulling the covers over her head. 'I think I might be about to die,' she muttered dramatically. 'Please tell me this is going to stop soon.'

Reassuring her it would soon be over, Roisin wet the flannel and fetched a glass of water. These she placed along with the barley sugar on the floor next to Ger. To her relief she noticed the sick bowl was empty. After a quick wash and a brush through her own hair she was ready to go back upstairs for dinner. Outside the dining room a sign had been placed on a stand and Roisin couldn't help but smile. Even some of the dining staff were indisposed it would appear.

Due to the extreme weather conditions, please serve yourself from the buffet this evening.

Helping herself to a plate of food, she took her seat at a table. With fewer passengers than normal in evidence, a solitary waiter struggled to maintain his balance whilst attempting to keep the lids from sliding off the dishes he was carrying. From the direction of the kitchen came the sound of breaking crockery and raised voices as the skeleton staff of chefs tried to maintain some semblance of order. Half a dozen hardy passengers were scattered around the room holding onto their plates and glasses to prevent them sliding off the tables. Tucking into her meal of braised lamb and vegetables, Roisin thought of her mother's words when she herself had a headache threatening or was feeling unwell. *You're a very fortunate girl Roisin. You never get sick. You have the constitution of an ox.*

The air felt stuffy and Roisin, eager to see the storm before it passed, knew she would have to get to the top of the ship without being observed. Anyone seeing her would think her unhinged, braving such tempestuous weather.

The promenade deck was now deserted and she climbed up to the small upper deck next to the bridge. Standing there, she braced herself against the power of the icy wind, feeling energised after being cooped up inside.

Below her the lifeboats were swinging and groaning

on their metal hawsers. Far off on the distant horizon, sheet lightning illuminated clouds heavy with sleet. From overhead, there came a deep rumble of thunder. The waves hitting the ship broadside were huge, rearing up over the handrail, then dropping into the vast yawning chasm of churning ocean. She wasn't alarmed, it was exhilarating to see the forces of nature at close hand. Leaning tight into the rail, Roisin stretched out her arms, just as she did at home when there was a storm, in awe at being part of such a unique spectacle.

Soaked to the skin she was about to leave when she noticed a pinpoint of light and a movement amongst the shadows. A whiff of cigarette smoke told her there was someone there. An innate sense of danger prickled her skin and she knew she was being watched.

She turned to go, but before she could move a figure stepped out and darted towards her. Strong arms twisted her around and pinned her against the rail. It was pointless crying out. There was no-one in sight and any sound she did make would not be heard above the creaking of the ship and the roar of the wind and waves.

A figure loomed above her, tall, thin and dark haired and smelling of cigarette smoke. It was a man she recognised, a man who was now tightening his hands around her throat.

She wasn't especially strong, but she was quick and sure footed. A knee to the groin and he relaxed his grip giving Roisin time to slide sideways out of his grasp. The events which then unfolded would remain forever etched in her memory.

Time seemed to stand still, as winded by her kick, the

man arched over the rail, his legs for one ghastly moment suspended in mid-air. As she watched in horror, a large wave broke against the side of the ship, swamping the bent figure. Within an instant, he was gone.

Chapter Ten

For a moment she stood as though paralysed, before she rushed forward to the spot where the man had disappeared. Scouring the darkness, there was no sign of him in the water. Snatching a lifebelt hanging from a hook she cast it into the wind–whipped waves. It was a pointless gesture she knew, but she had to try. Gathering her wits about her she ran, forcing her legs to carry her up the steps to the bridge where she hammered hard on the metal door with her fists until a uniformed officer appeared.

'A man has gone overboard. Come quickly.' Sobbing hysterically, she dragged the officer by his arm to the place where the man had disappeared. The red and white life ring was still there, cresting a wave, but there was no sign of the man.

From the bridge, the emergency siren sounded and the cry of '*Man overboard, Starboard side*' went up. Soon the area was swarming with crew members scanning the ocean with high powered binoculars and searchlights. Roisin was wrapped in a blanket and a nurse had been summoned to take her to the infirmary. Once the Captain was available, she would be asked for an account of events, the kindly nurse told her.

The next few hours passed in a daze. Following a muster drill it was established a man by the name of Patrick Higgins was missing. He hadn't been seen by his travelling companions since going for a cigarette after the evening meal. Many of the passengers were not best pleased to be roused from their sick beds to assemble at various points around the ship. They muttered peevishly at the inconvenience of it all until the news spread and a collective sense of shock replaced their irritation.

In the infirmary, Roisin, shaken and distressed, was handed a cup of sweet tea and a small glass of brandy. The alcohol burned her throat and made her splutter and wipe her eyes. Cocooned in blankets and seated in a chair close to the nurse's station, she was glad when Ger, still looking off colour, popped her head around the door to check if she was all right.

'Jeez girl, isn't it just awful. You know it was the fella who tried to attack me, don't you?'

Roisin nodded in response. She was too shaken to say more and had a feeling if she did she might cry.

'I'll see you in the morning, Roisin,' Ger said, giving her shoulder a rub. 'With a bit of luck everything will have calmed down by then, including the storm. By the way, what on earth were you doing all the way up there? You were lucky you weren't washed overboard too!'

Roisin shrugged her shoulders and lay her head against the back of the chair. She'd had a lucky escape. In more ways than one.

'Never mind. We'll talk tomorrow. Try and get some sleep.' Ger enveloped her in a hug and departed, blowing a kiss from the doorway. Roisin was left to contemplate the awful turn of events that had occurred. Eventually she dozed, waking some time later to the sounds of a murmured conversation taking place close by.

'The Captain has said it's not safe to turn the ship around in these conditions. To be brutally frank, the water is so cold the man would have died pretty quickly, even if it had been possiblc to locate him.'

Roisin recognised the voice of the officer she had encountered on the Bridge. He was talking to the nurse. 'How is the girl?' he was saying, 'it must have been terrible for her to see what happened.'

'She's doing well, physically. She hasn't said much, although it's hardly surprising. She's in shock. The captain will talk to her tomorrow. Would you like a nice cup of tea, I'm just about to make one?'

He must have agreed as the nurse took herself off to the little kitchenette to prepare a pot for both of them.

Morning came, and the ship was making steady progress. The worst of the storm was over and Roisin woke to the smell of frying bacon coming from the ship's kitchens. Her sleep had been fitful, interrupted by vivid nightmares.

Surveying her face in the nurse's wash room mirror, she looked puffy and exhausted. There were black circles under her eyes and her hair hung in straggly ringlets. How lovely it would be to have a soak in a nice hot bath, she thought. Before doing anything, she needed to find out the time of her interview with the Captain.

As if reading her mind, the nurse who had come to give her a quick check-up, handed her an envelope. 'They have to ask you a few questions about what happened. It's normal procedure in this sort of situation. Don't look so worried,' she said, observing Roisin's demeanour.

The letter was a request to attend an interview with the Captain and Chief Officer at 2 p.m. As she was a minor, a chaperone would have to be in attendance. Roisin hoped Ger was feeling well enough to accompany her. She felt overwhelmed by it all and knew she would get flustered if she was accompanied by a stranger.

When she got back to the cabin, Ger was up and looking reinvigorated. She had tidied the cramped space and everywhere was spick and span. Roisin was so relieved to be back in familiar surroundings, she burst into tears. Ger sat her down and placed an arm around her shoulders.

'Do you feel up to telling me what happened?'

At this, Roisin leant against her friend, sobbing her heart out. 'I think I killed him. What if they put me in prison?'

It took a great deal of patient coaxing before Ger got the full account. She listened without interruption, waiting for Roisin to finish before responding.

'Now you listen to me. You've had a horrible time, but that man was trying to assault you and the Lord only knows what he would have done if you hadn't escaped his clutches. You're not to blame and I'm going to come along and tell them what he did to me. They will see then what a disreputable character he was. But, before we do anything else, I'm going to run you a nice hot, relaxing bath. I've got some lovely bath oil. It will make you feel like a million dollars. Then we'll go and have breakfast. I don't know about you, but I'm famished!'

Roisin luxuriated in the bath Ger had run for her. She washed her hair first and then added some of Ger's foaming oil. It was heavenly and not at all what she was used to. At home she had to make do with the tin bath in front of the fire. After the bath she felt much better in herself. With a clean set of clothes and her hair brushed and plaited, she was ready to face the world.

'It's my mission to cheer you up young lady,' Ger said with conviction. 'After the interview I'll style your hair for dinner this evening. It'll make you look older and you can practise being aloof in front of all the gossips. They will be bursting to find out what went on.'

Ger held Roisin by the arm as they entered the dining room to have breakfast. It was crowded and heads turned as they entered. It was obvious to Roisin she was going to be the topic of conversation for some time to come.

'Just ignore them,' Ger said, 'they have nothing better to do than tittle-tattle.'

Fixing the other passengers with a steely glare, Ger steered Roisin in the direction of seats at a corner table. She then proceeded to order two portions of everything on the menu. After the porridge, grapefruit, cooked breakfast, toast, tea and coffee, they were stuffed to the gills. Ger even managed to get a laugh out of Roisin by puffing out her cheeks to show her how full she was.

'Now, can you face a walk or shall we read the papers?' Ger said, as they dodged a waiter balancing a basket of bread rolls. 'If you prefer we can just go back to the cabin. What do you feel like doing? I can see by your face you're dreading this afternoon, but I promise you everything will work out. You'll see.'

'A little walk will do me good I think,' Roisin said. She was glad to be in Ger's company. A reassuring presence was just what she needed.

They completed a circuit of the promenade deck in amiable silence. Following the storm, the sky was washed out and devoid of colour. A watery sun put in an appearance now and then, peeping from behind fluffy white clouds. It was a relief to see a moderate swell after the towering seas of the night before. Back inside they parted company, with Ger going off for a smoke, but only after assurances that Roisin was all right to be left by herself for a while.

'Come and find me if you're worried Ro. I won't be far away.'

They arranged to meet later in the foyer, allowing themselves enough time to have lunch if they could both face it. Roisin was unsettled and nervous. She was convinced that if she hung around in the more crowded areas, someone would want to talk to her about the previous evening and she kept her distance from the other passengers.

An exploration of the quieter part of the ship revealed a number of rooms she hadn't noticed previously. One was a wood panelled library. She spent a couple of hours there distracting herself by looking through a set of beautiful leather bound encyclopaedias, until the clock on the wall revealed it was time to leave.

Ger was waiting for her. 'Shall we have some soup to keep us going until dinner this evening?' Roisin suppressed a smile. It was hard not to laugh at the change in her appetite after her bout of seasickness.

It was a few minutes before two o'clock when they presented themselves at the main desk and were shown into a side room by a steward. Behind a large, polished table sat two men in full uniform with their braided caps lined up on the table in front of them. They stood as Ger and Roisin entered.

'Welcome Miss Flynn and Miss O'Connor.' The man speaking was the taller of the two and his white hair and bushy beard gave him a distinguished air. For an instant, Roisin was taken aback to hear herself addressed so formally. It was her mother who was usually referred to as Miss O'Connor. She also realised she hadn't been aware of Ger's surname until that moment.

'My name is Captain Harris and this is my Chief Officer Mr Owen,' he said, gesturing for them to take their seats. 'The seriousness of the situation necessitates this being a formal interview. Having said that, you can be assured you have nothing to concern yourself with Miss O'Connor. It is my duty to establish, as much as is humanly possible, the sequence of events leading to the unfortunate incident that occurred yesterday, which you were witness to.'

The Captain had a soft Canadian burr, which Roisin found reassuring, although she was still finding it hard to control her agitation. 'Mr Owen will record your statement and you can check its authenticity before signing it. Is that clear?' Roisin nodded in agreement, pushing her hands down on her knees to stop them from knocking.

Turning from Roisin, he addressed his next questions to Ger. 'Miss Flynn, I am given to understand you have some additional information pertinent to proceedings, in which case I must ask that you leave the room for the duration of this interview. Mr Owen will stand in as chaperone. When Miss O'Connor has given her account I will then hear from you. Do you understand?'

'I certainly do,' Ger declared, a tremble in her voice betraying her own nervousness.

Without Ger with her for support, re-living and recalling the awful events of the previous evening was harrowing, but unburdening herself to someone other than Ger was, to Roisin's surprise, a relief. When Captain Harris declared from the evidence provided that the event the previous night had been a very regrettable accident, Roisin almost wept with relief

'You are not in any way responsible for what happened in my estimation. However, I have to advise you that your mother and your guardians will be informed and that an enquiry will ensue. That is the correct procedure. You may be interviewed when you reach Canada, but it will be a mere formality, Roisin.' This was said kindly and tears pricked her eyes at his use of her first name.

With her account verified and signed, Roisin left Ger to volunteer evidence of her own encounter with the late Patrick Higgins.

The library seemed to Roisin to be the best place to take refuge and soon she was immersed in a book on natural history.

How wonderful it would be to study to become a naturalist, she thought. *You could spend all your time*

examining fossils and looking at plants and animals in their own environments.

Returning to the cabin she found Ger painting her nails with a pink, pearlised polish. The sharp tang of acetone hung in the air and Roisin felt her eyes start to smart. Ger had decided there was to be no further discussion on the subject of Patrick Higgins. Instead they spent a relaxing couple of hours chatting about inconsequential matters and experimenting with Ger's eye shadow palette, and powder and lipsticks.

In preparation for dinner, Ger swept Roisin's hair up into a fashionable French twist and secured it using some of her spare pins. A quick puff of something called Spray Net to hold it all in place and Roisin's new look, with the addition of a touch of make-up and a dab of Chanel No.5, was complete.

A glimpse in the mirror took Roisin by surprise, revealing an altogether more elegant version of herself despite her plain, woollen dress. Ger was right, she did look older with her hair up. She wasn't at all sure her mother would approve of this new level of sophistication, but it was temporary and not something she was going to do every day.

'You look stunning, Ro. You can be sure you'll turn heads this evening my girl.'

From her bag, Ger selected a soft, cashmere stole in a deep shade of emerald green and placed it around Roisin's shoulders. 'There, that's perfect,' she said, her ministrations complete.

It was obvious more than a few admiring glances were being directed at Roisin during dinner. At an adjoining table were the men who had been in her train carriage on the way to Cobh. She couldn't help but notice the younger of the three. He kept looking in her direction, egged on by his enthusiastic group of friends. It was a curious sensation to be stared at in that way. She hadn't really had much experience with boys and wasn't sure if she liked being the focus of attention. It felt like being studied as a specimen would under a microscope.

As she and Ger got up to leave at the end of the meal, the young lad made his way to their table. 'Would you be so kind as to accompany me on an evening stroll Miss?'

The request was obviously aimed at Roisin, but Ger couldn't resist a bit of teasing. 'Sure, I'm far too old for you young fella. Roisin on the other hand, would be more than happy to take the air with you, I feel sure of it.'

At that moment, had the ground opened up and swallowed her, Roisin would have been thankful. The boy she noticed was also blushing to the roots of his hair. She wasn't at all convinced it was a good idea, but she felt sorry for the boy, who by now was being teased mercilessly by his friends.

They were starting to attract attention from the other diners and Roisin was desperate to escape as quickly as possible. Nodding in his direction, she began to walk quickly towards the exit door, the boy running behind to catch her up.

'Now you take good care of that young woman,' Ger shouted after them with mock fierceness. 'I want her delivered safely back into my care by 10 o'clock. At the latest. '

With a wink and a wave to the boy's friends, sitting

open-mouthed at the adjoining table, she headed in the direction of the smoking room. Here a crowd of her admirers had assembled, hoping for a ballad or two before bedtime.

The lad was called Sean. He was eighteen and travelling to Canada to find work. He asked if Roisin would mind him taking her arm as they walked and she agreed.

'I have to confess I do know a bit about you, Roisin. The whole ship has been agog with curiosity since the Higgins fella went overboard. Now, you can talk about it if you want to, or we can avoid any mention of it if you prefer.'

She elected to stick to safer topics of conversation for the time being and asked Sean his reasons for travelling to Canada. He told her he was the oldest of seven children and his family had been plunged into poverty following the death of his father. With only a small pension, his mother was struggling to make ends meet. He was now head of the family, but finding work had not been easy. He had been planning to go to England, until he heard construction work was plentiful and well paid in Canada. After scraping together his fare he was going to chance his luck in Toronto. His plan was to work for a few years and send a regular amount home to his mother. Once he had made his fortune, he would return to Ireland and build his own house.

They had been on deck for the best part of an hour and Ger's stole was no substitute for a warm coat. Sean could see Roisin was starting to shiver with cold. Reaching out, he placed an arm around her shoulders then withdrew, unsure if it was acceptable behaviour. He was in awe of

Ger and aware he would get into trouble if he was too forward.

'I think we should go back inside before you catch your death,' he said, cupping his hands and blowing on them. 'The air is freezing. I suppose we will have to get used to it though. I've heard winters in Canada are brutal.'

The promenade deck was clearing of walkers and back in the entrance hall the clock was showing ten minutes to nine. Groups of people were milling around and the hum of conversation, punctuated by raucous laughter, was coming from the various lounges. The library was Roisin's favourite place and she suggested they go there where it would be quieter.

To her surprise, she was enjoying Sean's company. He had a good sense of humour and the combination of old fashioned manners and cheeky banter made her smile. He was also rather passable to look at, with his fine sandy hair, a dusting of freckles and twinkling blue eyes.

The library was unoccupied as Roisin hoped. Sean sat down on an overstuffed horsehair sofa in an alcove stacked ceiling high with books and patted the space next to him. Roisin paused, wondering if it would be better if she went to sit on one of the wing-backed chairs a few feet away. Sean was no threat to her, she decided, and sat alongside him with their knees almost touching.

'Now tell me all about yourself, Miss Roisin O'Connor.'

Sean was a relative stranger and talking about herself wasn't something she was used to, but he was a good listener. She even felt safe enough to cautiously volunteer a little information about Higgins' death, even though the memory caused a catch in her throat. Seeing she was upset, Sean's face reddened and he clicked his teeth in annoyance.

'I met the fella a few times and I can tell you he was a blackguard and a villain.'

At this Roisin managed a smile. Sean's choice of words echoed her mother's when describing any man she considered dishonourable.

'Even his friends didn't have a good word to say about him,' Sean was saying, 'especially when he had taken a drink. He could be very unpleasant and was always picking fights. From what I can gather he was escaping debts and a pregnant girlfriend at home. He was a bad lot and it's good riddance in my opinion.'

If Sean's intention was to comfort and reassure her, then he had succeeded. Even so, no words of consolation were ever going to erase the memory of that fateful night.

It was almost time to go and find Ger, but first she wanted to borrow a book. Selecting a volume at random from a set of encyclopaedias, she looked forward to reading a few pages before settling down to sleep.

'Bookworm are we? I'm not one for books meself.' Sean was studying her with a quizzical look on his face.

Roisin couldn't imagine anyone not being interested in reading. She remembered her mother saying 'you are never alone if you have a book.'

'Will you take a stroll with me again tomorrow evening?' Sean was saying, 'I'll see you after dinner if you like?'

He looked so eager, Roisin felt she couldn't refuse. 'That will be lovely,' she said, watching his face brighten in response.

After locating Ger and wishing Sean a goodnight they returned to the cabin. Before retiring Roisin had to face a quizzing about her escort for the evening.

'So, you're walking out with Sean again tomorrow? You must like him. Is he good boyfriend material?' Ger was in fine spirits and eager to hear all about Roisin's evening.

'I do like him, but I'm too young for a boyfriend. And, he doesn't like reading.'

This was too much for Ger who dissolved into gales of laughter. 'You are priceless Ro. I will really miss your funny little ways.'

Roisin felt sure Ger's interest in her was a sign of boredom from being cooped up onboard for so long. There didn't seem to be a better explanation. Ger was glamorous, amusing and popular. It was flattering to be seen as her friend and she appreciated being taken under her wing, especially in light of the Patrick Higgins affair. She was an amusing distraction, that was all. It was unlikely their paths would ever cross again. The Celtic Colleen had far more interesting things to see and do than bother with an unsophisticated country girl.

Chapter Eleven

The next morning dawned cold and bright. After breakfast Roisin went out onto the promenade deck where a group of children, supervised by the ship's onboard nanny, were playing quoits and skittles. Shrieking with excitement, the youngsters seemed carefree and Roisin looked at them with envy.

It wasn't that long ago she was as untroubled as they were. Now, with two full days ahead before they reached Halifax, it seemed to Roisin she had crossed an invisible line and adulthood was approaching all too quickly.

Was she missing out on an important part of her life? Some of her school friends had already started work, while others were returning to school to continue their education. Whether they envied or pitied her it was difficult to tell. They had seemed to dismiss her easily from their lives once they knew she was leaving. The leap she was taking into the unknown seemed of little consequence to them.

If her departure turned out to be a great adventure and the making of her, or a complete disaster, it didn't matter.

She had come to the to realisation she no longer belonged. That is if she ever had.

Reading always helped improve her mood and having returned the book she had borrowed the night before, Roisin spent a quiet afternoon in the library until it was time for dinner.

The random seating arrangements in the dining room meant she and Ger were at a table with a starry-eyed young couple. To Ger's disgust, they spent most of the time holding hands under the table and gazing into each other's eyes. Catching Roisin's eye, Ger pouted her lips and rolled her eyes when they weren't looking, which gave Roisin a fit of the giggles.

Sean joined them as they were leaving the dining room. He offered his arm to Roisin and they departed for their walk with exhortations from Ger to '*Behave*' and for there to be '*No canoodling*,' whatever that was. Following a bracing stroll Sean asked her if she had ever been to the games room. She had passed it a few times. It was populated mostly by older men and was noisy and fogged with smoke. Even though it wasn't a place she would go to on her own, she was curious and willing to venture inside with Sean.

'There's plenty to do. We can play cards or I'll teach you how to play shuffleboard if you like.'

Shuffleboard was new to her and Sean patiently explained the rules as they watched the end of a doubles game.

'See, you need to get your pucks as far down the table as possible into those numbered areas to win.'

For someone who had never played the game before,

Roisin caught on quickly. To everyone's surprise, her
own included, she won two games in succession. Sean
could only shake his head in disbelief.

'Well, that's a first for me,' he said, 'I've never been
beaten by a girl before!'

It was getting late and Sean escorted her back to the
smoking room. Ger for once was seated by herself and
looked weary. She raised a hand holding a cigarette in
welcome.

'I'm a little tired so I'm off to my bed,' she said,
staggering as she got to her feet. 'It's the gala concert
tomorrow evening and I need to catch up on my beauty
sleep.'

Roisin took Ger by the arm and, declining an offer of
help from Sean, led her back to the cabin and helped her
to undress. Up in her own bunk, she tried to read a book
of fairy tales chosen from the library. When she heard
Ger cry out in her sleep as though in discomfort, she
felt a wave of concern. She waited until Ger's breathing
became regular before turning off the overhead light. Her
own sleep was fitful, but by morning Ger seemed her old
self and was eagerly looking forward to her breakfast.

It was Friday, the last full day they would spend on the
ship. Time to organise their luggage and get ready for
disembarkation the following morning. A farewell dinner
had been arranged and with most of their packing done,
they were looking forward to the advertised *Gala Supper
With Music* later that evening. Ger seemed to have
recovered her spark and giggling like schoolgirls, they
spent most of the afternoon getting ready. Ger insisted on
lending Roisin one of her frocks. It was high necked and

made of Chinese silk in a beautiful shade of cobalt blue. The only problem was her shoes. The dress looked all wrong with her plain black brogues.

Like a magician pulling a rabbit out of a hat, Ger drew from a bag a pair of low heeled, suede pumps, adorned with a small bow.

'Now you just need a suspender belt and a pair of nylons and you'll be all set for tonight.'

The nylons were a revelation to someone who had always worn socks and Roisin was concerned she might ladder them.

'Don't you worry. I have plenty,' Ger said, 'now let's pin up your hair and make you the belle of the ball!'

In a corner of the dining room, a group of musicians were playing a selection of popular songs. When the meal was over, all five courses of it, the chairs and tables were pushed to one side to allow dancing. As usual, Ger, with her blonde curls framing her face and wearing a long, cream shift dress, was attracting a great deal of attention. A group of men huddled around pleading with her for a tune.

'Sing us one of the old ones,' cried out a plump, balding man, 'to remind us of home.'

Ger walked in the direction of the band and after a brief word with the violinist, took her place beside him. Someone handed her a microphone which she declined.

'This is an old love song from home you may be familiar with. It's one of my favourites and I hope you like it too. It's called *She Moved Through The Fair.*'

There was a brief ripple of applause. Then, with the mournful rise and fall of the violin introduction, the crowd fell silent. As Ger's flawless voice soared around the room, the words of the haunting lament wove its magic, capturing the emotions of all those assembled. Sean had slipped in quietly to stand alongside Roisin. Moved by the expressions of love and loss captured in the song, he reached for her hand and held it tightly.

My love said to me
My Mother won't mind
And me Father won't slight you
For your lack of kind
Then she stepped away from me
And this she did say
It will not be long love
'Til our wedding day.
She stepped away from me
And she moved through the Fair
And fondly I watched her
Move here and move there
And she went her way homeward
With one star awake
As the swans in the evening
Move over the lake

The song came to an end and Ger extended an arm in the direction of the violinist. Waving his violin bow in the air, he clicked his heels and bent his head forward in response to a round of applause from the crowd. Ger then curtsied in a theatrical way and walked back to her table. If you were to ask her, she would say she never tired of it. The heady rush that came with the rousing cheers, the clapping and foot stamping. There was nothing in the world to match the sounds of an appreciative audience ringing in your ears. It was her life blood.

As the evening drew to a close, Roisin knew she had to say goodbye to Sean and felt a pang of sadness at parting from him. It was unlikely they would meet again, but she liked him and would miss being in his company. He asked if he could escort her to her cabin and Roisin agreed.

Once again he took her hand. 'You are a lovely girl and one day someone will come along and make you very happy. I wish you all the luck in the world.'

With a kiss to her cheek and a cheery wave he was gone, leaving her bemused. Why would she need anyone else to make her happy? It was obviously important to lay claim to having had a boyfriend as it kept getting mentioned. Growing up was confusing. She had a lot to learn if she was to keep up with it all.

She was tucked up in her bunk checking through her documents for the morning when Ger knocked to be let in.

'My bloody feet are killing me,' she exclaimed, kicking off her shoes. 'What a night it was. You should have stayed Ro. You missed the Captain. He came to my table to congratulate me on my singing. I had no idea he was watching. He kissed my hand in front of everyone, can you believe it? Now what happened to you and that lovely boyfriend of yours?'

'He's a friend, that's all, and we have said our goodbyes. He's travelling on to Toronto so I won't see him again.' Roisin decided not to pursue the topic further and shuffled her papers and put them back into their envelope. 'Your singing was wonderful,' she continued. 'I'm not at all surprised the Captain was impressed. I really hope I get to see you perform the next time you are in Halifax.'

From a pocket inside her handbag, Ger took out a business card, and a small, leather covered notebook with a miniature pencil attached. She handed them to Roisin. The card was a pale lilac colour and edged in a border of forget-me-knots.

'My address at home in Ireland is on the card. Write down where you're staying in the notebook. You never know, we might meet up again. You've been a lot of fun Ro, and a good companion. It would be lovely to keep in touch. I'll even send you a postcard from wherever I am on my travels.'

With that promise, Ger declared she was exhausted and was soon fast asleep. Roisin's head was full of imaginings as to what lay ahead and she took longer to drift off. Her last thought before sleep took hold was the word *canoodle.* Rolling it around on her tongue, she vowed to make sure she asked Ger its meaning in the morning.

Chapter Twelve

The Mercinia was due to arrive in Halifax before midday. As Roisin peered through the porthole, she was disappointed to see the horizon was obscured by a dense mist. This meant there would be no clear view of the city as the ship made its approach to the port. Overhead a flock of seagulls could be heard, squawking loudly, a sure sign of approaching landfall.

The majority of passengers had turned up for breakfast, perhaps concerned it might be a while before they had the chance to eat again.

Roisin was pleased there was no sign of Sean and the other men. She had said her goodbyes and didn't want another conversation with him before leaving the ship. Instead, she focused on the breakfast menu with its cheery picture of flying Canada geese.

The menu offered the usual wide choice of items and Roisin selected the porridge, a boiled egg and toast and pancakes with maple syrup. 'They'll have to winch you off the ship after that lot,' Ger said in jest, picking a more modest plate of a grilled ham slice with poached eggs.

They noticed the young couple from the previous evening seated together, still gazing lovingly into each other's eyes over their breakfast dishes.

'Ah, that reminds me,' Roisin said. The sight of the two had jogged her memory, 'what exactly does canoodle mean? I'm guessing it's a lovey-dovey thing?'

Ger laughed at her choice of words. 'Well now young lady, when a couple are showing each other a bit of affection they are said to be canoodling. Is it safe to say you and Sean might have had a bit of a canoodle?'

Roisin thought for a moment, then drew her finger across her lips. 'Not telling,' she replied, much to Ger's amusement.

For those arriving in Eastern Canada by ship, entry was via Pier 21 with its 'Welcome Home To Canada' sign positioned above the lofty entrance doors. The waterfront ocean terminal, vast in size, had served to process the waves of immigrants entering the country since its inception in 1928. With the arrival of the Mercinia, its Great Hall was packed with disembarked passengers milling around in confusion.

The whole experience was overwhelming. Roisin was glad Ger was at her side as they waited to be called to have their hand luggage inspected by customs officers and their documents checked by immigration officials. Despite the initial chaos, order was quickly established as they were processed by the courteous and helpful staff.

The last stage of the procedure was to try and find her trunk, located in the downstairs baggage room. If all went to plan, Joe and Peggy would be waiting outside to pick her up.

Before that, Roisin and Ger needed to say their farewells. Ger had to find her driver as she was being picked up and taken by car to her hotel in the centre of Halifax.

'Roisin, you darling girl I'm going to say au revoir rather than goodbye. I feel we may meet again before too long.'

They hugged, and with her customary wink and a wave, Ger walked away, the clicking of her heels echoing in the vast and rapidly emptying space.

Roisin soon found the stairs leading down to the baggage collection area. Reunited with her trunk, she pulled her coat around her, straightened her beret and sat herself down on the trunk's hard surface. Her hands were cold and she looked in her pockets for her gloves. She was sure it was where she had them last. Or was it? They weren't in her bag either and she could feel a rising sense of panic. What would her mother say if she had mislaid them? With a start she remembered her mother was not there to scold her and anyway the gloves were packed in the trunk. Not much use to her when her fingertips were starting to turn blue with the cold. She consoled herself by breaking off a square of chocolate from the last bar at the bottom of her valise. The sweet milkiness, dissolving slowly on her tongue, was a balm to her frayed nerves.

The minutes ticked by. She could hear the shuffling of footsteps from the level above her. She imagined people were making their way to waiting trains or were being collected by family from the cold quayside. Why was nobody coming for her?

A sense of alarm was starting to turn to despair. What would happen to her if she was left here by herself? What would she do? Where would she go?

The man who had dragged her trunk out from a side-room was nowhere to be seen.

Debating whether she should go and try and find someone to ask, she gulped in relief when she heard a voice calling her name.

'Hey, hey Roisin.' The sturdily built man striding towards her looked very much like an older and slightly more rounded version of the Joe she had seen in photographs.

'I've been walking up and down looking for you. I should have realised you would be down here with your luggage.'

With the assistance of a porter requisitioned by Joe, the trunk was loaded onto the flat back of his pick-up truck and secured with a tarpaulin and ropes. Once her valise was stowed in the footwell, she jumped in alongside Joe to begin the final stage of her long journey. A new home and a new life beckoned. The idea of it filled her with trepidation.

'Peggy would have loved to have come to meet you, but she feels the cold now,' Joe was saying, interrupting her thoughts. 'We thought it best she waited at home for us.'

Joe was a great talker and he spoke of how he had departed from Pier 21 on a troopship destined to join Allied Forces during World War II. He had met Peggy in London and after a whirlwind romance, they had married. On his return to his home country he had bought a property and Peggy followed soon after, passing through Pier 21 as a young war bride.

Lulled by Joe's soft Canadian accent and the warmth of the cab, Roisin drifted off to sleep. She woke to find they had left the city behind. The earlier mist had cleared and they were no longer on the highway. The road was narrower and lined on either side by towering pine trees embedded at their base in a crust of whitish blue ice. A few miles on and the trees thinned, revealing glimpses of sparkling ocean, fringed by boulder-strewn beaches.

It wasn't long before they passed a metal sign hanging from a post that read 'Tigh na Coille' which Roisin recognised as the Gaelic for 'House in the Woods'. As they turned onto a rutted driveway, the fields, where there was no covering of ice, lay bare with the odd patch of brown grass. It was so unlike the lush pastures of home, green even in the deepest of winter, that Roisin couldn't help but wonder if the pictures she had seen of Canada were genuine.

The house, when it came into view, raised her spirits. It was just as she imagined. Painted white with numerous windows, including an oriel in the front gable, it stood in imposing grandeur, surrounded by spreading mature trees and encircled by a picket fence.

It's beautiful, she thought to herself, *just like a fairytale.* Joe could see she was impressed. He described to her the work he and Peggy had undertaken as the truck proceeded at a snail's pace up the track leading to the house.

'It was built in 1913 and was almost derelict when we took it on. It's taken years to renovate, but we have it as we want it now. There are seven acres of pasture, all overgrown when we came and ten acres of woodland needing constant attention. We have worked hard, it's been a labour of love. Unfortunately, Peggy is restricted now in what she can do, especially in the winter. I'm hoping you will be able to lend a hand. It looks a bit barren now, but you wait. It's beautiful in spring and summer, but when autumn comes it's spectacular in these parts. I think once you find your feet, you will love being here Roisin.'

Joe pulled in front of a set of steps leading to a wooden veranda complete with a swing seat. As they got out of the truck, the front door opened and a woman stepped out, wiping her hands on her apron. Roisin recognised her immediately. The O'Connor genes had handed down to the cousins the same hair colour and face shapes. Peggy was three years older and shorter and stockier than Theresa, but there could be no denying their shared lineage.

'Roisin, you're here at last,' Peggy said, wrapping her in a tight embrace.

Releasing her she took a step back and surveyed her niece. 'Will you let me look at you? Sure, the last time I saw you, you were just a little tot and now you're all grown up.'

Despite her many years in Canada, Peggy's accent had not faded and Roisin felt cheered by the sound of her Irish lilt.

With Joe tasked with getting a sack barrow for the trunk, Peggy led the way inside. Stepping into a wide hallway, Roisin could see a door located to the right and another ahead. A wooden staircase with a polished balustrade led to the upstairs. The room at the back of the house was a warm and cosy kitchen with a wooden dresser, easy chairs and a substantial scrubbed-top table laid with three place settings. The wood stove, positioned in a recess along the back wall, crackled with burning logs.

A delicious aroma was coming from a pan bubbling away on the stove top and Roisin realised she was hungry. She'd had nothing to eat, since breakfast apart from a square of chocolate.

Recognising the signs of tiredness, Peggy pointed to a chair next to the fireplace.

'Have a seat there in the warm. You look worn out. Joe won't be long. He needs to bed down the animals before it gets too dark. We'll eat when he comes in and then you can have a look around the house. When you unpack your luggage, you can take it upstairs. Your room is all ready for you. I hope you like it.'

'I'm sure I will,' Roisin said, already beginning to feel herself relax. She was looking forward to unpacking her trunk, but also keen to hear about the farm. 'What animals do you have?'

'It's just a small hobby farm in comparison to some of our neighbours. Joe will show you around in the morning. We don't have many animals, but there is an orchard and fields where we grow our own fruit and vegetables. We're lucky to have a stream and a well, with the sweetest water for miles around. If you want to get cleaned up before dinner, step through the door over on your right. Here in Canada it's called a mud room.'

With her trunk wheeled safely inside, the large pan of food was carried to the table with ceremony by Joe, while

Peggy set out some fresh bread and a bowl of butter alongside.

'In your honour, we have an old family favourite you might recognise.' With a flourish, Peggy took the lid off the pan. 'It's Irish Stew and soda bread to go with it. Your mam and I loved a bowl of stew when we were growing up. Afterwards, we can have some of my bottled peaches and cream.'

It wasn't difficult to imagine the two women as youngsters. Not only did they look alike, they had similar mannerisms, although Theresa's face was not etched with lines of pain like her cousin's. And while Theresa's hands were rough and sore from work, she didn't have the throbbing and swollen joints that made life so painful and difficult for Peggy.

The food was delicious, and once the table was cleared and the dishes washed, Peggy was eager to show Roisin around the house before she started her unpacking. Ushering Roisin back into the hall, Peggy pushed open the large panelled door opening off the hallway. It led into a more formal-looking room with stuffed velvet sofas, shelves stacked with china and an upright piano. It was old-fashioned but cosy, and in keeping with the age of house.

The centrepiece of the room was a rather grand fireplace in front of which lay an oriental rug. It was obviously the best room in the house and reserved for special occasions. Roisin couldn't see herself coming in here very often. That is until her gaze fell upon the alcoves on either side of the fireplace. They were crammed from floor to ceiling with books and journals of all shapes and sizes.

She couldn't believe her luck. She had access to her own personal library. It couldn't get any better than that, could it?

Chapter Thirteen

Her room was in the eaves. The sloping walls were supported by thick, wooden beams and the oriel window was the one she had seen from outside. Beneath the window was a recessed seat with patchwork cushions. The walls had been painted a shade of sea green, matching the background of the rosebud-sprigged curtains. Across the foot of the bed lay a brightly coloured patchwork coverlet.

'Is it all right? We were going to put you in the guest room as it's bigger, but Joe and I thought you might prefer this one with the window,' Peggy said.

She was so quiet, Peggy and Joe feared the worst. Had they got it wrong? Could it be that she didn't like the room?

As Roisin turned towards them, they saw tears in her eyes. 'What's wrong? We can put you into the other room if you would prefer.'

'No, I wouldn't want to be anywhere else. It's just perfect.'

The trunk was too heavy to bring upstairs and Peggy

told her to unpack her things and stack them on the table. They would all help take them up later. Roisin felt a wave of emotion as she opened the lid. The trunk had travelled so far and at times she had wondered if she would ever see it, or her possessions again.

To her surprise, the trunk yielded an unexpected offering. Nestling amongst her clothing was a rectangular box, wrapped in shiny pink tissue paper. She had no recollection of it being there when she was packing. Turning it over, she noticed a gift card with a message in her mother's handwriting:

To my darling girl. Do not open this box until Christmas morning. Love to you as always xxx

Soon everything was unpacked and laid out ready. With Joe and Peggy's assistance, she carried her belongings up to her room and before long everything had been tidied away. There was plenty of space in the wardrobe and chest of drawers for her clothes. Her collection of personal items and books she arranged neatly on shelves above the bed.

'I've had a thought,' said Joe, taking the cushions off the window seat. 'There's some spare wood in the barn. I can make an extension to go over the window ledge. You can pull it out to use it and slide it back in when you're ready. If I can find a chair to fit underneath, you can use it as a desk.'

Emptying her valise, she found the bag of sweets and the remains of the chocolate bar. They reminded her of her mother and she felt sad at not being able to see and talk to her.

The gift she had purchased for Joe and Peggy was

tucked in a corner of her valise. Alongside was a stick of barley sugar and the breakfast menu from the ship she had taken as a memento.

An image of Ger came to mind. They had been through such a lot together in just a few, short days. Only *she* could really understand what Roisin had endured at the height of that storm. Would she ever see Ger again, or her mother for that matter? Her mood of despondency was short-lived as she imagined Ger chiding her with a few choice words. *Come on now Ro, chin up my girl. The show must go on!*

She hesitated before offering her aunt and uncle the gift of the miniature model of the ship's bell. It was such a small and inadequate token after Joe and Peggy had already done so much for her. They did seem pleased with the gift, although she wondered if their enthusiasm might just have been for her benefit.

'How lovely?' Peggy said, holding the bell up to catch the light. Pulling on the rope clapper, she laughed heartily. 'See Joe, I can ring whenever I need you.'

The following morning Roisin woke to the sound of murmured voices and the enticing smell of frying bacon. Pulling back the curtains revealed a frosty scene with the ground still covered in ice. The trees, heavy with their burden of jagged icicles, drooped in melancholy solidarity. Beyond she caught sight of the ocean, glinting in the morning sun. She dressed hurriedly, aware she had overslept. In the back kitchen there was no sign of Joe, but Peggy was busy at the stove singing along to the radio. This explained the voices she had heard earlier from upstairs.

'I'm sorry Aunt Peggy, I must have overslept. I wanted to get up and see the animals with Uncle Joe but I've only just woken up.'

'I'm glad you had a good night. You must have needed the rest,' Peggy said. 'There's no need to worry. Joe is going to drive me to Mass and then I have a quilting bee to go to. He will show you everything when he gets back.'

'A quilting bee?'

Peggy laughed at her puzzlement. 'When I first came to Canada, I worked as a nurse, as you know. After I retired I felt a bit isolated and I joined the quilting bee. We meet in each other's homes to sew quilts. Did you notice the one on your bed? It was done by our group over one winter. I'm afraid I'm slow at sewing, but it's good for my hands and I enjoy the fellowship. I know your mammy says you're not one for going to church, Joe isn't either, but everyone is friendly and I know they all want to meet you. Now take a seat, and I'll get you some breakfast.'

With breakfast over and Peggy dressed for church in a smart wool coat and brown velvet hat, Joe brought the pick-up to the front of the house. The pair departed, the truck bouncing over ruts in the drive.

Alone in the house, Roisin washed and dried the dishes, stacking them in piles on the table, unsure of where they were kept.

A stack of magazines in a rack turned out to be copies of *Canadian Geographic.* So engrossed was she in a story about hibernating bears, she didn't notice Joe when he re-appeared.

'I see you found my magazines. We knew you were interested in nature so I kept some back copies for you to read. Canada is full of natural features and wildlife as you will discover, but first, the wonders of 'Tigh na Coille' await you.'

Peggy had left some clothing for her in the mud room. 'Don't worry about what you look like, We'll go to town and get you some work clothes during the week,' Joe said, stifling a grin.

The sight of his niece, wearing a battered pair of Peggy's boots on her feet and dressed in an old pair of his coveralls cinched at the waist with a belt, was truly a comedic sight to behold.

'Tie back that beautiful hair of yours though. There's machinery and Peggy will kill me if you're not in one piece when she gets back.'

The barn was sited close to the house. It was built of timber and painted brick red on the outside. Tall wooden doors swung outwards for access and inside the concrete floor was covered in straw. Wooden steps led up to a hayloft with small windows set on either side of the raised platform. A store room held apple barrels and boxes of winter vegetables. Suspended along the left wall was a hayrick. Various items of farm machinery and saddlery hung from iron hooks or were lined in some disarray against the walls. Roisin took a deep breath. The scent of sweet hay mingling with the faint odour of animal dung wasn't unpleasant. It reminded her of the summer, despite the bleak, frozen landscape outside.

'Is this where the animals sleep?' she asked.

'The hens and pigs have their own shelters outside, but the horse and cow come into the barn overnight during the winter months. Once the weather improves, we can take them down to graze in the lower pastures. Let me introduce you to our little family,' Joe said, giving her a cheery wink.

The paddock was to the rear of the barn and covered in a layer of sand. This was to help keep the area free from ice and made it easier when it came to clearing up, Joe explained.

'Feeding is usually done in the barn in winter. The most important thing to remember is that our livestock must have access to water at all times. I come out three or four times a day to break the ice when it's below freezing.' As he was speaking the horse and cow ambled over to investigate.

'This very handsome boy is Chester and he's twenty years young. He is unusual around these parts for a Canadian horse, being a chestnut with a flaxen mane.'

The horse nuzzled around his pocket for the carrot he knew was there.

'And this beauty is Bluebell, the nicest-natured Jersey you could ever meet. She's a great milker and loves to be petted. Sometimes I do believe she thinks she's a dog.'

Roisin hadn't been up close to animals this size before. To her relief the pair were more like pets and happily allowed Roisin to stroke their noses and rub their ears.

The pigs were in two separate pens. 'This is Clemmie and the bigger boy is Hector. I'm keeping them apart until she has her babies,' Joe explained. 'She is due to farrow any time and likes a little privacy. Some say the males eat the piglets, but I've never seen that happen. She does seem a bit crabby at the moment. Poor old Hec has had a couple of bites to his nose.'

The hens had their own section of yard and were pecking vigorously at some seed scattered on the frozen ground. A large brown rooster crowed heartily as they passed. Joe shooed him away as it took a dive at their feet.

'That's Artie the cockerel. He's a character. He and his wives are Le Grand chickens. Those ladies lay the best brown speckled eggs in the county. I picked up half a dozen earlier. We can have another look this evening to see if there are any more.'

Roisin paused, an expression of awe on her face. She was struggling to take everything in, The sounds and smells of the farmyard were making her senses tingle. It was almost overpowering. So much to see and do. She hoped she would not let her aunt and uncle down.

Everything about her new home was more, much more than she could ever have wished for.

Chapter Fourteen

There was a lot to remember, but Roisin was a quick learner. She made sure she rose at the same time as Joe each morning and once they had breakfast and the stove was alight, the chores began. They settled into an easy pattern of milking, feeding, watering and mucking out. Joe demonstrated the best way to attach a halter and lead line to Chester and a tether to Bluebell so they could be taken down to the paddock.

While she and Joe worked, Roisin made notes on the feeding schedules and supplements needed for each of the animals. She learned for Chester and Bluebell, it was necessary to add alfalfa hay with feed for protein and a salt lick for extra minerals during the winter months. That Clemmie needed lots of hay for warmth as well as extra food and plenty of water while she was farrowing. The days passed quickly and soon her little notebook was full.

'It's sooo much more interesting than school,' she declared, as she and Joe were walking back to the house for their coffee and biscuits one morning.

For Joe, the additional help was proving invaluable.

The girl was not only bright and interested in everything, she was a real hard worker. He and Peggy didn't have children and he often felt ill at ease with other people's offspring, but Roisin fitted right in and was a pleasure to have around. When she had asked about exploring the bay, Joe thought it only fair she had a break from work. He decided he would show her the paths to the beach that afternoon. For now though, it had been a long morning and he was hungry and ready for his midday meal.

Lunch was hunks of bread and creamy cheese with home-baked oat biscuits to follow. While they ate, Joe outlined some of the plans he had for the spring and summer planting. 'I'll take you down to the lower pastures when the weather improves. I'm going to build a deer-proof fence as soon as the ground thaws. They are beautiful animals, but they wreak havoc when the new shoots start to appear.'

He had sketched an outline of the area he hoped to cover with fencing and was showing it to Roisin. He would be using tall wooden stakes and maybe mesh, he told her. 'The problem is, if they can see through the gaps they may try to jump it anyway. We will give it a go to start with as it's a cheaper option than plank fencing.'

'Joe, the poor girl is full to the brim with facts and figures. You promised to take her to the beach and I think we could all do with a walk,' Peggy said, gathering together Joe's sketches and placing them in a pile on the sideboard.

The days had been so full Roisin had completely forgotten how close the property was to the ocean. From dawn until dusk there was always something to do.

As it was winter, once they had finished the evening feeding and milking and the animals had been tended to for the night, it was pitch black outside. After dinner they would sit listening to the radio with Peggy sewing or knitting and she and Joe reading until it was bedtime. It would be lovely to have some time off during the day. She couldn't wait to explore the beaches and feel the ocean wash over her bare feet. Two and a half thousand miles was a huge distance, but it was the same water that lapped the shores of her native land. The idea was comforting and putting her feet into the ocean she thought would somehow close the distance between her and her mother.

'As Peggy is coming with us, we will take the easiest path today. There are others you can take and I'll show you them another time. You do need to be careful where you walk when the bears come out of hibernation though. They are very protective of their cubs.' Joe was helping Peggy with her coat and was unaware of the effect his words were having on his niece.

'Really, there are bears?' Eyes wide with amazement, Roisin could hardly contain her excitement at the thought there were such interesting creatures virtually on the doorstep.

Under Peggy's instruction and despite her protestations that she was warm enough, she was persuaded to wear one of her aunt's old coats along with a pair of battered gumboots.

She hoped they wouldn't encounter anyone on their walk. She felt like an old farmer. Peggy and Joe had promised they would take her to town to buy some working clothes and boots later in the week and she was looking forward to it. Anything had to be an improvement on what she was wearing today.

She hid her impatience at Peggy's slow progress, eager to see the ocean close up.

Crossing the road at the bottom of the drive, they took a narrow track through a densely-packed pine forest. She could smell the ocean and the taste of salt was tangy on her tongue. The track widened to become a path strewn with small, moss-covered rocks and tree roots. This opened onto a long crescent of sandy beach dotted with large grey boulders.

The tide was out and it was some distance to the water's edge. To Joe and Peggy's astonishment and before either of them had time to utter a word, Roisin had discarded her coat and boots and was running towards the water, the wind whipping long strands of her hair around her face. Splashing through the breakers she suddenly stopped and held her arms out in front of her, almost in supplication.

'I can see now why some in Waterbridge believed the girl to be peculiar,' Peggy observed.

She thought back to when she and Theresa were teenagers. How different her cousin's life would have been without the child. Theresa herself was born when her mother was forty-two, a very welcome surprise her parents were at pains to tell her.

Peggy remembered how proud they were of their only daughter and her achievements. The unexpected pregnancy dashed their hopes for her future.

The inevitable gossip circulating in the town was hurtful, for all concerned.

When Theresa returned from having the child, her

parents planned to do all they could to help her pick up the pieces of her life. Eventually, they felt sure everything would return to normal.

With Theresa's consent, they made arrangements for her confinement at the Mother and Baby home. She would remain there for six weeks until her child was born and for a further six months afterwards, until the adoption. It never occurred to them that Theresa would change her mind about giving up her child.

'I'm keeping her,' she had said defiantly, 'please don't try and persuade me otherwise.'

Her parents were horrified, but their appeals did not shake her resolve. *She was stubborn and selfish*, they told her. *Didn't she care about the disgrace she was bringing on herself and on them? It was a reckless and stupid idea. She would never manage to bring up a child on her own. Why wouldn't she let Peggy and Joe take her? They could give the child a much better life than Theresa ever could. She would be a single mother. A sinner in the church's eyes. The shame of it!*

Finally, when all their entreaties failed, came the wounding barb to sever the relationship forever. 'If you do this, we will have nothing more to do with you. You will no longer be our daughter.'

Peggy turned from her musings to talk to Joe.

'What do you think of her? Have we bitten off more than we can chew? We only know what Theresa told us. Much as I love my cousin, I do wonder if she was finding her difficult and that's why she sent her to us. And, let's not forget what happened on the ship. We have yet to speak to her about it. I have to confess to feeling uneasy.

I'm worried about whether taking her on was the right thing to do. For all concerned.'

Joe didn't reply. He was already starting to collect Roisin's discarded clothing. When he had done so, they stood apart, each lost in their own thoughts, until an exhilarated and very bedraggled figure began to sprint back up the sand towards them. Despite not getting an answer to her questions, Peggy understood her husband only too well. It was plain to see the girl had captivated him.

Back at the house and with the animals locked up safely for the night, it was time to prepare the evening meal. They were having a pot roast and Roisin helped by peeling potatoes and scraping carrots to go with the beef joint. Thinking of Bluebell she felt a bit sorry when the meat came out of the oven. Her hunger soon got the better of her though, and she demolished what was on her plate with gusto.

'Hot milk and a bath for you, my girl. You look as though you have been dragged around the floor of the threshing barn.' Peggy's plain speaking made Roisin giggle and she agreed she was in need of a good clean up.

While Roisin went for her bath, Peggy took the opportunity to question Joe further. He was not a man to be pushed. She knew to tread carefully or he would just clam up. He was a thinker and never one for hasty decisions, but his judgement was usually sound and she valued this in him.

She waited for a response, as the wooden clock on the wall ticked away the minutes.

Eventually, she couldn't stand the silence any longer.

'For God's sake Joe. Will you tell me what in heaven's name you are thinking?

Joe was sitting in his favourite chair next to the stove, an unopened tractor magazine on his lap. He turned to face his wife, in no mood for a disagreement. Two religious references in one sentence were a measure of her impatience with him, and he didn't want to provoke her further.

'The truth of the matter is, the girl *is* unusual,' he volunteered. 'It's not just that she's a natural with the animals, she's whip-smart too and quick at picking things up. Look what happened when I gave her the plan of the field? In no time she had worked out how many posts and how much fencing we would need for the deer enclosure.'

Joe got up and added a log to the stove before continuing. 'And look at how she calculated a feeding plan for all the animals. It would have taken me days.'

Peggy attempted to interrupt and Joe put his hand up to silence her. 'There's something else. She's intuitive. The animals are drawn to her in a way I haven't seen before, and she has a sixth sense when it comes to changes in the weather. She told me earlier she can feel there is a bad storm coming. There's been nothing on the weather forecast, so we will have to wait and see whether it comes to pass.'

'Tsk. That sounds like mumbo-jumbo. You're getting soft in the head in your old age,' Peggy retorted dismissively.

'You asked for my opinion and you've had it,' Joe said, his tone sharper than usual. 'For the time being, this is the best place for her. We can protect her and she will thrive under our care. My concern is for the long term. This isn't going to be enough for her. We need to put our heads together Peg. That girl is going to need more than we can offer here.'

Peggy was taken aback. They had been together a long time and she had never heard Joe speak so eloquently or passionately on any subject. Hearing it said, she realised he was right. The girl was their responsibility now. What lay ahead was anybody's guess.

Chapter Fifteen

'Are we going into Halifax?' The shopping trip was arranged for the coming Friday and Roisin was keen to know if they were going to the city.

'No, we don't go into the city very often,' Peggy replied, 'there are stores in Lewistown. We can get everything we need there and it's only a few miles away.'

Crammed into the truck between her aunt and uncle, it was difficult for Roisin to see much from the windows. A few miles on she did catch sight of a diminutive white painted church with a bell tower. Peggy pointed at it, telling her it was the church she attended. A sharp turn in the road and they began to wind down a narrow street with houses on either side. Ahead, was a small harbour with a number of boats, each hitched to a wooden post.

The road curved to the right then opened into a wide, tree lined street. On either side was a mixture of buildings, some tall and gabled, others low and squat.

Parking the truck outside one bearing a sign saying 'Convenience Store', Joe dropped down the tailgate in preparation. He wanted to pick up some animal feed and the owner, Rich, usually had a bag of spent grain from home brewing, a treat all the animals loved. If he was lucky and Peggy didn't notice, he might even pick up a couple of bottles of beer for himself.

'Hi there young lady. So you're the Irish girl I've heard so much about.'

Roisin looked in surprise at the man addressing her. Rich had grown up in the town and he and his wife Marjie had run the store for over thirty years. It was a small community and the locals passed through on a regular basis, buying everything from household goods to horse liniment. Not much escaped their notice. She volunteered a shy hello, and while Peggy gossiped with Marjie, and Joe and Rich carried bags out to the truck, she took herself off to see what was on offer amongst the jumble of goods filling the store.

To the rear of the building was a workwear section and she tried on a few pairs of rubber boots until she found a pair that fitted. There were rows of workwear and waterproof clothing, all in sizes far too large for her. She spotted what she was looking for on an end rail sandwiched between lines of men's shirts and trousers. The sign above read 'Boys Sizes' and from here she selected a few items of clothing and took them to show Peggy.

'Can I have these for work please Aunt Peggy?' she said, holding the garments up for inspection.

Peggy and Marjie exchanged glances and each raised an eyebrow. From under the counter a sheet of brown paper and a ball of string were produced. Marjie carefully wrapped the two plaid work shirts and two pairs of denim overalls, complete with bib and brace, and handed the package along with the boots to one very satisfied customer.

～

The sky was darkening by the time the evening chores were completed and the animals had settled down for the night. They had left the job of emptying the truck until after dinner. After they had done so, they checked on Clemmie to see if the piglets had made an appearance.

'Still no sign. Let's give her a couple of handfuls of this grain mash and see if it helps her along.'

Joe was not surprised to hear the news on the radio warning of a bad nor'easter heading for the Maritimes. It was going to be a big storm, just as Roisin had predicted and he was hoping Clemmie would farrow before it landed.

'You were right Roisin, we are going to get a humdinger of a storm. We will just have to make sure everything is tied down. Those winds can be damaging and we wouldn't want to lose a roof.'

Peggy was studying her replenished kitchen cupboards, pleased their visit to town meant she now had all the essentials to last a few days.

'I'm glad we stocked up on provisions today. We need to make sure there's plenty of wood up by the house too Joe. You know the power can be knocked out for days if things get really bad.'

By morning the wind was gusting vigorously and flurries of wet snow were falling. After breakfast Joe and Roisin checked the barn.

'It's best the animals stay inside until this passes. I'll make sure everything is tied down outside,' Joe announced, leaving Roisin to milk Bluebell and muck out the barn.

Chester seemed a bit disgruntled at being kept inside. She fed him an apple from one of the barrels and ran her hand along his back. Stroking his muzzle, she whispered some lines from the Yeats poem into his ear, which seemed to soothe him.

When winds have gathered and sun and
moon burned dim.
Above its cloudy rim;
But let a gentle silence wrought with music flow
Whither her footsteps go.

Joe re-appeared a few moments later. 'Come and see what's arrived, young Roisin.'

She followed him outside to the pig pen. Tucked up in a nest of straw, Clemmie was lying on her side with seven little piglets sucking furiously at her teats.

'Now all we need to do is find out how many boys and girls we have when she allows us a look,' Joe said.

Roisin could barely contain her excitement and hopped from foot to foot. She had never seen a litter of piglets up close and the sight of the squirming little creatures delighted her.

The storm was like no other Roisin had encountered. The wind gained in strength throughout the day, whistling and howling and blowing the snow into drifts. Even the house shook alarmingly.

'There's sure to be a storm surge with this wind,' Joe said. 'Let's hope it's not too high. I've never known the water come up as far as the house, although we have found seaweed on the road before now.'

Peggy was baking a couple of meat pies and a batch of biscuits to see them over the worst of the weather. In the background the radio kept them updated on the progress of the nor'easter.

There was nothing for it but to hunker down for a couple of days until the worst was over. Joe regularly inspected the barn and outbuildings for any damage. Clemmie was kept warm and given extra feed and water and her pen kept clean and dry. Roisin did the rest of the feeding, the milking and fetched the eggs. Just getting to the barn was a trial. The wind speed was so intense the back door was pulled out of her hand.

Stepping outside, needles of icy snow burned her face and eyes. Despite the extremes of weather, the beauty of the landscape, even at its most inhospitable, was breathtaking.

As quickly as it had arrived the wind slowed, then subsided. The temperature dropped again overnight and the snow, now as powdery as icing sugar, drifted into banks along the walls of the house and barn. Joe's relief was evident. 'I think we've only lost a couple of roof shingles. I'll ask Cal to come over and help with the repair.'

'Who's Cal?' Roisin enquired and Joe told her he lived at the neighbouring property.

'We can take a walk there later and see if he needs a hand with anything. Is there any pie left Peg? He always enjoys your cooking. But, first we need to clear the paths of snow or we won't be going anywhere today.'

By mid morning they had a freshly cleared drive and Roisin had acquired a couple of blisters for her effort. Joe grinned when she held out her hands to show him.

'War wounds,' he said laughing. 'You can show Cal and he can see how hard we have been working you. There is a shorter way to get to Cal's house, but the drifts will be too deep today. The snow plows have been out clearing the main road. It will be quicker if we go that way.'

When they reached the road, the sun was out. Dressed in warm clothing and boots, they were both perspiring by the time they had walked the short distance to Cal's house.

Whoever Cal was, he obviously hadn't got around to clearing a path. It was an effort walking through the drifts and Roisin was panting from exertion by the time they reached the house. It was a smaller property than Peggy and Joe's and in a state of disrepair. It looked as though it needed new windows and a lick of paint.

'Hey, Cal. How are you doing?' Joe called out.

A figure appeared from inside a garage containing a rusty, flatbed truck.

To Roisin's surprise, Cal was a lot younger than she expected. Not that much older than her, she would guess. He approached, twisting his cap in his hands and glancing at her shyly, his blond hair falling across his face and covering his eyes. He was tall and thin. 'Lanky' her mother would have called him. As she handed him the bag containing a slice of pie and some biscuits, he pushed back a lock of hair and she noticed how blue his eyes were. The colour of summer cornflowers.

'This is my niece, Roisin,' Joe said by way of introduction. 'Remember I told you she was coming to stay with us? She travelled all the way here from Ireland on her own.'

Cal nodded, avoiding eye contact. He didn't appear very talkative and Roisin wondered if it was because he didn't have very many visitors. Peggy had mentioned he lived alone.

There was no time for further speculation. Joe was keen to find out if the storm had caused any damage to Cal's property.

'An old apple tree came down, that's all,' Cal said. 'It was pretty rotten at the base so I wasn't surprised when it fell. Once the snow clears, I'll chainsaw it up for logs. How about your place?'

'We lost a few roof shingles, but we were well prepared. Roisin here knew a storm was coming, ahead of the weather forecaster,' Joe said, with pride in his voice. 'Do you think you could come over and help? I'm not great at getting on the roof any more?'

'I have a shift at the mill tomorrow. I'll be over around two o'clock. Is that OK?

'Sure,' Joe replied, 'and stay for dinner. Peggy is always pleased to see you.'

On the walk back, Roisin was eager to know all about Cal. There was something about him that intrigued her and she wanted to find out as much as possible about him. He was shy, but there was more to it. Was he lonely?

Unhappy? Sad? She sensed it was all of those things combined.

'He didn't invite us in. Why was that uncle Joe?' From what Peggy had told her about the locals she knew this was not typical amongst neighbours in these parts and she thought it curious behaviour.

Joe looked pensive. When he did speak he chose his words carefully.

'It's a long and sorry story. That boy is nineteen years old and despite the awful things that have happened to him, he is brave and honest and he's kept going, even when the odds were stacked against him.'

Joe went on to explain how Cal's mother had found life in Canada too difficult. She had returned to her home in Ireland, leaving Cal and his father to manage on their own.

'Cal was only fourteen and he did his best. His father Mac was heartbroken and took to drinking. He became so depressed he couldn't see another way out'.

Joe paused and sighed deeply before continuing. 'As your Aunt Peggy would say, there's no way of sugarcoating this Roisin so I'm hoping it won't upset you, but Mac took a shotgun and killed himself inside the garage. Poor Cal was the one who found his body.'

Joe shook his head as if in disbelief. 'Since then he copes as best he can. He had to get rid of their animals, and now he just grows a few seasonal vegetables. He manages by doing odd jobs for people and a few shifts at the pulp mill to make ends meet. Cal's a good kid and folk around here help as much as they can. It's a very lonely existence for such a young man.'

Roisin appeared uncharacteristically subdued and Joe left her to her thoughts. It was understandable. He could tell she was deeply affected by what she had heard and he didn't press her.

His hunch was correct. Roisin was thinking about Cal, and how difficult it must be for him. At least she had a family while Cal had no-one. She wanted to get to know him, but knew instinctively she would have to tread carefully.

If Joe was to be believed, he was not the sort who would welcome sympathy. He was too fiercely independent for that. Any well-intentioned interference and he was sure to retreat into his shell.

What he really needed, she decided, was friendship. It was not going to be an easy task, that was clear, but she would take her time. She wasn't going anywhere soon and she needed a friend just as much as he did.

Chapter Sixteen

As much as Roisin was intrigued by Cal, he was curious about her. She was pretty, but it was more than looks. Yes, there was her wonderful black hair and those unusual smoke–grey eyes, full of curiosity and intelligence. She was certainly very pleasing to look at. He couldn't put his finger on it, but there was more to it than the purely superficial. There was an aura about her he found perplexing. The feeling unnerved him. Girls were a bit of a mystery to him and it had been a while since he had been in female company, that is if you didn't count Peggy.

At school he had kept to himself until, to his surprise, a girl in his year sought him out and they dated over the summer. They made love a few times, in that embarrassed, fumbling teenage way. He enjoyed her company, but wasn't sorry when she left in the fall to attend college.

He hadn't paid a great deal of attention when Joe had mentioned his niece was coming to live with them.

She was young, around sixteen he thought, and he remembered Joe saying she was interested in nature and loved to go running. Anything beyond that had passed over his head.

Now he found himself thinking of her steady gaze as she listened to him and Joe talking. Not only was she observing him, he felt she was weighing him up. As to the reason why, well that escaped him. Perhaps if he got to know her a little better it would become clearer? If nothing else, it would be good to talk to someone closer in age.

The last few years he had spent far too much time in his own company or with folk older than him. Whilst he was grateful for all the help he had received and the concern shown for his welfare, it would be refreshing to be around someone younger.

He laid the paper bag with Peggy's baking on a table cluttered with used crockery. Moving the dirty dishes into the sink, he filled the coffee pot. Being on his own meant it was difficult to find the motivation to keep the house clean and tidy.

The interaction with Joe and Roisin made him aware he really ought to be more hospitable when people called. He could tell the girl was puzzled by his lack of sociability and he vowed to make more effort in the future. After all, Peggy and Joe had always gone out of their way to look out for him. Nothing was too much trouble and he owed them so much.

It had been Peggy he turned to when his mother's behaviour became unpredictable enough to give cause for concern. She was tired all the time and losing interest, not only in what was going on around her, but also in her personal appearance. This worried Cal more than returning to a cold house with no food on the table. He became accustomed to coming home from school to find his mother still in bed, her face turned towards the wall. The lines on her cheeks carved by her tears, contrasted with the paleness of her face which over the weeks became ingrained with grime. After lighting the fire and preparing a meal, he would lead her to the bathroom where he would gently wash her hands and face and brush her wild, tangled hair. She refused to change out of her grubby nightgown. If he pleaded enough with her, she would allow him to steer her arms into one of his father's oversized sweaters and lead her downstairs. She wasn't eating enough to keep a bird alive and was rapidly losing weight. Something needed to be done, but what? His father seemed indifferent to her plight.

'Och, she'll get over it. You know she has these little bouts of homesickness. She's missing her home and family in Ireland, that's all. Don't you worry son, she will be all right.'

Mac had dismissed his concerns as Cal pleaded with him to call the doctor. He was not reassured by his father's nonchalance. The situation was much worse than anything that had happened before and he was worried. Very worried.

On the pretext of collecting eggs one Saturday morning, he took the back path to Joe and Peggy's property. A strong wind was blowing, and from the bottom field he could see Peggy. She was wrestling with the laundry as she tried to peg it out on the line. Increasing his pace he reached her just in time to grab one end of a sheet that was starting to trail on the ground.

'Oh, thank goodness you're here Cal. You've come just in time. I wouldn't want to wash it all again.'

Following her up to the house, he stopped to collect the eggs while she went ahead to make coffee.

There was no sign of Joe, and he sat in silence at the table as she prepared coffee and set out a plate of biscuits.

He couldn't help but notice how warm and homely the room was. It had been a long time since he had experienced anything close to the feeling of well-being he was experiencing at that moment.

Peggy had been talking to him, he realised. When he hadn't responded, she leaned forward and took his hand.

'It's not Joe you've come to see is it?'

Cal shook his head and she could see the purple shadows under his eyes.

'Is it about your mam? I haven't seen much of her for a while. Is she ill?'

Cal nodded and before he could stop himself, he had poured out the whole story, including his concerns about what his father would say if he knew he was confiding in Peggy.

He was going behind his back by being here and Mac had a temper.

Peggy poured them both another cup of coffee and placed a plate of cold cuts in front of Cal. The poor boy was too thin. He needed feeding up.

'You did the right thing in coming to tell me Cal,' she said. 'It sounds as though your mother needs to see a doctor. From what you have said, it's unlikely she will get better without medical intervention. And don't worry about your dad. We will get him to see reason. Joe will be back soon and he can drive me over. We will talk to him and get your mam the help she needs.'

True to her word, Peggy spoke to Mac, gaining his trust as she explained the gravity of the situation. She made no mention of Cal 's visit to see her.

With Mac's permission she arranged for the doctor to call.

To Cal's relief, slowly but surely, the prescribed medication began to take effect. His mother's mood lightened and she was almost her old self again. Cal felt as if a burden had been lifted from his shoulders.

That is until he awoke from a deep sleep one night to the sound of raised voices coming from downstairs. Creeping to the top stair, he sat shivering, holding onto the curved rail of the bannister while the argument raged below.

It was difficult to make out much of what was being said. He could hear the boom of his father's voice and the rattle of glass as he brought his fist down on the table. Not a sound was heard for a while and then his mother's voice drifted upwards. It was not her normal, timid tone. She sounded cool and measured. With increasing vigour, she made her point with a degree of determination Cal had not heard before.

'I'm going home Mac, the boy can stay with you. It's for the best. I cannot bear to be here any longer. I don't want to make idle threats.'

She hesitated and composed herself before continuing. 'But, if you try to prevent me from leaving the consequences will be dire, for us all.'

Cal had gripped the polished wood of the bannister

like a drowning man. He felt as though he had been cast adrift. It would be a bleak future with just him and his dad muddling along.

He couldn't have known a larger catastrophe loomed and that the worst was yet to come.

Chapter Seventeen

al was used to living alone, but of late found himself spending more time in the warmth of Peggy's kitchen. One freezing winter's morning he received the invitation he had hardly dared hope for.

'Will you come for Christmas dinner Cal?' Peggy had been making a Christmas cake and a plum pudding. The rich smell of dried fruits soaked in sugar and alcohol permeated the room.

'Thank you ma'am. I would like that very much,' he replied.

'You would be most welcome and, by the way, Cal...'

'Yes ma'am?'

'Please call me Peggy.'

'Yes ma'am.'

The work on the roof had taken a little longer than anticipated. When it was at last finished and had met Joe's exacting standards, Cal and Joe trooped in, famished after all their hard work.

Roisin had dealt with the animals then helped Peggy prepare a hearty stew with extra potatoes and vegetables.

To follow there was a home-baked apple pie with custard.

'Coffee for everyone?' Joe asked, when the meal was over. While he put the pot on the stove, Roisin and Cal washed and dried the dishes.

The coffee tasted good. Being an Irish girl, her drink of choice was usually strong tea or a glass of milk. Over the weeks she was getting used to the slightly bitter taste of coffee, as long as there was sugar to sweeten it.

'We'll make a good Canadian coffee drinker out of you before long,' Joe said with a laugh.

The evening passed pleasantly enough. There was talk of cars, farm machinery, stock and feed prices and the politics at the pulp mill. Roisin found her attention starting to wander until Cal interrupted her reverie.

'Would you like to come over and choose a Christmas tree tomorrow? Your aunt and uncle have said it's OK. I have some balsam firs growing on my land. I'll cut one down and we can bring it over on my truck.'

The days had been so busy and had passed so quickly she had almost forgotten it would soon be Christmas. She liked the idea of a real tree and she hoped her aunt and uncle would let her help with the decorations.

At home, the tree was small and artificial. It didn't matter. She had enjoyed the ritual of making paper chains and walking up the lane with her mother to collect sprigs of holly and trailing evergreen, before they sat down to eat Christmas dinner together.

Theresa, like her cousin, always made a Christmas pudding and hid a silver sixpence in the mix. Roisin remembered you had to be careful not to chip a tooth or swallow the coin if it was in your portion.

Even though there was never much spare money, it was a happy time.

She wondered if her mother would be on her own over the holiday. She hoped not. This was going to be their first Christmas apart and it was not going to be easy for either of them.

❧

Roisin felt a frisson of excitement as she walked to Cal's house. He was already waiting for her with a saw in one hand, and a rope and flour sack over his other arm. Together they trudged through deep snow drifts until they came to a plantation of firs, their branches dusted with snow. He pointed out a narrow track rutted with hoof marks, running through the trees.

'See the path. It's a deer run and it leads right into the lower pastures of Joe and Peggy's property. The deer have been using it for as long as I remember and, I would guess, even before that. If you feel like coming over at any time, it will take you about twenty minutes to walk along it, and less than ten if you run.'

It was apparent Joe had said something to him about her running and she felt the colour rise in her cheeks. The fact they had been discussing her made her feel uncomfortable. Putting aside her own feelings, it occurred to her there was more to it than that. Cal was extending an invitation. In his own quiet way, he was offering her the hand of friendship and she was happy to take it.

Cal paused by a group of taller firs standing close together. 'These were planted by my dad when I was a baby,' he said, sounding wistful. 'They are too big for what we want. We need one around my height or we won't get it through the door.'

With his guidance she selected a tree barely a few inches taller than he was. It wasn't too bushy at the base and had a good shape.

Urging her to stand back from where it would fall, he had soon sawn part way through the trunk. They watched as with a crack, the trunk snapped evenly and the tree landed with a gentle whoosh in a pile of snow. Cal then wrapped the base in the flour sack.

'This is for protection,' he explained. 'The resin is very sticky. You wouldn't want to get it on your hands or clothes.'

With a deft movement, he knotted the rope around the middle of the tree and together they dragged it through the snow and placed it on the back of the truck. Roisin inhaled the sharp, clean smell of the pine needles and resin. It was going to be her first Canadian Christmas and her excitement was mounting.

Leaving Joe and Cal to deal with the tree, Roisin joined her aunt back at the house. 'I've collected the mail and there's a letter for you,' Peggy said. 'It looks like it's from your mam,'

The envelope was propped up against the salt and pepper pots on the table. She recognised her mother's flowing handwriting on the front. Peggy had received one too, tucked inside a Christmas card. She waved her letter in the air enthusiastically.

'Would you believe it? Even with the storm the mail has still managed to get here, and in good time too,' she declared.

'Will it be all right if I take it up to my room to read?' Roisin asked.

'Of course,' Peggy said, 'and by the time you come down Joe will be back and I'll send him up to the attic to get the lights and decorations for the tree.'

Joe had made a pull-out desk for her room and found a chair to fit underneath. Roisin loved the oriel window and now she could sit and read or write her letters while looking out over the trees. If it was a clear day, she could see beyond the trees to the ocean glittering in the distance. As the light was now starting to fade, she pulled the curtains closed and sat for a few moments before carefully lifting the gummed flap. From the envelope she withdrew a card embellished with glitter to look like snowflakes. The picture on the front was of a skater on a frozen pond. The girl had long, dark hair and was wearing a red, fur-lined coat. Inside the card was her mother's letter.

My Darling Roisin

I trust you are well and recovering from that awful ordeal on the ship.

I received word of the events and my first reaction was to book a berth on the next boat out and come and bring you back home. I feel guilty for sending you away and cry myself to sleep most nights.

The woman you shared a cabin with sounds lovely and I was so pleased to hear she looked out for you. She is well known here and very popular in America and Canada, I believe. As you can imagine, the whole sorry state of affairs is the subject of gossip in the town.

*I have been informed you cannot be held accountable
in any way for what happened. It sounds as though
that appalling man brought it on himself. I have been
advised by the powers-that-be they may pay you a visit,
although I'm given to understand it's just a formality.
Peggy tells me you have settled well. She says you are
good with the animals and a real asset on the farm. I am
very proud of my girl.*

*As for my news? You will remember the couple who
took over the grocery store, the Hennesseys? They were
very kind to me when you left and we have become
friendly. They have invited me to spend Christmas
with them. I have also bought a second hand sewing
machine and taken on extra work making dresses for
half the women in the town. They choose an outfit from a
magazine and I adapt the pattern and run it up for them.
When the summer comes, perhaps you can get Peggy to
measure you and I will make you a lovely dress.*

*You are always in my thoughts. Please write again
soon. I loved the postcard you sent from the ship.
Sending all my love to you at Christmas xxx*

*PS Do you like the card?
PPS Talk to Peggy about the accident.*

Roisin re-read the letter before putting it back into the
envelope and placing it in the drawer of her night stand.
She took the Christmas card downstairs and joined Peggy,
who was sitting at the table drinking tea. Pouring another

cup she handed it to Roisin along with a chocolate biscuit.

'It's great to hear from your mam isn't it? She sounds well. Did she bring you up to date with all her news in your letter?'

Roisin nodded and held out the card. Peggy studied it. 'Ah, that's really lovely. The girl looks just like you.'

Peggy's card had a picture of sprigs of holly with '*Seasons Greetings*' written across the front. 'We'll put them on the mantle when the tree goes up tomorrow.'

The radio was on low and Peggy got up to switch it off. She moved stiffly as she made her way back to sit at the table. Roisin asked if she needed her tablets.

'I've taken them already, thanks. I'm not very good in the winter. The cold gets right into my bones.'

She pulled her cardigan tight against her chest as Roisin got up to add more logs to the stove.

She was about to put on her boots and join Joe outside, when Peggy stopped her by placing an arm gently on her shoulder. 'Your mother said she would like us to have a word with you about what happened on the ship.'

Roisin squirmed uncomfortably in response. 'I know it was very unsettling for you,' Peggy continued, 'but if we talk about it together, we can all understand what went on. Then, if we can, Joe and I will do our best to help you put it all behind you. It must be affecting you. You're having nightmares, we can hear you calling out in the night.'

She was having nightmares, it was true. She would wake in the early hours shaking and in a cold sweat. In one she was running and hands were reaching out trying to grab her, in another she was trapped in the house and the sea was rearing up and about to submerge her. She didn't think talking was going to do much good, but she knew her aunt had been a nurse and had treated soldiers suffering from shell shock. If anyone could help her it would be Aunt Peggy.

The back door opened and Joe could be heard stamping his feet before removing his coat and boots.

Roisin got up to put on a pot of coffee. She would make it strong, just the way he liked it. It was going to be a long evening ahead.

Chapter Eighteen

Sitting up in bed holding the cup of hot chocolate Peggy had made to help her sleep, Roisin felt weary. It had been emotionally draining having to speak once again about the incident on the ship, but Peggy and Joe had listened attentively to her account. She had considered the possibility they might judge her by her actions when they heard what she had to say. In a way, she *had* been responsible for Patrick Higgins death and a part of her felt the guilt associated with that fact.

Peggy and Joe had exchanged looks across the table as Roisin finished her stumbling explanation of what happened on the night in question. She was usually such a cheerful girl. Now, her head was down and she was rubbing at a knot in the wooden surface of the kitchen table. She was troubled, they could see that and they waited for her to compose herself.

It was Peggy who broke the silence when it became apparent Roisin had nothing more to say.

'You may well be thinking you will never recover, but let me tell you this. Without a shadow of doubt, you won't forget what happened, but you will get over it. You have to stop blaming yourself. Fear and guilt can eat you up and make you ill if you allow it to consume you. Do you understand what I'm saying?'

Roisin lifted a tear stained face and shrugged her shoulders. She thought she understood. It was just all so confusing.

Peggy handed her a handkerchief from her apron pocket and glanced beseechingly at Joe. He gave her a look and she knew it meant she was to carry on.

'One way to help you get through this is by forgiveness. You have to find it in your heart to forgive that man, and more importantly yourself. It may sound like a momentous task and it's true, many who have undergone trauma at the hands of someone else achieve neither of those things. Life can be unpredictable and difficult at times. Look at what Cal had to endure, and your Uncle Joe too. He doesn't say much about the war, even though he saw some awful things, just as I did when I was nursing. My best friend was killed by a soldier she was treating. He shot her in the head and then turned the gun on himself.'

Peggy paused and wiped away a tear on the corner of her apron before finally concluding: 'Dreadful events are a part of life and you can sink under the weight of the burden, or you can carry on with your life and try to be a better person because of it.'

Roisin listened carefully, attempting to take in everything being said. Peggy had spoken kindly and honestly. So much of what she said made sense. Up until she had left Ireland, her mother had been her protector, cushioning her from the harsher aspects of life. It had always been the two of them, united against the world. Now it was time to start facing up to reality. Peggy and Joe would be there to guide her until she was ready to make her own way in the world. Then, she would be on her own and if Ger were to be believed, she might even achieve something in her life.

After Roisin had gone to bed, Joe and Peggy sat talking for a while. 'Do you think I was too severe with her, Joe? She is still so young. I hope I haven't made things worse.'

Taking his wife's hand, Joe held it up against his cheek. 'No, I don't think you were harsh at all. What you said will have helped her a great deal. I thought she seemed a lot brighter in herself afterwards. She even reminded me I'd forgotten to get the tree decorations down.'

He chuckled at the prospect of having two women in the house to order him around. 'We'll keep an eye on her and listen out for any more nightmares. I think she's resilient and a lot tougher than you imagine Peg.'

Christmas was fast approaching and it was decided they should all go to town the following day. Lewistown was full of shoppers and while Peggy and Joe went to the store to buy Christmas food, Roisin explored the town. She was impressed by the large Christmas tree festooned with lights and the brightly decorated shop windows. She still had some of the money her mother had given her and was looking for last minute gifts. To get away from the crowds, she turned down a side road.

Here the stores were smaller and more specialised than

those on Main Street. One selling women's clothing caught her eye. The mannequins in the window were wearing rather stylish outfits. One dressed in a fawn coloured shift dress, had a contrasting chiffon scarf with brown polka dots placed casually around its neck. Roisin thought the scarf would go perfectly with Peggy's best coat and waited for the woman behind the counter to finish serving a customer.

Looking around it was plain to see the outfits were both fashionable and highly priced.

She hoped she had enough money and wouldn't have to leave without the scarf. The assistant, tall and slender looked like a fashion model herself, with her pencil skirt and crisp, white blouse.

'How much is the spotted scarf in the window please?' Roisin asked hesitantly.

'Are you from England?' the woman asked, noticing her accent.

'No, Ireland. I'm living with my aunt and uncle and I want to get them both something nice for Christmas. The scarf is lovely and the colours are a good match to go with my Aunt Peggy's coat.'

'Well you are in luck,' the woman said, coming out from behind the counter. 'I'm about to change the window display for the holidays and everything is being reduced. I can offer it to you at sale price. It's chiffon, not silk, but it's good quality. How does 75 cents sound?

Taking the scarf from the window the woman handed it to Roisin. On closer inspection she could see the dots were raised velvet, making the scarf look expensive. Eagerly, she handed over the money to the assistant who carefully wrapped it in tissue paper and placed it into a gift bag.

Across the street was an antique watch and clock repairers with a large clock positioned above the door. The sign on the window read 'Antiques and Collectibles' and as she pushed the door open, a bell clanged loudly from within. This alerted an elderly man who appeared from the rear of the building.

The shop was packed from floor to ceiling with books, pictures and china ware. Tall, glass cabinets displaying watches and jewellery lined the walls. It was very cluttered and smelled old and dusty. Roisin thought it charming. She was impressed by how much history was contained in such a small space.

'Are you looking for anything in particular?'

The shopkeeper was not Canadian, she could tell by his voice. Almost everyone she met noticed her accent and now she found herself doing the same.

'I'm looking for something for my uncle for Christmas. Are you Scottish?' As soon as the words were out, she wondered if she had spoken out of turn. The man seemed unperturbed and smiled at her.

'Ah, that's clever of you. I am originally from Scotland, but I have been here for over forty years now. Your accent tells me you're a long way from home too. Are you Irish?' he asked, looking at her over a pair of pince nez glasses perched on his nose.

'I am, and proud of it,' she said, peering into one of the glass cases. An item had caught her eye and she asked if she could have a closer look. It was a silver coloured duck's head.

'You have good taste young lady. That is French in origin. An art deco bottle opener from the 1920's. It might look like silver when in fact it's cast in metal. Look at how delicately it's been worked, the feathers appear almost real. It's the duck's bill you use to open the bottle.'

She thought her Uncle Joe would like it for his beers. The price on the ticket however, was more than she wanted to pay. Reluctantly she stepped back from the cabinet and was about to walk away when the man called out to her.

'You won't know this, but customers are never expected to pay the asking price,' he said. 'With antiques, the purchaser always makes an offer. How much would you want to pay?'

She was trying to think what might be a fair price when she noticed something else of interest. It occurred to her she had nothing to give Cal for Christmas.

'Is that a pocket knife?' she asked, pointing at the cabinet. 'Can I see it please?'

The man withdrew the knife from the glass case to give her a closer look. It was heavy in her hand and the outside casing was mother of pearl. 'You certainly have a good eye, young lady,' the man said. 'It's a well made piece, although not antique. I wouldn't be asking much for it.'

She wished Joe and Peggy were around to ask. She didn't want to make a fool of herself by offering too little. Anyway, Cal was unlikely to have got her a Christmas present. What if he was uncomfortable receiving a gift when he had nothing to give in return? It was a bit of a dilemma and she was running out of time. She needed to make a decision quickly.

'How much for both?' she asked, in her most confident voice.

Peggy and Joe were waiting for her at the store when she arrived, out of breath from running.

'Looks as though you've been busy, 'Joe said, eyeing her packages. 'Catch your breath and then we'll set off. Peg and I have everything we need'.

Laden with parcels, he signalled to Peggy who had been talking to Marjie at the counter, it was time to leave. Turning to walk to the truck, Roisin noticed he had a bottle of Rich's beer in each of his jacket pockets.

Back at the house they unpacked the groceries and Joe was dispatched to fetch a ladder to get into the attic and collect the Christmas decorations.

'Can I come and help?' Roisin said, keen to explore the attic.

'Of course.' Joe said, laughing at her eagerness. 'Put your work clothes on first. It's very dusty up there.'

Following Joe up the ladder and through the access hatch, she was surprised to see how cluttered the area was. Although the circular windows at either end let in some light, it was still difficult to see much in the winter gloom. Boxes stacked in corners and unwanted items of furniture covered in old sheets took up most of the space.

'This junk came from my parents home after they died,' Joe explained. 'I just haven't had the heart to sort through and get rid of it. Most of it can be thrown away or chopped up for firewood. It's a good job Peg doesn't come up here or she would be nagging me to clear the place out.'

It certainly could do with a clean, Roisin thought, as

cobwebs snagged in her hair and particles of dust got up her nose making her sneeze. On the rear facing window ledge she noticed a square, metal box. It was badly dented and the picture on the lid was faded. She could just make out what appeared to be a vase of flowers, the yellows, pinks and blues of the blooms barely discernible. She held it up to show Joe who was pulling the box of Christmas decorations across the floor.

'Well, well, it's been a long time since I've seen that. It's my mother's old sewing tin. Open it up and have a look inside.'

The lid had warped and it squeaked as she prised the catch apart. Inside were bits of ribbon, string and spools of different coloured threads, a felt needle-case and a large assortment of buttons.

'You can have it if you like, but we need to hurry up and get the tree decorated. I should have done it yesterday. I don't want to face the wrath of your Aunt Peggy if it's not sorted out today.'

With Roisin's help and under Peggy's watchful eye, Joe brought in the tree. He placed it in the window recess of the lounge in a tub disguised with wrapping paper. It was a relief to see the lights were working. It meant he didn't have to hunt around for spare bulbs. Balancing on a stepladder while Roisin handed him up the fragile, brightly coloured baubles and handfuls of silver tinsel, he caught Peggy's eye and nodded in her direction. From the box of decorations Peggy took an object wrapped in layers of newspaper. She passed it to Roisin who carefully uncovered it to reveal a beautiful glass star, sparkling as it reflected the light.

'Right my girl, this star is a family heirloom. I've had it since I was a child in Ireland and it's graced the tree every year since. This year I want you to do the honours.' Peggy said, her voice breaking with emotion. She wiped away a tear as she watched Roisin climb the ladder and stretch up to place the star on top of the tree.

'It's going to be a lovely Christmas,' Joe said, placing an arm around his wife's shoulder. 'Just like old times.'

Chapter Nineteen

The weather had been warmer for a few days. The sky, grey and overcast, had given the melting snow the appearance of wet papier mâché. On Christmas Eve the temperature dropped again, freezing everything and making it treacherous underfoot. At breakfast, Joe warned Peggy to stay inside. 'We'll bring the potatoes and vegetables for tomorrow up from the barn after we've fed the animals.'

Overhead the sky was clear with not a cloud to be seen. Roisin felt the familiar buzz running from her head to her feet that told her it was going to snow again. After milking Bluebell, she took the cow and Chester to the paddock. After collecting a bale of hay, she wheeled it down in the barrow before spreading it evenly over the hard ground. A high whinny and a pawing of the ground alerted her to the fact the water in the trough was frozen. Using a stone to break the ice, she was rewarded with a nuzzle of gratitude from Chester before the horse drank his fill.

Joe had moved the pigs out into the yard. He wanted

to clean and disinfect the pens once they were out of the way. The piglets had already started to put on weight and were tottering around after Clemmie. Hector surveyed the antics of his family with a baleful stare.

'We can start weaning them in a few weeks. It takes a bit of doing, but we'll introduce the feed gradually. Once they're off Clemmie they can go to their new homes.'

Joe had already sold the piglets. Each year he would keep one back to fatten up and slaughter in the autumn. Roisin couldn't help but feel concern for the fate of the remaining piglet, the runt of the litter.

Joe had said she mustn't get too attached to any of the animals. Even if they weren't part of the food chain, nature could be cruel and there was no room for sentimentality.

As her mother would say when she brought wounded creatures home to try and nurse them back to health: 'Death is a part of life and you have to become accustomed to it'.

She tried to accept what Theresa had told her. It didn't stop her being heartbroken when she heard of a neighbour up the lane who had drowned an unwanted litter of kittens in a bucket of water. And it was hard not to weep when the blackbird she found with a broken wing was eaten by a feral cat, leaving behind a few glossy, black feathers. She had fed the bird with an eye-dropper and although it couldn't fly, it would take nuts and berries from her hand and hop after the chickens, stealing their grain.

'No tears now,' Theresa chided her. 'Everyone and everything dies, it's nature's way. If there was no death, there would be no new life.'

It was true. Life could be unfair and death was a

certainty. She doubted it was something she would ever get used to, even if she lived to be one hundred.

'I can taste snow, Uncle Joe,' Roisin cried out.

Turning her face skywards, she put out her tongue to catch the first snowflake.

Joe shook his head in bafflement. 'You may be right about the snow, although there's not a cloud in the sky and there was nothing about it on the radio this morning,'

She was a strange girl, Joe mused. He watched as she wheeled the barrow back into the barn, marvelling at her determination. She was always so interested and eager to learn, she energised him with her enthusiasm. Sometimes he wondered what it would have been like if he and Peggy had children. It hadn't happened and it was perhaps as well with Peggy's condition. *This is it*, he thought, *the closest I am going to get to being a father and I am going to enjoy it while I can.*

The kitchen was warm and welcoming and there was a spicy, aromatic smell in the air. Peggy was making stuffing for the turkey and the table was covered in bowls and a scattering of breadcrumbs.

'Do you want the potatoes and vegetables yet Peg? Or shall I leave them outside for now?'

'Just put everything by the back door. We can peel them and put them in cold water once the turkey is prepared.

'Oh, what's this red stuff?' Roisin asked. Lifting the lid on one of the dishes had revealed a jam-like substance.

Peggy laughed. 'It's cranberry sauce. It's traditional here in Canada and goes with the turkey. You would have thought cranberries would be everywhere in Ireland as they grow in boggy ground. The truth is I never saw them until I came to this country. If I've got the balance right, and the sauce is not too sour, I think you'll like it with the turkey.'

Roisin was looking forward to an evening curled up with a book. She hoped her Uncle Joe would light the fire in the lounge. It would be cosy with the firelight and Christmas tree lights twinkling. Her best laid plans unravelled when it became apparent her Aunt Peggy had other ideas for Christmas Eve.

'I have a favour to ask Roisin. Will you come to Midnight Mass? It's a nice service and my friends would love to meet you?'

Roisin sighed inwardly, but didn't hesitate. Attending church now and again to keep her Aunt Peggy happy was no real hardship. 'Of course I will,' she said, with as much enthusiasm as she could summon.

With a pile of potatoes peeled and the carrots and parsnips scrubbed in readiness, Roisin watched with interest as Joe took a knife to a large vegetable the size of a football.

'You haven't had squash before have you? I can tell from the look on your face,' Joe said, as he scooped out a pile of seeds. 'We'll have it with dinner and then Peggy will make pumpkin pie with the rest. You are in for a treat without a doubt. Nobody makes a pie as good as your Aunt Peggy.'

Peggy rolled her eyes at the compliment and reminded Joe to make sure the seeds didn't end up in the slop bucket with the peelings. She would dry and roast the seeds once Christmas was over, she told Roisin. With a pinch of salt they made a lovely snack.

Roisin remembered she needed to wrap her Christmas gifts. 'Do you have any Christmas paper Aunt Peggy? I have presents to wrap for tomorrow.'

From a drawer Peggy produced a few sheets of festive paper, some sticky labels, a pair of scissors and a roll of sticky tape. Roisin took them to her room and sat at her desk.

Taking the gifts from the bag she had been given at the clothes shop, she examined each in turn before carefully wrapping and adding a label with the recipient's name written in her best handwriting. She remembered the box her mother had concealed in her luggage and carried it, and the packages, down to the kitchen.

'Why don't you put them under the tree?' Peggy was resting with her feet up listening to a carol service on the radio.

She watched Roisin stack the packages in a neat pile before taking them to the lounge room. The girl is so like her father, she observed, with that black hair and those grey eyes. She had met Greg a few times when he and Theresa were going out together. He was likeable enough, with an easy wit and a barrel load of charm. She didn't tell her cousin she thought him rather superficial and too much under his mother's thumb.

She was not really surprised by his behaviour when Theresa became pregnant. When he refused to have any contact with Theresa and his child afterwards, she thought it unforgivable. It was his loss and in Peggy's eyes, when he left for England, it was good riddance to bad rubbish. Still, there could be no denying Roisin looked like her father. Peggy made the sign of the cross and offered up a silent prayer of thanks, for that's where the resemblance ended. They were as different as chalk and cheese when it came to temperament.

To Roisin's surprise, Midnight Mass was scheduled to begin at 10 p.m. her usual bedtime. By 9.30 they were all dressed in their best clothes and ready to go. The tiny church, decorated with greenery and illuminated with candles, looked beautiful in their flickering glow. In front of the altar a nativity scene was lit from behind by a low electric light bulb. Most of the pews were already taken when they arrived and they just managed to squeeze into one at the rear of the church. It was already occupied by a family of four, a mother and father and twin girls dressed in identical outfits.

The service was brief, with just a few words reflecting on the meaning of Christmas, a selection of carols and a final blessing. It was very unlike church services back home. Father Kelly was well known for his long winded sermons that had everyone yawning and shuffling, eager for it to come to an end.

This priest was called Father Jack, and was younger than any priest Roisin had previously encountered.

When he shook her by the hand as they were leaving the church, she noticed his engaging smile and twinkling brown eyes.

'You are Roisin, I would guess? It's very good to meet you. Your aunt has told me all about you.'

Taken aback by his friendliness, she could only mumble her thanks for the 'nice' service, whilst hoping her Aunt Peggy hadn't asked him to try and persuade her to attend mass more frequently. As if reading her thoughts, Father

Jack placed an arm on her shoulder. 'At this church we welcome everyone. Some here tonight will probably not come again until next Christmas. Feel free to attend at any time Roisin. You will be made very welcome, even if it's only on high days and holidays.'

Peggy and Joe were talking in a group that included the parents of the twin girls. 'Ah here she is. Has Father Jack been turning on the charm again? He's lovely isn't he?' Peggy said. She was obviously not immune to his charm. Roisin noticed the flush to her aunt's cheeks when she mentioned his name.

'Now let me introduce you to everyone, Roisin. This is Joan and her husband John, and Mary and her husband Alec. I came over on the ship with Joan and Mary and we have been friends ever since. Laura joined our little group of quilters three years ago and her husband Felix is our local vet. The girls, as you have probably guessed, are twins.' Peggy hesitated for a second before pointing at each of them in turn. 'This is Eleanor and that's Evelyn, though they prefer to be called Ellie and Evie. As you can see, they are identical and difficult to tell apart.'

The twins looked to be around nine or ten and had their mother's pale colouring, and reddish blonde, shoulder-length curls. Up close, Roisin noticed slight contrasts in the shape of their faces and the distribution of freckles across their noses. What was more striking however, was that they clearly had very different characters. While one clung to her mother's arm and looked down at her feet when Roisin tried to speak to her, the other held her gaze without looking away, her bright blue eyes full of intelligence.

The snow began to fall as they arrived back at the house and were pulling into the drive.

'Just when it looked as though the last batch of snow was clearing,' Joe declared in mock annoyance. 'I should have listened to you, Roisin. We are going to have a white Christmas after all.'

Chapter Twenty

'Happy Christmas to you!' called out Peggy who was frying bacon and sausages in the pan as Roisin appeared at the breakfast table. 'There's quite a bit to do this morning. We will have to pull together to get the dinner ready for when Cal comes at two o'clock. The first job is to get this turkey in the oven or there will be no Christmas dinner. Can you give me a hand after breakfast please?'

Roisin was distracted. She was thinking about whether she had made the right decision in buying the gift for Cal.

'You know I got Cal something for Christmas?' Roisin said, wrestling the massive bird into the oven. 'The thing is, I don't want him to feel awkward if he hasn't got me anything in return. What should I do?'

Peggy was watching Roisin's struggles with amusement and spent a few moments considering the question.

'Mm, I see what you mean. In all honesty, I think Cal is going to just appreciate being here with us today. I have a few things wrapped up for him too. It never occurred to me that he might feel under obligation to bring anything in return. You really are a very considerate girl thinking of his feelings. I suspect he will be pleased you thought to get him something, so I wouldn't worry too much.'

Reassured by her aunt's reply, she joined Joe, who was collecting eggs in the yard. At his feet, Artie and the hens pecked eagerly at the corn scattered on the ground. The fresh fall of powder snow lay like a down coverlet. When caught by the icy wind, it whipped into peevish flurries or banked against the side of the farm buildings.

Joe decided the animals could be outside as long as they were brought back in by late afternoon. 'They hate being cooped up all day as you know,' he remarked. 'If you fetch the barrow, we can take them some fresh vegetables along with their hay as a treat. It is Christmas after all.'

A few minutes before two o'clock, Cal arrived carrying a tin of biscuits and a package loosely wrapped in crinkled brown paper. He had slicked his hair down with water and the sweater he was wearing over his shirt was unravelling around his thin wrists.

'Sure smells good,' he remarked.

He handed the tin of biscuits to Peggy. 'I'm sorry it's not much. I chose the tin to remind you of Ireland.'

The picture on the front was of a whitewashed cottage with a thatched roof, not unlike Theresa's cottage in Waterbridge.

Thanking him, for his kindness, she placed the tin on a high shelf. Christmas was such an emotional time and she didn't want Roisin upset by a reminder of home on this of all days.

'And this is for you.' Shyly, he handed the brown paper parcel to Roisin.

'You really didn't have to bring anything Cal. We are pleased you can join and share in our meal,' Peggy said, as she stirred gravy at the stove. 'Why don't you show Cal where to put it with the other presents under the tree Roisin? Dinner is almost ready and we can open them together once we have eaten.'

Roisin had never seen so much food in her life. While Joe carved the turkey at the table, Peggy served from dishes piled high with mashed potatoes, carrots, roasted parsnips and squash mashed with butter. Cal, she noticed, ate slowly, savouring each mouthful and gladly accepting whatever was placed in front of him.

'Remind me to make up a plate for you to take back home Cal,' Peggy said, pleased to see him tucking into the food with such relish. 'We'll be eating leftovers ourselves for a few days by the looks of it. And, there's still the Christmas pudding to come.We will have to wait for our dinners to go down before I even think about serving it.'

When dinner was over, Joe lit the fire in the lounge and sent Peggy there with instructions to rest while the table was cleared and the dishes washed and put away.

'I guess you must be missing your mother today?' Cal asked Roisin as they stood at the sink together, tackling the mountain of dirty crockery.

'I am missing her. It was always just the two of us. It takes a bit of getting used to, but who knows, it might be the making of me. That's what my friend Ger said anyway!'

Cal laughed, then looked serious. 'I've almost forgotten my mother, it's so long since she left. I miss my dad too, even though he could get nasty with the drink. I don't mind being on my own usually. It's just Christmas can be a really lonely time.'

Joe had banked the fire and the embers glowed white-hot in the hearth. The tree looked spectacular, glimmering in the shadow of the bay window.

'Time to open the Christmas presents,' Joe declared, rubbing his hands together in anticipation. 'Are you going to hand out yours first Roisin?'

Peggy seemed thrilled with her scarf. 'That's really lovely Roisin, and the colour is just right. It will match my good coat and hat perfectly. What have you got there Joe?'

Joe seemed perplexed by his gift and surveyed it from all angles. 'I'm not really sure. It's a duck's head I think.'

Roisin showed him how the opener worked. 'It's for your beer. See, you put the bottle cap into the duck's bill then pull.'

Joe roared with laughter. 'Well, I have to admit, I've never seen anything quite like it. It's magnificent. I think I need to try it though. Now where are my beers? I'm sure Cal will have a bottle with me.'

'You're very quiet Cal,' Peggy said, looking concerned. 'Is everything all right?'

Cal had unwrapped Roisin's gift and was turning the pocket knife over and over in his hands. He looked over at Roisin and the expression on his face made her heart sink. She could see he was upset. *He doesn't like it*, she thought in dismay.

'How did you know?' Cal asked, his eyes wet with tears.

'Know what Cal? Have I done something wrong?' Roisin was at a loss as to what he meant.

'The penknife,' he said, his voice barely audible, 'I can't believe it.'

'I don't understand. I just thought....' her voice tailed off, and she looked crestfallen.

Seeing her confusion he swiftly regained his composure. 'This knife is almost exactly the same as the one I lost last year. It was my dad's and he'd had it since he was a boy. I felt really guilty afterwards, losing it like that. It was as though I'd let him down. I couldn't have asked for anything better. You did good Roisin, really good.'

Roisin felt a curious mix of embarrassment and pleasure at his reaction which she tried to hide by gathering up some of the used wrapping paper.

Darting forward, Cal retrieved his gift to Roisin from under the tree and handed it to her. She pulled aside the crinkled paper to reveal a block of bleached driftwood. Suspended by fishing wire were pieces of brightly coloured glass. As she held it up to catch the light, the movement caused the glass to jingle melodiously. Looking closely, she could see lines and irregular shapes etched into the frosted surfaces of the individual pieces.

'It's not much,' Cal said softly. 'I made it myself from flotsam on the beach. The coloured pebbles are sea glass. Have you heard of it?'

Roisin shook her head.

'It's bits of old glass tumbled and weathered by the ocean that get washed up onshore. See the different colours? The greens and browns are common, while others like the orange are rarer. I actually like the blues and turquoise colours best. Just imagine, one of those pieces might have started off as a medicine bottle many years ago.'

'It's beautiful, thank you,' Roisin said, genuinely touched by the effort he had made. 'Do you think you could show me where you found the glass?

'Sure. If it's all right with Peggy and Joe, we can walk up to the lighthouse one day next week. There's usually plenty of sea glass on the beach below.'

'That's a really fine bit of work young man,' Joe said. 'It's deserving of a place in your window, do you agree Roisin?'

'Oh, yes please. I'd like that very much.'

Peggy had spent the long winter evenings knitting a sweater for Joe. They rarely exchanged gifts at Christmas. It had always been a very quiet affair with just the two of them, once they moved to Canada. She was taken aback when Joe produced a gift bag with the name of a down-town department store on its side.

'I got this for you when I collected Roisin from Halifax. That's why I was a bit late in picking her up. I hope it's the right one.'

Inside the bag was a bottle of perfume, the stopper in the shape of folded swans wings.

'Oh Joe, you remembered. It's my favourite. I haven't had scent for years.'

All the hard work leading up to the holiday had been a pleasure not a burden for Peggy. She enjoyed knitting and it helped with the stiffness in her fingers. Along with Joe's sweater she had made a warm, winter hat and gloves for Cal in the same navy blue wool. There was also a knitted

Christmas stocking for him containing a couple of bars of chocolate, a pair of warm socks, a pack of playing cards and an instruction book on how to whittle wood.

For her niece there were fleecy pyjamas, sheepskin lined slippers, a nature book, a set of leather-bound mystery stories, bath salts in a pretty floral tin and a snow globe, inside of which was a miniature cottage surrounded by trees.

As Roisin and Cal locked the animals away for the night, Peggy and Joe sat in companionable silence, watching the flames flicker in the hearth. As the sky dimmed, Joe got up to draw the curtains and light the lamps. Looking around at the piles of discarded paper, Peggy heaved a contented sigh. 'What a grand day it's been. The house has really come to life this year.'

'It's been marvellous, and it's all down to you. Come here and give me a kiss for Christmas,' Joe said, merry after a glass of beer.

'For heaven's sake, will you behave yourself Joe. Those two could come back at any moment,' Peggy protested, wriggling from his grasp.

Joe looked downcast at being rebuffed. Feeling guilty, she took his arm and rested her head on his shoulder. 'Is it just me or have you noticed they are getting close?'

'I thought that too. Are you concerned?'

'Maybe a little,' Peggy said, shifting her position to get comfortable. 'She's still very young. It's easy to forget she's only sixteen. It's been good for Cal though, having her here. He seems so much happier.'

Joe nodded in agreement. 'We do have to bear in mind that she is under our guardianship. Theresa would be distraught if anything happened to her. You know what I'm talking about don't you Peg? Perhaps you need to have a quiet word with her on the subject of the 'birds and the bees.'

'I will, of course,' Peggy replied, 'although I don't suppose she'll thank me for it. She's had her period since being here so it's probably best to have a talk as soon as possible. Maybe you ought to have a word with Cal too? By the way, did you notice she didn't open the present from her mother? I think she took it back upstairs before she went outside.'

There was the sound of voices and a stamping of feet. Cal and Roisin appeared together at the back door just as Peggy was putting out portions of Christmas pudding topped with brandy butter.

'Look out for the sixpence. We don't want anyone choking or swallowing it,' Peggy said. 'Oh, and, don't forget, whoever gets it has to make a wish.'

They had almost finished eating when Cal grimaced and carefully removed the silver coin from his mouth and placed it at the side of his bowl.

'Make a wish, make a wish. You can't say it out loud though or it won't come true,' Roisin cried out, clapping her hands in excitement.

Cal sat for a moment looking thoughtful, then turned to face Peggy, 'I'm not good with words as you know. I just want to say thank you, all of you, for including me. I couldn't have wished for a better day.'

'But, have you made a wish on the sixpence?' Roisin said.

'Yes,' he said emphatically. 'Yes I have.'

Later, when Cal had gone home and Peggy and Joe had retired, Roisin sat up in bed reading one of her new books. Although it was late, and the house was cooling down, she was warm and snug in her new pyjamas. At her side was the box holding the gift from her mother. She had meant to open it earlier, but was reluctant to do so, fearing she might cry in front of Cal. *Come on now, don't be a baby*, she scolded herself. *She wanted you to have it today. Get on and open it while it's still Christmas Day.*

Gently pulling away the tissue paper she opened up the lid. Nestled inside was a silver, heart – shaped locket hanging from a delicate chain. Lifting it carefully, she held it under the reading lamp for a closer look. It had been engraved on both sides. She had to screw up her eyes to make out what was written. *Macushla,* her lips formed the familiar endearment. A tear ran down her cheek as with trembling hands, she turned the locket over. *Beat of my heart*. Bringing the locket to her lips, she allowed her tears to run unchecked. 'Happy Christmas Mammy,' she whispered.

Chapter Twenty One

In the weeks since she had arrived in Canada, the pattern of her days and the rhythm of the tasks were becoming second nature. It didn't feel like any kind of hardship to be outdoors. It was wonderful breathing in the fresh air and taking care of the animals, however severe the weather. Better than being stuck in a fusty old classroom with the nuns always scolding her. At home in Ireland, it seemed as though she was always wanting to escape. To run away, whether from school or the confines of the cottage.

When her mother had at last explained what Sister Agnes had in store for her if she stayed in Waterbridge, Roisin had shuddered at the idea. Even if she hadn't taken up the offer of work from Sister Agnes, what else would she have done with her life without an education? Got a job in a shop or a hotel? She couldn't see herself being happy in either of those situations. Here, she had space and an unanticipated sense of freedom. For now it was the right place to be.

It was the start of a new year and a new life for her. As

for the future, a germ of a plan was beginning to take root.

She just needed to work it out in her head before putting it to Peggy and Joe.

'Is that from your mammy?' Peggy had noticed the locket around Roisin's neck.

'It is. I thought I'd put it on for a while then just wear it on special occasions. Look, she had it engraved,' Roisin said, holding it out for her aunt to read the words.

'Well, isn't that just gorgeous? Your mam always had a way with words. You must be missing her?'

'I am missing her. I do think she made the right decision sending me here though,' Roisin said with conviction, 'and it got me thinking. I have something I'd like to discuss with you and Uncle Joe when he gets back.'

Peggy was intrigued. Joe had gone into town for animal feed and was calling at the vet's for some Nitro ointment to treat a sore on Chester's leg. She hoped he wouldn't get distracted and take too long. She was eager to hear all about this idea.

'He shouldn't be that long. Unless he gets talking, in which case, who knows...!' Peggy said with a resigned shrug. 'While I've got you to myself, I wanted to have a word. It's nothing serious. Joe and I have picked up on something and it concerns you and Cal.'

Roisin felt her face go scarlet at the mention of Cal. Biting her lip, she waited, sure she knew what was coming.

'You like him, don't you?' Peggy said.

Roisin nodded, rubbing the side of her face.

Peggy could see her niece was uncomfortable and

decided beating around the bush would only prolong the agony.

Better by far to get straight to the point.

'The fact of the matter is, when a boy and a girl are friendly with each other, they can have feelings that are, you know, enjoyable. Nothing wrong with that. It's just that when you are young, as you and Cal are, it can be difficult to keep your emotions under control.

Damn, Peggy thought to herself, *I'm making a right mess of this. The girl has probably no idea what I'm getting at.*

'What I'm trying to say is, you know how your mammy came to have you?'

'Yes, I do.' By now Roisin had her hand across her mouth and was suppressing a bubble of laughter rising up in her throat..

'Well, heaven help us,' Peggy cried out in frustration, 'she will kill all of us if the same thing happens to you!'

With her own face also starting to flush with embarrassment, Peggy looked across at her niece. She could see her shoulders were shaking.

'I'm so sorry Aunt Peg.' Biting on her fist, Roisin was finding it hard to stop laughing.

'I know I should be taking this seriously. It's just you looked so stern and then you started talking really fast…. about sex!'

Joe walked in to find the two of them convulsed with laughter.

'Don't ask. Whatever you do, don't ask,' Peggy managed to gasp, tears rolling down her cheeks.

When they had composed themselves, they informed

a bemused Joe it was the birds and bees talk that was responsible for their fit of the giggles.

'You do understand the reasons we might have worries about you and Cal, don't you?' Joe said, his tone serious.

'Yes, I do know what you are saying. Cal and I are both in need of a friend at the moment. He's interesting and I like talking to him, that's all. Don't worry. I've seen how hard it's been for my mam and I wouldn't want that for myself.'

Joe felt put in his place, but he didn't mind. She could be curt. It was part of her personality, and after all, she knew her own mind. That much was abundantly clear.

'Can we change the subject now, please?' she said, going to the dresser and picking up a newspaper cutting, 'I've got an idea I'd like to speak to you both about it.'

She had seen the article before Christmas. Joe had kept back a copy of the newspaper to light the fire and she had cut out the piece she wanted and set it aside. Since then, she had gone over in her head the best way to broach the subject to Peggy and Joe. Her mother, she supposed, would need to be consulted too.

'Um, I saw this a while ago and wondered if it might be something I could try? It's a distance learning course. It means I can still help Uncle Joe during the day and do coursework in the evenings. It doesn't start until September and it looks as though I would just have to pay for the books. I can do that myself with my pocket money.'

Unsure of the reaction she was going to get, she waited, pushing the piece of paper from side to side.

'Your Aunt Peggy will have her own thoughts on this,'

Joe said. 'As for me, I think it's a terrific suggestion. Would you agree, Peg?'

Peggy nodded in encouragement, content to let Joe take the lead for once.

'You're an intelligent girl,' Joe continued, scanning the newspaper cutting, 'and this will give you the equivalent of a high school education. Who knows, you might even end up going to university. Felix mentioned the universities are encouraging more women to take up places, especially in the sciences.'

'All right Joe,' Peggy interjected, 'let's not get carried away. It is a good idea, and I'm sure your mam will be pleased when we tell her. She was quite concerned about you missing out on your education. She has banked some money with us to help with anything you might need. I'll write to her tomorrow and ask if we can use some of that. If she agrees, and I think she will, you can send off for the application form.'

It was a mixture of excitement and anticipation that kept Roisin awake that night. Whilst she hadn't been missing school at all, she had always enjoyed studying. In the early hours she finally slept, but not before it entered her head that she would like to tell Cal her news. *I'll go and see him tomorrow, when he gets back from work,* she thought, before drifting off into an untroubled and dreamless slumber.

Chapter Twenty Two

With two slices of Peggy's cake tucked into the pocket of a pair of Joe's coveralls, Roisin followed the stream that ran down past the paddock. Passing Chester and Bluebell, she paused to give each of them a carrot and a few minutes of fussing. Crossing the lower pastures, still covered in layers of snowfall, she kicked off her boots and socks, eager to feel the soft cushion of snow beneath her bare feet. Back home, it rarely snowed and even when it did, it would be unusual for it to lay for any length of time. Here, the drifts deepened with each new fall and it seemed to her as though she was living in a perpetual winter wonderland.

Leaving her boots behind, she took the deer path that led to Cal's property. It appeared she wasn't the only one to have taken the track recently, if the fresh hoof marks and pellets of dung were anything to go by. Reaching the copse of balsam firs where Cal had cut down the Christmas tree, she noticed movement amongst the lower branches of one of the loftier trees.

Sheltering in a patch of pale, winter sunlight stood a

grey-brown doe and her fawn. The doe was aware of her, cupping her large ears in Roisin's direction, though seemingly untroubled by her presence. A few minutes passed as Roisin stood with bated breath, not wanting to break the spell. Then, startled by a noise somewhere in the forest, the doe bolted, her bushy, white tail erect and her baby scampering after her on spindly legs.

Cal's pick-up was parked outside the house which meant he was back from work. He must have noticed her approach, as he was there to greet her by the time she reached the house.

'Hi there. Where are your boots? Your feet must be freezing.'

'Nope. I rarely feel the cold. I have to wear boots when I'm working, otherwise I prefer being barefoot.'

Cal looked amused. 'Are you just exploring, or have you come to see me for a reason?'

'I wanted to tell you my news. Peggy has sent cake,' she said, taking the wrapped slices from her pocket. 'Oh, and I just saw a mum and baby deer really close up. Do hunters actually shoot them? They are so gentle. Why would anyone want to kill such beautiful animals?'

'You would need to talk to the farmers around here. White-tailed deer cause a lot of damage to crops. That's why your uncle is going to build a fence to try and keep them out. You had better come inside before your feet turn to blocks of ice.'

He led the way into the kitchen where he had just lit the stove. He had obviously been having lunch. There was a plate of half eaten bread and cheese and a discarded apple core on the rickety table.

'Coffee?' he asked, 'I was just about to make a pot.'

Roisin nodded in agreement. Glancing around, she noticed how shabby and uncared for everything looked. No wonder he hadn't wanted her and Joe to come into the house when they visited after the storm.

He put a coffee cup down in front of her and handed her a plate containing a slice of bread and a wedge of cheese. Taking the knife she had given him at Christmas from his pocket, he cored an apple and sliced it into segments before placing it in a dainty, flower-painted bowl. Searching through the dresser, he found a blue and white plate onto which he put the two portions of cake.

'I'm not one for entertaining, as you've probably gathered. I only get the plates out when I have visitors. In other words, not very often. They are from a set my parents were given when they got married.'

Even though he spoke in a matter of fact way, she could feel his sadness. 'It must be lonely, living here on your own surrounded by all their belongings.' As soon as the words were out of her mouth, she regretted them.

'I'm so sorry Cal. Me and my big mouth. My mother says I have a habit of speaking without thinking, and she's right.'

Cal turned to her and his voice was surprisingly upbeat. 'Do you know, you are a genius?'

'I am?' she said, puzzled by his reaction.

'Yes, you are.' Grabbing her by the arm he whirled her around the room.

He stopped when they were both out of breath. 'You know, I hadn't realised this up until now. I've been living with ghosts for the last few years. You can be too full of grief and burdened with memories to get on with the task of living. I've just been existing and it stops. Now!'

She jumped in response as he raised his voice in emphasis.

'I'm going to clear out their possessions and re-organise the house. Do you think you could have a word with your Aunt Peggy? She will probably know somewhere I can take my dad's clothes and whatever my mom left behind. Now, what was it you came over to tell me?'

'Oh, nothing much. It can wait. You are invited to dinner on Sunday. Can you take me to the sea glass beach afterwards? I'd really like to see it.'

He agreed he would, and Roisin retraced her steps. This time there was no sign of the deer. She came upon her socks and boots where she had left them. Once she had them back on, she ran up to the barn where Joe was laying out straw and filling the troughs with hay.

'There you are,' he said. ' I was beginning to think you had got lost. Did you see Cal?'

'I did. I even got lunch. He said something a bit odd though. Perhaps you can explain what he meant?'

Joe listened, leaning his chin on a pitchfork, as she told him what Cal had said.

'It sounds like you did him a good turn today young lady.'

'I wasn't aware I did anything.' She was still baffled by Cal's behaviour and keen to know what she had done to have such an effect on him.

Joe paused and scratched the bristles on his chin, before replying.'Sometimes it isn't anything in particular that you do. It's simply getting a person to see things for themselves from a different viewpoint. That's what makes all the difference.'

'I *think* I see,' she said. 'I was just worried I'd done something wrong.'

Peggy was waiting for them, the lunchtime meal ready in the oven. It smelled good and Roisin felt hungry. She had eaten with Cal, but the run back had given her an appetite. While Roisin and Joe were out, Peggy had written to Theresa. The letter was on the table, left unsealed in case there was anything Roisin wanted to add.

'Just give her my love and tell her I will write soon. Oh, and could you mention how much I love the necklace?'

'I will of course. Did you tell Cal your plans?' Peggy asked.

'I didn't get the chance. He said I was a genius. I'm not really sure why. Uncle Joe said it was a good thing, though. Cal has decided to sort out the house and was asking if you knew somewhere he could take his dad's clothes and the stuff his mother left behind.'

'Well, whatever you said must have inspired him. It's not good for him having constant reminders of a mother who abandoned him and a father who chose to end his life so violently,' Peggy said, tutting at the unfairness of it all. 'Now, if my memory serves me right there is a thrift store in Halifax,' she continued. 'If we help him to bag everything up, I'm sure they will be glad to receive it. I might even get Joe to clear out the attic. He thinks I don't know how much rubbish is up there.'

Joe raised his eyes heavenwards in mock indignation.

'Despite what you say Peg, it was my intention to clear

out the attic before we start work on the deer fence and spring planting begins.'

Roisin remembered the arrangement she had made with Cal for the following day.

'Is it all right if Cal takes me to the sea glass beach after dinner tomorrow? He said he will help me with the evening chores to make up for it and to give you a rest, Uncle Joe.'

'There you go Peggy, someone is looking out for my welfare,' Joe said, grinning at his wife. 'That will suit me just fine, Roisin. I'm sure you will find the beach interesting. It's not the easiest of walks to get to it, but you will see the lighthouse and the washed up sea glass is a sight to behold.'

'By the way,' he added, 'I forgot to mention it earlier. I put your chimes up while you were out. When it's warmer and you have your window open, they will make a lovely sound as the wind moves through them.'

Chapter Twenty Three

Before Cal could say a word, she had taken off at speed along the beach, kicking off her boots in the process. 'Come on, I'll race you,' she shouted over her shoulder.

Stopping only to retrieve her discarded boots, he chased after her, following the indentations made by her feet in the wet sand.

'You're such a slowcoach,' she called out, streaking ahead and leaving him gasping for breath in her wake.

Clambering onto a large, granite rock, she waited for him to catch up. The rock felt warm to her touch, its smooth polished surface the result of glacial weathering. From her vantage point she could see the full sweep of the crescent bay, framed on one side by dense forest and on the other by the curving shoreline lapped by rolling breakers.

Cal joined her, and they sat watching a group of sandpipers skittering amongst the waves and digging for clams in the surf.

The run had warmed him and he took off the hat and

gloves Peggy had knitted for him for Christmas. His face no longer looked sallow and the hollows of his cheeks had filled out, thanks in part to Peggy's cooking.

'What was it you were going to tell me yesterday?'

'It's nothing really,' she said, shrugging her shoulders. 'I'm going to apply to do some classes in September. It's a distance learning course run by the college so I can still help Uncle Joe with the farm. Felix said if I get good grades it will get me into university. I was so excited, I couldn't sleep for thinking about it.'

Cal was quiet for a while, unable to push aside the implications for the future. There was more than one way of losing someone you cared about.

He chose his words with care. 'I can't really say I have much interest in education,' he said. 'I didn't even get to finish my high school diploma. I know how much you like finding out about things. You're a smart girl. It will be good for you to study again and who knows where it will take you. I've heard it mentioned that a good education is a passport to the world.'

'Oh I don't know about that,' she said, hugging her knees. 'That's way ahead in the future. I have to finish this course first before I can make any plans beyond that.'

With his face turned away from her, she wasn't able to read his expression.

'Would you be sad if I went away?'

He handed her boots to her without answering the question.

'You will be needing these,' he said, his voice husky, 'the path is rough and the rocks can be slippery. Your aunt and uncle will not be pleased if I don't get you home in one piece.' He pointed in the direction of an outcrop at the end of the beach.

'See the path going up the side of that big rock? We have to climb that and then walk for another mile along the coastal track that leads to the lighthouse. It's a bit of a scramble down to the beach from there. If we time it right, we should have about an hour before the tide turns.'

The climb was steep, but soon they were at the top of the promontory. Here they had a view of the lighthouse, silhouetted against the winter sky.

Extending towards the horizon, was the wide expanse of blue -green ocean. The last part of the walk was the most difficult to negotiate. The access from the lighthouse down to the beach was no more than a narrow track, overgrown with spiky bushes.

Occasionally she had to reach for Cal's arm to steady herself as they dislodged small rocks, or the loose sand shifted beneath their feet.

The path petered out at an outcrop of large boulders. Clambering over these brought them into a small cove. A strip of golden sand was just visible, littered with brown rock-weed dislodged from underwater boulders and washed up on the shore. It would have been an insignificant beach without the presence of the pieces of smooth, frosted glass nestling amongst the muted greys and browns of the beach pebbles.

The sea glass glinted in the afternoon sunlight. It reminded Roisin of brightly coloured jewels, discarded by a hard-to-please suitor, seeking to impress his beloved.

'It's just magical,' she exclaimed, clapping her hands in delight. 'I didn't realise there would be so much of it.'

'Nature sure can be amazing at times," Cal said, delighted by her response. 'My mom told me sailors used to call the glass mermaid tears. When someone is lost at sea, it's said mermaids cry and their tears wash up as sea glass.'

It was a lovely myth. Better than the more mundane explanation she knew to be the truth. They were reverse gems, it said in one of Joe's books. Broken bottles and jars, man-made in origin, then dumped into the ocean. It took the mighty force of the waves to change them into a thing of beauty.

Gathering together a small selection, she placed them in her pockets, careful not to take too many. She wondered if she were to return, many years into the future, would there be any remaining.

It made her sad to think of the possibility that there would be no more of these gifts from the sea to enjoy.

'C'mon,' Cal said, reaching for her hand, 'we'd better be making our way back. Tide's starting to come in.'

He was right. She saw the line of sand had disappeared and the water was beginning to creep up onto the shingle. Clambering over the boulders, already damp from sea spray, she struggled to remain upright on their slippery surface.

It wouldn't be long before the tide was fully in and the rocks they were standing on would be pummelled by the incoming waves before becoming submerged.

'Do people ever get cut off by the tide?' Roisin asked, a shiver running down her spine at the thought.

'It does happen. Most Maritime folk know to pay heed to the information on tides. A couple of people drowned in the cove a few years back. They were here for the summer vacation and hadn't checked out the tide times.'

The sun was already low by the time they had scrambled back up to the lighthouse. She shivered again, thinking how awful it must be to drown. They stood for a few minutes watching the sky, streaked with bands of violet, orange, yellow and palest pink, before joining the coastal path that would return them to the crescent beach. The light was fading fast when they at last arrived and with the tide still high, they kept close to the treeline. Reaching the path that would bring them back to the road, the snap of a twig and a rustling in the undergrowth stopped them dead in their tracks. Cal put a finger to his lips.

'Ssh,' he whispered.

Holding her breath in anticipation, her heart started to thump a little faster. What on earth was it? Much to her surprise, what looked like an especially large hedgehog with a spreading fan of quills across its back, began to amble across their path.

Cal held her arm in his. 'It's a porcupine. Keep very still until it passes. They can get aggressive and release a very noxious odour if they feel threatened.'

They stood side by side, trying not to move or make a sound. To their relief the animal seemed unperturbed by their presence. It strolled past them and made its way back into the forest, looking for all the world as if out for an evening stroll.

Chapter Twenty Four

It hadn't been easy for Cal, having to sort through his father's clothes and personal effects, and the few items left behind by his mother. Peggy and Roisin had spent the morning at his house and under Cal's supervision, had filled three old suitcases and a number of strong bags ready to take to the thrift store in Halifax.

He elected to keep some of his dad's personal belongings, including his fountain pen, a pair of silver cufflinks and a pocket-watch. He also set aside some workwear and a couple of pairs of work boots he would be able to make use of.

'Are you feeling all right Cal?' Peggy asked, placing an arm on his shoulder. 'It's not the easiest task to tackle at the best of times.'

'It's been difficult,' he agreed, 'but I feel better for having done it. I'm really glad of the help. From both of you. It would have been so much harder if I had to do it by myself.'

The clearing out of his parents' belongings was not entirely to blame for the unsettling feeling that had descended on him. He'd had a restless night dissecting every word of Roisin's plans.

He didn't want to dampen her enthusiasm, but he felt awkward and uncomfortable about what lay ahead. Where exactly did he fit into her future, if at all? She had helped him exorcise the ghosts of his past and to see everything differently. Would he just return to the way things were before once she left the farm? The very idea of it made him uneasy. It was true he wanted what was best for her... but in that moment, the image of them together on the sea glass beach was what was offering him reassurance and gladdening his heart.

Cal snapped out of his reverie as Peggy cheerfully brought him back to the matter in hand.

'It's been a very productive morning,' she said, wiping her hands on her apron. 'Let's go and get a cup of tea and see how that uncle of yours is getting on, Roisin. He promised me he would have the attic cleared by the time we got back.'

They found Joe at the back of the house surrounded by bags and boxes. Wielding an axe he was breaking up a set of rickety dining chairs.

'I'm going to have a bonfire later and burn most of this old furniture. It's not good for anything else. Some of it has woodworm and it's not worth keeping. I just hope the worm hasn't found its way into the roof gables. Now, are my ears deceiving me or did I hear mention of a cup of tea?'

The following Saturday, with Roisin's help, Cal loaded the back of the pick-up and placed a tarpaulin over it as protection from the weather.

Though never one for big cities, Roisin was excited to be visiting Halifax.

They had been given permission to go to a showing at the movie theatre once they had dropped everything off at the thrift store.

The drive to the outskirts of the town took less than an hour and Cal made a slight detour to the Hydrostone neighbourhood. He wanted to show Roisin the pretty tree-lined streets of houses so loved by his mother. Constructed after the Harbour explosion of 1917, they were built to replace the wooden constructions obliterated by the blast and were designed in the style of an English garden suburb.

'My mom loved these houses,' he said, remembering happier times. 'I sometimes wonder if she would have stayed if we had lived somewhere like this rather than out in the country. Maybe if she'd been here she wouldn't have felt so isolated.'

'It must be difficult not having her around.'

Cal thought for a minute. 'I guess it is, but if she is content where she is, then I'm OK with that.'

'Does she keep in touch?'

'She writes every now and then. I haven't heard much from her since my dad died though. I think she feels guilty about not being here for the funeral.'

Roisin felt the invisible link between them strengthen as they sat together, each wrapped up in their own thoughts. They were both without parents, even if their absences were for different reasons.

She knew she was lucky to have Peggy and Joe. It meant she wasn't entirely alone.

Unbidden, the memory of her own mother came to her. There were so many things she missed about her, including her warmth, intelligence, her humour and her kindness.

The recollection caused an unexpected jolt of pain that took her by surprise. Cal saw her look of distress and reached for her hand.

Swallowing hard, she sniffed away the hot tears that threatened to spill down her cheeks.

In contrast to the tranquillity of Hydrostone, the streets surrounding the thrift store were bustling, the pavements crowded with people walking purposefully. Cars honked their horns and yellow trolley buses click-clacked as they passed, drawing power from the electrically charged wires overhead.

Cal parked the pick-up in a side road and they carried the bulging bags and suitcases into the store, where they were accepted by an appreciative member of staff. Back on the streets Roisin recoiled from the noise and commotion swirling around her. She felt suddenly overwhelmed by the sheer numbers of people jostling for space on the side-walk.

Fur-coated women office workers and men in suits and trilby hats darted between housewives carrying baskets laden with groceries. Children in school uniforms holding bundles of books stood in small groups chattering together about the day's events.

Being so close to the port brought large groups of uniformed soldiers and seamen of all nationalities into the city, raucous in their excitement as they savoured their few brief hours of shore leave.

The line for the movie theatre was already beginning to snake around the block and they tagged on the end. The afternoon matinee was due to start and the waiting crowd advanced, eager to take their seats.

To Roisin's surprise, the Art Deco interior was more stylish than what was promised by the rather drab exterior.

Despite her protests, Cal insisted on purchasing their tickets, although she bought a large bag of popcorn to share during the movie.

Sinking into the plush velvet seats, they awaited the start of the film, a courtroom drama. As the lights dimmed, she glanced around.

Many of the couples were already entwined in each other's arms, their attention on each other, rather than on the screen.

'I don't think they are going to see much of the film,' she whispered to Cal as the ruched curtains rolled back with a loud swish.

When the film finished, they exited, blinking as their eyes adjusted to the mid afternoon glare. They were deep in discussion about the film when, passing an empty store, Roisin backtracked having caught a brief glimpse of a concert poster pasted to the outside of one of the windows. The photograph on the front was unmistakable and she peered closer to see what was written below.

In large letters it read: 'Presenting The Celtic Colleen herself Miss Geraldine Flynn'.

Underneath was a list of concert dates and venues in various parts of the province.

'Look, it's Ger,' she said, pulling at his arm in excitement. 'I shared a cabin with her on the ship. She was a real friend to me when all that happened with that man Patrick Higgins.'

'I remember you mentioning her,' Cal said, squinting at the small text. 'It says she's starting a tour in April. She'll be performing at our theatre in Lewistown. It's a real pity my mom isn't around. She loved to hear her sing.'

As they left the city, Roisin was glad to escape and was full of exuberant chatter on the drive home. They came off the freeway and left behind the outer suburbs. Soon they would be back at the farm, where Peggy and Joe would be waiting to hear about her day.

'Would it be all right if I open the window?'

The heater was throwing out humid air and she felt hot and grubby from the city dust.

'Sure,' Cal said, 'are you wanting to blow the cobwebs away?'

She looked at him quizzically.

'It's something my mom used to say. It means to clear your head.'

With her arm resting on top of the open window, she felt the cool wind ripple across her face.

It occurred to her she never really felt muddled, not up to now anyway. As far as she was aware, she didn't have any cobwebs to blow away. Taking a deep breath, she inhaled the scent of pine carried on the breeze. The air was clear and she could taste the wind-borne salt on her lips.

The road ahead shimmered in the fading, afternoon light.

She was looking forward to getting back to the farm. More than that, she was looking forward to going home.

Chapter Twenty Five

A warm wind blew in off the land. It carried a soft rain that dissolved the last of the piles of grit-laced snow. The days grew longer and lighter. Unfolding pink mayflowers trailed along the banks of the stream and fat green buds appeared on the trees, heralding the start of spring.

When work began on the deer fence it was not a moment too soon for Joe. The fruit trees along the edges of the field were already showing signs of being gnawed and nibbled.

Chester, overweight and a little lazy after winter, reluctantly drew the log sled laden with fence stakes down to the lower meadows. Once unharnessed, he happily munched on the newly emerging grass that had lain dormant during the coldest months. At the end of the day, Joe re-filled the sled with fallen branches and brought them back to be sawn into logs and stacked, ready for the following winter.

It took almost a week to complete the fence to Joe's satisfaction and they both had calluses on their hands from digging holes deep enough to hold the eight-foot high stakes.

When he could, Cal came to help after work, a very welcome extra pair of hands. Once the mesh had been fixed in place, Joe got Roisin to tie pieces of ribbon and wool from his mother's sewing box to deter the hungry and inquisitive animals.

'We need to keep an eye out just to make sure they don't try to jump the fence or break it down,' Joe said. 'Hopefully they will create a new path for themselves a way away and we won't need to worry about them destroying our summer planting.'

It was warm enough to sit outside and Peggy came to join them carrying an old blanket and a basket covered with a red and white tea towel. From inside she produced bottles of ginger beer and freshly baked oatcakes. They were still warm from the oven and melted on the tongue. Overhead a pair of song sparrows chittered, fluttering their wings in flight as they searched for air-borne insects.

Roisin felt drowsy and lay back on the rough square of blanket, squinting up at the sky. Constructing the fence had not been easy. Her muscles ached and her hands were rough and blemished. Even so, she felt a sense of accomplishment at the end of what had been a hard and tiring week.

Joe was glad of her help and together they were planning the summer planting. He had also sold the piglets. Over the coming weeks they would be going to their new homes.

There was sure to be a lot of extra work over the summer months, but Roisin was looking forward to the longer, sun-filled days, after months of snow and freezing temperatures.

She must have drifted off to sleep for a while. When she opened her eyes, Joe and Peggy were nowhere to be seen.

'They've gone back to the house.' Cal's voice came from alongside her.

He was propped up on one arm watching her. 'Sleepy head. Snoring your head off, you were,' he teased.

'I was not,' she said, indignant at the very notion, 'I don't snore.'

Laughing out loud at her outrage, he stood and stretched out his arm to pull her to her feet. Together they rolled up the blanket and walked to the house.

'There's a parcel for you,' Peggy said pointing to a large package wrapped in brown paper on the kitchen table.

'Ooh, I wonder what it can be.' Roisin noticed the Irish stamps and knew it must be from her mother.

Cal was going to help a neighbour knock down an old barn and was saying his goodbyes. 'See you young fella,' Joe said, patting Cal on the back, 'and many thanks. You were a great help with the fence. I owe you a couple of beers.'

'Humph, a couple of beers indeed! The boy needs something more substantial than alcohol,' Peggy said, fixing Joe with one of her looks. 'You'll come for your dinner tomorrow Cal and I'll hear no more about it. Beer indeed!'

The kitchen table was cluttered and Roisin took the parcel to her room. She tore open the layers of brown paper to find a letter from her mother nestling on top of a layer of pale pink tissue paper. Putting the letter to one side, she pushed aside the tissue paper to reveal an expanse of silky fabric. It was a dress made from the softest satin and the colour of the inside of a shell. It had a full net underskirt and pearl buttons at the neck and sleeves. The material was so beautiful and delicate, she was concerned it would tear if she tried it on with her rough hands and split nails. Carefully placing it onto a clothes hanger, she hung it on the outside of her wardrobe.

As she opened her mother's letter, she wondered where on earth she could go that would justify wearing something so exquisite.

Hello again my darling girl,

I do hope you like the dress and that it fits you. Peggy took some measurements from your clothes and I have left the seams wide so they can be let out if need be. The style is all the rage here and I thought the pale pink colour would suit your complexion my little Rose. You may be wondering when you will get the opportunity to wear the dress. Well, Peggy said you were going to see The 'Celtic Colleen' in concert and we plotted together to make sure you will look glamorous. I'm glad you liked the locket too. Wear it and think of me when you are out having a lovely time.

I have some exciting news! The Hennesseys have bought a house and I have moved into the flat above the shop. Can you believe it? It's huge with two bedrooms and a box-room where I have set up my sewing machine. The Hennesseys have been wonderful. They painted the rooms before I moved in and I made the curtains. It all looks very smart. They have said I can take in a lodger

to help with the rent. I am so busy with all the work
coming in, I don't think I need to just at the moment. It's
marvellous that you are thinking of starting the course
in September. You have my blessing. I am so proud of
you. Please let me know if there is anything else you
need.
   I hope to hear from you very soon.
   Your loving Mam xxx

Roisin took the dress downstairs to show Peggy, who
was elbow deep in flour from baking.

'Isn't it just divine?' Peggy said, wiping her forehead
with the back of her hand. 'Your mam has done you
proud. Are you going to try it on?'

'I can't. Look at my hands.' Roisin held them out
for scrutiny. 'They're all rough and my nails are in a
state. I don't want to damage the material.' She looked
downhearted at the thought.

'Don't you worry now. I'll get some oatmeal to soak
your hands and I have a nail file. We'll soon have them
looking splendid,' Peggy said. 'And Cal has asked if I
can trim his hair. If you like I can do yours too. A couple
of inches off the ends will tidy it up.'

That evening Roisin sat at her desk and began a letter
of thanks to her mother. Her fingernails looked almost
normal again, after the home-made manicure. As she
tried on the dress in front of the full length mirror in Joe
and Peggy's bedroom, it came as a surprise to her, not
only that the dress fitted perfectly, but that she actually
looked passably elegant. Especially if she followed Ger's
example and held her hair up and away from her face.

'I know you like your coveralls and work shirts, but it's nice to look stylish occasionally. The dress really suits you,' Peggy remarked. 'We just need to get you some shoes to go with it. You can't be wearing galoshes or going barefoot to the theatre.'

I don't suppose so, Roisin thought, but the image made her giggle. Writing her thank you note, she included a little drawing of herself in the dress and wearing galoshes. Alongside she wrote: *Aunt Peggy says no to bare feet or boots,* which she knew would make her mother laugh.

There was still light in the sky and from her window she could see the outline of the Brandywine maple with its clusters of red flowers. She had read about maples in Joe's book of trees. With summer approaching, lush green leaves would appear on the branches. Then in autumn, as winter beckoned, the trees begin to store sugars in their leaves, causing the colour changes the Canadians call 'The Fall'.

How beautiful it will be to see it, she thought, as she put the finishing touches to her letter. Her only regret was that her mother, who loved nature as much as she did, would not be with her to share the experience.

Chapter Twenty Six

A change in the weather meant spring planting could begin, but not before the ground was prepared ready for seeding. Joe showed Roisin how to place the collar and frame around Chester to enable the cultivator to be attached in preparation for ploughing. Once the first furrow had been cut, the job became easier, and with Joe leading Chester, Roisin had soon mastered the technique of maintaining a straight line. It was hot and sweaty work and very tiring. By the end of the day, the first stage of the job was completed.

The next task would be to break up the clods of earth using the harrow. Compost made from food scraps would then be added by the barrow load and once the soil was raked and the drills prepared, the seeds could be sown directly into the ground. First to be planted would be the onions, lettuce, spinach and turnips. Later, when the sun warmed the ground, beets, carrots, potatoes, broccoli, cabbage and cauliflower could be sown, followed in early summer by more tender plants like the squashes, peppers, pumpkins and tomatoes.

Looking at the empty fields of soft brown earth, it was difficult to imagine the abundance that was to come once the rain and sunshine worked their magic.

One by one the piglets, now weaned and substantially bigger, went off to their new homes leaving the yard a cleaner and quieter place. Even Artie and the rest of the chickens looked happier now they could peck and scratch at the dirt without being disturbed by gangs of raucous piglets. The one remaining piglet, who was being fattened for slaughter, seemed unfazed by the departure of his brothers and sisters. He could be found happily rooting around the yard, accepting a back scratch from anyone passing.

'You can give him a name if you want to. He's going to be here until the end of the summer,' Joe said.

Roisin thought for a minute. 'He looks a bit like our milkman back home and he was called Fergus,' she volunteered.

'Fergus it is. I think it suits him just fine,' Joe declared.

Peggy put her head around the back door to call them in for lunch.

'Meet Fergus,' Joe said. 'Roisin says he reminds her of the milkman back home in Ireland.'

Peggy studied the piglet. He was looking up at her in anticipation, convinced she had some scraps for him in her apron pocket.

'Oh God, you're right! I remember that milkman from when we were young. He was awful. Always trying to grab a kiss off the girls. Your mam and I called him Roly Poly because his stomach bulged over his trousers.' She laughed out loud at the memory. 'Fergus, oh my goodness he's the spit of him. Wait 'til I write and tell Theresa. She'll remember him I'm sure.'

The day of the concert was drawing near and Roisin felt a growing sense of excitement at the thought of seeing Ger again. She hoped it would be possible to talk to her afterwards. Ger was a popular figure. A rising star. Would she even want to have anything to do with her again? She was only a young kid, and the shared memory of what had happened on the ship might be one Ger would prefer to forget.

'Do you think Ger will want to see me Aunt Peggy?'

Peggy knew her niece was nervous at the thought of the reception she might get from the woman. The girl had only known her for a short time. It was possible Roisin had built up some sort of fanciful notion about their friendship, although she wasn't generally one for being over imaginative.

'Let's just wait and see. I know we are all looking forward to the performance. We can focus on that for now.'

Along with Roisin, she and Joe, Cal, and the quilting bee ladies and their husbands were all going to the concert. Peggy, not usually one for showing off, secretly thought how envious her friends would be if the Celtic Colleen recognised her niece and as a consequence she, Peggy, could bask in the reflected glory.

'If there is an opportunity to meet with her, then all well and good. If not, then so be it,' she said. 'Now, I haven't forgotten you need shoes my girl. There is a good shoe shop in Lewistown. We'll go tomorrow and get you fixed up.'

Joe was attending a get-together at Felix the veterinarian's house where there was a meeting for those involved in organising a charity fund-raising dinner. He dropped Peggy and Roisin off in the town. Once they had done their shopping, they would walk back to the house for their ride back.

The store was reminiscent of the one patronised by her mother when the time came to buy school shoes. This was usually a fraught occasion and one of the rare times Theresa had her patience tested. There was never a pair made that would suit her daughter. Roisin hated wearing anything on her feet, especially the stiff, black leather lace-ups that were part of her school uniform.

'We want something fashionable, not too rigid, not too high and not too restricting. The girl is like Goldilocks with her feet. The shoes have to be just right.' Peggy said this with conviction while her niece looked on, embarrassed at the thought that she might be seen as difficult.

The woman assistant, grey-haired and good-natured, had dealt with a generation of townspeople's feet. The youngsters, who had come to be measured for boots and shoes in the winter and sandals in the summer, were now grown up and entrusting their own children's feet to her expert hands.

'Let's measure you first,' the woman said, 'then we can have a look at what we have in your size. Do you have a colour in mind?'

'Um, not really. My dress is very pale pink. Any colour

that would go with that, I suppose,' Roisin sighed, anticipating a long, drawn-out ordeal.

A variety of shoes in different styles and colours were produced, none of which appealed. She could sense her aunt's growing exasperation and was about to resign herself to choosing a pair that were the best of a bad job, when the assistant disappeared into the back of the shop. She re-appeared a few minutes later, holding a white box.

'What do you think of these?' she asked, taking out a pair of cream-coloured ballerina flats with a tiny heel. 'The leather is butter soft. You won't even know you are wearing them.'

The shoes weighed next to nothing and were the most comfortable Roisin had ever tried on. It did indeed feel as though she had nothing on her feet.

With encouragement from the two women, she walked around the shop and then did a little pirouette in front of a full length mirror before declaring the shoes 'ideal', much to the relief of both Peggy and the shop assistant.

The short walk to Felix and Laura's house took them along roads lined with elegant and stately properties once owned by merchants and dignitaries of the town. Birdsong filled the air and sprinkler systems hissed, spraying a mist of droplets across acres of velvet grass.

The house, set back from the road on an expansive tree-lined plot, was large and imposing. It was built in the Victorian Gothic style, with dormer windows and a distinctive gingerbread lattice trim under the eaves. A willow tree on the manicured lawn, dipped its silver – grey fronds into a pond surrounded by pale, grey stones.

To one side of the main house, a set of steps led to a

carriage house serving as an office for Felix. This was where the meeting was being held. Peggy sent Roisin ahead to knock and see if Joe was ready. It was Felix who answered and apologising for the delay, he directed them to the house where Laura was waiting.

Although from the outside the house had an air of refinement, the interior was worn and shabby. Shoes littered the hallway and discarded books and toys were scattered about, ready to trip up an unwary visitor. Laura opened the door looking flustered and Peggy and Roisin accompanied her to the rear kitchen, trying to avoid the piles of abandoned items. Laura put the kettle on to make tea whilst the twins squabbled on the veranda at the back of the house.

'They have been terribly rowdy today,' Laura said in exasperation, tucking a stray strand of hair behind her ear. 'I had to attend to a lot of calls this morning for the practice and I haven't had time to do much of anything else.' She looked in dismay at the state of disarray around her as if realising for the first time the extent of the chaos.

Peggy was not the sort of person who could stand by when someone was obviously in a predicament, and this was no exception.

Rolling up her sleeves, she sent Roisin to bring the twins in from outside. Leaving Laura to sort the laundry, she cleared the table and piled the heap of dirty dishes into the sink. The girls, with Roisin's assistance, were instructed to pick up their belongings, take them to their room and tidy them away.

Reluctantly, the girls complied, one stomping up the stairs balancing an armful of toys and games while the other dawdled behind, carrying one or two items at a time. Before long, order was restored to both levels of the house and Peggy and Laura were able to relax with a well-earned cup of tea.

'Phew,' Roisin exclaimed as she surveyed the twins' bedroom, 'you do have a lot of things.'

The room was painted bright pink and crammed with soft toys and books. Two white metal beds with patchwork coverlets stood on either side of a cream fluffy rug. Above each of the beds was a painted sign, one saying 'Evie' and the other 'Ellie'.

'So which of you is Ellie and which of you is Evie?'

'I'm Evie.' Roisin noticed it was the twin she had picked out at church as the more confident of the two, who spoke first.

'And I'm Ellie,' the other twin volunteered, holding a battered teddy bear against her cheek.

Evie fixed Roisin with a steady stare. It was a little disconcerting coming from a child. Roisin returned her gaze until the younger girl was forced to look away.

'Do you have a boyfriend?' Evie asked, looking at her slyly.

'Well I have a friend, and he's a boy. Does that count?'

'Is it Cal, the boy who lives next door to you?' Evie said, and Roisin noticed two patches of colour had appeared high up on the girl's pale cheeks.

'Cal is a friend nothing more than that. There's lots I want to do before I settle down and have a steady relationship, if that's what you're asking.'

'Mm, I guess so,' Evie replied.

Roisin was sure she detected a look of relief on Evie's

face. *She's infatuated*, she thought, trying to conceal a smile. Not wanting to hurt her feelings, Roisin made no comment. The girl was only a youngster after all.

'Anyway, my mom says I have to marry someone with lots of money and a big house if I'm to be happy,' Evie declared, regaining her composure.

That certainly won't be Cal, Roisin muttered to herself.

'I am never going to get married,' Ellie announced quietly. 'I'm going to stay at home with my mom and dad until I'm old and grey.'

With the meeting in the carriage house over, Joe and Felix arrived to find the house an oasis of calm. There was no sign of the twins and Laura had brushed her hair and put on a clean blouse.

'The twins are upstairs. Roisin is keeping them amused,' she said by way of explanation to her husband.

'Well, she can come by any time if she is able to keep them quiet and in their room,' Felix said, obviously impressed by the turn of events.

'It was down to Peggy really,' Laura said, 'she got us all organised. She is an absolute whizz at getting stuck in and sorting things out. It's made me realise that I have to concede defeat and not try to do everything by myself. The house, the girls and the administration work for the practice are too much to cope with. If it's all right with you Felix, I'm going to get someone in to help in the house.'

In the truck on the way home, Joe noticed that Peggy looked worn out.

'Have you been doing too much, old girl?' he said, his voice tinged with concern.

'Not really. Laura just seemed a bit overwhelmed. It didn't take long with all of us pitching in, did it Roisin?'

'No, not once the girls realised you meant business Aunt Peggy!'

'Those girls are a handful it has to be said. Were you able to work out which was Evie and which was Ellie?' Peggy said.

'Evie is the one who thinks she has to marry a rich man to be happy,' Roisin replied with a giggle. 'Mind you,' she added mischievously, 'she also has a massive crush on Cal. I can't wait to tell him.'

It wasn't until they were about to turn into the drive that Joe spoke again.

'It was your idea, wasn't it Peg. Laura getting some extra help?'

He patted his wife's knee. He was not expecting a reply, and sure enough he didn't get one.

Peggy could be a formidable woman when she put her mind to it. Even after all the years spent together he had to admit it to himself. He was still in awe of her.

Chapter Twenty Seven

The concert was due to start at eight o'clock and despite Peggy's best efforts they were running behind schedule. She had got herself ready, anticipating Joe would be the one to hold up proceedings. Sure enough, he was still seated at the table polishing his best brogues when she came down.

'Come on, will you? We need to get a move on. And make sure you don't get polish on that clean shirt or there will be hell to pay,' she said through a mouthful of bobby pins.

Her attempts at rolling Roisin's hair into a French twist were proving difficult as she had trimmed a little too much off the length. Eventually she got it to her liking. Teasing a few tendrils from the sides to soften the effect, she took a container of hair spray and shook a mist of fine droplets over it to hold the style in place. After applying a quick file and a coat of clear nail varnish to her niece's fingernails, she began to shoo her upstairs to change into her dress.

'Did you say Cal is picking you up at seven?'

Roisin nodded. Joe and Peggy were going in their pick-up and she and Cal were travelling together in his truck.

'I hope he has cleared out the front seat. We don't want your dress to be ruined,' Peggy exclaimed with a worried frown.

On the dot of seven, Cal arrived. He was wearing a clean white shirt and a dark suit, only slightly too big for him. His freshly washed hair was brushed to one side giving him a dapper look which was somewhat at odds with his apparent nervousness. He stood in the doorway clenching and unclenching his fists, an obvious sign of unease. Peggy beckoned him in, patting Joe on the shoulder to indicate he should go and finish getting ready.

'Well I never,' Peggy said, 'you look very smart Cal. There's many a young lady who would be proud to be on your arm this evening.'

Cal ran his fingers through his hair and blushed.

'I wasn't sure what to wear,' he murmured, 'this is my dad's suit and shirt. They are a bit too big for me. Are you sure they look all right?'

'More than all right,' Peggy replied, 'now where the hell are Joe and Roisin? They had better get here quick sticks or we will be late for the start of the concert.'

Roisin had spent some time studying her appearance in the long mirror. She wasn't sure how she felt about the rather sophisticated figure looking back at her. On the ship, when she had borrowed Ger's clothes and allowed her to apply make-up, it had felt like play acting. This was different. Her mother was right, the shade of the dress did suit her colouring and the sheer material revealed curves she wasn't aware she possessed. The shoes were also having an interesting effect on her legs, making them look longer and slimmer. True, she would have preferred to be barefoot and have her hair hanging loose, but this was a formal occasion and she couldn't let anyone down, including herself. Anyway, if she did get to see Ger, her friend would surely have something to say if she turned up looking like a farmhand.

Shyly she hung back in the kitchen doorway scuffing the toe of her shoe on the wooden boards and waiting for a reaction.

She had placed her mother's locket around her neck and there was a faint rasping noise as she moved it backwards and forwards on its chain.

Joe gave an appraising whistle and held out an arm to draw her into the room.

'You look a picture. Here, let's have a look at you in the light,' he said, spinning her around on the spot.

Peggy's eyes were moist. 'You look adorable and so grown up. Your mam would have loved to have seen you in your frock. She knows you so well to have chosen that colour for you. What do you think of her Cal?'

The flush had returned to Cal's cheeks. 'I, I don't know what to say,' he stammered.

He seemed to be searching for the right words 'Er, um...' Eventually he recovered his composure and swallowing hard said firmly, 'You look like a movie star. It's you who should be up on the stage, not Ger.'

'Well I was on stage once for an Irish dancing contest,' Roisin divulged with a grin. 'You should have heard the racket when we were practising. We learned the steps by dancing on a tin tray!'

The two couples linked arms and made their way to their respective vehicles.

'Your carriage awaits my lady,' Cal said with exaggerated formality as he opened the door of the pick-up for her.

'I hope the seats are clean. Aunt Peggy will be very upset if anything happens to this dress.'

Cal had only remembered the state of the truck's interior as he was leaving the house. The floor was easy enough to clear, but the seats were grubby with patches of oil. At a loss he was resigned to admitting defeat and ready to face Peggy's wrath when he had a brainwave. Taking a clean sheet from his mother's linen cupboard, he placed it over the passenger seat. Pleased with his handiwork, he pointed at the snow white sheet.

'Even your Aunt Peggy can't complain. It's Irish linen!'

'No she can't,' she replied. 'Oh, and by the way, you look very handsome. You had better hope the Scott twins aren't there this evening. You have a secret admirer in Evie.'

'What? The pair of them must be all of ten years old,' Cal said, looking aghast.

'Nine actually. Now, don't you even think of breaking that girl's heart or you will have me to reckon with.'

Roisin was wagging her finger at him in mock indignation, giving a passable impression of Peggy.

When they reached Lewistown it looked as though every occupant of the town had turned up for the performance. The little theatre was full to capacity and it took them a while to make their way to their seats, especially with Peggy pausing to exchange pleasantries along the way.

Joe had purchased the tickets with instruction from Peggy that they should be positioned, in her words, 'In the middle and close to the stage.' Fortunately for him, he had got it right. Looking around, Roisin was pleased she was wearing her new dress. The Celtic Colleen had a far-reaching following in the province. It was apparent everyone had made an effort and turned up in their finery to see her.

The stage was a raised wooden platform, bare apart from a microphone on a stand and a padded stool at the centre. Midnight blue velvet drapes served as a backdrop. As the lights dimmed, the material, illuminated with tiny points of light, created the impression of a night sky. A single spotlight pointing at the stool, cast a pool of white light.

A figure hesitated in the wings and then came to the centre of the stage to a rousing round of applause.

The long, silver-coloured evening gown Ger was wearing sparkled, as though studded with diamonds. A circle of diamanté at her neck glittered, caught in the shaft of light.

With a wave, Ger stepped up and perched on the stool. Shading her eyes with one hand, she peered out into the audience who clapped again, their enthusiasm undimmed. The applause subsided and she took the microphone from its stand.

'Good evening ladies and gentlemen and thank you for coming this evening,' she began, before clearing her throat and continuing. 'My name is Geraldine Flynn, although most of you know me as The Celtic Colleen. As you will be aware, this is the first time I have performed in your lovely little town, and if I am honest, I am shocked by how many of you have turned up to see little old me.'

She flicked her curls girlishly and a ripple of laughter spread throughout the theatre.

'I have a set of songs planned for tonight, but if anyone has a special request, please shout out.'

With that the evening unfolded, Ger weaving her magic on her captivated listeners. The occupants of the town, many of Irish and Scottish descent, maintained strong sentimental and emotional ties to both countries. Some could trace their ancestry back over many generations, whilst others were more recent émigrés. All were united in their love of their respective 'old country' whichever it was. The ballads, with their tales of hardship, lost love, supernatural events, or rebellion, were a unifying force, whatever their origins.

The songs certainly aroused strong emotions in the assembled audience. Many wept openly or blew their noses self-consciously. Next to Roisin, Peggy sat with tears running down her cheeks. Even the normally practical and unemotional Joe was dabbing at his eyes with a handkerchief. Alongside her Cal sat upright in his seat, gripping the arms and looking straight ahead. Roisin assumed he too was struggling to control his feelings.

As the evening began drawing to a close, and the last flawless note of the final song echoed around the theatre, the audience rose as one.

Looking overwhelmed, Ger blew a kiss to her admiring crowd and with her customary wave, departed from the stage. A stamping of feet and clapping of hands brought her back for an encore and then it was over. The overhead lights were switched on and everyone got to their feet and began heading for the exits.

Cal slipped out of his seat and strode ahead of Roisin, but not before she noticed he was using the sleeve of his shirt to wipe away a tear from the corner of his eye.

Chapter Twenty Eight

As the audience slowly filed out of the theatre, it took some time to get back to the lobby area and Roisin could hardly contain her impatience. To make matters worse, her aunt was in earnest conversation with a group of her friends. Hopping from foot to foot, Roisin waited for a pause in their chatter. 'Can I go and look for Ger please Aunt Peggy?' she pleaded. 'I noticed the stage door as we came in. Come and find us when you have finished talking and I'll introduce you to her.'

Grabbing Cal's arm, she pulled him out of the main entrance and around the corner to the side of the building. A line of excited fans holding printed photographs of Ger, had already gathered at the stage door. The photo had been shot in a studio and Ger looked like a Hollywood starlet. Just then the door opened and she emerged, still wearing her long gown, and with a coat thrown over her shoulders to ward off the evening chill. As the crowd surged forward, eager to have their photographs signed. Roisin waited, chewing her fingernails and holding onto Cal's arm.

Ger looked up and catching sight of her called out, 'Ro, is that you? I thought you might be here. I was blinded by the lights when I was onstage and couldn't see a thing.'

Stepping forward, she encircled Roisin in a hug.

'And who is this good-looking young man?' She said, noticing Roisin wasn't alone.

Roisin couldn't look at Cal knowing he would be the colour of beetroot. 'This is my friend Cal. He owns the neighbouring farm.'

'It's very nice to meet you, Roisin's friend. If the pair of you go off and find my dressing room, I'll be with you in a while. Tell Lanie you are friends of mine. She'll make you a drink.'

The dressing room was situated at the end of a long, gloomy corridor lit by shell-shaped uplighters. A narrow strip of brightness shone from beneath a door adorned with a gold star.

Roisin tapped on the door, hoping they were in the right place.

'Who is it?' The voice was throaty and low with an accent Roisin couldn't place. Spanish or Italian?

'It's er, Roisin O'Connor and I'm with my friend Cal. Ger told us to come and wait for her,' she said, before adding. 'We met on the Mercinia. I shared a cabin with her on the voyage over.'

The door was opened by a slight figure, with a helmet of dark hair. Her skin was tanned and she had large striking eyes. They looked almost black with the light shining behind her.

'Come in. I am Eleni but you can call me Lanie. Would you like some tea? Or I have Turkish coffee if you prefer.'

'I'd like tea please. What about you Cal? Are you going to try the coffee?'

Cal nodded. 'That would be good. Thanks.'

Lanie boiled enough water for a single cup of tea on a small portable gas ring. After straining the leaves, she added milk before handing it to Roisin and offering her a bowl of sugar. She then placed coffee and water into a flat bottomed copper pot with a long handle. As it came to the boil, she lowered the heat, letting it simmer for a few minutes before pouring the liquid into a tiny, patterned cup and handing it to Cal.

The sound of voices could be heard in the corridor and Ger entered the room with Joe and Peggy in tow.

'Look who I found by the stage door,' Ger said. 'They've been telling me all about your antics Roisin, it sounds as though you have become a real little farmer since I last saw you. Now let me look at you properly.'

She took hold of Roisin's hands and held her at arm's length.

'I have to say my girl, you look wonderful. You're as pretty as a picture in that dress and it's nice to see you with some colour in your cheeks. You were all washed out when I saw you last. The lifestyle here must be agreeing with you.'

Her gaze swivelled pointedly in Cal's direction and he reddened once again.

Tossing her coat onto the back of a chair, she sat at a dressing table in front of a mirror framed with light bulbs and began removing her make-up. An attentive Lanie busied herself, making sure everything Ger needed was to hand. As she changed her clothes behind an ornate screen in the corner of the room, much to the embarrassment of Joe and Cal, Ger chattered eagerly about what a success the evening had been.

'Such a warm and appreciative audience,' she enthused. 'I will definitely be coming back. Everyone made me feel so welcome.'

Lanie was instructed to pour a tot of whiskey each for Peggy and Joe.

'It's Irish, and purely medicinal of course,' Ger said with a grin.

'I've been thinking,' she added. 'As tomorrow is Sunday and I don't have another show until Monday, what do you say we drive over to see you all at the farm? Joe was telling me you are close to the ocean. We can spend some time with you all, go for our drive and come back and do a spot of beach-combing. It's been years since I paddled in rock pools and collected shells.'

Ger looked wistful as she spoke. It had been a successful start to this tour which was pleasing. However, the packed itinerary and constant travel meant she had little time to relax and unwind. She felt tired and out of sorts and definitely in need of a short break.

Talk of the beach reminded Roisin of the walk with Cal to look for sea glass. It was on the tip of her tongue to mention it to Ger, when she happened to glance in Cal's direction. He was sipping his coffee and listening to the conversation swirling around him. If Ger's singing had stirred up painful memories for him, she needed to find out how he was feeling. Not now though. It wasn't the right time. It was reassuring to see he looked relaxed and not all dejected. He even seemed to be enjoying himself and she felt a wave of affection wash over her. She was glad she hadn't mentioned the visit to the beach. It was her and Cal's special place and she wasn't ready to share it with anyone else.

Her daydreaming was interrupted by Peggy who was extending an invitation to Ger and Lanie. 'Why don't you join us for Sunday dinner before your drive?' she was saying. 'Come after I get back from church. Shall we say one o'clock?'

Peggy was a generous host and in previous years had enjoyed entertaining. It had become a less regular occurrence as her health deteriorated. Although she prided herself on being modest, there was a part of her that couldn't wait to tell her friends the news. She could only imagine their response when she told them 'The Celtic Colleen' was coming to dinner.

On the drive home with Cal, Roisin was in high spirits. 'Did you like the concert? Ger's a bit of a character, don't you think?'

Cal peered into the darkness. On the road ahead he could just about make out the two points of light from Joe's pick-up. As was his way, he chose his words carefully before replying.

'It was a first-rate evening and Ger seems like a nice person. Very down to earth. I'm not so sure about that woman, Lanie. She was friendly enough. Just a bit wary and on edge, don't you think? She did make good coffee though. It was strong, just how I like it.'

He was right about Lanie. There was something about her Roisin couldn't pinpoint. Perhaps when they came tomorrow it would become clearer.

'Cal? I've been thinking.'

'You have? About what?'

'Driving. How old do you have to be to learn to drive in Canada?'

'You can have a learner's licence at sixteen. Why?

'I'd like to learn, that's why,' she said, 'and, I'd like you to teach me.'

Chapter Twenty Nine

The following Sunday morning, Roisin awoke early to a faint clinking of glass as her wind chimes swayed gently in the morning breeze. Her room had been stuffy the night before and she had opened the window a crack to let in the night air. She remembered Ger was coming and felt excited at the prospect of seeing her friend again. Jumping out of bed, she washed and dressed quickly. On her chair she set out fresh clothing to change into after her chores. She wolfed down her breakfast and joined Joe in the yard where they fed and watered the animals and swept and hosed down the barn and its surrounds in preparation for their visitors.

Peggy had placed a roasting joint in the oven. While Joe took Peggy to church, Roisin was left to peel vegetables and set the table with a white linen cloth and the best cutlery. On his return, Joe and Roisin had a cup of coffee together and he read his newspaper before going back out to pick up Peggy. He left her to check on the meat roasting in the oven and to get changed into fresh clothing.

Just before the women were due to arrive, Cal arrived

and Roisin sat with him on the old swing seat watching the tree swallows swoop in their search for airborne insects.

It was a warm spring day in April and the sun, already high in a sky studded with cotton wool clouds, shone through the trees, heating up the wooden boards at their feet. The smell of resin from the knots in the wood was sharp and aromatic.

From the direction of a sugar maple planted by Joe soon after he and Peggy bought the house, came the low hum of bees collecting pollen to take back to their hives. It would be many years before the tree could be tapped for its syrup. Probably around another thirty years, Cal estimated. He told Roisin about the native peoples of Canada, who lived on the land long before the European settlers came. They were the first to make holes in the trunks of maple trees allowing them to collect the sweet syrup.

'You'll never be a Canadian unless you develop a taste for maple syrup,' he teased, knowing she had a sweet tooth but wasn't partial to the taste of maple syrup.

Rolling her eyes, she pulled a face and stuck out her tongue at him.

Suddenly a loud, discordant noise made them both jump.

A car had turned into the driveway, the driver honking the horn repeatedly. It was cherry red in colour; an American convertible, smooth and glossy, its whitewall tyres gleaming in the sunlight. At the wheel was Lanie and in the passenger seat sat Ger, wearing a large pair of sunglasses. With a headscarf wrapped around her hair as protection against the wind, she looked as though she had stepped off a film set.

'Yoohoo! We're here.' Ger got out of the car and reaching into the rear seat, retrieved a leather clutch bag, a large bunch of exotic flowers wrapped in clear cellophane and a bottle shaped package.

Hearing the commotion, Peggy and Joe come out onto the verandah to welcome their guests. Ger handed the flowers to Peggy, and the package containing a bottle of Irish whiskey to a delighted Joe.

'They are gorgeous Ger, thanks so much,' Peggy said, almost dwarfed by the blooms. 'Now please, come in. Dinner is almost ready. Roisin will show you where to wash up while I put these in water. Then we'll eat.'

The mud room was off limits to their guests. Instead, under instruction from her aunt, Roisin led the way to the upstairs bathroom. It had been scrubbed clean and scented soap and fresh towels had been laid out in honour of their special visitors.

'We are being well looked after. Your aunt and uncle are very hospitable,' Ger said surveying the immaculate layout.

'Come and see where I sleep,' Roisin said, excited to show them her room. The door creaked on its hinges as she stepped in, followed by Ger and Lanie. The sight greeting them was ethereal. Lanie let out a long low whistle and Ger gasped in delight.

Roisin, rooted to the spot, could only watch as her wind chimes, as if moved by an unseen hand, created a swirling dapple of blue, yellow, green and red on the wall above her bed.

'Will you look at that? It's like magic,' Ger said as she sat down on the bed to watch. Roisin joined her while Lanie stood propped against the door frame with her arms folded. Within minutes the display was over.

'It's such a darling room and Peggy and Joe are very fond of you, I can tell. You must miss your mam though?'

'There are times when I do. We write often and she knows I've settled well here and I'm happy. She's moved into the town and started a dressmaking business. She's doing really well. She made the frock I was wearing last night.'

'My goodness, she has a real eye for cut and style. She should be working for a fashion house!' Ger proclaimed.

Roisin could tell that Ger was impressed and felt proud of her talented mother and her many achievements.

'I've just had a brainwave,' Ger said, clapping her hand to her forehead. 'Give me your mam's address and I'll call in on her at Waterbridge when I get back home. She can give me some advice on style and colour and maybe even make some outfits for my next tour.'

She lay back on the bed and yawned lazily. 'Oh, and by the way, the dress suited you perfectly. We weren't the only ones to notice, were we Lanie?'

She turned to look at Lanie who smiled for the first time, showing even, white teeth.

'The boy? What's his name, Cal? He's obviously smitten with you girl.'

Chuckling to herself, Ger rose from the bed stretching like a drowsy cat.

'You could do worse you know, Miss Picky. He's a lovely fella and rather nice looking too.'

Hearing Joe calling her name, Roisin, glad of the diversion, escorted the pair downstairs.

Ger as usual, was getting too close to reading her thoughts.

Cal had been tasked with carving the meat onto a platter and Joe was filling the best crystal glasses with water from a jug. The vegetables had been ladled into large tureens and Peggy had placed her best silver serving spoons alongside.

'Come on in and take a seat, it doesn't matter where. We don't stand on ceremony here.'

Joe looked over his wife's head at Roisin and winked, causing her to giggle.

The conversation at the table flowed easily, with even Lanie moved to comment on the food. 'Is very good,' she said in her husky voice, waving her fork in the air, much to Peggy's disapproval.

'It is good,' Ger agreed. 'Lanie is an excellent cook too, Peggy. She is Greek and makes wonderful dishes when she can get the ingredients. There really is nothing quite like home-cooked food. I miss it when I'm on the road. Even the best hotel meals can't compare with this. Thank you for inviting us and making us so welcome.'

Peggy beamed broadly at the compliment. 'You are very welcome. I thought you might like something to remind you of home so I've made a fruit trifle for dessert. The topping is made from cream from our own cow. I hope you enjoy it.'

While everyone pitched in to clear the table, Peggy took a large bowl of trifle from the refrigerator. Lanie looked unsure, but Ger oohed and ahhed in delight at the sight of the layers of sponge, jelly, and custard topped with a thick swirl of cream.

'My favourite. It was always a special treat when I was a child. You must have some Lanie, it's delicious.'

'Just this amount to try please,' Lanie said, her reluctance obvious.

She held up a finger and thumb to indicate a small portion. Looking anxious, she dipped her spoon into the dish Peggy handed her and sampled a minuscule amount while everyone waited in anticipation. A look of satisfaction crossed her face. Licking her lips with relish, she scooped the remaining trifle into her mouth, clearing her bowl in record time.

'Is excellent. Please, I have recipe?' she asked, appearing puzzled by the roars of laughter that followed.

When the meal was over, Peggy took her guests into the lounge while Joe made coffee and Cal and Roisin tackled the mountain of dishes.

'They said they are going to drive along the coast road and will be back later. They want to meet us at the beach. Will you come?'

Cal was elbow deep in sudsy water while Roisin was drying and stacking the dishes ready to be put away.

'Maybe, but don't you want to talk to Ger without me around?'

'No, of course not. Anyway, Lanie is always there like a spare wheel.'

Everything had been tidied away and she was in the process of putting the vase of Ger's flowers onto the table, when she stopped what she was doing, a worried look crossing her face,

'I want to take back what I said just now about Lanie being a spare wheel. It was mean and unkind of me. I'm pleased Ger has a good friend. I'm not too sure what it is that Lanie does though. An assistant of some kind, would you say?'

Cal shrugged his shoulders. He had an idea, but wasn't prepared to say anything. Not without knowing for sure.

'I'll go and thank Peggy for dinner,' he said, 'and I'll see you down at the beach later.'

While Peggy put her feet up and had a rest, Roisin and Joe took the two women on a tour of the farm. When they got to the yard, Fergus trotted up to them and Roisin told the story of how the piglet got his name.

'Fergus the milkman. That's just precious,' Ger said laughing out loud. 'He has very human features, for sure.'

They walked down to the pasture where Chester and Bluebell were grazing in the warm, afternoon sun. Joe had carrots and leftover green beans in his pocket and Chester trotted across the field eager to see the visitors, especially as there were snacks on offer. Joe pointed out the fence he and Roisin had built and the fields they had cultivated. The ground was already covered in green shoots, a sign that in just a few weeks the growing crops would be ready for picking.

Putting an arm around his niece, Joe gave her shoulder a squeeze.

'She's been a real asset, this young 'un. We've grown very fond of her. Has she told you she is going to take up her studies again in September?'

'I'm pleased to hear it,' Ger said. 'I've already told her how special she is. She can make a great success of her life as long as she doesn't let anything stand in her way.'

Roisin felt her face flush. She wondered if the remark was directed at Cal. Rather than reply, she scrutinised her fingernails in great detail.

I'm right, it's the boy, Ger thought to herself. *He's important to her and she's confused.*

Ger was right. It was all getting too complicated. Roisin wasn't sure she liked the indecision of it all.

Why couldn't life be straightforward? Growing up was proving to have a lot to answer for!

Chapter Thirty

Joe told Roisin she could leave early and with no sign of Cal, she decided she would go to the beach ahead of him. She was still wearing her work clothes. It had been her plan to get changed but saw little point if she was going to be paddling about in salt water and getting sand everywhere. Anyway, she didn't think Ger would object too much knowing she had been working.

Taking off her boots, she left them on the veranda for later. The feeling she got barefoot, when stretching her toes and flexing her feet, was delicious. She never tired of the sensation.

Springing up onto the balls of her feet, she felt the familiar rush of anticipation and then a moment of suspension, as though she was at the still centre of a vortex. The first step resulted in an eruption of energy as she propelled herself forwards. The rush of wind hitting her face and the trill of birdsong ringing in her ears was exhilarating.

Slowing briefly to check for traffic, she crossed the road, her feet barely making contact with the ground. She ran until she reached the beach. It was empty, aside from a flock of herring gulls bobbing on the breaking waves on the shore.

Pausing only to roll up the trouser legs of her coveralls, she sprinted down the beach until she reached the large rock where she and Cal had climbed before their walk to the sea glass beach.

Roisin lay back for a while, the sun on her face. She must have dozed for a while as she woke when the sun disappeared behind a cloud. Sitting up, she could see three tiny figures in the distance. Standing to wave at them, she jumped down to head back in their direction.

'There you are Ro,' Ger called out, stubbing a cigarette into the sand with her shoe. 'Cal said you had left your boots behind so you were probably running along the beach. He knows you too well.'

The sprinkling of freckles across the bridge of her nose was a sign Ger had caught the sun. She still looked cool and elegant, having changed into a white linen blouse and wide legged pants.

Lighting another cigarette, she stood surveying Roisin with an amused look on her face.

'Jeez girl, what on earth are you wearing?'

'These are my work clothes. Do you like them?' Roisin flicked back her tangled hair and put her hand on her hip, posing like the models she had seen in fashion magazines.

'Well, if the street urchin look ever becomes fashionable, I know where to come for advice.'

Returning from their drive, Ger and Lanie had parked the car on the drive and bumped into Cal. He had been coming from the house carrying a rug and blankets and

Joe's old canvas knapsack into which Peggy had put a Thermos of coffee and a slab of her tea bread.

'The woman has a heart of gold,' Ger exclaimed. 'You'd never starve with her around. Shall we find a nice, shaded spot? I think Lanie is tired after driving all afternoon.'

Lanie did look weary. Cal spread the rug and she lay down, her head resting on the knapsack. While Cal went to search for wood to make a fire, Ger and Roisin walked along the shoreline looking for shells and bits of driftwood.

In a tide pool between two bulbous rocks, periwinkles and sea snails grazed on patches of algae. Amongst floating fronds of seaweed, clusters of sea urchins, and red starfish, sheltered sand dollars, their shells etched with a motif of petals. When they both dangled their feet into the clear water it disturbed rock crabs, who scuttled away to find a hiding place, safe from their human intruders.

Are you happy, Ro?' Ger asked, tracing a pattern on the surface of the water with her fingers.

'Um, yes, I think so.' She had never been asked the question before and was unsure how she was supposed to respond. She wasn't unhappy so this probably meant she was, whatever being happy meant.

'And the incident on the ship with the Higgins fella. Does it still trouble you?'

Roisin looked ahead at the rippled surface of the ocean. Despite the offshore breeze, beads of moisture formed along her top lip. When she first arrived, she had woken most nights bathed in a cold sweat and with her heart pounding. Running to the window, she would peer out into the darkness, convinced a thunderous wall of water was heading towards the house and she would be dragged into the depths of the ocean, never to be seen again.

'Nightmares?' Ger asked softly, seeing the pain of memory etched on her features.

'Yes, but they've stopped now. Peggy helped me to see you can get over horrible things happening to you. I do think it was my fault he fell into the ocean though. If I hadn't kicked him…!' She shrugged her shoulders leaving the sentence unfinished.

'You know it could easily have been you instead of him,' Ger said in a rare burst of anger. 'I don't think we should waste any more oxygen talking about the rotten swine. Tell me about Cal instead. Are you in love?'

As once again the colour rose in her face, it occurred to Roisin she could jump up and take off down the beach to avoid the question. It was impossible to hide anything from Ger and she wondered how long she herself could put aside the inescapable truth.

She was falling for Cal.

The problem was, the timing was all wrong. She wasn't yet seventeen. A serious relationship was for the future. She wanted an education, a job and perhaps to see the world. Why couldn't it be simple like it was before? It was all so bewildering.

'You know Ro, I think if he really loves you, he'll wait for you.' Ger always seemed capable of picking up on her thoughts.

'Do you think so?'

'I do. But first, those things in life calling to you? If you let them slip through your fingers you will always regret it, and life is too short for regrets.'

On their walk back, Ger picked up a selection of shells washed in by the tide and put them into the pocket of her shirt. A piece of driftwood, bleached white as bone, caught her eye. Bending to retrieve it, she dislodged a hermit crab that had taken up residence in a discarded whelk shell. It scuttled off in the direction of the ocean, waving a claw as if in annoyance at being disturbed.

'What about you Ger? Everything seems to be going well with your singing and the touring. You look very content. Have you found a nice man?' Roisin asked, conscious it was a bold question.

The question stopped Ger in her tracks and Roisin waited for the rebuke that would tell her she had overstepped the mark. It took a few minutes for Ger to regain her composure and her response when it came, took Roisin by surprise.

'Oh, Ro, you darling girl. I thought you knew.'

'What would I know?' she asked, confused by Ger's reaction.

'It's not men I'm attracted to you goose, it's women. The reason I am so content is down to Lanie. We love each other Ro. Even though the church and some sections of the community disapprove of who and what we are, we are together. Do you understand?'

It was all beginning to make sense.

If she had spent time thinking about it, the clues were there from the start when she and Ger first met. She just hadn't pieced them together. It explained Lanie's behaviour too. No wonder she came across as wary and a bit aloof.

'You're quiet Ro. Are you shocked?'

'Not shocked, no. I'm glad you've found someone who makes you happy.'

'It's never easy telling people and it's only those we trust who know. I must admit I thought you would have guessed, although I forget how young you are. Sometimes you are wise beyond your years.'

From further up the beach came the sound of voices and laughter. Drawing near they saw Cal and Lanie. They had dug a depression in the sand and surrounded it with small boulders to create a fire pit. Into the hollow they were piling layers of brushwood gathcrcd at the edge of the beach. Lanie, flushed from her exertions, gave them a wave as they approached.

'You and Cal seem to be getting on famously,' Ger said, throwing herself down onto the rug.

She lay the piece of driftwood she had found next to her and arranged the shells in a line across its smooth surface.

'You're not the only ones to have been busy. Look at my treasures.'

'Very nice. Now we have coffee and Peggy cake?' Lanie said, abrupt as always.

'Yes, but first a cigarette Lanie. I have been so good. It's been ages since I had one. Please,' Ger said, in a wheedling voice.

Lanie made a clicking noise of displeasure with her tongue. She took a pack of cigarettes and a lighter from Ger's bag and handed them to her.

'Bad for you, bad for your voice,' she said sternly.

Lying back on the rug, Ger lit her cigarette and inhaled deeply.

'Today has been great, hasn't it?' she said, blowing a smoke ring into the air. 'Life is good, don't you think?' The question was addressed to no-one in particular.

Roisin observed Cal, as he sat opposite her. His hair was getting long again after Peggy's trim and the sun had lightened it a shade. It fell across his eyes and she wasn't able to read his expression, but he was watching her too.

'You having a good time. Not bored?' she asked.

'Sure I'm having a good time. It's been a lot of fun, and no, I'm not bored. Lanie's been telling me all about Greece. I'd love to go visit there someday,' he said.

Lanie was pouring coffee and slicing Peggy's tea bread. 'Is beautiful country, Greece. You all come one day. I have big family. They very happy to meet you.'

The sun, a ball of orange light, was sinking fast, turning the ocean to liquid gold. Seabirds hovered, poised to skim the surface for their last meal of the day. With the air beginning to cool, Cal borrowed Ger's lighter. Igniting the twigs in the fire pit, he added pieces of moss and dry seaweed until the fire was crackling.

Lanie and Ger sat close, a blanket across their knees. They were watching the sunset and although they had their backs to her, Roisin knew their hands were interlocked.

The dusk deepened, turning the sky from purple to navy, then to black. One by one the stars appeared and soon the whole sky was illuminated with twinkling points of light. Cal reached across to grab a log which he placed on top of the glowing embers. He gave Roisin a gentle nudge as she sat with her head on her knees, deep in thought.

'You cold?' he asked, reaching for the spare blanket.

She shook her head, but he tucked it around her anyway.

Lifting a corner, she gestured for him to come and sit alongside her. As he did so, she could feel the warmth from his body and despite her reservations, rested her head in the curve of his arm. He smelled of sawdust and soap. Through his shirt she could feel the steady rhythm of his heart. She felt slightly breathless and her own heart began to beat faster.

'Ro?' he said quietly.

Ger's diminutive name for her sounded unfamiliar coming from him and she lifted her head to look up at his face. He rarely called her by her name. She had wondered if it was his way of keeping her at a distance.

'Can I kiss you?'

She nodded, and he bent to put his lips against hers with the gentlest of touches. With her eyes closed, she felt the world spin. As he went to draw away, she reached up and pulled him to her, kissing him back with a fierce intensity that left them both reeling. Her hands were shaking and she was sure if she tried to stand, her legs would not support her.

She was sixteen and it was her first real kiss. She felt elated and sad at the same time.

This changed everything and not necessarily for the better.

'We should probably talk,' Cal said.

'I know we should, but not yet.'

She leant into him, not wanting the moment to end. He stroked her hair, then put his arm around her shoulder, before pulling the blanket around them. Overhead, a piece of cosmic dust blazed a fleeting trail through the atmosphere.

'Oh look,' Ger cried out in excitement, breaking the spell, 'a shooting star. Make a wish everyone.'

The air sharpened. Soon the tide would come in. It was time to leave. Cal kicked sand over the glowing ashes of the fire.

In high spirits, they walked back to the house. Peggy and Joe must have heard their approach and were sitting out on the verandah waiting for them.

'We were about to send out a search party,' Joe said with a grin.

'Thank you so much for your hospitality today. Lanie and I have had the most wonderful time,' Ger said, hugging Peggy before planting a kiss on Joe's cheek.

While Lanie pulled the car's retractable roof back into position, Ger got into the passenger seat. From there she called to Roisin who came over and leaned her head in through the open window.

Whatever Ger whispered to her it was for Roisin's ears only. Lanie jumped into the driver's side and started the engine. It purred into life, and the car glided down a driveway now bathed in moonlight.

After Peggy and Joe retired, she and Cal sat on the swing, listening to the eerie hoot of an owl in a distant tree.

He reached for her hand. 'Was it important, what Ger said to you before she left?'

His unease was palpable. He desperately wanted to know if it was about him. She knew she couldn't lie, even if it caused him pain.

'She told me I was to follow my dreams and not let anything, even you, hold me back.'

The right words of encouragement eluded him. Imagining a future without her opened up a hollowness in the pit of his stomach. The possibility of her leaving loomed, a shadow at his back. He couldn't allow it to darken and spoil this moment. Not when everything felt right.

If he closed his eyes he could almost pretend the ground was still solid and not shifting beneath his feet.

Chapter Thirty One

In mid June a south westerly weather system brought with it winds and heavy rain lasting for a number of days. Joe was pleased they had baled the hay and brought it up to the barn before the rains came. A surplus from the spring planting was exchanged with a neighbouring farmer for bedding straw. This they stacked in the barn and covered with a large tarpaulin. The weeks of sunshine that followed produced an abundance of growth and the long hot summer days were spent weeding, watering, picking, storing and helping Peggy to bottle fruit and vegetables for winter.

An experimental patch of sweet corn, planted alongside rows of field corn grown for animal feed, ripened in the sun and yielded a bountiful harvest. Pulling aside the fibrous leaves revealed the husk, studded with golden kernels and topped with a silk tassel, the sweet nutty earthiness a welcome taste of summer.

The demands of the farm meant Roisin had little time to herself and with Cal busy working, she hadn't seen much of him. When her learner's licence came, she remembered she had asked him to teach her to drive. On a humid Saturday afternoon she walked over to see him, having not been to the house since their trip to the city. She was surprised to see the clapboard outside had been given a fresh coat of paint and on the veranda, red geraniums tumbled over the sides of battered clay pots.

Cal's pick-up was parked on the drive. With no sign of him, she banged on the door a few times then sat on the step waiting for him to appear. When he did, his just washed hair was still dripping wet.

As he buttoned up a blue denim shirt that matched the colour of his eyes, she felt the now familiar tingle of excitement at seeing him. Feeling self-conscious, she wished she had cleaned herself up before coming over. She was hot and dusty from the morning's work and her plait hung limply over her shoulder. An attempt at wiping the perspiration from her face, resulted in a brown, muddy streak across her cheek.

'Hi there. It's been a while,' he said.

'I got my licence, look.' She held it out and he took it, studying the document carefully before handing it back to her.

'And you want me to teach you to drive. Am I right?'

He looked serious and she nodded, feeling unsure. Maybe he had changed his mind.

Realising his teasing had gone far enough, he moved towards her, wrapping his arms around her, inhaling the scent of earth and sun on the skin at the back of her neck.

'Of course I'll teach you, although we will have to warn everyone to keep off the roads,' he said playfully, trying to get her to smile.

'It's what Joe said too,' she said, ducking away from him in mock annoyance.

'When do you want to start?'

'Aunt Peggy wants you to come to dinner tomorrow, if you are free. We could have a lesson afterwards, if that's all right.'

'Sure. Just one thing. Have you said anything to them about us Ro?'

'No, I haven't because I don't really know what to say. What is us? What does it mean?'

The words came tumbling out and she paused for breath, chewing her lip as she always did when she was worried.

'We have to talk to them,' Cal said, his face serious. 'I promised there was nothing going on, and although we haven't done anything to be ashamed of, they need to know things have changed between us.'

It was going to be an awkward conversation, Cal realised. Peggy and Joe had been good to him and he really didn't want to disrespect them in any way. When Joe had taken him aside and asked if he had feelings for 'the girl' he had said no. Echoing what Roisin had already told her aunt, he maintained they were friends and that was all there was to it. Now, it was becoming apparent their feelings for each other were deepening. What was developing between them couldn't be kept a secret for much longer.

'Come inside.' Taking her arm, he drew her into the cool of the house. The kitchen was clean and tidy, unlike the last time she had visited. Pulling up a chair for her he handed her a glass of water.

'We need to get everything straightened out between

us before we speak with them,' he said gently, aware she was anxious.

'Yes, I suppose we do.'

'You go first,' he said, sitting down alongside her.

The glass felt cold to her touch. She placed it against her cheek, glad of its cooling effect. She felt awkward in his presence, unsure of her feelings and what she was expected to say. He got up and went to the cupboard underneath the sink where he found a square of cloth. After running it under the tap, he handed it to her.

'What's that for?'

'You have mud on your face.'

She dabbed furiously at her cheeks, missing the brown smudge. Taking the cloth from her, he tenderly wiped away the streak of dirt from the side of her nose.

'All this is making me nervous. What do you think we should say to them?' she asked.

'We have to be truthful. After all, we haven't done anything wrong. If we reassure them you are going ahead with your plans for school, I think they will understand.' His reply was as much to reassure himself. He wasn't feeling confident about facing up to Joe and Peggy.

'You know they feel responsible for you, don't you? If they do get angry it's because they want to protect you. They have your best interests at heart. You are very young after all.'

It took him by surprise to see her hands clench and her mouth tighten. Usually she was cheerful and even-tempered. He'd never seen her get angry. About anything. Now she looked furious.

'I am nearly seventeen. I have come to the other side

of the world on my own to make a new life with people who were virtually strangers. I'm grateful for everything that's been done for me, but I can look after myself you know? I'm not helpless.' She paused, lowering her voice as the wave of emotion washed over her. 'And, I'll tell you something for nothing, witnessing the death of another person, makes you grow up. Fast!'

She looked fierce, and before Cal could say anything, she had walked out onto the verandah where she stood, drawing in deep breaths. Following, he watched and waited until her shoulders slumped and her fingers, gripping the handrail, relaxed.

Reaching for her, he turned her to face him. The set of her mouth and her red rimmed eyes told him all he needed to know.

He had upset her and he needed to make amends.

Tilting her chin upwards, he kissed her nose, her forehead, each of her sunburned cheeks and her full mouth.

Releasing her, he held her at arm's length. 'I kinda know what you are saying,' he said. 'My dad. . .?'

'Cal, I ….!' her words trailed off. In the heat of the moment, she had forgotten about his dad and felt ashamed at her over-reaction.

He kissed her again to reassure her, and she felt the tingling sensation again, like an electric current passing between them.

Her heart felt as if it was trying to beat its way out of her chest and her legs were buckling under her. She thought back to what the girls at school used to say about the boys they came into contact with. It had all seemed rather crude and not very romantic. The boys sounded immature and awkward, masking their inexperience with coarse words and pranks.

She looked up at Cal. He was different. He was strong, gentle and considerate as well as being good looking and she admired him as well as loved him. It occurred to her that those girls might envy her. *If only they could see me now*, she thought, with a growing sense of satisfaction.

'Are you feeling better after your outburst?' I've never seen you so riled up.'

'Oh, Cal, I'm so sorry. Please forgive me. I don't know what came over me. How could I be so stupid, forgetting about the terrible way your dad died?'

Peggy and Joe must have told her about the suicide, he realised. Given a choice, he would have liked to have spared her the awful reality of the situation.

The note had been on the table when he returned from school. The words, in his father's handwriting, were big and bold, sloping off shakily towards the end.

Don't go into the barn. Get Joe. I'm sorry son.

He had hesitated for a moment. Then, with his heart thumping and his hands shaking, he ran, terror turning his legs to water.

He found his dad leaning back against an old fermentation barrel draped with a grain sack. The body was slumped sideways, one hand holding the trigger while the other still gripped the gun barrel jammed into his mouth.

Averting his eyes from the hessian sack, soaked in

bloody tissue and fragments of bone, Cal moved the gun to the floor and felt for a pulse.

Nothing.

He placed his head against his Dad's chest and thought he heard a faint gurgle. '*Dad, dad.*'

No response.

There was nothing else for it. He had to go and find Joe.

෨

Roisin was waiting for him to respond, a worried frown furrowing her brow. He drew her closer, offering and seeking comfort. 'I didn't say it because I wanted you to feel guilty. It was just to let you know I understand what you went through.'

The full horror of that day was for him alone. He couldn't describe to her how awful it had been. Not now. Perhaps not ever.

The intimacy between them had left her feeling drained and a bit unsteady on her feet. It helped that he wasn't angry at her thoughtlessness because there was something she wanted to ask him.

Since the day at the beach with Ger and Lanie, a thought had been buzzing around in her head. Now felt as good a time as any to mention it.

'Do you mind if I ask you something?' she murmured. 'It's a bit personal and you don't have to answer if you don't want to.'

'Whoa, that sounds serious. What is it Ro?'

Her mouth felt dry and she took a step back so she could look straight at him. Holding his gaze, her grey eyes were unwavering.

'Have you ever slept with anyone?' she said.

Taken aback by her bluntness, he batted an imaginary fly away from his face.

'How important is it for you to know?' he said.

'I think it must be important, because it's been going round and round in my head for weeks.'

The warmth flooded his face at the memory of one long, hot summer.

Embarrassment made his hands clammy. 'Yes, when I was sixteen. It was a girl I knew from school. We dated over a summer and then she went to college.'

It was a surprise to her to find she felt a pang of jealousy at the thought of him with another girl. Why was that? It was ridiculous. He was a young man of nineteen. Why wouldn't he have had that sort of relationship?

'How about you? You must have had lots of boyfriends.'

It was difficult for her to work out if he was teasing or not. The very idea of boys being interested in her she thought ridiculous. Back home, to her mother's great relief, she generally avoided them like the plague.

'No, I've never really had much to do with boys if I'm honest. Don't forget I went to an all girls school. Anyway, my mother would have killed me if she'd found me with a fella. She would never want me to end up with a baby like she did.'

She paused, remembering the looks she was getting from men on the Mercinia after Ger's ministrations. And, of course there was Sean. 'There was someone recently. I met him on the ship coming over. We spent a couple of days together. I don't think you could call him a boyfriend.'

'Is he in Halifax?' Cal asked.

'No, he went on to Toronto. He wanted to make his fortune and then go back home.'

Cal exhaled deeply and turned his head away.

He didn't want her to see the look of relief on his face.

Chapter Thirty Two

After a night spent tossing and turning she woke early. Drawing back the curtains revealed a pale sun hovering above a low lying mist. The trees, grey green in the washed out light, looked ghostly and she shuddered at the sight, anxiety causing her mind to work overtime.

All the defiance and bravado of the previous day had dissipated, and she felt uncharacteristically vulnerable. In general, her aunt and uncle were good-hearted, generous people. For the life of her she couldn't gauge what their reaction might be when they found out what was happening between her and Cal. And then there was her mother. No doubt she would have to be told as well. What if they were all angry and disappointed? Worse, what if Peggy and Joe wanted to send her away? This had become her home now and she wanted to stay.

'You're quiet, young lady.'

She had come to help Joe bag vegetables to take to the farmers' market the following weekend and he could see she wasn't herself. Peggy was going to cook hodge podge for their dinner and Roisin was adding a selection of potatoes, carrots, peas and green beans to a bowl to take up to the house.

'Do you know it was me who taught Peg how to make the dish?' Joe said proudly, hoping he might cheer her up. 'It's a family recipe. My mother used to make it. Peg's a great cook, but she's had to learn how to adapt her cooking to what's available. Hodge podge is a great way to use up seasonal vegetables.'

The morning seemed to drag and for once her chores seemed tedious. She was even grouchy with Fergus, who trotted up to see if she had any tidbits for him. She immediately felt ashamed at being cross with him. The following week Joe was taking him to the local butcher. It almost broke her heart to think the poor little piglet was going to be turned into sausages and chops. Contrite, she rewarded him with a carrot and a scratch along his bristly back.

With their meal prepared and waiting on the stove to be heated later, Joe drove Peggy to church. Feeling listless, Roisin sat flicking through back copies of *Canadian Geographic*.

Her whirring brain was preventing her from concentrating and she considered writing to her mother, but couldn't think what to say.

I'll hear from her soon enough, she thought. *Peggy is sure to write and tell her what's going on.*

She walked down to the lower paddock to kill time. Like an old married couple, Chester and Bluebell stood close together, grazing in the sunshine. She had brought chunks of apple and carrot and fresh corn husks and these she fed to them through the bars of the gate. When there was nothing else on offer, Bluebell ambled off to locate a fresh patch of grass to munch on. Feeling weary, Roisin leant on the gate resting her head on her folded arms. Appearing to sense her unease, Chester gave a little nicker in greeting and dropped his head to lean in over her shoulder as if in sympathy.

'You know something's going on, don't you boy?' she said, giving him a scratch in his favourite spot behind his ears.

She hoped Cal was on time. It would be good to get the meal over with before they faced the music. She wasn't looking forward to it. Not one little bit.

When Cal did arrive, they sat at the table and Joe told him the origins of hodge podge whilst Roisin chased vegetables around her plate with a fork.

'You'd better not leave any on your plate or he'll be mortally offended. I suppose he's told you it's his mother's recipe?' Peggy said.

She was in high spirits after being paid a compliment by Father Jack. 'He said it was lovely to hear I hadn't lost my wonderful Irish accent after being in Canada for so long.'

She straightened her apron and patted her hair self-consciously, as though worried he might walk in and find her looking untidy.

Joe shook his head, chuckling to himself. The only time his wife ever showed a modicum of vanity was when a Catholic priest paid her a compliment.

'Are you looking forward to your driving lesson, Roisin?' Joe said, changing the subject.

She nodded and when she began to collect the dishes, Cal took her arm.

'Come and sit down. We need to tell them now,' he said gently.

'Tell us what?' Joe looked bemused and glanced over at Peggy, who was pursing her mouth.

'Oh, Jesus, Mary and Joseph, you're not pregnant are you?' she cried out, looking shocked.

To ward off any bad news, she made a quick sign of the cross and muttered a short prayer under her breath.

Roisin was mentally preparing herself for the storm she felt sure was about to be unleashed.

Struggling to find the right words, she looked across at Cal for guidance.

'Shall I?' He had been waiting for her to speak, not wanting to appear pushy by taking the lead. She nodded, mute with anxiety.

'To reassure you,' he began quietly, 'Ro is not pregnant.'

Peggy had been leaning forward, twisting her gnarled hands in front of her.

'Well, thank the good Lord for his mercy,' she said, sounding greatly relieved.

'I just want you to know that we haven't let you down in any way and we haven't been dishonest,' Cal went on. 'When we told you that we were friends, well, that was true, at that time. It's just over the last few weeks our feelings have changed and we have grown closer.'

'Go on,' Joe said, his expression inscrutable.

Cal reached across the table for Roisin's hand. It trembled in his like a trapped bird.

'You need to have your say now,' he said, nodding in

encouragement. He knew if she didn't speak soon she would lose her nerve.

Listening to Cal, she realised how proud she was of him.

He had shown maturity, and she didn't want to let him down by coming across as a silly child who didn't know her own mind.

'What Cal has said is right. We wanted to tell you because we didn't want you thinking we were going behind your backs. I am so thankful for all you've done for me. For us,' she said, correcting herself and looking at Cal for approval.

'Go on,' he mouthed at her.

'If it's all right with you, we would like everything to carry on as before until I finish my course. I've been reading up on grants and endowments. I've decided once I have my diploma, I want to apply to go to university. We have talked about it and Cal knows how important it is to me. He's going to help out here as much as he can and I will be back at weekends and during the holidays, so you really don't have to worry about anything.'

Her aunt and uncle allowed her to speak without interruption. They still had concerns they wanted to discuss, without Cal and Roisin present. Picking up his car keys, Joe handed them to Cal.

'She can have her driving lesson in my pick-up. Give us about an hour will you? And don't let her hit anything or we will have words,' Joe quipped, easing the tension around the table.

Joe's truck was still parked at the front of the house and they walked to it holding hands.

'I think that went well. Feels good huh, not having to sneak around?' Cal said.

'Phew, yes. I'm glad it's over. Be prepared for a lecture when we get back though.'

They climbed into the pick-up with Roisin in the driving seat. Cal showed her how to start the engine and how much choke to use until it stopped sputtering and began running smoothly. He went through all the features on the instrument panel, from how to switch on the lights and wipers, to what to do if the oil or engine lights were to come on. He got her to open the hood and locate where the oil reservoir was, and showed her how to check it using the dip-stick.

When he was sure she had grasped the basics, he turned the truck to face in the direction of the road.

'You need to practise using the pedals and get used to turning the steering wheel in the right direction. It takes a while to get the coordination right, so don't get discouraged.'

After a few faltering starts and a number of engine stalls, she got the hang of it. 'Remember it's ABC: accelerator, brake, clutch,' Cal reminded her, 'and don't forget to think of the clutch as like a spring you are holding under your foot. Select your gear and bring it up smoothly until you hear the engine noise change. When you hear the engine race, it's telling you to change gear.'

He was a patient teacher and she was a quick and eager learner. Soon she was driving down to the main road and back up the drive, although she hadn't yet mastered the more difficult task of reversing.

'You're doing well Ro. I think that's enough for today

though. It's time we went back to see what your aunt and uncle have in store for us.'

Peggy and Joe were still sitting at opposite ends of the kitchen table when they returned. All seemed serene. The only sounds were coming from the coffee pot bubbling away on the stove and the kettle whistling quietly to itself. One of Peggy's chocolate cakes rested on a paper doily on top of a willow pattern plate.

'How was your lesson Roisin? Is my truck still in one piece?'

'It was great, I was really driving,' she said, unable to conceal her excitement. 'I can take you to the farmers' market next week if you like.'

'She'll soon pick it up,' Cal said. 'I just need to teach her how to reverse and go around corners.'

Peggy got up to make tea and pour coffee. She didn't seem cross, just preoccupied. She cut the cake and passed a slice to each of them before taking her her place once again at the table

'I'll have to write and tell your mam you know?'

This came as no surprise to Roisin. She had been expecting exactly that response.

Peggy glanced in Joe's direction. 'We've been talking, Joe and I, and to be frank we aren't really surprised. It was clear from the start there was a spark between you two. Now, you might think we are old fuddy-duddies and too old to know anything, but let me tell you, we haven't forgotten what it's like to be young and love-struck, have we?'

'No, we haven't,' Joe said, with a wistful sigh.

Peggy shot him a look of exasperation, before turning

her attention back to Cal and Roisin. 'All things considered, we are going to trust you to do the right thing. You're both level-headed and entitled to a private life, we recognise that. All we ask is that you are careful and don't get yourselves into a mess. You do know what I'm saying, don't you? Joe and I are your guardians Roisin, so please don't let us down'

'We won't let you down. We promise, don't we Cal?'

Cal felt under pressure to back her up. He wished he had a bit more time to think. Eventually he found what he hoped were the right words.

'Thank you for putting your trust in us,' he said. 'Roisin knows her own mind and I admire her for that. As for me, I just want to reassure you I will do my best for her. You have my word.'

'Then that's good enough for us,' Peggy said. 'Now, Joe has some news for you about the latest addition to the family.'

Joe opened a drawer and taking out a small booklet, he held it up for them to see. On the front was a picture of a tractor.

'This is our new baby,' he said proudly. 'Even though it's second hand, it runs like a dream. Felix found it at a farm auction. It means there will be less manual work to do. Chester is starting to slow down and this little beaut will do as much as he does, and more. The time has come for a change. For all of us.'

Chapter Thirty Three

With the days becoming shorter and the first hint of cold in the air, the surrounding trees, in an attempt to conserve energy, prepared to lose their leaves. First came the dazzling display of fiery red, russet orange and gold. As the weeks passed there came the dramatic shedding that left the ground overlain with a shifting tapestry of colour.

Sitting at her desk doing her homework, Roisin watched as the Brandywine maple outside her window began to turn from the deepest red to darkest purple. She had begun her college studies early in September and found the work effortless.

To Peggy and Joe's combined relief, her first set of grades were well above average. Had she been attending Community College she would have been top in her year. They had feared her attention might wander with Cal around. Instead he turned out to be a surprisingly hard taskmaster, ensuring her homework was completed before he would walk with her to the beach or take her for a driving lesson.

Peggy had done a good job reassuring Theresa, who wrote to say how proud and happy she was to hear Roisin was handling everything in such a grown- up way.

If Theresa needed further confirmation of Cal's good character, it came from an unexpected source.

Wanting to discuss ideas for outfits for her next tour, Ger had called in to see Theresa at Waterbridge. This had set the whole town agog when she turned up in a fancy car with a woman driver at the wheel.

Still fizzing with excitement following the visit, Theresa wrote to Roisin immediately afterwards.

Ger is such an interesting person and a complete hoot. She had me in stitches with stories about her life on the road. The woman with her was a bit quiet.

We had a great morning choosing styles and materials and the orders have been pouring in ever since.

Ger said they had spent some time with you all and that you are blossoming. She tells me Cal is a steadying influence. I trust her judgement as she seems very protective of you.

She sees herself as your Fairy Godmother. Isn't that funny?

Did I mention I have a lodger? He's a lovely man with a PHD so he's a doctor. His name is Steven Crawford. He is over here from an English university researching a book he is writing on Irish folk tales. I was escorted to a choral concert by him in the city last week. As you can imagine, it set tongues wagging!

What with Ger and her friend and now Steven, your mother is the talk of the town.

Keep studying hard.
I will send something over for your birthday.

Your loving Mam.
PS Are my eyes deceiving me? Did Peggy really say
you were learning to drive, Macushla?

The letter was a breath of fresh air.

Roisin felt relieved her mother had taken the news of her and Cal so well.

There was even a suggestion of a new man in her own life. Someone interested in the folk tales Theresa loved so much. He sounded perfect for her.

Her driving lessons were progressing well and before long she would be ready to take her test. Joe had also shown her how to drive the tractor. She giggled to herself as she thought of the expression on her mother's face when she learned of that fact. She would be astonished if she could see her daughter in the cab, expertly ploughing the bottom field in preparation for the winter.

On the rare occasions when she had the time and inclination to sit and think back over the last year, it occurred to Roisin she had come a long way, and not just in terms of distance. She was almost seventeen and no longer felt like a child.

So much of what had happened since leaving Ireland had contributed towards her growing up. Not least the event on the ship with Patrick Higgins. It had been so awful and had affected her so badly, she knew it was a time in her life she would never forget. Despite this she had much to be thankful for. On reflection, it had been a good year and there wasn't much else she wanted or needed.

With her birthday approaching, she wasn't surprised she had items of mail. There was a long narrow parcel, a card from her mother, and a letter addressed to her in handwriting she didn't recognise.

'Looks interesting,' Peggy said, as she sat knitting by the fire.

'Very formal style of writing,' Joe said, leaning over Roisin's shoulder to check for clues to the identity of the writer. 'Bold strokes. I'd say it's a man's hand.'

Roisin felt a flutter of anxiety as she picked up the thick vellum envelope.

She had never had an official letter addressed to her before. What if it was something from the police in relation to Patrick Higgins?

'Go on, open it. It could be good news,' Peggy urged her.

Her hands shook as she tore open the envelope. She read only a few lines before throwing the letter back onto the table.

'Oh no, no, no.' she wailed, 'It can't be true. She can't be dead.'

'Who is dead?' Peggy said, shocked by the outburst.

'It's Ger,' Roisin sobbed. 'Lanie says she's dead.'

Peggy tried to take her by the arm, but she ducked under and slipped from her grasp.

Distraught, she ran out through the door, wailing like a banshee at the top of her lungs.

As Joe went to follow, Peggy took his arm to restrain him.

'It's Cal she needs, not us. Go and fetch him,' she said, her voice cracking with emotion.

Chapter Thirty Four

B linded by tears and the setting sun, Roisin ran on, with no idea where she was headed. Past the paddock, through the freshly ploughed field, across the meadows that in summer swayed with sweet-scented grass and were now covered in sharp stubble that scratched her legs. On and on she ran. Eventually, she reached the forest and pushed her way through a gap in the trees, branches slapping against her face and catching in her hair. In parts it was so densely packed with ancient firs, it was almost impenetrable. Some of the trees had uprooted or been struck by lightning and she jumped over them as they lay at angles, their limbs brown and lifeless. Stripped of their green covering of needles, they resembled abandoned pirate vessels, the tracery of their branches poking out like rigging, awaiting the unfurling of sails.

There was no real path to follow and it grew darker as scudding clouds obscured the moon. She sensed the storm was imminent and still she zigzagged through the trees, slowing only to leap over a dead branch or push aside a pile of shrubby vegetation that closed behind her like a green curtain.

She ran until her heart felt as though it would burst from her chest and her legs were unable to carry her any further.

Collapsing onto the forest floor, sobs wracked her whole body.

'No, no, no. Not Ger, NOT GER,' she screamed at the sky as the first streak of lightning forked overhead. It was followed by a distant rumble of thunder and a deluge of fat raindrops.

Exhausted, she dropped to the ground and curled into a tight ball as the storm grew in intensity. When it was directly above her, she knew both she and the trees around her were in danger of being struck by lightning, yet she felt no fear. Nature was unforgiving, it was the way the universe worked. Praying or bargaining was of no use. What was it her mother said? *Death is a part of life and you have to accept the inevitability of it.*

At last the storm retreated. She stood, stretching her arms and legs, stiff from being in one position for too long. There was nothing to be gained from remaining where she was. She needed to be sensible and try and retrace her steps.

The problem was, she had no sense of where she was or from which direction she had come. She knew a stream ran close to the edge of the property. *If I find it, I can follow that back to the farm, s*he thought.

Walking for what seemed like hours, her concern increased. Everything looked the same. She couldn't distinguish one fallen tree trunk from another. Even with the odd glimpse of light from the moon as it appeared from behind a cloud, nothing looked familiar.

The forest, extending beyond the boundaries of Joe and Peggy's land for many miles, had no paths or markers. Now bone weary and soaked to the skin, she realised she was hopelessly lost. There were also bears to consider. It was too early for them to be in hibernation. Although generally wary of humans and only aggressive if they had cubs or there was food, it would serve her right if she was eaten and not a trace of her remained for anyone to find.

Her senses were alert and tuned to every movement of the trees and every crack of a twig on the forest floor. She could tell she was surrounded by nocturnal creatures who could see her, even if she couldn't see them in the darkness.

Resigning herself to whatever fate awaited her, she sat, with her back propped against a tree.

The thud of approaching footsteps and a pencil thin flash of light through the trees, set her heart thumping and she scrabbled for a branch to defend herself. Peering into the blackness, there was no sign of the light. Whatever it was had disappeared, or it was her mind playing tricks? Moments passed and there it was again. Someone was out there, she was sure of it.

With her throat dry and her voice already hoarse from sobbing she managed a feeble cry. 'I'm over here.'

To her relief, she heard Cal's voice. 'Keep shouting Ro, I'm coming to get you!'

When he appeared from behind a thorny thicket of brambles, his concern turned to exasperation. 'What the hell were you thinking, running off like that?'

He placed his jacket around her shoulders and shone the torch into her face. Apart from a gash across her forehead and superficial scratches to her hands and arms, she was relatively unscathed. He hugged her tightly, smoothing her tangled hair.

'I'm so sorry about Ger,' he murmured. 'Now let's get you back. It's past ten o'clock. You've been out here for hours.'

Peggy and Joe were waiting by the door. Joe looked haggard and close to exhaustion himself. He had searched the farm and walked up and down the beach looking for her. It was Cal who guessed her headlong flight would have taken her in the direction of the forest.

'Oh, my dear girl, will you look at the state of you. Come here and let's get you cleaned up and into bed,' Peggy said, wrapping her in a soft blanket.

Despite his protests, Cal was sent home with instructions to come back the following day after work.

'Thanks for all your help,' Peggy told him. 'She'll be grand. We'll take care of her. You need to get yourself off to bed. It's been a long night.'

Filling a basin with warm soapy water, Peggy washed Roisin's face and hands then dressed her cuts, before brushing twigs and some pine needles from her knotted hair.

While she busied herself warming milk on the stove, she didn't notice Roisin slide Lanie's letter across the table and place it into her pocket.

After Peggy and Joe had gone to bed, she sat propped up against downy pillows. It felt good to be in a warm bed. If Cal hadn't found her when he did, her resting

place for the night might have been the hard forest floor,
instead of a comfortable mattress and fresh linens.

The writing style was italic, the bold strokes accentuated
by the use of black ink. She had only read the first line
before taking flight. Now as she studied it more closely, it
was apparent the tone of the letter was stilted and formal.

My dear Roisin (Ro)

*These words come to you with much pain and sadness
for Ger is dead.*

*As my English is not good, I have asked the executor
of Ger's will to write to you on my behalf.*

*It was all so quick which somehow makes it harder to
bear. She had a cough for many months that would not
go away. By the time she sought treatment the doctors
said it was too late to do anything. It was a tumour on
her lung and it had probably been there for some time.
Her mother and I were with her when she died. It was
very peaceful. My heart is broken.*

*You are the only person I will write to. She was very
fond of you and spoke of you often. She was so happy
on the day we spent with you and Cal on the beach. It is
the best memory for me and my eyes are full of tears as I
dictate these words.*

*I suspect she may have known something was wrong
as she made a will a few months ago.*

*Her estate is to be divided between me and her mother
with some money going to you.*

*The solicitor advised it should be put into a trust until
you are twenty-one.*

Ger said no, you were to have it as soon as the law in

Canada allows it. This is eighteen, the solicitor says.

I am returning to my family in Greece after the funeral. Ger is going to be buried next to her father in the churchyard in her hometown..

Forgive me. I cannot say any more.

Eleni Kefalas (Lanie)

For now there would be no more tears. Just a numbness, as though all emotion had been compressed out of her body, leaving her a dry husk. She imagined the wind could whirl her around and deposit her wherever it saw fit.

Re-reading the letter over and over again, she became convinced she would find it was all a mistake. Ger couldn't be dead.

It was wrong for someone so young and talented and so full of life to suddenly disappear from the lives of those who loved her. It was inconceivable.

Chapter Thirty Five

Joe and Peggy were concerned for her welfare. Roisin seemed to have lost interest in everything. Most mornings she came down to breakfast, her face pale and tear-stained. She wasn't eating properly and her clothes were beginning to hang in loose folds from her thin frame.

Throughout the day she worked with Joe, preparing for the coming winter, a quiet and listless shadow of her former self. She even avoided Cal on the pretext that she had homework.

'I'm worried about her Peg. She isn't herself.'

Joe had tried his best to cheer her up but nothing seemed to work.

'You know full well she's grieving Joe,' Peggy said, not unkindly. 'Nothing any of us can say or do can change that fact. It takes time, we know that. I was thinking I would prepare a little tea party for her birthday? Cal is going to come over. Perhaps she will have brightened up by then.'

They were doing everything they could to help her,

Roisin could see that. She tried to shake off the feeling of emptiness in the pit of her stomach. She was even irritable with Cal when he tried to comfort her. Even though she knew what he had been through with his dad, she didn't want to discuss it with him or anyone else.

When she thought about Ger, which was often, a lump forced its way up into her throat preventing her from talking and large tear drops rolled down her cheeks. It was, she thought, better for both of them if Cal stayed away. She didn't want him to see her when she was so upset.

Peggy had baked a cake and iced it, writing across the top in pink letters *Happy Birthday Roisin.* There were piped red roses, a shiny number seventeen and seventeen pink candles. Cal had blown up some balloons and tied them to the kitchen chairs with string. Roisin sat in obedient silence, nibbling at the edges of a sandwich. As she blew out her candles, they sang Happy Birthday and she forced a smile. She didn't feel in the least bit happy and doubted she ever would again.

'Make a wish,' Cal said, although he knew her heart wasn't in it.

Once the table had been cleared, Joe brought over her cards and presents. The oblong box from her mother was a fountain pen engraved with her name. On the card Theresa had written, *With all good wishes my darling. Never forget the power of the written word.*

The parcel from Joe and Peggy was bulky and had obviously been difficult to wrap. She pulled the paper aside to reveal a large shoulder bag made from the softest calf leather.

'It's for your books when you go off to college. Joe saw it in that store in Lewistown. The one that sells leather goods. Do you like it?'

'It's beautiful. Thank you so much. It will be really useful to keep all my books and papers together in one place,' she said, hugging her aunt and uncle.

Cal was empty-handed. It serves *me right for being so foul to him*, she thought.

'I do have something for you, it's just not here. I want you to come somewhere with me tomorrow. You don't mind waiting until then do you?' he said, his expression inscrutable.

Roisin didn't respond, just shrugged her shoulders. It was Peggy who broke the awkward silence.

'Oh, I almost forgot. This came yesterday.' From her apron pocket Peggy pulled out a letter.

Roisin's heart skipped a beat. The expensive looking envelope had the same handwriting as the one bearing the terrible news of Ger's death.

This time it was addressed to Joe and Peggy and it had already been opened.

'Go on, look inside.' Peggy handed it to her and with fumbling fingers Roisin pulled out the contents. A rectangle of paper fluttered onto the table.

'It's from Ger's solicitor,' Peggy declared. 'It's a cheque from her estate. It amounts to almost $500 Canadian dollars. You are a very fortunate girl.'

She didn't feel fortunate. It was a lot of money and it would mean she had choices otherwise not available to her. It was a lovely gesture and so typical of Ger's generosity. She wished she felt more appreciative. Excusing herself, she took refuge in the bathroom, where she rinsed and dried her face. Opening the door to a tentative knock, she saw Cal, sent to check up on her no doubt. He stood in the hallway, at a loss as to what he should say or do.

'Do you feel up to coming back down?' he said.

'Can you just give me a minute?'

'Sure,' he said, turning to go downstairs.

'Cal?'

'Yes?'

'Thank you.'

'For what?' He looked perplexed.

'For being you. That's all.'

She reached for his hand and he lifted hers, touching it to his lips in a chivalrous manner that made her smile, despite herself.

When he'd gone, she sat on her bed trying to gather her thoughts. They had all worked so hard to give her a lovely birthday and she was wretched and unappreciative of their efforts. It wasn't like her to be so ungrateful. After all, she hadn't known Ger for long. It must have been much worse for Cal, finding his father the way he did. Knowing this, she still couldn't shake off the feeling that nothing would ever be the same again.

Closing her eyes momentarily, she heard the faint sound of tinkling glass. Sitting up with a start, she noticed her chimes were stirring, as if moved by a breeze. She checked to see if she had left the window ajar. It was shut tight, as was her door. Drawing the curtains against the fading light, she turned and gasped out loud. The wall behind her bed was dancing with light, the shifting shapes reflecting the coloured pieces of glass in her chimes. It was the same effect as when Ger and Lanie had been in her room. She stood for a few minutes watching, until eventually the image faded, then ceased as quickly as it had begun.

She didn't believe in supernatural events, yet felt comforted by the spectacle. There would be an explanation for it, she was pretty sure. Although she had to admit even science didn't have an answer for everything.

She decided for the moment she would keep it to herself. When the time was right, she would tell Cal. See what he had to say about it.

For now it was important she go and make amends for her behaviour. Ger, she felt sure, would have had something to say about how she had been acting.

Don't you dare use me as an excuse to be miserable Ro, or I'll come back and haunt you.

Chapter Thirty Six

Roisin sat outside, rocking back and forth on the swing while she waited for Cal to arrive. His mysterious invitation from the day before had both worried and intrigued her. Unsure of where he was taking her, she had pinned up her hair and was wearing her flat shoes and a floral, calf-length dress passed onto her by Laura, the twins mother. The dress was loose and floaty in contrast to the one Theresa had made for her and she liked the sensation of freedom it gave her after months spent wearing her coveralls.

Although it was Sunday, Cal was working an extra shift at the mill as there was a big order to fill. Peggy, concerned he might fade away altogether without food, had made sandwiches with leftover chicken and prepared a flask of coffee. He had been evasive when Roisin questioned him. She was concerned he might have spent money on her in an effort to make her feel better. It would explain all the extra shifts he had taken on over the last few weeks. She hoped he knew she didn't like grand gestures. It would be preferable if he had planned something simple they could enjoy doing together. A distraction to stop her from thinking too much,

When his pick-up turned in off the road, she watched as it bounced up the drive, swerving to avoid the worst of the ruts. He jumped out of the cab wearing his favourite denim shirt, along with shorts and sandals.

'Go and get your bathing suit,' he said, pointing in the direction of the house.

Peggy had appeared in the doorway holding a bag with towels peeping out of the top which she handed to Roisin.

'Please tell me you're not taking me swimming, Cal. Surely, the sea must be much too cold at this time of the year.'

'Ah yes, but you don't feel the cold, remember?'

It was true. She couldn't deny it.

'You're driving,' he told her, handing her the truck keys.

' I'd like to know where we are going. What if I get lost?'

Cal grinned and hopped into the passenger seat. 'Just head in the direction of the lighthouse.'

She felt relieved. He hadn't planned anything fancy after all. They were going to the sea glass beach. A box on the dashboard caught her eye. Before she could question him on its contents, he took it and placed it in the bag in the footwell.

There was very little traffic on the road and it wasn't long before Cal pointed out the sign for the track that would lead them to the lighthouse. She brought the truck to a halt on a grass verge and together they walked down the steep path to the deserted beach.

With the tide out and the sun high, a faint haze lay over

the water. There would be no rush to leave today. It would be hours before the tide turned. Roisin placed her shoes next to the bag then ran ahead to the waters edge while Cal spread the towels on the shingle and stretched out, looking up at the sky. When she returned, her hair had worked loose and the bottom of her dress was soaked in seawater and clung to her legs.

'Beautiful here, isn't it?' he said, averting his gaze.

'It is,' she agreed, joining him on the adjacent towel. 'I think it's one of the loveliest places I have ever seen.'

They lay side by side, fingers intertwined, listening to the cry of the seabirds and the lapping waves.

'Something just occurred to me,' she said, sitting up suddenly.

The realisation she had missed something so important was upsetting. It was typical of him not to have said anything. Surely there must have been a clue? If only she had been paying attention.

'You've had another of your brainwaves?' Cal said, teasing her.

She ignored the remark. 'How old are you now?'

'I've turned twenty. Why do you need to know?'

'It means you've had your birthday. When was it?'

'July 4th. Good old American Independence Day.'

'Why didn't you tell me?'

'No need. It's not that important. I stopped celebrating my birthday years ago.'

'Well, let me tell you Callum Anderson,' she said, waggling her finger at him, 'that will not happen ever again. Not as long as I'm around.'

He smiled to himself, amused by her bossiness. It felt

good to have someone care about him again. He hadn't realised how lonely an existence it had been. Not until this beautiful, dark haired, mystifying young woman had swept into his life like a whirlwind, driving away all the hurt and pain and giving him new hope for the future. The dawning realisation that whatever lay ahead, she would always be a part of his life, felt to him like a wonderful gift.

For the first time in many years he experienced a deep sense of contentment. A feeling all would be well.

The sun had begun to burn off the mist to reveal a searingly bright blue sky. The sea, topped with white horses, glinted in the autumn sunlight.

'Time to go and look for some glass,' he said, pulling her to her feet.

'No, I have plenty,' she protested. 'If it keeps getting taken away there will be no sea glass beach to come and visit.'

'Just one piece. Try and find something unusual or distinctive if you can.'

Scouring through the glass pebbles, she rejected each of the most common colours. Turning over a small boulder and almost buried by the sand, she uncovered a diamond shaped piece. The colour was iridescent, a mixture of teal and deep cerulean blue.

'Look Cal,' she cried out in excitement, holding it up to the light, 'this has to be the loveliest piece of sea glass in the whole world.'

He stood, cupping the box he had brought with him in his hands. She looked puzzled when he passed it to her.

'Go on,' he urged, 'open it.'

Inside lay a sheet of writing paper and the pen her mother had sent for her birthday.

'Take out the paper and pen. See what's underneath.'

She did so and lifted out a perfectly carved model of a fishing boat, complete with a wheelhouse.

'Did you make this for me?'

'Yes and no. I made it using the penknife you bought for me at Christmas. And no, it's not just for you. It's for you *and* Ger. It's a way for you to say goodbye. You're going to write a message to her and put it into the boat with the sea glass. We're going to swim out into the ocean and send it on its way.'

She didn't protest when he held the towel around her while she slipped out of her dress. Her bathing suit was tight over her hips and breasts and it had been a struggle to get into it. She hadn't worn it since the previous summer when she had gone swimming in the river with some of the older girls from her school. Then she had been flat chested with no shape to speak of. Now, the material clung to her newly acquired curves and she felt self-conscious in his presence.

'Hey, no peeking,' she chided.

He turned his head away, but not before she noticed the expression on his face.

It was difficult to gauge exactly what he was thinking. She just knew she liked the way he was looking at her, even if it gave her goosebumps.

She sat back down on a towel, her toes digging into the warm pebbles. The pen and paper lay on top of the box in front of her. It took her a good few minutes before she located the right words. Using the surface of the box to lean on, she wrote her message then carefully wrapped the sheet of paper around the piece of sea glass. With great care, she tucked the package into the carved-out hollow of the boat.

Taking off his shirt and sandals, Cal picked up the little craft and cradled it in the crook of his arm. He reached for her hand and they walked to the edge of the water. Shivering in the breeze, Cal held on tight to her hand and together they jumped the incoming foam-crested breakers. When the shoreline shelved, they began swimming, each now holding onto a side of the little vessel. Reaching the point where he knew the rip current would carry it out to sea, Cal placed the boat on the rippling surface of the ocean. Treading water, they watched as the undertow pulled it further and further away from them. Before long it had disappeared from view.

Back on the beach, Roisin sat resting her chin on her knees, scanning the choppy surface for the tiny boat. All she could see was the vast expanse of deep water stretching as far as the horizon.

She imagined having wings and joining the migratory birds on their journey across miles of ocean. Some landing for a while to rest and replenish in preparation for their journey further south, others remaining for the winter to nest in the fresh water reed beds and boglands of her homeland

She thought of her mother. They both had new lives and their journeys were taking them in different directions. Despite the physical distance between them, the bond they shared was unbreakable.

She thought of Ger, slumbering in a churchyard for all

eternity. *How cruel is death, severing forever the link connecting you to life.* If there was any comfort to be had, it was in knowing nothing could take away the precious memories and the love she carried, safe within her heart.

Cal picked up the sandwiches and flask. 'Hey dreamer, are you hungry?' he asked.

For the first time in weeks she felt the weight of sorrow lift.

'I'm starving.'

They dressed and shared the sandwiches and coffee in silence. Soon the tide would start to turn and it would be time to leave.

'I have a question for you,' she said. 'Do you believe in an afterlife?'

She told him what had occurred in her room with her wind chimes, hoping he wouldn't think her foolish.

'I agree it does sound strange,' Cal said, looking pensive. 'I guess some would say it's more to do with grieving and knowing you won't see the person again? A sort of wish fulfilment?' He pulled her close, thinking he couldn't bear it if he were never to see *her* again. 'Some weird things happened after my dad died and I can't explain them either.'

She waited, willing him to continue speaking. He was looking into the distance and she sensed he wasn't ready to tell her the full story of that terrible, dark time in his life.

'Thank you for helping me today. I feel so much better now that I've said my goodbye to Ger. What you did for us was perfect.' She planted a kiss on his cheek and went to stand up.

'Oh no you don't,' he said, pulling her back down beside him, 'you haven't had your birthday present yet.'

'Oh, but I...' she started to say, before he put a finger to her lips to silence her.

He held out his hand. Resting in the centre of his palm was a circle of gold with a crowned heart held by two hands. She recognised the design immediately.

'I don't have to tell you it's a Claddagh ring,' he said. 'I wanted you to have a reminder of what we mean to one another. As you know, the hands represent friendship, the heart love and the crown loyalty. I wonder if you will do me the honour of wearing it?'

She smiled at his formality. Stretching out her right hand, she let him slip the ring onto her ring finger.

'This is for now,' he said, a catch in his throat. 'Ger told you it's important to follow your dreams, wherever they may take you and you need to do that. If, or when you are ready to come back to me, I will be here, waiting for you.'

'Callum Anderson. I do believe that I'm a little bit in love with you.'

'Well, Miss Roisin O'Connor, I *know* I love you.'

They packed the bag and hand in hand began the climb back up to the truck. Away from the shore, the sun was warm at their backs and Roisin turned to see if there was any sign of the boat. It was nowhere in sight, but now the sea was flat and calm, as though placated by their offering. Soon the beach would be underwater once more. The tide would come in and go out as it always did, bringing with it more of the brightly coloured pieces of glass that gave the beach its name.

It occurred to her that one day she would return to find a piece of iridescent, crystalline glass, dazzling in its brightness and vivid as the eye in a peacock's tail feather.

Prologue

Waterbridge

Theresa climbed the back stairs and clicked on the overhead light. Crossing to the window she closed the wooden shutters before drawing the curtains against the evening gloom. The wind was increasing and she could hear the window panes rattle as if warning of the deluge soon to arrive. Steven would be drenched as he walked the mile back from the train station.

She had been down to the shop earlier to pick up some bread and loose tea. Sarah had been eager for a chat and she had sat with her for a while.

Against all the odds and following repeated miscarriages, Sarah was now eight months pregnant and glad to take advantage of any opportunity to elevate her swollen ankles and take the weight off her aching back. While John set about cleaning the bacon slicer, she and Theresa shared a pot of tea and a leftover custard slice each.

'Your apron is getting a bit tight. I've got a few scraps

of leftover material. I'll measure you tomorrow and run up a couple of pinnies to keep you going until the baby comes,' Theresa told her.

Sarah had been a good friend to her and she was happy to help out in any way she could. She knew both John and Sarah were concerned about the possibility of something going wrong and hadn't bought much in preparation for the arrival of the baby.

Theresa had kept a few of Roisin's baby clothes and set about knitting some matinee jackets. She was keeping them in a layette basket she had purchased until the child's safe arrival. She had also found a roll end of Winceyette which she intended to make into a couple of nightdresses for Sarah for her hospital stay.

Sarah shifted in her seat in an effort to get comfortable. 'You won't be walking to meet Steven tonight, I trust? The weather has turned filthy since this morning and there's no point in both of you getting soaked.'

Theresa shook her head and sipped her tea. She was always glad of Sarah's company and enjoyed their chats together. Sarah was no gossip, but as a shopkeeper she was party to most of the comings and goings in the small town.

When she and John first came to Waterbridge, she was aware of some tittle tattle about Theresa's decision to keep her child.

More recently the talk centred around Theresa's male lodger. When visiting the store most kept their counsel in her presence, knowing she and Theresa were close. There had though, been an incident recently that made her blood boil. She overheard a snippet of conversation between two of her customers as she swilled the outside step with a bucket of soapy water. At the mention of Theresa's name, she had paused, the steam rising from the hot suds sloshing from side to side in the galvanised pail.

'You know she has a man living up there with her don't you?' one of the women was saying.

Her friend tutted in response. 'I know. You would think she would have learned her lesson after the last time, although I do hear he is a well respected academic from England.'

'He is,' said the first woman, 'but it's a disgrace all the same. Them not being married an' all. The Hennesseys should know better than to allow such behaviour under their roof.'

Sarah had heard enough. On the pretext of being unaware of their presence, she stepped out and swung the contents of the bucket in the direction of the women, dousing their feet in hot foaming water. There was a screech and a cry of anger 'Jesus Sarah, will you be careful! These are new leather shoes and the stockings are just out of the packet.'

'Oh, I'm so sorry,' Sarah said, wiping her hands on her apron. 'I didn't see the two of ye'. I thought I heard a couple of cats hissing at each other.'

When the tale was relayed back to her, Theresa had laughed until her jaw ached. John had looked on, feigning disapproval at his wife's antics. He couldn't keep up the pretence for too long though and he was soon laughing along with the pair of them.

'You will lose me customers, woman,' he said, shaking his head in mock exasperation.

Theresa hesitated, placed her cup down in front of her and said, 'Steven's asked me to marry him.'

She waited for Sarah's reaction.

'What wonderful news! Why are you looking so glum?'

It had been a surprise to Theresa when Steven proposed. On Sundays, if the weather was fair, they walked through the town and crossed the ancient stone bridge that gave Waterbridge its name. A path ran along the side of the river for a couple of miles before it turned inland and became a narrow track running through a patch of muddy farmland. It opened up again to cross verdant fields before following a gentle slope upwards, rising to ascend to an ancient drumlin enclosed by Scotch pines. She had walked here with Roisin on many occasions, her daughter sprinting ahead and waving excitedly at her from the top of the hill. During the last few weeks the autumn rains, combined with the hooves from a herd of cows, had turned the field into a quagmire. They had paused, and leaned on the gate leading into the field. There would be no climb to the top today.

Steven knew she was thinking of her daughter and held back from posing the question he was so desperate to hear the answer to. Instead, he waited until she began to rub her frozen hands together.

He was tall, over six feet, and he bent to take her fingers in his, blowing on them to give them warmth. She looked up at him in surprise for he was not normally a demonstrative man.

'I have something to ask you, Theresa. Before I do,

I need to tell you my tenure here is up and I will be returning to England for the winter term.'

Theresa had known the time was approaching when he would be leaving and felt sad at being left on her own once again. His absence would certainly leave a void in her life. They had so much in common and enjoyed each other's company. She would miss him reading chapters from his book to her, their walks, the trips to the theatre and to musical performances, the talking together about everything under the sun.

It will be no real hardship, she reasoned, *My life is not so bad. I have my work and Sarah will need me when the baby comes.*

She looked down at his long, slender fingers cupping her hands and then up at his face, his eyes shielded by his round spectacles.

'What was it you wanted to ask me?' she said.

He cleared his throat nervously. 'Since I've been in Ireland I've been thinking very seriously about my future. It has become obvious to me we get on well and have many of the same interests. I hope I don't sound too forward, but would you consider becoming my wife and accompanying me back to England? I have no ring to give you. I thought if your answer is yes, we can choose one together? I'm asking you to marry me, Theresa.'

Sarah poured them both another cup of tea from the pot and sat back in her chair, arms folded across her bulging stomach. 'And what did you say to him, girl?'

'Well, I was dumbfounded as you can imagine.' Theresa

took a sip of the hot, sweet beverage before continuing. 'I said I would think about it and let him know this evening.'

'What?' Sarah spluttered into her cup, 'that man is offering you the chance of a wonderful new life away from this hotbed of small-minded eejits and you're making him wait for an answer? You need your head examined. If it was me I'd be off like a shot!'

John looked up from his task and smiled in his wife's direction. 'You wouldn't get very far in your condition, now would you Mrs Hennessey?'

The notion of Sarah doing anything at speed had them all laughing again.

It was getting late and Theresa, aware Steven would soon be home, took the cups to wash at the back sink. The conversation with Sarah had got her thinking. Once back in her own flat, she decided against spending more time with her sewing. Instead, she cleared everything away, lit the fire and switched on the lamps to create a cosy glow in the room.

She spread the heavy gold chenille cloth with the tassels across the table and laid out a plate of ham sandwiches and a home-made seed cake in preparation for Steven's return. He ate his midday meal at the university and usually they had a light tea together in the evening. Sarah's comment had made her uneasy. She was worried that in delaying her answer his feelings might have been hurt.

She couldn't work out why she wasn't jumping at the chance he was offering. After all, as Sarah had pointed out, it was a great opportunity and she wasn't getting any younger. There had been no further contact with her own parents and Roisin was establishing a life for herself in Canada. Theresa thought it unlikely her girl would want to return to Ireland considering the distance and how well she had settled. Waterbridge, it had to be said, was no great shakes. It was a small town with too many petty-minded individuals. In addition, the church still dominated and held sway over people's morals and behaviour, as she knew all too well.

Why then was it so difficult to leave the place? Was it just habit and familiarity, or fear of the unknown? After all, it was hypocritical of her to resist change, for hadn't she packed her own daughter off to the other side of the world. It was luck rather than good management on her part that it had turned out to be a success.

The truth of the matter was she hadn't done too badly on her own. Over the years it had been a struggle to lift herself out of a situation with the potential to pull anyone under. Now being self -reliant meant there was no going back. In spite of the mealy-mouthed gossips, she commanded a level of respect in the town. Ger's visit had helped enormously on that score. Being a successful woman in her own right with a business, and a lovely home and supportive friends was gratifying. Why give it all up for a man she liked and respected, but didn't love?

Hearing Steven's footsteps on the stairs, she walked to the door to greet him. He had left before breakfast to catch the train and was back later than usual. Was he avoiding her? He was wearing a shower-proof overcoat having anticipated the change in the weather. Even with the addition of an umbrella, he was still sodden.

Taking a warm towel from the airing cupboard, she

handed it to him to rub through his dripping hair. After taking his coat to hang it on the back of the door to dry, she shook the umbrella in the hallway.

'Sit by the fire and warm yourself. You must be frozen. I'll make some tea and bring you a plate of sandwiches.' A mixture of guilt and anxiety was causing her to fuss over him.

'Will you come and sit with me for a while first?' he said. 'I've been thinking about this all day and I have a different proposition to the one already made. I want you to hear me out before you say anything. Is that all right with you?'

Theresa nodded in agreement. How domestic this scene must look, she thought, sitting opposite him. Anyone who didn't know us would think we had been married for years. Lifting the poker she raked the coals until they glowed. The fire soon became red-hot. It was almost impossible to look into its depths and it forced her to face him.

Taking off his glasses to rub his eyes, Steven folded the wire arms and placed them, lenses up, on the mantle shelf before arranging his long limbs in the armchair. He was older than Theresa, close to fifty and still looked boyish. A calf lick caused his hair to fall forwards and he had a habit of brushing it to the side, only for it to fall back immediately onto his face, giving him a distracted look. She got up and went to the table, returning with the plate of sandwiches. He took one, and when he spoke again Theresa thought how much she liked his voice, the tones rich and modulated from a lifetime of public speaking.

'I knew when you didn't agree immediately to my offer

of marriage that you had doubts. Would that be fair to say?' he asked.

There was no point in pretending otherwise and Theresa nodded in agreement.

'I think it's also fair to say that my feelings for you are not reciprocated. In other words, I have strong feelings for you, and although you care for me and we get on famously, you do not feel as I do?'

'That is so.' She wanted to elaborate, to explain herself, but kept her counsel, somewhat in awe of his formal tone.

'Well, here is my suggestion. I hope it's mutually agreeable. You are an independent woman Theresa and I value that in you very highly. I certainly wouldn't want you to change to please me. We are well suited in so many ways and I feel bereft at the thought of losing your companionship. I even hold a vain hope that you might grow to love me in time.'

He propped his elbows on his knees and leaned forward, steepling his fingers before continuing.

'Would you take a chance and marry me anyway? My house in England has plenty of room and you could set yourself up to continue with your sewing if that's what you want to do. The village is a short train ride from London and I know you could forge contacts there and be successful. You are very talented. In fact I do believe you could be a success at anything you set your mind to. And, if it doesn't work out, I promise I will bring you back here and make sure you are well provided for.'

The heat from the fire was making her face burn and Theresa stood and took a few steps back until she was standing in a current of cold air.

'Do you mind if I make a pot of tea?' She needed to do something with her hands as a distraction.

He nodded in agreement and she went into the little kitchenette glad of a break and the opportunity to order her thoughts.

By the time the kettle had boiled and she had placed the teapot and cups on the tray, she had reached a decision.

Steven stood when Theresa came back into the room. He looked apprehensive as he watched her set the tray down on the table. An age seemed to pass before she at last turned towards him, a shy smile playing on her lips. 'The answer is yes, Steven. I will marry you.' She put a finger to his lips as he was about to speak. 'I do have a few conditions though.'

Steven's long legs looked as though they might buckle under him and he resumed his place in the chair beside the fire.

'First of all, I don't want any fuss.' This was delivered so emphatically Steven could only nod mutely in agreement. 'The other stipulations are,' Theresa continued, 'I would like us to have a simple ceremony at a Register Office in England, and no engagement ring, just a plain gold wedding band. I also want to be here for a few weeks after Sarah has her baby. I can help out and it will give me time to wind everything down here. A spring wedding will be nice don't you think? Does that fit in with your plans?'

'Is that all?' he said, grinning like a Cheshire cat.

'That's it. If you are in agreement we can set the wheels in motion as soon as possible. Tomorrow, Sarah and I will look at dress patterns together. I need to make a wedding outfit that befits the wife of a distinguished academic such as yourself.'

In her gentle way, she was making fun of him he knew, but for once in his life he couldn't think of a suitable retort, amusing or otherwise. Instead, he stood and held out his arms to her. She moved towards him and he held her close, fearful that if he let her go she would change her mind.

'Thank you,' he said, burying his face in her hair. They stood, wrapped in each other's arms for a few minutes until Theresa gently disentangled herself.

'I know it's getting late, but there's someone I really need to tell and it won't keep.'

Going to the sideboard she withdrew her red, leather covered writing box and placed it on the table. Removing the lid, she took out her pen and a sheet of paper. As she was about to start writing, Steven came over and placed a hand over hers.

'In all the excitement I forgot to mention something very important,' he said, eagerness making his voice quiver.' I didn't want to say anything before in case you thought I was offering you an inducement to marry me.'

She was intrigued he could tell and he savoured the moment, rehearsing the words in his head, knowing they would bring her so much joy in the telling.

'My publisher has been in contact. I have been asked to undertake a book and lecture tour of universities on the East coast of America. It's during the last two weeks of next year's summer term. We can travel on to Canada afterwards and have a late honeymoon in Nova Scotia. What do you think?'

Later, when her legs felt less unsteady, her heart had stopped fluttering and her breathing was restored to some semblance of normality, she returned to sit at the table. Looking at her writing box, she remembered a time when she had lifted it down from a shelf in her cottage. Then it had felt as though her heart would break with the weight of the decision she was having to make.

Now, just over a year later, a new life beckoned. Deep within the core of her being, she recognised that whatever the future held, she would face it with equanimity. Knowing she and her daughter shared the same capacity for resilience filled her with an immense sense of pride. She could hardly contain her excitement at the thought of seeing Roisin once again. As she began to write, the words flowed with ease from her pen.

My dearest girl
I hope you are well and happy.
It's very late at night here, but I wanted to put this letter in the post first thing in the morning. I have some very exciting news to tell you...!

THE END

Back to the beginning...

When Tina Pritchard set out to write The Sea Glass Beach she did so with some experience of the heartache associated with the Irish institutions that made life so hard for unmarried mothers.
Here she describes her own close call with the seemingly inevitable solution - adoption.

The young woman in this picture is my mother. She looks beautiful, like a 1950's starlet. Seemingly carefree, she smiles happily into the camera. Alongside her is a dapper man I know very little about. My father. Less than a year later my mother gave birth to me and 'my father' disappeared from my life forever. She was sent to have me in Sean Ross Abbey, a Mother and Baby Home now legendary in the annals of recent Irish history. Like many similar institutions it has gained notoriety as a consequence of its treatment of unmarried mothers and its adoption practices.

In those far off days the church with all its accumulated power held sway in such matters. Girls and women who had 'sinned' by becoming pregnant before marriage, were sent to institutions such as these. The church and its attendants soon realised they had a potential income stream for the church coffers and adoptions were arranged and babies taken from their mothers and sent primarily to the USA and Canada.

Raising a child alone, with the opprobrium of the church to contend with, the shame visited on the women and their families, and with no social security or child care support, for the majority of women there simply was no alternative except to sign away their child for adoption.

I too could have easily become another 'adoption story' if it hadn't been for the tenacity of my grandmother, a widow with only a railway pension. She somehow managed to raise the money asked for by the nuns, ostensibly for the board provided for my mother whilst in their care.

Unlike many of my crib mates, I returned to the family home in Sunday's Well, Cork City.

I am four months old in the photograph (above right) and aged around two in the picture where I am holding my mothers hand and looking sombre. She was probably on a flying visit to Cork as by this time she had begun a new life in England. It would be another year before she sent for me to join her.

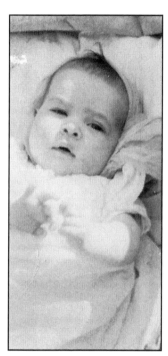 

The Catholic Church has much to answer for, but I have refused to allow my past to define me. All experience contributes to forming our character and personality, but we can also take control and make our own choices. Of course it is important to attempt to find out who we are and where we came from. To grow we need roots and our past is central to our identity. It is also important to acknowledge that the distant past is in part a product of our longings and imaginings viewed through the prism of our present. In going back we are time travellers bringing our own wants, needs and expectations with us and this voyage can turn out to be both unsatisfactory and disappointing in the extreme. We need to be realistic and have our eyes firmly open on our future, because as LP Hartley wrote *'The past is a foreign country; they do things differently there.'*

The Author

Tina Pritchard spent most of her life engaged in bringing up a family, taking a social science degree, working as a lecturer, a trainer and more recently as an independent celebrant conducting funerals, weddings and naming ceremonies.

Her first book, a psychological thriller, *In A Deep Dark Wood,* was published in 2021. *The Sea Glass Beach* is a departure in genre and started life as a short story morphing over the years into a novel. It is a work of fiction inspired in part by her own mother's experience of giving birth to a child at Sean Ross Abbey Mother and Baby Home in the 1950's. That child, born all those years ago in Co Tipperary, Ireland, is the author of this book.

Tina loves to write and has won competitions for both her short stories and her poetry. She lives in a beautiful part of the world and gains much of her inspiration from walking her badly behaved terrier, Horace, in the Derbyshire countryside.

What reviewers said about Tina Pritchard's
debut novel *In a Deep Dark Wood*

Kay Adams

A truly fantastic, gripping read and my thanks and
congratulations go out to this fantastic author Tina
Pritchard. A highly recommended 5 star book to read.

Rebecca Bagnall

Tina Pritchard has the knack of making you keep this
book in your hands until it's finished. Unputdownable
books are the best kind and this one had me gripped
from start to finish.

Ginger Book Geek

I will certainly be reading more of Tina's work in the
future. The score on the Ginger Book Geek board is a
very well deserved 5 stars out of 5.

Heather Hardie

Can't wait to read another book by Tina Pritchard.
A future bestselling author.

The Sea Glass Beach
is also available as an
Amazon ebook

Printed in Great Britain
by Amazon